Family Maps
of
Sanilac County, Michigan
Deluxe Edition

With Homesteads, Roads, Waterways, Towns, Cemeteries, Railroads, and More

Family Maps of Sanilac County, Michigan

Deluxe Edition

With Homesteads, Roads, Waterways, Towns, Cemeteries, Railroads, and More

by Gregory A. Boyd, J.D.

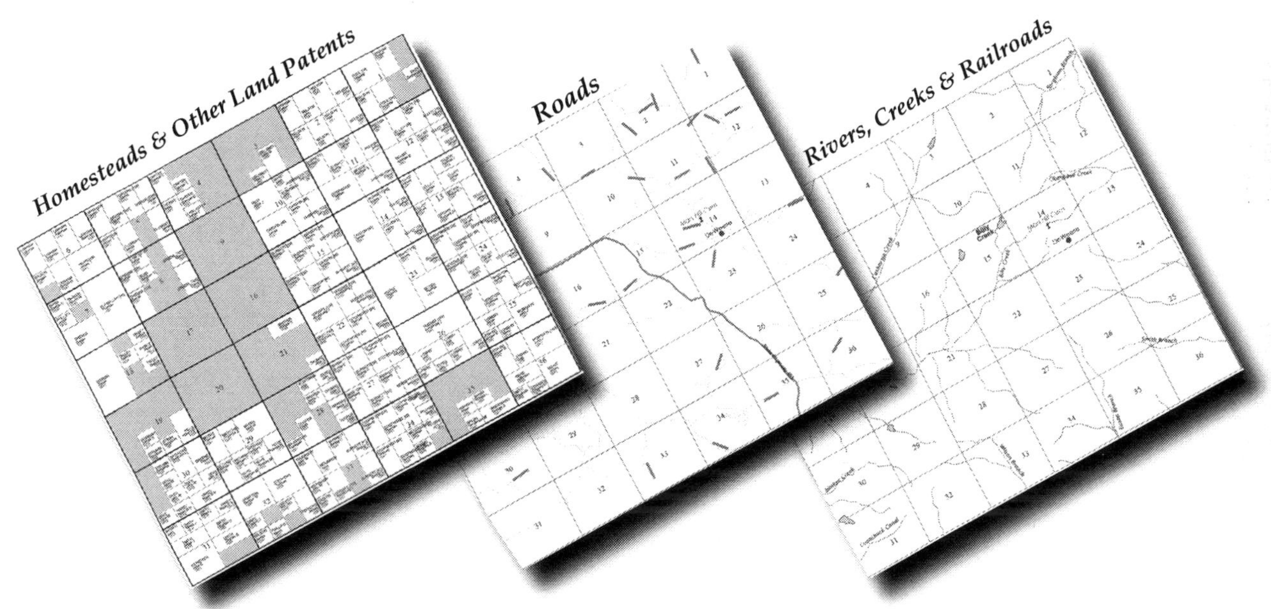

Featuring 3 Maps Per Township...

Arphax Publishing Co.
www.arphax.com

Family Maps of Sanilac County, Michigan, Deluxe Edition: With Homesteads, Roads, Waterways, Towns, Cemeteries, Railroads, and More.
by Gregory A. Boyd, J.D.

ISBN 1-4203-1334-7

Printed in the United States of America

Published by Arphax Publishing Co., 2210 Research Park Blvd., Norman, Oklahoma, USA 73069
www.arphax.com

First Edition

This book is dedicated to my wonderful family:

Vicki, Jordan, & Amy Boyd

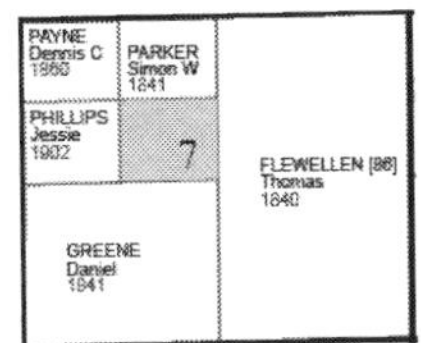

Contents

Preface 1
How to Use this Book - A Graphical Summary 2
How to Use This Book 3

- Part I -

The Big Picture

Map **A** - Where Sanilac County, Michigan Lies Within the State 11
Map **B** - Sanilac County, Michigan and Surrounding Counties 12
Map **C** - Congressional Townships of Sanilac County, Michigan 13
Map **D** - Cities & Towns of Sanilac County, Michigan 14
Map **E** - Cemeteries of Sanilac County, Michigan 16
Surnames in Sanilac County, Michigan Patents 18
Surname/Township Index 23

- Part II -

Township Map Groups

(each Map Group contains a Patent Index, Patent Map, Road Map, & Historical Map)

Map Group **1** - Township 14-N Range 12-E 54
Map Group **2** - Township 14-N Range 13-E 64
Map Group **3** - Township 14-N Range 14-E 74
Map Group **4** - Township 14-N Range 15-E 82
Map Group **5** - Township 14-N Range 16-E 92
Map Group **6** - Township 13-N Range 12-E 96
Map Group **7** - Township 13-N Range 13-E. 106
Map Group **8** - Township 13-N Range 14-E 116
Map Group **9** - Township 13-N Range 15-E 124
Map Group **10** - Township 13-N Range 16-E 134
Map Group **11** - Township 12-N Range 12-E 142
Map Group **12** - Township 12-N Range 13-E 150
Map Group **13** - Township 12-N Range 14-E 160
Map Group **14** - Township 12-N Range 15-E 168
Map Group **15** - Township 12-N Range 16-E 178
Map Group **16** - Township 11-N Range 12-E 186
Map Group **17** - Township 11-N Range 13-E 196
Map Group **18** - Township 11-N Range 14-E 206
Map Group **19** - Township 11-N Range 15-E 214

Map Group **20** - Township 11-N Range 16-E....224
Map Group **21** - Township 10-N Range 12-E....234
Map Group **22** - Township 10-N Range 13-E....240
Map Group **23** - Township 10-N Range 14-E....248
Map Group **24** - Township 10-N Range 15-E....258
Map Group **25** - Township 10-N Range 16-E....268
Map Group **26** - Township 10-N Range 17-E....278
Map Group **27** - Township 9-N Range 13-E....282
Map Group **28** - Township 9-N Range 14-E....290
Map Group **29** - Township 9-N Range 15-E....300
Map Group **30** - Township 9-N Range 16-E....310
Map Group **31** - Township 9-N Range 17-E....320

Appendices

Appendix A - Congressional Authority for Land Patents....326
Appendix B - Section Parts (Aliquot Parts)....327
Appendix C - Multi-Patentee Groups in Sanilac County....331

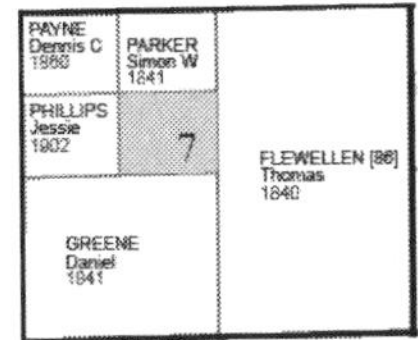

Preface

The quest for the discovery of my ancestors' origins, migrations, beliefs, and life-ways has brought me rewards that I could never have imagined. The *Family Maps* series of books is my first effort to share with historical and genealogical researchers, some of the tools that I have developed to achieve my research goals. I firmly believe that this effort will allow many people to reap the same sorts of treasures that I have.

Our Federal government's General Land Office of the Bureau of Land Management (the "GLO") has given genealogists and historians an incredible gift by virtue of its enormous database housed on its web-site at glorecords.blm.gov. Here, you can search for and find millions of parcels of land purchased by our ancestors in about thirty states.

This GLO web-site is one of the best FREE on-line tools available to family researchers. But, it is not for the faint of heart, nor is it for those unwilling or unable to to sift through and analyze the thousands of records that exist for most counties.

My immediate goal with this series is to spare you the hundreds of hours of work that it would take you to map the Land Patents for this county. Every Sanilac County homestead or land patent that I have gleaned from public GLO databases is mapped here. Consequently, I can usually show you in an instant, where your ancestor's land is located, as well as the names of nearby land-owners.

Originally, that was my primary goal. But after speaking to other genealogists, it became clear that there was much more that they wanted. Taking their advice set me back almost a full year, but I think you will agree it was worth the wait. Because now, you can learn so much more.

Now, this book answers these sorts of questions:

- Are there any variant spellings for surnames that I have missed in searching GLO records?
- Where is my family's traditional home-place?
- What cemeteries are near Grandma's house?
- My Granddad used to swim in such-and-such-Creek—where is that?
- How close is this little community to that one?
- Are there any other people with the same surname who bought land in the county?
- How about cousins and in-laws—did they buy land in the area?

And these are just for starters!

The rules for using the *Family Maps* books are simple, but the strategies for success are many. Some techniques are apparent on first use, but many are gained with time and experience. Please take the time to notice the roads, cemeteries, creek-names, family names, and unique first-names throughout the whole county. You cannot imagine what YOU might be the first to discover.

I hope to learn that many of you have answered age-old research questions within these pages or that you have discovered relationships previously not even considered. When these sorts of things happen to you, will you please let me hear about it? I would like nothing better. My contact information can always be found at www.arphax.com.

One more thing: please read the "How To Use This Book" chapter; it starts on the next page. This will give you the very best chance to find the treasures that lie within these pages.

My family and I wish you the very best of luck, both in life, and in your research. Greg Boyd

How to Use This Book - A Graphical Summary

Part I
"The Big Picture"

Map A ▸ *Counties in the State*
Map B ▸ *Surrounding Counties*
Map C ▸ *Congressional Townships (Map Groups) in the County*
Map D ▸ *Cities & Towns in the County*
Map E ▸ *Cemeteries in the County*
Surnames in the County ▸ *Number of Land-Parcels for Each Surname*
Surname/Township Index ▸ Directs you to Township Map Groups in Part II

The Surname/Township Index can direct you to any number of **Township Map Groups**

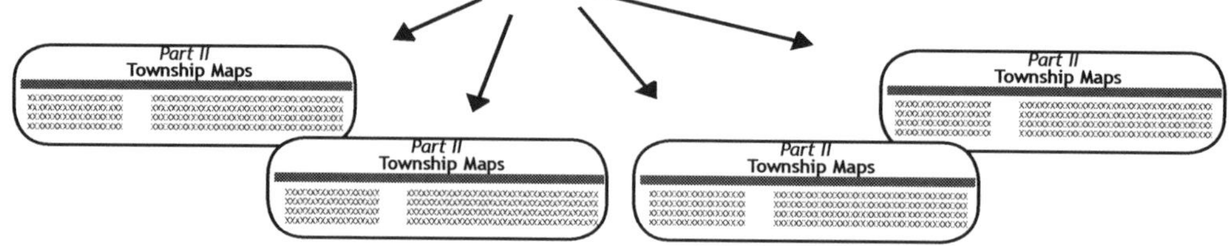

Part II
Township Map Groups
(1 for each Township in the County)

Each Township Map Group contains all four of of the following tools . . .

Land Patent Index ▸ *Every-name Index of Patents Mapped in this Township*
Land Patent Map ▸ *Map of Patents as listed in above Index*
Road Map ▸ *Map of Roads, City-centers, and Cemeteries in the Township*
Historical Map ▸ *Map of Railroads, Lakes, Rivers, Creeks, City-Centers, and Cemeteries*

Appendices

Appendix A ▸ *Congressional Authority enabling Patents within our Maps*
Appendix B ▸ *Section-Parts / Aliquot Parts (a comprehensive list)*
Appendix C ▸ *Multi-patentee Groups (Individuals within Buying Groups)*

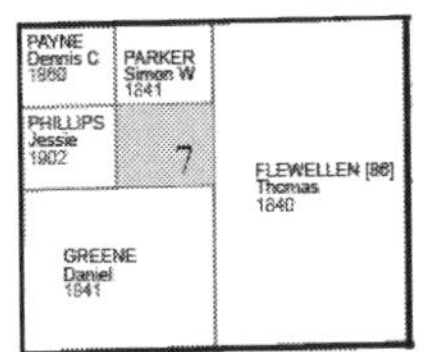

How to Use This Book

The two "Parts" of this *Family Maps* volume seek to answer two different types of questions. Part I deals with broad questions like: what counties surround Sanilac County, are there any ASHCRAFTs in Sanilac County, and if so, in which Townships or Maps can I find them? Ultimately, though, Part I should point you to a particular Township Map Group in Part II.

Part II concerns itself with details like: where exactly is this family's land, who else bought land in the area, and what roads and streams run through the land, or are located nearby. The Chart on the opposite page, and the remainder of this chapter attempt to convey to you the particulars of these two "parts", as well as how best to use them to achieve your research goals.

Part I
"The Big Picture"

Within Part I, you will find five "Big Picture" maps and two county-wide surname tools.

These include:

- Map A - Where Sanilac County lies within the state
- Map B - Counties that surround Sanilac County
- Map C - Congressional Townships of Sanilac County (+ Map Group Numbers)
- Map D - Cities & Towns of Sanilac County (with Index)
- Map E - Cemeteries of Sanilac County (with Index)
- Surnames in Sanilac County Patents (with Parcel-counts for each surname)
- Surname/Township Index (with Parcel-counts for each surname by Township)

The five "Big-Picture" Maps are fairly self-explanatory, yet should not be overlooked. This is particularly true of Maps "C", "D", and "E", all of which show Sanilac County and its Congressional Townships (and their assigned Map Group Numbers).

Let me briefly explain this concept of Map Group Numbers. These are a device completely of our own invention. They were created to help you quickly locate maps without having to remember the full legal name of the various Congressional Townships. It is simply easier to remember "Map Group 1" than a legal name like: "Township 9-North Range 6-West, 5th Principal Meridian." But the fact is that the TRUE legal name for these Townships IS terribly important. These are the designations that others will be familiar with and you will need to accurately record them in your notes. This is why both Map Group numbers AND legal descriptions of Townships are almost always displayed together.

Map "C" will be your first intoduction to "Map Group Numbers", and that is all it contains: legal Township descriptions and their assigned Map Group Numbers. Once you get further into your research, and more immersed in the details, you will likely want to refer back to Map "C" from time to time, in order to regain your bearings on just where in the county you are researching.

Remember, township boundaries are a completely artificial device, created to standardize land descriptions. But do not let them become a boundary in your mind when choosing which townships to research. Your relative's in-laws, children, cousins, siblings, and mamas and papas, might just as easily have lived in the township next to the one your grandfather lived in—rather than in the one where he actually lived. So Map "C" can be your guide to which other Townships/ Map Groups you likewise ought to analyze.

Of course, the same holds true for County lines; this is the purpose behind Map "B". It shows you surrounding counties that you may want to consider for further reserarch.

Map "D", the Cities and Towns map, is the first map with an index. Map "E" is the second (Cemeteries). Both, Maps "D" and "E" give you broad views of City (or Cemetery) locations in the County. But they go much further by pointing you toward pertinent Township Map Groups so you can locate the patents, roads, and waterways located near a particular city or cemetery.

Once you are familiar with these *Family Maps* volumes and the county you are researching, the "Surnames In Sanilac County" chapter (or its sister chapter in other volumes) is where you'll likely start your future research sessions. Here, you can quickly scan its few pages and see if anyone in the county possesses the surnames you are researching. The "Surnames in Sanilac County" list shows only two things: surnames and the number of parcels of land we have located for that surname in Sanilac County. But whether or not you immediately locate the surnames you are researching, please do not go any further without taking a few moments to scan ALL the surnames in these very few pages.

You cannot imagine how many lost ancestors are waiting to be found by someone willing to take just a little longer to scan the "Surnames In Sanilac County" list. Misspellings and typographical errors abound in most any index of this sort. Don't miss out on finding your Kinard that was written Rynard or Cox that was written Lox. If it looks funny or wrong, it very often is. And one of those little errors may well be your relative.

Now, armed with a surname and the knowledge that it has one or more entries in this book, you are ready for the "Surname/Township Index." Unlike the "Surnames In Sanilac County", which has only one line per Surname, the "Surname/Township Index" contains one line-item for each Township Map Group in which each surname is found. In other words, each line represents a different Township Map Group that you will need to review.

Specifically, each line of the Surname/Township Index contains the following four columns of information:

1. Surname
2. Township Map Group Number (these Map Groups are found in Part II)
3. Parcels of Land (number of them with the given Surname within the Township)
4. Meridian/Township/Range (the legal description for this Township Map Group)

The key column here is that of the Township Map Group Number. While you should definitely record the Meridian, Township, and Range, you can do that later. Right now, you need to dig a little deeper. That Map Group Number tells you where in Part II that you need to start digging.

But before you leave the "Surname/Township Index", do the same thing that you did with the "Surnames in Sanilac County" list: take a moment to scan the pages of the Index and see if there are similarly spelled or misspelled surnames that deserve your attention. Here again, is an easy opportunity to discover grossly misspelled family names with very little effort. Now you are ready to turn to . . .

Part II
"Township Map Groups"

You will normally arrive here in Part II after being directed to do so by one or more "Map Group Numbers" in the Surname/Township Index of Part I.

Each Map Group represents a set of four tools dedicated to a single Congressional Township that is either wholly or partially within the county. If you are trying to learn all that you can about a particular family or their land, then these tools should usually be viewed in the order they are presented.

These four tools include:

1. a Land Patent Index
2. a Land Patent Map
3. a Road Map, and
4. an Historical Map

As I mentioned earlier, each grouping of this sort is assigned a Map Group Number. So, let's now move on to a discussion of the four tools that make up one of these Township Map Groups.

Land Patent Index

Each Township Map Group's Index begins with a title, something along these lines:

MAP GROUP 1: Index to Land Patents
Township 16-North Range 5-West (2nd PM)

The Index contains seven (7) columns. They are:

1. ID (a unique ID number for this Individual and a corresponding Parcel of land in this Township)
2. Individual in Patent (name)
3. Sec. (Section), and
4. Sec. Part (Section Part, or Aliquot Part)
5. Date Issued (Patent)
6. Other Counties (often means multiple counties were mentioned in GLO records, or the section lies within multiple counties).
7. For More Info . . . (points to other places within this index or elsewhere in the book where you can find more information)

While most of the seven columns are self-explanatory, I will take a few moments to explain the "Sec. Part." and "For More Info" columns.

The "Sec. Part" column refers to what surveryors and other land professionals refer to as an Aliquot Part. The origins and use of such a term mean little to a non-surveyor, and I have chosen to simply call these sub-sections of land what they are: a "Section Part". No matter what we call them, what we are referring to are things like a quarter-section or half-section or quarter-quarter-section. See Appendix "B" for most of the "Section Parts" you will come across (and many you will not) and what size land-parcel they represent.

The "For More Info" column of the Index may seem like a small appendage to each line, but please recognize quickly that this is not so. And to understand the various items you might find here, you need to become familiar with the Legend that appears at the top of each Land Patent Index.

Here is a sample of the Legend . . .

LEGEND

"For More Info . . . " column

A = Authority (Legislative Act, See Appendix "A")
B = Block or Lot (location in Section unknown)
C = Cancelled Patent
F = Fractional Section
G = Group (Multi-Patentee Patent, see Appendix "C")
V = Overlaps another Parcel
R = Re-Issued (Parcel patented more than once)

Most parcels of land will have only one or two of these items in their "For More Info" columns, but when that is not the case, there is often some valuable information to be gained from further investigation. Below, I will explain what each of these items means to you you as a researcher.

A = Authority
(Legislative Act, See Appendix "A")

All Federal Land Patents were issued because some branch of our government (usually the U.S. Congress) passed a law making such a transfer of title possible. And therefore every patent within these pages will have an "A" item next to it in the index. The number after the "A" indicates which item in Appendix "A" holds the citation to the particular law which authorized the transfer of land to the public. As it stands, most of the Public Land data compiled and released by our government, and which serves as the basis for the patents mapped here, concerns itself with "Cash Sale" homesteads. So in some Counties, the law which authorized cash sales will be the primary, if not the only, entry in the Appendix.

B = Block or Lot (location in Section unknown)

A "B" designation in the Index is a tip-off that the EXACT location of the patent within the map is not apparent from the legal description. This Patent will nonetheless be noted within the proper

Section along with any other Lots purchased in the Section. Given the scope of this project (many states and many Counties are being mapped), trying to locate all relevant plats for Lots (if they even exist) and accurately mapping them would have taken one person several lifetimes. But since our primary goal from the onset has been to establish relationships between neighbors and families, very little is lost to this goal since we can still observe who all lived in which Section.

C = Cancelled Patent

A Cancelled Patent is just that: cancelled. Whether the original Patentee forfeited his or her patent due to fraud, a technicality, non-payment, or whatever, the fact remains that it is significant to know who received patents for what parcels and when. A cancellation may be evidence that the Patentee never physically re-located to the land, but does not in itself prove that point. Further evidence would be required to prove that. *See also*, Re-issued Patents, *below*.

F = Fractional Section

A Fractional Section is one that contains less than 640 acres, almost always because of a body of water. The exact size and shape of land-parcels contained in such sections may not be ascertainable, but we map them nonetheless. Just keep in mind that we are not mapping an actual parcel to scale in such instances. Another point to consider is that we have located some fractional sections that are not so designated by the Bureau of Land Management in their data. This means that not all fractional sections have been so identified in our indexes.

G = Group

(Multi-Patentee Patent, see Appendix "C")

A "G" designation means that the Patent was issued to a GROUP of people (Multi-patentees). The "G" will always be followed by a number. Some such groups were quite large and it was impractical if not impossible to display each individual in our maps without unduly affecting readability. EACH person in the group is named in the Index, but they won't all be found on the Map. You will find the name of the first person in such a Group on the map with the Group number next to it, enclosed in [square brackets].

To find all the members of the Group you can either scan the Index for all people with the same Group Number or you can simply refer to Appendix "C" where all members of the Group are listed next to their number.

O = Overlaps another Parcel

An Overlap is one where PART of a parcel of land gets issued on more than one patent. For genealogical purposes, both transfers of title are important and both Patentees are mapped. If the ENTIRE parcel of land is re-issued, that is what we call it, a Re-Issued Patent (*see below*). The number after the "O" indicates the ID for the overlapping Patent(s) contained within the same Index. Like Re-Issued and Cancelled Patents, Overlaps may cause a map-reader to be confused at first, but for genealogical purposes, all of these parties' relationships to the underlying land is important, and therefore, we map them.

R = Re-Issued (Parcel patented more than once)

The label, "Re-issued Patent" describes Patents which were issued more than once for land with the EXACT SAME LEGAL DESCRIPTION. Whether the original patent was cancelled or not, there were a good many parcels which were patented more than once. The number after the "R" indicates the ID for the other Patent contained within the same Index that was for the same land. A quick glance at the map itself within the relevant Section will be the quickest way to find the other Patentee to whom the Parcel was transferred. They should both be mapped in the same general area.

I have gone to some length describing all sorts of anomalies either in the underlying data or in their representation on the maps and indexes in this book. Most of this will bore the most ardent reseracher, but I do this with all due respect to those researchers who will inevitably (and rightfully) ask: *"Why isn't so-and-so's name on the exact spot that the index says it should be?"*

In most cases it will be due to the existence of a Multi-Patentee Patent, a Re-issued Patent, a Cancelled Patent, or Overlapping Parcels named in separate Patents. I don't pretend that this discussion will answer every question along these lines, but I hope it will at least convince you of the complexity of the subject.

Not to despair, this book's companion web-site will offer a way to further explain "odd-ball" or errant data. Each book (County) will have its own web-page or pages to discuss such situations. You can go to www.arphax.com to find the relevant web-page for Sanilac County.

Land Patent Map

On the first two-page spread following each Township's Index to Land Patents, you'll find the corresponding Land Patent Map. And here lies the real heart of our work. For the first time anywhere, researchers will be able to observe and analyze, on a grand scale, most of the original land-owners for an area AND see them mapped in proximity to each one another.

We encourage you to make vigorous use of the accompanying Index described above, but then later, to abandon it, and just stare at these maps for a while. This is a great way to catch misspellings or to find collateral kin you'd not known were in the area.

Each Land Patent Map represents one Congressional Township containing approximately 36-square miles. Each of these square miles is labeled by an accompanying Section Number (1 through 36, in most cases). Keep in mind, that this book concerns itself solely with Sanilac County's patents. Townships which creep into one or more other counties will not be shown in their entirety in any one book. You will need to consult other books, as they become available, in order to view other countys' patents, cities, cemeteries, etc.

But getting back to Sanilac County: each Land Patent Map contains a Statistical Chart that looks like the following:

Township Statistics

Parcels Mapped	:	173
Number of Patents	:	163
Number of Individuals	:	152
Patentees Identified	:	151
Number of Surnames	:	137
Multi-Patentee Parcels	:	4
Oldest Patent Date	:	11/27/1820
Most Recent Patent	:	9/28/1917
Block/Lot Parcels	:	0
Parcels Re-Issued	:	3
Parcels that Overlap	:	8
Cities and Towns	:	6
Cemeteries	:	6

This information may be of more use to a social statistician or historian than a genealogist, but I think all three will find it interesting.

Most of the statistics are self-explanatory, and what is not, was described in the above discussion of the Index's Legend, but I do want to mention a few of them that may affect your understanding of the Land Patent Maps.

First of all, Patents often contain more than one Parcel of land, so it is common for there to be more Parcels than Patents. Also, the Number of Individuals will more often than not, not match the number of Patentees. A Patentee is literally the person or PERSONS named in a patent. So, a Patent may have a multi-person Patentee or a single-person patentee. Nonetheless, we account for all these individuals in our indexes.

On the lower-righthand side of the Patent Map is a Legend which describes various features in the map, including Section Boundaries, Patent (land) Boundaries, Lots (numbered), and Multi-Patentee Group Numbers. You'll also find a "Helpful Hints" Box that will assist you.

One important note: though the vast majority of Patents mapped in this series will prove to be reasonably accurate representations of their actual locations, we cannot claim this for patents lying along state and county lines, or waterways, or that have been platted (lots).

Shifting boundaries and sparse legal descriptions in the GLO data make this a reality that we have nonetheless tried to overcome by estimating these patents' locations the best that we can.

Road Map

On the two-page spread following each Patent Map you will find a Road Map covering the exact same area (the same Congressional Township).

For me, fully exploring the past means that every once in a while I must leave the library and travel to the actual locations where my ancestors once walked and worked the land. Our Township Road Maps are a great place to begin such a quest.

Keep in mind that the scaling and proportion of these maps was chosen in order to squeeze hundreds of people-names, road-names, and place-names into tinier spaces than you would traditionally see. These are not professional road-maps, and like any secondary genealogical source, should be looked upon as an entry-way to original sources—in this case, original patents and applications, professionally produced maps and surveys, etc.

Both our Road Maps and Historical Maps contain cemeteries and city-centers, along with a listing of these on the left-hand side of the map. I should note that I am showing you city center-points, rather than city-limit boundaries, because in many instances, this will represent a place where settlement began. This may be a good time to mention that many cemeteries are located on private property, Always check with a local historical or genealogical society to see if a particular cemetery is publicly accessible (if it is not obviously so). As a final point, look for your surnames among the road-names. You will often be surprised by what you find.

Historical Map

The third and final map in each Map Group is our attempt to display what each Township might have looked like before the advent of modern roads. In frontier times, people were usually more determined to settle near rivers and creeks than they were near roads, which were often few and far between. As was the case with the Road Map, we've included the same cemeteries and city-centers. We've also included railroads, many of which came along before most roads.

While some may claim "Historical Map" to be a bit of a misnomer for this tool, we settled for this label simply because it was almost as accurate as saying "Railroads, Lakes, Rivers, Cities, and Cemeteries," and it is much easier to remember.

In Closing . . .

By way of example, here is *A Really Good Way to Use a Township Map Group*. First, find the person you are researching in the Township's Index to Land Patents, which will direct you to the proper Section and parcel on the Patent Map. But before leaving the Index, scan all the patents within it, looking for other names of interest. Now, turn to the Patent Map and locate your parcels of land. Pay special attention to the names of patent-holders who own land surrounding your person of interest. Next, turn the page and look at the same Section(s) on the Road Map. Note which roads are closest to your parcels and also the names of nearby towns and cemeteries. Using other resources, you may be able to learn of kin who have been buried here, plus, you may choose to visit these cemeteries the next time you are in the area.

Finally, turn to the Historical Map. Look once more at the same Sections where you found your research subject's land. Note the nearby streams, creeks, and other geographical features. You may be surprised to find family names were used to name them, or you may see a name you haven't heard mentioned in years and years—and a new research possibility is born.

Many more techniques for using these *Family Maps* volumes will no doubt be discovered. If from time to time, you will navigate to Sanilac County's web-page at www.arphax.com (use the "Research" link), you can learn new tricks as they become known (or you can share ones you have employed). But for now, you are ready to get started. So, go, and good luck.

– Part I –

The Big Picture

Map A - Where Sanilac County, Michigan Lies Within the State

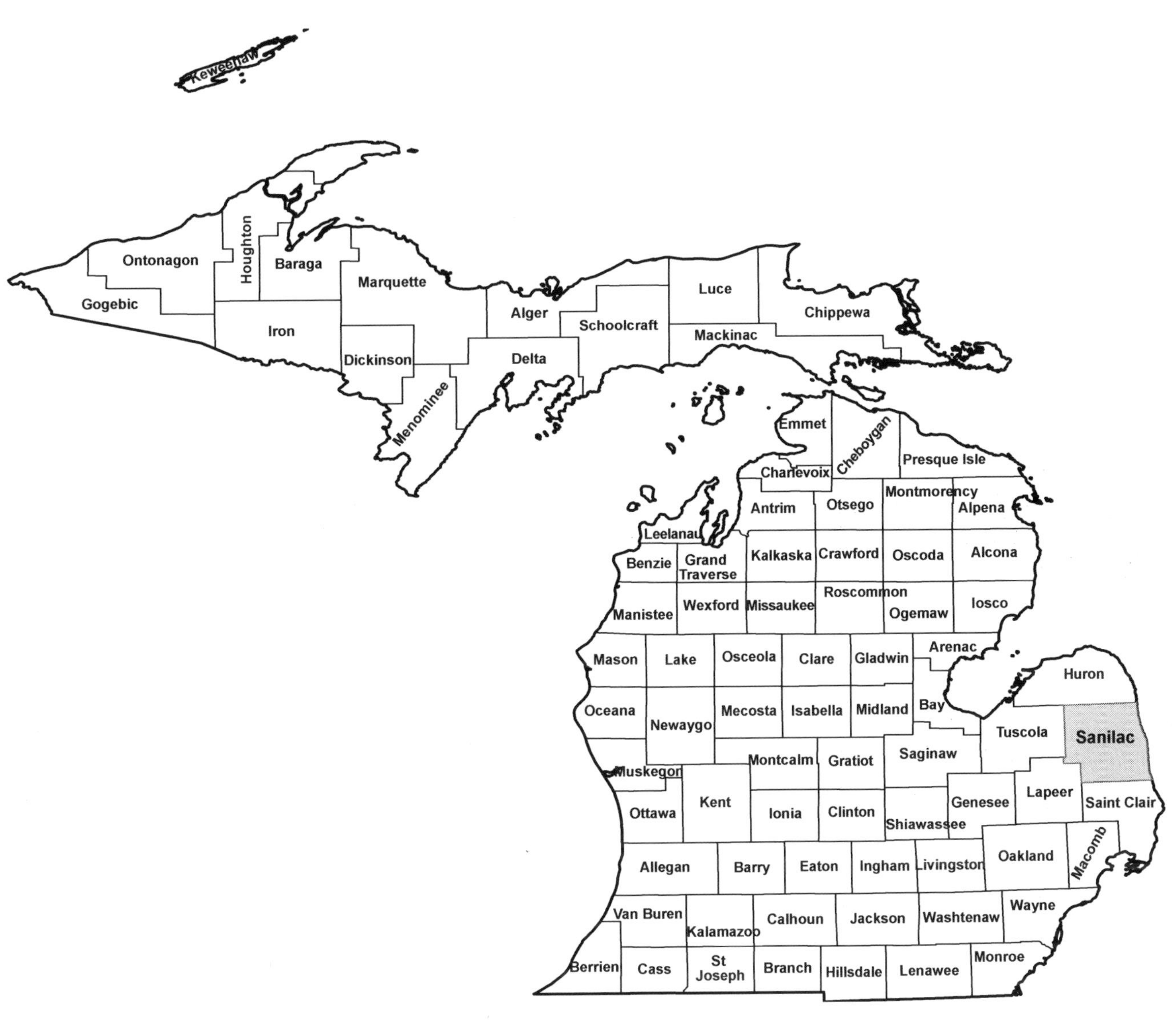

Legend

State Boundary

County Boundaries

Sanilac County, Michigan

Helpful Hints

1 We start with Map "A" which simply shows us where within the State this county lies.

2 Map "B" zooms in further to help us more easily identify surrounding Counties.

3 Map "C" zooms in even further to reveal the Congressional Townships that either lie within or intersect Sanilac County.

Map B - Sanilac County, Michigan and Surrounding Counties

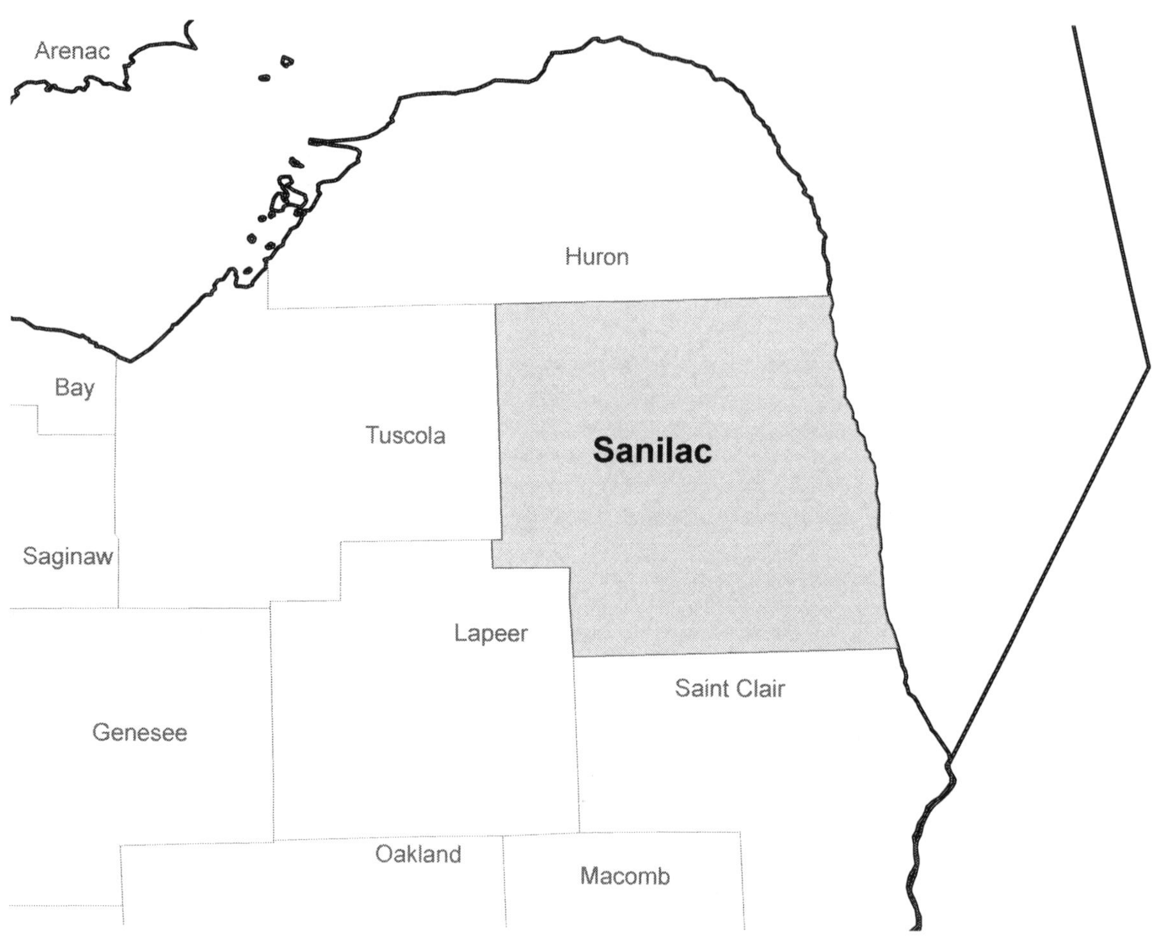

Legend

State Boundaries (when applicable)

County Boundaries

Helpful Hints

1 Many Patent-holders and their families settled across county lines. It is always a good idea to check nearby counties for your families.

2 Refer to Map "A" to see a broader view of where this County lies within the State, and Map "C" to see which Congressional Townships lie within Sanilac County.

Map C - Congressional Townships of Sanilac County, Michigan

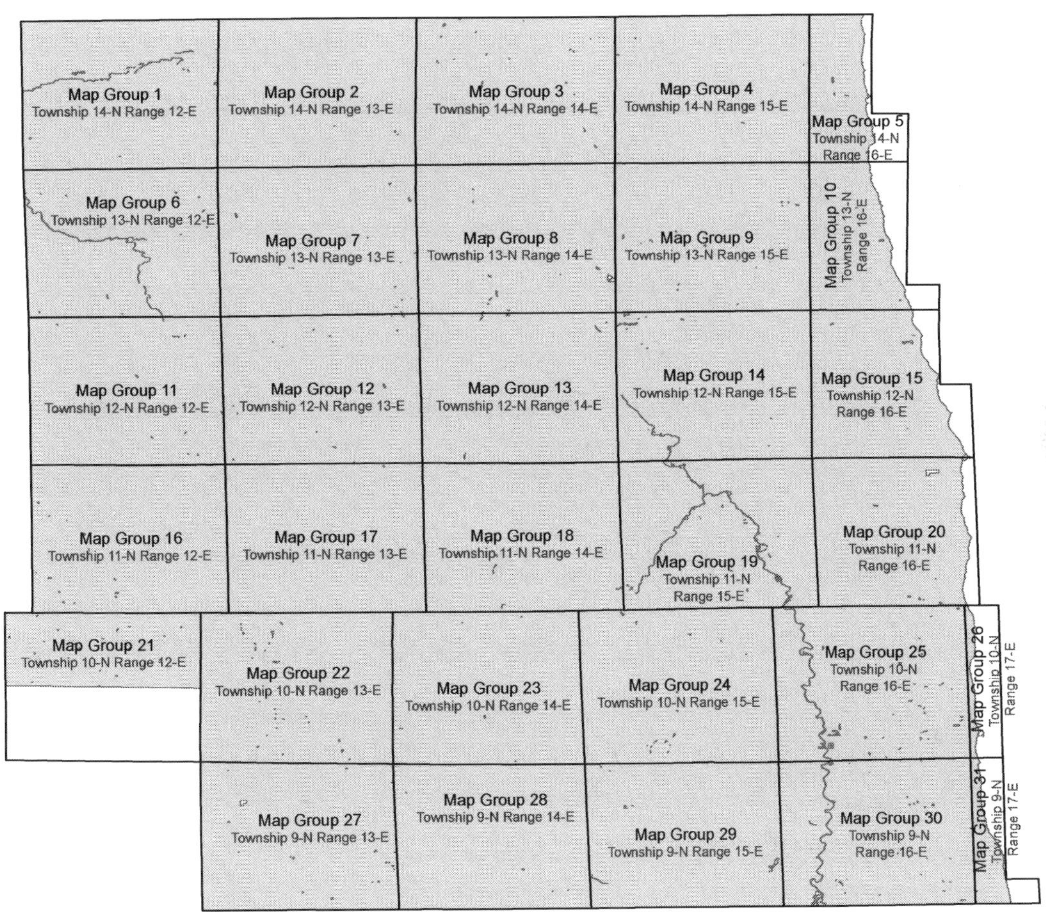

Legend

Sanilac County, Michigan

Congressional Townships

Helpful Hints

1 Many Patent-holders and their families settled across county lines. It is always a good idea to check nearby counties for your families (See Map "B").

2 Refer to Map "A" to see a broader view of where this county lies within the State, and Map "B" for a view of the counties surrounding Sanilac County.

Map D Index: Cities & Towns of Sanilac County, Michigan

The following represents the Cities and Towns of Sanilac County (along with the corresponding Map Group in which each is *found). Cities and Towns are displayed in both the Road and Historical maps in the Group.*

City/Town	Map Group No.
Amadore	30
Applegate	19
Argyle	7
Austin Center	2
Birch Beach	31
Blue Water Beach	31
Brown City	27
Carsonville	14
Cash	18
Charleston	4
Croswell	25
Cumber	2
Decker	11
Deckerville	9
Elmer	12
Forester	15
Forestville	5
Freidberger	2
Great Lakes Beach	31
Hemans	11
Huronia Heights	31
Juhl	17
Laing	7
Lexington	26
Lexington Heights	31
Marlette	21
McGregor	14
Melvin	28
Minden City	3
New Greenleaf	1
Palms	3
Peatville	3
Peck	23
Pine Hill (historical)	20
Port Sanilac	15
Richmondville	10
Roseburg	29
Sandusky	18
Shabbona	6
Snover	12
Speaker	28
Tyre	2
Valley Center	27
Watertown	18
Wickware	1

Map D - Cities & Towns of Sanilac County, Michigan

New Greenleaf
Map Group 1
Township 14-N Range 12-E
Wickware

Tyre
Map Group 2
Township 14-N Range 13-E
Cumber
Austin Center
Freidberger

Minden City
Map Group 3
Township 14-N Range 14-E
Peatville
Palms

Charleston
Map Group 4
Township 14-N Range 15-E

Forestville
Map Group 5
Township 14-N Range 16-E

Map Group 6
Township 13-N Range 12-E
Shabbona

Argyle
Map Group 7
Township 13-N Range 13-E
Laing

Map Group 8
Township 13-N Range 14-E

Map Group 9
Township 13-N Range 15-E
Deckerville

Map Group 10
Township 13-N
Range 16-E
Richmondville

Hemans
Decker
Map Group 11
Township 12-N Range 12-E

Map Group 12
Township 12-N Range 13-E
Snover
Elmer

Map Group 13
Township 12-N Range 14-E

McGregor
Map Group 14
Township 12-N Range 15-E
Carsonville

Forester
Map Group 15
Township 12-N
Range 16-E
Port Sanilac

Map Group 16
Township 11-N Range 12-E

Map Group 17
Township 11-N Range 13-E
Juhl

Sandusky
Map Group 18
Township 11-N Range 14-E
Cash
Watertown

Map Group 19
Township 11-N Range 15-E
Applegate

Map Group 20
Township 11-N
Range 16-E
Pine Hill (historical)

Marlette
Map Group 21
Township 10-N Range 12-E

Map Group 22
Township 10-N Range 13-E

Map Group 23
Township 10-N Range 14-E
Peck

Map Group 24
Township 10-N Range 15-E

Map Group 25
Township 10-N Range 16-E
Croswell

Map Group 26
Township 10-N
Range 17-E
Lexington

Map Group 27
Township 9-N Range 13-E
Brown City
Valley Center

Map Group 28
Township 9-N Range 14-E
Speaker
Melvin

Map Group 29
Township 9-N Range 15-E
Roseburg

Map Group 30
Township 9-N Range 16-E
Lexington Heights
Great Lakes Beach
Huronia Heights
Blue Water Beach
Birch Beach
Amadore

Map Group 31
Township 9-N Range 17-E

Legend

Sanilac County, Michigan

Congressional Townships

Helpful Hints

1 Cities and towns are marked only at their center-points as published by the USGS and/or NationalAtlas.gov. This often enables us to more closely approximate where these might have existed when first settled.

2 To see more specifically where these Cities & Towns are located within the county, refer to both the Road and Historical maps in the Map-Group referred to above. See also, the Map "D" Index on the opposite page.

Map E Index: Cemeteries of Sanilac County, Michigan

The following represents many of the Cemeteries of Sanilac County, along with the corresponding Township Map Group in which each *is found. Cemeteries are displayed in both the Road and Historical maps in the Map Groups referred to below.*

Cemetery	Map Group No.
Argyle Cem.	7
Carmen Cem.	30
Delaware Cem.	4
Downing Cem.	8
East Marion Cem.	9
Evergreen Cem.	6
Fremont Cem.	29
Germania Cem.	16
Greenwood Cem.	18
Hoppenworth Cem.	20
Huckins Cem.	25
Hyslop Cem.	17
Johnson Cem.	11
Juhl Cem.	17
Kerr Cem.	21
Lakeview Cem.	30
Lee Cem.	19
Linwood Cem.	4
Long Cem.	25
Marlette Cem.	21
McLeish Cem.	16
Mills Cem.	9
Minden City Cem.	3
Moore Cem.	12
Moshier Cem.	11
Mount Hope Cem.	23
Mount Hope Cem.	25
Mount Lion Cem.	14
Mount Pleasant Cem.	2
Omard Cem.	22
Ridge Cem.	20
Rosbury Cem.	14
Saint Denis Cem.	25
Saint Elizabeth Cem.	21
Saint John Cem.	20
Saint Johns Cem.	5
Saint Marys Cem.	19
Saint Marys Cem.	20
Saint Marys Cem.	27
Saint Patricks Cem.	3
Snover Memorial Park	12
Steckley Cem.	19
Valley Center Cem.	27
West Delaware Cem.	4
Wheatland Cem.	7
Wixson Cem.	30
Worth Township Cem.	30
Wright Cem.	9
Zion Cem.	18

Map E - Cemeteries of Sanilac County, Michigan

Minden City
Map Group 1
Township 14-N Range 12-E
Map Group 2
Township 14-N Range 13-E
Mount Pleasant
Map Group 3
Township 14-N Range 14-E
Saint Patricks
West Delaware
Linwood
Map Group 4
Township 14-N Range 15-E
Delaware
Saint Johns
Map Group 5
Township 14-N
Range 16-E
Map Group 6
Township 13-N Range 12-E
Evergreen
Wheatland
Map Group 7
Township 13-N Range 13-E
Argyle
Map Group 8
Township 13-N Range 14-E
Downing
Mills
Map Group 9
Township 13-N Range 15-E
Wright
East Marion
Map Group 10
Township 13-N
Range 16-E
Johnson
Moshier
Map Group 11
Township 12-N Range 12-E
Map Group 12
Township 12-N Range 13-E
Moore
Snover Memorial Park
Map Group 13
Township 12-N Range 14-E
Rosbury
Mount Lion
Map Group 14
Township 12-N Range 15-E
Map Group 15
Township 12-N
Range 16-E
Saint Marys
Germania
McLeish
Map Group 16
Township 11-N Range 12-E
Hyslop
Map Group 17
Township 11-N Range 13-E
Juhl
Greenwood
Map Group 18
Township 11-N Range 14-E
Zion
Saint Marys
Lee
Map Group 19
Township 11-N Range 15-E
Steckley
Map Group 20
Township 11-N
Range 16-E
Ridge
Saint John
Hoppenworth
Saint Elizabeth
Marlette
Kerr
Map Group 21
Township 10-N Range 12-E
Map Group 22
Township 10-N Range 13-E
Omard
Map Group 23
Township 10-N Range 14-E
Mount Hope
Map Group 24
Township 10-N Range 15-E
Map Group 25
Township 10-N Range 16-E
Long
Saint Denis
Huckins
Mount Hope
Map Group 26
Township 10-N
Range 17-E
Wixson
Lakeview
Evergreen Saint Marys
Map Group 27
Township 9-N Range 13-E
Valley Center
Map Group 28
Township 9-N Range 14-E
Fremont
Map Group 29
Township 9-N Range 15-E
Map Group 30
Township 9-N Range 16-E
Carmen
Worth Township
Map Group 31
Township 9-N
Range 17-E

Legend

Sanilac County, Michigan

Congressional Townships

Helpful Hints

1 Cemeteries are marked at locations as published by the USGS and/or NationalAtlas.gov.

2 To see more specifically where these Cemeteries are located, refer to the Road & Historical maps in the Map-Group referred to above. See also, the Map "E" Index on the opposite page to make sure you don't miss any of the Cemeteries located within this Congressional township.

Surnames in Sanilac County, Michigan Patents

The following list represents the ***surnames*** that we have located in Sanilac County, Michigan Patents and the number of parcels that we have mapped for each one. Here is a quick way to determine the existence (or not) of Patents to be found in the subsequent indexes and maps of this volume.

Surname	# of Land Parcels
ABBIHL	1
ABBOTT	7
ABEL	2
ACHESON	3
AHEARN	3
AITKEN	2
AITKIN	1
ALCORN	1
ALDERTON	2
ALEXANDER	1
ALLAN	2
ALLEN	8
ALLMAN	3
ALWAY	2
ANDERSON	6
ANDREWS	4
ARMSTED	1
ARMSTRONG	4
ASH	7
ASHLEY	2
ATKINSON	1
AUBLE	1
AVERY	11
AYLSWORTH	1
AYRAULT	6
BABCOCK	2
BACKUS	1
BACON	1
BADGERS	1
BADGROW	1
BAER	1
BAGG	1
BAILEY	4
BAILIE	3
BAKER	5
BALDWIN	4
BALL	2
BANCROFT	4
BANKS	3
BARBER	2
BARDWELL	5
BARNARD	10
BARRY	2
BARSTOW	2
BARTLETT	2
BARWICK	4
BASHFORD	1
BATCHELDER	11
BAUGHMAN	1
BEACH	42
BEAL	11
BEARD	7
BEATYS	4
BECKETT	2
BECKWITH	39
BEHR	1
BEISANG	1
BELDEN	2
BELL	4
BENNAWAY	1
BENNET	3
BENNETT	4
BERDEN	2
BERNEY	1
BETTERMANN	1
BEZEMEK	2
BEZENEK	1
BHONONE	1
BIEBER	3
BIGNEY	1
BINNINGA	1
BISBEE	1
BISHOP	5
BLACKMAIR	1
BLACKMAR	2
BLAKE	2
BLAKESLEY	2
BLASHILL	1
BLINDBERRY	1
BLINDBURY	2
BODDY	3
BOGERT	1
BOISE	2
BOND	4
BOOTHBY	1
BORLAND	2
BOTSFORD	2
BOTTOMLEY	4
BOUTAIGER	1
BOWMAN	2
BOWSER	3
BOYD	3
BOYS	1
BRABBS	5
BRACKENRIDGE	1
BRADBEK	1
BRADEN	1
BRADLEY	1
BRADY	5
BRANAGAN	2
BRANNAGAN	1
BRASEBRIDGE	2
BRAUN	3
BREADER	1
BRENNAN	1
BRENNEN	1
BRIGHT	3
BRIMLEY	1
BROADBRIDGE	2
BROCKELSBY	1
BROCKWAY	5
BRODIE	1
BROOKS	3
BROWN	19
BROWNE	1
BROWNING	2
BRUCE	1
BRYANT	5
BRYCE	3
BUCHANAN	1
BUEL	6
BUELL	2
BUGBEE	5
BUNKER	22
BURCH	2
BURCHAM	1
BURGER	1
BURGESS	1
BURK	2
BURLINGGAME	1
BURMEISTER	1
BURNHAM	1
BURNS	2
BURT	2
BURTCH	4
BURTON	1
BURTT	1
BUTHE	1
BUTLER	8
BUTTERFIELD	1
BYERS	1
BYRNE	1
BYRNES	1
CADY	1
CALHOUN	2
CALKINS	1
CAMERON	3
CAMP	2
CAMPBELL	13
CANEDY	2
CANHAM	3
CARLETON	3
CARLISLE	1
CARLTON	1
CARNEY	2
CARPENTER	2
CARRINGTON	4
CARROLAN	1
CARROLL	13
CARSON	2
CARTER	1
CARWELL	1
CARY	3
CASE	1
CASH	5
CASLER	1
CASTER	1
CATALINE	1
CAVE	1
CAVEN	1
CAWOOD	3
CHAPEL	1
CHASE	27
CHIPMAN	4
CHRIST	1
CHRISTIAN	1
CICOTT	1
CICOTTE	6
CLAPSADDLE	2
CLARK	12
CLARKE	3
CLARY	4
CLAYTON	3
CLEAVELAND	1
CLELAND	9
CLENDENIN	1
CLIFFORD	1
CLIFTON	1
CLINE	1
COALTER	2
COBURN	42
COCHRAN	1
COCOMAN	3
CODDINGTON	2
COE	7
COFFEY	1
COFFINGER	1
COFFY	1
COLBORN	5
COLE	6
COLLINA	1
COLLINGS	2
COLMAN	1
COMMER	1
COMPANY	13
COMSTOCK	2
CONANT	2
CONAT	2
CONDON	1
CONNOR	1
COOK	6
COREY	3
CORNELL	1
COURTNEY	1
COUSE	1
COVIL	3
COXE	1
CRAIG	3
CRAMPTON	5
CRANDALL	1
CROCKER	3
CROCKERD	1
CROCKET	1
CRORY	2
CROSS	2
CROWELL	1
CROWLEY	1
CUMMINGS	14
CUNNINGHAM	1
CURN	4
CURRIE	2
CURTIS	3
CURWELL	4
DALE	3
DANCEY	2
DARCY	2
DAVENPORT	1
DAVIS	37
DE GROAT	1
DE GROATE	1
DEAN	1
DECKER	7
DEEGAN	4
DEGRAW	2
DEIGAN	1
DELAVAN	10
DELL	2
DENSHAM	1

Surname	# of Land Parcels
DENSHAW	1
DERING	2
DERR	2
DESOTELL	1
DEUSHAM	1
DEVAL	2
DEVINE	1
DEWEY	2
DEY	1
DEYOE	2
DIAMOND	2
DICKINSON	51
DICKSON	2
DIETER	1
DIMOND	5
DOAN	1
DODGE	3
DOERING	2
DOLE	1
DONAHUE	1
DONALD	1
DONALLAN	2
DONELLAN	1
DONELLY	1
DONNAVAN	2
DONNELLAN	3
DONNER	2
DONOLON	1
DOPP	1
DORING	1
DOUGLASS	5
DOWLING	4
DOWNING	2
DOZING	2
DROWN	1
DUCAT	1
DUDLEY	1
DUNLAP	1
DUNLEY	1
DUNLOP	3
DURR	3
DUVAL	1
DWIGHT	7
DYER	3
EARLES	3
EASTMAN	2
EATON	1
ECKARDT	2
EDDY	3
EDMONDS	7
EDWARDS	3
EINSIDER	1
ELDRED	1
ELLIS	1
ELWIN	1
ENNEST	5
ERBE	1
ERITY	2
ERSKIN	1
ERSKINE	13
ESELE	1
EVOY	1
EWER	22
FALKENBURY	4
FARNSWORTH	20
FARRELL	1
FAY	3
FEAD	1
FENTON	4
FERGUSON	4

Surname	# of Land Parcels
FERRIS	1
FIELD	2
FIFIELD	3
FIKE	2
FINLAYSON	1
FINLEY	3
FISH	11
FISHER	5
FITCH	2
FITZPATRICK	1
FLEMING	2
FLETCHER	4
FOELSZ	1
FOLEY	3
FORBES	4
FORD	3
FOSTER	1
FOX	6
FRALICK	1
FRANKE	3
FREHSE	2
FRENCH	3
FYE	1
GALBRAITH	11
GALLEY	1
GARA	1
GARDNER	1
GARVIN	2
GECK	1
GEEL	7
GEORGE	1
GETTY	2
GIBSON	3
GILBRAITH	1
GILL	3
GILLETT	1
GILLIGAN	1
GINSBIGLER	1
GLENNIE	1
GLOVER	8
GOETCHINS	4
GOIT	1
GOODRICH	7
GOODWIN	5
GORDON	4
GOULD	5
GRAHAM	3
GRANDY	1
GRANGER	4
GRANT	2
GRAVES	2
GRAY	7
GREAVES	2
GREEN	4
GREENLEAF	3
GREENMAN	2
GREGG	4
GRICE	1
GRIGG	1
GROW	2
GUTHRIE	3
GYSTER	1
HACKER	1
HACKETT	1
HADDOW	3
HADLEY	9
HAEBERLE	1
HAGER	1
HAGGERTY	1
HAIGHT	1

Surname	# of Land Parcels
HAILFAX	2
HALE	1
HALFMANN	1
HALL	16
HALWERSON	2
HAMILTON	8
HAMMOND	3
HAMPTMAN	1
HANDY	1
HANES	3
HANNA	1
HANSEN	1
HARDEN	1
HARDER	3
HARDING	1
HARDY	1
HARKER	1
HARLOW	2
HARNACK	1
HARPER	5
HARRINGTON	1
HARRIS	3
HARTEE	3
HARTEN	1
HARTSHORN	1
HARTWELL	2
HARTWICK	1
HATHAWAY	2
HAWKS	2
HAY	19
HAYES	4
HAYNES	5
HAZEN	2
HEARN	3
HEATHCOTE	3
HEBENTON	1
HEDRICK	1
HEEBENER	1
HEIDE	1
HEILIG	1
HENDERSON	1
HENRY	3
HERRICK	1
HERTEL	2
HEYMAN	1
HICKEY	2
HIGGINS	1
HILL	9
HILLEBRAND	2
HILLS	1
HINKSON	3
HIRSCHMAN	2
HOBSON	2
HOCHSTETTER	1
HODGKINS	1
HOFFMAN	1
HOFFMANN	2
HOGAN	4
HOLBERT	2
HOLCOMB	4
HOLLISTER	2
HOLLSTEIN	3
HOLMES	1
HOMER	1
HOMUTH	4
HOOLE	2
HOPKINS	1
HOSACK	1
HOUSE	6
HOUSELL	1

Surname	# of Land Parcels
HOWARD	28
HOWELL	1
HOWEY	1
HOWIE	1
HOYT	5
HUBBARD	40
HUBEL	2
HUBINGER	3
HUCKINS	5
HUGHES	1
HULSART	3
HULVERSON	1
HULVORSON	2
HUNT	4
HUNTER	11
HURD	15
HURLEY	2
HUSBAND	1
HYSLOP	2
INGRAHAM	1
IRVING	1
IRWIN	5
JENNY	1
JEX	1
JOHNS	1
JOHNSON	21
JOINER	1
JOLLY	2
JONES	22
JORDAN	9
JOWETT	1
JURN	1
JURY	1
KAUFMANN	1
KE_Y_KE_SIK	1
KELLAND	1
KELLEY	7
KELLY	3
KELSEY	1
KELSO	1
KENGOTT	2
KENNY	1
KENYON	1
KERCHEVAL	2
KEYS	2
KEYWORTH	1
KIBBEE	11
KIDD	3
KING	18
KINNE	2
KINSLEY	4
KINY	1
KIPP	1
KIPPER	2
KIRBY	1
KIRKBRIDE	3
KIRKPATRICK	2
KIRKWOOD	3
KLEIN	3
KLINGHAMER	1
KLOSTERMANN	1
KNAPP	1
KNIGHT	3
KNOX	2
KOLAR	1
KOLTS	3
KOTZKE	2
KRITZMANN	1
KROETSCH	4
KRUPP	1

Surname	# of Land Parcels
KURTZ	1
LACASSE	2
LAKE	2
LAMB	7
LAMBERT	1
LANCASTER	1
LANE	2
LANGE	1
LANGENBUCK	3
LAPPIN	2
LAUREL	3
LAVIN	4
LAW	1
LECHTENBURG	1
LEE	6
LEEPLA	2
LEINS	3
LEITCH	4
LENNON	1
LENSE	1
LENTY	1
LEONARD	14
LEONHARD	2
LESTER	3
LEVAGOOD	1
LEWIS	2
LICHTENBERG	7
LIDDELL	2
LINCE	1
LINDNER	2
LINDSAY	2
LINDSEY	1
LINK	2
LITT	2
LITTLE	1
LIVINGWAY	2
LOCK	1
LOCKE	1
LOOBY	1
LOSAYA	1
LOUNT	1
LOWE	1
LUCAS	1
LUCE	15
LYNN	1
LYON	27
MACLACHLAN	3
MACOMBER	5
MACY	9
MAHON	1
MAIRE	3
MALONE	3
MANION	1
MANNEY	3
MANS	1
MANSS	2
MANWARING	2
MARECK	3
MARIN	1
MARREDETH	7
MARRELL	1
MARRIOTT	3
MARSHALL	2
MARTINDALE	4
MARVIN	2
MASDAN	1
MASDEN	1
MASKELL	2
MASON	24
MASSEY	4

Surname	# of Land Parcels
MASTEN	1
MASTERSON	1
MATTESON	1
MATTISON	1
MAXSON	1
MAY	1
MAYES	1
MAYNARD	1
MCALPIN	3
MCALPINE	3
MCBRIDE	3
MCCABE	1
MCCARTHY	3
MCCLURE	6
MCCOLLOM	1
MCCONNELL	5
MCCORMACK	1
MCCORMICK	8
MCCREDIE	1
MCDONALD	6
MCDOUGALL	4
MCEACHIN	3
MCFARLAND	3
MCGILL	2
MCGINN	14
MCGINNIS	1
MCGRATH	3
MCGREGOR	4
MCGUGAN	2
MCHUGH	1
MCINNIS	1
MCINTOSH	6
MCINTYRE	3
MCKAY	3
MCKELLAR	1
MCKENZIE	4
MCKIE	6
MCLACHLAN	5
MCLACHLIN	1
MCLAREN	1
MCLEAN	5
MCLEISH	2
MCLELLAN	3
MCMAHON	3
MCMILLAN	2
MCMILLEN	1
MCMULDROCH	2
MCPHAIL	12
MCPHEE	2
MCRAE	8
MCRAY	3
MCVANE	1
MEEHAN	1
MELVILLE	3
MERCHANT	3
MEREDEN	1
MERREDETH	1
MERRILL	36
MERRILLS	1
MERRIMAN	5
METCALF	2
MICHIGAN	1
MIDDAUGH	2
MILES	3
MILLER	26
MILLS	38
MINARD	2
MINER	1
MITCHELL	1
MIZNER	20

Surname	# of Land Parcels
MOFFAT	7
MOLLOY	1
MONTGOMERY	3
MONTNEY	1
MOODY	1
MOONY	5
MOORE	25
MORELL	1
MORGAN	5
MORRILL	1
MORRIS	1
MORRISON	1
MORSE	33
MORTON	1
MOSHIER	10
MOSS	1
MUDGE	1
MULLINS	1
MUMA	1
MUNFORD	1
MUNRO	2
MURDOCK	1
MURPHY	5
MURRAY	3
MYERS	2
NAGESIK	1
NESTER	3
NEUMANN	2
NEVILLE	1
NEWMAN	3
NEWTON	1
NICHOL	3
NICHOLS	2
NICHOLSON	1
NICOL	3
NICOLL	1
NISBET	1
NIXON	4
NOBLE	4
NOLAN	2
NORMANDIE	2
NORRIS	1
NORTHRUP	1
NOTLEY	1
NYE	3
OAKES	3
OBRIEN	1
OCALLAGHAN	1
ODLAUM	1
OGDEN	3
OLDFIELD	1
ORTON	3
ORVIS	6
OSEWALD	1
OSGOOD	2
OSWALD	1
OWEN	2
PACE	1
PACK	16
PAGANETTI	2
PAISLEY	1
PAKE	3
PALMER	4
PALMS	3
PAPST	1
PARKER	27
PARKIN	2
PARKINSON	1
PARMELY	1
PARTRIDGE	4

Surname	# of Land Parcels
PATTERSON	1
PATTISON	2
PATTON	1
PAUL	1
PEASLEE	1
PEGSHA	2
PENSIONNAL	3
PERKINS	8
PERRET	1
PETER	8
PETERS	2
PETTY	1
PHELPS	4
PHILIPS	2
PHILLIPS	2
PICKARD	1
PIERCE	1
PIFER	1
PITTS	3
POLAND	1
POLLARD	5
PORTER	5
POST	5
POTTS	5
POWER	1
PRATT	4
PRESLEY	1
PREVOST	1
PROCTOR	1
PROVOST	1
PURMAN	1
PURMANN	1
PUTNAM	2
QUAY	1
RAMSAY	1
RATTRAY	1
RAUH	1
RAYMOND	3
READ	3
REDPATH	2
REED	1
REEVE	57
REINELT	10
REMICK	2
REYNOLDS	1
RIBBEL	1
RICE	4
RICHARDS	1
RITTENDORF	1
ROADHOUSE	3
ROBB	1
ROBERTS	2
ROBERTSON	1
ROBINSON	7
ROBISON	2
ROBSON	3
ROCKWELL	4
ROGERS	1
ROLLAS	2
ROSBERRY	1
ROSE	1
ROSS	9
ROTH	1
ROVOLT	1
RUDD	1
RUDEL	1
RUMNEY	1
RUNKWITZ	2
RUSSELSMITH	2
RUST	9

Surname	# of Land Parcels
RYAN	3
RYANS	2
RYCKMAN	4
RYEN	1
SABIN	2
SALSBURY	2
SAMPLE	5
SANBORN	39
SANDERSON	2
SANSBURN	2
SARGENT	2
SARSFIELD	1
SARTWELL	1
SAUDER	2
SAUNDERS	5
SAWYER	1
SCHAFER	1
SCHAGENE	3
SCHEDINA	4
SCHLEGEL	2
SCHMELZ	1
SCHNEIDER	4
SCHOLTZ	1
SCHOLZ	1
SCHREIN	2
SCHUBEL	1
SCHULZ	1
SCHUMACHER	1
SCHWEIZER	5
SCHWIGART	2
SCOLLAY	4
SCOTT	5
SEAL	2
SEAMAN	1
SEAMANS	1
SEARS	3
SEBOLD	1
SEDER	5
SEGRET	1
SELLARS	2
SELTZER	1
SEYMOUR	2
SHANE	1
SHARLOW	1
SHARP	1
SHARRARD	2
SHEA	2
SHEFFER	2
SHEIBLE	1
SHELDEN	1
SHELDON	3
SHELL	13
SHEPHARD	2
SHERWOOD	1
SHILL	2
SHIRLEY	2
SHRIGLEY	1
SIBLEY	22
SILBEY	1
SILVERTHORN	1
SIMMS	3
SIMONS	3
SINCLAIR	3
SISCHO	1
SKINNER	1
SLADE	1
SLY	3
SMITH	42
SNAY	1
SNELL	7
SNOVER	3
SNOWDEN	1
SNOWDIN	1
SNYDER	1
SOMERVILLE	1
SOMMERHALDER	1
SOMMERVILLE	4
SON	1
SOPER	2
SOULE	1
SPARLING	2
SPEARMAN	1
SPENCER	5
SPRING	4
STACEY	1
STACUM	2
STAFFORD	1
STEBBINS	3
STEEL	3
STEENSON	1
STEEVENS	19
STEINER	1
STEINHOFF	2
STENSON	1
STEPHENS	9
STEVENS	35
STEVENSON	15
STEWARD	1
STEWART	3
STILSON	16
STILWELL	6
STINSON	2
STOCKWELL	1
STOVER	1
STOWELL	1
STRONG	1
STROUD	2
STUART	1
SULLIVAN	1
SULLIVIN	1
SUMNER	1
SUTTON	2
SWAFFER	1
SWART	1
SWEETSER	4
SWIFT	3
SWINSTON	1
TAMBURAT	3
TATE	3
TAYLOR	10
TEMISON	1
TEMPLE	3
TERRIL	1
THAYER	10
THEABO	1
THEBOULT	1
THIBODEAU	1
THOMAS	5
THOMPSON	2
THOMSON	1
THORNTON	2
THROOP	3
TOBIN	3
TODD	10
TOOL	5
TOWER	1
TRAINER	2
TRATHEN	1
TRAVIS	1
TROWBRIDGE	24
TUCKER	2
TWISS	5
TWIST	2
TYLDEN	1
TYLER	3
UHL	1
URIDGE	5
VACHI	3
VAN ALLEN	4
VAN CAMP	8
VAN DUSEN	2
VAN LOAN	2
VAN NEST	1
VAN SICKLE	1
VANDERBURGH	9
VANDUSEN	1
VARNUM	1
VARTY	3
VARTZ	1
VATER	1
VERDRIES	1
VIETS	1
VINCENT	2
VOGAL	1
WAHLY	4
WALDO	3
WALDON	1
WALKER	14
WALLACE	8
WALLIS	2
WALSH	9
WARD	24
WARING	1
WARNER	3
WARPOOL	1
WARREN	13
WATERBURY	4
WATERS	4
WATKINS	1
WATROUS	3
WATSON	5
WAY	3
WEBSTER	4
WEHR	2
WEISEMBERGER	1
WEITZEL	1
WELCH	2
WELLES	2
WELLS	28
WELSH	2
WESLEY	1
WHALES	1
WHEELER	14
WHEELOCK	4
WHITAKER	2
WHITE	10
WHITMAN	12
WHITNEY	5
WIGGINS	1
WIGHT	19
WILDFONG	3
WILKINSON	1
WILLCOX	3
WILLERTON	1
WILLIAMS	6
WILLIS	3
WILLITS	1
WILLITTS	1
WILLOUGHBY	1
WILLSON	2
WILSON	17
WILTSIE	2
WING	3
WISSON	1
WITHAM	1
WIXSON	37
WODRASKA	1
WOOD	4
WOODRUFF	1
WOODS	55
WOODWARD	1
WOOLLEY	1
WRACHA	1
WRESCHE	1
WRIGHT	12
WYMAN	5
YAKE	3
YATES	1
YORKE	2
YOUNG	5
ZAUNER	2
ZOLL	1

Surname/Township Index

This Index allows you to determine which *Township Map Group(s)* contain individuals with the following surnames. Each *Map Group* has a corresponding full-name index of all individuals who obtained patents for land within its Congressional township's borders. After each index you will find the Patent Map to which it refers, and just thereafter, you can view the township's Road Map and Historical Map, with the latter map displaying streams, railroads, and more.

So, once you find your Surname here, proceed to the Index at the beginning of the **Map Group** indicated below.

Surname	Map Group	Parcels of Land	Meridian/Township/Range		
ABBIHL	**24**	1	Michigan-Toledo Strip	10-N	15-E
ABBOTT	**21**	2	Michigan-Toledo Strip	10-N	12-E
" "	**20**	2	Michigan-Toledo Strip	11-N	16-E
" "	**9**	2	Michigan-Toledo Strip	13-N	15-E
" "	**8**	1	Michigan-Toledo Strip	13-N	14-E
ABEL	**21**	1	Michigan-Toledo Strip	10-N	12-E
" "	**22**	1	Michigan-Toledo Strip	10-N	13-E
ACHESON	**24**	3	Michigan-Toledo Strip	10-N	15-E
AHEARN	**21**	3	Michigan-Toledo Strip	10-N	12-E
AITKEN	**29**	2	Michigan-Toledo Strip	9-N	15-E
AITKIN	**29**	1	Michigan-Toledo Strip	9-N	15-E
ALCORN	**11**	1	Michigan-Toledo Strip	12-N	12-E
ALDERTON	**9**	2	Michigan-Toledo Strip	13-N	15-E
ALEXANDER	**13**	1	Michigan-Toledo Strip	12-N	14-E
ALLAN	**30**	2	Michigan-Toledo Strip	9-N	16-E
ALLEN	**15**	3	Michigan-Toledo Strip	12-N	16-E
" "	**23**	2	Michigan-Toledo Strip	10-N	14-E
" "	**30**	2	Michigan-Toledo Strip	9-N	16-E
" "	**5**	1	Michigan-Toledo Strip	14-N	16-E
ALLMAN	**12**	3	Michigan-Toledo Strip	12-N	13-E
ALWAY	**4**	2	Michigan-Toledo Strip	14-N	15-E
ANDERSON	**30**	2	Michigan-Toledo Strip	9-N	16-E
" "	**16**	1	Michigan-Toledo Strip	11-N	12-E
" "	**20**	1	Michigan-Toledo Strip	11-N	16-E
" "	**3**	1	Michigan-Toledo Strip	14-N	14-E
" "	**28**	1	Michigan-Toledo Strip	9-N	14-E
ANDREWS	**30**	2	Michigan-Toledo Strip	9-N	16-E
" "	**23**	1	Michigan-Toledo Strip	10-N	14-E
" "	**27**	1	Michigan-Toledo Strip	9-N	13-E
ARMSTED	**7**	1	Michigan-Toledo Strip	13-N	13-E
ARMSTRONG	**25**	2	Michigan-Toledo Strip	10-N	16-E
" "	**20**	1	Michigan-Toledo Strip	11-N	16-E
" "	**12**	1	Michigan-Toledo Strip	12-N	13-E
ASH	**23**	3	Michigan-Toledo Strip	10-N	14-E
" "	**18**	2	Michigan-Toledo Strip	11-N	14-E
" "	**17**	1	Michigan-Toledo Strip	11-N	13-E
" "	**19**	1	Michigan-Toledo Strip	11-N	15-E
ASHLEY	**25**	2	Michigan-Toledo Strip	10-N	16-E
ATKINSON	**27**	1	Michigan-Toledo Strip	9-N	13-E
AUBLE	**1**	1	Michigan-Toledo Strip	14-N	12-E
AVERY	**29**	5	Michigan-Toledo Strip	9-N	15-E
" "	**12**	2	Michigan-Toledo Strip	12-N	13-E
" "	**30**	2	Michigan-Toledo Strip	9-N	16-E
" "	**6**	1	Michigan-Toledo Strip	13-N	12-E

Surname	Map Group	Parcels of Land	Meridian/Township/Range		
AVERY (Cont'd)	**27**	1	Michigan-Toledo Strip	9-N	13-E
AYLSWORTH	**23**	1	Michigan-Toledo Strip	10-N	14-E
AYRAULT	**31**	3	Michigan-Toledo Strip	9-N	17-E
" "	**26**	2	Michigan-Toledo Strip	10-N	17-E
" "	**30**	1	Michigan-Toledo Strip	9-N	16-E
BABCOCK	**23**	1	Michigan-Toledo Strip	10-N	14-E
" "	**18**	1	Michigan-Toledo Strip	11-N	14-E
BACKUS	**2**	1	Michigan-Toledo Strip	14-N	13-E
BACON	**23**	1	Michigan-Toledo Strip	10-N	14-E
BADGERS	**4**	1	Michigan-Toledo Strip	14-N	15-E
BADGROW	**13**	1	Michigan-Toledo Strip	12-N	14-E
BAER	**3**	1	Michigan-Toledo Strip	14-N	14-E
BAGG	**20**	1	Michigan-Toledo Strip	11-N	16-E
BAILEY	**23**	1	Michigan-Toledo Strip	10-N	14-E
" "	**19**	1	Michigan-Toledo Strip	11-N	15-E
" "	**13**	1	Michigan-Toledo Strip	12-N	14-E
" "	**5**	1	Michigan-Toledo Strip	14-N	16-E
BAILIE	**23**	3	Michigan-Toledo Strip	10-N	14-E
BAKER	**25**	3	Michigan-Toledo Strip	10-N	16-E
" "	**30**	2	Michigan-Toledo Strip	9-N	16-E
BALDWIN	**10**	2	Michigan-Toledo Strip	13-N	16-E
" "	**21**	1	Michigan-Toledo Strip	10-N	12-E
" "	**15**	1	Michigan-Toledo Strip	12-N	16-E
BALL	**23**	2	Michigan-Toledo Strip	10-N	14-E
BANCROFT	**25**	2	Michigan-Toledo Strip	10-N	16-E
" "	**24**	1	Michigan-Toledo Strip	10-N	15-E
" "	**7**	1	Michigan-Toledo Strip	13-N	13-E
BANKS	**17**	3	Michigan-Toledo Strip	11-N	13-E
BARBER	**8**	2	Michigan-Toledo Strip	13-N	14-E
BARDWELL	**1**	3	Michigan-Toledo Strip	14-N	12-E
" "	**30**	2	Michigan-Toledo Strip	9-N	16-E
BARNARD	**23**	3	Michigan-Toledo Strip	10-N	14-E
" "	**27**	3	Michigan-Toledo Strip	9-N	13-E
" "	**28**	3	Michigan-Toledo Strip	9-N	14-E
" "	**29**	1	Michigan-Toledo Strip	9-N	15-E
BARRY	**13**	2	Michigan-Toledo Strip	12-N	14-E
BARSTOW	**6**	2	Michigan-Toledo Strip	13-N	12-E
BARTLETT	**19**	1	Michigan-Toledo Strip	11-N	15-E
" "	**9**	1	Michigan-Toledo Strip	13-N	15-E
BARWICK	**2**	4	Michigan-Toledo Strip	14-N	13-E
BASHFORD	**11**	1	Michigan-Toledo Strip	12-N	12-E
BATCHELDER	**21**	3	Michigan-Toledo Strip	10-N	12-E
" "	**17**	3	Michigan-Toledo Strip	11-N	13-E
" "	**19**	2	Michigan-Toledo Strip	11-N	15-E
" "	**22**	1	Michigan-Toledo Strip	10-N	13-E
" "	**16**	1	Michigan-Toledo Strip	11-N	12-E
" "	**12**	1	Michigan-Toledo Strip	12-N	13-E
BAUGHMAN	**23**	1	Michigan-Toledo Strip	10-N	14-E
BEACH	**14**	20	Michigan-Toledo Strip	12-N	15-E
" "	**15**	9	Michigan-Toledo Strip	12-N	16-E
" "	**9**	7	Michigan-Toledo Strip	13-N	15-E
" "	**10**	2	Michigan-Toledo Strip	13-N	16-E
" "	**30**	2	Michigan-Toledo Strip	9-N	16-E
" "	**23**	1	Michigan-Toledo Strip	10-N	14-E
" "	**20**	1	Michigan-Toledo Strip	11-N	16-E
BEAL	**28**	11	Michigan-Toledo Strip	9-N	14-E
BEARD	**23**	2	Michigan-Toledo Strip	10-N	14-E
" "	**19**	2	Michigan-Toledo Strip	11-N	15-E
" "	**28**	2	Michigan-Toledo Strip	9-N	14-E
" "	**14**	1	Michigan-Toledo Strip	12-N	15-E

Surname	Map Group	Parcels of Land	Meridian/Township/Range		
BEATYS	**14**	4	Michigan-Toledo Strip	12-N	15-E
BECKETT	**27**	2	Michigan-Toledo Strip	9-N	13-E
BECKWITH	**14**	20	Michigan-Toledo Strip	12-N	15-E
" "	**15**	9	Michigan-Toledo Strip	12-N	16-E
" "	**9**	7	Michigan-Toledo Strip	13-N	15-E
" "	**10**	2	Michigan-Toledo Strip	13-N	16-E
" "	**20**	1	Michigan-Toledo Strip	11-N	16-E
BEHR	**7**	1	Michigan-Toledo Strip	13-N	13-E
BEISANG	**21**	1	Michigan-Toledo Strip	10-N	12-E
BELDEN	**16**	2	Michigan-Toledo Strip	11-N	12-E
BELL	**2**	2	Michigan-Toledo Strip	14-N	13-E
" "	**21**	1	Michigan-Toledo Strip	10-N	12-E
" "	**18**	1	Michigan-Toledo Strip	11-N	14-E
BENNAWAY	**30**	1	Michigan-Toledo Strip	9-N	16-E
BENNET	**2**	3	Michigan-Toledo Strip	14-N	13-E
BENNETT	**1**	2	Michigan-Toledo Strip	14-N	12-E
" "	**24**	1	Michigan-Toledo Strip	10-N	15-E
" "	**18**	1	Michigan-Toledo Strip	11-N	14-E
BERDEN	**13**	2	Michigan-Toledo Strip	12-N	14-E
BERNEY	**19**	1	Michigan-Toledo Strip	11-N	15-E
BETTERMANN	**3**	1	Michigan-Toledo Strip	14-N	14-E
BEZEMEK	**3**	2	Michigan-Toledo Strip	14-N	14-E
BEZENEK	**3**	1	Michigan-Toledo Strip	14-N	14-E
BHONONE	**30**	1	Michigan-Toledo Strip	9-N	16-E
BIEBER	**16**	3	Michigan-Toledo Strip	11-N	12-E
BIGNEY	**13**	1	Michigan-Toledo Strip	12-N	14-E
BINNINGA	**20**	1	Michigan-Toledo Strip	11-N	16-E
BISBEE	**25**	1	Michigan-Toledo Strip	10-N	16-E
BISHOP	**16**	3	Michigan-Toledo Strip	11-N	12-E
" "	**11**	1	Michigan-Toledo Strip	12-N	12-E
" "	**14**	1	Michigan-Toledo Strip	12-N	15-E
BLACKMAIR	**15**	1	Michigan-Toledo Strip	12-N	16-E
BLACKMAR	**1**	2	Michigan-Toledo Strip	14-N	12-E
BLAKE	**25**	1	Michigan-Toledo Strip	10-N	16-E
" "	**16**	1	Michigan-Toledo Strip	11-N	12-E
BLAKESLEY	**18**	2	Michigan-Toledo Strip	11-N	14-E
BLASHILL	**12**	1	Michigan-Toledo Strip	12-N	13-E
BLINDBERRY	**20**	1	Michigan-Toledo Strip	11-N	16-E
BLINDBURY	**15**	2	Michigan-Toledo Strip	12-N	16-E
BODDY	**20**	1	Michigan-Toledo Strip	11-N	16-E
" "	**15**	1	Michigan-Toledo Strip	12-N	16-E
" "	**9**	1	Michigan-Toledo Strip	13-N	15-E
BOGERT	**1**	1	Michigan-Toledo Strip	14-N	12-E
BOISE	**29**	2	Michigan-Toledo Strip	9-N	15-E
BOND	**6**	3	Michigan-Toledo Strip	13-N	12-E
" "	**1**	1	Michigan-Toledo Strip	14-N	12-E
BOOTHBY	**22**	1	Michigan-Toledo Strip	10-N	13-E
BORLAND	**2**	1	Michigan-Toledo Strip	14-N	13-E
" "	**3**	1	Michigan-Toledo Strip	14-N	14-E
BOTSFORD	**25**	1	Michigan-Toledo Strip	10-N	16-E
" "	**30**	1	Michigan-Toledo Strip	9-N	16-E
BOTTOMLEY	**22**	2	Michigan-Toledo Strip	10-N	13-E
" "	**16**	1	Michigan-Toledo Strip	11-N	12-E
" "	**29**	1	Michigan-Toledo Strip	9-N	15-E
BOUTAIGER	**4**	1	Michigan-Toledo Strip	14-N	15-E
BOWMAN	**21**	2	Michigan-Toledo Strip	10-N	12-E
BOWSER	**9**	3	Michigan-Toledo Strip	13-N	15-E
BOYD	**18**	3	Michigan-Toledo Strip	11-N	14-E
BOYS	**23**	1	Michigan-Toledo Strip	10-N	14-E
BRABBS	**21**	5	Michigan-Toledo Strip	10-N	12-E

Surname	Map Group	Parcels of Land	Meridian/Township/Range		
BRACKENRIDGE	**15**	1	Michigan-Toledo Strip	12-N	16-E
BRADBEK	**4**	1	Michigan-Toledo Strip	14-N	15-E
BRADEN	**3**	1	Michigan-Toledo Strip	14-N	14-E
BRADLEY	**27**	1	Michigan-Toledo Strip	9-N	13-E
BRADY	**3**	4	Michigan-Toledo Strip	14-N	14-E
" "	**21**	1	Michigan-Toledo Strip	10-N	12-E
BRANAGAN	**29**	2	Michigan-Toledo Strip	9-N	15-E
BRANNAGAN	**29**	1	Michigan-Toledo Strip	9-N	15-E
BRASEBRIDGE	**23**	2	Michigan-Toledo Strip	10-N	14-E
BRAUN	**21**	3	Michigan-Toledo Strip	10-N	12-E
BREADER	**20**	1	Michigan-Toledo Strip	11-N	16-E
BRENNAN	**24**	1	Michigan-Toledo Strip	10-N	15-E
BRENNEN	**1**	1	Michigan-Toledo Strip	14-N	12-E
BRIGHT	**13**	3	Michigan-Toledo Strip	12-N	14-E
BRIMLEY	**4**	1	Michigan-Toledo Strip	14-N	15-E
BROADBRIDGE	**13**	2	Michigan-Toledo Strip	12-N	14-E
BROCKELSBY	**2**	1	Michigan-Toledo Strip	14-N	13-E
BROCKWAY	**28**	2	Michigan-Toledo Strip	9-N	14-E
" "	**23**	1	Michigan-Toledo Strip	10-N	14-E
" "	**18**	1	Michigan-Toledo Strip	11-N	14-E
" "	**29**	1	Michigan-Toledo Strip	9-N	15-E
BRODIE	**12**	1	Michigan-Toledo Strip	12-N	13-E
BROOKS	**23**	3	Michigan-Toledo Strip	10-N	14-E
BROWN	**27**	6	Michigan-Toledo Strip	9-N	13-E
" "	**2**	5	Michigan-Toledo Strip	14-N	13-E
" "	**11**	2	Michigan-Toledo Strip	12-N	12-E
" "	**6**	2	Michigan-Toledo Strip	13-N	12-E
" "	**24**	1	Michigan-Toledo Strip	10-N	15-E
" "	**7**	1	Michigan-Toledo Strip	13-N	13-E
" "	**29**	1	Michigan-Toledo Strip	9-N	15-E
" "	**30**	1	Michigan-Toledo Strip	9-N	16-E
BROWNE	**27**	1	Michigan-Toledo Strip	9-N	13-E
BROWNING	**30**	2	Michigan-Toledo Strip	9-N	16-E
BRUCE	**24**	1	Michigan-Toledo Strip	10-N	15-E
BRYANT	**20**	3	Michigan-Toledo Strip	11-N	16-E
" "	**25**	2	Michigan-Toledo Strip	10-N	16-E
BRYCE	**27**	2	Michigan-Toledo Strip	9-N	13-E
" "	**23**	1	Michigan-Toledo Strip	10-N	14-E
BUCHANAN	**11**	1	Michigan-Toledo Strip	12-N	12-E
BUEL	**24**	3	Michigan-Toledo Strip	10-N	15-E
" "	**25**	1	Michigan-Toledo Strip	10-N	16-E
" "	**19**	1	Michigan-Toledo Strip	11-N	15-E
" "	**30**	1	Michigan-Toledo Strip	9-N	16-E
BUELL	**25**	1	Michigan-Toledo Strip	10-N	16-E
" "	**19**	1	Michigan-Toledo Strip	11-N	15-E
BUGBEE	**25**	4	Michigan-Toledo Strip	10-N	16-E
" "	**15**	1	Michigan-Toledo Strip	12-N	16-E
BUNKER	**20**	15	Michigan-Toledo Strip	11-N	16-E
" "	**25**	7	Michigan-Toledo Strip	10-N	16-E
BURCH	**30**	2	Michigan-Toledo Strip	9-N	16-E
BURCHAM	**15**	1	Michigan-Toledo Strip	12-N	16-E
BURGER	**16**	1	Michigan-Toledo Strip	11-N	12-E
BURGESS	**4**	1	Michigan-Toledo Strip	14-N	15-E
BURK	**15**	2	Michigan-Toledo Strip	12-N	16-E
BURLINGGAME	**25**	1	Michigan-Toledo Strip	10-N	16-E
BURMEISTER	**16**	1	Michigan-Toledo Strip	11-N	12-E
BURNHAM	**7**	1	Michigan-Toledo Strip	13-N	13-E
BURNS	**29**	2	Michigan-Toledo Strip	9-N	15-E
BURT	**11**	1	Michigan-Toledo Strip	12-N	12-E
" "	**6**	1	Michigan-Toledo Strip	13-N	12-E

Surname	Map Group	Parcels of Land	Meridian/Township/Range		
BURTCH	**30**	4	Michigan-Toledo Strip	9-N	16-E
BURTON	**23**	1	Michigan-Toledo Strip	10-N	14-E
BURTT	**1**	1	Michigan-Toledo Strip	14-N	12-E
BUTHE	**3**	1	Michigan-Toledo Strip	14-N	14-E
BUTLER	**15**	5	Michigan-Toledo Strip	12-N	16-E
" "	**31**	3	Michigan-Toledo Strip	9-N	17-E
BUTTERFIELD	**28**	1	Michigan-Toledo Strip	9-N	14-E
BYERS	**29**	1	Michigan-Toledo Strip	9-N	15-E
BYRNE	**16**	1	Michigan-Toledo Strip	11-N	12-E
BYRNES	**16**	1	Michigan-Toledo Strip	11-N	12-E
CADY	**12**	1	Michigan-Toledo Strip	12-N	13-E
CALHOUN	**28**	2	Michigan-Toledo Strip	9-N	14-E
CALKINS	**15**	1	Michigan-Toledo Strip	12-N	16-E
CAMERON	**24**	2	Michigan-Toledo Strip	10-N	15-E
" "	**2**	1	Michigan-Toledo Strip	14-N	13-E
CAMP	**12**	2	Michigan-Toledo Strip	12-N	13-E
CAMPBELL	**12**	8	Michigan-Toledo Strip	12-N	13-E
" "	**21**	1	Michigan-Toledo Strip	10-N	12-E
" "	**23**	1	Michigan-Toledo Strip	10-N	14-E
" "	**20**	1	Michigan-Toledo Strip	11-N	16-E
" "	**9**	1	Michigan-Toledo Strip	13-N	15-E
" "	**1**	1	Michigan-Toledo Strip	14-N	12-E
CANEDY	**22**	2	Michigan-Toledo Strip	10-N	13-E
CANHAM	**4**	3	Michigan-Toledo Strip	14-N	15-E
CARLETON	**27**	2	Michigan-Toledo Strip	9-N	13-E
" "	**23**	1	Michigan-Toledo Strip	10-N	14-E
CARLISLE	**20**	1	Michigan-Toledo Strip	11-N	16-E
CARLTON	**28**	1	Michigan-Toledo Strip	9-N	14-E
CARNEY	**20**	1	Michigan-Toledo Strip	11-N	16-E
" "	**3**	1	Michigan-Toledo Strip	14-N	14-E
CARPENTER	**16**	2	Michigan-Toledo Strip	11-N	12-E
CARRINGTON	**25**	2	Michigan-Toledo Strip	10-N	16-E
" "	**30**	1	Michigan-Toledo Strip	9-N	16-E
" "	**31**	1	Michigan-Toledo Strip	9-N	17-E
CARROLAN	**3**	1	Michigan-Toledo Strip	14-N	14-E
CARROLL	**30**	12	Michigan-Toledo Strip	9-N	16-E
" "	**16**	1	Michigan-Toledo Strip	11-N	12-E
CARSON	**19**	2	Michigan-Toledo Strip	11-N	15-E
CARTER	**27**	1	Michigan-Toledo Strip	9-N	13-E
CARWELL	**1**	1	Michigan-Toledo Strip	14-N	12-E
CARY	**2**	3	Michigan-Toledo Strip	14-N	13-E
CASE	**25**	1	Michigan-Toledo Strip	10-N	16-E
CASH	**18**	4	Michigan-Toledo Strip	11-N	14-E
" "	**24**	1	Michigan-Toledo Strip	10-N	15-E
CASLER	**11**	1	Michigan-Toledo Strip	12-N	12-E
CASTER	**25**	1	Michigan-Toledo Strip	10-N	16-E
CATALINE	**8**	1	Michigan-Toledo Strip	13-N	14-E
CAVE	**27**	1	Michigan-Toledo Strip	9-N	13-E
CAVEN	**11**	1	Michigan-Toledo Strip	12-N	12-E
CAWOOD	**16**	3	Michigan-Toledo Strip	11-N	12-E
CHAPEL	**1**	1	Michigan-Toledo Strip	14-N	12-E
CHASE	**29**	6	Michigan-Toledo Strip	9-N	15-E
" "	**23**	4	Michigan-Toledo Strip	10-N	14-E
" "	**19**	4	Michigan-Toledo Strip	11-N	15-E
" "	**30**	4	Michigan-Toledo Strip	9-N	16-E
" "	**24**	3	Michigan-Toledo Strip	10-N	15-E
" "	**28**	3	Michigan-Toledo Strip	9-N	14-E
" "	**25**	1	Michigan-Toledo Strip	10-N	16-E
" "	**18**	1	Michigan-Toledo Strip	11-N	14-E
" "	**31**	1	Michigan-Toledo Strip	9-N	17-E

Surname	Map Group	Parcels of Land	Meridian/Township/Range		
CHIPMAN	**13**	4	Michigan-Toledo Strip	12-N	14-E
CHRIST	**4**	1	Michigan-Toledo Strip	14-N	15-E
CHRISTIAN	**9**	1	Michigan-Toledo Strip	13-N	15-E
CICOTT	**26**	1	Michigan-Toledo Strip	10-N	17-E
CICOTTE	**25**	5	Michigan-Toledo Strip	10-N	16-E
" "	**30**	1	Michigan-Toledo Strip	9-N	16-E
CLAPSADDLE	**12**	2	Michigan-Toledo Strip	12-N	13-E
CLARK	**1**	3	Michigan-Toledo Strip	14-N	12-E
" "	**4**	2	Michigan-Toledo Strip	14-N	15-E
" "	**30**	2	Michigan-Toledo Strip	9-N	16-E
" "	**31**	2	Michigan-Toledo Strip	9-N	17-E
" "	**20**	1	Michigan-Toledo Strip	11-N	16-E
" "	**6**	1	Michigan-Toledo Strip	13-N	12-E
" "	**2**	1	Michigan-Toledo Strip	14-N	13-E
CLARKE	**30**	2	Michigan-Toledo Strip	9-N	16-E
" "	**15**	1	Michigan-Toledo Strip	12-N	16-E
CLARY	**4**	4	Michigan-Toledo Strip	14-N	15-E
CLAYTON	**28**	3	Michigan-Toledo Strip	9-N	14-E
CLEAVELAND	**30**	1	Michigan-Toledo Strip	9-N	16-E
CLELAND	**1**	6	Michigan-Toledo Strip	14-N	12-E
" "	**2**	2	Michigan-Toledo Strip	14-N	13-E
" "	**12**	1	Michigan-Toledo Strip	12-N	13-E
CLENDENIN	**6**	1	Michigan-Toledo Strip	13-N	12-E
CLIFFORD	**2**	1	Michigan-Toledo Strip	14-N	13-E
CLIFTON	**15**	1	Michigan-Toledo Strip	12-N	16-E
CLINE	**30**	1	Michigan-Toledo Strip	9-N	16-E
COALTER	**9**	2	Michigan-Toledo Strip	13-N	15-E
COBURN	**30**	22	Michigan-Toledo Strip	9-N	16-E
" "	**25**	15	Michigan-Toledo Strip	10-N	16-E
" "	**28**	3	Michigan-Toledo Strip	9-N	14-E
" "	**31**	2	Michigan-Toledo Strip	9-N	17-E
COCHRAN	**23**	1	Michigan-Toledo Strip	10-N	14-E
COCOMAN	**14**	3	Michigan-Toledo Strip	12-N	15-E
CODDINGTON	**18**	2	Michigan-Toledo Strip	11-N	14-E
COE	**27**	3	Michigan-Toledo Strip	9-N	13-E
" "	**28**	3	Michigan-Toledo Strip	9-N	14-E
" "	**29**	1	Michigan-Toledo Strip	9-N	15-E
COFFEY	**16**	1	Michigan-Toledo Strip	11-N	12-E
COFFINGER	**28**	1	Michigan-Toledo Strip	9-N	14-E
COFFY	**16**	1	Michigan-Toledo Strip	11-N	12-E
COLBORN	**28**	3	Michigan-Toledo Strip	9-N	14-E
" "	**29**	2	Michigan-Toledo Strip	9-N	15-E
COLE	**16**	3	Michigan-Toledo Strip	11-N	12-E
" "	**20**	1	Michigan-Toledo Strip	11-N	16-E
" "	**7**	1	Michigan-Toledo Strip	13-N	13-E
" "	**8**	1	Michigan-Toledo Strip	13-N	14-E
COLLINA	**2**	1	Michigan-Toledo Strip	14-N	13-E
COLLINGS	**1**	2	Michigan-Toledo Strip	14-N	12-E
COLMAN	**6**	1	Michigan-Toledo Strip	13-N	12-E
COMMER	**9**	1	Michigan-Toledo Strip	13-N	15-E
COMPANY	**19**	6	Michigan-Toledo Strip	11-N	15-E
" "	**24**	2	Michigan-Toledo Strip	10-N	15-E
" "	**20**	1	Michigan-Toledo Strip	11-N	16-E
" "	**6**	1	Michigan-Toledo Strip	13-N	12-E
" "	**8**	1	Michigan-Toledo Strip	13-N	14-E
" "	**1**	1	Michigan-Toledo Strip	14-N	12-E
" "	**28**	1	Michigan-Toledo Strip	9-N	14-E
COMSTOCK	**29**	2	Michigan-Toledo Strip	9-N	15-E
CONANT	**12**	2	Michigan-Toledo Strip	12-N	13-E
CONAT	**31**	2	Michigan-Toledo Strip	9-N	17-E

Surname	Map Group	Parcels of Land	Meridian/Township/Range		
CONDON	**28**	1	Michigan-Toledo Strip	9-N	14-E
CONNOR	**14**	1	Michigan-Toledo Strip	12-N	15-E
COOK	**28**	3	Michigan-Toledo Strip	9-N	14-E
" "	**16**	2	Michigan-Toledo Strip	11-N	12-E
" "	**30**	1	Michigan-Toledo Strip	9-N	16-E
COREY	**18**	3	Michigan-Toledo Strip	11-N	14-E
CORNELL	**30**	1	Michigan-Toledo Strip	9-N	16-E
COURTNEY	**25**	1	Michigan-Toledo Strip	10-N	16-E
COUSE	**11**	1	Michigan-Toledo Strip	12-N	12-E
COVIL	**16**	3	Michigan-Toledo Strip	11-N	12-E
COXE	**30**	1	Michigan-Toledo Strip	9-N	16-E
CRAIG	**20**	2	Michigan-Toledo Strip	11-N	16-E
" "	**8**	1	Michigan-Toledo Strip	13-N	14-E
CRAMPTON	**16**	3	Michigan-Toledo Strip	11-N	12-E
" "	**30**	2	Michigan-Toledo Strip	9-N	16-E
CRANDALL	**4**	1	Michigan-Toledo Strip	14-N	15-E
CROCKER	**10**	3	Michigan-Toledo Strip	13-N	16-E
CROCKERD	**29**	1	Michigan-Toledo Strip	9-N	15-E
CROCKET	**30**	1	Michigan-Toledo Strip	9-N	16-E
CRORY	**14**	2	Michigan-Toledo Strip	12-N	15-E
CROSS	**14**	1	Michigan-Toledo Strip	12-N	15-E
" "	**4**	1	Michigan-Toledo Strip	14-N	15-E
CROWELL	**15**	1	Michigan-Toledo Strip	12-N	16-E
CROWLEY	**2**	1	Michigan-Toledo Strip	14-N	13-E
CUMMINGS	**16**	6	Michigan-Toledo Strip	11-N	12-E
" "	**9**	3	Michigan-Toledo Strip	13-N	15-E
" "	**27**	3	Michigan-Toledo Strip	9-N	13-E
" "	**21**	1	Michigan-Toledo Strip	10-N	12-E
" "	**30**	1	Michigan-Toledo Strip	9-N	16-E
CUNNINGHAM	**27**	1	Michigan-Toledo Strip	9-N	13-E
CURN	**13**	4	Michigan-Toledo Strip	12-N	14-E
CURRIE	**15**	1	Michigan-Toledo Strip	12-N	16-E
" "	**2**	1	Michigan-Toledo Strip	14-N	13-E
CURTIS	**11**	3	Michigan-Toledo Strip	12-N	12-E
CURWELL	**6**	2	Michigan-Toledo Strip	13-N	12-E
" "	**1**	2	Michigan-Toledo Strip	14-N	12-E
DALE	**16**	3	Michigan-Toledo Strip	11-N	12-E
DANCEY	**27**	2	Michigan-Toledo Strip	9-N	13-E
DARCY	**18**	2	Michigan-Toledo Strip	11-N	14-E
DAVENPORT	**15**	1	Michigan-Toledo Strip	12-N	16-E
DAVIS	**25**	6	Michigan-Toledo Strip	10-N	16-E
" "	**28**	5	Michigan-Toledo Strip	9-N	14-E
" "	**24**	4	Michigan-Toledo Strip	10-N	15-E
" "	**17**	3	Michigan-Toledo Strip	11-N	13-E
" "	**18**	3	Michigan-Toledo Strip	11-N	14-E
" "	**6**	3	Michigan-Toledo Strip	13-N	12-E
" "	**19**	2	Michigan-Toledo Strip	11-N	15-E
" "	**1**	2	Michigan-Toledo Strip	14-N	12-E
" "	**29**	2	Michigan-Toledo Strip	9-N	15-E
" "	**30**	2	Michigan-Toledo Strip	9-N	16-E
" "	**22**	1	Michigan-Toledo Strip	10-N	13-E
" "	**20**	1	Michigan-Toledo Strip	11-N	16-E
" "	**11**	1	Michigan-Toledo Strip	12-N	12-E
" "	**12**	1	Michigan-Toledo Strip	12-N	13-E
" "	**4**	1	Michigan-Toledo Strip	14-N	15-E
DE GROAT	**27**	1	Michigan-Toledo Strip	9-N	13-E
DE GROATE	**30**	1	Michigan-Toledo Strip	9-N	16-E
DEAN	**27**	1	Michigan-Toledo Strip	9-N	13-E
DECKER	**25**	3	Michigan-Toledo Strip	10-N	16-E
" "	**14**	2	Michigan-Toledo Strip	12-N	15-E

Surname	Map Group	Parcels of Land	Meridian/Township/Range		
DECKER (Cont'd)	**24**	1	Michigan-Toledo Strip	10-N	15-E
" "	**27**	1	Michigan-Toledo Strip	9-N	13-E
DEEGAN	**3**	4	Michigan-Toledo Strip	14-N	14-E
DEGRAW	**28**	2	Michigan-Toledo Strip	9-N	14-E
DEIGAN	**3**	1	Michigan-Toledo Strip	14-N	14-E
DELAVAN	**30**	10	Michigan-Toledo Strip	9-N	16-E
DELL	**27**	2	Michigan-Toledo Strip	9-N	13-E
DENSHAM	**24**	1	Michigan-Toledo Strip	10-N	15-E
DENSHAW	**24**	1	Michigan-Toledo Strip	10-N	15-E
DERING	**13**	2	Michigan-Toledo Strip	12-N	14-E
DERR	**12**	2	Michigan-Toledo Strip	12-N	13-E
DESOTELL	**27**	1	Michigan-Toledo Strip	9-N	13-E
DEUSHAM	**22**	1	Michigan-Toledo Strip	10-N	13-E
DEVAL	**6**	2	Michigan-Toledo Strip	13-N	12-E
DEVINE	**30**	1	Michigan-Toledo Strip	9-N	16-E
DEWEY	**7**	2	Michigan-Toledo Strip	13-N	13-E
DEY	**13**	1	Michigan-Toledo Strip	12-N	14-E
DEYOE	**15**	2	Michigan-Toledo Strip	12-N	16-E
DIAMOND	**24**	1	Michigan-Toledo Strip	10-N	15-E
" "	**31**	1	Michigan-Toledo Strip	9-N	17-E
DICKINSON	**14**	20	Michigan-Toledo Strip	12-N	15-E
" "	**15**	13	Michigan-Toledo Strip	12-N	16-E
" "	**9**	9	Michigan-Toledo Strip	13-N	15-E
" "	**10**	8	Michigan-Toledo Strip	13-N	16-E
" "	**20**	1	Michigan-Toledo Strip	11-N	16-E
DICKSON	**25**	1	Michigan-Toledo Strip	10-N	16-E
" "	**17**	1	Michigan-Toledo Strip	11-N	13-E
DIETER	**3**	1	Michigan-Toledo Strip	14-N	14-E
DIMOND	**15**	3	Michigan-Toledo Strip	12-N	16-E
" "	**30**	2	Michigan-Toledo Strip	9-N	16-E
DOAN	**13**	1	Michigan-Toledo Strip	12-N	14-E
DODGE	**22**	1	Michigan-Toledo Strip	10-N	13-E
" "	**14**	1	Michigan-Toledo Strip	12-N	15-E
" "	**9**	1	Michigan-Toledo Strip	13-N	15-E
DOERING	**17**	2	Michigan-Toledo Strip	11-N	13-E
DOLE	**22**	1	Michigan-Toledo Strip	10-N	13-E
DONAHUE	**22**	1	Michigan-Toledo Strip	10-N	13-E
DONALD	**16**	1	Michigan-Toledo Strip	11-N	12-E
DONALLAN	**3**	2	Michigan-Toledo Strip	14-N	14-E
DONELLAN	**2**	1	Michigan-Toledo Strip	14-N	13-E
DONELLY	**20**	1	Michigan-Toledo Strip	11-N	16-E
DONNAVAN	**3**	2	Michigan-Toledo Strip	14-N	14-E
DONNELLAN	**4**	3	Michigan-Toledo Strip	14-N	15-E
DONNER	**3**	2	Michigan-Toledo Strip	14-N	14-E
DONOLON	**3**	1	Michigan-Toledo Strip	14-N	14-E
DOPP	**20**	1	Michigan-Toledo Strip	11-N	16-E
DORING	**17**	1	Michigan-Toledo Strip	11-N	13-E
DOUGLASS	**24**	3	Michigan-Toledo Strip	10-N	15-E
" "	**23**	2	Michigan-Toledo Strip	10-N	14-E
DOWLING	**28**	3	Michigan-Toledo Strip	9-N	14-E
" "	**29**	1	Michigan-Toledo Strip	9-N	15-E
DOWNING	**25**	1	Michigan-Toledo Strip	10-N	16-E
" "	**13**	1	Michigan-Toledo Strip	12-N	14-E
DOZING	**14**	2	Michigan-Toledo Strip	12-N	15-E
DROWN	**25**	1	Michigan-Toledo Strip	10-N	16-E
DUCAT	**14**	1	Michigan-Toledo Strip	12-N	15-E
DUDLEY	**28**	1	Michigan-Toledo Strip	9-N	14-E
DUNLAP	**9**	1	Michigan-Toledo Strip	13-N	15-E
DUNLEY	**23**	1	Michigan-Toledo Strip	10-N	14-E
DUNLOP	**20**	2	Michigan-Toledo Strip	11-N	16-E

Surname	Map Group	Parcels of Land	Meridian/Township/Range		
DUNLOP (Cont'd)	**9**	1	Michigan-Toledo Strip	13-N	15-E
DURR	**7**	2	Michigan-Toledo Strip	13-N	13-E
" "	**30**	1	Michigan-Toledo Strip	9-N	16-E
DUVAL	**7**	1	Michigan-Toledo Strip	13-N	13-E
DWIGHT	**19**	5	Michigan-Toledo Strip	11-N	15-E
" "	**10**	2	Michigan-Toledo Strip	13-N	16-E
DYER	**4**	3	Michigan-Toledo Strip	14-N	15-E
EARLES	**27**	3	Michigan-Toledo Strip	9-N	13-E
EASTMAN	**8**	1	Michigan-Toledo Strip	13-N	14-E
" "	**27**	1	Michigan-Toledo Strip	9-N	13-E
EATON	**15**	1	Michigan-Toledo Strip	12-N	16-E
ECKARDT	**27**	2	Michigan-Toledo Strip	9-N	13-E
EDDY	**25**	1	Michigan-Toledo Strip	10-N	16-E
" "	**6**	1	Michigan-Toledo Strip	13-N	12-E
" "	**1**	1	Michigan-Toledo Strip	14-N	12-E
EDMONDS	**10**	6	Michigan-Toledo Strip	13-N	16-E
" "	**20**	1	Michigan-Toledo Strip	11-N	16-E
EDWARDS	**13**	2	Michigan-Toledo Strip	12-N	14-E
" "	**23**	1	Michigan-Toledo Strip	10-N	14-E
EINSIDER	**20**	1	Michigan-Toledo Strip	11-N	16-E
ELDRED	**20**	1	Michigan-Toledo Strip	11-N	16-E
ELLIS	**16**	1	Michigan-Toledo Strip	11-N	12-E
ELWIN	**29**	1	Michigan-Toledo Strip	9-N	15-E
ENNEST	**13**	4	Michigan-Toledo Strip	12-N	14-E
" "	**15**	1	Michigan-Toledo Strip	12-N	16-E
ERBE	**20**	1	Michigan-Toledo Strip	11-N	16-E
ERITY	**29**	1	Michigan-Toledo Strip	9-N	15-E
" "	**30**	1	Michigan-Toledo Strip	9-N	16-E
ERSKIN	**12**	1	Michigan-Toledo Strip	12-N	13-E
ERSKINE	**24**	4	Michigan-Toledo Strip	10-N	15-E
" "	**12**	4	Michigan-Toledo Strip	12-N	13-E
" "	**17**	2	Michigan-Toledo Strip	11-N	13-E
" "	**13**	2	Michigan-Toledo Strip	12-N	14-E
" "	**18**	1	Michigan-Toledo Strip	11-N	14-E
ESELE	**16**	1	Michigan-Toledo Strip	11-N	12-E
EVOY	**16**	1	Michigan-Toledo Strip	11-N	12-E
EWER	**20**	15	Michigan-Toledo Strip	11-N	16-E
" "	**25**	7	Michigan-Toledo Strip	10-N	16-E
FALKENBURY	**22**	4	Michigan-Toledo Strip	10-N	13-E
FARNSWORTH	**25**	8	Michigan-Toledo Strip	10-N	16-E
" "	**19**	8	Michigan-Toledo Strip	11-N	15-E
" "	**20**	2	Michigan-Toledo Strip	11-N	16-E
" "	**9**	1	Michigan-Toledo Strip	13-N	15-E
" "	**30**	1	Michigan-Toledo Strip	9-N	16-E
FARRELL	**27**	1	Michigan-Toledo Strip	9-N	13-E
FAY	**9**	2	Michigan-Toledo Strip	13-N	15-E
" "	**8**	1	Michigan-Toledo Strip	13-N	14-E
FEAD	**25**	1	Michigan-Toledo Strip	10-N	16-E
FENTON	**14**	2	Michigan-Toledo Strip	12-N	15-E
" "	**1**	2	Michigan-Toledo Strip	14-N	12-E
FERGUSON	**16**	4	Michigan-Toledo Strip	11-N	12-E
FERRIS	**15**	1	Michigan-Toledo Strip	12-N	16-E
FIELD	**11**	2	Michigan-Toledo Strip	12-N	12-E
FIFIELD	**21**	3	Michigan-Toledo Strip	10-N	12-E
FIKE	**17**	1	Michigan-Toledo Strip	11-N	13-E
" "	**12**	1	Michigan-Toledo Strip	12-N	13-E
FINLAYSON	**20**	1	Michigan-Toledo Strip	11-N	16-E
FINLEY	**14**	3	Michigan-Toledo Strip	12-N	15-E
FISH	**28**	8	Michigan-Toledo Strip	9-N	14-E
" "	**23**	1	Michigan-Toledo Strip	10-N	14-E

Surname	Map Group	Parcels of Land	Meridian/Township/Range		
FISH (Cont'd)	**29**	1	Michigan-Toledo Strip	9-N	15-E
" "	**30**	1	Michigan-Toledo Strip	9-N	16-E
FISHER	**3**	3	Michigan-Toledo Strip	14-N	14-E
" "	**16**	1	Michigan-Toledo Strip	11-N	12-E
" "	**6**	1	Michigan-Toledo Strip	13-N	12-E
FITCH	**22**	2	Michigan-Toledo Strip	10-N	13-E
FITZPATRICK	**16**	1	Michigan-Toledo Strip	11-N	12-E
FLEMING	**18**	1	Michigan-Toledo Strip	11-N	14-E
" "	**1**	1	Michigan-Toledo Strip	14-N	12-E
FLETCHER	**13**	2	Michigan-Toledo Strip	12-N	14-E
" "	**3**	2	Michigan-Toledo Strip	14-N	14-E
FOELSZ	**25**	1	Michigan-Toledo Strip	10-N	16-E
FOLEY	**27**	3	Michigan-Toledo Strip	9-N	13-E
FORBES	**28**	3	Michigan-Toledo Strip	9-N	14-E
" "	**29**	1	Michigan-Toledo Strip	9-N	15-E
FORD	**9**	2	Michigan-Toledo Strip	13-N	15-E
" "	**4**	1	Michigan-Toledo Strip	14-N	15-E
FOSTER	**16**	1	Michigan-Toledo Strip	11-N	12-E
FOX	**22**	4	Michigan-Toledo Strip	10-N	13-E
" "	**11**	2	Michigan-Toledo Strip	12-N	12-E
FRALICK	**30**	1	Michigan-Toledo Strip	9-N	16-E
FRANKE	**7**	3	Michigan-Toledo Strip	13-N	13-E
FREHSE	**2**	2	Michigan-Toledo Strip	14-N	13-E
FRENCH	**12**	1	Michigan-Toledo Strip	12-N	13-E
" "	**6**	1	Michigan-Toledo Strip	13-N	12-E
" "	**2**	1	Michigan-Toledo Strip	14-N	13-E
FYE	**13**	1	Michigan-Toledo Strip	12-N	14-E
GALBRAITH	**30**	9	Michigan-Toledo Strip	9-N	16-E
" "	**29**	2	Michigan-Toledo Strip	9-N	15-E
GALLEY	**21**	1	Michigan-Toledo Strip	10-N	12-E
GARA	**3**	1	Michigan-Toledo Strip	14-N	14-E
GARDNER	**20**	1	Michigan-Toledo Strip	11-N	16-E
GARVIN	**15**	2	Michigan-Toledo Strip	12-N	16-E
GECK	**4**	1	Michigan-Toledo Strip	14-N	15-E
GEEL	**30**	5	Michigan-Toledo Strip	9-N	16-E
" "	**25**	2	Michigan-Toledo Strip	10-N	16-E
GEORGE	**7**	1	Michigan-Toledo Strip	13-N	13-E
GETTY	**2**	2	Michigan-Toledo Strip	14-N	13-E
GIBSON	**20**	2	Michigan-Toledo Strip	11-N	16-E
" "	**4**	1	Michigan-Toledo Strip	14-N	15-E
GILBRAITH	**29**	1	Michigan-Toledo Strip	9-N	15-E
GILL	**18**	3	Michigan-Toledo Strip	11-N	14-E
GILLETT	**28**	1	Michigan-Toledo Strip	9-N	14-E
GILLIGAN	**21**	1	Michigan-Toledo Strip	10-N	12-E
GINSBIGLER	**4**	1	Michigan-Toledo Strip	14-N	15-E
GLENNIE	**9**	1	Michigan-Toledo Strip	13-N	15-E
GLOVER	**20**	8	Michigan-Toledo Strip	11-N	16-E
GOETCHINS	**21**	4	Michigan-Toledo Strip	10-N	12-E
GOIT	**16**	1	Michigan-Toledo Strip	11-N	12-E
GOODRICH	**9**	4	Michigan-Toledo Strip	13-N	15-E
" "	**15**	3	Michigan-Toledo Strip	12-N	16-E
GOODWIN	**13**	2	Michigan-Toledo Strip	12-N	14-E
" "	**28**	2	Michigan-Toledo Strip	9-N	14-E
" "	**8**	1	Michigan-Toledo Strip	13-N	14-E
GORDON	**1**	3	Michigan-Toledo Strip	14-N	12-E
" "	**18**	1	Michigan-Toledo Strip	11-N	14-E
GOULD	**15**	4	Michigan-Toledo Strip	12-N	16-E
" "	**6**	1	Michigan-Toledo Strip	13-N	12-E
GRAHAM	**30**	2	Michigan-Toledo Strip	9-N	16-E
" "	**7**	1	Michigan-Toledo Strip	13-N	13-E

Surname	Map Group	Parcels of Land	Meridian/Township/Range		
GRANDY	**28**	1	Michigan-Toledo Strip	9-N	14-E
GRANGER	**30**	4	Michigan-Toledo Strip	9-N	16-E
GRANT	**29**	2	Michigan-Toledo Strip	9-N	15-E
GRAVES	**9**	2	Michigan-Toledo Strip	13-N	15-E
GRAY	**2**	5	Michigan-Toledo Strip	14-N	13-E
" "	**29**	2	Michigan-Toledo Strip	9-N	15-E
GREAVES	**9**	2	Michigan-Toledo Strip	13-N	15-E
GREEN	**16**	1	Michigan-Toledo Strip	11-N	12-E
" "	**6**	1	Michigan-Toledo Strip	13-N	12-E
" "	**7**	1	Michigan-Toledo Strip	13-N	13-E
" "	**3**	1	Michigan-Toledo Strip	14-N	14-E
GREENLEAF	**1**	3	Michigan-Toledo Strip	14-N	12-E
GREENMAN	**1**	2	Michigan-Toledo Strip	14-N	12-E
GREGG	**6**	3	Michigan-Toledo Strip	13-N	12-E
" "	**7**	1	Michigan-Toledo Strip	13-N	13-E
GRICE	**14**	1	Michigan-Toledo Strip	12-N	15-E
GRIGG	**8**	1	Michigan-Toledo Strip	13-N	14-E
GROW	**1**	2	Michigan-Toledo Strip	14-N	12-E
GUTHRIE	**30**	3	Michigan-Toledo Strip	9-N	16-E
GYSTER	**27**	1	Michigan-Toledo Strip	9-N	13-E
HACKER	**2**	1	Michigan-Toledo Strip	14-N	13-E
HACKETT	**9**	1	Michigan-Toledo Strip	13-N	15-E
HADDOW	**19**	2	Michigan-Toledo Strip	11-N	15-E
" "	**16**	1	Michigan-Toledo Strip	11-N	12-E
HADLEY	**20**	4	Michigan-Toledo Strip	11-N	16-E
" "	**2**	3	Michigan-Toledo Strip	14-N	13-E
" "	**25**	2	Michigan-Toledo Strip	10-N	16-E
HAEBERLE	**28**	1	Michigan-Toledo Strip	9-N	14-E
HAGER	**20**	1	Michigan-Toledo Strip	11-N	16-E
HAGGERTY	**10**	1	Michigan-Toledo Strip	13-N	16-E
HAIGHT	**12**	1	Michigan-Toledo Strip	12-N	13-E
HAILFAX	**4**	2	Michigan-Toledo Strip	14-N	15-E
HALE	**24**	1	Michigan-Toledo Strip	10-N	15-E
HALFMANN	**8**	1	Michigan-Toledo Strip	13-N	14-E
HALL	**19**	5	Michigan-Toledo Strip	11-N	15-E
" "	**2**	3	Michigan-Toledo Strip	14-N	13-E
" "	**30**	2	Michigan-Toledo Strip	9-N	16-E
" "	**25**	1	Michigan-Toledo Strip	10-N	16-E
" "	**20**	1	Michigan-Toledo Strip	11-N	16-E
" "	**14**	1	Michigan-Toledo Strip	12-N	15-E
" "	**15**	1	Michigan-Toledo Strip	12-N	16-E
" "	**28**	1	Michigan-Toledo Strip	9-N	14-E
" "	**31**	1	Michigan-Toledo Strip	9-N	17-E
HALWERSON	**24**	2	Michigan-Toledo Strip	10-N	15-E
HAMILTON	**23**	3	Michigan-Toledo Strip	10-N	14-E
" "	**24**	3	Michigan-Toledo Strip	10-N	15-E
" "	**16**	2	Michigan-Toledo Strip	11-N	12-E
HAMMOND	**25**	1	Michigan-Toledo Strip	10-N	16-E
" "	**26**	1	Michigan-Toledo Strip	10-N	17-E
" "	**20**	1	Michigan-Toledo Strip	11-N	16-E
HAMPTMAN	**6**	1	Michigan-Toledo Strip	13-N	12-E
HANDY	**9**	1	Michigan-Toledo Strip	13-N	15-E
HANES	**30**	3	Michigan-Toledo Strip	9-N	16-E
HANNA	**7**	1	Michigan-Toledo Strip	13-N	13-E
HANSEN	**30**	1	Michigan-Toledo Strip	9-N	16-E
HARDEN	**20**	1	Michigan-Toledo Strip	11-N	16-E
HARDER	**20**	2	Michigan-Toledo Strip	11-N	16-E
" "	**25**	1	Michigan-Toledo Strip	10-N	16-E
HARDING	**30**	1	Michigan-Toledo Strip	9-N	16-E
HARDY	**23**	1	Michigan-Toledo Strip	10-N	14-E

Surname	Map Group	Parcels of Land	Meridian/Township/Range		
HARKER	**2**	1	Michigan-Toledo Strip	14-N	13-E
HARLOW	**3**	2	Michigan-Toledo Strip	14-N	14-E
HARNACK	**21**	1	Michigan-Toledo Strip	10-N	12-E
HARPER	**13**	4	Michigan-Toledo Strip	12-N	14-E
" "	**17**	1	Michigan-Toledo Strip	11-N	13-E
HARRINGTON	**30**	1	Michigan-Toledo Strip	9-N	16-E
HARRIS	**17**	1	Michigan-Toledo Strip	11-N	13-E
" "	**1**	1	Michigan-Toledo Strip	14-N	12-E
" "	**29**	1	Michigan-Toledo Strip	9-N	15-E
HARTEE	**7**	3	Michigan-Toledo Strip	13-N	13-E
HARTEN	**29**	1	Michigan-Toledo Strip	9-N	15-E
HARTSHORN	**12**	1	Michigan-Toledo Strip	12-N	13-E
HARTWELL	**4**	2	Michigan-Toledo Strip	14-N	15-E
HARTWICK	**1**	1	Michigan-Toledo Strip	14-N	12-E
HATHAWAY	**6**	2	Michigan-Toledo Strip	13-N	12-E
HAWKS	**18**	2	Michigan-Toledo Strip	11-N	14-E
HAY	**12**	11	Michigan-Toledo Strip	12-N	13-E
" "	**6**	7	Michigan-Toledo Strip	13-N	12-E
" "	**11**	1	Michigan-Toledo Strip	12-N	12-E
HAYES	**23**	4	Michigan-Toledo Strip	10-N	14-E
HAYNES	**28**	2	Michigan-Toledo Strip	9-N	14-E
" "	**29**	2	Michigan-Toledo Strip	9-N	15-E
" "	**30**	1	Michigan-Toledo Strip	9-N	16-E
HAZEN	**12**	2	Michigan-Toledo Strip	12-N	13-E
HEARN	**21**	3	Michigan-Toledo Strip	10-N	12-E
HEATHCOTE	**9**	2	Michigan-Toledo Strip	13-N	15-E
" "	**6**	1	Michigan-Toledo Strip	13-N	12-E
HEBENTON	**6**	1	Michigan-Toledo Strip	13-N	12-E
HEDRICK	**30**	1	Michigan-Toledo Strip	9-N	16-E
HEEBENER	**28**	1	Michigan-Toledo Strip	9-N	14-E
HEIDE	**9**	1	Michigan-Toledo Strip	13-N	15-E
HEILIG	**4**	1	Michigan-Toledo Strip	14-N	15-E
HENDERSON	**18**	1	Michigan-Toledo Strip	11-N	14-E
HENRY	**13**	2	Michigan-Toledo Strip	12-N	14-E
" "	**12**	1	Michigan-Toledo Strip	12-N	13-E
HERRICK	**20**	1	Michigan-Toledo Strip	11-N	16-E
HERTEL	**7**	2	Michigan-Toledo Strip	13-N	13-E
HEYMAN	**14**	1	Michigan-Toledo Strip	12-N	15-E
HICKEY	**20**	1	Michigan-Toledo Strip	11-N	16-E
" "	**30**	1	Michigan-Toledo Strip	9-N	16-E
HIGGINS	**20**	1	Michigan-Toledo Strip	11-N	16-E
HILL	**18**	3	Michigan-Toledo Strip	11-N	14-E
" "	**8**	2	Michigan-Toledo Strip	13-N	14-E
" "	**27**	2	Michigan-Toledo Strip	9-N	13-E
" "	**22**	1	Michigan-Toledo Strip	10-N	13-E
" "	**4**	1	Michigan-Toledo Strip	14-N	15-E
HILLEBRAND	**16**	2	Michigan-Toledo Strip	11-N	12-E
HILLS	**4**	1	Michigan-Toledo Strip	14-N	15-E
HINKSON	**24**	1	Michigan-Toledo Strip	10-N	15-E
" "	**20**	1	Michigan-Toledo Strip	11-N	16-E
" "	**15**	1	Michigan-Toledo Strip	12-N	16-E
HIRSCHMAN	**18**	1	Michigan-Toledo Strip	11-N	14-E
" "	**20**	1	Michigan-Toledo Strip	11-N	16-E
HOBSON	**21**	1	Michigan-Toledo Strip	10-N	12-E
" "	**16**	1	Michigan-Toledo Strip	11-N	12-E
HOCHSTETTER	**13**	1	Michigan-Toledo Strip	12-N	14-E
HODGKINS	**27**	1	Michigan-Toledo Strip	9-N	13-E
HOFFMAN	**19**	1	Michigan-Toledo Strip	11-N	15-E
HOFFMANN	**16**	2	Michigan-Toledo Strip	11-N	12-E
HOGAN	**20**	3	Michigan-Toledo Strip	11-N	16-E

Surname	Map Group	Parcels of Land	Meridian/Township/Range		
HOGAN (Cont'd)	**31**	1	Michigan-Toledo Strip	9-N	17-E
HOLBERT	**28**	2	Michigan-Toledo Strip	9-N	14-E
HOLCOMB	**12**	4	Michigan-Toledo Strip	12-N	13-E
HOLLISTER	**30**	1	Michigan-Toledo Strip	9-N	16-E
" "	**31**	1	Michigan-Toledo Strip	9-N	17-E
HOLLSTEIN	**7**	3	Michigan-Toledo Strip	13-N	13-E
HOLMES	**1**	1	Michigan-Toledo Strip	14-N	12-E
HOMER	**15**	1	Michigan-Toledo Strip	12-N	16-E
HOMUTH	**16**	4	Michigan-Toledo Strip	11-N	12-E
HOOLE	**24**	2	Michigan-Toledo Strip	10-N	15-E
HOPKINS	**25**	1	Michigan-Toledo Strip	10-N	16-E
HOSACK	**13**	1	Michigan-Toledo Strip	12-N	14-E
HOUSE	**18**	3	Michigan-Toledo Strip	11-N	14-E
" "	**12**	2	Michigan-Toledo Strip	12-N	13-E
" "	**22**	1	Michigan-Toledo Strip	10-N	13-E
HOUSELL	**4**	1	Michigan-Toledo Strip	14-N	15-E
HOWARD	**18**	9	Michigan-Toledo Strip	11-N	14-E
" "	**8**	9	Michigan-Toledo Strip	13-N	14-E
" "	**25**	3	Michigan-Toledo Strip	10-N	16-E
" "	**17**	3	Michigan-Toledo Strip	11-N	13-E
" "	**7**	2	Michigan-Toledo Strip	13-N	13-E
" "	**21**	1	Michigan-Toledo Strip	10-N	12-E
" "	**20**	1	Michigan-Toledo Strip	11-N	16-E
HOWELL	**11**	1	Michigan-Toledo Strip	12-N	12-E
HOWEY	**6**	1	Michigan-Toledo Strip	13-N	12-E
HOWIE	**16**	1	Michigan-Toledo Strip	11-N	12-E
HOYT	**6**	3	Michigan-Toledo Strip	13-N	12-E
" "	**7**	1	Michigan-Toledo Strip	13-N	13-E
" "	**4**	1	Michigan-Toledo Strip	14-N	15-E
HUBBARD	**7**	16	Michigan-Toledo Strip	13-N	13-E
" "	**8**	6	Michigan-Toledo Strip	13-N	14-E
" "	**18**	3	Michigan-Toledo Strip	11-N	14-E
" "	**12**	3	Michigan-Toledo Strip	12-N	13-E
" "	**13**	3	Michigan-Toledo Strip	12-N	14-E
" "	**6**	3	Michigan-Toledo Strip	13-N	12-E
" "	**27**	2	Michigan-Toledo Strip	9-N	13-E
" "	**22**	1	Michigan-Toledo Strip	10-N	13-E
" "	**23**	1	Michigan-Toledo Strip	10-N	14-E
" "	**19**	1	Michigan-Toledo Strip	11-N	15-E
" "	**2**	1	Michigan-Toledo Strip	14-N	13-E
HUBEL	**1**	1	Michigan-Toledo Strip	14-N	12-E
" "	**2**	1	Michigan-Toledo Strip	14-N	13-E
HUBINGER	**6**	3	Michigan-Toledo Strip	13-N	12-E
HUCKINS	**25**	5	Michigan-Toledo Strip	10-N	16-E
HUGHES	**25**	1	Michigan-Toledo Strip	10-N	16-E
HULSART	**21**	3	Michigan-Toledo Strip	10-N	12-E
HULVERSON	**24**	1	Michigan-Toledo Strip	10-N	15-E
HULVORSON	**24**	2	Michigan-Toledo Strip	10-N	15-E
HUNT	**2**	2	Michigan-Toledo Strip	14-N	13-E
" "	**4**	1	Michigan-Toledo Strip	14-N	15-E
" "	**28**	1	Michigan-Toledo Strip	9-N	14-E
HUNTER	**24**	7	Michigan-Toledo Strip	10-N	15-E
" "	**16**	4	Michigan-Toledo Strip	11-N	12-E
HURD	**10**	8	Michigan-Toledo Strip	13-N	16-E
" "	**15**	3	Michigan-Toledo Strip	12-N	16-E
" "	**5**	3	Michigan-Toledo Strip	14-N	16-E
" "	**20**	1	Michigan-Toledo Strip	11-N	16-E
HURLEY	**9**	2	Michigan-Toledo Strip	13-N	15-E
HUSBAND	**7**	1	Michigan-Toledo Strip	13-N	13-E
HYSLOP	**17**	2	Michigan-Toledo Strip	11-N	13-E

Surname	Map Group	Parcels of Land	Meridian/Township/Range		
INGRAHAM	**12**	1	Michigan-Toledo Strip	12-N	13-E
IRVING	**28**	1	Michigan-Toledo Strip	9-N	14-E
IRWIN	**2**	5	Michigan-Toledo Strip	14-N	13-E
JENNY	**22**	1	Michigan-Toledo Strip	10-N	13-E
JEX	**20**	1	Michigan-Toledo Strip	11-N	16-E
JOHNS	**9**	1	Michigan-Toledo Strip	13-N	15-E
JOHNSON	**17**	5	Michigan-Toledo Strip	11-N	13-E
" "	**21**	3	Michigan-Toledo Strip	10-N	12-E
" "	**12**	3	Michigan-Toledo Strip	12-N	13-E
" "	**23**	2	Michigan-Toledo Strip	10-N	14-E
" "	**19**	2	Michigan-Toledo Strip	11-N	15-E
" "	**15**	2	Michigan-Toledo Strip	12-N	16-E
" "	**22**	1	Michigan-Toledo Strip	10-N	13-E
" "	**16**	1	Michigan-Toledo Strip	11-N	12-E
" "	**11**	1	Michigan-Toledo Strip	12-N	12-E
" "	**3**	1	Michigan-Toledo Strip	14-N	14-E
JOINER	**15**	1	Michigan-Toledo Strip	12-N	16-E
JOLLY	**24**	2	Michigan-Toledo Strip	10-N	15-E
JONES	**3**	4	Michigan-Toledo Strip	14-N	14-E
" "	**30**	4	Michigan-Toledo Strip	9-N	16-E
" "	**9**	3	Michigan-Toledo Strip	13-N	15-E
" "	**28**	3	Michigan-Toledo Strip	9-N	14-E
" "	**29**	3	Michigan-Toledo Strip	9-N	15-E
" "	**24**	1	Michigan-Toledo Strip	10-N	15-E
" "	**19**	1	Michigan-Toledo Strip	11-N	15-E
" "	**12**	1	Michigan-Toledo Strip	12-N	13-E
" "	**15**	1	Michigan-Toledo Strip	12-N	16-E
" "	**7**	1	Michigan-Toledo Strip	13-N	13-E
JORDAN	**2**	9	Michigan-Toledo Strip	14-N	13-E
JOWETT	**20**	1	Michigan-Toledo Strip	11-N	16-E
JURN	**13**	1	Michigan-Toledo Strip	12-N	14-E
JURY	**29**	1	Michigan-Toledo Strip	9-N	15-E
KAUFMANN	**19**	1	Michigan-Toledo Strip	11-N	15-E
KE_Y_KE_SIK	**30**	1	Michigan-Toledo Strip	9-N	16-E
KELLAND	**12**	1	Michigan-Toledo Strip	12-N	13-E
KELLEY	**4**	5	Michigan-Toledo Strip	14-N	15-E
" "	**11**	1	Michigan-Toledo Strip	12-N	12-E
" "	**6**	1	Michigan-Toledo Strip	13-N	12-E
KELLY	**11**	2	Michigan-Toledo Strip	12-N	12-E
" "	**12**	1	Michigan-Toledo Strip	12-N	13-E
KELSEY	**31**	1	Michigan-Toledo Strip	9-N	17-E
KELSO	**14**	1	Michigan-Toledo Strip	12-N	15-E
KENGOTT	**22**	2	Michigan-Toledo Strip	10-N	13-E
KENNY	**13**	1	Michigan-Toledo Strip	12-N	14-E
KENYON	**4**	1	Michigan-Toledo Strip	14-N	15-E
KERCHEVAL	**5**	2	Michigan-Toledo Strip	14-N	16-E
KEYS	**16**	2	Michigan-Toledo Strip	11-N	12-E
KEYWORTH	**6**	1	Michigan-Toledo Strip	13-N	12-E
KIBBEE	**12**	8	Michigan-Toledo Strip	12-N	13-E
" "	**18**	2	Michigan-Toledo Strip	11-N	14-E
" "	**3**	1	Michigan-Toledo Strip	14-N	14-E
KIDD	**14**	3	Michigan-Toledo Strip	12-N	15-E
KING	**24**	5	Michigan-Toledo Strip	10-N	15-E
" "	**12**	3	Michigan-Toledo Strip	12-N	13-E
" "	**18**	2	Michigan-Toledo Strip	11-N	14-E
" "	**7**	2	Michigan-Toledo Strip	13-N	13-E
" "	**22**	1	Michigan-Toledo Strip	10-N	13-E
" "	**23**	1	Michigan-Toledo Strip	10-N	14-E
" "	**14**	1	Michigan-Toledo Strip	12-N	15-E
" "	**8**	1	Michigan-Toledo Strip	13-N	14-E

Surname	Map Group	Parcels of Land	Meridian/Township/Range		
KING (Cont'd)	**9**	1	Michigan-Toledo Strip	13-N	15-E
" "	**30**	1	Michigan-Toledo Strip	9-N	16-E
KINNE	**30**	2	Michigan-Toledo Strip	9-N	16-E
KINSLEY	**7**	4	Michigan-Toledo Strip	13-N	13-E
KINY	**24**	1	Michigan-Toledo Strip	10-N	15-E
KIPP	**11**	1	Michigan-Toledo Strip	12-N	12-E
KIPPER	**4**	2	Michigan-Toledo Strip	14-N	15-E
KIRBY	**12**	1	Michigan-Toledo Strip	12-N	13-E
KIRKBRIDE	**17**	3	Michigan-Toledo Strip	11-N	13-E
KIRKPATRICK	**16**	2	Michigan-Toledo Strip	11-N	12-E
KIRKWOOD	**8**	3	Michigan-Toledo Strip	13-N	14-E
KLEIN	**16**	2	Michigan-Toledo Strip	11-N	12-E
" "	**7**	1	Michigan-Toledo Strip	13-N	13-E
KLINGHAMER	**8**	1	Michigan-Toledo Strip	13-N	14-E
KLOSTERMANN	**4**	1	Michigan-Toledo Strip	14-N	15-E
KNAPP	**19**	1	Michigan-Toledo Strip	11-N	15-E
KNIGHT	**16**	3	Michigan-Toledo Strip	11-N	12-E
KNOX	**30**	2	Michigan-Toledo Strip	9-N	16-E
KOLAR	**3**	1	Michigan-Toledo Strip	14-N	14-E
KOLTS	**22**	3	Michigan-Toledo Strip	10-N	13-E
KOTZKE	**17**	2	Michigan-Toledo Strip	11-N	13-E
KRITZMANN	**7**	1	Michigan-Toledo Strip	13-N	13-E
KROETSCH	**7**	4	Michigan-Toledo Strip	13-N	13-E
KRUPP	**2**	1	Michigan-Toledo Strip	14-N	13-E
KURTZ	**9**	1	Michigan-Toledo Strip	13-N	15-E
LACASSE	**27**	2	Michigan-Toledo Strip	9-N	13-E
LAKE	**4**	2	Michigan-Toledo Strip	14-N	15-E
LAMB	**11**	7	Michigan-Toledo Strip	12-N	12-E
LAMBERT	**23**	1	Michigan-Toledo Strip	10-N	14-E
LANCASTER	**9**	1	Michigan-Toledo Strip	13-N	15-E
LANE	**14**	1	Michigan-Toledo Strip	12-N	15-E
" "	**15**	1	Michigan-Toledo Strip	12-N	16-E
LANGE	**21**	1	Michigan-Toledo Strip	10-N	12-E
LANGENBUCK	**7**	3	Michigan-Toledo Strip	13-N	13-E
LAPPIN	**20**	2	Michigan-Toledo Strip	11-N	16-E
LAUREL	**14**	3	Michigan-Toledo Strip	12-N	15-E
LAVIN	**3**	4	Michigan-Toledo Strip	14-N	14-E
LAW	**2**	1	Michigan-Toledo Strip	14-N	13-E
LECHTENBURG	**4**	1	Michigan-Toledo Strip	14-N	15-E
LEE	**28**	4	Michigan-Toledo Strip	9-N	14-E
" "	**17**	1	Michigan-Toledo Strip	11-N	13-E
" "	**9**	1	Michigan-Toledo Strip	13-N	15-E
LEEPLA	**1**	2	Michigan-Toledo Strip	14-N	12-E
LEINS	**24**	3	Michigan-Toledo Strip	10-N	15-E
LEITCH	**9**	3	Michigan-Toledo Strip	13-N	15-E
" "	**8**	1	Michigan-Toledo Strip	13-N	14-E
LENNON	**16**	1	Michigan-Toledo Strip	11-N	12-E
LENSE	**14**	1	Michigan-Toledo Strip	12-N	15-E
LENTY	**18**	1	Michigan-Toledo Strip	11-N	14-E
LEONARD	**11**	3	Michigan-Toledo Strip	12-N	12-E
" "	**12**	3	Michigan-Toledo Strip	12-N	13-E
" "	**7**	3	Michigan-Toledo Strip	13-N	13-E
" "	**6**	2	Michigan-Toledo Strip	13-N	12-E
" "	**23**	1	Michigan-Toledo Strip	10-N	14-E
" "	**8**	1	Michigan-Toledo Strip	13-N	14-E
" "	**4**	1	Michigan-Toledo Strip	14-N	15-E
LEONHARD	**30**	2	Michigan-Toledo Strip	9-N	16-E
LESTER	**20**	1	Michigan-Toledo Strip	11-N	16-E
" "	**4**	1	Michigan-Toledo Strip	14-N	15-E
" "	**30**	1	Michigan-Toledo Strip	9-N	16-E

Surname	Map Group	Parcels of Land	Meridian/Township/Range		
LEVAGOOD	**29**	1	Michigan-Toledo Strip	9-N	15-E
LEWIS	**12**	2	Michigan-Toledo Strip	12-N	13-E
LICHTENBERG	**18**	5	Michigan-Toledo Strip	11-N	14-E
" "	**24**	1	Michigan-Toledo Strip	10-N	15-E
" "	**19**	1	Michigan-Toledo Strip	11-N	15-E
LIDDELL	**21**	2	Michigan-Toledo Strip	10-N	12-E
LINCE	**14**	1	Michigan-Toledo Strip	12-N	15-E
LINDNER	**7**	2	Michigan-Toledo Strip	13-N	13-E
LINDSAY	**2**	2	Michigan-Toledo Strip	14-N	13-E
LINDSEY	**2**	1	Michigan-Toledo Strip	14-N	13-E
LINK	**3**	2	Michigan-Toledo Strip	14-N	14-E
LITT	**2**	2	Michigan-Toledo Strip	14-N	13-E
LITTLE	**8**	1	Michigan-Toledo Strip	13-N	14-E
LIVINGWAY	**8**	2	Michigan-Toledo Strip	13-N	14-E
LOCK	**28**	1	Michigan-Toledo Strip	9-N	14-E
LOCKE	**28**	1	Michigan-Toledo Strip	9-N	14-E
LOOBY	**24**	1	Michigan-Toledo Strip	10-N	15-E
LOSAYA	**20**	1	Michigan-Toledo Strip	11-N	16-E
LOUNT	**30**	1	Michigan-Toledo Strip	9-N	16-E
LOWE	**2**	1	Michigan-Toledo Strip	14-N	13-E
LUCAS	**14**	1	Michigan-Toledo Strip	12-N	15-E
LUCE	**30**	7	Michigan-Toledo Strip	9-N	16-E
" "	**25**	4	Michigan-Toledo Strip	10-N	16-E
" "	**19**	3	Michigan-Toledo Strip	11-N	15-E
" "	**24**	1	Michigan-Toledo Strip	10-N	15-E
LYNN	**30**	1	Michigan-Toledo Strip	9-N	16-E
LYON	**10**	13	Michigan-Toledo Strip	13-N	16-E
" "	**4**	6	Michigan-Toledo Strip	14-N	15-E
" "	**9**	4	Michigan-Toledo Strip	13-N	15-E
" "	**25**	2	Michigan-Toledo Strip	10-N	16-E
" "	**5**	2	Michigan-Toledo Strip	14-N	16-E
MACLACHLAN	**7**	3	Michigan-Toledo Strip	13-N	13-E
MACOMBER	**23**	4	Michigan-Toledo Strip	10-N	14-E
" "	**16**	1	Michigan-Toledo Strip	11-N	12-E
MACY	**5**	7	Michigan-Toledo Strip	14-N	16-E
" "	**4**	2	Michigan-Toledo Strip	14-N	15-E
MAHON	**3**	1	Michigan-Toledo Strip	14-N	14-E
MAIRE	**30**	3	Michigan-Toledo Strip	9-N	16-E
MALONE	**4**	3	Michigan-Toledo Strip	14-N	15-E
MANION	**19**	1	Michigan-Toledo Strip	11-N	15-E
MANNEY	**6**	3	Michigan-Toledo Strip	13-N	12-E
MANS	**16**	1	Michigan-Toledo Strip	11-N	12-E
MANSS	**16**	2	Michigan-Toledo Strip	11-N	12-E
MANWARING	**11**	1	Michigan-Toledo Strip	12-N	12-E
" "	**6**	1	Michigan-Toledo Strip	13-N	12-E
MARECK	**29**	3	Michigan-Toledo Strip	9-N	15-E
MARIN	**27**	1	Michigan-Toledo Strip	9-N	13-E
MARREDETH	**2**	7	Michigan-Toledo Strip	14-N	13-E
MARRELL	**18**	1	Michigan-Toledo Strip	11-N	14-E
MARRIOTT	**2**	3	Michigan-Toledo Strip	14-N	13-E
MARSHALL	**20**	1	Michigan-Toledo Strip	11-N	16-E
" "	**27**	1	Michigan-Toledo Strip	9-N	13-E
MARTINDALE	**15**	2	Michigan-Toledo Strip	12-N	16-E
" "	**27**	2	Michigan-Toledo Strip	9-N	13-E
MARVIN	**16**	2	Michigan-Toledo Strip	11-N	12-E
MASDAN	**27**	1	Michigan-Toledo Strip	9-N	13-E
MASDEN	**27**	1	Michigan-Toledo Strip	9-N	13-E
MASKELL	**20**	2	Michigan-Toledo Strip	11-N	16-E
MASON	**17**	6	Michigan-Toledo Strip	11-N	13-E
" "	**24**	4	Michigan-Toledo Strip	10-N	15-E

Surname	Map Group	Parcels of Land	Meridian/Township/Range		
MASON (Cont'd)	**18**	2	Michigan-Toledo Strip	11-N	14-E
" "	**7**	2	Michigan-Toledo Strip	13-N	13-E
" "	**9**	2	Michigan-Toledo Strip	13-N	15-E
" "	**22**	1	Michigan-Toledo Strip	10-N	13-E
" "	**23**	1	Michigan-Toledo Strip	10-N	14-E
" "	**19**	1	Michigan-Toledo Strip	11-N	15-E
" "	**14**	1	Michigan-Toledo Strip	12-N	15-E
" "	**8**	1	Michigan-Toledo Strip	13-N	14-E
" "	**27**	1	Michigan-Toledo Strip	9-N	13-E
" "	**29**	1	Michigan-Toledo Strip	9-N	15-E
" "	**30**	1	Michigan-Toledo Strip	9-N	16-E
MASSEY	**4**	4	Michigan-Toledo Strip	14-N	15-E
MASTEN	**20**	1	Michigan-Toledo Strip	11-N	16-E
MASTERSON	**30**	1	Michigan-Toledo Strip	9-N	16-E
MATTESON	**25**	1	Michigan-Toledo Strip	10-N	16-E
MATTISON	**25**	1	Michigan-Toledo Strip	10-N	16-E
MAXSON	**14**	1	Michigan-Toledo Strip	12-N	15-E
MAY	**9**	1	Michigan-Toledo Strip	13-N	15-E
MAYES	**13**	1	Michigan-Toledo Strip	12-N	14-E
MAYNARD	**19**	1	Michigan-Toledo Strip	11-N	15-E
MCALPIN	**16**	3	Michigan-Toledo Strip	11-N	12-E
MCALPINE	**11**	3	Michigan-Toledo Strip	12-N	12-E
MCBRIDE	**7**	1	Michigan-Toledo Strip	13-N	13-E
" "	**9**	1	Michigan-Toledo Strip	13-N	15-E
" "	**4**	1	Michigan-Toledo Strip	14-N	15-E
MCCABE	**27**	1	Michigan-Toledo Strip	9-N	13-E
MCCARTHY	**29**	3	Michigan-Toledo Strip	9-N	15-E
MCCLURE	**18**	3	Michigan-Toledo Strip	11-N	14-E
" "	**30**	2	Michigan-Toledo Strip	9-N	16-E
" "	**24**	1	Michigan-Toledo Strip	10-N	15-E
MCCOLLOM	**2**	1	Michigan-Toledo Strip	14-N	13-E
MCCONNELL	**6**	3	Michigan-Toledo Strip	13-N	12-E
" "	**1**	2	Michigan-Toledo Strip	14-N	12-E
MCCORMACK	**18**	1	Michigan-Toledo Strip	11-N	14-E
MCCORMICK	**1**	7	Michigan-Toledo Strip	14-N	12-E
" "	**2**	1	Michigan-Toledo Strip	14-N	13-E
MCCREDIE	**22**	1	Michigan-Toledo Strip	10-N	13-E
MCDONALD	**29**	2	Michigan-Toledo Strip	9-N	15-E
" "	**24**	1	Michigan-Toledo Strip	10-N	15-E
" "	**12**	1	Michigan-Toledo Strip	12-N	13-E
" "	**13**	1	Michigan-Toledo Strip	12-N	14-E
" "	**3**	1	Michigan-Toledo Strip	14-N	14-E
MCDOUGALL	**2**	4	Michigan-Toledo Strip	14-N	13-E
MCEACHIN	**1**	3	Michigan-Toledo Strip	14-N	12-E
MCFARLAND	**24**	1	Michigan-Toledo Strip	10-N	15-E
" "	**18**	1	Michigan-Toledo Strip	11-N	14-E
" "	**19**	1	Michigan-Toledo Strip	11-N	15-E
MCGILL	**21**	2	Michigan-Toledo Strip	10-N	12-E
MCGINN	**13**	7	Michigan-Toledo Strip	12-N	14-E
" "	**8**	6	Michigan-Toledo Strip	13-N	14-E
" "	**27**	1	Michigan-Toledo Strip	9-N	13-E
MCGINNIS	**1**	1	Michigan-Toledo Strip	14-N	12-E
MCGRATH	**23**	2	Michigan-Toledo Strip	10-N	14-E
" "	**30**	1	Michigan-Toledo Strip	9-N	16-E
MCGREGOR	**22**	1	Michigan-Toledo Strip	10-N	13-E
" "	**20**	1	Michigan-Toledo Strip	11-N	16-E
" "	**14**	1	Michigan-Toledo Strip	12-N	15-E
" "	**9**	1	Michigan-Toledo Strip	13-N	15-E
MCGUGAN	**13**	2	Michigan-Toledo Strip	12-N	14-E
MCHUGH	**6**	1	Michigan-Toledo Strip	13-N	12-E

Surname	Map Group	Parcels of Land	Meridian/Township/Range		
MCINNIS	**29**	1	Michigan-Toledo Strip	9-N	15-E
MCINTOSH	**6**	2	Michigan-Toledo Strip	13-N	12-E
" "	**1**	2	Michigan-Toledo Strip	14-N	12-E
" "	**15**	1	Michigan-Toledo Strip	12-N	16-E
" "	**9**	1	Michigan-Toledo Strip	13-N	15-E
MCINTYRE	**2**	2	Michigan-Toledo Strip	14-N	13-E
" "	**7**	1	Michigan-Toledo Strip	13-N	13-E
MCKAY	**1**	3	Michigan-Toledo Strip	14-N	12-E
MCKELLAR	**2**	1	Michigan-Toledo Strip	14-N	13-E
MCKENZIE	**7**	3	Michigan-Toledo Strip	13-N	13-E
" "	**2**	1	Michigan-Toledo Strip	14-N	13-E
MCKIE	**6**	4	Michigan-Toledo Strip	13-N	12-E
" "	**11**	2	Michigan-Toledo Strip	12-N	12-E
MCLACHLAN	**7**	5	Michigan-Toledo Strip	13-N	13-E
MCLACHLIN	**7**	1	Michigan-Toledo Strip	13-N	13-E
MCLAREN	**23**	1	Michigan-Toledo Strip	10-N	14-E
MCLEAN	**7**	4	Michigan-Toledo Strip	13-N	13-E
" "	**21**	1	Michigan-Toledo Strip	10-N	12-E
MCLEISH	**16**	2	Michigan-Toledo Strip	11-N	12-E
MCLELLAN	**23**	3	Michigan-Toledo Strip	10-N	14-E
MCMAHON	**28**	3	Michigan-Toledo Strip	9-N	14-E
MCMILLAN	**19**	2	Michigan-Toledo Strip	11-N	15-E
MCMILLEN	**25**	1	Michigan-Toledo Strip	10-N	16-E
MCMULDROCH	**15**	1	Michigan-Toledo Strip	12-N	16-E
" "	**9**	1	Michigan-Toledo Strip	13-N	15-E
MCPHAIL	**2**	8	Michigan-Toledo Strip	14-N	13-E
" "	**7**	3	Michigan-Toledo Strip	13-N	13-E
" "	**1**	1	Michigan-Toledo Strip	14-N	12-E
MCPHEE	**11**	2	Michigan-Toledo Strip	12-N	12-E
MCRAE	**2**	5	Michigan-Toledo Strip	14-N	13-E
" "	**27**	3	Michigan-Toledo Strip	9-N	13-E
MCRAY	**1**	3	Michigan-Toledo Strip	14-N	12-E
MCVANE	**1**	1	Michigan-Toledo Strip	14-N	12-E
MEEHAN	**1**	1	Michigan-Toledo Strip	14-N	12-E
MELVILLE	**8**	2	Michigan-Toledo Strip	13-N	14-E
" "	**14**	1	Michigan-Toledo Strip	12-N	15-E
MERCHANT	**1**	2	Michigan-Toledo Strip	14-N	12-E
" "	**15**	1	Michigan-Toledo Strip	12-N	16-E
MEREDEN	**2**	1	Michigan-Toledo Strip	14-N	13-E
MERREDETH	**2**	1	Michigan-Toledo Strip	14-N	13-E
MERRILL	**28**	23	Michigan-Toledo Strip	9-N	14-E
" "	**24**	4	Michigan-Toledo Strip	10-N	15-E
" "	**17**	4	Michigan-Toledo Strip	11-N	13-E
" "	**29**	3	Michigan-Toledo Strip	9-N	15-E
" "	**19**	2	Michigan-Toledo Strip	11-N	15-E
MERRILLS	**4**	1	Michigan-Toledo Strip	14-N	15-E
MERRIMAN	**9**	3	Michigan-Toledo Strip	13-N	15-E
" "	**10**	2	Michigan-Toledo Strip	13-N	16-E
METCALF	**2**	2	Michigan-Toledo Strip	14-N	13-E
MICHIGAN	**14**	1	Michigan-Toledo Strip	12-N	15-E
MIDDAUGH	**25**	1	Michigan-Toledo Strip	10-N	16-E
" "	**9**	1	Michigan-Toledo Strip	13-N	15-E
MILES	**29**	2	Michigan-Toledo Strip	9-N	15-E
" "	**30**	1	Michigan-Toledo Strip	9-N	16-E
MILLER	**7**	5	Michigan-Toledo Strip	13-N	13-E
" "	**29**	5	Michigan-Toledo Strip	9-N	15-E
" "	**23**	3	Michigan-Toledo Strip	10-N	14-E
" "	**19**	3	Michigan-Toledo Strip	11-N	15-E
" "	**12**	3	Michigan-Toledo Strip	12-N	13-E
" "	**11**	2	Michigan-Toledo Strip	12-N	12-E

Surname	Map Group	Parcels of Land	Meridian/Township/Range		
MILLER (Cont'd)	**6**	2	Michigan-Toledo Strip	13-N	12-E
" "	**13**	1	Michigan-Toledo Strip	12-N	14-E
" "	**28**	1	Michigan-Toledo Strip	9-N	14-E
" "	**30**	1	Michigan-Toledo Strip	9-N	16-E
MILLS	**23**	10	Michigan-Toledo Strip	10-N	14-E
" "	**17**	10	Michigan-Toledo Strip	11-N	13-E
" "	**22**	5	Michigan-Toledo Strip	10-N	13-E
" "	**27**	4	Michigan-Toledo Strip	9-N	13-E
" "	**9**	3	Michigan-Toledo Strip	13-N	15-E
" "	**25**	2	Michigan-Toledo Strip	10-N	16-E
" "	**24**	1	Michigan-Toledo Strip	10-N	15-E
" "	**19**	1	Michigan-Toledo Strip	11-N	15-E
" "	**11**	1	Michigan-Toledo Strip	12-N	12-E
" "	**31**	1	Michigan-Toledo Strip	9-N	17-E
MINARD	**17**	2	Michigan-Toledo Strip	11-N	13-E
MINER	**4**	1	Michigan-Toledo Strip	14-N	15-E
MITCHELL	**19**	1	Michigan-Toledo Strip	11-N	15-E
MIZNER	**20**	4	Michigan-Toledo Strip	11-N	16-E
" "	**4**	4	Michigan-Toledo Strip	14-N	15-E
" "	**5**	3	Michigan-Toledo Strip	14-N	16-E
" "	**19**	2	Michigan-Toledo Strip	11-N	15-E
" "	**14**	2	Michigan-Toledo Strip	12-N	15-E
" "	**15**	2	Michigan-Toledo Strip	12-N	16-E
" "	**25**	1	Michigan-Toledo Strip	10-N	16-E
" "	**26**	1	Michigan-Toledo Strip	10-N	17-E
" "	**13**	1	Michigan-Toledo Strip	12-N	14-E
MOFFAT	**25**	3	Michigan-Toledo Strip	10-N	16-E
" "	**18**	3	Michigan-Toledo Strip	11-N	14-E
" "	**29**	1	Michigan-Toledo Strip	9-N	15-E
MOLLOY	**4**	1	Michigan-Toledo Strip	14-N	15-E
MONTGOMERY	**16**	2	Michigan-Toledo Strip	11-N	12-E
" "	**21**	1	Michigan-Toledo Strip	10-N	12-E
MONTNEY	**6**	1	Michigan-Toledo Strip	13-N	12-E
MOODY	**3**	1	Michigan-Toledo Strip	14-N	14-E
MOONY	**3**	4	Michigan-Toledo Strip	14-N	14-E
" "	**16**	1	Michigan-Toledo Strip	11-N	12-E
MOORE	**12**	10	Michigan-Toledo Strip	12-N	13-E
" "	**17**	5	Michigan-Toledo Strip	11-N	13-E
" "	**13**	4	Michigan-Toledo Strip	12-N	14-E
" "	**28**	3	Michigan-Toledo Strip	9-N	14-E
" "	**18**	1	Michigan-Toledo Strip	11-N	14-E
" "	**11**	1	Michigan-Toledo Strip	12-N	12-E
" "	**1**	1	Michigan-Toledo Strip	14-N	12-E
MORELL	**2**	1	Michigan-Toledo Strip	14-N	13-E
MORGAN	**3**	3	Michigan-Toledo Strip	14-N	14-E
" "	**21**	2	Michigan-Toledo Strip	10-N	12-E
MORRILL	**18**	1	Michigan-Toledo Strip	11-N	14-E
MORRIS	**16**	1	Michigan-Toledo Strip	11-N	12-E
MORRISON	**1**	1	Michigan-Toledo Strip	14-N	12-E
MORSE	**7**	20	Michigan-Toledo Strip	13-N	13-E
" "	**6**	8	Michigan-Toledo Strip	13-N	12-E
" "	**13**	5	Michigan-Toledo Strip	12-N	14-E
MORTON	**8**	1	Michigan-Toledo Strip	13-N	14-E
MOSHIER	**11**	10	Michigan-Toledo Strip	12-N	12-E
MOSS	**22**	1	Michigan-Toledo Strip	10-N	13-E
MUDGE	**3**	1	Michigan-Toledo Strip	14-N	14-E
MULLINS	**23**	1	Michigan-Toledo Strip	10-N	14-E
MUMA	**2**	1	Michigan-Toledo Strip	14-N	13-E
MUNFORD	**15**	1	Michigan-Toledo Strip	12-N	16-E
MUNRO	**25**	2	Michigan-Toledo Strip	10-N	16-E

Surname	Map Group	Parcels of Land	Meridian/Township/Range		
MURDOCK	**3**	1	Michigan-Toledo Strip	14-N	14-E
MURPHY	**3**	2	Michigan-Toledo Strip	14-N	14-E
" "	**12**	1	Michigan-Toledo Strip	12-N	13-E
" "	**6**	1	Michigan-Toledo Strip	13-N	12-E
" "	**1**	1	Michigan-Toledo Strip	14-N	12-E
MURRAY	**21**	3	Michigan-Toledo Strip	10-N	12-E
MYERS	**17**	2	Michigan-Toledo Strip	11-N	13-E
NAGESIK	**30**	1	Michigan-Toledo Strip	9-N	16-E
NESTER	**19**	2	Michigan-Toledo Strip	11-N	15-E
" "	**20**	1	Michigan-Toledo Strip	11-N	16-E
NEUMANN	**16**	2	Michigan-Toledo Strip	11-N	12-E
NEVILLE	**1**	1	Michigan-Toledo Strip	14-N	12-E
NEWMAN	**16**	3	Michigan-Toledo Strip	11-N	12-E
NEWTON	**27**	1	Michigan-Toledo Strip	9-N	13-E
NICHOL	**14**	3	Michigan-Toledo Strip	12-N	15-E
NICHOLS	**14**	1	Michigan-Toledo Strip	12-N	15-E
" "	**29**	1	Michigan-Toledo Strip	9-N	15-E
NICHOLSON	**30**	1	Michigan-Toledo Strip	9-N	16-E
NICOL	**1**	3	Michigan-Toledo Strip	14-N	12-E
NICOLL	**1**	1	Michigan-Toledo Strip	14-N	12-E
NISBET	**30**	1	Michigan-Toledo Strip	9-N	16-E
NIXON	**17**	3	Michigan-Toledo Strip	11-N	13-E
" "	**4**	1	Michigan-Toledo Strip	14-N	15-E
NOBLE	**12**	2	Michigan-Toledo Strip	12-N	13-E
" "	**4**	2	Michigan-Toledo Strip	14-N	15-E
NOLAN	**1**	2	Michigan-Toledo Strip	14-N	12-E
NORMANDIE	**29**	2	Michigan-Toledo Strip	9-N	15-E
NORRIS	**17**	1	Michigan-Toledo Strip	11-N	13-E
NORTHRUP	**30**	1	Michigan-Toledo Strip	9-N	16-E
NOTLEY	**16**	1	Michigan-Toledo Strip	11-N	12-E
NYE	**4**	3	Michigan-Toledo Strip	14-N	15-E
OAKES	**22**	1	Michigan-Toledo Strip	10-N	13-E
" "	**17**	1	Michigan-Toledo Strip	11-N	13-E
" "	**18**	1	Michigan-Toledo Strip	11-N	14-E
OBRIEN	**29**	1	Michigan-Toledo Strip	9-N	15-E
OCALLAGHAN	**19**	1	Michigan-Toledo Strip	11-N	15-E
ODLAUM	**19**	1	Michigan-Toledo Strip	11-N	15-E
OGDEN	**4**	2	Michigan-Toledo Strip	14-N	15-E
" "	**9**	1	Michigan-Toledo Strip	13-N	15-E
OLDFIELD	**15**	1	Michigan-Toledo Strip	12-N	16-E
ORTON	**7**	2	Michigan-Toledo Strip	13-N	13-E
" "	**24**	1	Michigan-Toledo Strip	10-N	15-E
ORVIS	**31**	3	Michigan-Toledo Strip	9-N	17-E
" "	**30**	2	Michigan-Toledo Strip	9-N	16-E
" "	**25**	1	Michigan-Toledo Strip	10-N	16-E
OSEWALD	**4**	1	Michigan-Toledo Strip	14-N	15-E
OSGOOD	**9**	2	Michigan-Toledo Strip	13-N	15-E
OSWALD	**4**	1	Michigan-Toledo Strip	14-N	15-E
OWEN	**31**	2	Michigan-Toledo Strip	9-N	17-E
PACE	**11**	1	Michigan-Toledo Strip	12-N	12-E
PACK	**22**	9	Michigan-Toledo Strip	10-N	13-E
" "	**18**	4	Michigan-Toledo Strip	11-N	14-E
" "	**24**	1	Michigan-Toledo Strip	10-N	15-E
" "	**19**	1	Michigan-Toledo Strip	11-N	15-E
" "	**12**	1	Michigan-Toledo Strip	12-N	13-E
PAGANETTI	**15**	2	Michigan-Toledo Strip	12-N	16-E
PAISLEY	**28**	1	Michigan-Toledo Strip	9-N	14-E
PAKE	**9**	3	Michigan-Toledo Strip	13-N	15-E
PALMER	**24**	2	Michigan-Toledo Strip	10-N	15-E
" "	**14**	2	Michigan-Toledo Strip	12-N	15-E

Surname	Map Group	Parcels of Land	Meridian/Township/Range		
PALMS	**5**	3	Michigan-Toledo Strip	14-N	16-E
PAPST	**6**	1	Michigan-Toledo Strip	13-N	12-E
PARKER	**10**	13	Michigan-Toledo Strip	13-N	16-E
" "	**4**	6	Michigan-Toledo Strip	14-N	15-E
" "	**9**	4	Michigan-Toledo Strip	13-N	15-E
" "	**5**	2	Michigan-Toledo Strip	14-N	16-E
" "	**25**	1	Michigan-Toledo Strip	10-N	16-E
" "	**29**	1	Michigan-Toledo Strip	9-N	15-E
PARKIN	**23**	1	Michigan-Toledo Strip	10-N	14-E
" "	**19**	1	Michigan-Toledo Strip	11-N	15-E
PARKINSON	**18**	1	Michigan-Toledo Strip	11-N	14-E
PARMELY	**30**	1	Michigan-Toledo Strip	9-N	16-E
PARTRIDGE	**6**	3	Michigan-Toledo Strip	13-N	12-E
" "	**13**	1	Michigan-Toledo Strip	12-N	14-E
PATTERSON	**20**	1	Michigan-Toledo Strip	11-N	16-E
PATTISON	**8**	2	Michigan-Toledo Strip	13-N	14-E
PATTON	**2**	1	Michigan-Toledo Strip	14-N	13-E
PAUL	**24**	1	Michigan-Toledo Strip	10-N	15-E
PEASLEE	**30**	1	Michigan-Toledo Strip	9-N	16-E
PEGSHA	**3**	2	Michigan-Toledo Strip	14-N	14-E
PENSIONNAL	**7**	3	Michigan-Toledo Strip	13-N	13-E
PERKINS	**21**	4	Michigan-Toledo Strip	10-N	12-E
" "	**28**	4	Michigan-Toledo Strip	9-N	14-E
PERRET	**3**	1	Michigan-Toledo Strip	14-N	14-E
PETER	**2**	8	Michigan-Toledo Strip	14-N	13-E
PETERS	**15**	1	Michigan-Toledo Strip	12-N	16-E
" "	**2**	1	Michigan-Toledo Strip	14-N	13-E
PETTY	**20**	1	Michigan-Toledo Strip	11-N	16-E
PHELPS	**25**	1	Michigan-Toledo Strip	10-N	16-E
" "	**26**	1	Michigan-Toledo Strip	10-N	17-E
" "	**20**	1	Michigan-Toledo Strip	11-N	16-E
" "	**27**	1	Michigan-Toledo Strip	9-N	13-E
PHILIPS	**25**	1	Michigan-Toledo Strip	10-N	16-E
" "	**11**	1	Michigan-Toledo Strip	12-N	12-E
PHILLIPS	**12**	2	Michigan-Toledo Strip	12-N	13-E
PICKARD	**14**	1	Michigan-Toledo Strip	12-N	15-E
PIERCE	**25**	1	Michigan-Toledo Strip	10-N	16-E
PIFER	**9**	1	Michigan-Toledo Strip	13-N	15-E
PITTS	**28**	3	Michigan-Toledo Strip	9-N	14-E
POLAND	**19**	1	Michigan-Toledo Strip	11-N	15-E
POLLARD	**2**	3	Michigan-Toledo Strip	14-N	13-E
" "	**1**	2	Michigan-Toledo Strip	14-N	12-E
PORTER	**26**	3	Michigan-Toledo Strip	10-N	17-E
" "	**25**	1	Michigan-Toledo Strip	10-N	16-E
" "	**31**	1	Michigan-Toledo Strip	9-N	17-E
POST	**1**	3	Michigan-Toledo Strip	14-N	12-E
" "	**7**	2	Michigan-Toledo Strip	13-N	13-E
POTTS	**23**	3	Michigan-Toledo Strip	10-N	14-E
" "	**24**	1	Michigan-Toledo Strip	10-N	15-E
" "	**30**	1	Michigan-Toledo Strip	9-N	16-E
POWER	**18**	1	Michigan-Toledo Strip	11-N	14-E
PRATT	**11**	2	Michigan-Toledo Strip	12-N	12-E
" "	**25**	1	Michigan-Toledo Strip	10-N	16-E
" "	**20**	1	Michigan-Toledo Strip	11-N	16-E
PRESLEY	**9**	1	Michigan-Toledo Strip	13-N	15-E
PREVOST	**27**	1	Michigan-Toledo Strip	9-N	13-E
PROCTOR	**6**	1	Michigan-Toledo Strip	13-N	12-E
PROVOST	**25**	1	Michigan-Toledo Strip	10-N	16-E
PURMAN	**4**	1	Michigan-Toledo Strip	14-N	15-E
PURMANN	**4**	1	Michigan-Toledo Strip	14-N	15-E

Surname	Map Group	Parcels of Land	Meridian/Township/Range		
PUTNAM	**8**	2	Michigan-Toledo Strip	13-N	14-E
QUAY	**13**	1	Michigan-Toledo Strip	12-N	14-E
RAMSAY	**21**	1	Michigan-Toledo Strip	10-N	12-E
RATTRAY	**16**	1	Michigan-Toledo Strip	11-N	12-E
RAUH	**4**	1	Michigan-Toledo Strip	14-N	15-E
RAYMOND	**15**	2	Michigan-Toledo Strip	12-N	16-E
" "	**20**	1	Michigan-Toledo Strip	11-N	16-E
READ	**8**	2	Michigan-Toledo Strip	13-N	14-E
" "	**9**	1	Michigan-Toledo Strip	13-N	15-E
REDPATH	**3**	2	Michigan-Toledo Strip	14-N	14-E
REED	**9**	1	Michigan-Toledo Strip	13-N	15-E
REEVE	**17**	35	Michigan-Toledo Strip	11-N	13-E
" "	**19**	10	Michigan-Toledo Strip	11-N	15-E
" "	**18**	4	Michigan-Toledo Strip	11-N	14-E
" "	**12**	3	Michigan-Toledo Strip	12-N	13-E
" "	**22**	2	Michigan-Toledo Strip	10-N	13-E
" "	**24**	1	Michigan-Toledo Strip	10-N	15-E
" "	**13**	1	Michigan-Toledo Strip	12-N	14-E
" "	**30**	1	Michigan-Toledo Strip	9-N	16-E
REINELT	**8**	7	Michigan-Toledo Strip	13-N	14-E
" "	**7**	3	Michigan-Toledo Strip	13-N	13-E
REMICK	**7**	1	Michigan-Toledo Strip	13-N	13-E
" "	**1**	1	Michigan-Toledo Strip	14-N	12-E
REYNOLDS	**31**	1	Michigan-Toledo Strip	9-N	17-E
RIBBEL	**6**	1	Michigan-Toledo Strip	13-N	12-E
RICE	**19**	4	Michigan-Toledo Strip	11-N	15-E
RICHARDS	**7**	1	Michigan-Toledo Strip	13-N	13-E
RITTENDORF	**2**	1	Michigan-Toledo Strip	14-N	13-E
ROADHOUSE	**9**	2	Michigan-Toledo Strip	13-N	15-E
" "	**3**	1	Michigan-Toledo Strip	14-N	14-E
ROBB	**24**	1	Michigan-Toledo Strip	10-N	15-E
ROBERTS	**20**	1	Michigan-Toledo Strip	11-N	16-E
" "	**13**	1	Michigan-Toledo Strip	12-N	14-E
ROBERTSON	**3**	1	Michigan-Toledo Strip	14-N	14-E
ROBINSON	**29**	3	Michigan-Toledo Strip	9-N	15-E
" "	**2**	2	Michigan-Toledo Strip	14-N	13-E
" "	**7**	1	Michigan-Toledo Strip	13-N	13-E
" "	**28**	1	Michigan-Toledo Strip	9-N	14-E
ROBISON	**23**	1	Michigan-Toledo Strip	10-N	14-E
" "	**20**	1	Michigan-Toledo Strip	11-N	16-E
ROBSON	**17**	2	Michigan-Toledo Strip	11-N	13-E
" "	**2**	1	Michigan-Toledo Strip	14-N	13-E
ROCKWELL	**22**	2	Michigan-Toledo Strip	10-N	13-E
" "	**27**	2	Michigan-Toledo Strip	9-N	13-E
ROGERS	**16**	1	Michigan-Toledo Strip	11-N	12-E
ROLLAS	**3**	2	Michigan-Toledo Strip	14-N	14-E
ROSBERRY	**14**	1	Michigan-Toledo Strip	12-N	15-E
ROSE	**7**	1	Michigan-Toledo Strip	13-N	13-E
ROSS	**22**	3	Michigan-Toledo Strip	10-N	13-E
" "	**14**	3	Michigan-Toledo Strip	12-N	15-E
" "	**9**	2	Michigan-Toledo Strip	13-N	15-E
" "	**8**	1	Michigan-Toledo Strip	13-N	14-E
ROTH	**4**	1	Michigan-Toledo Strip	14-N	15-E
ROVOLT	**13**	1	Michigan-Toledo Strip	12-N	14-E
RUDD	**16**	1	Michigan-Toledo Strip	11-N	12-E
RUDEL	**25**	1	Michigan-Toledo Strip	10-N	16-E
RUMNEY	**10**	1	Michigan-Toledo Strip	13-N	16-E
RUNKWITZ	**20**	2	Michigan-Toledo Strip	11-N	16-E
RUSSELSMITH	**22**	2	Michigan-Toledo Strip	10-N	13-E
RUST	**23**	2	Michigan-Toledo Strip	10-N	14-E

Surname	Map Group	Parcels of Land	Meridian/Township/Range		
RUST (Cont'd)	**24**	2	Michigan-Toledo Strip	10-N	15-E
" "	**18**	1	Michigan-Toledo Strip	11-N	14-E
" "	**12**	1	Michigan-Toledo Strip	12-N	13-E
" "	**6**	1	Michigan-Toledo Strip	13-N	12-E
" "	**28**	1	Michigan-Toledo Strip	9-N	14-E
" "	**29**	1	Michigan-Toledo Strip	9-N	15-E
RYAN	**15**	2	Michigan-Toledo Strip	12-N	16-E
" "	**23**	1	Michigan-Toledo Strip	10-N	14-E
RYANS	**23**	2	Michigan-Toledo Strip	10-N	14-E
RYCKMAN	**3**	4	Michigan-Toledo Strip	14-N	14-E
RYEN	**30**	1	Michigan-Toledo Strip	9-N	16-E
SABIN	**27**	2	Michigan-Toledo Strip	9-N	13-E
SALSBURY	**28**	2	Michigan-Toledo Strip	9-N	14-E
SAMPLE	**9**	3	Michigan-Toledo Strip	13-N	15-E
" "	**25**	2	Michigan-Toledo Strip	10-N	16-E
SANBORN	**23**	7	Michigan-Toledo Strip	10-N	14-E
" "	**18**	5	Michigan-Toledo Strip	11-N	14-E
" "	**20**	5	Michigan-Toledo Strip	11-N	16-E
" "	**28**	5	Michigan-Toledo Strip	9-N	14-E
" "	**29**	5	Michigan-Toledo Strip	9-N	15-E
" "	**19**	4	Michigan-Toledo Strip	11-N	15-E
" "	**30**	3	Michigan-Toledo Strip	9-N	16-E
" "	**25**	2	Michigan-Toledo Strip	10-N	16-E
" "	**12**	2	Michigan-Toledo Strip	12-N	13-E
" "	**6**	1	Michigan-Toledo Strip	13-N	12-E
SANDERSON	**30**	1	Michigan-Toledo Strip	9-N	16-E
" "	**31**	1	Michigan-Toledo Strip	9-N	17-E
SANSBURN	**1**	2	Michigan-Toledo Strip	14-N	12-E
SARGENT	**8**	2	Michigan-Toledo Strip	13-N	14-E
SARSFIELD	**29**	1	Michigan-Toledo Strip	9-N	15-E
SARTWELL	**6**	1	Michigan-Toledo Strip	13-N	12-E
SAUDER	**21**	2	Michigan-Toledo Strip	10-N	12-E
SAUNDERS	**29**	5	Michigan-Toledo Strip	9-N	15-E
SAWYER	**8**	1	Michigan-Toledo Strip	13-N	14-E
SCHAFER	**11**	1	Michigan-Toledo Strip	12-N	12-E
SCHAGENE	**7**	3	Michigan-Toledo Strip	13-N	13-E
SCHEDINA	**3**	4	Michigan-Toledo Strip	14-N	14-E
SCHLEGEL	**16**	2	Michigan-Toledo Strip	11-N	12-E
SCHMELZ	**4**	1	Michigan-Toledo Strip	14-N	15-E
SCHNEIDER	**2**	3	Michigan-Toledo Strip	14-N	13-E
" "	**9**	1	Michigan-Toledo Strip	13-N	15-E
SCHOLTZ	**16**	1	Michigan-Toledo Strip	11-N	12-E
SCHOLZ	**21**	1	Michigan-Toledo Strip	10-N	12-E
SCHREIN	**16**	2	Michigan-Toledo Strip	11-N	12-E
SCHUBEL	**4**	1	Michigan-Toledo Strip	14-N	15-E
SCHULZ	**30**	1	Michigan-Toledo Strip	9-N	16-E
SCHUMACHER	**4**	1	Michigan-Toledo Strip	14-N	15-E
SCHWEIZER	**22**	5	Michigan-Toledo Strip	10-N	13-E
SCHWIGART	**4**	2	Michigan-Toledo Strip	14-N	15-E
SCOLLAY	**7**	3	Michigan-Toledo Strip	13-N	13-E
" "	**23**	1	Michigan-Toledo Strip	10-N	14-E
SCOTT	**29**	3	Michigan-Toledo Strip	9-N	15-E
" "	**10**	1	Michigan-Toledo Strip	13-N	16-E
" "	**5**	1	Michigan-Toledo Strip	14-N	16-E
SEAL	**24**	2	Michigan-Toledo Strip	10-N	15-E
SEAMAN	**3**	1	Michigan-Toledo Strip	14-N	14-E
SEAMANS	**3**	1	Michigan-Toledo Strip	14-N	14-E
SEARS	**12**	1	Michigan-Toledo Strip	12-N	13-E
" "	**6**	1	Michigan-Toledo Strip	13-N	12-E
" "	**7**	1	Michigan-Toledo Strip	13-N	13-E

Surname	Map Group	Parcels of Land	Meridian/Township/Range		
SEBOLD	**4**	1	Michigan-Toledo Strip	14-N	15-E
SEDER	**7**	5	Michigan-Toledo Strip	13-N	13-E
SEGRET	**3**	1	Michigan-Toledo Strip	14-N	14-E
SELLARS	**17**	2	Michigan-Toledo Strip	11-N	13-E
SELTZER	**16**	1	Michigan-Toledo Strip	11-N	12-E
SEYMOUR	**22**	2	Michigan-Toledo Strip	10-N	13-E
SHANE	**7**	1	Michigan-Toledo Strip	13-N	13-E
SHARLOW	**13**	1	Michigan-Toledo Strip	12-N	14-E
SHARP	**25**	1	Michigan-Toledo Strip	10-N	16-E
SHARRARD	**6**	2	Michigan-Toledo Strip	13-N	12-E
SHEA	**2**	2	Michigan-Toledo Strip	14-N	13-E
SHEFFER	**1**	2	Michigan-Toledo Strip	14-N	12-E
SHEIBLE	**4**	1	Michigan-Toledo Strip	14-N	15-E
SHELDEN	**25**	1	Michigan-Toledo Strip	10-N	16-E
SHELDON	**12**	2	Michigan-Toledo Strip	12-N	13-E
" "	**7**	1	Michigan-Toledo Strip	13-N	13-E
SHELL	**30**	7	Michigan-Toledo Strip	9-N	16-E
" "	**29**	5	Michigan-Toledo Strip	9-N	15-E
" "	**25**	1	Michigan-Toledo Strip	10-N	16-E
SHEPHARD	**25**	1	Michigan-Toledo Strip	10-N	16-E
" "	**2**	1	Michigan-Toledo Strip	14-N	13-E
SHERWOOD	**12**	1	Michigan-Toledo Strip	12-N	13-E
SHILL	**28**	2	Michigan-Toledo Strip	9-N	14-E
SHIRLEY	**20**	2	Michigan-Toledo Strip	11-N	16-E
SHRIGLEY	**29**	1	Michigan-Toledo Strip	9-N	15-E
SIBLEY	**19**	9	Michigan-Toledo Strip	11-N	15-E
" "	**25**	8	Michigan-Toledo Strip	10-N	16-E
" "	**30**	3	Michigan-Toledo Strip	9-N	16-E
" "	**20**	2	Michigan-Toledo Strip	11-N	16-E
SILBEY	**30**	1	Michigan-Toledo Strip	9-N	16-E
SILVERTHORN	**11**	1	Michigan-Toledo Strip	12-N	12-E
SIMMS	**8**	2	Michigan-Toledo Strip	13-N	14-E
" "	**27**	1	Michigan-Toledo Strip	9-N	13-E
SIMONS	**4**	2	Michigan-Toledo Strip	14-N	15-E
" "	**5**	1	Michigan-Toledo Strip	14-N	16-E
SINCLAIR	**1**	2	Michigan-Toledo Strip	14-N	12-E
" "	**7**	1	Michigan-Toledo Strip	13-N	13-E
SISCHO	**28**	1	Michigan-Toledo Strip	9-N	14-E
SKINNER	**19**	1	Michigan-Toledo Strip	11-N	15-E
SLADE	**16**	1	Michigan-Toledo Strip	11-N	12-E
SLY	**30**	2	Michigan-Toledo Strip	9-N	16-E
" "	**29**	1	Michigan-Toledo Strip	9-N	15-E
SMITH	**11**	5	Michigan-Toledo Strip	12-N	12-E
" "	**28**	5	Michigan-Toledo Strip	9-N	14-E
" "	**30**	5	Michigan-Toledo Strip	9-N	16-E
" "	**22**	4	Michigan-Toledo Strip	10-N	13-E
" "	**18**	4	Michigan-Toledo Strip	11-N	14-E
" "	**23**	3	Michigan-Toledo Strip	10-N	14-E
" "	**16**	3	Michigan-Toledo Strip	11-N	12-E
" "	**21**	2	Michigan-Toledo Strip	10-N	12-E
" "	**19**	2	Michigan-Toledo Strip	11-N	15-E
" "	**13**	2	Michigan-Toledo Strip	12-N	14-E
" "	**3**	2	Michigan-Toledo Strip	14-N	14-E
" "	**26**	1	Michigan-Toledo Strip	10-N	17-E
" "	**17**	1	Michigan-Toledo Strip	11-N	13-E
" "	**8**	1	Michigan-Toledo Strip	13-N	14-E
" "	**2**	1	Michigan-Toledo Strip	14-N	13-E
" "	**27**	1	Michigan-Toledo Strip	9-N	13-E
SNAY	**4**	1	Michigan-Toledo Strip	14-N	15-E
SNELL	**22**	4	Michigan-Toledo Strip	10-N	13-E

Surname	Map Group	Parcels of Land	Meridian/Township/Range		
SNELL (Cont'd)	**1**	3	Michigan-Toledo Strip	14-N	12-E
SNOVER	**21**	3	Michigan-Toledo Strip	10-N	12-E
SNOWDEN	**19**	1	Michigan-Toledo Strip	11-N	15-E
SNOWDIN	**14**	1	Michigan-Toledo Strip	12-N	15-E
SNYDER	**9**	1	Michigan-Toledo Strip	13-N	15-E
SOMERVILLE	**24**	1	Michigan-Toledo Strip	10-N	15-E
SOMMERHALDER	**11**	1	Michigan-Toledo Strip	12-N	12-E
SOMMERVILLE	**2**	3	Michigan-Toledo Strip	14-N	13-E
" "	**1**	1	Michigan-Toledo Strip	14-N	12-E
SON	**7**	1	Michigan-Toledo Strip	13-N	13-E
SOPER	**11**	1	Michigan-Toledo Strip	12-N	12-E
" "	**12**	1	Michigan-Toledo Strip	12-N	13-E
SOULE	**2**	1	Michigan-Toledo Strip	14-N	13-E
SPARLING	**2**	2	Michigan-Toledo Strip	14-N	13-E
SPEARMAN	**9**	1	Michigan-Toledo Strip	13-N	15-E
SPENCER	**9**	2	Michigan-Toledo Strip	13-N	15-E
" "	**23**	1	Michigan-Toledo Strip	10-N	14-E
" "	**25**	1	Michigan-Toledo Strip	10-N	16-E
" "	**15**	1	Michigan-Toledo Strip	12-N	16-E
SPRING	**12**	3	Michigan-Toledo Strip	12-N	13-E
" "	**29**	1	Michigan-Toledo Strip	9-N	15-E
STACEY	**2**	1	Michigan-Toledo Strip	14-N	13-E
STACUM	**9**	1	Michigan-Toledo Strip	13-N	15-E
" "	**4**	1	Michigan-Toledo Strip	14-N	15-E
STAFFORD	**25**	1	Michigan-Toledo Strip	10-N	16-E
STEBBINS	**14**	2	Michigan-Toledo Strip	12-N	15-E
" "	**19**	1	Michigan-Toledo Strip	11-N	15-E
STEEL	**25**	2	Michigan-Toledo Strip	10-N	16-E
" "	**11**	1	Michigan-Toledo Strip	12-N	12-E
STEENSON	**21**	1	Michigan-Toledo Strip	10-N	12-E
STEEVENS	**4**	6	Michigan-Toledo Strip	14-N	15-E
" "	**10**	5	Michigan-Toledo Strip	13-N	16-E
" "	**15**	4	Michigan-Toledo Strip	12-N	16-E
" "	**30**	4	Michigan-Toledo Strip	9-N	16-E
STEINER	**23**	1	Michigan-Toledo Strip	10-N	14-E
STEINHOFF	**27**	2	Michigan-Toledo Strip	9-N	13-E
STENSON	**21**	1	Michigan-Toledo Strip	10-N	12-E
STEPHENS	**28**	5	Michigan-Toledo Strip	9-N	14-E
" "	**18**	2	Michigan-Toledo Strip	11-N	14-E
" "	**7**	1	Michigan-Toledo Strip	13-N	13-E
" "	**30**	1	Michigan-Toledo Strip	9-N	16-E
STEVENS	**29**	13	Michigan-Toledo Strip	9-N	15-E
" "	**30**	8	Michigan-Toledo Strip	9-N	16-E
" "	**24**	6	Michigan-Toledo Strip	10-N	15-E
" "	**27**	3	Michigan-Toledo Strip	9-N	13-E
" "	**28**	3	Michigan-Toledo Strip	9-N	14-E
" "	**23**	1	Michigan-Toledo Strip	10-N	14-E
" "	**25**	1	Michigan-Toledo Strip	10-N	16-E
STEVENSON	**25**	11	Michigan-Toledo Strip	10-N	16-E
" "	**24**	3	Michigan-Toledo Strip	10-N	15-E
" "	**7**	1	Michigan-Toledo Strip	13-N	13-E
STEWARD	**1**	1	Michigan-Toledo Strip	14-N	12-E
STEWART	**24**	3	Michigan-Toledo Strip	10-N	15-E
STILSON	**17**	8	Michigan-Toledo Strip	11-N	13-E
" "	**22**	2	Michigan-Toledo Strip	10-N	13-E
" "	**23**	2	Michigan-Toledo Strip	10-N	14-E
" "	**18**	2	Michigan-Toledo Strip	11-N	14-E
" "	**11**	1	Michigan-Toledo Strip	12-N	12-E
" "	**7**	1	Michigan-Toledo Strip	13-N	13-E
STILWELL	**3**	6	Michigan-Toledo Strip	14-N	14-E

Surname	Map Group	Parcels of Land	Meridian/Township/Range		
STINSON	**21**	1	Michigan-Toledo Strip	10-N	12-E
" "	**22**	1	Michigan-Toledo Strip	10-N	13-E
STOCKWELL	**13**	1	Michigan-Toledo Strip	12-N	14-E
STOVER	**13**	1	Michigan-Toledo Strip	12-N	14-E
STOWELL	**20**	1	Michigan-Toledo Strip	11-N	16-E
STRONG	**12**	1	Michigan-Toledo Strip	12-N	13-E
STROUD	**2**	2	Michigan-Toledo Strip	14-N	13-E
STUART	**1**	1	Michigan-Toledo Strip	14-N	12-E
SULLIVAN	**24**	1	Michigan-Toledo Strip	10-N	15-E
SULLIVIN	**3**	1	Michigan-Toledo Strip	14-N	14-E
SUMNER	**27**	1	Michigan-Toledo Strip	9-N	13-E
SUTTON	**20**	1	Michigan-Toledo Strip	11-N	16-E
" "	**1**	1	Michigan-Toledo Strip	14-N	12-E
SWAFFER	**30**	1	Michigan-Toledo Strip	9-N	16-E
SWART	**8**	1	Michigan-Toledo Strip	13-N	14-E
SWEETSER	**23**	2	Michigan-Toledo Strip	10-N	14-E
" "	**18**	2	Michigan-Toledo Strip	11-N	14-E
SWIFT	**10**	3	Michigan-Toledo Strip	13-N	16-E
SWINSTON	**11**	1	Michigan-Toledo Strip	12-N	12-E
TAMBURAT	**16**	3	Michigan-Toledo Strip	11-N	12-E
TATE	**8**	2	Michigan-Toledo Strip	13-N	14-E
" "	**16**	1	Michigan-Toledo Strip	11-N	12-E
TAYLOR	**2**	5	Michigan-Toledo Strip	14-N	13-E
" "	**13**	2	Michigan-Toledo Strip	12-N	14-E
" "	**19**	1	Michigan-Toledo Strip	11-N	15-E
" "	**20**	1	Michigan-Toledo Strip	11-N	16-E
" "	**4**	1	Michigan-Toledo Strip	14-N	15-E
TEMISON	**20**	1	Michigan-Toledo Strip	11-N	16-E
TEMPLE	**29**	3	Michigan-Toledo Strip	9-N	15-E
TERRIL	**30**	1	Michigan-Toledo Strip	9-N	16-E
THAYER	**8**	4	Michigan-Toledo Strip	13-N	14-E
" "	**3**	3	Michigan-Toledo Strip	14-N	14-E
" "	**4**	2	Michigan-Toledo Strip	14-N	15-E
" "	**27**	1	Michigan-Toledo Strip	9-N	13-E
THEABO	**30**	1	Michigan-Toledo Strip	9-N	16-E
THEBOULT	**30**	1	Michigan-Toledo Strip	9-N	16-E
THIBODEAU	**29**	1	Michigan-Toledo Strip	9-N	15-E
THOMAS	**2**	3	Michigan-Toledo Strip	14-N	13-E
" "	**17**	2	Michigan-Toledo Strip	11-N	13-E
THOMPSON	**1**	1	Michigan-Toledo Strip	14-N	12-E
" "	**3**	1	Michigan-Toledo Strip	14-N	14-E
THOMSON	**1**	1	Michigan-Toledo Strip	14-N	12-E
THORNTON	**8**	2	Michigan-Toledo Strip	13-N	14-E
THROOP	**25**	1	Michigan-Toledo Strip	10-N	16-E
" "	**20**	1	Michigan-Toledo Strip	11-N	16-E
" "	**5**	1	Michigan-Toledo Strip	14-N	16-E
TOBIN	**23**	2	Michigan-Toledo Strip	10-N	14-E
" "	**9**	1	Michigan-Toledo Strip	13-N	15-E
TODD	**20**	5	Michigan-Toledo Strip	11-N	16-E
" "	**29**	3	Michigan-Toledo Strip	9-N	15-E
" "	**15**	2	Michigan-Toledo Strip	12-N	16-E
TOOL	**28**	5	Michigan-Toledo Strip	9-N	14-E
TOWER	**7**	1	Michigan-Toledo Strip	13-N	13-E
TRAINER	**28**	2	Michigan-Toledo Strip	9-N	14-E
TRATHEN	**1**	1	Michigan-Toledo Strip	14-N	12-E
TRAVIS	**6**	1	Michigan-Toledo Strip	13-N	12-E
TROWBRIDGE	**25**	11	Michigan-Toledo Strip	10-N	16-E
" "	**19**	10	Michigan-Toledo Strip	11-N	15-E
" "	**20**	2	Michigan-Toledo Strip	11-N	16-E
" "	**30**	1	Michigan-Toledo Strip	9-N	16-E

Surname	Map Group	Parcels of Land	Meridian/Township/Range		
TUCKER	**14**	2	Michigan-Toledo Strip	12-N	15-E
TWISS	**16**	5	Michigan-Toledo Strip	11-N	12-E
TWIST	**16**	1	Michigan-Toledo Strip	11-N	12-E
" "	**11**	1	Michigan-Toledo Strip	12-N	12-E
TYLDEN	**16**	1	Michigan-Toledo Strip	11-N	12-E
TYLER	**6**	2	Michigan-Toledo Strip	13-N	12-E
" "	**7**	1	Michigan-Toledo Strip	13-N	13-E
UHL	**4**	1	Michigan-Toledo Strip	14-N	15-E
URIDGE	**4**	5	Michigan-Toledo Strip	14-N	15-E
VACHI	**14**	3	Michigan-Toledo Strip	12-N	15-E
VAN ALLEN	**1**	3	Michigan-Toledo Strip	14-N	12-E
" "	**4**	1	Michigan-Toledo Strip	14-N	15-E
VAN CAMP	**31**	4	Michigan-Toledo Strip	9-N	17-E
" "	**30**	2	Michigan-Toledo Strip	9-N	16-E
" "	**23**	1	Michigan-Toledo Strip	10-N	14-E
" "	**9**	1	Michigan-Toledo Strip	13-N	15-E
VAN DUSEN	**27**	2	Michigan-Toledo Strip	9-N	13-E
VAN LOAN	**1**	2	Michigan-Toledo Strip	14-N	12-E
VAN NEST	**23**	1	Michigan-Toledo Strip	10-N	14-E
VAN SICKLE	**8**	1	Michigan-Toledo Strip	13-N	14-E
VANDERBURGH	**18**	8	Michigan-Toledo Strip	11-N	14-E
" "	**19**	1	Michigan-Toledo Strip	11-N	15-E
VANDUSEN	**27**	1	Michigan-Toledo Strip	9-N	13-E
VARNUM	**23**	1	Michigan-Toledo Strip	10-N	14-E
VARTY	**4**	3	Michigan-Toledo Strip	14-N	15-E
VARTZ	**4**	1	Michigan-Toledo Strip	14-N	15-E
VATER	**7**	1	Michigan-Toledo Strip	13-N	13-E
VERDRIES	**21**	1	Michigan-Toledo Strip	10-N	12-E
VIETS	**12**	1	Michigan-Toledo Strip	12-N	13-E
VINCENT	**18**	1	Michigan-Toledo Strip	11-N	14-E
" "	**20**	1	Michigan-Toledo Strip	11-N	16-E
VOGAL	**4**	1	Michigan-Toledo Strip	14-N	15-E
WAHLY	**20**	4	Michigan-Toledo Strip	11-N	16-E
WALDO	**10**	3	Michigan-Toledo Strip	13-N	16-E
WALDON	**1**	1	Michigan-Toledo Strip	14-N	12-E
WALKER	**21**	8	Michigan-Toledo Strip	10-N	12-E
" "	**16**	4	Michigan-Toledo Strip	11-N	12-E
" "	**17**	1	Michigan-Toledo Strip	11-N	13-E
" "	**1**	1	Michigan-Toledo Strip	14-N	12-E
WALLACE	**29**	5	Michigan-Toledo Strip	9-N	15-E
" "	**24**	3	Michigan-Toledo Strip	10-N	15-E
WALLIS	**11**	2	Michigan-Toledo Strip	12-N	12-E
WALSH	**6**	6	Michigan-Toledo Strip	13-N	12-E
" "	**7**	2	Michigan-Toledo Strip	13-N	13-E
" "	**16**	1	Michigan-Toledo Strip	11-N	12-E
WARD	**4**	13	Michigan-Toledo Strip	14-N	15-E
" "	**19**	4	Michigan-Toledo Strip	11-N	15-E
" "	**20**	3	Michigan-Toledo Strip	11-N	16-E
" "	**30**	2	Michigan-Toledo Strip	9-N	16-E
" "	**9**	1	Michigan-Toledo Strip	13-N	15-E
" "	**29**	1	Michigan-Toledo Strip	9-N	15-E
WARING	**15**	1	Michigan-Toledo Strip	12-N	16-E
WARNER	**18**	3	Michigan-Toledo Strip	11-N	14-E
WARPOOL	**16**	1	Michigan-Toledo Strip	11-N	12-E
WARREN	**6**	12	Michigan-Toledo Strip	13-N	12-E
" "	**23**	1	Michigan-Toledo Strip	10-N	14-E
WATERBURY	**15**	2	Michigan-Toledo Strip	12-N	16-E
" "	**20**	1	Michigan-Toledo Strip	11-N	16-E
" "	**4**	1	Michigan-Toledo Strip	14-N	15-E
WATERS	**27**	4	Michigan-Toledo Strip	9-N	13-E

Surname	Map Group	Parcels of Land	Meridian/Township/Range		
WATKINS	**20**	1	Michigan-Toledo Strip	11-N	16-E
WATROUS	**7**	2	Michigan-Toledo Strip	13-N	13-E
" "	**6**	1	Michigan-Toledo Strip	13-N	12-E
WATSON	**1**	3	Michigan-Toledo Strip	14-N	12-E
" "	**6**	1	Michigan-Toledo Strip	13-N	12-E
" "	**2**	1	Michigan-Toledo Strip	14-N	13-E
WAY	**1**	3	Michigan-Toledo Strip	14-N	12-E
WEBSTER	**30**	3	Michigan-Toledo Strip	9-N	16-E
" "	**2**	1	Michigan-Toledo Strip	14-N	13-E
WEHR	**4**	2	Michigan-Toledo Strip	14-N	15-E
WEISEMBERGER	**3**	1	Michigan-Toledo Strip	14-N	14-E
WEITZEL	**7**	1	Michigan-Toledo Strip	13-N	13-E
WELCH	**18**	1	Michigan-Toledo Strip	11-N	14-E
" "	**9**	1	Michigan-Toledo Strip	13-N	15-E
WELLES	**8**	2	Michigan-Toledo Strip	13-N	14-E
WELLS	**7**	7	Michigan-Toledo Strip	13-N	13-E
" "	**28**	6	Michigan-Toledo Strip	9-N	14-E
" "	**1**	5	Michigan-Toledo Strip	14-N	12-E
" "	**3**	3	Michigan-Toledo Strip	14-N	14-E
" "	**20**	2	Michigan-Toledo Strip	11-N	16-E
" "	**14**	2	Michigan-Toledo Strip	12-N	15-E
" "	**24**	1	Michigan-Toledo Strip	10-N	15-E
" "	**17**	1	Michigan-Toledo Strip	11-N	13-E
" "	**29**	1	Michigan-Toledo Strip	9-N	15-E
WELSH	**16**	1	Michigan-Toledo Strip	11-N	12-E
" "	**29**	1	Michigan-Toledo Strip	9-N	15-E
WESLEY	**15**	1	Michigan-Toledo Strip	12-N	16-E
WHALES	**9**	1	Michigan-Toledo Strip	13-N	15-E
WHEELER	**7**	12	Michigan-Toledo Strip	13-N	13-E
" "	**23**	2	Michigan-Toledo Strip	10-N	14-E
WHEELOCK	**28**	4	Michigan-Toledo Strip	9-N	14-E
WHITAKER	**22**	2	Michigan-Toledo Strip	10-N	13-E
WHITE	**2**	4	Michigan-Toledo Strip	14-N	13-E
" "	**29**	4	Michigan-Toledo Strip	9-N	15-E
" "	**10**	2	Michigan-Toledo Strip	13-N	16-E
WHITMAN	**27**	11	Michigan-Toledo Strip	9-N	13-E
" "	**28**	1	Michigan-Toledo Strip	9-N	14-E
WHITNEY	**28**	3	Michigan-Toledo Strip	9-N	14-E
" "	**14**	2	Michigan-Toledo Strip	12-N	15-E
WIGGINS	**16**	1	Michigan-Toledo Strip	11-N	12-E
WIGHT	**19**	4	Michigan-Toledo Strip	11-N	15-E
" "	**14**	4	Michigan-Toledo Strip	12-N	15-E
" "	**23**	2	Michigan-Toledo Strip	10-N	14-E
" "	**9**	2	Michigan-Toledo Strip	13-N	15-E
" "	**27**	2	Michigan-Toledo Strip	9-N	13-E
" "	**28**	2	Michigan-Toledo Strip	9-N	14-E
" "	**24**	1	Michigan-Toledo Strip	10-N	15-E
" "	**25**	1	Michigan-Toledo Strip	10-N	16-E
" "	**20**	1	Michigan-Toledo Strip	11-N	16-E
WILDFONG	**17**	2	Michigan-Toledo Strip	11-N	13-E
" "	**12**	1	Michigan-Toledo Strip	12-N	13-E
WILKINSON	**6**	1	Michigan-Toledo Strip	13-N	12-E
WILLCOX	**6**	3	Michigan-Toledo Strip	13-N	12-E
WILLERTON	**7**	1	Michigan-Toledo Strip	13-N	13-E
WILLIAMS	**12**	3	Michigan-Toledo Strip	12-N	13-E
" "	**21**	2	Michigan-Toledo Strip	10-N	12-E
" "	**2**	1	Michigan-Toledo Strip	14-N	13-E
WILLIS	**9**	3	Michigan-Toledo Strip	13-N	15-E
WILLITS	**30**	1	Michigan-Toledo Strip	9-N	16-E
WILLITTS	**30**	1	Michigan-Toledo Strip	9-N	16-E

Surname	Map Group	Parcels of Land	Meridian/Township/Range		
WILLOUGHBY	**27**	1	Michigan-Toledo Strip	9-N	13-E
WILLSON	**23**	2	Michigan-Toledo Strip	10-N	14-E
WILSON	**21**	12	Michigan-Toledo Strip	10-N	12-E
" "	**27**	2	Michigan-Toledo Strip	9-N	13-E
" "	**23**	1	Michigan-Toledo Strip	10-N	14-E
" "	**25**	1	Michigan-Toledo Strip	10-N	16-E
" "	**6**	1	Michigan-Toledo Strip	13-N	12-E
WILTSIE	**4**	2	Michigan-Toledo Strip	14-N	15-E
WING	**7**	3	Michigan-Toledo Strip	13-N	13-E
WISSON	**25**	1	Michigan-Toledo Strip	10-N	16-E
WITHAM	**20**	1	Michigan-Toledo Strip	11-N	16-E
WIXSON	**30**	19	Michigan-Toledo Strip	9-N	16-E
" "	**25**	6	Michigan-Toledo Strip	10-N	16-E
" "	**9**	5	Michigan-Toledo Strip	13-N	15-E
" "	**4**	3	Michigan-Toledo Strip	14-N	15-E
" "	**14**	2	Michigan-Toledo Strip	12-N	15-E
" "	**24**	1	Michigan-Toledo Strip	10-N	15-E
" "	**19**	1	Michigan-Toledo Strip	11-N	15-E
WODRASKA	**3**	1	Michigan-Toledo Strip	14-N	14-E
WOOD	**16**	3	Michigan-Toledo Strip	11-N	12-E
" "	**6**	1	Michigan-Toledo Strip	13-N	12-E
WOODRUFF	**30**	1	Michigan-Toledo Strip	9-N	16-E
WOODS	**7**	24	Michigan-Toledo Strip	13-N	13-E
" "	**6**	13	Michigan-Toledo Strip	13-N	12-E
" "	**1**	5	Michigan-Toledo Strip	14-N	12-E
" "	**25**	3	Michigan-Toledo Strip	10-N	16-E
" "	**20**	2	Michigan-Toledo Strip	11-N	16-E
" "	**9**	2	Michigan-Toledo Strip	13-N	15-E
" "	**22**	1	Michigan-Toledo Strip	10-N	13-E
" "	**23**	1	Michigan-Toledo Strip	10-N	14-E
" "	**17**	1	Michigan-Toledo Strip	11-N	13-E
" "	**12**	1	Michigan-Toledo Strip	12-N	13-E
" "	**4**	1	Michigan-Toledo Strip	14-N	15-E
" "	**29**	1	Michigan-Toledo Strip	9-N	15-E
WOODWARD	**30**	1	Michigan-Toledo Strip	9-N	16-E
WOOLLEY	**16**	1	Michigan-Toledo Strip	11-N	12-E
WRACHA	**3**	1	Michigan-Toledo Strip	14-N	14-E
WRESCHE	**3**	1	Michigan-Toledo Strip	14-N	14-E
WRIGHT	**1**	4	Michigan-Toledo Strip	14-N	12-E
" "	**30**	3	Michigan-Toledo Strip	9-N	16-E
" "	**20**	2	Michigan-Toledo Strip	11-N	16-E
" "	**9**	2	Michigan-Toledo Strip	13-N	15-E
" "	**25**	1	Michigan-Toledo Strip	10-N	16-E
WYMAN	**25**	2	Michigan-Toledo Strip	10-N	16-E
" "	**20**	2	Michigan-Toledo Strip	11-N	16-E
" "	**26**	1	Michigan-Toledo Strip	10-N	17-E
YAKE	**24**	2	Michigan-Toledo Strip	10-N	15-E
" "	**29**	1	Michigan-Toledo Strip	9-N	15-E
YATES	**20**	1	Michigan-Toledo Strip	11-N	16-E
YORKE	**27**	2	Michigan-Toledo Strip	9-N	13-E
YOUNG	**11**	3	Michigan-Toledo Strip	12-N	12-E
" "	**2**	1	Michigan-Toledo Strip	14-N	13-E
" "	**3**	1	Michigan-Toledo Strip	14-N	14-E
ZAUNER	**22**	2	Michigan-Toledo Strip	10-N	13-E
ZOLL	**24**	1	Michigan-Toledo Strip	10-N	15-E

– Part II –

Township Map Groups

Map Group 1: Index to Land Patents

Township 14-North Range 12-East (Michigan-Toledo Strip)

After you locate an individual in this Index, take note of the Section and Section Part then proceed to the Land Patent map on the pages immediately following. You should have no difficulty locating the corresponding parcel of land.

The "For More Info" Column will lead you to more information about the underlying Patents. See the *Legend* at right, and the "How to Use this Book" chapter, for more information.

LEGEND

"For More Info . . . " column

A = Authority (Legislative Act, See Appendix "A")
B = Block or Lot (location in Section unknown)
C = Cancelled Patent
F = Fractional Section
G = Group (Multi-Patentee Patent, see Appendix "C")
V = Overlaps another Parcel
R = Re-Issued (Parcel patented more than once)

(A & G items require you to look in the Appendixes referred to above. All other Letter-designations followed by a number require you to locate line-items in this index that possess the ID number found after the letter).

ID	Individual in Patent	Sec.	Sec. Part	Date Issued	Other Counties	For More Info . . .
32	AUBLE, George	22	E½NW	1859-05-09		A1
55	BARDWELL, Jerusha	20	N½SE	1877-04-05		A2
56	" "	21	NWSW	1877-04-05		A2
57	" "	21	SWNW	1877-04-05		A2
124	BENNETT, William	25	N½NE	1860-05-01		A1
125	" "	25	SWNE	1860-05-01		A1
65	BLACKMAR, John M	20	S½SE	1870-05-20		A2
66	" "	29	N½NE	1870-05-20		A2
81	BOGERT, Leonard P	7	W½SW	1871-06-15		A2
33	BOND, George	33	SW	1877-07-20		A2
58	BRENNEN, John	33	SENW	1866-09-03		A1
91	BURTT, Mortamer	36	SWNE	1885-07-27		A2
14	CAMPBELL, Archibald	7	NWNE	1872-04-15		A1
126	CARWELL, William	22	SESE	1868-08-20		A1
17	CHAPEL, Charles	2	E½NW	1860-05-01		A1
28	CLARK, Elias D	13	NE	1860-05-01		A1
29	" "	13	NENW	1860-05-01		A1
30	" "	13	S½NW	1860-05-01		A1
4	CLELAND, Alexander	11	SESE	1897-01-29		A1
5	" "	13	NWNW	1897-01-29		A1
104	CLELAND, Robert	1	SESW	1870-10-01		A1
105	CLELAND, Robert M	15	NESW	1872-03-20		A2
106	" "	15	NWSE	1872-03-20		A2
107	" "	15	S½SE	1872-03-20		A2
59	COLLINGS, John	2	NWSW	1860-05-01		A1
60	" "	3	NESE	1860-05-01		A1
37	COMPANY, H M Bradley And	11	NWSW	1869-07-01		A1
127	CURWELL, William	26	N½SE	1871-09-30		A2
128	" "	26	SWNE	1871-09-30		A2
23	DAVIS, Ebenezer R	33	W½NW	1872-07-01		A2
116	DAVIS, Sidney W	28	NESE	1873-04-25		A2
27	EDDY, Edwin	12	SWNW	1868-08-20		A1
130	FENTON, William M	7	SWNW	1855-10-01		A1 F
131	" "	9	SESW	1855-10-01		A1
129	FLEMING, William	6	NENE	1867-07-01		A1 G40
82	GORDON, Lewis	28	S½SE	1859-10-10		A1
83	" "	28	SESW	1871-02-10		A2
84	" "	33	NENW	1871-02-10		A2
9	GREENLEAF, Alfred	21	NESW	1870-05-20		A2
10	" "	21	NWSE	1870-05-20		A2
11	" "	21	S½SW	1870-05-20		A2
117	GREENMAN, Stephen	26	S½NW	1860-05-01		A1
118	" "	26	SW	1860-05-01		A1
89	GROW, Marion M	27	S½NE	1860-05-01		A1
90	" "	27	SE	1860-05-01		A1
31	HARRIS, Francis J	11	S½NE	1884-08-09		A2

ID	Individual in Patent	Sec.	Sec. Part	Date Issued	Other Counties	For More Info . . .
46	HARTWICK, James	21	SENW	1872-08-10		A1
16	HOLMES, Caleb	1	W½SW	1859-05-09		A1
15	HUBEL, Bethel	14	NESW	1872-03-20		A2
111	LEEPLA, Samuel	18	SESW	1875-09-01		A2
112	" "	18	W½SW	1875-09-01		A2
19	MCCONNELL, Consider A	32	SESW	1868-08-20		A1
88	MCCONNELL, Luther E	32	SWSE	1872-12-30		A2 F
53	MCCORMICK, James	6	W½SW	1864-09-15		A1 F
41	MCCORMICK, James F	10	NWNE	1864-01-05		A1 C R47
42	" "	3	SWSE	1864-01-05		A1 C R48
43	" "	4	NWSW	1864-01-05		A1 C R49
44	" "	5	NESE	1864-01-05		A1 C R50
45	" "	6	NESW	1864-01-05		A1 C R51
52	MCCORMICK, James J	8	NESW	1866-09-01		A1
47	" "	10	NWNE	1882-10-20		A1 R41
48	" "	3	SWSE	1882-10-20		A1 R42
49	" "	4	NWSW	1882-10-20		A1 R43
50	" "	5	NESE	1882-10-20		A1 R44
51	" "	6	NESW	1882-10-20		A1 R45
92	MCEACHIN, Neil	6	NWSE	1879-06-30		A2
93	" "	6	S½SE	1879-06-30		A2
94	" "	6	SESW	1879-06-30		A2
123	MCGINNIS, Thomas Z	15	S½NW	1871-09-30		A2
67	MCINTOSH, John	5	NE	1859-10-10		A1 F
95	MCINTOSH, Neil	5	NENW	1859-10-10		A1 F
132	MCKAY, William	25	SWSW	1878-07-15		A1 R135
133	" "	36	SENW	1878-07-15		A1 R136
134	" "	36	W½NW	1878-07-15		A1 R137
68	MCPHAIL, John	34	NE	1870-05-20		A2
135	MCRAY, William	25	SWSW	1860-11-21		A1 C R132
136	" "	36	SENW	1860-11-21		A1 C R133
137	" "	36	W½NW	1860-11-21		A1 C R134
108	MCVANE, Robert	34	SW	1871-06-15		A2
96	MEEHAN, Patrick	25	E½SE	1860-05-01		A1
20	MERCHANT, David	25	E½SW	1860-05-01		A1
21	" "	25	W½SE	1860-05-01		A1
129	MOORE, Franklin	6	NENE	1867-07-01		A1 G40
129	MOORE, Stephen	6	NENE	1867-07-01		A1 G40
22	MORRISON, Donald	6	SWNW	1867-07-01		A1
18	MURPHY, Christopher	34	NW	1871-06-15		A2
80	NEVILLE, Lawrence	36	N½NE	1860-05-01		A1
120	NICOL, Thomas	35	E½NE	1861-12-03		A1 V98
121	" "	35	SWSE	1861-12-03		A1
122	NICOL, Thomas Y	35	NWSE	1867-07-01		A1
6	NICOLL, Alexander	25	NW	1860-05-01		A1
97	NOLAN, Patrick	26	S½SE	1859-10-10		A1
98	" "	35	NE	1859-10-10		A1 V120
138	POLLARD, William	14	SENE	1862-05-15		A1
139	" "	14	W½NE	1862-05-15		A1
100	POST, Richard M	10	E½SW	1857-10-30		A1 C
101	" "	15	N½NE	1857-10-30		A1 C
102	" "	15	NENW	1857-10-30		A1 C
110	REMICK, Royal C	18	NESW	1869-07-01		A1
25	SANSBURN, Edward	27	E½SW	1861-07-01		A1
26	" "	27	W½SW	1861-12-03		A1
12	SHEFFER, Alonzo	4	N½SE	1872-03-20		A2
13	" "	4	NESW	1872-03-20		A2
69	SINCLAIR, John	24	N½SE	1860-05-01		A1
70	" "	24	S½NE	1860-05-01		A1
38	SNELL, Hezekiah	32	N½SE	1877-07-20		A2
39	" "	32	SENE	1877-07-20		A2
40	" "	32	SESE	1877-07-20		A2
71	SOMMERVILLE, John	24	NWNE	1868-08-20		A1
34	STEWARD, George H	17	NE	1876-09-06		A2
72	STUART, John T	4	NW	1870-05-20		A2
103	SUTTON, Robert B	18	SENE	1872-04-15		A1
119	THOMPSON, Thomas G	20	SW	1871-09-30		A2
109	THOMSON, Robert	3	W½NW	1872-07-01		A2 F
73	TRATHEN, John	2	SWNE	1878-02-13		A2
1	VAN ALLEN, ABRAM	21	NESE	1870-11-18		A2
2	" "	22	N½SW	1870-11-18		A2
3	" "	22	NWSE	1870-11-18		A2
8	VAN LOAN, ALEXANDER	34	NESE	1866-09-03		A1

ID	Individual in Patent	Sec.	Sec. Part	Date Issued	Other Counties	For More Info . . .
7	VAN LOAN, ALEXANDER (Cont'd)	33	SE	1871-06-15		A2
74	WALDON, John	33	NE	1871-06-15		A2
140	WALKER, William	19	NW	1875-02-05		A2 F
54	WATSON, James	35	SW	1870-05-20		A2
75	WATSON, John	34	SESE	1871-02-10		A2
76	" "	34	W½SE	1871-02-10		A2
86	WAY, Lewis	2	N½NE	1857-02-20		A1 F
87	" "	2	SENE	1857-02-20		A1 F
85	" "	1	NW	1857-07-01		A1 F
24	WELLS, Edgar P	31	S½SW	1871-02-10		A2 F
35	WELLS, George P	5	W½NW	1860-05-01		A1 F
77	WELLS, John	12	N½SW	1859-05-09		A1
78	" "	12	SE	1859-05-09		A1
79	" "	12	SESW	1859-05-09		A1
36	WOODS, George	9	SWSE	1876-11-03		A2
61	WOODS, John L	11	N½NE	1855-10-01		A1
62	" "	17	SESW	1855-10-01		A1
63	" "	17	SWSE	1855-10-01		A1
64	" "	19	N½NE	1855-10-01		A1
99	WRIGHT, Philip	29	N½NW	1870-05-20		A2
113	WRIGHT, Sarah J	17	E½SE	1877-07-20		A2
114	" "	17	NESW	1877-07-20		A2
115	" "	17	NWSE	1877-07-20		A2

Patent Map

T14-N R12-E
Michigan-Toledo Strip Meridian

Map Group 1

Township Statistics

Parcels Mapped	:	140
Number of Patents	:	98
Number of Individuals	:	84
Patentees Identified	:	82
Number of Surnames	:	70
Multi-Patentee Parcels	:	1
Oldest Patent Date	:	10/1/1855
Most Recent Patent	:	1/29/1897
Block/Lot Parcels	:	0
Parcels Re - Issued	:	8
Parcels that Overlap	:	2
Cities and Towns	:	2
Cemeteries	:	0

6
FLEMING [40] William 1867
MORRISON Donald 1867
MCCORMICK James F 1864
MCCORMICK James J 1882
MCEACHIN Neil 1879
MCCORMICK James 1864
MCEACHIN Neil 1879
MCEACHIN Neil 1879

5
WELLS George P 1860
MCINTOSH Neil 1859
MCINTOSH John 1859
MCCORMICK James J 1882
MCCORMICK James F 1864

4
STUART John T 1870
MCCORMICK James F 1864
MCCORMICK James J 1882
SHEFFER Alonzo 1872
SHEFFER Alonzo 1872

7
CAMPBELL Archibald 1872
FENTON William M 1855
BOGERT Leonard P 1871

8
MCCORMICK James J 1866

9
FENTON William M 1855
WOODS George 1876

18
SUTTON Robert B 1872
LEEPLA Samuel 1875
REMICK Royal C 1869
LEEPLA Samuel 1875

17
STEWARD George H 1876
WRIGHT Sarah J 1877
WRIGHT Sarah J 1877
WOODS John L 1855
WOODS John L 1855
WRIGHT Sarah J 1877

16

19
WALKER William 1875
WOODS John L 1855

20
THOMPSON Thomas G 1871
BARDWELL Jerusha 1877
BLACKMAR John M 1870

21
BARDWELL Jerusha 1877
HARTWICK James 1872
BARDWELL Jerusha 1877
GREENLEAF Alfred 1870
GREENLEAF Alfred 1870
ALLEN Abram Van 1870
GREENLEAF Alfred 1870

30

29
WRIGHT Philip 1870
BLACKMAR John M 1870

28
DAVIS Sidney W 1873
GORDON Lewis 1871
GORDON Lewis 1859

31
WELLS Edgar P 1871

32
SNELL Hezekiah 1877
SNELL Hezekiah 1877
MCCONNELL Consider A 1868
MCCONNELL Luther E 1872
SNELL Hezekiah 1877

33
DAVIS Ebenezer R 1872
GORDON Lewis 1871
BRENNEN John 1866
WALDON John 1871
LOAN Alexander Van 1871
BOND George 1877

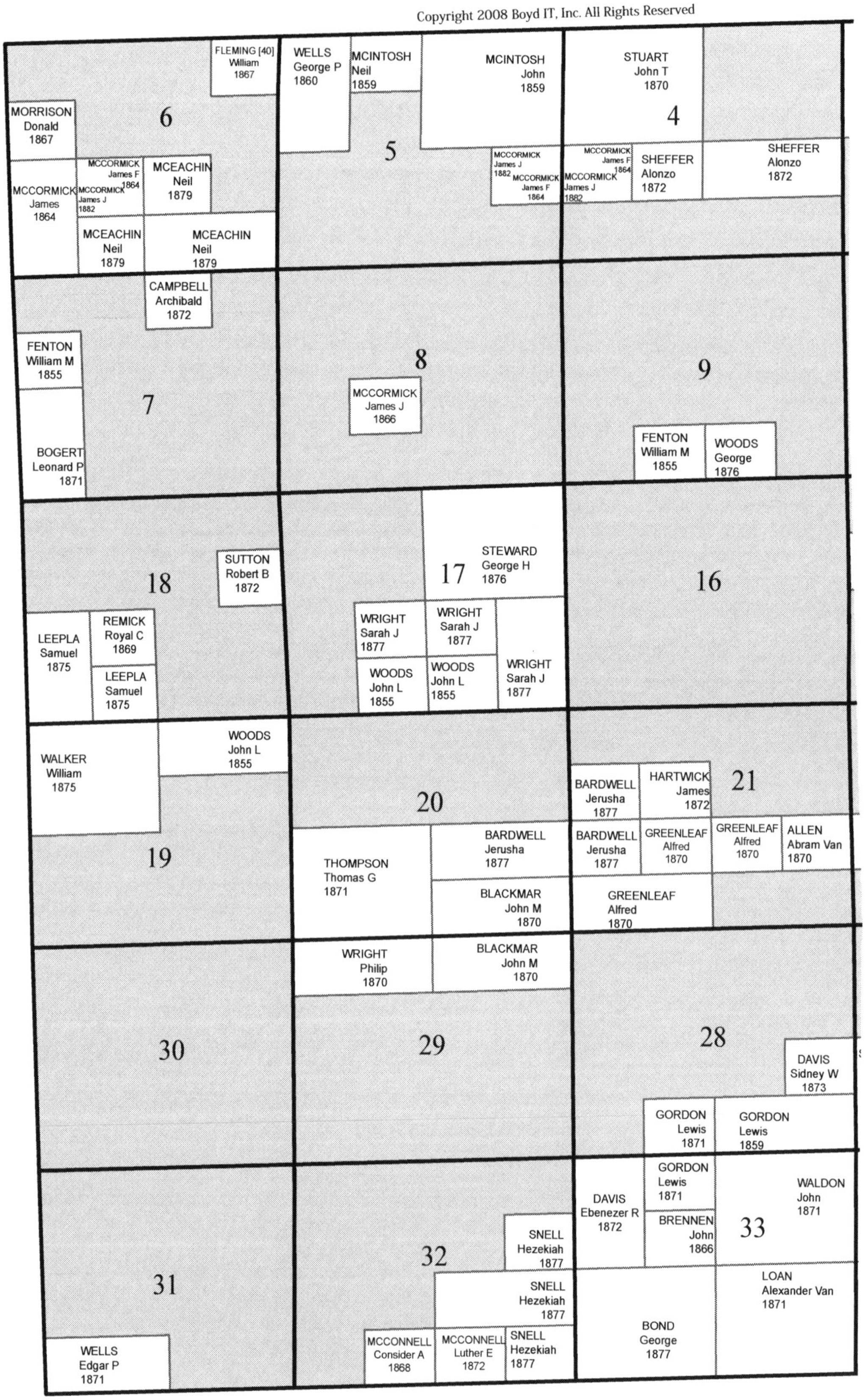

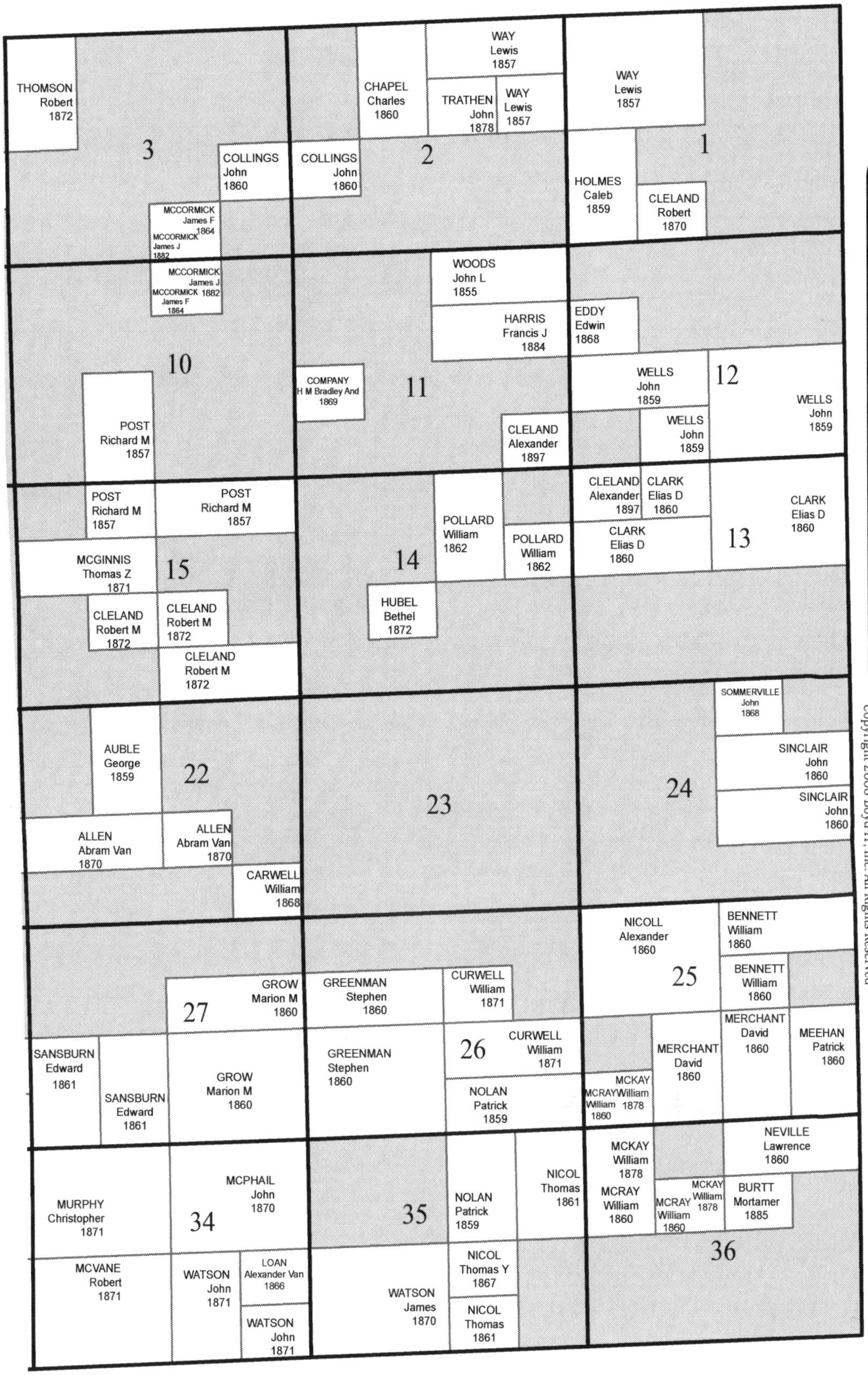

THOMSON Robert 1872
CHAPEL Charles 1860
WAY Lewis 1857
TRATHEN John 1878
WAY Lewis 1857
WAY Lewis 1857
3
COLLINGS John 1860
COLLINGS John 1860
2
1
HOLMES Caleb 1859
CLELAND Robert 1870
MCCORMICK James F 1864
MCCORMICK James J 1882
MCCORMICK James J 1882
MCCORMICK James F 1864
WOODS John L 1855
HARRIS Francis J 1884
EDDY Edwin 1868
10
COMPANY H M Bradley And 1869
11
WELLS John 1859
12
WELLS John 1859
POST Richard M 1857
CLELAND Alexander 1897
WELLS John 1859
POST Richard M 1857
POST Richard M 1857
CLELAND Alexander 1897
CLARK Elias D 1860
CLARK Elias D 1860
POLLARD William 1862
POLLARD William 1862
CLARK Elias D 1860
13
MCGINNIS Thomas Z 1871
15
14
HUBEL Bethel 1872
CLELAND Robert M 1872
CLELAND Robert M 1872
CLELAND Robert M 1872
SOMMERVILLE John 1868
AUBLE George 1859
22
SINCLAIR John 1860
23
24
SINCLAIR John 1860
ALLEN Abram Van 1870
ALLEN Abram Van 1870
CARWELL William 1868
NICOLL Alexander 1860
BENNETT William 1860
25
BENNETT William 1860
GROW Marion M 1860
27
GREENMAN Stephen 1860
CURWELL William 1871
MERCHANT David 1860
MEEHAN Patrick 1860
SANSBURN Edward 1861
GREENMAN Stephen 1860
26
CURWELL William 1871
MERCHANT David 1860
GROW Marion M 1860
SANSBURN Edward 1861
NOLAN Patrick 1859
MCKAY William 1878
MCRAY William 1860
NEVILLE Lawrence 1860
MCKAY William 1878
MCPHAIL John 1870
NICOL Thomas 1861
MURPHY Christopher 1871
34
35
NOLAN Patrick 1859
MCRAY William 1860
MCKAY William 1878
MCRAY William 1860
BURTT Mortamer 1885
36
NICOL Thomas Y 1867
MCVANE Robert 1871
WATSON John 1871
LOAN Alexander Van 1866
WATSON James 1870
WATSON John 1871
NICOL Thomas 1861

Helpful Hints

1. This Map's INDEX can be found on the preceding pages.
2. Refer to Map "C" to see where this Township lies within Sanilac County, Michigan.
3. Numbers within square brackets [ ] denote a multi-patentee land parcel (multi-owner). Refer to Appendix "C" for a full list of members in this group.
4. Areas that look to be crowded with Patentees usually indicate multiple sales of the same parcel (Re-issues) or Overlapping parcels. See this Township's Index for an explanation of these and other circumstances that might explain "odd" groupings of Patentees on this map.

Legend

Patent Boundary
Section Boundary
No Patents Found (or Outside County)
1., 2., 3., ... Lot Numbers (when beside a name)
[ ] Group Number (see Appendix "C")

Scale: Section = 1 mile X 1 mile (generally, with some exceptions)

Road Map

T14-N R12-E
Michigan-Toledo Strip Meridian

Map Group 1

Cities & Towns

New Greenleaf
Wickware

Cemeteries

None

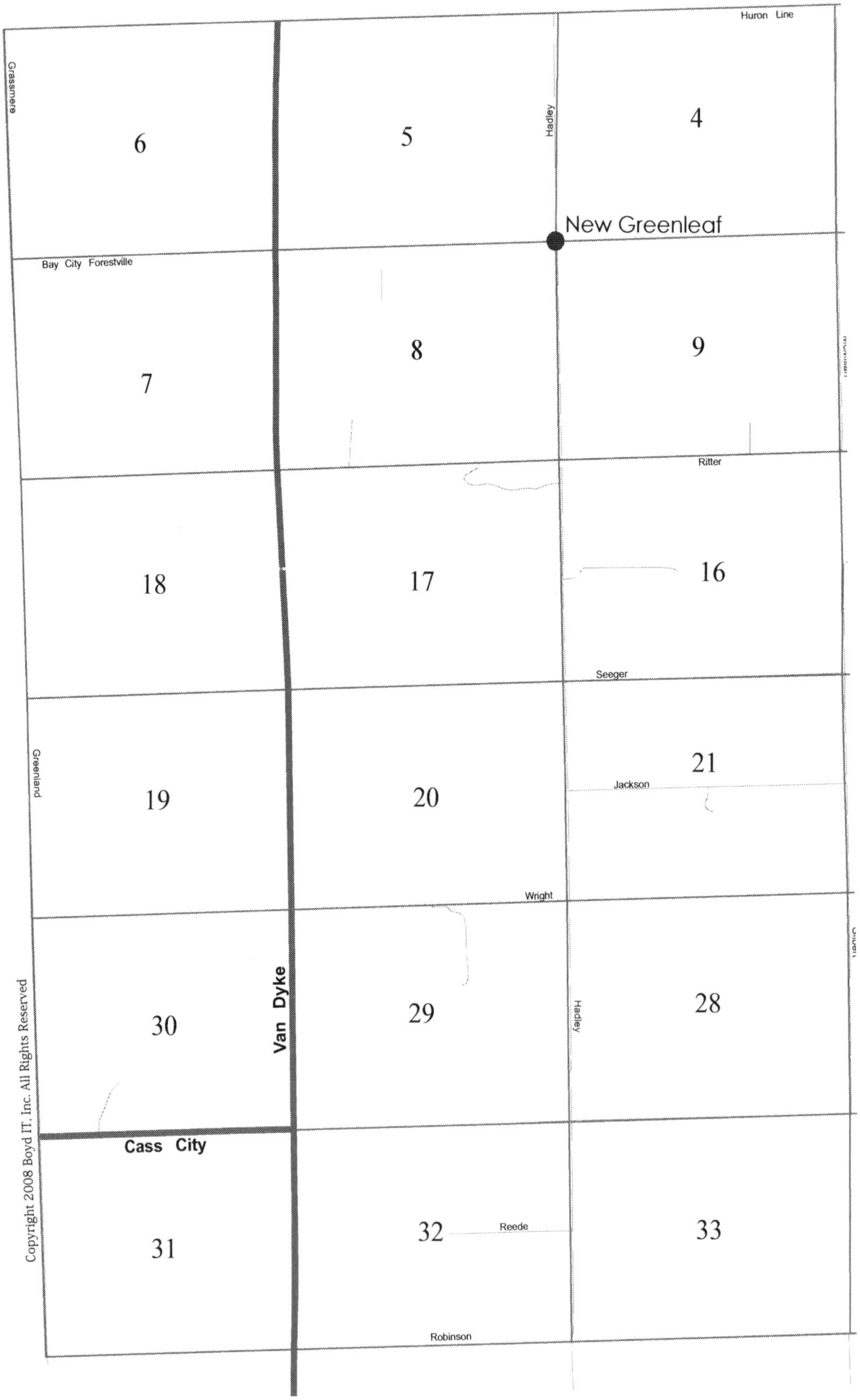

Huron Line
Grassmere
Hadley
6
5
4
New Greenleaf
Bay City Forestville
7
8
9
Ritter
18
17
16
Seeger
Greenland
19
20
21
Jackson
Wright
Van Dyke
30
29
Hadley
28
Cass City
31
32
Reede
33
Robinson

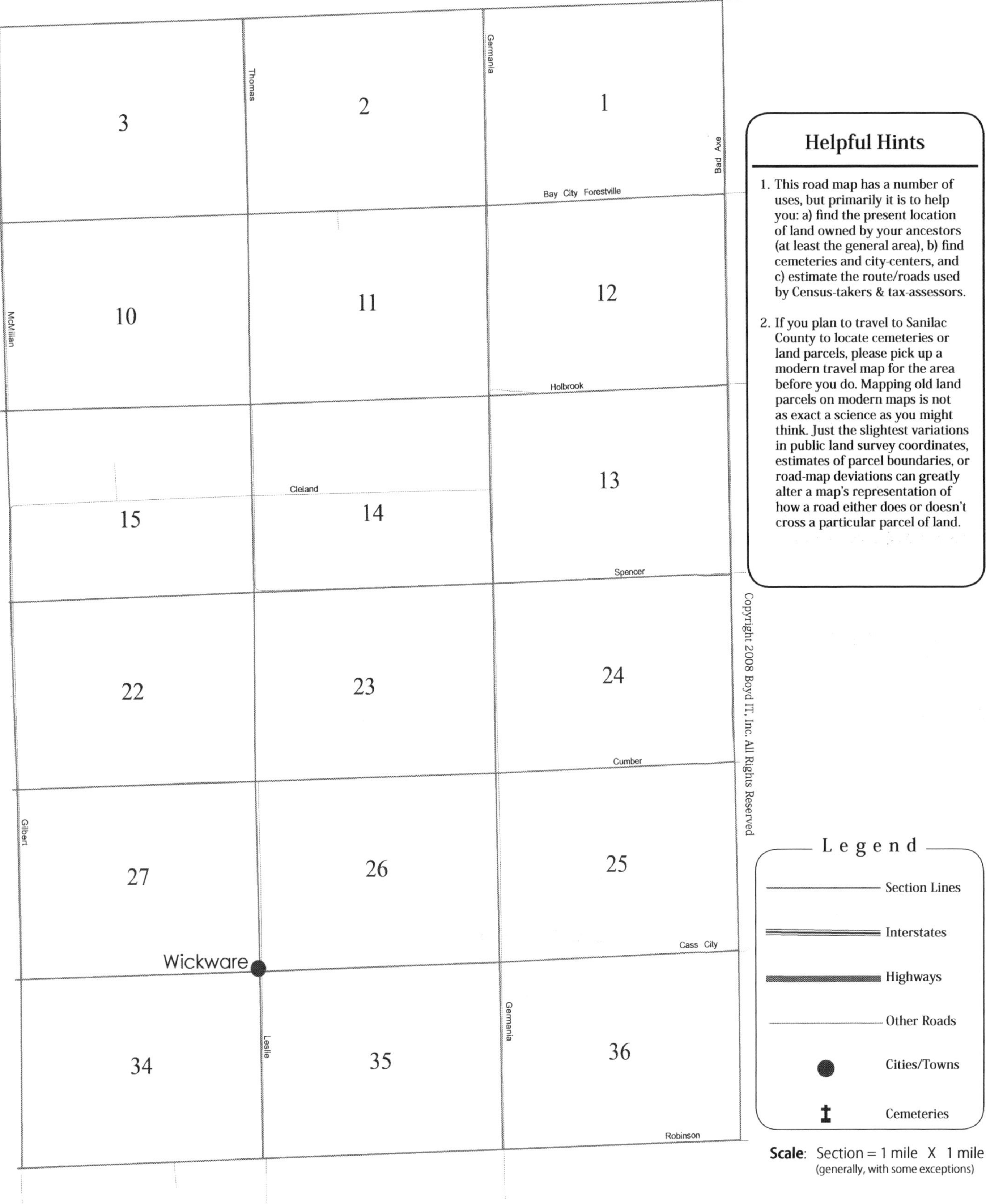

Helpful Hints

1. This road map has a number of uses, but primarily it is to help you: a) find the present location of land owned by your ancestors (at least the general area), b) find cemeteries and city-centers, and c) estimate the route/roads used by Census-takers & tax-assessors.

2. If you plan to travel to Sanilac County to locate cemeteries or land parcels, please pick up a modern travel map for the area before you do. Mapping old land parcels on modern maps is not as exact a science as you might think. Just the slightest variations in public land survey coordinates, estimates of parcel boundaries, or road-map deviations can greatly alter a map's representation of how a road either does or doesn't cross a particular parcel of land.

Legend

- Section Lines
- Interstates
- Highways
- Other Roads
- Cities/Towns
- Cemeteries

Scale: Section = 1 mile X 1 mile
(generally, with some exceptions)

Cities & Towns

New Greenleaf
Wickware

Cemeteries

None

6 5 4
New Greenleaf
7 8 9
North Branch Cass River
18 17 16
19 20 21
30 29 28
Greenman Creek
31 32 33

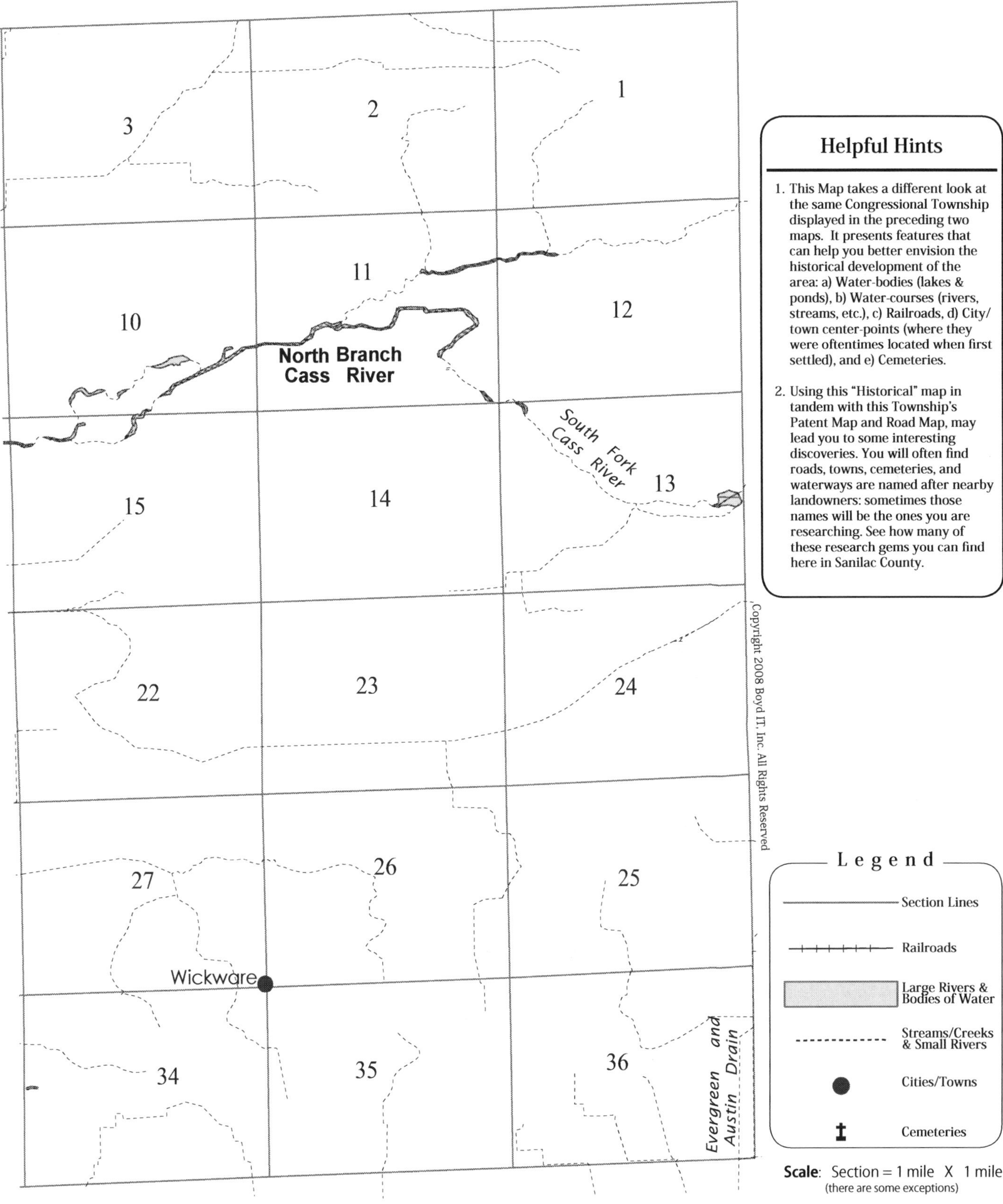

Helpful Hints

1. This Map takes a different look at the same Congressional Township displayed in the preceding two maps. It presents features that can help you better envision the historical development of the area: a) Water-bodies (lakes & ponds), b) Water-courses (rivers, streams, etc.), c) Railroads, d) City/town center-points (where they were oftentimes located when first settled), and e) Cemeteries.

2. Using this "Historical" map in tandem with this Township's Patent Map and Road Map, may lead you to some interesting discoveries. You will often find roads, towns, cemeteries, and waterways are named after nearby landowners: sometimes those names will be the ones you are researching. See how many of these research gems you can find here in Sanilac County.

Legend

- Section Lines
- Railroads
- Large Rivers & Bodies of Water
- Streams/Creeks & Small Rivers
- Cities/Towns
- Cemeteries

Scale: Section = 1 mile X 1 mile
(there are some exceptions)

Map Group 2: Index to Land Patents

Township 14-North Range 13-East (Michigan-Toledo Strip)

After you locate an individual in this Index, take note of the Section and Section Part then proceed to the Land Patent map on the pages immediately following. You should have no difficulty locating the corresponding parcel of land.

The "For More Info" Column will lead you to more information about the underlying Patents. See the *Legend* at right, and the "How to Use this Book" chapter, for more information.

LEGEND

"For More Info . . . " column

A = Authority (Legislative Act, See Appendix "A")
B = Block or Lot (location in Section unknown)
C = Cancelled Patent
F = Fractional Section
G = Group (Multi-Patentee Patent, see Appendix "C")
V = Overlaps another Parcel
R = Re-Issued (Parcel patented more than once)

(A & G items require you to look in the Appendixes referred to above. All other Letter-designations followed by a number require you to locate line-items in this index that possess the ID number found after the letter).

ID	Individual in Patent	Sec.	Sec. Part	Date Issued	Other Counties	For More Info . . .
202	BACKUS, James W	1	SENE	1859-10-10		A1 F
245	BARWICK, Nelson	3	NWSE	1860-11-21		A1
246	" "	3	SWNE	1860-11-21		A1
278	BARWICK, Thomas	10	NWNE	1860-11-21		A1
279	" "	3	SWSE	1860-11-21		A1
287	BELL, William	14	NENE	1859-10-10		A1
288	" "	14	W½NE	1859-10-10		A1
186	BENNET, James	29	SWSW	1859-10-10		A1
187	" "	31	E½NE	1859-10-10		A1
188	" "	32	NWNW	1859-10-10		A1
289	BORLAND, William	1	S½SW	1870-05-10		A1
291	BROCKELSBY, William L	10	N½NW	1861-12-03		A1
232	BROWN, Joseph	19	E½SW	1859-10-10		A1
233	" "	19	W½SW	1859-10-10		A1
234	" "	30	E½NW	1859-10-10		A1
235	" "	30	W½NW	1859-10-10		A1
236	" "	31	SWNW	1866-06-20		A1
220	CAMERON, John M	18	NW	1875-02-05		A2
284	CARY, Timothy	23	N½SE	1860-10-01		A1
286	" "	24	NWSW	1860-10-01		A1
285	" "	23	NESW	1860-11-21		A1
252	CLARK, Robert	21	W½SW	1862-02-01		A1
189	CLELAND, James	5	SENW	1877-03-20		A2
190	" "	5	W½NW	1877-03-20		A2
241	CLIFFORD, Michael	25	NW	1859-10-10		A1
251	COLLINA, Richard	3	SESE	1861-12-10		A1
242	CROWLEY, Michael	2	S½SW	1859-10-10		A1
212	CURRIE, John	7	NE	1857-10-30		A1
243	DONELLAN, Michael	9	NW	1857-02-16		A1
213	FREHSE, John	5	NENW	1859-10-10		A1 F
214	" "	5	NWNE	1859-10-10		A1 F
159	FRENCH, Charles H	15	NESE	1881-08-20		A2
215	GETTY, John	1	NENW	1857-07-01		A1
216	" "	1	NWNE	1857-07-01		A1
157	GRAY, Archibald	21	SWNE	1860-11-21		A1
156	" "	21	SENE	1862-02-01		A1
169	GRAY, Duncan	21	E½SW	1860-11-21		A1
170	" "	21	W½SE	1860-11-21		A1
253	GRAY, Robert	21	NW	1861-07-01		A1
207	HACKER, Joachim H	5	E½NE	1859-10-10		A1 F
160	HADLEY, Clark	14	SWNW	1857-02-20		A1
161	" "	32	NWSE	1857-02-20		A1
162	" "	32	SENE	1857-02-20		A1
142	HALL, Alexander	24	SESE	1875-07-30		A2
143	" "	25	NENE	1875-07-30		A2
144	" "	25	W½NE	1875-07-30		A2

ID	Individual in Patent	Sec.	Sec. Part	Date Issued	Other Counties	For More Info . . .
208	HARKER, Joachim	5	SWNE	1870-05-10		A1
263	HUBBARD, Rollin B	4	NWNW	1867-07-01		A1 V296
165	HUBEL, Dexter	4	SWNE	1875-05-10		A1
175	HUNT, Edward	24	E½NW	1870-05-20		A2
176	" "	24	W½NE	1870-05-20		A2
269	IRWIN, Septimus	23	NENW	1859-05-09		A1
271	" "	23	W½NE	1859-05-09		A1
268	" "	23	E½NE	1859-10-10		A1
270	" "	23	SENW	1859-10-10		A1
272	" "	23	W½NW	1859-10-10		A1 R225
192	JORDAN, James	17	N½SW	1860-05-01		A1
193	" "	17	S½SE	1860-05-01		A1
194	" "	17	SESW	1860-05-01		A1
195	" "	20	N½NE	1860-05-01		A1
196	" "	20	NENW	1860-05-01		A1
197	" "	20	S½SW	1860-05-01		A1
198	" "	29	N½NW	1860-05-01		A1
199	" "	30	NE	1860-05-01		A1
290	JORDAN, William	19	E½	1860-05-01		A1
203	KRUPP, James W	9	SE	1857-07-01		A1
254	LAW, Robert	10	SE	1860-05-01		A1
145	LINDSAY, Alexander	3	SW	1857-10-30		A1
146	" "	4	SE	1857-10-30		A1
280	LINDSEY, Thomas	19	S½NW	1861-12-03		A1 F
217	LITT, John	34	NENE	1861-12-10		A1
218	" "	34	W½NE	1861-12-10		A1
219	LOWE, John	32	SENW	1889-01-31		A2
141	MARREDETH, Abram	28	NW	1860-11-21		A1
205	MARREDETH, Jessee	28	SENE	1861-12-03		A1
206	" "	28	W½NE	1861-12-03		A1
292	MARREDETH, William	20	E½SE	1861-07-01		A1
295	" "	29	E½NE	1861-07-01		A1
293	" "	20	S½NE	1862-02-01		A1
294	" "	20	W½SE	1862-02-01		A1
265	MARRIOTT, Samuel	14	SW	1860-05-01		A1
264	" "	14	SESE	1861-07-01		A1
266	" "	14	W½SE	1861-07-01		A1
244	MCCOLLOM, Neil	17	N½SE	1861-12-03		A1
191	MCCORMICK, James J	3	E½NW	1866-06-20		A1
171	MCDOUGALL, Duncan	32	E½SW	1870-05-20		A2
172	" "	32	S½SE	1870-05-20		A2
177	MCDOUGALL, George	28	SW	1862-02-01		A1
221	MCDOUGALL, John	33	E½SW	1862-02-01		A1
239	MCINTYRE, Malcolm	18	S½SW	1859-10-10		A1 F
240	" "	19	N½NW	1859-10-10		A1 F
173	MCKELLAR, Duncan	31	SW	1861-12-03		A1
182	MCKENZIE, Hugh	30	SW	1861-07-01		A1 F
153	MCPHAIL, Angus	34	NESW	1872-12-30		A2
154	" "	34	SENW	1872-12-30		A2
155	" "	34	W½SW	1872-12-30		A2
158	MCPHAIL, Archibald	33	SE	1861-12-10		A1
166	MCPHAIL, Dugald	34	E½SE	1861-12-03		A1
167	" "	35	NWSW	1861-12-03		A1
168	" "	35	SWNW	1861-12-03		A1
222	MCPHAIL, John	32	SWSW	1874-07-15		A1
148	MCRAE, Alexander	21	SESE	1860-10-01		A1
149	" "	27	NWNW	1860-10-01		A1
150	" "	28	NENE	1860-10-01		A1
147	" "	15	SWSW	1870-05-20		A2
174	MCRAE, Duncan	21	NESE	1883-11-20		A2
200	MEREDEN, James	12	E½SE	1859-10-10		A1
223	MERREDETH, John	20	N½SW	1873-04-25		A2
255	METCALF, Robert	4	E½NE	1859-10-10		A1
256	" "	4	NWNE	1859-10-10		A1
237	MORELL, Joseph	28	SESE	1885-01-30		A2
152	MUMA, Alman	24	NENE	1867-07-01		A1
224	PATTON, John	2	SE	1870-11-18		A2
163	PETER, Constantine	27	N½SE	1862-05-15		A1
164	" "	27	SWSE	1862-05-15		A1
225	PETER, John	23	W½NW	1860-10-01		A1 R272
274	PETER, Stephen	27	SESE	1860-11-21		A1
273	" "	26	S½SW	1861-12-10		A1
275	" "	35	N½NW	1861-12-10		A1

ID	Individual in Patent	Sec.	Sec. Part	Date Issued	Other Counties	For More Info . . .
276	PETER, Stephen (Cont'd)	35	SENW	1861-12-10		A1
277	" "	35	W½NE	1861-12-10		A1
238	PETERS, Joseph	27	N½SW	1881-01-20		A2
281	POLLARD, Thomas	22	SESE	1879-06-13		A2
282	" "	22	W½SE	1879-06-13		A2
283	" "	23	SWSW	1879-06-13		A2
209	RITTENDORF, Johann	6	N½NW	1859-10-10		A1 F
178	ROBINSON, George	31	E½NW	1860-11-21		A1
179	" "	31	W½NE	1860-11-21		A1
211	ROBSON, John C	30	SE	1859-10-10		A1
183	SCHNEIDER, Jacob	32	NENE	1861-12-10		A1
184	" "	32	W½NE	1861-12-10		A1
185	" "	33	NWNW	1861-12-10		A1
247	SHEA, Patrick	25	N½SE	1859-10-10		A1
248	" "	25	N½SW	1859-10-10		A1
296	SHEPHARD, William	4	NW	1862-02-01		A1 V263
201	SMITH, James	28	NWSE	1883-06-07		A2
226	SOMMERVILLE, John	18	N½SW	1860-11-21		A1 F
227	" "	18	NWSE	1860-11-21		A1 F
228	" "	18	SWNE	1860-11-21		A1 F
151	SOULE, Alexander	13	E½NE	1859-10-10		A1
249	SPARLING, Peter	1	SESE	1860-10-01		A1
250	" "	1	SWSE	1861-12-03		A1
181	STACEY, Herbert	33	E½NE	1861-07-01		A1
180	STROUD, George	4	SW	1857-07-01		A1
229	STROUD, John	8	NE	1857-02-16		A1
257	TAYLOR, Robert	11	S½NE	1860-05-01		A1
258	" "	11	SENW	1860-05-01		A1
259	" "	12	SENW	1860-05-01		A1
260	" "	12	W½NW	1860-05-01		A1
261	" "	12	W½SW	1860-05-01		A1
297	THOMAS, William	12	E½SW	1860-05-01		A1
298	" "	12	W½SE	1860-05-01		A1
299	" "	13	NWNE	1860-05-01		A1
204	WATSON, Jeptha	1	NENE	1857-07-01		A1
210	WEBSTER, John B	14	E½NW	1879-06-30		A2
231	WHITE, John	8	NW	1859-10-10		A1
230	" "	17	NENE	1875-02-05		A2
300	WHITE, William	7	NWSW	1860-11-21		A1
301	" "	7	SESW	1873-01-20		A1
267	WILLIAMS, Samuel	7	S½NW	1859-10-10		A1 F
262	YOUNG, Robert	3	W½NW	1857-10-30		A1

Patent Map

T14-N R13-E
Michigan-Toledo Strip Meridian

Map Group 2

Township Statistics

Parcels Mapped	:	161
Number of Patents	:	103
Number of Individuals	:	89
Patentees Identified	:	89
Number of Surnames	:	73
Multi-Patentee Parcels	:	0
Oldest Patent Date	:	2/16/1857
Most Recent Patent	:	1/31/1889
Block/Lot Parcels	:	0
Parcels Re - Issued	:	1
Parcels that Overlap	:	2
Cities and Towns	:	4
Cemeteries	:	1

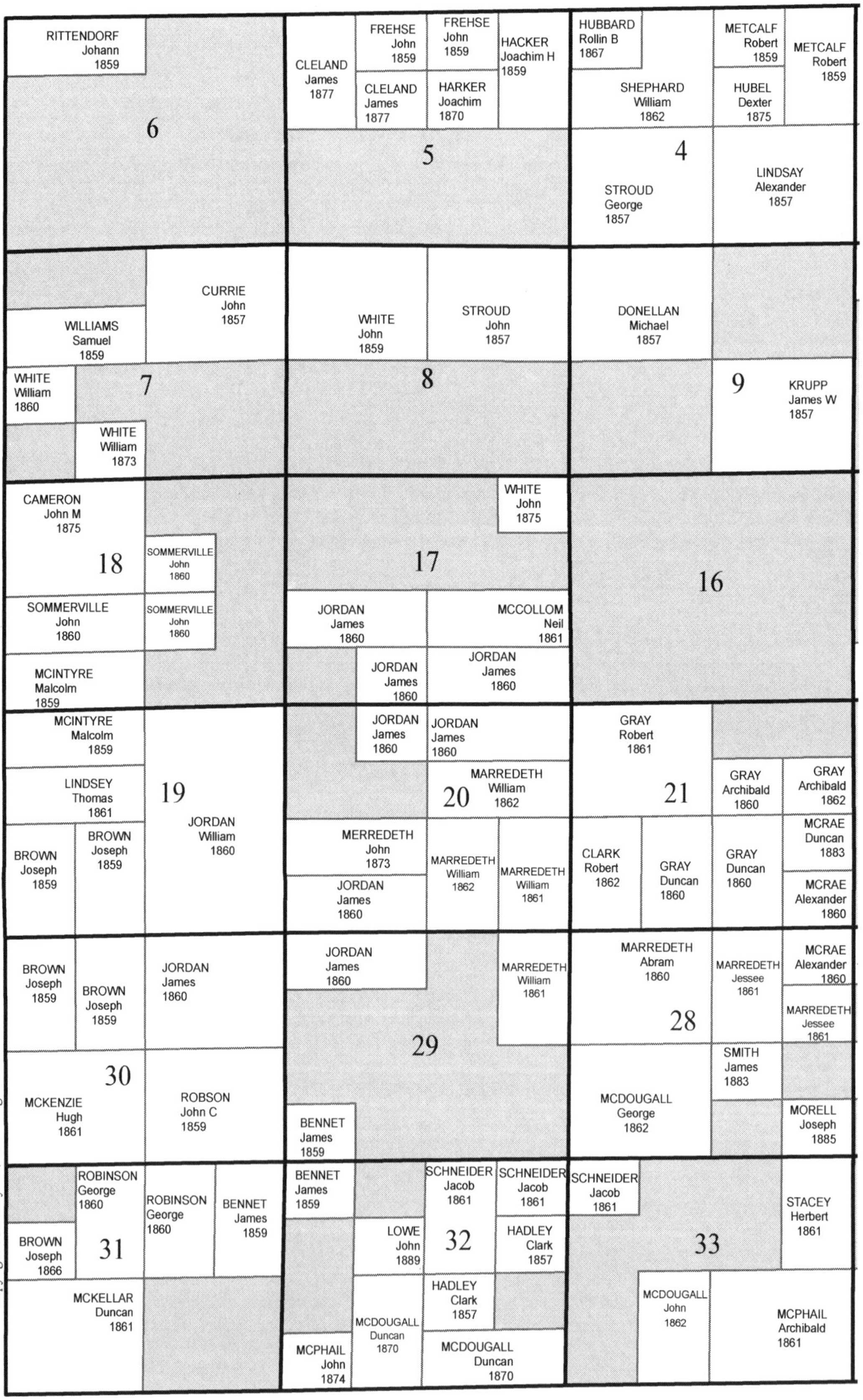

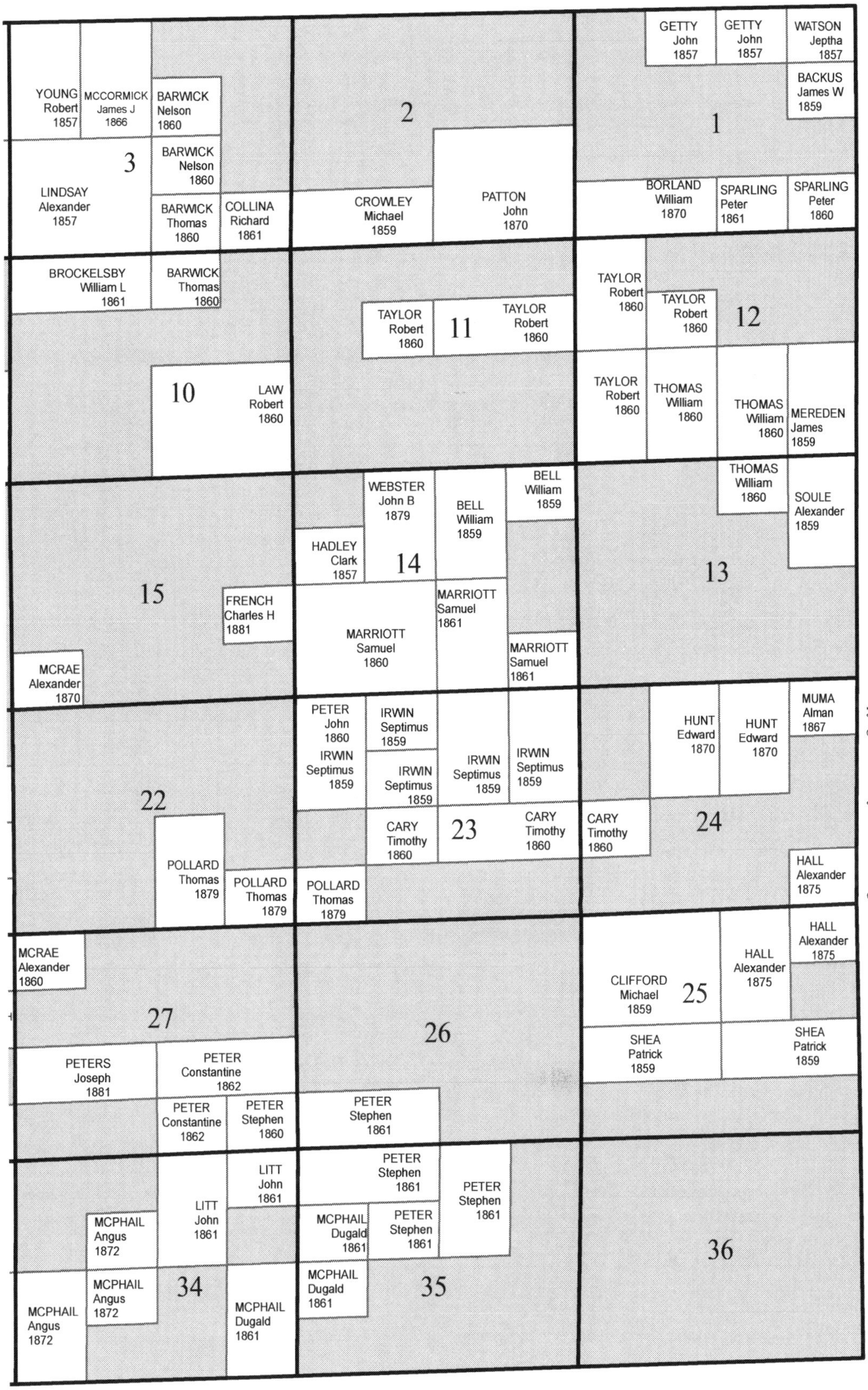

YOUNG Robert 1857
MCCORMICK James J 1866
BARWICK Nelson 1860
3
LINDSAY Alexander 1857
BARWICK Nelson 1860
BARWICK Thomas 1860
COLLINA Richard 1861
2
CROWLEY Michael 1859
PATTON John 1870
GETTY John 1857
GETTY John 1857
WATSON Jeptha 1857
BACKUS James W 1859
1
BORLAND William 1870
SPARLING Peter 1861
SPARLING Peter 1860
BROCKELSBY William L 1861
BARWICK Thomas 1860
10
LAW Robert 1860
TAYLOR Robert 1860
11
TAYLOR Robert 1860
TAYLOR Robert 1860
TAYLOR Robert 1860
12
TAYLOR Robert 1860
THOMAS William 1860
THOMAS William 1860
MEREDEN James 1859
15
FRENCH Charles H 1881
MCRAE Alexander 1870
WEBSTER John B 1879
BELL William 1859
BELL William 1859
HADLEY Clark 1857
14
MARRIOTT Samuel 1860
MARRIOTT Samuel 1861
MARRIOTT Samuel 1861
THOMAS William 1860
SOULE Alexander 1859
13
22
POLLARD Thomas 1879
POLLARD Thomas 1879
PETER John 1860
IRWIN Septimus 1859
IRWIN Septimus 1859
IRWIN Septimus 1859
IRWIN Septimus 1859
IRWIN Septimus 1859
CARY Timothy 1860
23
CARY Timothy 1860
POLLARD Thomas 1879
HUNT Edward 1870
HUNT Edward 1870
MUMA Alman 1867
CARY Timothy 1860
24
HALL Alexander 1875
MCRAE Alexander 1860
27
PETERS Joseph 1881
PETER Constantine 1862
PETER Constantine 1862
PETER Stephen 1860
26
PETER Stephen 1861
CLIFFORD Michael 1859
25
HALL Alexander 1875
HALL Alexander 1875
SHEA Patrick 1859
SHEA Patrick 1859
MCPHAIL Angus 1872
LITT John 1861
LITT John 1861
MCPHAIL Angus 1872
34
MCPHAIL Angus 1872
MCPHAIL Dugald 1861
PETER Stephen 1861
MCPHAIL Dugald 1861
PETER Stephen 1861
PETER Stephen 1861
MCPHAIL Dugald 1861
35
36

Helpful Hints

1. This Map's INDEX can be found on the preceding pages.
2. Refer to Map "C" to see where this Township lies within Sanilac County, Michigan.
3. Numbers within square brackets [ ] denote a multi-patentee land parcel (multi-owner). Refer to Appendix "C" for a full list of members in this group.
4. Areas that look to be crowded with Patentees usually indicate multiple sales of the same parcel (Re-issues) or Overlapping parcels. See this Township's Index for an explanation of these and other circumstances that might explain "odd" groupings of Patentees on this map.

Legend

Patent Boundary

Section Boundary

No Patents Found (or Outside County)

1., 2., 3., ... Lot Numbers (when beside a name)

[ ] Group Number (see Appendix "C")

Scale: Section = 1 mile X 1 mile (generally, with some exceptions)

Road Map

T14-N R13-E
Michigan-Toledo Strip Meridian

Map Group 2

Cities & Towns

Austin Center
Cumber
Freidberger
Tyre

Cemeteries

Mount Pleasant Cemetery

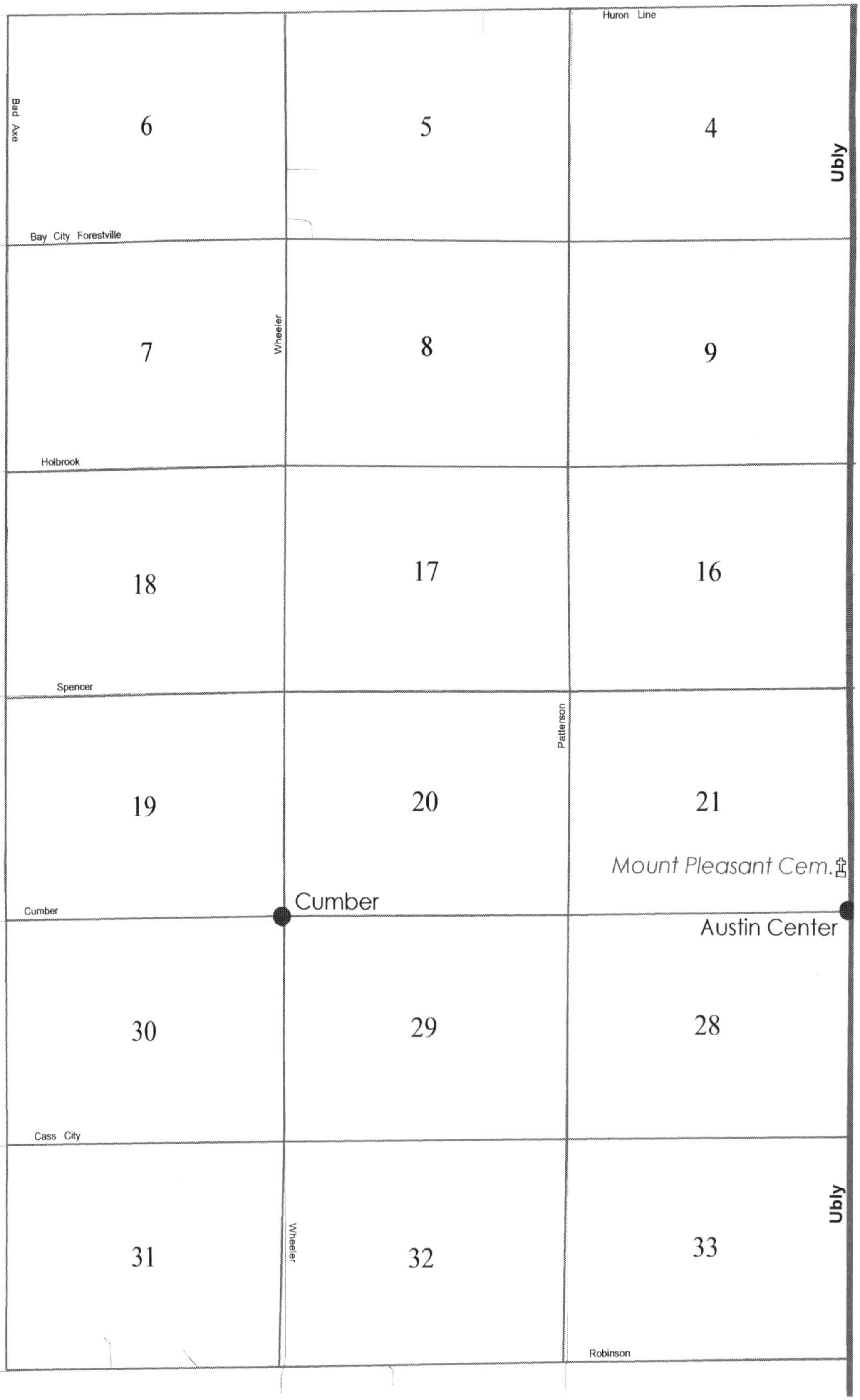

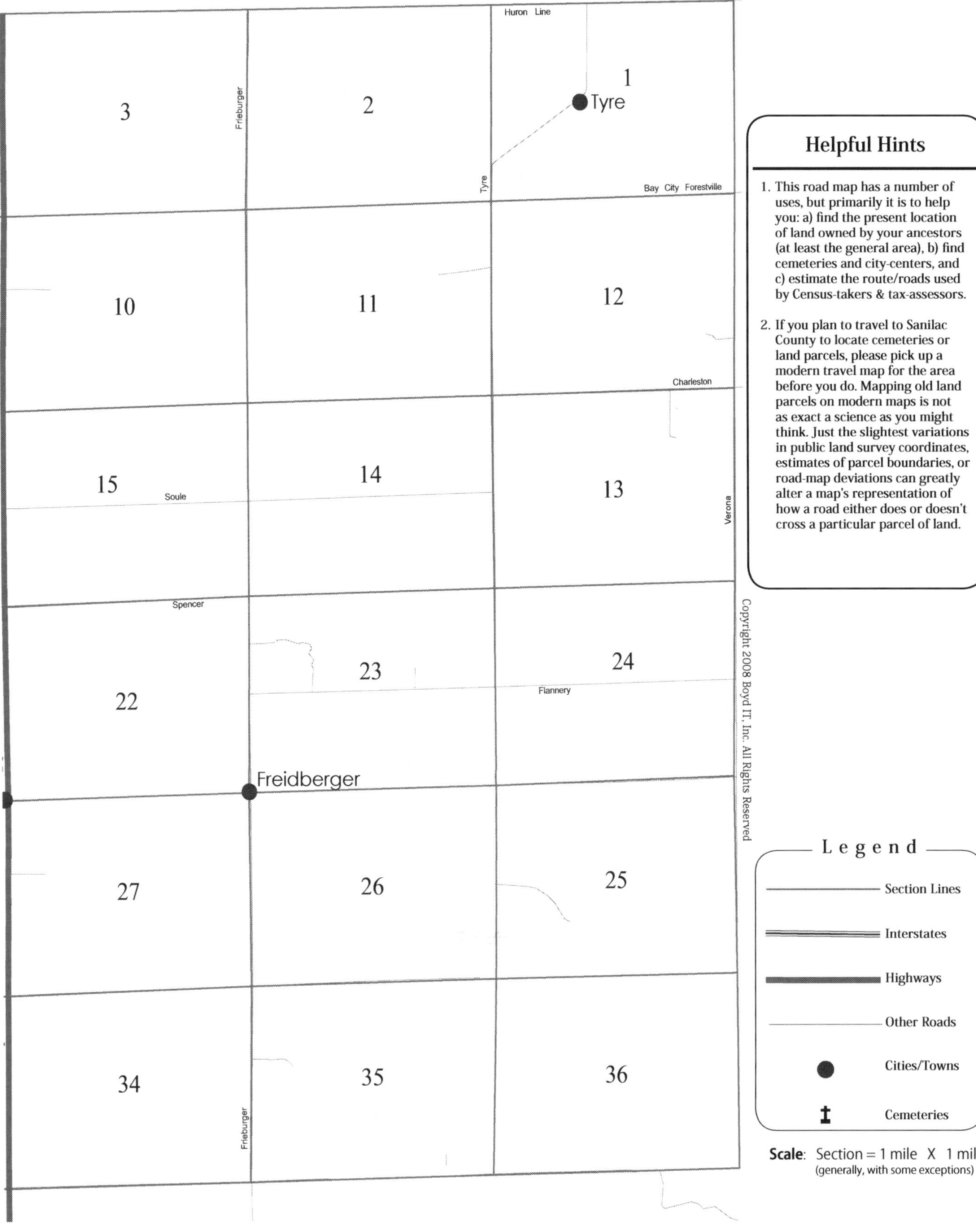

Helpful Hints

1. This road map has a number of uses, but primarily it is to help you: a) find the present location of land owned by your ancestors (at least the general area), b) find cemeteries and city-centers, and c) estimate the route/roads used by Census-takers & tax-assessors.
2. If you plan to travel to Sanilac County to locate cemeteries or land parcels, please pick up a modern travel map for the area before you do. Mapping old land parcels on modern maps is not as exact a science as you might think. Just the slightest variations in public land survey coordinates, estimates of parcel boundaries, or road-map deviations can greatly alter a map's representation of how a road either does or doesn't cross a particular parcel of land.

Scale: Section = 1 mile X 1 mile
(generally, with some exceptions)

Historical Map

T14-N R13-E
Michigan-Toledo Strip Meridian

Map Group 2

Cities & Towns

Austin Center
Cumber
Freidberger
Tyre

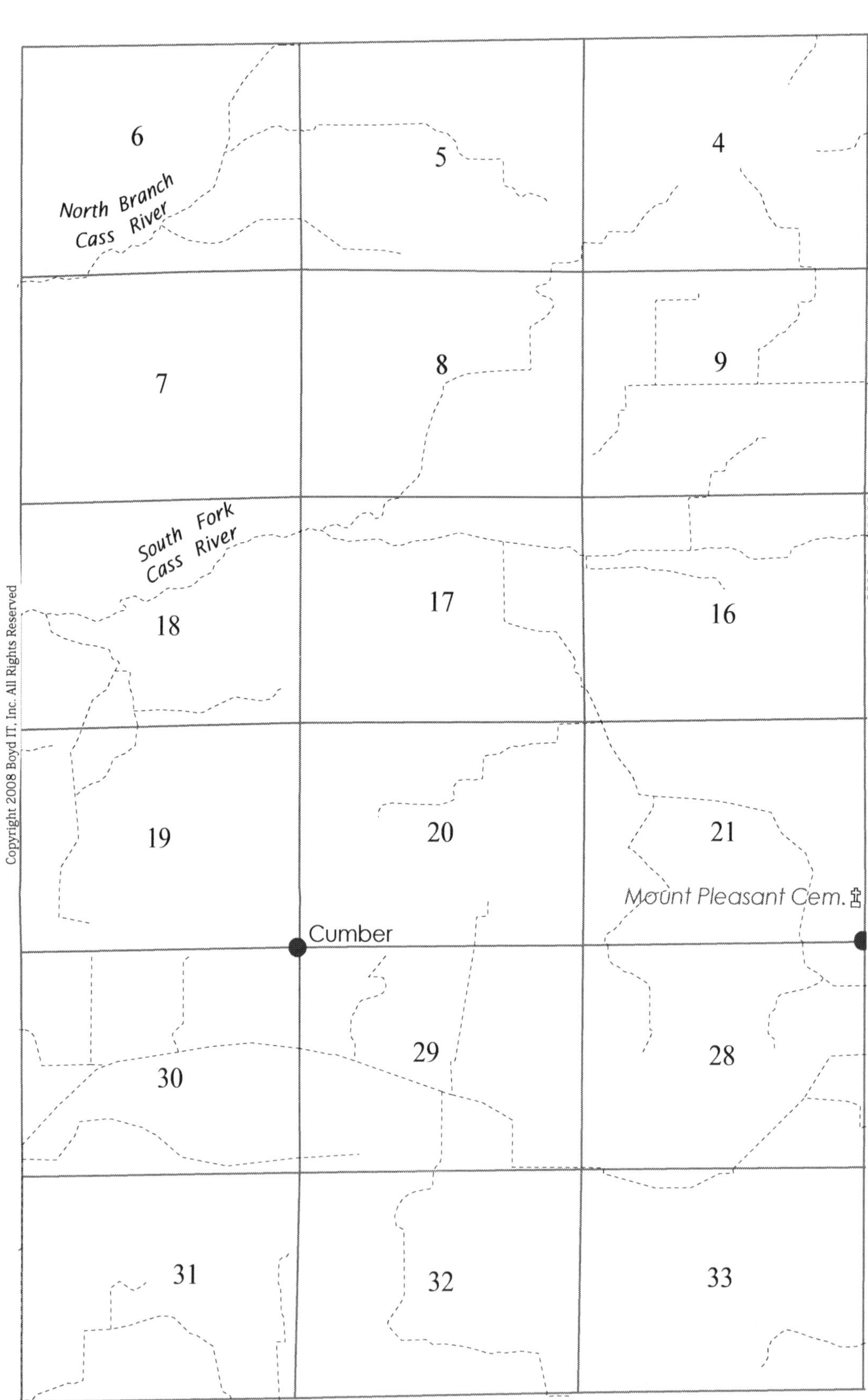

Cemeteries

Mount Pleasant Cemetery

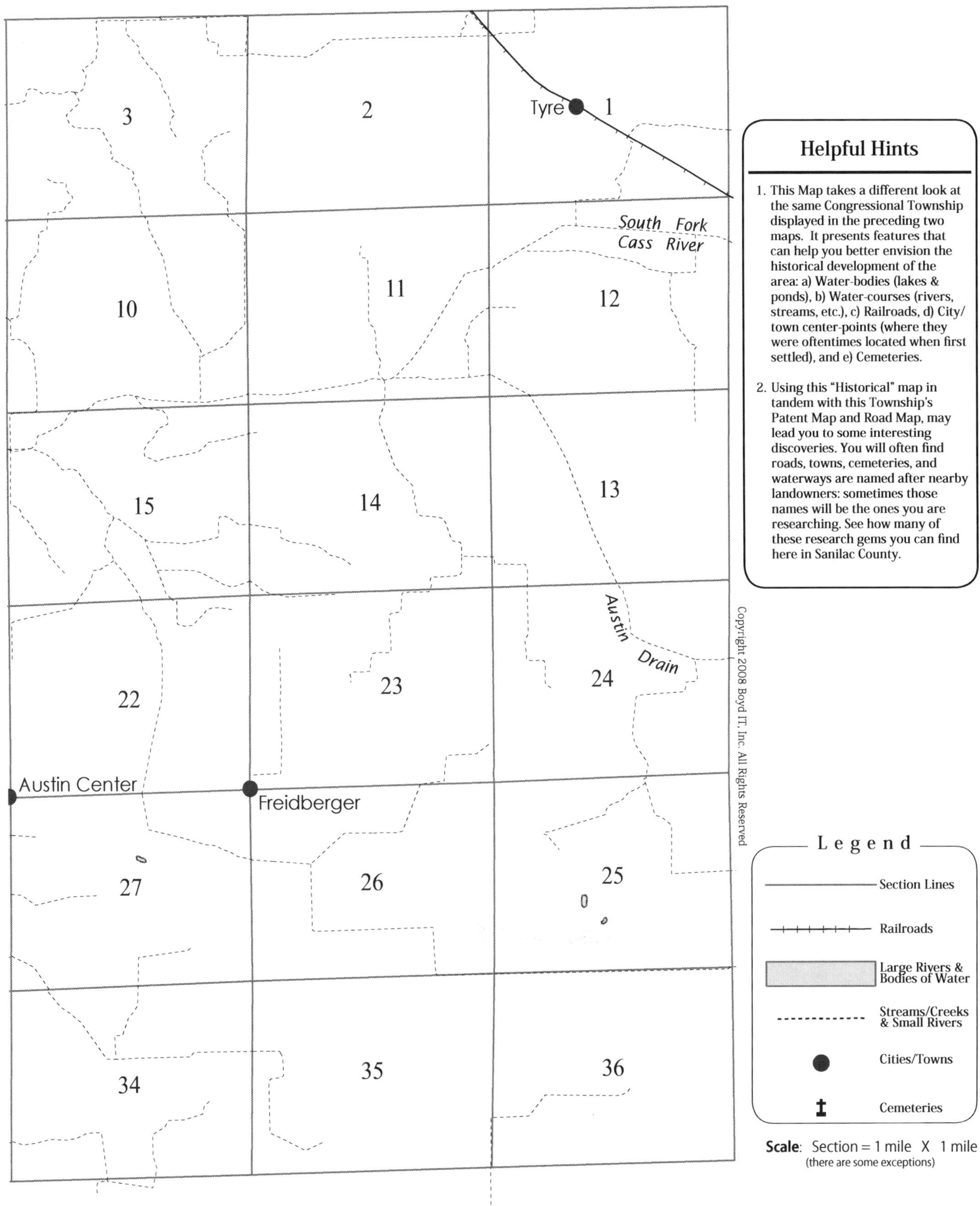

Helpful Hints

1. This Map takes a different look at the same Congressional Township displayed in the preceding two maps. It presents features that can help you better envision the historical development of the area: a) Water-bodies (lakes & ponds), b) Water-courses (rivers, streams, etc.), c) Railroads, d) City/town center-points (where they were oftentimes located when first settled), and e) Cemeteries.

2. Using this "Historical" map in tandem with this Township's Patent Map and Road Map, may lead you to some interesting discoveries. You will often find roads, towns, cemeteries, and waterways are named after nearby landowners: sometimes those names will be the ones you are researching. See how many of these research gems you can find here in Sanilac County.

Map Group 3: Index to Land Patents

Township 14-North Range 14-East (Michigan-Toledo Strip)

After you locate an individual in this Index, take note of the Section and Section Part then proceed to the Land Patent map on the pages immediately following. You should have no difficulty locating the corresponding parcel of land.

The "For More Info" Column will lead you to more information about the underlying Patents. See the *Legend* at right, and the "How to Use this Book" chapter, for more information.

LEGEND

"For More Info . . . " column

A = Authority (Legislative Act, See Appendix "A")
B = Block or Lot (location in Section unknown)
C = Cancelled Patent
F = Fractional Section
G = Group (Multi-Patentee Patent, see Appendix "C")
V = Overlaps another Parcel
R = Re-Issued (Parcel patented more than once)

(A & G items require you to look in the Appendixes referred to above. All other Letter-designations followed by a number require you to locate line-items in this index that possess the ID number found after the letter).

ID	Individual in Patent	Sec.	Sec. Part	Date Issued	Other Counties	For More Info . . .
347	ANDERSON, John	3	NW	1857-10-30		A1
320	BAER, Conrad	10	SW	1859-10-10		A1
388	BETTERMANN, Robert	13	NESE	1860-05-01		A1
364	BEZEMEK, Mathias	6	N½SW	1862-10-01		A1 F
365	" "	6	SENW	1862-10-01		A1 F
366	BEZENEK, Mathias	6	NENE	1867-07-01		A1 F
321	BORLAND, Daniel	14	E½NW	1857-07-01		A1
317	BRADEN, Caspar	11	NE	1855-10-01		A1
369	BRADY, Michael	23	N½SE	1857-07-01		A1
370	" "	23	SESE	1857-07-01		A1
371	" "	24	SW	1857-07-01		A1
372	" "	26	NENE	1857-07-01		A1
315	BUTHE, Augustus	1	NW	1857-02-20		A1 F
340	CARNEY, James	14	NE	1860-05-01		A1
346	CARROLAN, Jane	15	SE	1869-11-15		A1 C R380
380	CARROLAN, Patrick	15	SE	1857-07-01		A1 R346
348	DEEGAN, John	25	E½SW	1857-02-20		A1
349	" "	25	SWSE	1857-02-20		A1
381	DEEGAN, Patrick	13	SW	1857-07-01		A1
382	" "	24	NW	1857-07-01		A1
383	DEIGAN, Patrick	25	W½NW	1860-05-01		A1
350	DIETER, John	2	NW	1857-10-30		A1
341	DONALLAN, James	25	NWSW	1860-11-21		A1
342	" "	26	NESE	1860-11-21		A1
327	DONNAVAN, Dennis	18	W½NW	1859-10-10		A1
328	" "	7	SWSW	1859-10-10		A1
396	DONNER, William	17	NE	1859-05-09		A1
397	" "	17	NENW	1861-07-01		A1
398	DONOLON, William	25	E½NW	1857-10-30		A1
308	FISHER, Anthony	9	E½NE	1860-05-01		A1
309	" "	9	E½SE	1860-05-01		A1
310	" "	9	SWSW	1865-10-02		A1
336	FLETCHER, George S	3	N½NE	1857-07-01		A1 F
337	" "	3	SENE	1857-07-01		A1 F
351	GARA, John	22	E½NE	1859-10-10		A1
339	GREEN, Isaac	2	NE	1857-07-01		A1 F
353	HARLOW, John	1	S½SW	1857-07-01		A1
352	" "	1	N½SW	1857-10-30		A1
374	JOHNSON, Moses N	31	W½SE	1898-07-27		A2
303	JONES, Albert	3	S½SE	1857-02-20		A1
302	" "	3	E½SW	1859-05-09		A1
323	JONES, David B	10	NE	1857-02-20		A1
324	JONES, David D	10	NW	1857-02-16		A1
338	KIBBEE, Henry C	25	SWSW	1865-10-02		A1
304	KOLAR, Albert	7	NENE	1870-10-05		A2
343	LAVIN, James	14	N½SE	1857-02-20		A1

ID	Individual in Patent	Sec.	Sec. Part	Date Issued	Other Counties	For More Info . . .
344	LAVIN, James (Cont'd)	14	S½SE	1857-02-20		A1
354	LAVIN, John	23	NE	1857-10-30		A1
373	LAVIN, Michael	14	SWSW	1860-10-01		A1
386	LINK, Philip	2	SE	1857-02-16		A1
387	LINK, Philipp	12	NW	1857-10-30		A1
384	MAHON, Peter	36	SE	1857-10-30		A1
306	MCDONALD, Alexander	12	SE	1857-02-20		A1
325	MOODY, David	34	NESE	1861-07-01		A1
378	MOONY, Nicholas	35	W½NW	1857-10-30		A1
379	" "	35	W½SW	1857-10-30		A1
376	" "	27	E½SE	1859-05-09		A1
377	" "	34	E½NE	1859-05-09		A1
322	MORGAN, Daniel	15	NENW	1861-07-01		A1
335	MORGAN, George	11	SWSE	1857-02-20		A1
334	" "	11	E½SE	1857-10-30		A1
355	MUDGE, John	1	E½	1857-02-20		A1 F
326	MURDOCK, David	12	SW	1857-10-30		A1
399	MURPHY, William	36	N½SW	1859-10-10		A1
400	" "	36	NW	1859-10-10		A1
367	PEGSHA, Mathias	4	NESE	1861-09-02		A1
368	" "	4	W½SE	1861-09-02		A1
307	PERRET, Alexander	13	S½SE	1857-10-30		A1
389	REDPATH, Robert	8	SESW	1859-10-10		A1
390	" "	8	SWSE	1859-10-10		A1
345	ROADHOUSE, James	3	N½SE	1857-02-20		A1
356	ROBERTSON, John	5	NWNW	1856-01-10		A1
361	ROLLAS, Josef	3	W½SW	1859-10-10		A1
362	" "	4	SESE	1859-10-10		A1
305	RYCKMAN, Albert	6	SENE	1911-09-11		A1
385	RYCKMAN, Peter	6	W½NE	1857-02-20		A1 F
402	RYCKMAN, William	5	E½NE	1857-02-20		A1 F
401	" "	4	W½NW	1860-05-01		A1 F
311	SCHEDINA, Anton	5	SWSE	1860-11-21		A1
312	" "	8	NESW	1860-11-21		A1
313	" "	8	NWSE	1860-11-21		A1
314	" "	8	W½NE	1860-11-21		A1
403	SEAMAN, William	12	S½NE	1857-10-30		A1
330	SEAMANS, Ely	12	N½NE	1857-10-30		A1
363	SEGRET, Mathew	15	NWNW	1861-12-03		A1
318	SMITH, Catharine	24	NE	1857-07-01		A1 G57
357	SMITH, John	24	SE	1856-01-10		A1
318	" "	24	NE	1857-07-01		A1 G57
329	STILWELL, Elisha	10	SE	1857-07-01		A1
394	STILWELL, Susanna	14	E½SW	1857-02-16		A1
395	" "	14	NWSW	1857-02-16		A1
404	STILWELL, William	14	W½NW	1859-10-10		A1
405	" "	15	NENE	1859-10-10		A1
406	" "	15	SENE	1859-10-10		A1
358	SULLIVIN, John	26	SENE	1861-07-01		A1
375	THAYER, Nelson O	36	SESW	1860-11-21		A1
392	THAYER, Simeon M	15	NWNE	1869-07-01		A1
393	" "	3	SWNE	1870-05-10		A1
407	THOMPSON, William	36	NE	1856-09-01		A1
316	WEISEMBERGER, Benet	8	W½NW	1859-05-09		A1
331	WELLS, Fred L	22	NWNE	1872-08-10		A1
332	WELLS, Fred S	15	E½SW	1872-08-10		A1
359	WELLS, John	13	NWSE	1861-09-02		A1
360	WODRASKA, John	17	NESE	1878-02-13		A2
333	WRACHA, Frederick	2	SW	1857-02-16		A1
319	WRESCHE, Christian	11	NWSE	1859-10-10		A1
391	YOUNG, Robert	13	NW	1857-02-20		A1

Patent Map

T14-N R14-E
Michigan-Toledo Strip Meridian

Map Group 3

Township Statistics

Parcels Mapped	:	106
Number of Patents	:	83
Number of Individuals	:	75
Patentees Identified	:	75
Number of Surnames	:	59
Multi-Patentee Parcels	:	1
Oldest Patent Date	:	10/1/1855
Most Recent Patent	:	9/11/1911
Block/Lot Parcels	:	0
Parcels Re - Issued	:	1
Parcels that Overlap	:	0
Cities and Towns	:	3
Cemeteries	:	2

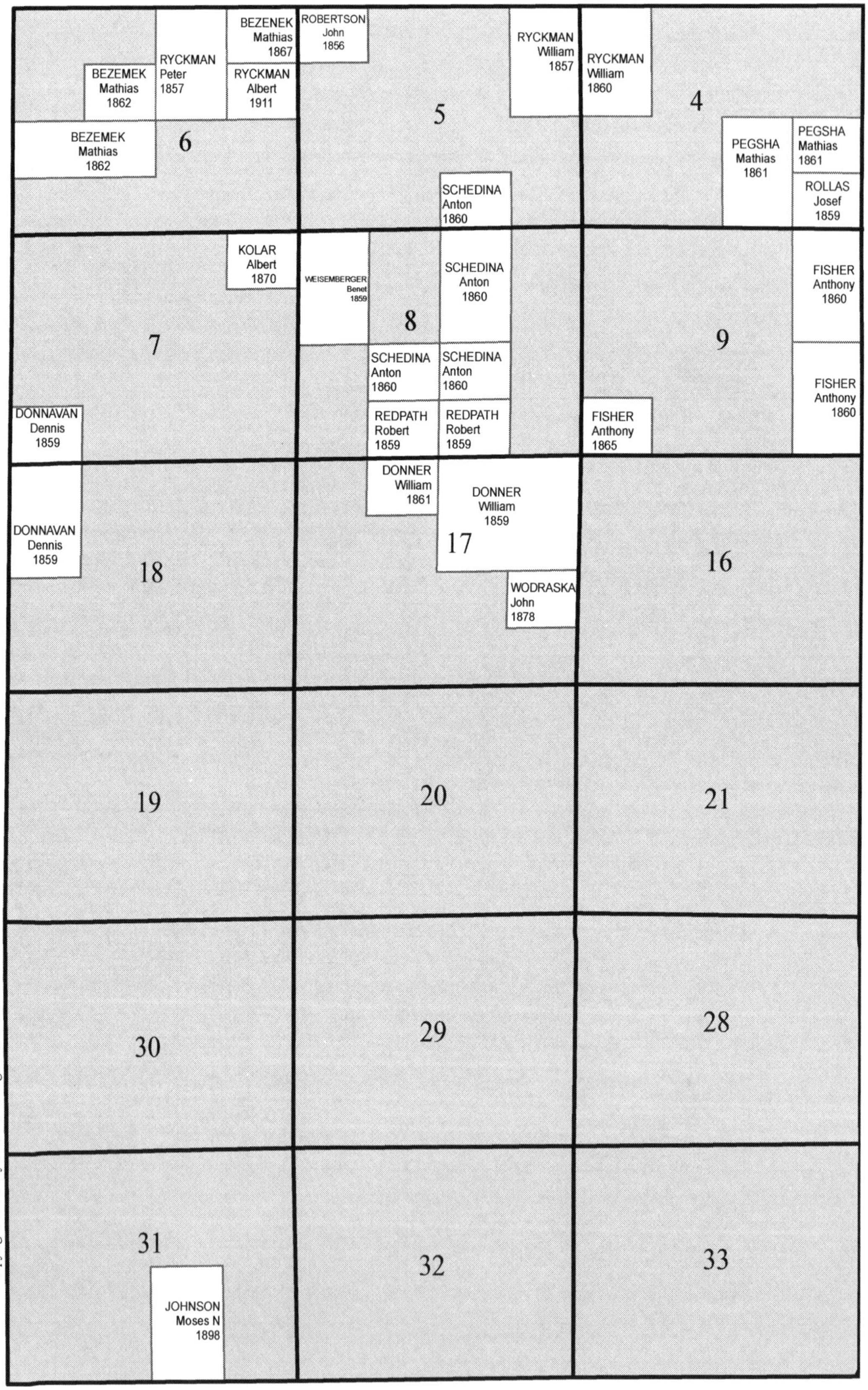

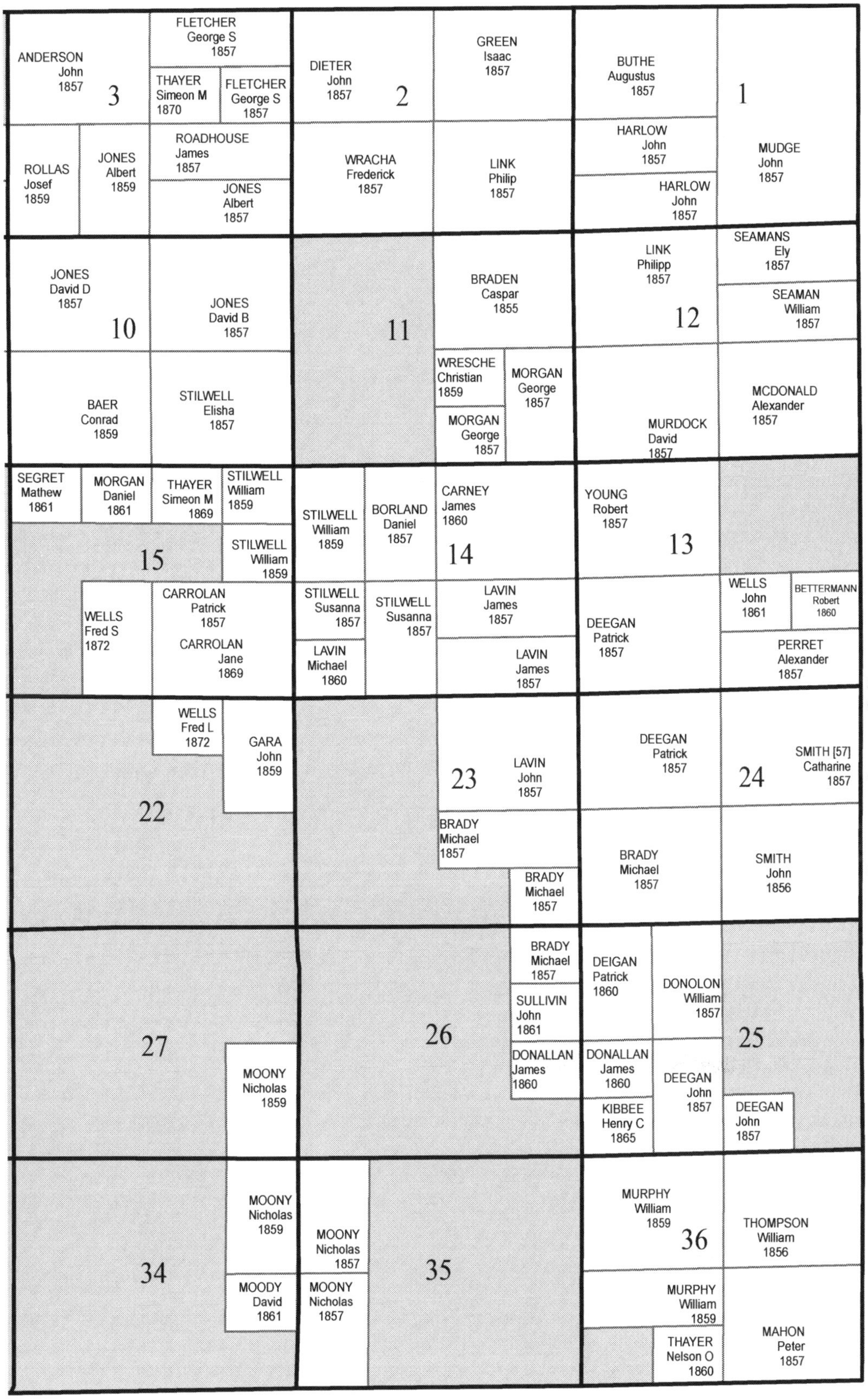

Helpful Hints

1. This Map's INDEX can be found on the preceding pages.
2. Refer to Map "C" to see where this Township lies within Sanilac County, Michigan.
3. Numbers within square brackets [ ] denote a multi-patentee land parcel (multi-owner). Refer to Appendix "C" for a full list of members in this group.
4. Areas that look to be crowded with Patentees usually indicate multiple sales of the same parcel (Re-issues) or Overlapping parcels. See this Township's Index for an explanation of these and other circumstances that might explain "odd" groupings of Patentees on this map.

Legend

Patent Boundary

Section Boundary

No Patents Found (or Outside County)

1., 2., 3., ... Lot Numbers (when beside a name)

[ ] Group Number (see Appendix "C")

Scale: Section = 1 mile X 1 mile (generally, with some exceptions)

Road Map

T14-N R14-E
Michigan-Toledo Strip Meridian

Map Group 3

Cities & Towns

- Minden City
- Palms
- Peatville

Cemeteries

- Minden City Cemetery
- Saint Patricks Cemetery

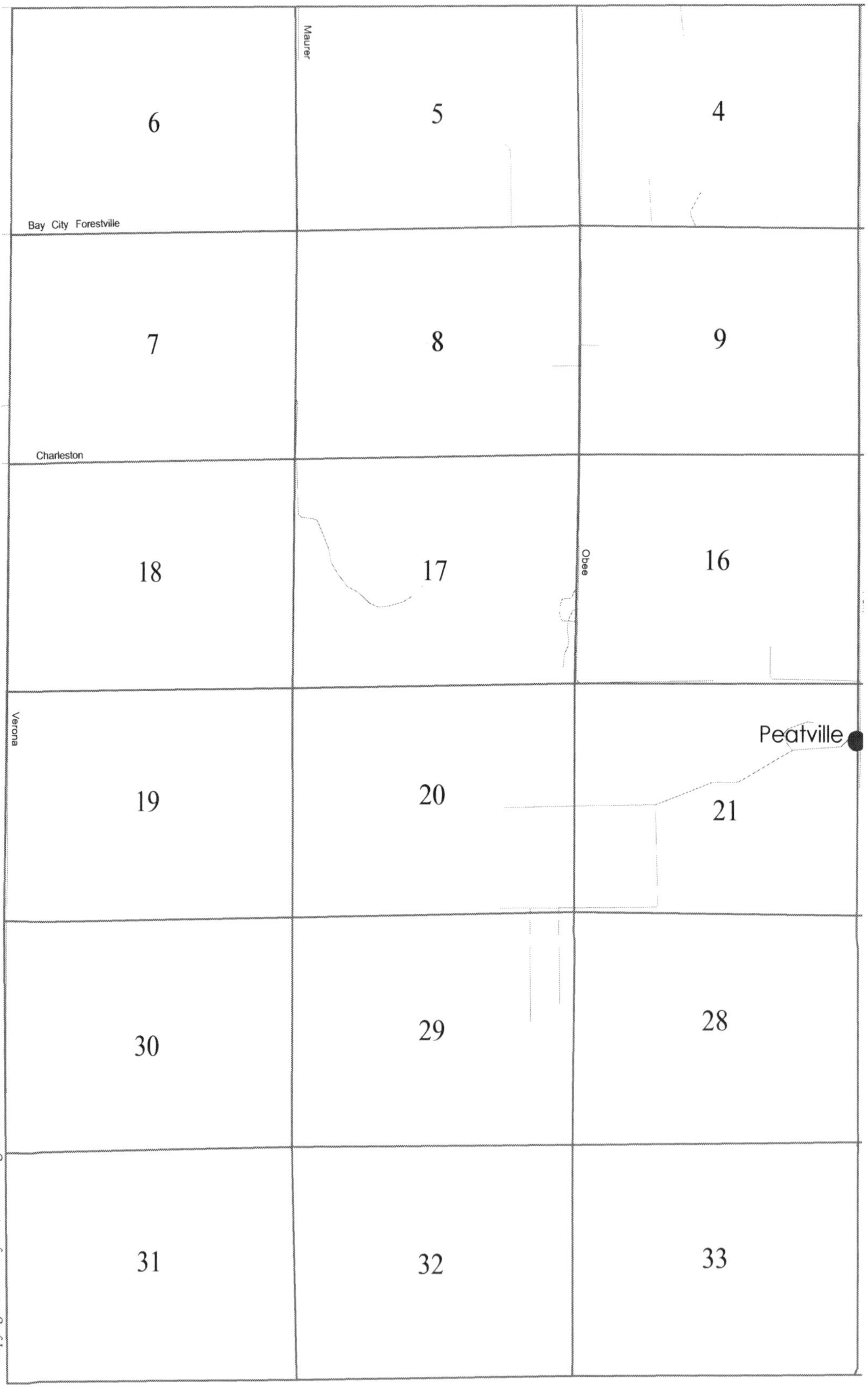

Maurer
6
5
4
Bay City Forestville
7
8
9
Charleston
18
17
Obee
16
Verona
19
20
Peatville
21
30
29
28
31
32
33

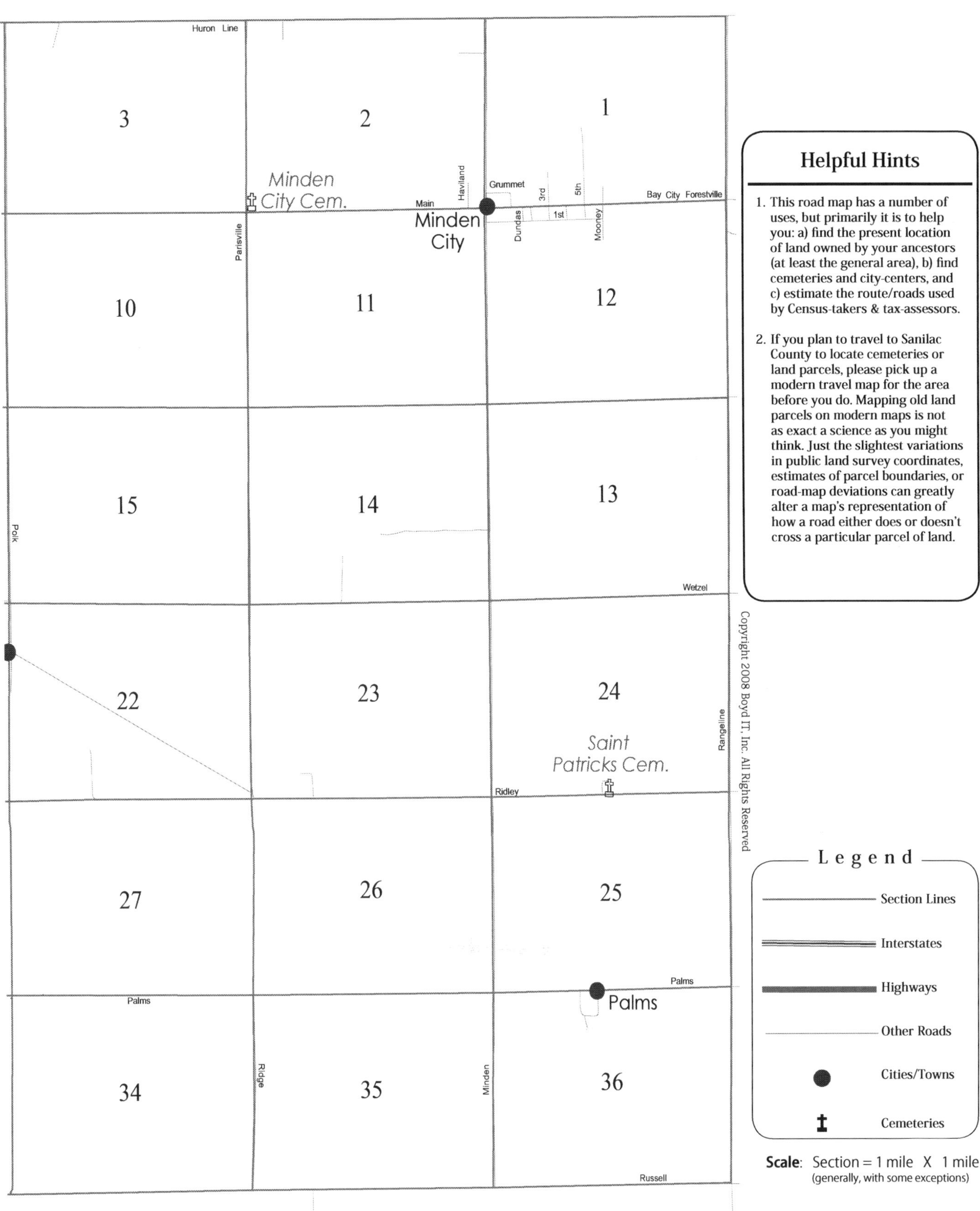
Huron Line
3
2
1
Minden City Cem.
Haviland
Grummet
3rd
5th
Bay City Forestville
Main
Minden City
Dundas
1st
Mooney
Parisville
10
11
12
15
14
13
Polk
Wetzel
22
23
24
Saint Patricks Cem.
Rangeline
Ridley
27
26
25
Palms
Palms
Palms
34
Ridge
35
Minden
36
Russell
Helpful Hints
1. This road map has a number of uses, but primarily it is to help you: a) find the present location of land owned by your ancestors (at least the general area), b) find cemeteries and city-centers, and c) estimate the route/roads used by Census-takers & tax-assessors.
2. If you plan to travel to Sanilac County to locate cemeteries or land parcels, please pick up a modern travel map for the area before you do. Mapping old land parcels on modern maps is not as exact a science as you might think. Just the slightest variations in public land survey coordinates, estimates of parcel boundaries, or road-map deviations can greatly alter a map's representation of how a road either does or doesn't cross a particular parcel of land.
Copyright 2008 Boyd IT, Inc. All Rights Reserved
Legend
Section Lines
Interstates
Highways
Other Roads
Cities/Towns
Cemeteries
Scale: Section = 1 mile X 1 mile
(generally, with some exceptions)

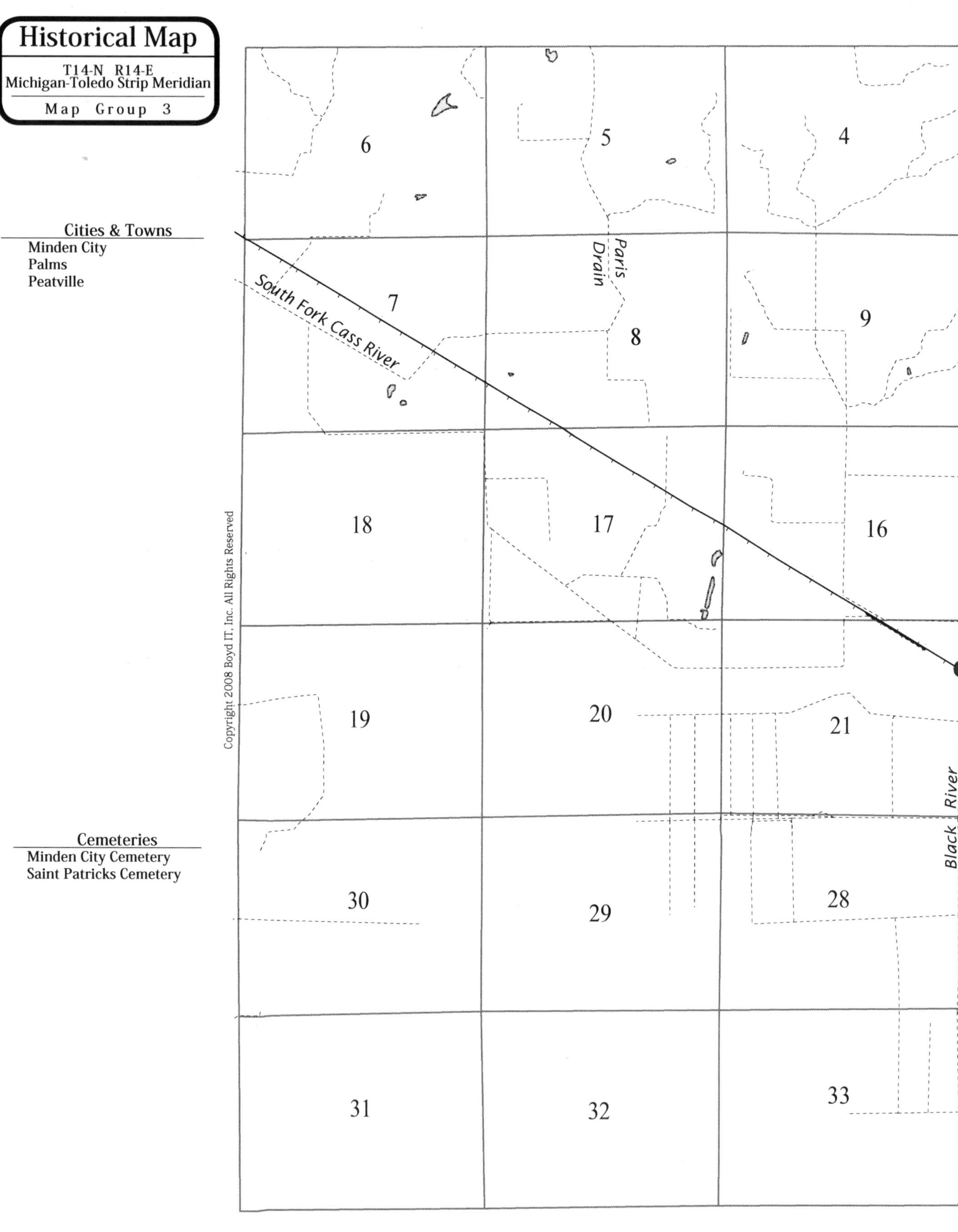
Historical Map
T14-N R14-E
Michigan-Toledo Strip Meridian
Map Group 3
Cities & Towns
Minden City
Palms
Peatville
Cemeteries
Minden City Cemetery
Saint Patricks Cemetery
6
5
4
7
8
9
18
17
16
19
20
21
30
29
28
31
32
33
Paris Drain
South Fork Cass River
Black River
Copyright 2008 Boyd IT, Inc. All Rights Reserved

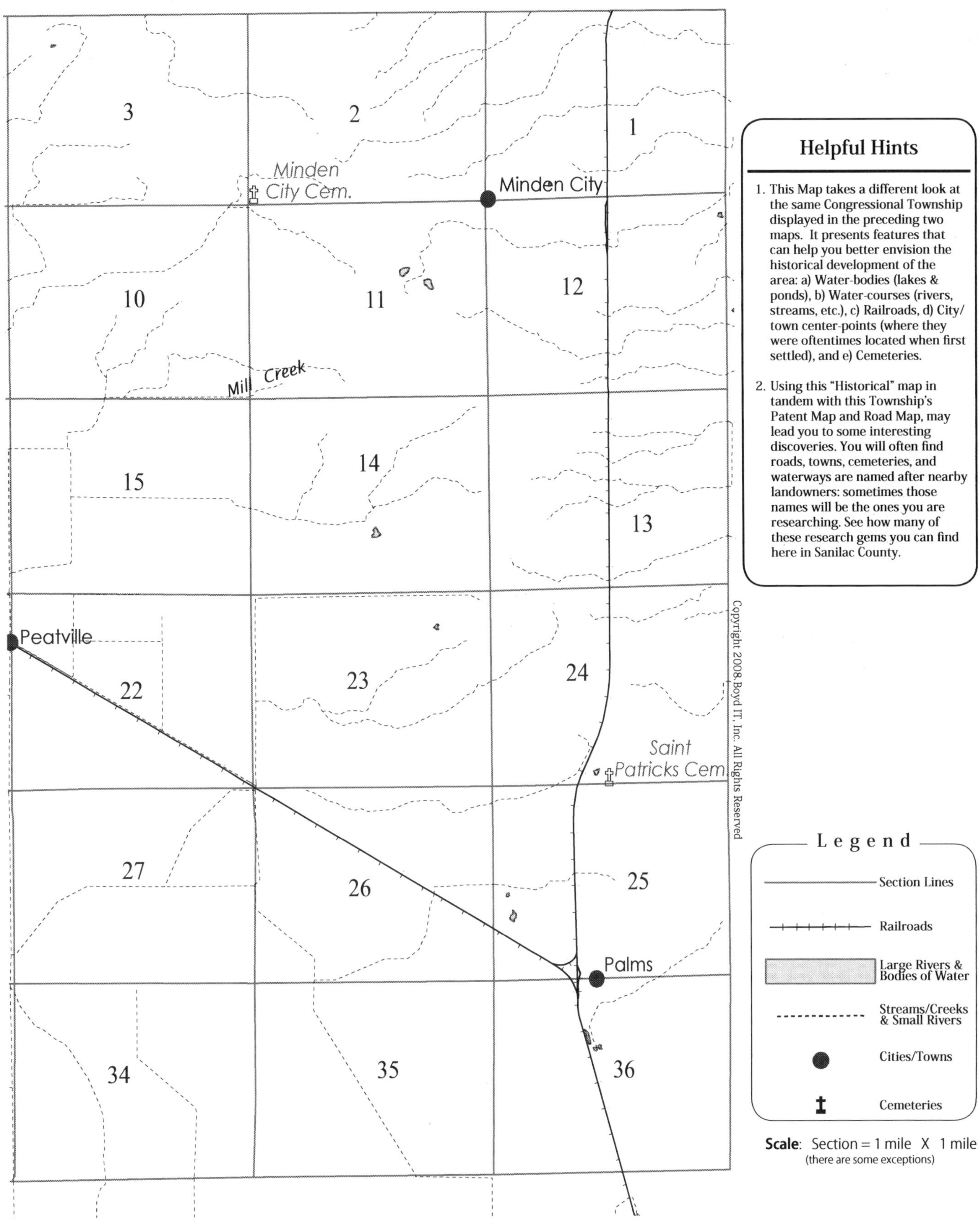

Helpful Hints

1. This Map takes a different look at the same Congressional Township displayed in the preceding two maps. It presents features that can help you better envision the historical development of the area: a) Water-bodies (lakes & ponds), b) Water-courses (rivers, streams, etc.), c) Railroads, d) City/town center-points (where they were oftentimes located when first settled), and e) Cemeteries.

2. Using this "Historical" map in tandem with this Township's Patent Map and Road Map, may lead you to some interesting discoveries. You will often find roads, towns, cemeteries, and waterways are named after nearby landowners: sometimes those names will be the ones you are researching. See how many of these research gems you can find here in Sanilac County.

Map Group 4: Index to Land Patents

Township 14-North Range 15-East (Michigan-Toledo Strip)

After you locate an individual in this Index, take note of the Section and Section Part then proceed to the Land Patent map on the pages immediately following. You should have no difficulty locating the corresponding parcel of land.

The "For More Info" Column will lead you to more information about the underlying Patents. See the *Legend* at right, and the "How to Use this Book" chapter, for more information.

LEGEND

"For More Info . . . " column

A = Authority (Legislative Act, See Appendix "A")
B = Block or Lot (location in Section unknown)
C = Cancelled Patent
F = Fractional Section
G = Group (Multi-Patentee Patent, see Appendix "C")
V = Overlaps another Parcel
R = Re-Issued (Parcel patented more than once)

(A & G items require you to look in the Appendixes referred to above. All other Letter-designations followed by a number require you to locate line-items in this index that possess the ID number found after the letter).

ID	Individual in Patent	Sec.	Sec. Part	Date Issued	Other Counties	For More Info . . .
446	ALWAY, George C	25	N½SW	1856-01-10		A1
447	" "	25	NWNW	1857-07-01		A1
459	BADGERS, Hiram	28	NESW	1862-05-15		A1
516	BOUTAIGER, Piere	18	NESW	1860-05-01		A1
468	BRADBEK, John	6	E½SE	1857-02-20		A1
445	BRIMLEY, George	20	NWSW	1859-10-10		A1
523	BURGESS, Samuel	1	NW	1861-12-03		A1 F
521	CANHAM, Robert	5	W½SW	1857-10-30		A1
524	CANHAM, Samuel	2	E½SW	1857-02-20		A1 C
525	" "	5	E½SW	1858-08-12		A1
470	CHRIST, John	19	SWSW	1857-10-30		A1
478	CLARK, John P	24	S½SW	1855-10-01		A1
479	" "	25	S½NE	1855-10-01		A1
502	CLARY, Michael	31	NW	1857-02-16		A1 V461, 462
499	" "	20	S½NE	1857-02-20		A1
500	" "	21	SW	1857-02-20		A1
501	" "	28	NWNW	1859-05-09		A1
430	CRANDALL, Edmond F	2	NENE	1857-10-30		A1
415	CROSS, Cyrenius S	27	E½SE	1867-02-16		A1
508	DAVIS, Orrice	27	NWNE	1859-10-10		A1
461	DONNELLAN, James	31	SENW	1857-10-30		A1 V502
462	" "	31	W½NW	1857-10-30		A1 V502
471	DONNELLAN, John	29	E½SW	1859-10-10		A1
503	DYER, Michael	30	NESW	1856-09-01		A1 F
505	" "	30	W½SW	1856-09-01		A1 F
504	" "	30	NW	1857-02-16		A1
489	FORD, Lorinda	25	SWNW	1855-06-15		A1
453	GECK, Henry	13	W½SW	1859-10-10		A1
416	GIBSON, David	33	NENE	1859-10-10		A1
472	GINSBIGLER, John	8	SWSW	1857-07-01		A1
473	HAILFAX, John	17	SW	1857-07-01		A1
474	" "	18	S½SE	1857-07-01		A1
532	HARTWELL, Thomas H	36	NESE	1859-10-10		A1
533	" "	36	SENE	1859-10-10		A1
483	HEILIG, Joseph	6	E½NE	1857-02-20		A1 F
522	HILL, Rodney D	15	SW	1852-02-10		A1
460	HILLS, Ira H	26	W½SW	1857-02-16		A1
507	HOUSELL, Obadiah	5	SWNW	1857-10-30		A1
411	HOYT, Asahel	22	N½NW	1857-02-20		A1
463	HUNT, James	20	S½NW	1859-10-10		A1
409	KELLEY, Alvah	4	SW	1856-01-10		A1
413	KELLEY, Charles H	5	NE	1847-02-20		A1 F
466	KELLEY, James W	8	N½NE	1857-02-16		A1
497	KELLEY, Michael B	8	NENW	1857-02-16		A1
498	" "	8	W½NW	1857-02-16		A1
464	KENYON, James	4	NW	1857-02-20		A1

ID	Individual in Patent	Sec.	Sec. Part	Date Issued	Other Counties	For More Info . . .
510	KIPPER, Peter	19	NWSW	1860-05-01		A1 F
511	" "	19	SWNW	1860-05-01		A1
541	KLOSTERMANN, Wilhelm	2	NWNE	1860-05-01		A1
481	LAKE, John W	27	SENW	1857-02-16		A1
506	LAKE, Nicholas	26	SWNW	1857-02-16		A1
454	LECHTENBURG, Henry	6	E½SW	1860-05-01		A1
509	LEONARD, Patrick	30	W½NE	1857-07-01		A1
449	LESTER, George S	35	NWSE	1855-10-01		A1
490	LYON, Lucius	10	E½SE	1839-04-10		A1 G49
491	" "	11	SW	1839-04-10		A1 G49
492	" "	14	NW	1839-04-10		A1 G49
493	" "	14	SW	1839-04-10		A1 G49
494	" "	15	E½NE	1839-04-10		A1 G49
495	" "	15	E½SE	1839-04-10		A1 G49
432	MACY, Francis G	13	E½SW	1837-08-05		A1
433	" "	13	SE	1837-08-05		A1
537	MALONE, Timothy F	21	SE	1857-07-01		A1
539	" "	22	W½SW	1857-07-01		A1
538	" "	21	SWNE	1860-05-01		A1
543	MASSEY, William	18	E½NW	1857-07-01		A1
544	" "	18	N½SE	1857-07-01		A1
546	" "	18	W½NE	1857-07-01		A1
545	" "	18	NWNW	1857-10-30		A1
476	MCBRIDE, John	34	SESW	1859-05-09		A1
527	MERRILLS, Silas	5	SE	1857-02-16		A1
467	MINER, Jedediah	22	NENE	1854-06-15		A1
455	MIZNER, Henry	28	E½NE	1855-10-01		A1
456	" "	28	E½SE	1855-10-01		A1
457	MIZNER, Henry R	28	NENW	1855-10-01		A1
536	MIZNER, Thomas W	13	S½NW	1914-01-16		A1
412	MOLLOY, Bernard	28	NWNE	1859-05-09		A1
465	NIXON, James	27	SWSW	1860-05-01		A1
530	NOBLE, Simon	31	SWNE	1861-07-01		A1
534	NOBLE, Thomas	31	NWNE	1859-10-10		A1
518	NYE, Richard	14	N½SE	1859-10-10		A1
519	" "	14	SENE	1859-10-10		A1
520	" "	14	SESE	1859-10-10		A1
410	OGDEN, Anthony	27	NWSW	1857-02-16		A1
477	OGDEN, John	27	W½SE	1857-02-16		A1
414	OSEWALD, Christian	7	S½SE	1857-07-01		A1
486	OSWALD, Joseph	7	NE	1857-02-20		A1
490	PARKER, Daniel	10	E½SE	1839-04-10		A1 G49
491	" "	11	SW	1839-04-10		A1 G49
492	" "	14	NW	1839-04-10		A1 G49
493	" "	14	SW	1839-04-10		A1 G49
494	" "	15	E½NE	1839-04-10		A1 G49
495	" "	15	E½SE	1839-04-10		A1 G49
531	PURMAN, Theodor	2	SW	1870-06-20		A1
431	PURMANN, Ferdienand	12	NW	1859-10-10		A1
452	RAUH, Hartman	11	NE	1859-10-10		A1
448	ROTH, George	6	W½SE	1857-02-12		A1
515	SCHMELZ, Philipp	6	S½NW	1857-02-20		A1 F
441	SCHUBEL, Frederick J	12	NE	1857-02-20		A1
450	SCHUMACHER, George	6	W½NE	1857-02-20		A1 F
444	SCHWIGART, Gabriel	7	NW	1857-10-30		A1
535	SCHWIGART, Thomas	7	SW	1857-10-30		A1
540	SEBOLD, Vincent	6	W½SW	1857-07-01		A1 F
451	SHEIBLE, Goatleip	11	N½SE	1857-02-20		A1
517	SIMONS, Reuben	26	NENE	1856-09-01		A1
547	SIMONS, William	25	SENW	1853-11-01		A1
434	SNAY, Francis	27	SENE	1857-02-16		A1
496	STACUM, Martin	35	SWSE	1857-07-01		A1 F
435	STEEVENS, Frederick H	26	E½SW	1837-08-07		A1
436	" "	26	SE	1837-08-07		A1
437	" "	35	E½SW	1837-08-07		A1
438	" "	35	NE	1837-08-07		A1
439	" "	35	NW	1837-08-07		A1
440	" "	36	NW	1837-08-07		A1
542	TAYLOR, William L	28	SWNE	1913-08-27		A1
529	THAYER, Simeon	31	SW	1857-02-16		A1
528	THAYER, Simeon M	20	NESW	1870-06-01		A1
487	UHL, Joseph	7	N½SE	1857-02-20		A1
512	URIDGE, Philip	28	SWSW	1859-10-10		A1

ID	Individual in Patent	Sec.	Sec. Part	Date Issued	Other Counties	For More Info . . .
513	URIDGE, Philip (Cont'd)	29	S½SE	1859-10-10		A1
514	" "	32	N½NE	1859-10-10		A1
548	URIDGE, William	3	N½NE	1859-10-10		A1 F
549	" "	3	NENW	1859-10-10		A1 F
408	VAN ALLEN, ABRAM	34	NWNE	1862-05-15		A1
552	VARTY, William	34	NW	1860-05-01		A1
550	" "	33	SENE	1860-10-01		A1
551	" "	33	W½NE	1860-10-01		A1
480	VARTZ, John	25	NWNE	1860-10-01		A1
526	VOGAL, Sebastian	6	N½NW	1857-10-30		A1 F
418	WARD, Eber B	15	NENW	1852-12-01		A1
419	" "	17	NESE	1852-12-01		A1
429	" "	8	SWNE	1852-12-01		A1
417	" "	13	S½NE	1855-10-01		A1
420	" "	17	S½SE	1855-10-01		A1
421	" "	20	N½NE	1855-10-01		A1
422	" "	20	N½NW	1855-10-01		A1
423	" "	20	N½SE	1855-10-01		A1
424	" "	27	NENW	1855-10-01		A1
425	" "	29	N½SE	1855-10-01		A1
426	" "	34	NESW	1855-10-01		A1
427	" "	34	SWNE	1855-10-01		A1
428	" "	34	W½SW	1855-10-01		A1
469	WATERBURY, John C	25	NENE	1853-11-01		A1
442	WEHR, Frederick	19	E½NE	1857-07-01		A1
443	" "	19	NESE	1857-07-01		A1
458	WILTSIE, Henry	22	NWNE	1855-06-15		A1
482	WILTSIE, John	35	E½SE	1888-05-16		A2
488	WIXSON, Joseph	32	NWSW	1857-02-20		A1
484	WIXSON, Joseph L	31	SE	1857-10-30		A1
485	" "	32	SWSW	1857-10-30		A1
475	WOODS, John L	30	SESE	1855-10-01		A1

Patent Map

T14-N R15-E
Michigan-Toledo Strip Meridian

Map Group 4

Township Statistics

Parcels Mapped	:	145
Number of Patents	:	115
Number of Individuals	:	95
Patentees Identified	:	94
Number of Surnames	:	79
Multi-Patentee Parcels	:	6
Oldest Patent Date	:	8/5/1837
Most Recent Patent	:	1/16/1914
Block/Lot Parcels	:	0
Parcels Re - Issued	:	0
Parcels that Overlap	:	3
Cities and Towns	:	1
Cemeteries	:	3

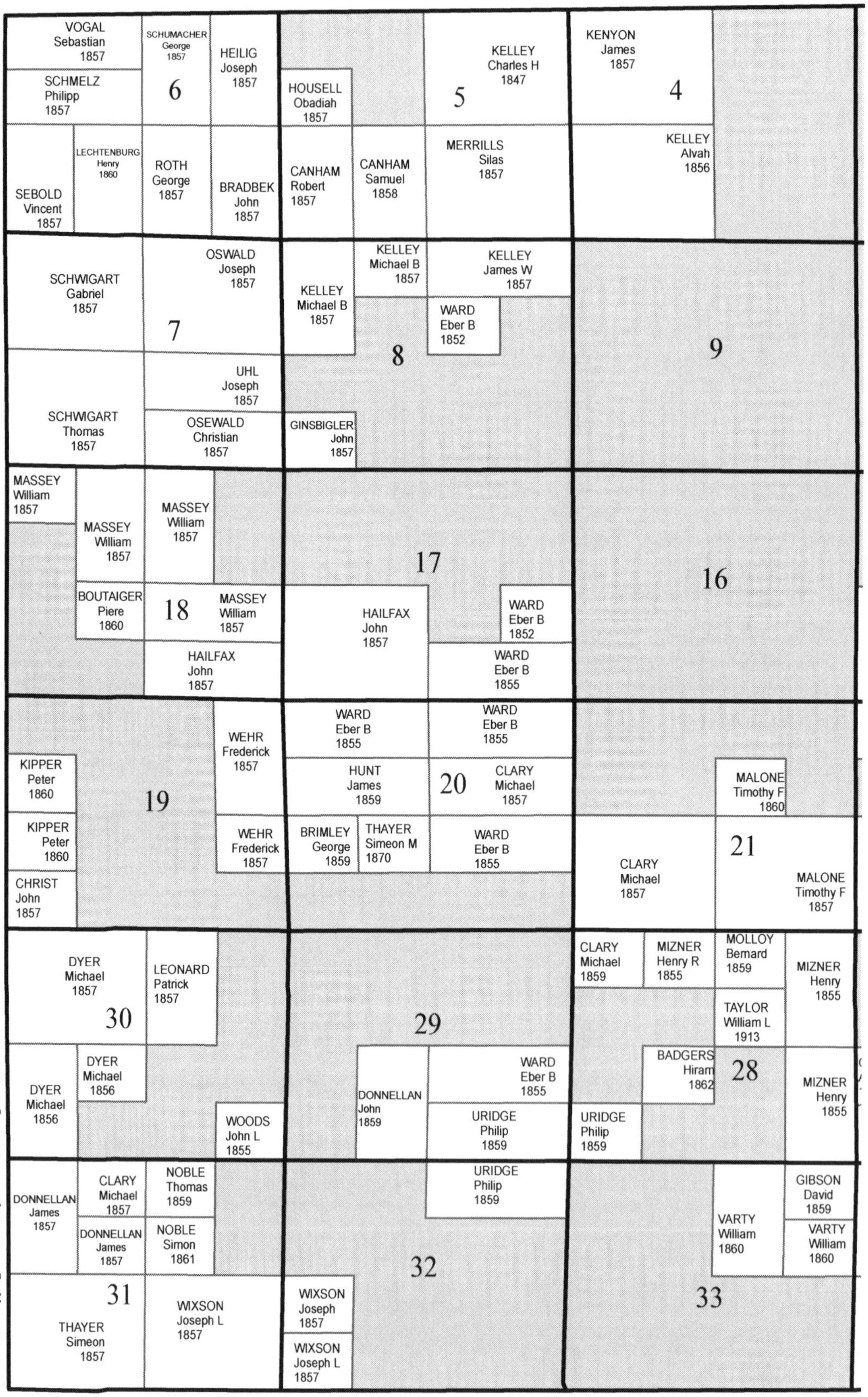

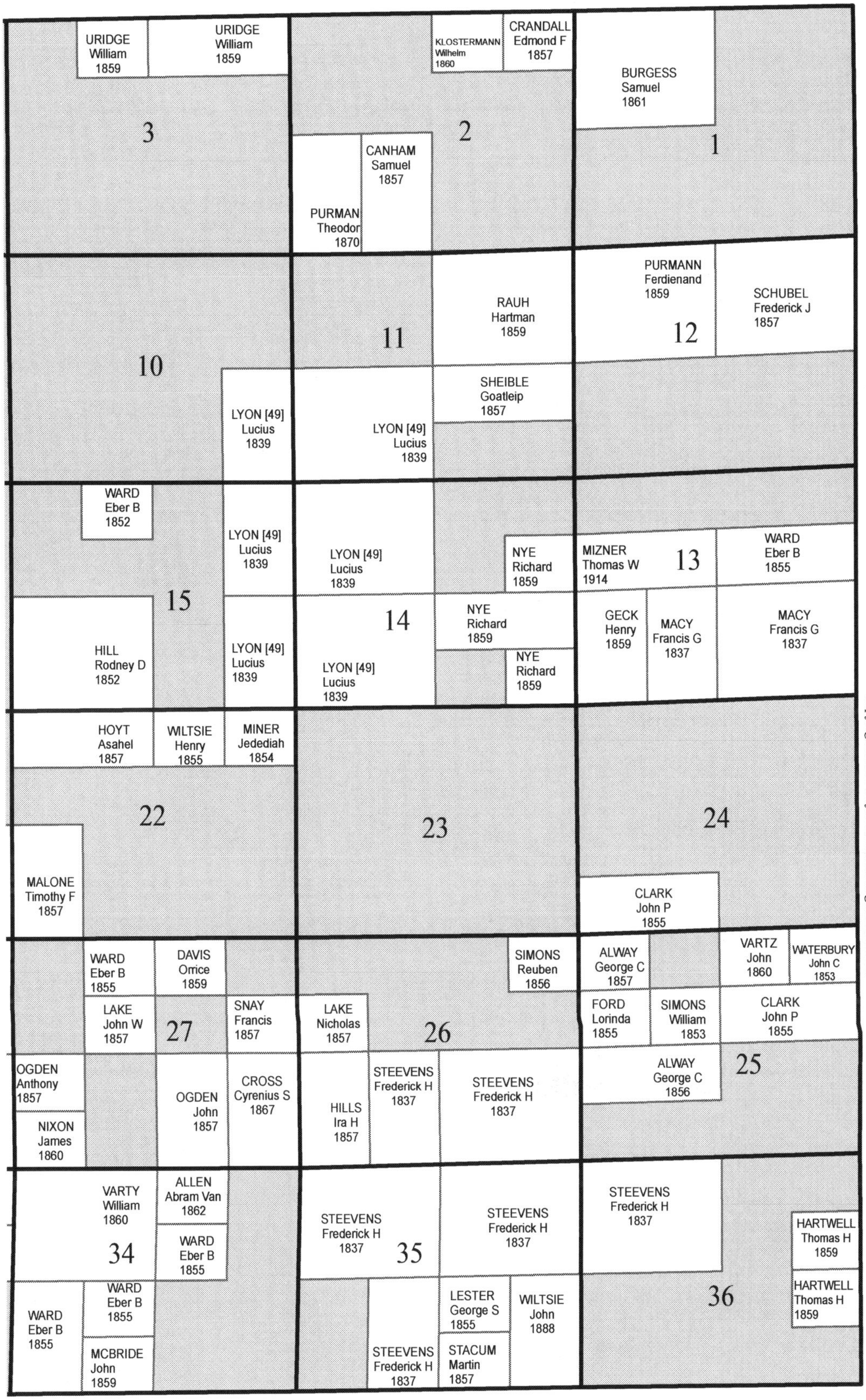

Helpful Hints

1. This Map's INDEX can be found on the preceding pages.
2. Refer to Map "C" to see where this Township lies within Sanilac County, Michigan.
3. Numbers within square brackets [ ] denote a multi-patentee land parcel (multi-owner). Refer to Appendix "C" for a full list of members in this group.
4. Areas that look to be crowded with Patentees usually indicate multiple sales of the same parcel (Re-issues) or Overlapping parcels. See this Township's Index for an explanation of these and other circumstances that might explain "odd" groupings of Patentees on this map.

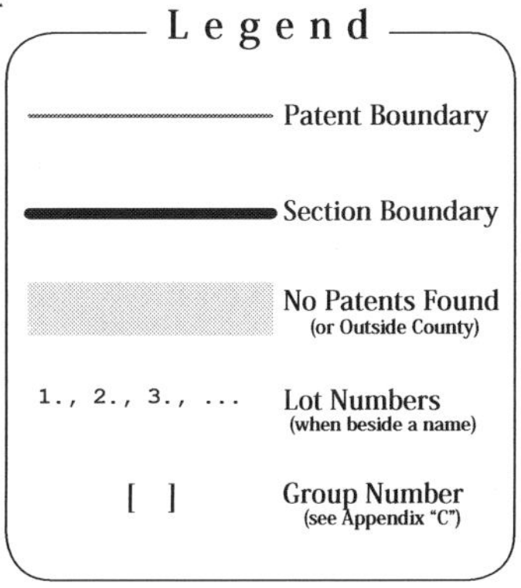

Legend

- Patent Boundary
- Section Boundary
- No Patents Found (or Outside County)
- 1., 2., 3., ... Lot Numbers (when beside a name)
- [ ] Group Number (see Appendix "C")

Scale: Section = 1 mile X 1 mile (generally, with some exceptions)

Road Map

T14-N R15-E
Michigan-Toledo Strip Meridian

Map Group 4

Cities & Towns

Charleston

Cemeteries

Delaware Cemetery
Linwood Cemetery
West Delaware Cemetery

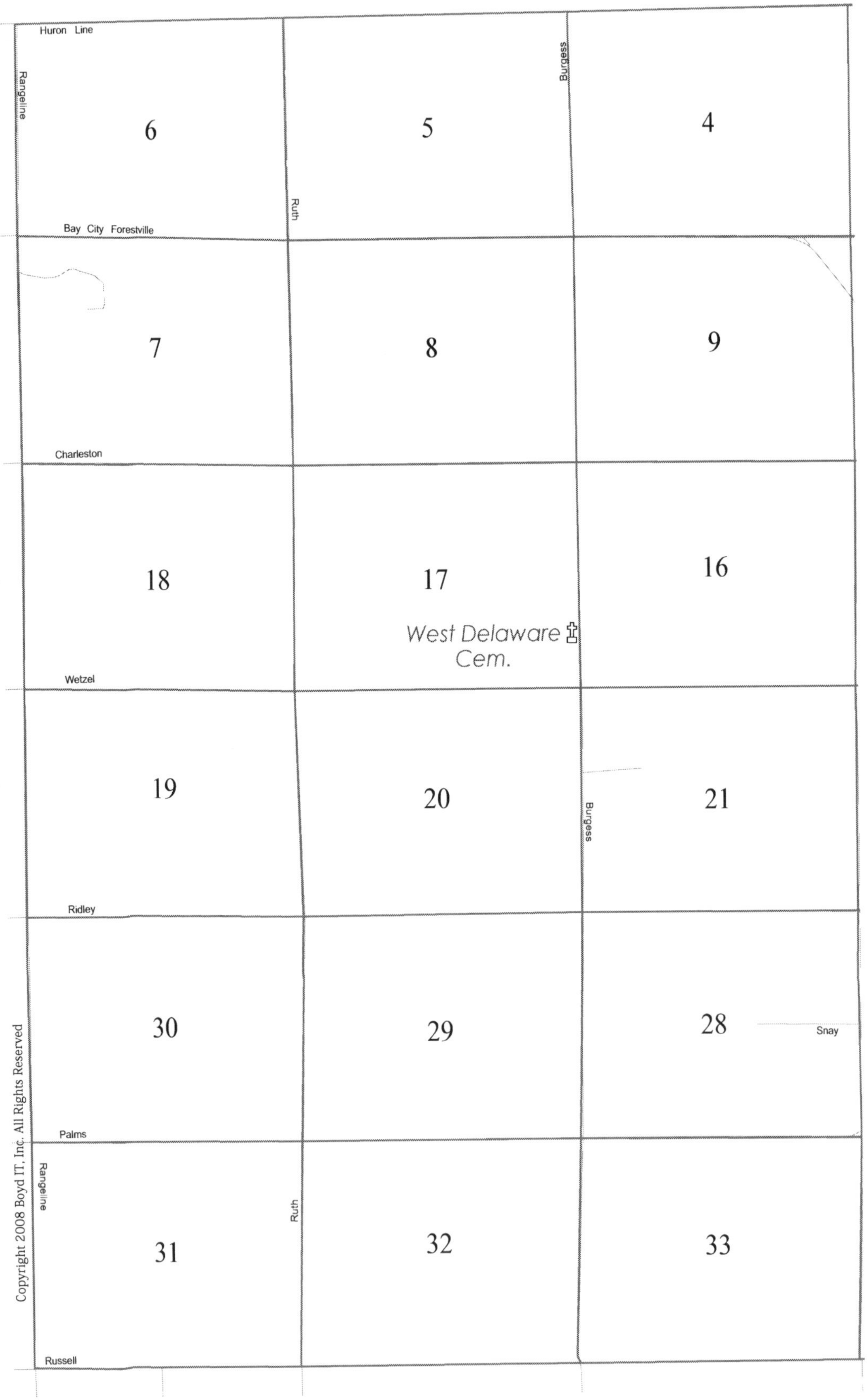

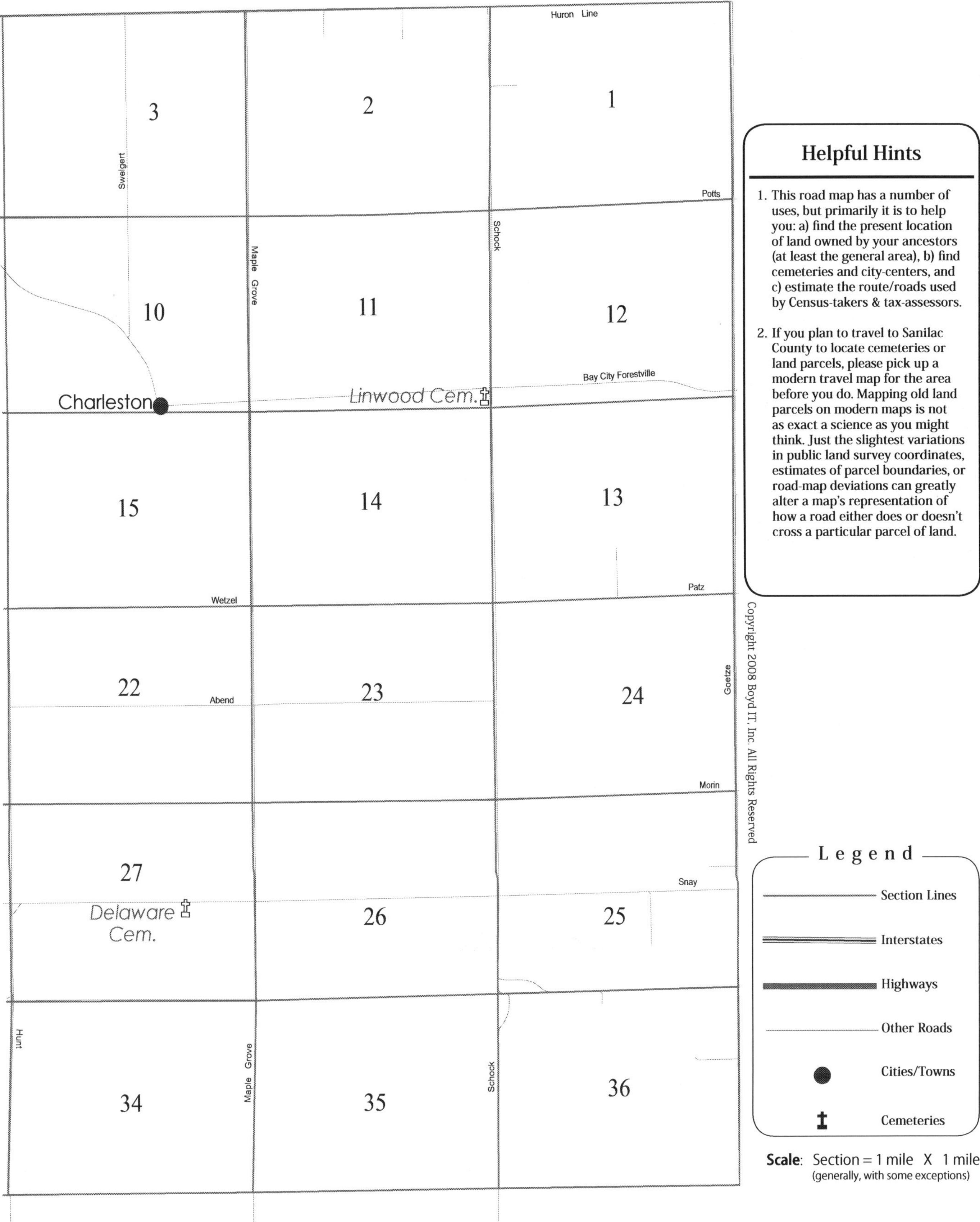

Helpful Hints

1. This road map has a number of uses, but primarily it is to help you: a) find the present location of land owned by your ancestors (at least the general area), b) find cemeteries and city-centers, and c) estimate the route/roads used by Census-takers & tax-assessors.

2. If you plan to travel to Sanilac County to locate cemeteries or land parcels, please pick up a modern travel map for the area before you do. Mapping old land parcels on modern maps is not as exact a science as you might think. Just the slightest variations in public land survey coordinates, estimates of parcel boundaries, or road-map deviations can greatly alter a map's representation of how a road either does or doesn't cross a particular parcel of land.

Legend

- Section Lines
- Interstates
- Highways
- Other Roads
- Cities/Towns
- Cemeteries

Scale: Section = 1 mile X 1 mile
(generally, with some exceptions)

Historical Map

T14-N R15-E
Michigan-Toledo Strip Meridian

Map Group 4

Cities & Towns

Charleston

Cemeteries

Delaware Cemetery
Linwood Cemetery
West Delaware Cemetery

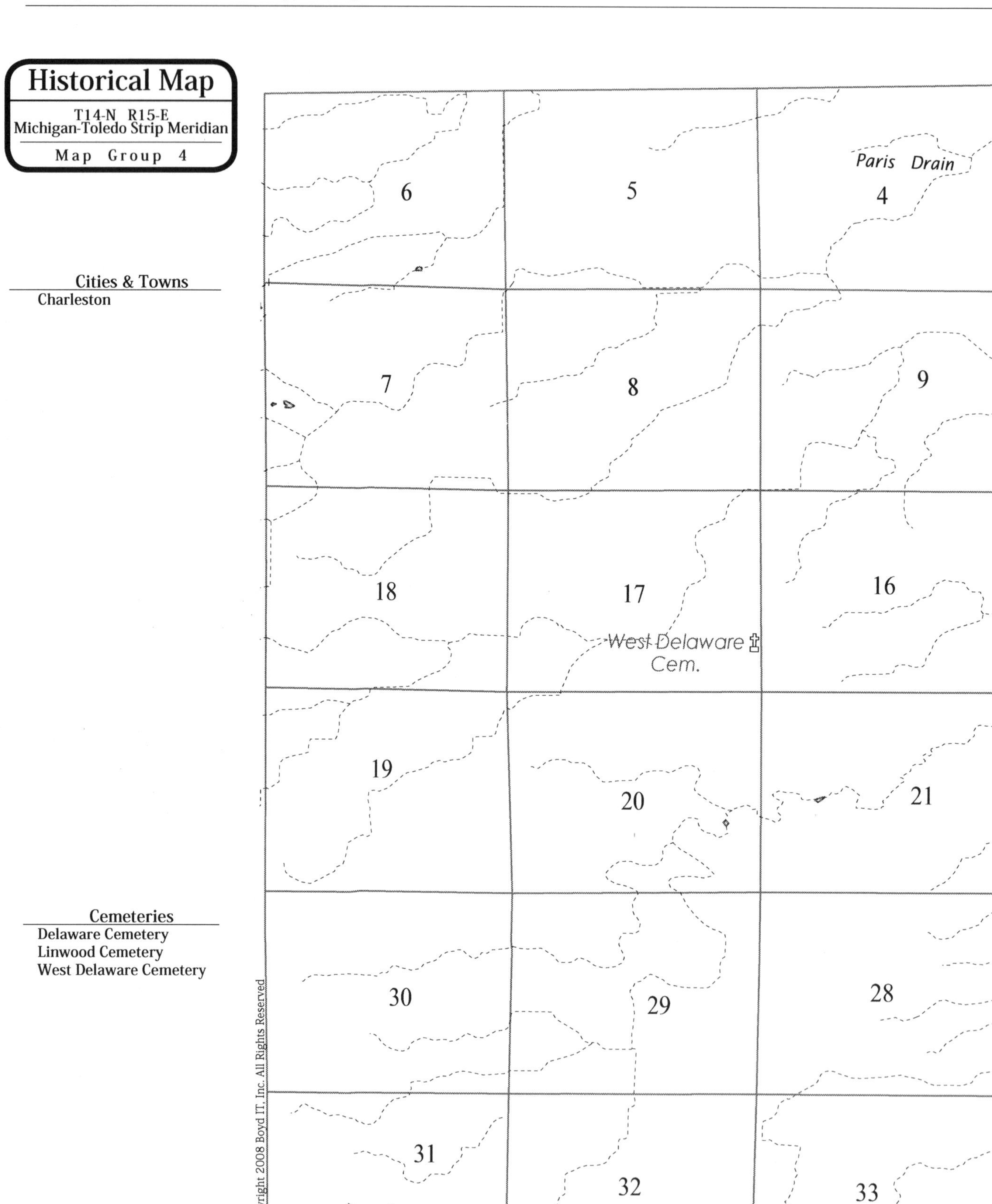

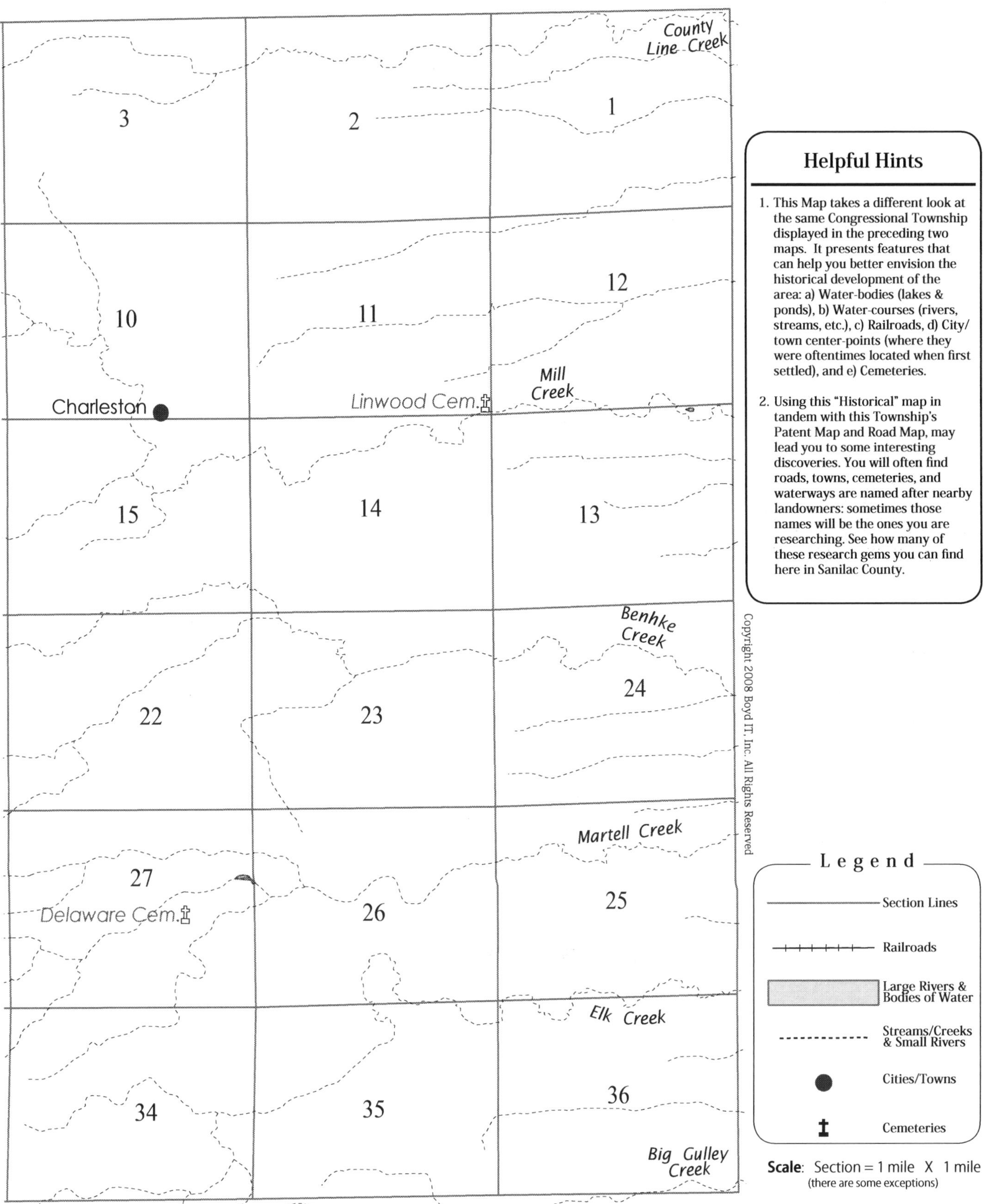

Helpful Hints

1. This Map takes a different look at the same Congressional Township displayed in the preceding two maps. It presents features that can help you better envision the historical development of the area: a) Water-bodies (lakes & ponds), b) Water-courses (rivers, streams, etc.), c) Railroads, d) City/town center-points (where they were oftentimes located when first settled), and e) Cemeteries.
2. Using this "Historical" map in tandem with this Township's Patent Map and Road Map, may lead you to some interesting discoveries. You will often find roads, towns, cemeteries, and waterways are named after nearby landowners: sometimes those names will be the ones you are researching. See how many of these research gems you can find here in Sanilac County.

Scale: Section = 1 mile X 1 mile
(there are some exceptions)

Map Group 5: Index to Land Patents

Township 14-North Range 16-East (Michigan-Toledo Strip)

After you locate an individual in this Index, take note of the Section and Section Part then proceed to the Land Patent map on the pages immediately following. You should have no difficulty locating the corresponding parcel of land.

The "For More Info" Column will lead you to more information about the underlying Patents. See the *Legend* at right, and the "How to Use this Book" chapter, for more information.

LEGEND

"For More Info . . . " column

A = Authority (Legislative Act, See Appendix "A")
B = Block or Lot (location in Section unknown)
C = Cancelled Patent
F = Fractional Section
G = Group (Multi-Patentee Patent, see Appendix "C")
V = Overlaps another Parcel
R = Re-Issued (Parcel patented more than once)

(A & G items require you to look in the Appendixes referred to above. All other Letter-designations followed by a number require you to locate line-items in this index that possess the ID number found after the letter).

ID	Individual in Patent	Sec.	Sec. Part	Date Issued	Other Counties	For More Info . . .
571	ALLEN, John	5	1NE	1848-06-01		A1 F
555	BAILEY, Calvin P	19	N½SE	1848-09-01		A1 G7
555	HURD, Jarvis	19	N½SE	1848-09-01		A1 G7
570	" "	30	SENE	1852-02-10		A1
569	" "	19	S½SE	1852-11-01		A1
553	KERCHEVAL, Benjamin B	29	NE	1837-08-18		A1 F
554	" "	32	NE	1837-08-18		A1
575	LYON, Lucius	17	NE	1839-04-10		A1 G49 F
576	" "	17	NW	1839-04-10		A1 G49
557	MACY, Francis G	17	SE	1837-08-05		A1
558	" "	17	SW	1837-08-05		A1
559	" "	18	SE	1837-08-05		A1
560	" "	18	SW	1837-08-05		A1
561	" "	19	NE	1837-08-05		A1
562	" "	19	NW	1837-08-05		A1
563	" "	20		1837-08-05		A1
567	MIZNER, Henry R	31	SW	1856-09-01		A1
573	MIZNER, Lansing B	29	E½SE	1837-11-02		A1
574	" "	31	W½SE	1855-10-01		A1
564	PALMS, Francis	5	N½SW	1856-01-10		A1
565	" "	6	N½SE	1856-01-10		A1
566	" "	6	SW	1856-01-10		A1
575	PARKER, Daniel	17	NE	1839-04-10		A1 G49 F
576	" "	17	NW	1839-04-10		A1 G49
568	SCOTT, Henry	6	N½NE	1855-10-01		A1
572	SIMONS, John	30	SENW	1855-10-01		A1
556	THROOP, Cornelia G	7	NWNE	1857-02-20		A1

SCOTT
Henry
1855

6

PALMS
Francis
1856

PALMS
Francis
1856

Lots-Sec. 5

1 ALLEN, John 1848

5

PALMS
Francis
1856

THROOP
Cornelia G
1857

7

8

18

LYON [49]
Lucius
1839

17

LYON [49]
Lucius
1839

MACY
Francis G
1837

MACY
Francis G
1837

MACY
Francis G
1837

MACY
Francis G
1837

MACY
Francis G
1837

MACY
Francis G
1837

19

BAILEY [7]
Calvin P
1848

HURD
Jarvis
1852

20

MACY
Francis G
1837

KERCHEVAL
Benjamin B
1837

SIMONS
John
1855

HURD
Jarvis
1852

29

30

MIZNER
Lansing B
1837

31

MIZNER
Henry R
1856

MIZNER
Lansing B
1855

32

KERCHEVAL
Benjamin B
1837

Patent Map

T14-N R16-E
Michigan-Toledo Strip Meridian

Map Group 5

Township Statistics

Parcels Mapped	:	24
Number of Patents	:	15
Number of Individuals	:	13
Patentees Identified	:	12
Number of Surnames	:	12
Multi-Patentee Parcels	:	3
Oldest Patent Date	:	8/5/1837
Most Recent Patent	:	2/20/1857
Block/Lot Parcels	:	1
Parcels Re - Issued	:	0
Parcels that Overlap	:	0
Cities and Towns	:	1
Cemeteries	:	1

Note: the area contained in this map amounts to far less than a full Township. Therefore, its contents are completely on this single page (instead of a "normal" 2-page spread).

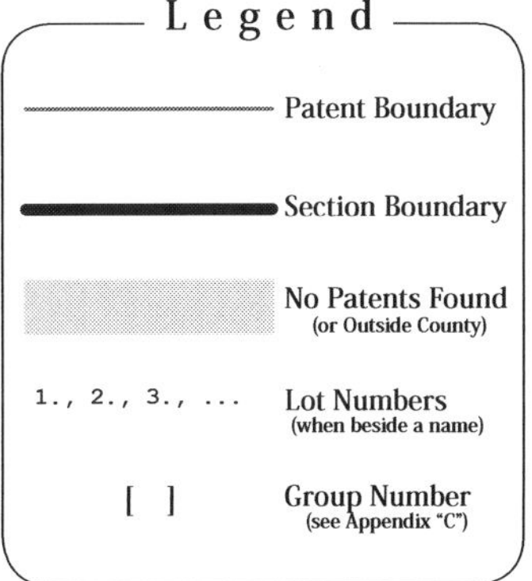

Scale: Section = 1 mile X 1 mile
(generally, with some exceptions)

Road Map

T14-N R16-E
Michigan-Toledo Strip Meridian

Map Group 5

Note: the area contained in this map amounts to far less than a full Township. Therefore, its contents are completely on this single page (instead of a "normal" 2-page spread).

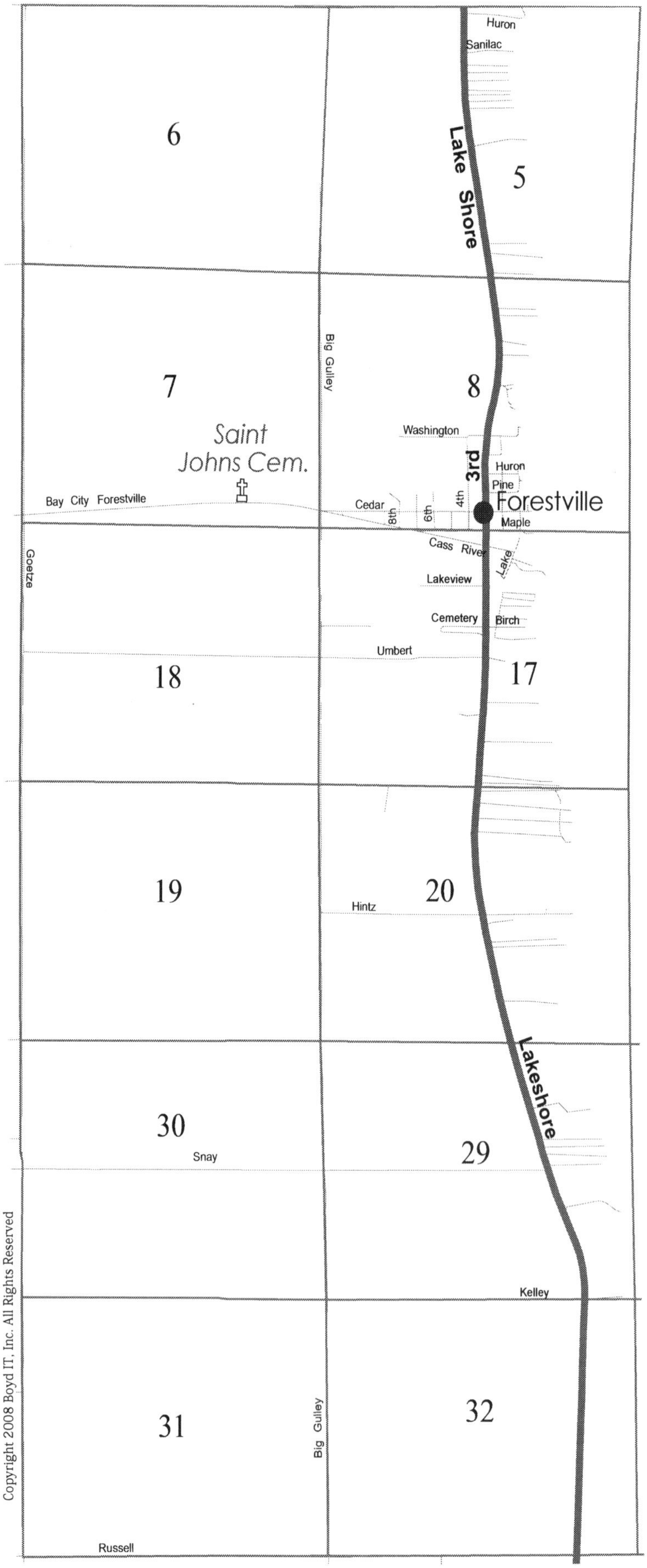

Cities & Towns

Forestville

Cemeteries

Saint Johns Cemetery

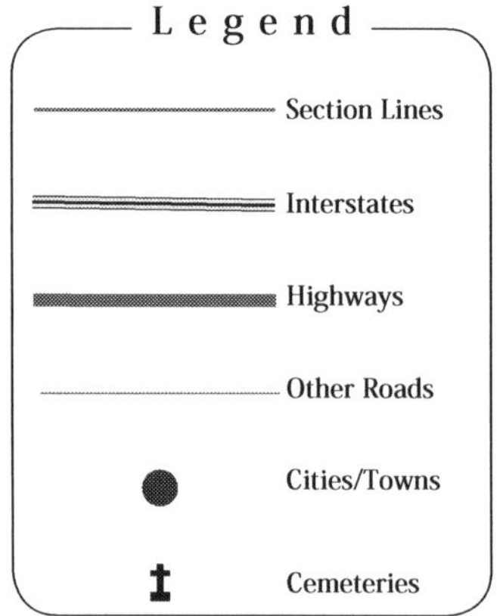

Scale: Section = 1 mile X 1 mile
(generally, with some exceptions)

6
5
Huron
Sanilac
Lake Shore
7
8
Big Gulley
Saint Johns Cem.
Washington
3rd
Huron
Pine
Forestville
Maple
Bay City Forestville
Cedar
8th
6th
4th
Cass River
Lake
Goetze
Lakeview
Cemetery
Birch
Umbert
18
17
19
20
Hintz
Lakeshore
30
Snay
29
Kelley
31
32
Big Gulley
Russell

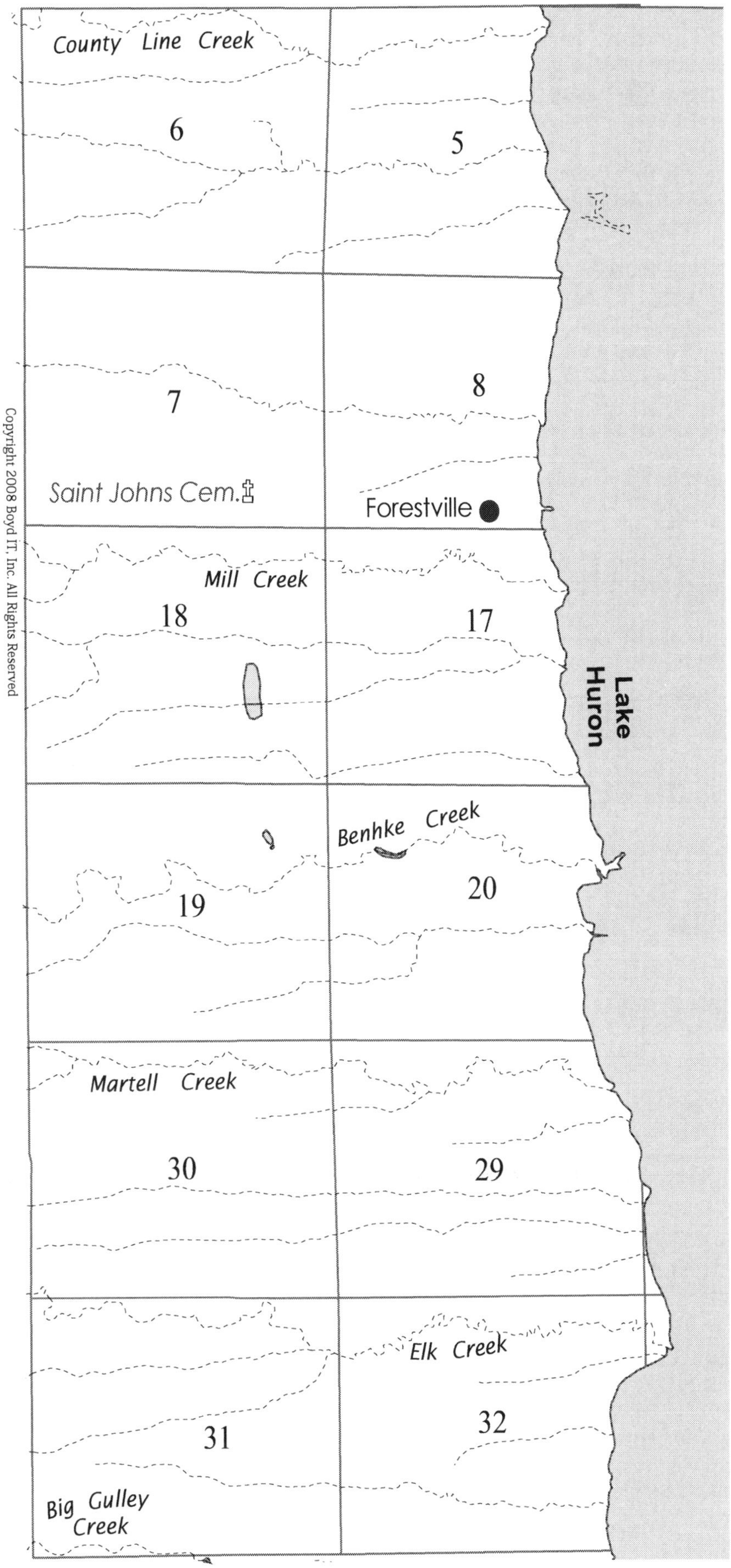

County Line Creek
6
5
7
8
Saint Johns Cem.
Forestville
Mill Creek
18
17
Lake Huron
Benhke Creek
19
20
Martell Creek
30
29
Elk Creek
31
32
Big Gulley Creek

Historical Map

T14-N R16-E
Michigan-Toledo Strip Meridian

Map Group 5

Note: the area contained in this map amounts to far less than a full Township. Therefore, its contents are completely on this single page (instead of a "normal" 2-page spread).

Cities & Towns

Forestville

Cemeteries

Saint Johns Cemetery

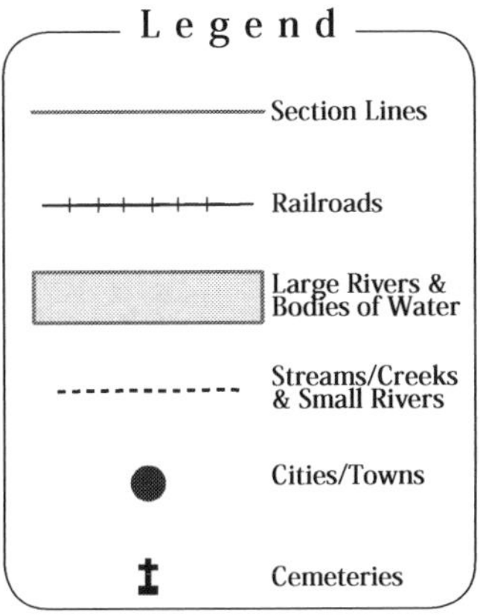

Scale: Section = 1 mile X 1 mile
(there are some exceptions)

Map Group 6: Index to Land Patents

Township 13-North Range 12-East (Michigan-Toledo Strip)

After you locate an individual in this Index, take note of the Section and Section Part then proceed to the Land Patent map on the pages immediately following. You should have no difficulty locating the corresponding parcel of land.

The "For More Info" Column will lead you to more information about the underlying Patents. See the *Legend* at right, and the "How to Use this Book" chapter, for more information.

LEGEND

"For More Info . . . " column

A = Authority (Legislative Act, See Appendix "A")
B = Block or Lot (location in Section unknown)
C = Cancelled Patent
F = Fractional Section
G = Group (Multi-Patentee Patent, see Appendix "C")
V = Overlaps another Parcel
R = Re-Issued (Parcel patented more than once)

(A & G items require you to look in the Appendixes referred to above. All other Letter-designations followed by a number require you to locate line-items in this index that possess the ID number found after the letter).

ID	Individual in Patent	Sec.	Sec. Part	Date Issued	Other Counties	For More Info . . .
669	AVERY, Sewell	28	NESE	1869-07-01		A1 G5
665	BARSTOW, Samuel	6	SESW	1855-10-01		A1 F
666	" "	6	SWSE	1855-10-01		A1
644	BOND, Joseph	1	N½SE	1876-01-20		A2
645	" "	1	SESW	1876-01-20		A2
646	" "	1	SWSE	1876-01-20		A2
647	BROWN, Joseph	1	NENW	1868-08-20		A1
648	" "	12	NENE	1869-07-01		A1
682	BURT, Wellington	12	W½NE	1872-04-15		A1
592	CLARK, David J	19	N½SE	1884-08-09		A2
587	CLENDENIN, Clarisa	35	SE	1875-09-01		A2
649	COLMAN, Joseph	23	NWSE	1859-05-09		A1
605	COMPANY, H M Bradley And	30	NENE	1866-06-20		A1
609	CURWELL, Hiram	4	E½NW	1885-01-13		A2
610	" "	4	E½SW	1885-01-13		A2
577	DAVIS, Alfred	10	SESW	1868-08-20		A1 G26
578	" "	28	SWSE	1868-08-20		A1 G26
579	" "	30	S½SW	1868-08-20		A1 G26
606	DEVAL, Henry	26	NWNW	1870-06-10		A1
607	" "	26	NWSW	1870-06-10		A1
669	EDDY, Edwin	28	NESE	1869-07-01		A1 G5
628	FISHER, James J	3	NW	1872-12-30		A2
585	FRENCH, Charles J	27	NESE	1875-05-10		A1 G41
670	GOULD, Syrenous	2	NE	1872-12-30		A2 F
612	GREEN, Isaac	2	NWSE	1868-08-20		A1
589	GREGG, David	24	SWNE	1869-07-01		A1 G43
590	" "	25	SENW	1869-07-01		A1 G43
591	" "	30	S½NW	1869-07-01		A1 G43 F
604	HAMPTMAN, George N	11	S½SW	1867-07-01		A1
667	HATHAWAY, Samuel G	22	NENW	1852-02-10		A1
668	" "	22	NWNE	1852-02-10		A1
625	HAY, James	27	SWSE	1855-10-01		A1
626	" "	34	SWSE	1855-10-01		A1
627	" "	36	SESW	1855-10-01		A1
684	HAY, William	35	NESW	1860-10-01		A1
686	" "	35	W½SW	1860-10-01		A1
685	" "	35	SENW	1869-07-01		A1
683	" "	34	SESE	1870-09-20		A2
650	HEATHCOTE, Joseph	11	NWNW	1868-08-20		A1
603	HEBENTON, George	10	NENE	1885-01-30		A2
611	HOWEY, Ira	25	SWNW	1895-05-28		A2
589	HOYT, William	24	SWNE	1869-07-01		A1 G43
590	" "	25	SENW	1869-07-01		A1 G43
591	" "	30	S½NW	1869-07-01		A1 G43 F
600	HUBBARD, Frederick	36	NWSE	1864-01-05		A1
601	" "	36	SENW	1864-01-05		A1

ID	Individual in Patent	Sec.	Sec. Part	Date Issued	Other Counties	For More Info . . .
602	HUBBARD, Frederick (Cont'd)	36	SESE	1864-01-05		A1
577	HUBINGER, John J	10	SESW	1868-08-20		A1 G26
578	" "	28	SWSE	1868-08-20		A1 G26
579	" "	30	S½SW	1868-08-20		A1 G26
593	KELLEY, David	36	SWSW	1891-10-13		A2
651	KEYWORTH, Joseph J	26	NENW	1888-10-18		A2
629	LEONARD, James	35	NENW	1867-07-01		A1
630	" "	36	NWSW	1867-07-01		A1
679	MANNEY, Uriah H	34	E½NE	1875-09-01		A2
680	" "	34	NESE	1875-09-01		A2
681	" "	35	SWNW	1875-09-01		A2
652	MANWARING, Joshua	31	N½SW	1868-08-20		A1
588	MCCONNELL, Consider A	6	NWNE	1866-06-20		A1 F
655	MCCONNELL, Luther E	5	N½NE	1872-12-30		A2 F
656	" "	5	NENW	1872-12-30		A2 F
631	MCHUGH, James	19	NE	1878-11-05		A2
594	MCINTOSH, Donald	3	NENW	1859-10-10		A1 F
595	" "	3	NWNE	1859-10-10		A1 F
687	MCKIE, William	21	NENW	1852-02-10		A1
688	" "	21	NWNE	1852-02-10		A1
689	" "	27	E½SW	1852-02-10		A1
690	" "	27	SENW	1852-02-10		A1
641	MILLER, John	26	S½NW	1864-01-05		A1
633	MILLER, John B	32	NESW	1875-05-10		A1
608	MONTNEY, Henry	20	SENE	1872-04-15		A1
671	MORSE, Timothy	1	SESE	1855-10-01		A1 G54
672	" "	1	SWSW	1855-10-01		A1 G54
673	" "	1	W½NW	1855-10-01		A1 G54 F
674	" "	2	NESE	1855-10-01		A1 G54
675	" "	2	SWSE	1855-10-01		A1 G54
676	" "	5	SESW	1855-10-01		A1 G54
677	" "	5	SWSE	1855-10-01		A1 G54
678	" "	8	NENW	1855-10-01		A1 G54
596	MURPHY, Edward W	2	SESE	1868-08-20		A1
585	PAPST, R	27	NESE	1875-05-10		A1 G41
582	PARTRIDGE, Benjamin F	18	N½NW	1855-10-01		A1 F
583	" "	19	S½SE	1855-10-01		A1
584	" "	20	SWSW	1855-10-01		A1
634	PROCTOR, John B	22	SE	1876-09-06		A2
586	RIBBEL, Charles J	26	E½SW	1869-11-15		A1
642	RUST, John	25	S½NE	1885-01-30		A2
691	SANBORN, William	32	N½SE	1860-05-01		A1
635	SARTWELL, John E	30	N½NW	1872-04-15		A1 F
599	SEARS, Franklin	28	SESE	1872-04-15		A1
653	SHARRARD, Joshua	27	SWNW	1885-01-30		A2
654	" "	28	SENE	1885-01-30		A2
598	TRAVIS, Elizabeth	35	W½NE	1895-11-25		A2
580	TYLER, Asher	24	NWNE	1852-11-01		A1
581	" "	24	SENE	1852-11-01		A1
660	WALSH, Patrick	24	SWNW	1874-03-10		A1
658	" "	23	E½SE	1876-11-03		A2
659	" "	23	SWSE	1876-11-03		A2
661	" "	24	SWSW	1876-11-03		A2
662	WALSH, Redmond	24	N½SE	1880-10-01		A2
663	" "	24	N½SW	1880-10-01		A2
613	WARREN, Isaiah	18	NE	1857-02-20		A1 F
614	" "	18	S½NW	1857-02-20		A1 F
615	" "	18	W½SE	1857-02-20		A1 F
616	" "	19	W	1857-02-20		A1 F
617	" "	5	N½SE	1857-02-20		A1 F
618	" "	5	NESW	1857-02-20		A1 F
619	" "	5	NWNW	1857-02-20		A1
620	" "	5	S½NE	1857-02-20		A1 F
621	" "	5	S½NW	1857-02-20		A1 F
622	" "	5	SESE	1857-02-20		A1 F
623	" "	6	N½NW	1857-02-20		A1 F
624	" "	6	SWSW	1857-02-20		A1 F
657	WATROUS, Martin	15	SWNW	1856-09-01		A1
643	WATSON, John	3	NWSE	1885-01-30		A2
632	WILKINSON, James T	32	NW	1876-11-03		A2
577	WILLCOX, Byron	10	SESW	1868-08-20		A1 G26
578	" "	28	SWSE	1868-08-20		A1 G26
579	" "	30	S½SW	1868-08-20		A1 G26

ID	Individual in Patent	Sec.	Sec. Part	Date Issued	Other Counties	For More Info . . .
577	WILLCOX, George	10	SESW	1868-08-20		A1 G26
578	" "	28	SWSE	1868-08-20		A1 G26
579	" "	30	S½SW	1868-08-20		A1 G26
664	WILSON, Robert	2	NW	1859-10-10		A1 F
597	WOOD, Edwin M	27	NE	1860-05-01		A1
671	WOODS, John L	1	SESE	1855-10-01		A1 G54
672	" "	1	SWSW	1855-10-01		A1 G54
673	" "	1	W½NW	1855-10-01		A1 G54 F
636	" "	10	SESE	1855-10-01		A1
637	" "	15	W½NE	1855-10-01		A1
674	" "	2	NESE	1855-10-01		A1 G54
675	" "	2	SWSE	1855-10-01		A1 G54
676	" "	5	SESW	1855-10-01		A1 G54
677	" "	5	SWSE	1855-10-01		A1 G54
678	" "	8	NENW	1855-10-01		A1 G54
638	" "	22	NWNW	1868-08-20		A1
639	" "	30	SWSE	1868-08-20		A1
640	" "	36	NWNE	1868-08-20		A1

Patent Map

T13-N R12-E
Michigan-Toledo Strip Meridian

Map Group 6

Township Statistics

Parcels Mapped	:	115
Number of Patents	:	88
Number of Individuals	:	65
Patentees Identified	:	59
Number of Surnames	:	60
Multi-Patentee Parcels	:	16
Oldest Patent Date	:	2/10/1852
Most Recent Patent	:	11/25/1895
Block/Lot Parcels	:	0
Parcels Re - Issued	:	0
Parcels that Overlap	:	0
Cities and Towns	:	1
Cemeteries	:	1

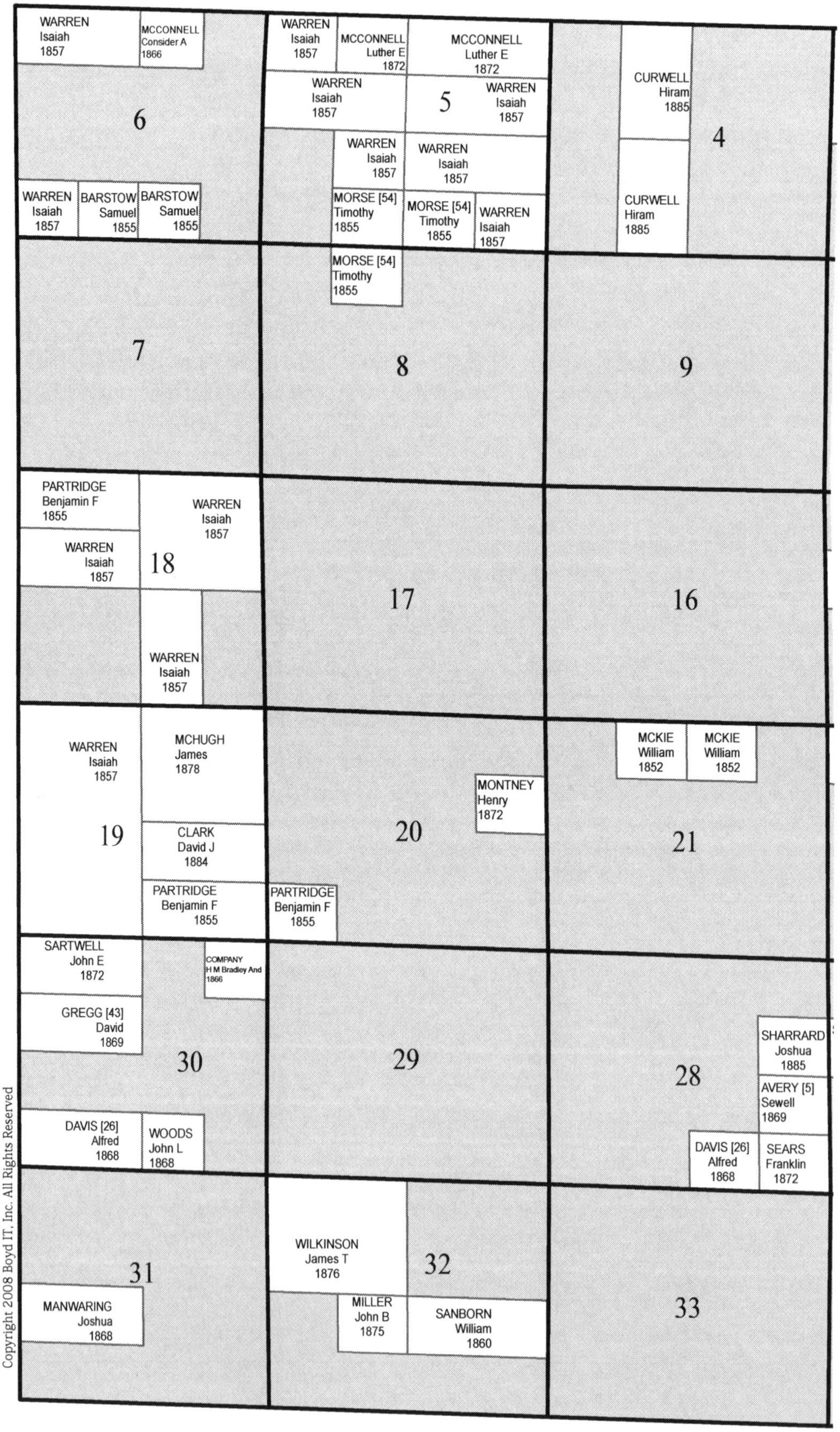

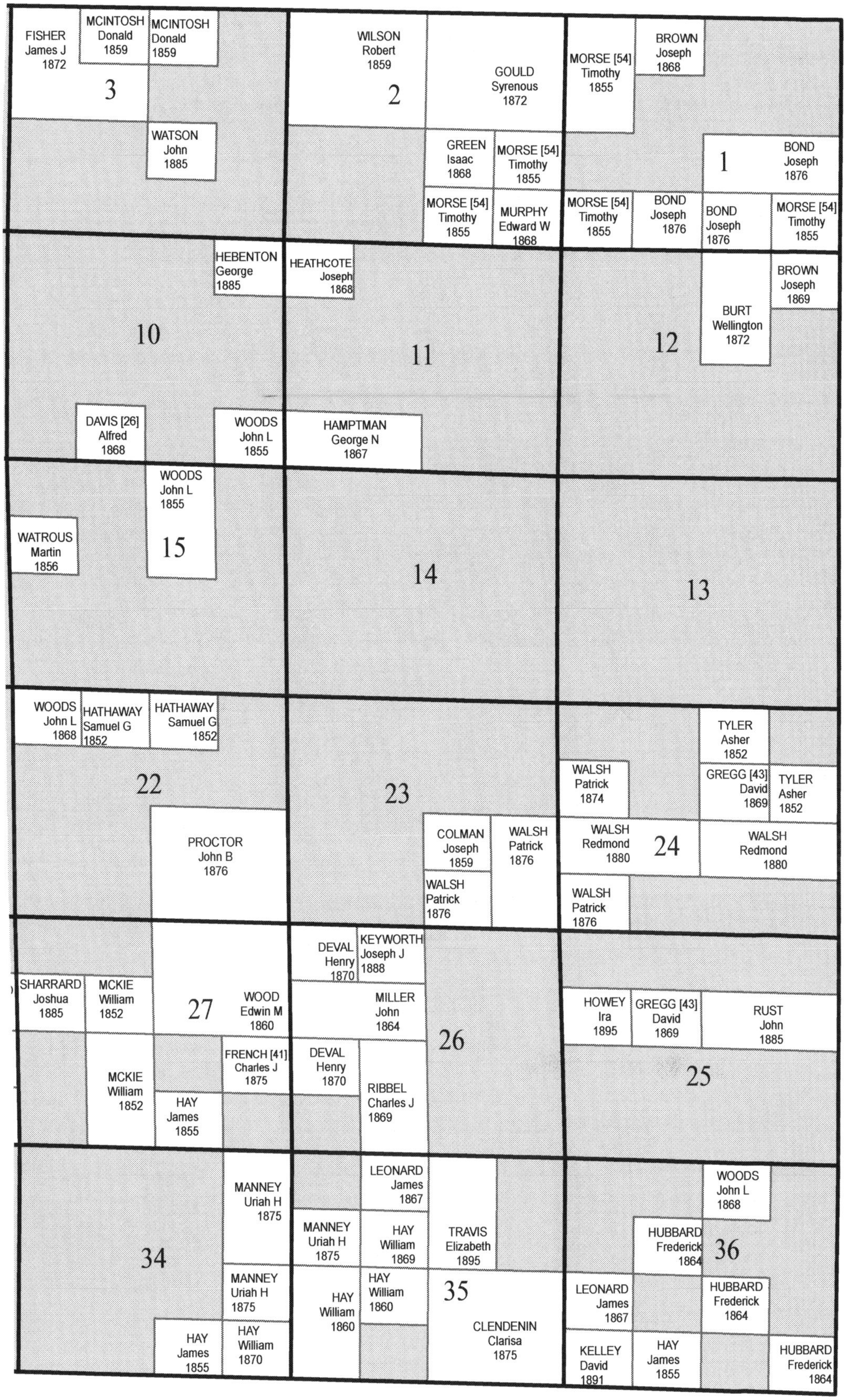

Helpful Hints

1. This Map's INDEX can be found on the preceding pages.
2. Refer to Map "C" to see where this Township lies within Sanilac County, Michigan.
3. Numbers within square brackets [ ] denote a multi-patentee land parcel (multi-owner). Refer to Appendix "C" for a full list of members in this group.
4. Areas that look to be crowded with Patentees usually indicate multiple sales of the same parcel (Re-issues) or Overlapping parcels. See this Township's Index for an explanation of these and other circumstances that might explain "odd" groupings of Patentees on this map.

Legend

- Patent Boundary
- Section Boundary
- No Patents Found (or Outside County)
- 1., 2., 3., ... Lot Numbers (when beside a name)
- [ ] Group Number (see Appendix "C")

Scale: Section = 1 mile X 1 mile (generally, with some exceptions)

Road Map

T13-N R12-E
Michigan-Toledo Strip Meridian

Map Group 6

Cities & Towns
Shabbona

Cemeteries
Evergreen Cemetery

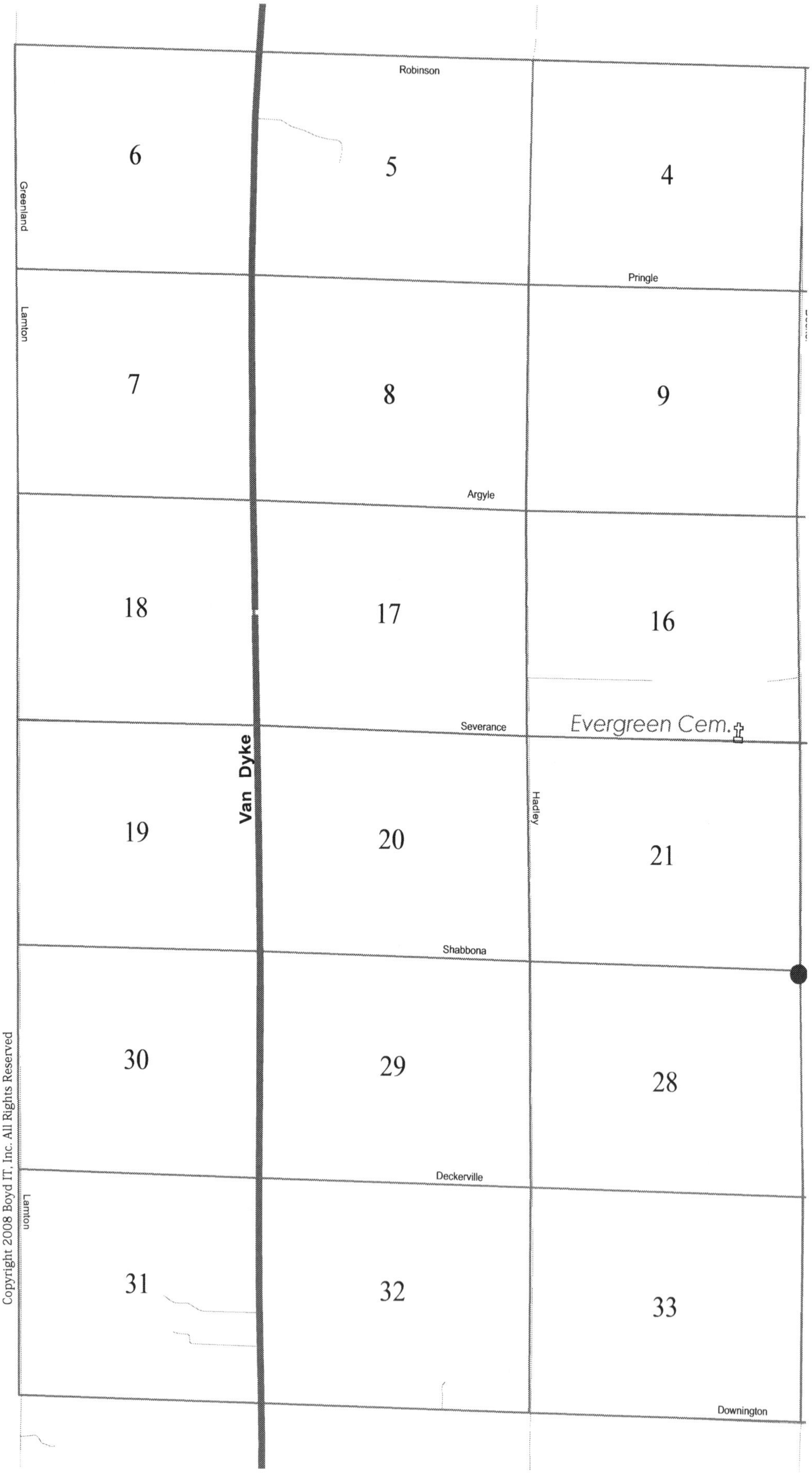

Robinson
Greenland
Pringle
Lamton
Argyle
Severance
Evergreen Cem.
Van Dyke
Hadley
Shabbona
Deckerville
Lamton
Downington

6 5 4
7 8 9
18 17 16
19 20 21
30 29 28
31 32 33

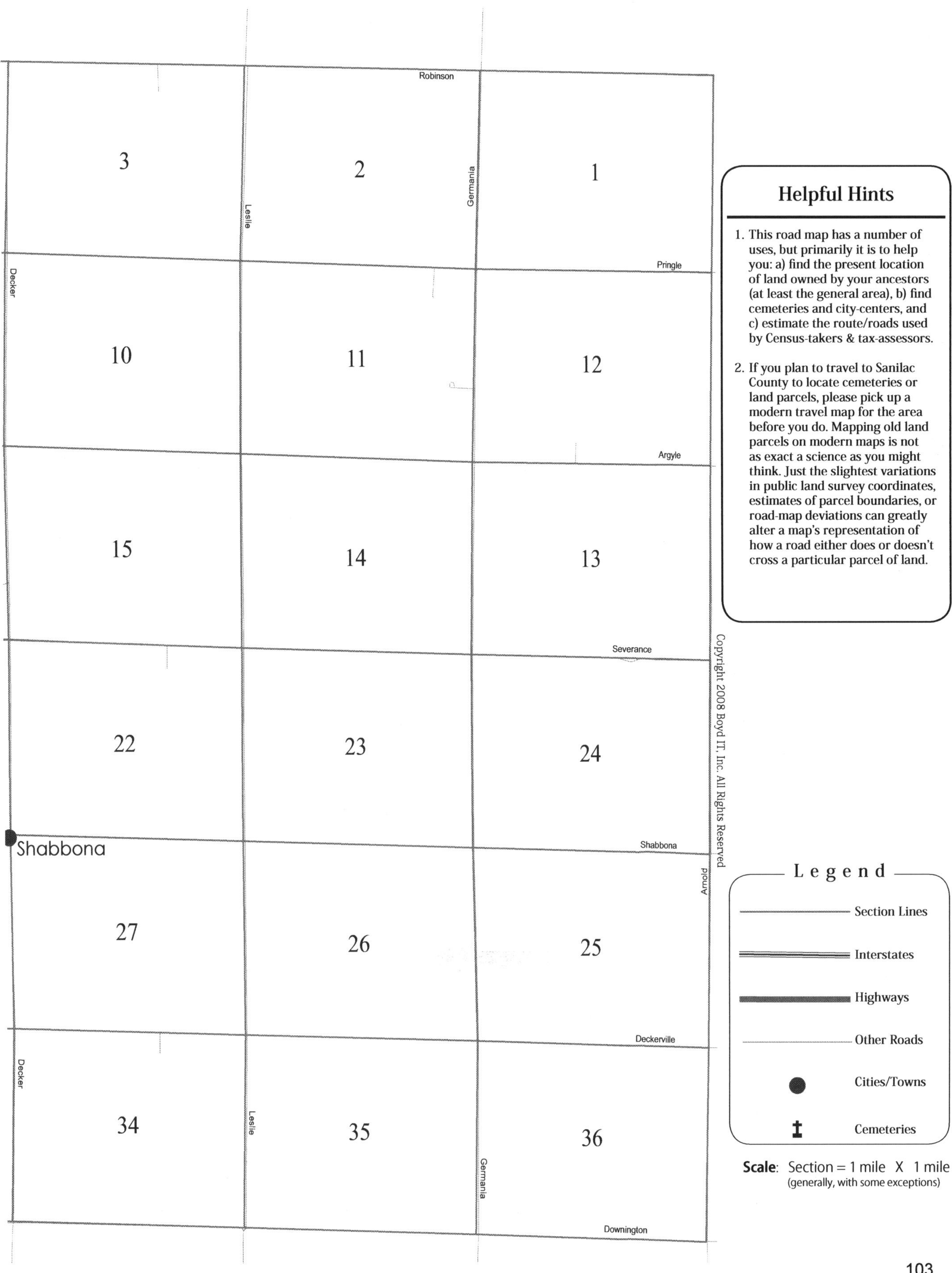

Helpful Hints

1. This road map has a number of uses, but primarily it is to help you: a) find the present location of land owned by your ancestors (at least the general area), b) find cemeteries and city-centers, and c) estimate the route/roads used by Census-takers & tax-assessors.

2. If you plan to travel to Sanilac County to locate cemeteries or land parcels, please pick up a modern travel map for the area before you do. Mapping old land parcels on modern maps is not as exact a science as you might think. Just the slightest variations in public land survey coordinates, estimates of parcel boundaries, or road-map deviations can greatly alter a map's representation of how a road either does or doesn't cross a particular parcel of land.

Legend

- Section Lines
- Interstates
- Highways
- Other Roads
- Cities/Towns
- Cemeteries

Scale: Section = 1 mile X 1 mile
(generally, with some exceptions)

Historical Map

T13-N R12-E
Michigan-Toledo Strip Meridian

Map Group 6

Cities & Towns

Shabbona

Cemeteries

Evergreen Cemetery

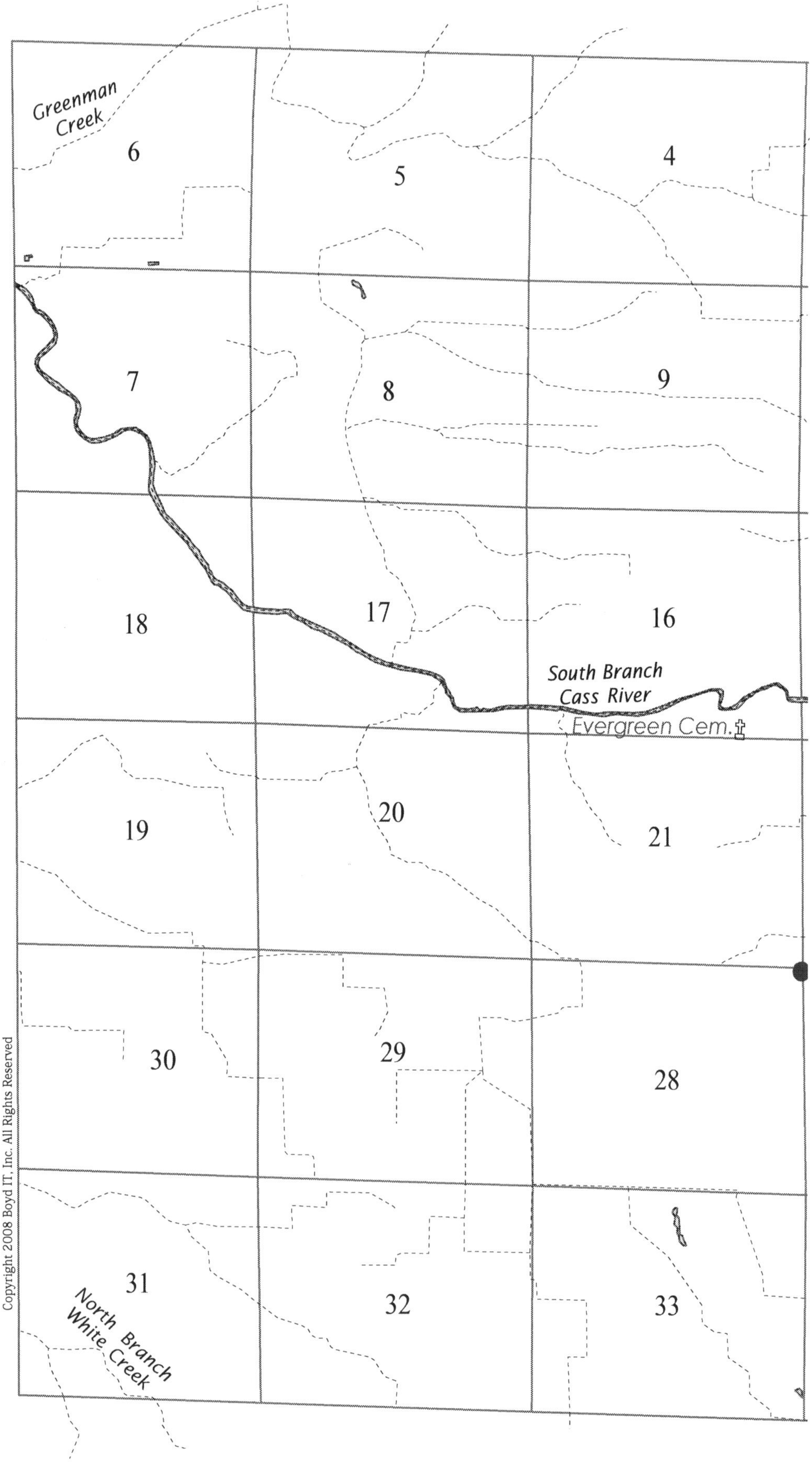

Greenman Creek

6 5 4

7 8 9

18 17 16

South Branch Cass River

Evergreen Cem.

19 20 21

30 29 28

31 32 33

North Branch White Creek

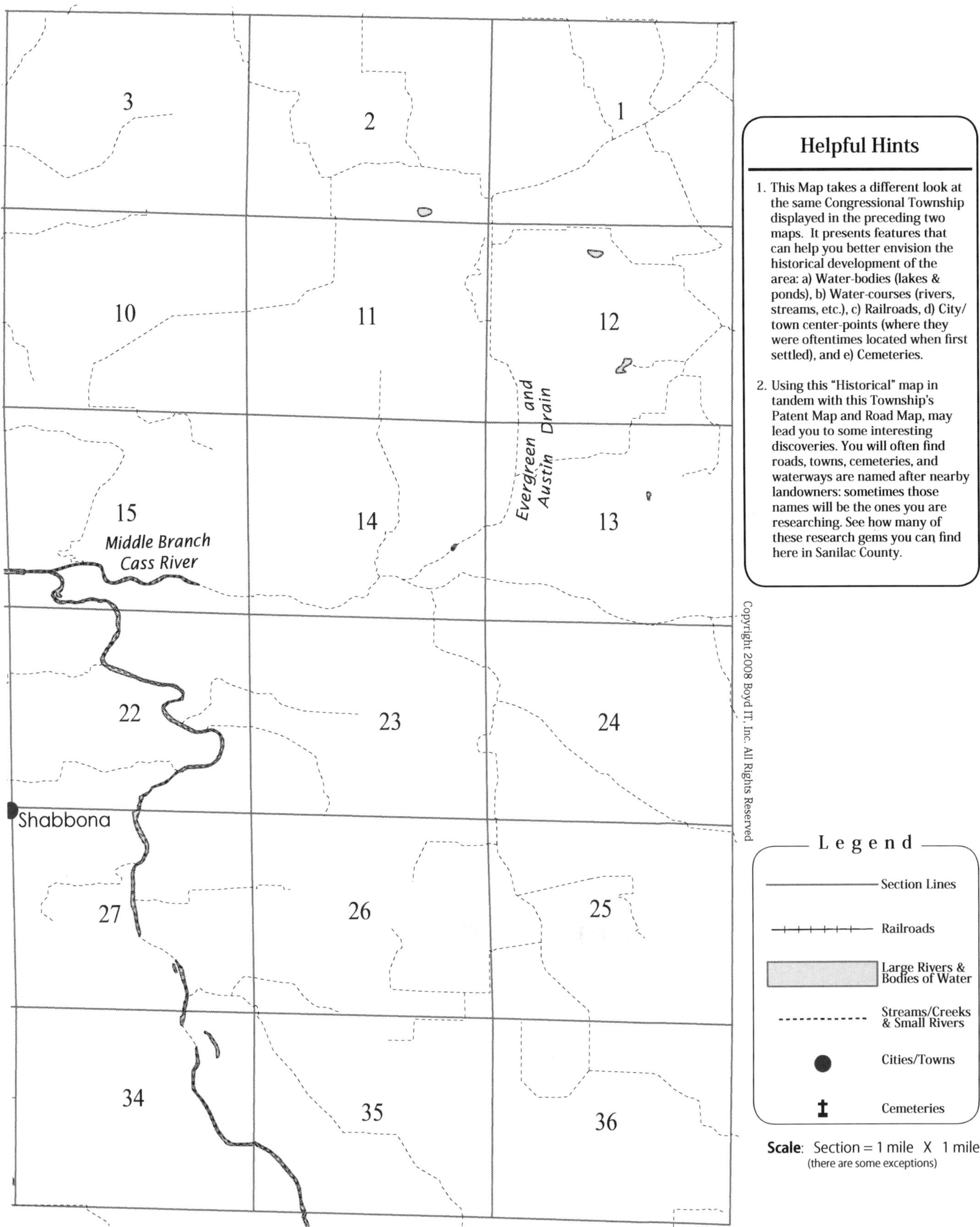

Helpful Hints

1. This Map takes a different look at the same Congressional Township displayed in the preceding two maps. It presents features that can help you better envision the historical development of the area: a) Water-bodies (lakes & ponds), b) Water-courses (rivers, streams, etc.), c) Railroads, d) City/town center-points (where they were oftentimes located when first settled), and e) Cemeteries.
2. Using this "Historical" map in tandem with this Township's Patent Map and Road Map, may lead you to some interesting discoveries. You will often find roads, towns, cemeteries, and waterways are named after nearby landowners: sometimes those names will be the ones you are researching. See how many of these research gems you can find here in Sanilac County.

Legend

- Section Lines
- Railroads
- Large Rivers & Bodies of Water
- Streams/Creeks & Small Rivers
- Cities/Towns
- Cemeteries

Scale: Section = 1 mile X 1 mile
(there are some exceptions)

Map Group 7: Index to Land Patents

Township 13-North Range 13-East (Michigan-Toledo Strip)

After you locate an individual in this Index, take note of the Section and Section Part then proceed to the Land Patent map on the pages immediately following. You should have no difficulty locating the corresponding parcel of land.

The "For More Info" Column will lead you to more information about the underlying Patents. See the *Legend* at right, and the "How to Use this Book" chapter, for more information.

LEGEND

"For More Info . . . " column

A = Authority (Legislative Act, See Appendix "A")
B = Block or Lot (location in Section unknown)
C = Cancelled Patent
F = Fractional Section
G = Group (Multi-Patentee Patent, see Appendix "C")
V = Overlaps another Parcel
R = Re-Issued (Parcel patented more than once)

(A & G items require you to look in the Appendixes referred to above. All other Letter-designations followed by a number require you to locate line-items in this index that possess the ID number found after the letter).

ID	Individual in Patent	Sec.	Sec. Part	Date Issued	Other Counties	For More Info . . .
718	ARMSTED, Christopher	35	SENE	1885-01-30		A2
860	BANCROFT, W L	1	SESE	1866-06-20		A1
865	BEHR, Wilhelm	21	NWNE	1889-01-31		A2
816	BROWN, Joseph	6	W½SW	1869-07-01		A1 F
793	BURNHAM, John	22	NWNW	1883-06-07		A2
803	COLE, John M	12	E½NE	1871-09-30		A2
764	DEWEY, George	28	SENE	1860-11-21		A1
770	DEWEY, George W	28	NESE	1860-11-21		A1
716	DURR, Caspar	15	N½SE	1861-12-03		A1
717	" "	15	N½SW	1861-12-03		A1
817	DUVAL, Joseph	21	NENE	1869-11-15		A1
698	FRANKE, Albert	14	SWSE	1869-07-01		A1
699	" "	23	N½NE	1869-07-01		A1
700	" "	23	SWNE	1869-07-01		A1
720	GEORGE, Daniel	25	N½NE	1885-01-30		A2
861	GRAHAM, Warren	12	NWNE	1882-12-01		A2
780	GREEN, Isaac	7	NWSW	1871-06-15		A1 F
721	GREGG, David	19	SWSW	1869-07-01		A1 G43 F
866	HANNA, William	11	SENE	1869-07-01		A1
867	HARTEE, William	14	NESW	1869-07-01		A1
868	" "	14	NWSE	1869-07-01		A1
869	" "	14	W½SW	1869-07-01		A1
826	HERTEL, Michael	15	S½SE	1870-05-20		A2
827	" "	15	S½SW	1870-05-20		A2
730	HOLLSTEIN, Ferdinand	22	E½NW	1871-09-30		A2
731	" "	22	NESW	1871-09-30		A2
732	" "	22	NWSE	1871-09-30		A2
778	HOWARD, Henry	11	W½NE	1868-08-20		A1
813	HOWARD, John T	24	SENE	1870-09-20		A1 G46
721	HOYT, William	19	SWSW	1869-07-01		A1 G43 F
715	HUBBARD, Bela	36	SENW	1868-08-20		A1 G47
714	" "	35	SWNE	1869-07-01		A1 G47
747	HUBBARD, Frederick	21	SENW	1864-01-05		A1
748	" "	23	NWNW	1864-01-05		A1
750	" "	28	SWSE	1864-01-05		A1 R805
751	" "	31	NWSE	1864-01-05		A1
752	" "	32	SWNE	1864-01-05		A1 R753
752	" "	32	SWNE	1864-01-05		A1 C R753
753	" "	32	SWNE	1864-01-05		A1 R752
753	" "	32	SWNE	1864-01-05		A1 C R752
754	" "	32	SWNW	1864-01-05		A1
745	" "	14	NENW	1866-09-03		A1
749	" "	25	SWSW	1866-09-03		A1
757	" "	36	NENW	1866-09-03		A1
758	" "	36	NESW	1866-09-03		A1
759	" "	36	SWNW	1866-09-03		A1

ID	Individual in Patent	Sec.	Sec. Part	Date Issued	Other Counties	For More Info . . .
746	HUBBARD, Frederick (Cont'd)	14	SESW	1868-08-20		A1
755	" "	34	NESE	1868-08-20		A1
756	" "	34	SESE	1868-08-20		A1
839	HUSBAND, Thomas	5	NW	1862-02-01		A1
795	JONES, John	20	NESW	1868-08-20		A1
715	KING, John E	36	SENW	1868-08-20		A1 G47
714	" "	35	SWNE	1869-07-01		A1 G47
765	KINSLEY, George	5	E½SE	1861-07-01		A1
766	" "	5	NESW	1861-07-01		A1
767	" "	5	NWSE	1861-07-01		A1
836	KINSLEY, Peter	9	N½SE	1861-07-01		A1
796	KLEIN, John	5	NWSW	1889-01-31		A2
760	KRITZMANN, Frederick	27	NW	1872-12-30		A2
703	KROETSCH, Ambrose	27	W½NE	1882-12-01		A2
710	KROETSCH, Annie	33	S½NE	1882-12-01		A2
768	KROETSCH, George	29	NE	1875-11-20		A2
837	KROETSCH, Philip	28	SWNW	1885-07-27		A1
775	LANGENBUCK, Gustavus	22	N½NE	1869-07-01		A1
776	" "	22	NESE	1869-07-01		A1
777	" "	22	SENE	1869-07-01		A1
787	LEONARD, James	17	NWSE	1867-07-01		A1
788	" "	29	NESE	1867-07-01		A1
789	" "	29	SWSE	1867-07-01		A1
761	LINDNER, Frederick	27	N½SE	1872-12-30		A2
762	" "	27	N½SW	1872-12-30		A2
790	MACLACHLAN, John B	11	NENE	1861-12-03		A1
791	" "	11	SW	1861-12-03		A1
792	" "	11	W½SE	1861-12-03		A1
821	MASON, Lorenzo M	13	NENE	1864-01-05		A1
822	" "	13	NENW	1864-01-05		A1
709	MCBRIDE, Angus	35	NWNE	1885-07-27		A2
722	MCINTYRE, Dugald	5	NE	1860-11-21		A1
870	MCKENZIE, William	6	N½NW	1860-11-21		A1 F
871	" "	6	NWNE	1860-11-21		A1 F
872	" "	6	SENW	1860-11-21		A1 F
704	MCLACHLAN, Andrew	26	SENE	1870-05-10		A1 G52
705	" "	28	SWSW	1870-05-10		A1 G52
706	" "	28	W½NE	1870-05-10		A1 G52
707	" "	33	NWNE	1870-05-10		A1 G52
708	" "	33	NWNW	1870-05-10		A1 G52
701	MCLACHLIN, Alexander	10	E½	1861-07-01		A1
723	MCLEAN, Duncan	4	NESW	1861-07-01		A1
728	" "	4	W½SW	1861-07-01		A1
724	" "	4	SENW	1861-12-03		A1 C R725
726	" "	4	W½NW	1861-12-03		A1 C R727
725	" "	4	SENW	1863-09-22		A1 F R724
727	" "	4	W½NW	1863-09-22		A1 F R726
711	MCPHAIL, Archibald	4	N½NE	1860-11-21		A1
712	" "	4	NWNW	1860-11-21		A1
828	MCPHAIL, Neil	4	SENE	1870-05-20		A2
804	MILLER, John	17	NESE	1864-01-05		A1
805	" "	28	SWSE	1864-01-05		A1 R750
806	" "	31	NENE	1864-01-05		A1
807	" "	31	NESE	1864-01-05		A1
808	" "	32	NWNW	1864-01-05		A1
840	MORSE, Timothy	2	NWNW	1855-10-01		A1 F
843	" "	23	NWSE	1855-10-01		A1 G54
844	" "	24	E½NW	1855-10-01		A1 G54
847	" "	24	W½NE	1855-10-01		A1 G54
848	" "	28	SESW	1855-10-01		A1 G54
849	" "	29	SESE	1855-10-01		A1 G54
850	" "	3	NENE	1855-10-01		A1 G54
851	" "	3	SWSW	1855-10-01		A1 G54
852	" "	30	SWSE	1855-10-01		A1 G54
853	" "	31	NWNE	1855-10-01		A1 G54
854	" "	32	NENE	1855-10-01		A1 G54
855	" "	35	NENE	1855-10-01		A1 G54
856	" "	6	SESW	1855-10-01		A1 G54
841	" "	6	SWSE	1855-10-01		A1
857	" "	7	E½NE	1855-10-01		A1 G54
858	" "	7	SENW	1855-10-01		A1 G54
859	" "	7	W½NW	1855-10-01		A1 G54
842	" "	9	SWNW	1855-10-01		A1

ID	Individual in Patent	Sec.	Sec. Part	Date Issued	Other Counties	For More Info . . .
845	MORSE, Timothy (Cont'd)	24	E½SW	1856-01-10		A1 G54
846	" "	24	NWSE	1856-01-10		A1 G54
809	ORTON, John	1	E½NW	1885-01-30		A1 F
810	" "	1	W½NE	1885-01-30		A1 F
733	PENSIONNAL, Fitzhaus	3	E½SE	1861-12-10		A1
734	" "	3	SESW	1861-12-10		A1
735	" "	3	SWSE	1861-12-10		A1
782	POST, Israel	35	E½SE	1883-06-07		A2
783	" "	36	W½SW	1883-06-07		A2
862	REINELT, Westley	13	NESE	1881-08-20		A2
863	" "	13	SENE	1881-08-20		A2
864	" "	13	W½NE	1881-08-20		A2
838	REMICK, R C	7	NESW	1867-07-01		A1 F
744	RICHARDS, Frederick B	33	SESE	1882-10-20		A2
719	ROBINSON, D J	33	NESE	1864-01-05		A1
771	ROSE, George W	4	SESW	1888-10-18		A2
818	SCHAGENE, Joseph	11	NW	1861-12-10		A1
819	" "	2	SESW	1861-12-10		A1
820	" "	2	W½SW	1861-12-10		A1
772	SCOLLAY, Grover	26	NESW	1882-04-20		A2
773	" "	26	S½SW	1882-04-20		A2
774	" "	26	SWSE	1882-04-20		A2
736	SEARS, Frank P	32	SENW	1869-07-01		A1
785	SEDER, Jacob	10	NW	1861-07-01		A1
786	" "	10	SW	1861-07-01		A1
825	SEDER, Matthew	9	E½NE	1883-06-07		A2
832	SEDER, Nelson	9	E½NW	1875-05-05		A2
833	" "	9	W½NE	1875-05-05		A2
811	SHANE, John	34	E½SW	1882-10-20		A2
779	SHELDON, Henry	33	NENW	1883-11-20		A2
813	SINCLAIR, Alexander	24	SENE	1870-09-20		A1 G46
794	SON, John Howard And	13	SESW	1870-06-10		A1
834	STEPHENS, Orlando	30	NENE	1880-11-20		A1
769	STEVENSON, George R	9	NWNW	1896-01-22		A2
812	STILSON, John	28	NENE	1864-01-05		A1
781	TOWER, Isaac W	25	NWSW	1883-01-20		A1
713	TYLER, Asher	20	E½NW	1852-11-01		A1
763	VATER, Friedrich	15	N½	1861-12-03		A1
814	WALSH, John	30	W½SW	1881-01-20		A2 F
815	" "	31	NWNW	1881-01-20		A2 F
823	WATROUS, Martin	18	S½NW	1856-01-10		A1
824	" "	31	SESE	1868-08-20		A1
835	WEITZEL, Paul	35	W½SW	1882-12-01		A2
737	WELLS, Fred L	12	S½SW	1868-08-20		A1
738	" "	13	NESW	1868-08-20		A1
739	" "	13	SENW	1868-08-20		A1
740	" "	23	SENE	1868-08-20		A1
741	" "	23	SWSE	1868-08-20		A1
742	" "	25	SESE	1868-08-20		A1
743	" "	26	NWNE	1868-08-20		A1
692	WHEELER, Albert A	19	SENE	1869-07-01		A1
696	" "	32	NENW	1870-05-10		A1
697	" "	32	NWNE	1870-05-10		A1
693	" "	29	N½SW	1871-06-15		A2
694	" "	29	NWSE	1871-06-15		A2
695	" "	29	SESW	1871-06-15		A2
704	WHEELER, Alonzo	26	SENE	1870-05-10		A1 G52
705	" "	28	SWSW	1870-05-10		A1 G52
706	" "	28	W½NE	1870-05-10		A1 G52
707	" "	33	NWNE	1870-05-10		A1 G52
708	" "	33	NWNW	1870-05-10		A1 G52
702	WHEELER, Alonzo E	29	NW	1871-02-10		A2
729	WILLERTON, Edward	6	E½NE	1888-10-18		A2 F
829	WING, Nelson H	31	SWSE	1856-09-01		A1
830	" "	33	SENW	1856-09-01		A1
831	" "	36	SESW	1856-09-01		A1
784	WOODS, J L	28	NENW	1868-08-20		A1
797	WOODS, John L	19	E½SW	1855-10-01		A1
798	" "	19	NWSW	1855-10-01		A1
799	" "	19	SWNW	1855-10-01		A1
843	" "	23	NWSE	1855-10-01		A1 G54
844	" "	24	E½NW	1855-10-01		A1 G54
847	" "	24	W½NE	1855-10-01		A1 G54

ID	Individual in Patent	Sec.	Sec. Part	Date Issued	Other Counties	For More Info . . .
848	WOODS, John L (Cont'd)	28	SESW	1855-10-01		A1 G54
849	" "	29	SESE	1855-10-01		A1 G54
850	" "	3	NENE	1855-10-01		A1 G54
851	" "	3	SWSW	1855-10-01		A1 G54
800	" "	30	NESW	1855-10-01		A1
801	" "	30	NWSE	1855-10-01		A1
852	" "	30	SWSE	1855-10-01		A1 G54
853	" "	31	NWNE	1855-10-01		A1 G54
854	" "	32	NENE	1855-10-01		A1 G54
855	" "	35	NENE	1855-10-01		A1 G54
802	" "	36	NWNW	1855-10-01		A1
856	" "	6	SESW	1855-10-01		A1 G54
857	" "	7	E½NE	1855-10-01		A1 G54
858	" "	7	SENW	1855-10-01		A1 G54
859	" "	7	W½NW	1855-10-01		A1 G54
845	" "	24	E½SW	1856-01-10		A1 G54
846	" "	24	NWSE	1856-01-10		A1 G54

Patent Map

T13-N R13-E
Michigan-Toledo Strip Meridian

Map Group 7

Township Statistics

Parcels Mapped	:	181
Number of Patents	:	129
Number of Individuals	:	85
Patentees Identified	:	82
Number of Surnames	:	72
Multi-Patentee Parcels	:	26
Oldest Patent Date	:	11/1/1852
Most Recent Patent	:	1/22/1896
Block/Lot Parcels	:	0
Parcels Re - Issued	:	4
Parcels that Overlap	:	0
Cities and Towns	:	2
Cemeteries	:	2

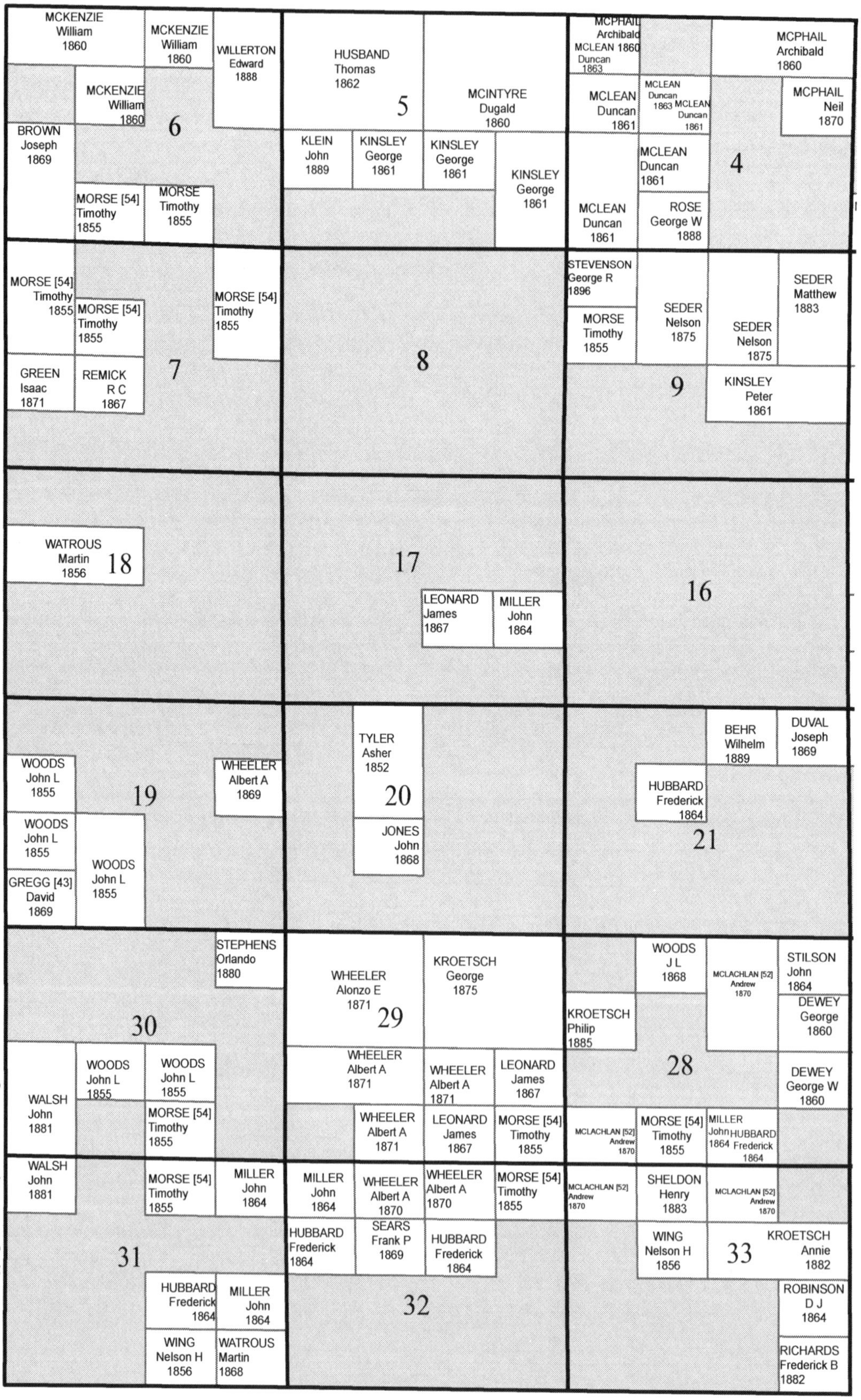

Helpful Hints

1. This Map's INDEX can be found on the preceding pages.
2. Refer to Map "C" to see where this Township lies within Sanilac County, Michigan.
3. Numbers within square brackets [ ] denote a multi-patentee land parcel (multi-owner). Refer to Appendix "C" for a full list of members in this group.
4. Areas that look to be crowded with Patentees usually indicate multiple sales of the same parcel (Re-issues) or Overlapping parcels. See this Township's Index for an explanation of these and other circumstances that might explain "odd" groupings of Patentees on this map.

Legend

- Patent Boundary
- Section Boundary
- No Patents Found (or Outside County)
- 1., 2., 3., ... Lot Numbers (when beside a name)
- [ ] Group Number (see Appendix "C")

Scale: Section = 1 mile X 1 mile (generally, with some exceptions)

Road Map

T13-N R13-E
Michigan-Toledo Strip Meridian

Map Group 7

Cities & Towns

Argyle
Laing

Cemeteries

Argyle Cemetery
Wheatland Cemetery

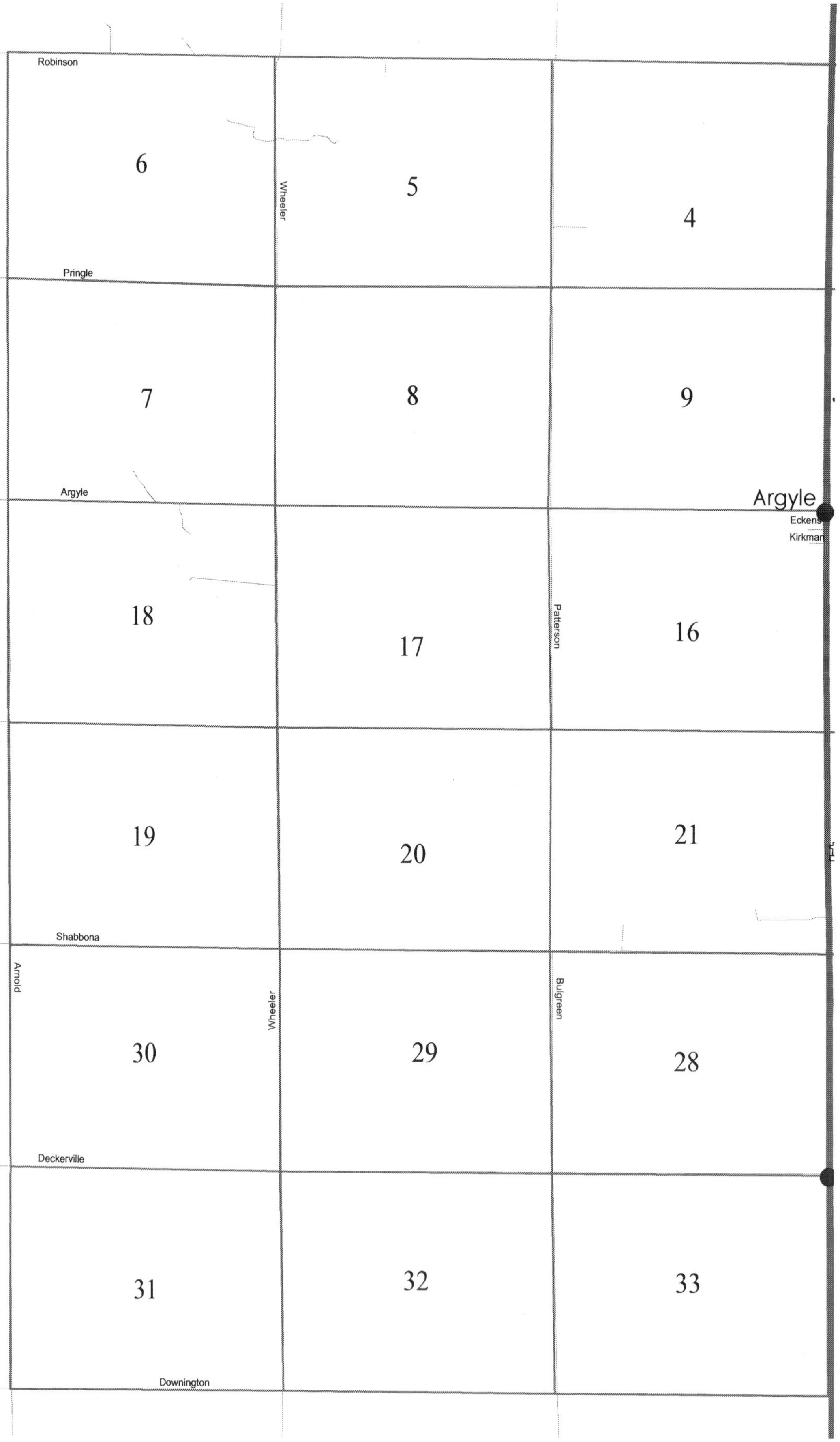

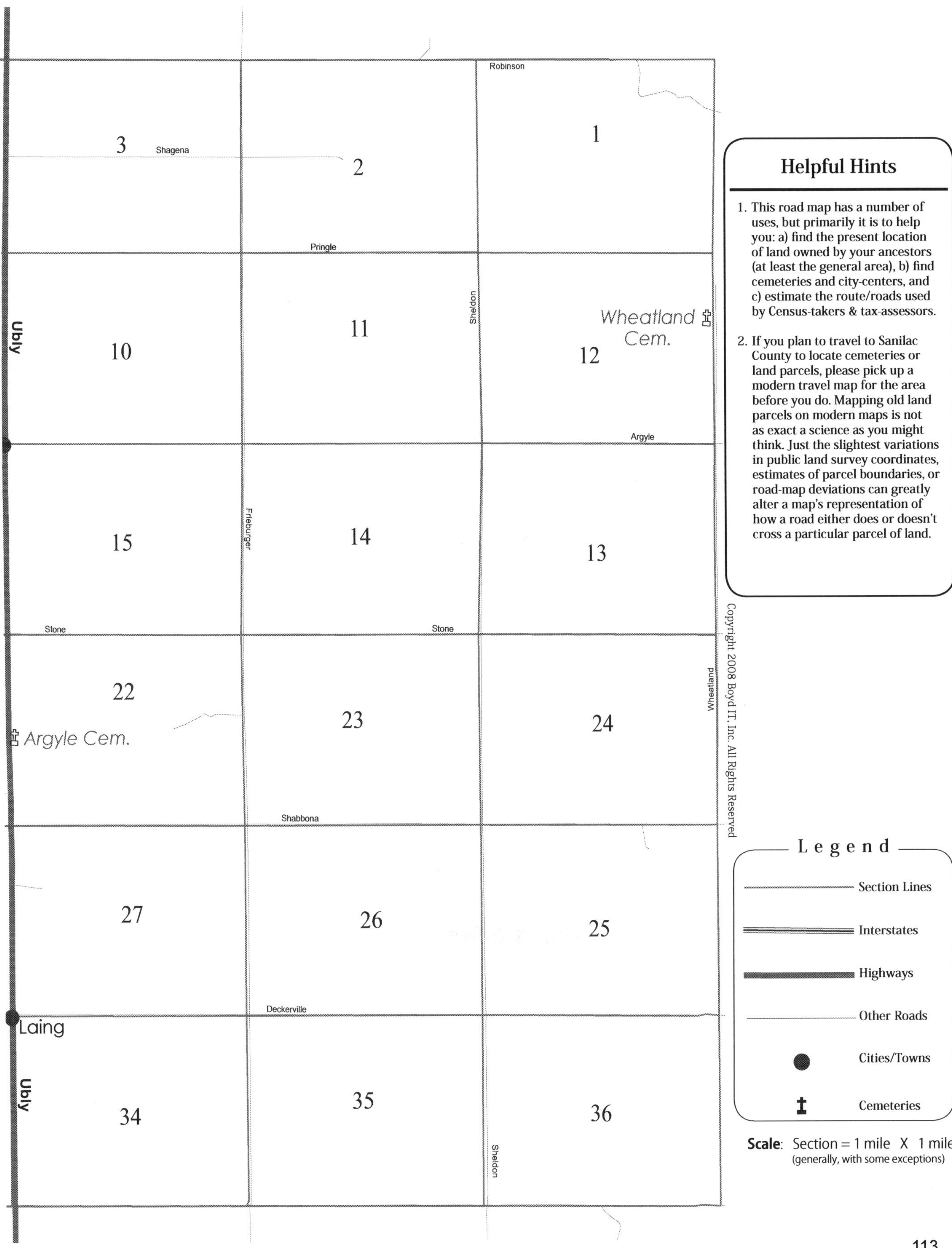
Robinson
3
Shagena
2
1
Pringle
Sheldon
11
Wheatland
Cem.
Ubly
10
12
Argyle
15
Frieburger
14
13
Stone
Stone
22
Argyle Cem.
23
Wheatland
24
Shabbona
27
26
25
Deckerville
Laing
Ubly
34
35
36
Sheldon
Helpful Hints
1. This road map has a number of uses, but primarily it is to help you: a) find the present location of land owned by your ancestors (at least the general area), b) find cemeteries and city-centers, and c) estimate the route/roads used by Census-takers & tax-assessors.
2. If you plan to travel to Sanilac County to locate cemeteries or land parcels, please pick up a modern travel map for the area before you do. Mapping old land parcels on modern maps is not as exact a science as you might think. Just the slightest variations in public land survey coordinates, estimates of parcel boundaries, or road-map deviations can greatly alter a map's representation of how a road either does or doesn't cross a particular parcel of land.
Legend
Section Lines
Interstates
Highways
Other Roads
Cities/Towns
Cemeteries
Scale: Section = 1 mile X 1 mile
(generally, with some exceptions)

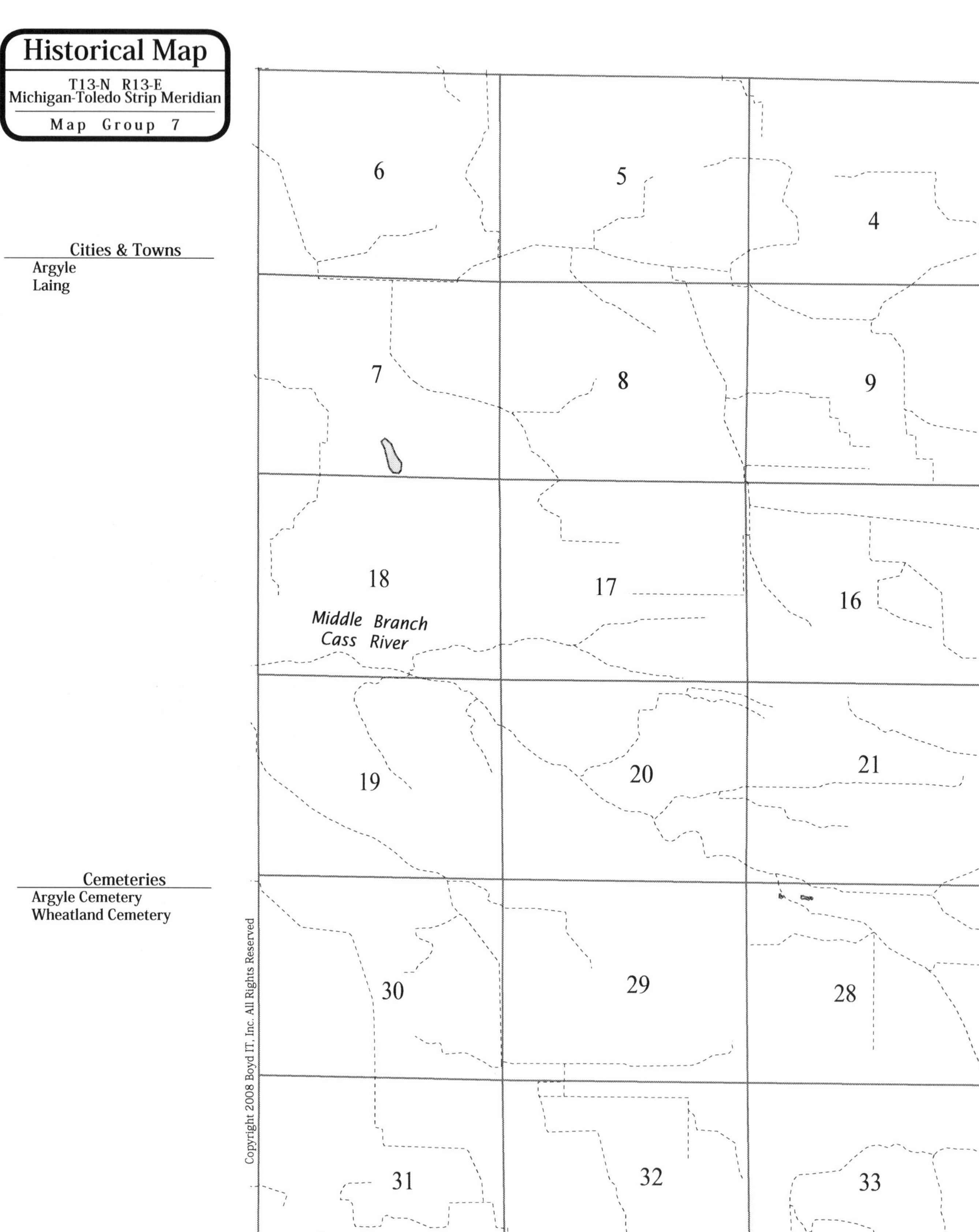
Historical Map
T13-N R13-E
Michigan-Toledo Strip Meridian
Map Group 7
Cities & Towns
Argyle
Laing
Cemeteries
Argyle Cemetery
Wheatland Cemetery
6
5
4
7
8
9
18
17
16
Middle Branch
Cass River
19
20
21
30
29
28
31
32
33
Copyright 2008 Boyd IT, Inc. All Rights Reserved

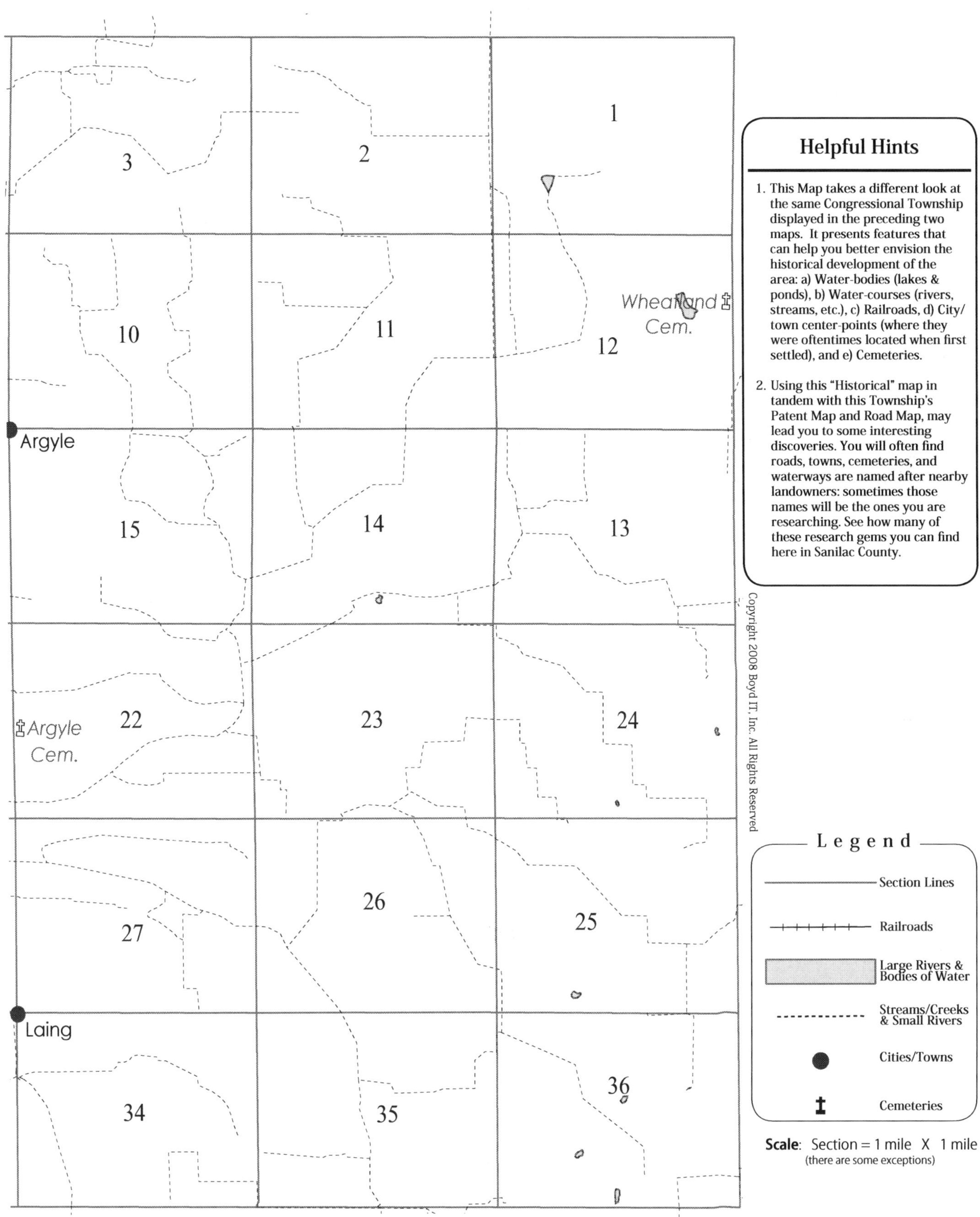
1
2
3
10
11
12
Wheatland
Cem.
Argyle
13
14
15
22
23
24
Argyle
Cem.
25
26
27
Laing
34
35
36
Helpful Hints
1. This Map takes a different look at the same Congressional Township displayed in the preceding two maps. It presents features that can help you better envision the historical development of the area: a) Water-bodies (lakes & ponds), b) Water-courses (rivers, streams, etc.), c) Railroads, d) City/town center-points (where they were oftentimes located when first settled), and e) Cemeteries.
2. Using this "Historical" map in tandem with this Township's Patent Map and Road Map, may lead you to some interesting discoveries. You will often find roads, towns, cemeteries, and waterways are named after nearby landowners: sometimes those names will be the ones you are researching. See how many of these research gems you can find here in Sanilac County.
Legend
Section Lines
Railroads
Large Rivers & Bodies of Water
Streams/Creeks & Small Rivers
Cities/Towns
Cemeteries
Scale: Section = 1 mile X 1 mile
(there are some exceptions)

Map Group 8: Index to Land Patents

Township 13-North Range 14-East (Michigan-Toledo Strip)

After you locate an individual in this Index, take note of the Section and Section Part then proceed to the Land Patent map on the pages immediately following. You should have no difficulty locating the corresponding parcel of land.

The "For More Info" Column will lead you to more information about the underlying Patents. See the *Legend* at right, and the "How to Use this Book" chapter, for more information.

LEGEND

"For More Info . . . " column

A = Authority (Legislative Act, See Appendix "A")
B = Block or Lot (location in Section unknown)
C = Cancelled Patent
F = Fractional Section
G = Group (Multi-Patentee Patent, see Appendix "C")
V = Overlaps another Parcel
R = Re-Issued (Parcel patented more than once)

(A & G items require you to look in the Appendixes referred to above. All other Letter-designations followed by a number require you to locate line-items in this index that possess the ID number found after the letter).

ID	Individual in Patent	Sec.	Sec. Part	Date Issued	Other Counties	For More Info . . .
877	ABBOTT, Charles A	12	SENE	1860-11-21		A1
909	BARBER, James	11	NWNE	1859-10-10		A1
910	" "	11	W½SE	1859-10-10		A1
911	CATALINE, James	1	NENE	1859-10-10		A1 F
924	COLE, John M	7	W½NW	1871-09-30		A2
942	COMPANY, S Rothschild And	35	S½SE	1865-10-02		A1
908	CRAIG, James A	1	E½SE	1861-12-03		A1
881	EASTMAN, David C	21	W½NE	1889-06-16		A2
950	FAY, William E	28	W½NE	1867-07-01		A1
941	GOODWIN, Philip H	35	S½NW	1860-11-21		A1
898	GRIGG, George	30	NW	1874-03-10		A1
933	HALFMANN, Mary C	8	SWSW	1868-08-20		A1
943	HILL, Silas	14	E½SE	1861-12-10		A1
944	" "	14	SENE	1861-12-10		A1
901	HOWARD, Henry	19	SESW	1868-08-20		A1
902	" "	19	SWSE	1868-08-20		A1
903	" "	21	SENE	1868-08-20		A1
904	" "	27	SWSW	1868-08-20		A1
905	" "	6	SWSE	1872-04-15		A1 G45
906	" "	7	NWNE	1872-04-15		A1 G45
917	HOWARD, Jand H	29	NESE	1867-07-01		A1
918	" "	29	NWNE	1867-07-01		A1
919	" "	29	SENE	1867-07-01		A1
905	HOWARD, John	6	SWSE	1872-04-15		A1 G45
906	" "	7	NWNE	1872-04-15		A1 G45
874	HUBBARD, Bela	31	NWNW	1869-07-01		A1 G47
892	HUBBARD, Frederick	6	NWSE	1865-10-02		A1
893	" "	8	NWSW	1865-10-02		A1
889	" "	21	SWSE	1867-07-01		A1
890	" "	29	SESE	1867-07-01		A1
891	" "	32	NWSW	1867-07-01		A1
874	KING, John E	31	NWNW	1869-07-01		A1 G47
912	KIRKWOOD, James	26	SWNW	1861-07-01		A1
913	" "	27	E½NE	1861-07-01		A1
914	" "	27	NESE	1861-07-01		A1
922	KLINGHAMER, John	18	SE	1883-06-07		A2
934	LEITCH, Neil	21	NENW	1867-07-01		A1
915	LEONARD, James	18	S½SW	1867-07-01		A1 F
916	LITTLE, James S	28	SENE	1888-10-18		A2
880	LIVINGWAY, Daniel	35	N½SE	1860-05-01		A1
923	LIVINGWAY, John	35	S½NE	1860-10-01		A1
932	MASON, Lorenzo M	21	NESE	1864-01-05		A1
927	MCGINN, John W	30	SWNE	1867-07-01		A1 G51
926	" "	6	N½NW	1868-08-20		A1
928	" "	31	NWSW	1869-07-01		A1 G51 F
945	MCGINN, Simms And	19	E½NW	1867-07-01		A1

ID	Individual in Patent	Sec.	Sec. Part	Date Issued	Other Counties	For More Info . . .
946	MCGINN, Simms And (Cont'd)	30	NESW	1867-07-01		A1
947	" "	30	SWSW	1867-07-01		A1
896	MELVILLE, George B	35	N½SW	1860-05-01		A1
897	" "	35	SESW	1860-05-01		A1
907	MORTON, Isaac	12	NENE	1859-10-10		A1
939	PATTISON, Oliver J	1	NWSE	1878-02-13		A1
940	" "	1	S½NE	1878-02-13		A1
894	PUTNAM, Frederick J	11	NESW	1859-10-10		A1
895	" "	11	SENW	1859-10-10		A1
948	READ, Thomas	2	N½NW	1861-12-03		A1 C F
949	" "	2	W½NW	1867-05-11		A1 F
879	REINELT, Charles	7	SE	1870-05-20		A2
878	" "	18	NE	1883-01-20		A1
884	REINELT, Emery	7	E½SW	1878-11-05		A2
885	" "	7	NENW	1878-11-05		A2
886	" "	7	SWNE	1878-11-05		A2
921	REINELT, Johann	7	SWSW	1865-10-02		A1
920	" "	18	NW	1870-05-20		A2 F
882	ROSS, David	6	W½NE	1885-04-15		A1 F
937	SARGENT, Noah	35	NENW	1859-05-09		A1
938	" "	35	NWNE	1859-05-09		A1
873	SAWYER, Alson	11	NENW	1861-07-01		A1
927	SIMMS, Walter	30	SWNE	1867-07-01		A1 G51
928	" "	31	NWSW	1869-07-01		A1 G51 F
883	SMITH, Edward	27	NWSW	1868-08-20		A1
931	SWART, Leyman	32	W½NW	1861-07-01		A1
929	TATE, Joseph	2	SESW	1859-10-10		A1
930	" "	2	W½SW	1859-10-10		A1
899	THAYER, Halsey	5	NWSW	1869-07-01		A1
900	" "	5	W½NW	1869-07-01		A1
935	THAYER, Nelson O	1	NENW	1860-11-21		A1
936	" "	1	NWNE	1860-11-21		A1
875	THORNTON, Chancy	2	NESW	1860-10-01		A1
876	" "	2	SENW	1860-10-01		A1
925	VAN SICKLE, JOHN	17	NW	1877-05-15		A1
887	WELLES, Fred L	28	NESE	1867-07-01		A1
888	" "	28	SESW	1867-07-01		A1

Patent Map

T13-N R14-E
Michigan-Toledo Strip Meridian

Map Group 8

Township Statistics

Parcels Mapped	:	78
Number of Patents	:	59
Number of Individuals	:	48
Patentees Identified	:	47
Number of Surnames	:	40
Multi-Patentee Parcels	:	5
Oldest Patent Date	:	5/9/1859
Most Recent Patent	:	6/16/1889
Block/Lot Parcels	:	0
Parcels Re - Issued	:	0
Parcels that Overlap	:	0
Cities and Towns	:	0
Cemeteries	:	1

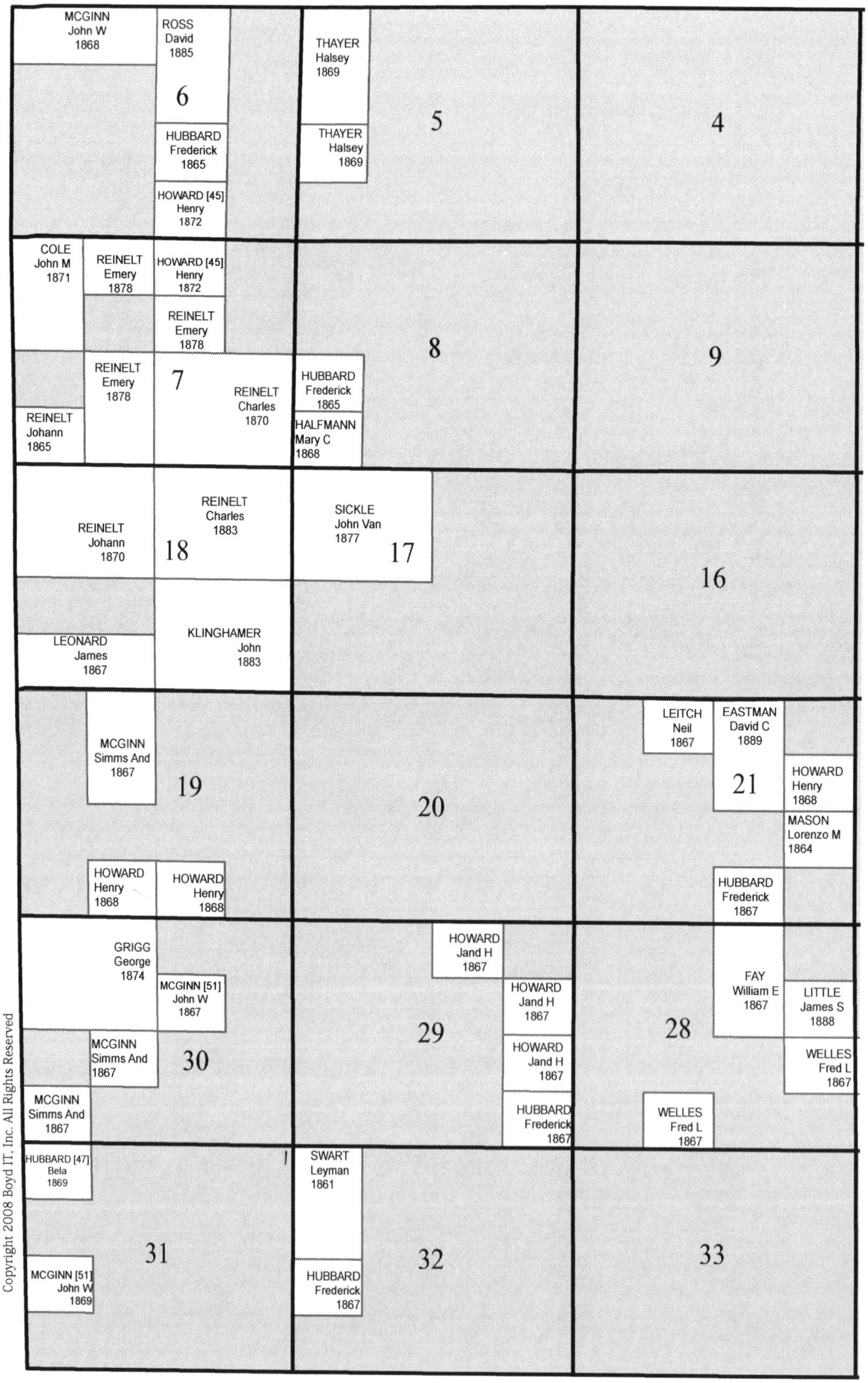

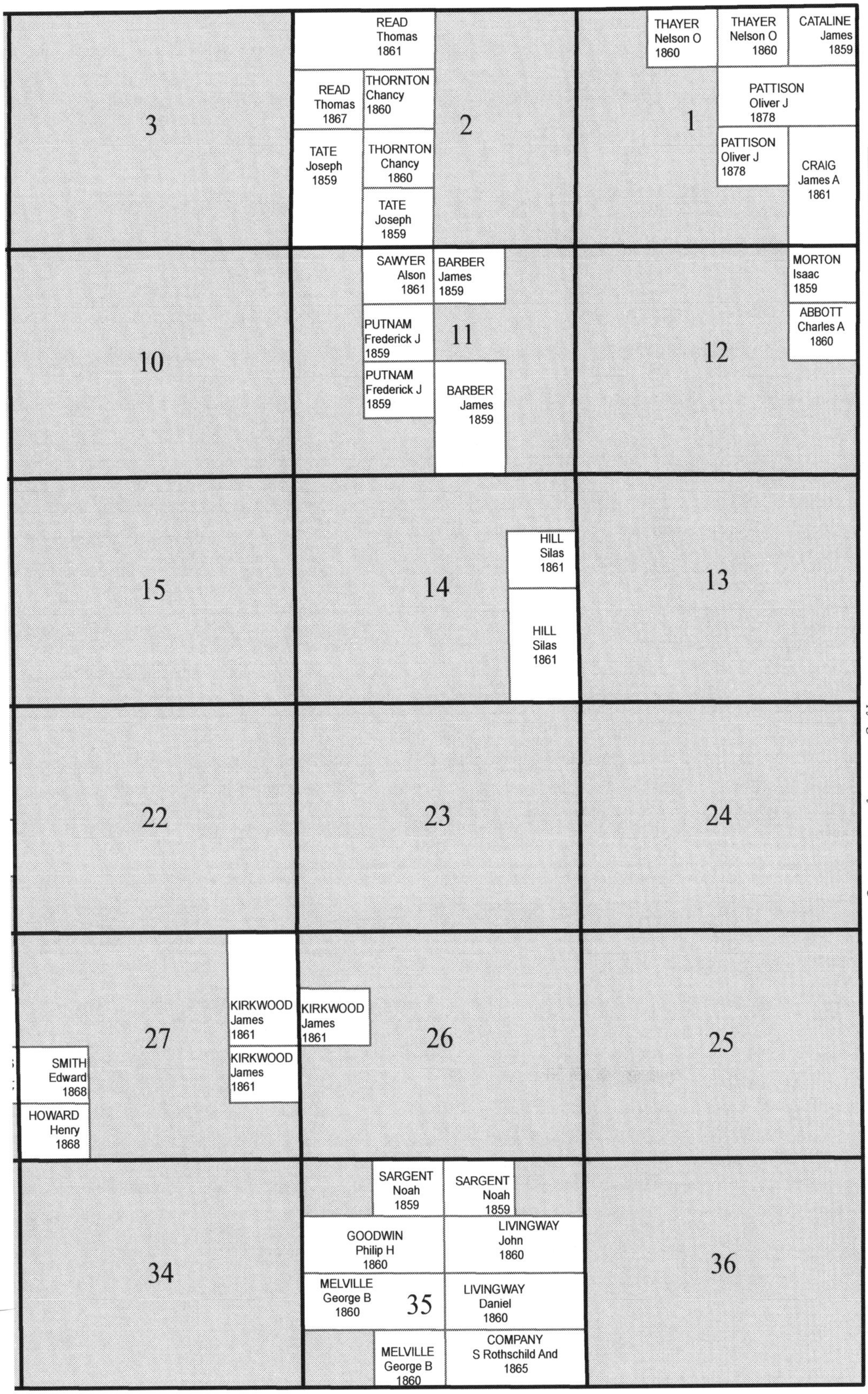

3

READ Thomas 1861

READ Thomas 1867

THORNTON Chancy 1860

TATE Joseph 1859

THORNTON Chancy 1860

TATE Joseph 1859

2

THAYER Nelson O 1860

THAYER Nelson O 1860

CATALINE James 1859

PATTISON Oliver J 1878

PATTISON Oliver J 1878

CRAIG James A 1861

1

10

SAWYER Alson 1861

BARBER James 1859

PUTNAM Frederick J 1859

11

PUTNAM Frederick J 1859

BARBER James 1859

MORTON Isaac 1859

ABBOTT Charles A 1860

12

15

14

HILL Silas 1861

HILL Silas 1861

13

22

23

24

27

KIRKWOOD James 1861

KIRKWOOD James 1861

KIRKWOOD James 1861

SMITH Edward 1868

HOWARD Henry 1868

26

25

34

SARGENT Noah 1859

SARGENT Noah 1859

GOODWIN Philip H 1860

LIVINGWAY John 1860

MELVILLE George B 1860

35

LIVINGWAY Daniel 1860

MELVILLE George B 1860

COMPANY S Rothschild And 1865

36

Helpful Hints

1. This Map's INDEX can be found on the preceding pages.
2. Refer to Map "C" to see where this Township lies within Sanilac County, Michigan.
3. Numbers within square brackets [ ] denote a multi-patentee land parcel (multi-owner). Refer to Appendix "C" for a full list of members in this group.
4. Areas that look to be crowded with Patentees usually indicate multiple sales of the same parcel (Re-issues) or Overlapping parcels. See this Township's Index for an explanation of these and other circumstances that might explain "odd" groupings of Patentees on this map.

Legend

Patent Boundary

Section Boundary

No Patents Found (or Outside County)

1., 2., 3., ... Lot Numbers (when beside a name)

[ ] Group Number (see Appendix "C")

Scale: Section = 1 mile X 1 mile (generally, with some exceptions)

Road Map

T13-N R14-E
Michigan-Toledo Strip Meridian

Map Group 8

Cities & Towns

None

Cemeteries

Downing Cemetery

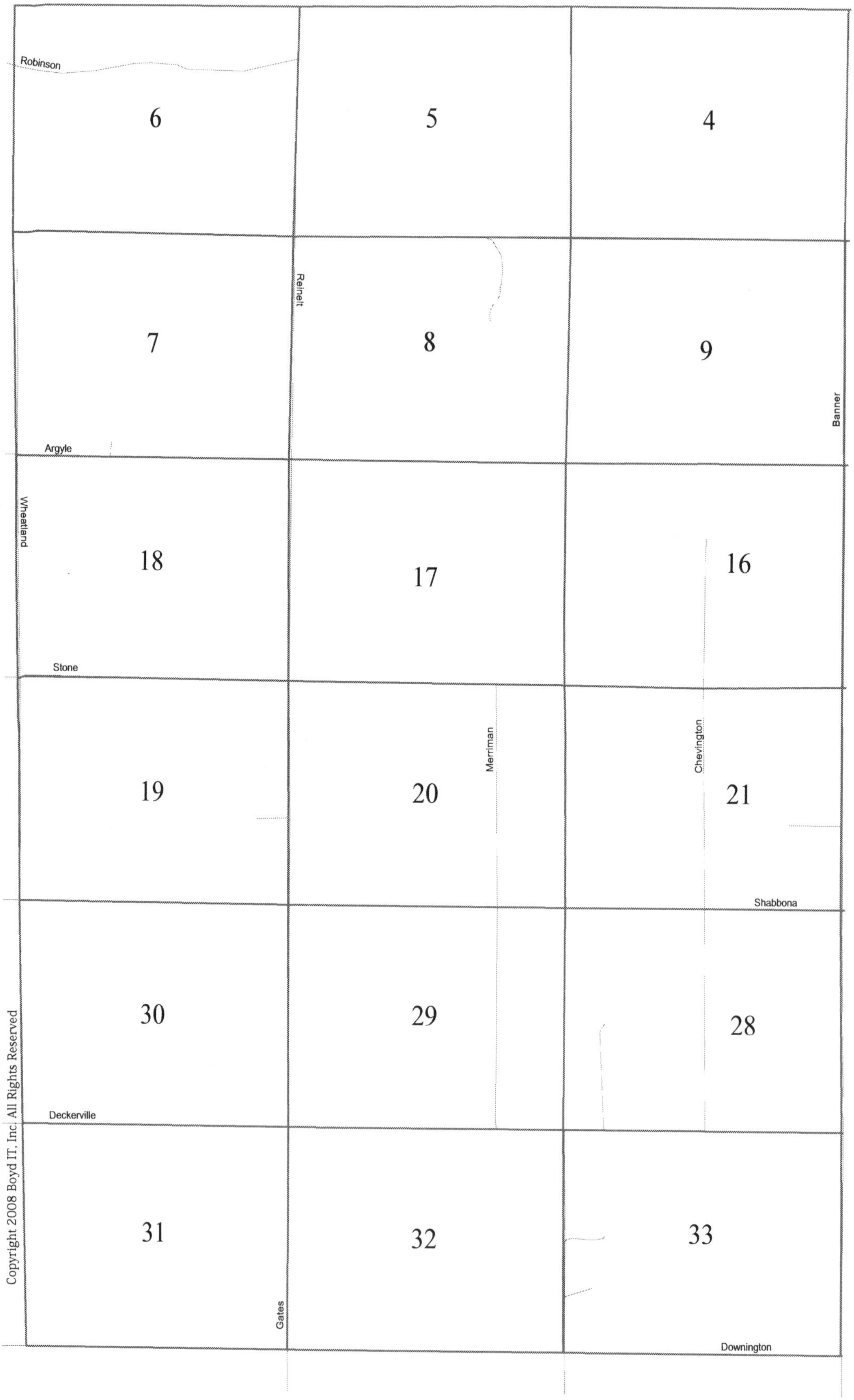

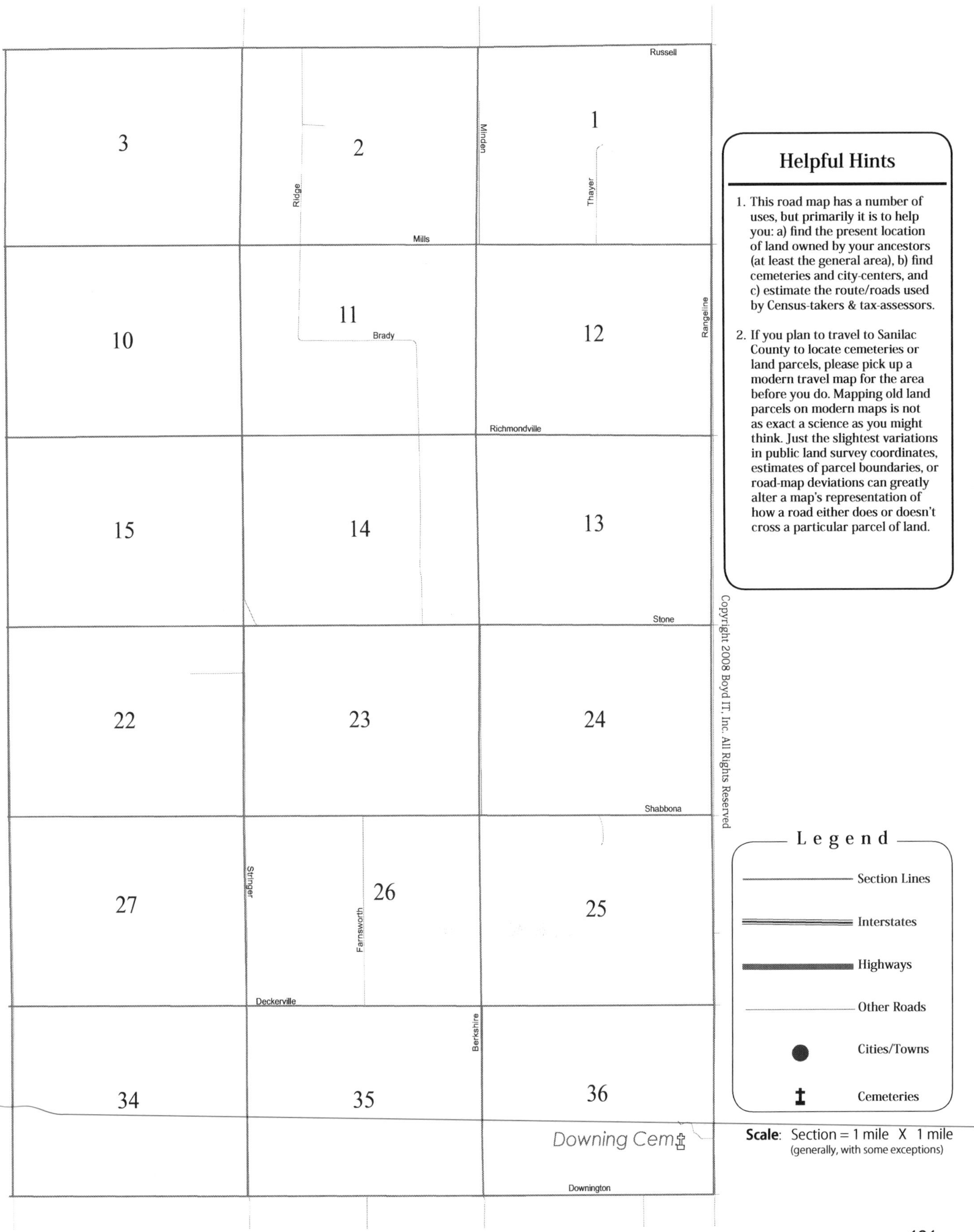

Helpful Hints

1. This road map has a number of uses, but primarily it is to help you: a) find the present location of land owned by your ancestors (at least the general area), b) find cemeteries and city-centers, and c) estimate the route/roads used by Census-takers & tax-assessors.
2. If you plan to travel to Sanilac County to locate cemeteries or land parcels, please pick up a modern travel map for the area before you do. Mapping old land parcels on modern maps is not as exact a science as you might think. Just the slightest variations in public land survey coordinates, estimates of parcel boundaries, or road-map deviations can greatly alter a map's representation of how a road either does or doesn't cross a particular parcel of land.

Legend

- Section Lines
- Interstates
- Highways
- Other Roads
- Cities/Towns
- Cemeteries

Scale: Section = 1 mile X 1 mile
(generally, with some exceptions)

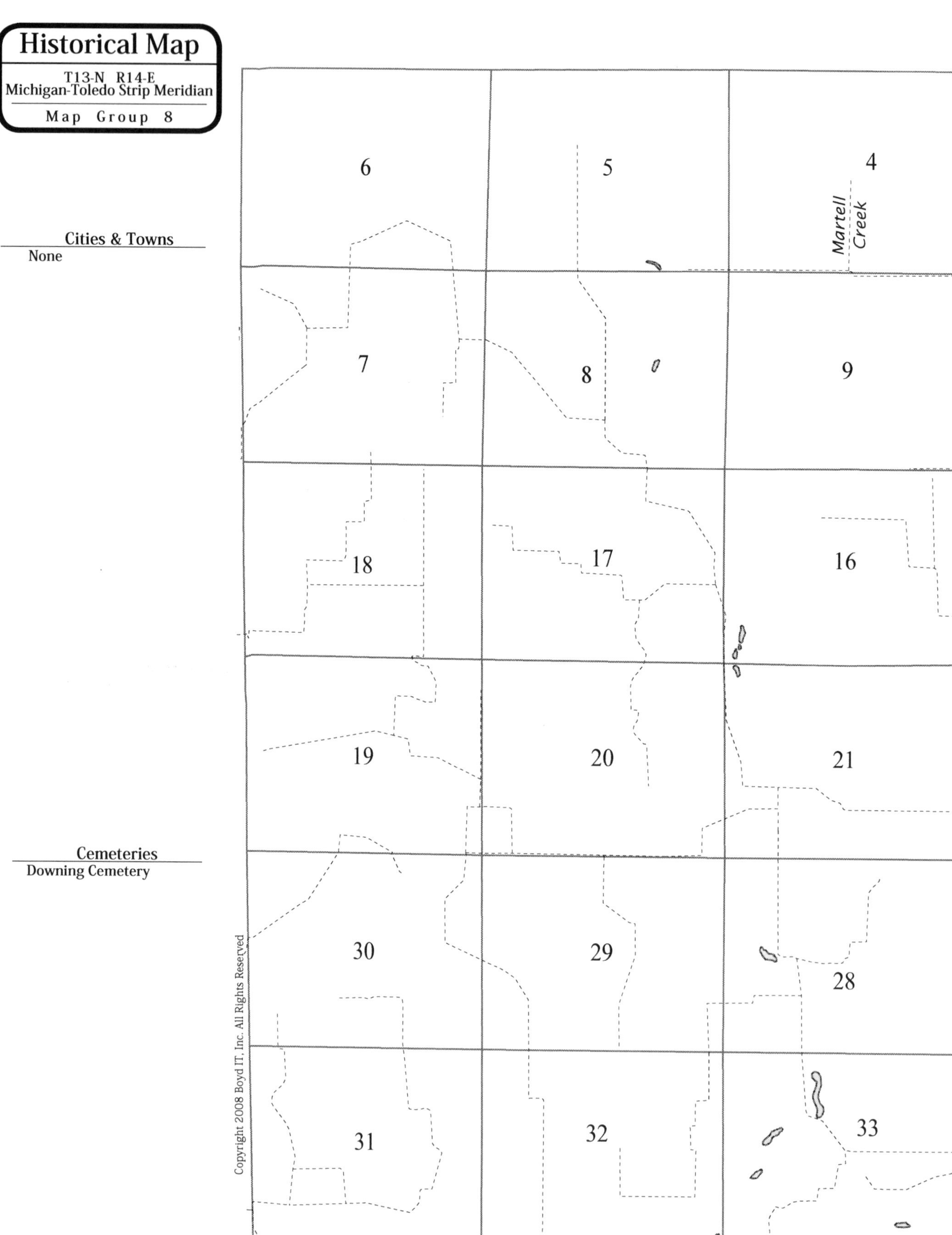
Historical Map
T13-N R14-E
Michigan-Toledo Strip Meridian
Map Group 8
Cities & Towns
None
Cemeteries
Downing Cemetery
6
5
4
Martell Creek
7
8
9
18
17
16
19
20
21
30
29
28
31
32
33
Copyright 2008 Boyd IT, Inc. All Rights Reserved

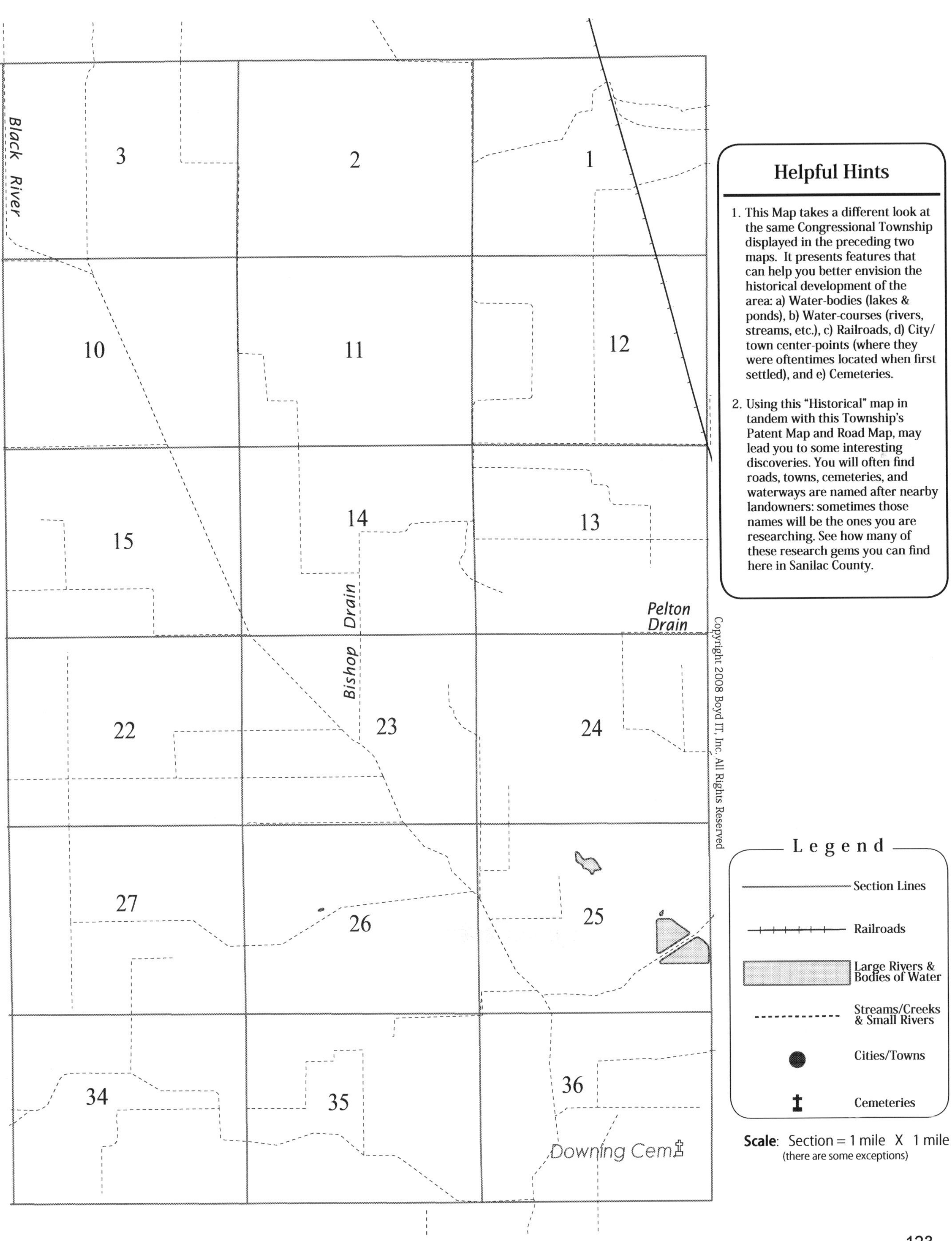
Black River
3
2
1
10
11
12
15
14
13
Bishop Drain
Pelton Drain
22
23
24
27
26
25
34
35
36
Downing Cem
Copyright 2008 Boyd IT, Inc. All Rights Reserved
Helpful Hints
1. This Map takes a different look at the same Congressional Township displayed in the preceding two maps. It presents features that can help you better envision the historical development of the area: a) Water-bodies (lakes & ponds), b) Water-courses (rivers, streams, etc.), c) Railroads, d) City/town center-points (where they were oftentimes located when first settled), and e) Cemeteries.
2. Using this "Historical" map in tandem with this Township's Patent Map and Road Map, may lead you to some interesting discoveries. You will often find roads, towns, cemeteries, and waterways are named after nearby landowners: sometimes those names will be the ones you are researching. See how many of these research gems you can find here in Sanilac County.
Legend
Section Lines
Railroads
Large Rivers & Bodies of Water
Streams/Creeks & Small Rivers
Cities/Towns
Cemeteries
Scale: Section = 1 mile X 1 mile
(there are some exceptions)

Map Group 9: Index to Land Patents

Township 13-North Range 15-East (Michigan-Toledo Strip)

After you locate an individual in this Index, take note of the Section and Section Part then proceed to the Land Patent map on the pages immediately following. You should have no difficulty locating the corresponding parcel of land.

The "For More Info" Column will lead you to more information about the underlying Patents. See the *Legend* at right, and the "How to Use this Book" chapter, for more information.

LEGEND

"For More Info . . . " column

A = Authority (Legislative Act, See Appendix "A")
B = Block or Lot (location in Section unknown)
C = Cancelled Patent
F = Fractional Section
G = Group (Multi-Patentee Patent, see Appendix "C")
V = Overlaps another Parcel
R = Re-Issued (Parcel patented more than once)

(A & G items require you to look in the Appendixes referred to above. All other Letter-designations followed by a number require you to locate line-items in this index that possess the ID number found after the letter).

ID	Individual in Patent	Sec.	Sec. Part	Date Issued	Other Counties	For More Info . . .
1054	ABBOTT, Samuel H	7	E½NW	1857-07-01		A1
1055	" "	7	NWNW	1857-07-01		A1
997	ALDERTON, Jacob	20	W½NE	1857-07-01		A1
999	ALDERTON, James	21	SESW	1861-12-03		A1
1038	BARTLETT, Lovett	5	W½NW	1857-07-01		A1
976	BEACH, George	11	SE	1838-09-04		A1 G12
977	" "	12	SW	1838-09-04		A1 G12
978	" "	13	NW	1838-09-04		A1 G12
979	" "	35	E½SW	1838-09-04		A1 G12
980	" "	35	SE	1838-09-04		A1 G12
981	" "	36	NW	1838-09-04		A1 G12
982	" "	36	W½SW	1838-09-04		A1 G12
976	BECKWITH, Alonzo S	11	SE	1838-09-04		A1 G12
977	" "	12	SW	1838-09-04		A1 G12
978	" "	13	NW	1838-09-04		A1 G12
979	" "	35	E½SW	1838-09-04		A1 G12
980	" "	35	SE	1838-09-04		A1 G12
981	" "	36	NW	1838-09-04		A1 G12
982	" "	36	W½SW	1838-09-04		A1 G12
971	BODDY, Edward	2	SESW	1859-10-10		A1
974	BOWSER, George A	27	NESW	1857-02-20		A1
975	" "	27	SWNW	1857-02-20		A1
973	" "	27	E½NW	1857-10-30		A1
992	CAMPBELL, Horatio	33	SENW	1857-10-30		A1
951	CHRISTIAN, Adolphus B	31	SE	1857-02-16		A1
1025	COALTER, Joseph	10	NESW	1857-10-30		A1
1026	" "	10	NWSE	1857-10-30		A1
1051	COMMER, Peter	26	W½SW	1857-10-30		A1
1001	CUMMINGS, James	11	W½NW	1857-02-16		A1
1000	" "	11	NWSW	1857-02-20		A1
1012	CUMMINGS, John	10	E½SE	1857-02-16		A1
1045	DICKINSON, Nathan	1	E½SE	1837-08-05		A1
1046	" "	12	E½NE	1837-08-05		A1
976	" "	11	SE	1838-09-04		A1 G12
977	" "	12	SW	1838-09-04		A1 G12
978	" "	13	NW	1838-09-04		A1 G12
979	" "	35	E½SW	1838-09-04		A1 G12
980	" "	35	SE	1838-09-04		A1 G12
981	" "	36	NW	1838-09-04		A1 G12
982	" "	36	W½SW	1838-09-04		A1 G12
986	DODGE, Hezekiah	3	E½SW	1859-10-10		A1
1013	DUNLAP, John	12	W½NE	1875-07-30		A2
1014	DUNLOP, John	3	SWNE	1860-05-01		A1
1015	FARNSWORTH, John	29	SESE	1875-02-05		A2
995	FAY, Israel	3	N½SE	1859-10-10		A1
996	" "	3	SWSE	1859-10-10		A1

ID	Individual in Patent	Sec.	Sec. Part	Date Issued	Other Counties	For More Info . . .
990	FORD, Hiram R	30	N½NE	1857-10-30		A1
991	" "	30	SWNE	1857-10-30		A1
983	GLENNIE, George	5	E½NW	1860-05-01		A1
952	GOODRICH, Alanson	30	E½SE	1857-02-16		A1
954	" "	31	NE	1857-02-16		A1
955	" "	36	SWSE	1857-10-30		A1
953	" "	30	SWSE	1868-08-20		A1
993	GRAVES, Ira	17	E½NE	1860-05-01		A1
994	" "	8	SESE	1860-05-01		A1
1033	GREAVES, Josiah	15	SESW	1859-10-10		A1
1034	" "	15	W½SW	1859-10-10		A1
1050	HACKETT, Patrick	3	SENW	1857-10-30		A1
1007	HANDY, Jesse	3	N½NW	1857-07-01		A1 F
1027	HEATHCOTE, Joseph	29	SESW	1859-05-09		A1
1028	" "	29	SWSW	1870-10-01		A1
1011	HEIDE, John C	27	SE	1857-10-30		A1
1008	HURLEY, Joel	20	E½NE	1859-05-09		A1
1009	" "	20	N½SE	1859-05-09		A1
965	JOHNS, Daniel	12	NENW	1859-10-10		A1
956	JONES, Alfred	6	E½SE	1857-02-16		A1
957	" "	6	NE	1857-02-16		A1 F
958	" "	6	SWSE	1857-02-16		A1
1049	KING, Orson W	10	SWSE	1856-09-01		A1
1060	KURTZ, William	11	NENW	1859-10-10		A1
1029	LANCASTER, Joseph	4	S½SE	1860-05-01		A1
1056	LEE, Shepard	17	NENW	1857-10-30		A1
1018	LEITCH, John	27	SESW	1861-04-10		A1
1019	" "	34	E½NW	1861-04-10		A1
1020	" "	34	SWNW	1861-04-10		A1
1039	LYON, Lucius	12	SE	1839-04-10		A1 G49
1040	" "	13	NE	1839-04-10		A1 G49
1041	" "	13	SE	1839-04-10		A1 G49
1042	" "	24	NE	1839-04-10		A1 G49
1036	MASON, Lorenzo M	28	E½NW	1854-06-15		A1
1037	" "	28	W½SE	1854-06-15		A1
984	MAY, George	11	NESW	1857-10-30		A1
1021	MCBRIDE, John	3	SWNW	1859-05-09		A1
1061	MCGREGOR, William	6	NWNW	1857-02-20		A1 F
1068	MCINTOSH, William W	32	NWSE	1859-05-09		A1
1062	MCMULDROCH, William	7	SE	1857-10-30		A1
987	MERRIMAN, Hiram	36	NESE	1852-02-10		A1
988	" "	36	NESW	1852-02-10		A1
989	" "	36	NWSE	1852-02-10		A1
1023	MIDDAUGH, John W	20	SW	1857-10-30		A1
1022	MILLS, John	10	E½NW	1859-05-09		A1
1063	MILLS, William	10	NE	1857-07-01		A1
1064	MILLS, William P	22	SWNE	1861-07-01		A1
1002	OGDEN, James	2	N½NW	1859-05-09		A1
963	OSGOOD, Crague	32	E½NW	1859-05-09		A1
964	" "	32	W½NE	1859-05-09		A1
1058	PAKE, Urias	29	N½NW	1857-10-30		A1
1059	" "	29	SENW	1857-10-30		A1
1065	PAKE, William	32	W½NW	1859-05-09		A1
1039	PARKER, Daniel	12	SE	1839-04-10		A1 G49
1040	" "	13	NE	1839-04-10		A1 G49
1041	" "	13	SE	1839-04-10		A1 G49
1042	" "	24	NE	1839-04-10		A1 G49
1030	PIFER, Joseph	19	SE	1857-02-16		A1
1066	PRESLEY, William	32	SWSE	1860-05-01		A1
1003	READ, James	26	W½SE	1857-07-01		A1
985	REED, Henry	26	E½SW	1860-05-01		A1
1004	ROADHOUSE, James	18	E½NW	1860-05-01		A1
1005	" "	18	E½SW	1860-05-01		A1
1047	ROSS, Nelson F	10	NWSW	1859-10-10		A1
1048	" "	10	W½NW	1859-10-10		A1
966	SAMPLE, David N	17	SESW	1859-05-09		A1
967	" "	17	SWSE	1860-05-01		A1
1043	SAMPLE, Martin	18	SE	1857-10-30		A1
1010	SCHNEIDER, Johann	3	SENE	1859-10-10		A1 F
998	SNYDER, Jacob	6	NWSE	1860-10-01		A1
1006	SPEARMAN, James	11	SENW	1857-07-01		A1
1031	SPENCER, Joshua	8	N½SE	1857-07-01		A1
1032	" "	8	S½NE	1857-10-30		A1

ID	Individual in Patent	Sec.	Sec. Part	Date Issued	Other Counties	For More Info . . .
1044	STACUM, Martin	2	NWNE	1857-07-01		A1 F
1067	TOBIN, William	5	NWNE	1865-10-02		A1 F
972	VAN CAMP, ELIJAH	4	N½SE	1859-10-10		A1
970	WARD, Eber B	9	SWSW	1869-07-01		A1
1069	WELCH, William	17	W½SW	1857-07-01		A1
1024	WHALES, John	3	W½SW	1859-10-10		A1
961	WIGHT, Buckminster	31	SESW	1852-02-10		A1 F
962	" "	31	SWSW	1852-02-10		A1 F
1057	WILLIS, Thomas	35	N½NW	1855-10-01		A1
1070	WILLIS, William	35	NE	1855-10-01		A1
1071	" "	35	S½NW	1855-10-01		A1
968	WIXSON, Dennis	8	E½NW	1857-07-01		A1
969	" "	8	E½SW	1857-07-01		A1
1035	WIXSON, Lemuel	7	NE	1867-02-16		A1
1052	WIXSON, Randal	8	W½NW	1857-07-01		A1
1053	" "	8	W½SW	1857-07-01		A1
1016	WOODS, John L	33	E½SE	1854-06-15		A1
1017	" "	33	SWSE	1854-06-15		A1
960	WRIGHT, Andrew	19	E½NE	1857-02-20		A1
959	WRIGHT, Andrew J	20	NW	1857-10-30		A1

Patent Map

T13-N R15-E
Michigan-Toledo Strip Meridian

Map Group 9

Township Statistics

Parcels Mapped	:	121
Number of Patents	:	87
Number of Individuals	:	81
Patentees Identified	:	79
Number of Surnames	:	71
Multi-Patentee Parcels	:	11
Oldest Patent Date	:	8/5/1837
Most Recent Patent	:	7/30/1875
Block/Lot Parcels	:	0
Parcels Re - Issued	:	0
Parcels that Overlap	:	0
Cities and Towns	:	1
Cemeteries	:	3

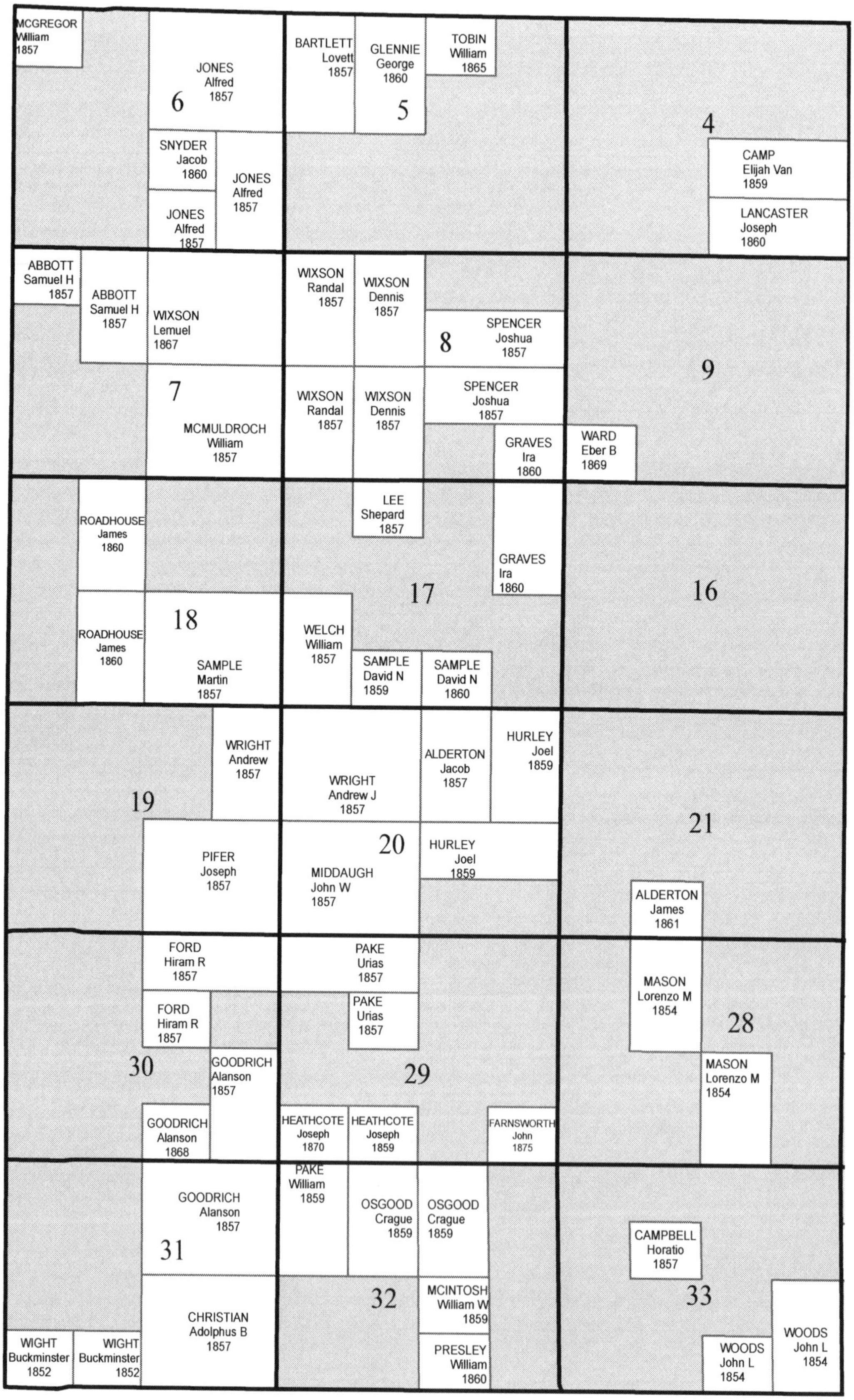

MCGREGOR William 1857
JONES Alfred 1857
6
SNYDER Jacob 1860
JONES Alfred 1857
JONES Alfred 1857
BARTLETT Lovett 1857
GLENNIE George 1860
TOBIN William 1865
5
4
CAMP Elijah Van 1859
LANCASTER Joseph 1860
ABBOTT Samuel H 1857
ABBOTT Samuel H 1857
WIXSON Lemuel 1867
7
MCMULDROCH William 1857
WIXSON Randal 1857
WIXSON Dennis 1857
SPENCER Joshua 1857
8
WIXSON Randal 1857
WIXSON Dennis 1857
SPENCER Joshua 1857
GRAVES Ira 1860
9
WARD Eber B 1869
ROADHOUSE James 1860
ROADHOUSE James 1860
18
SAMPLE Martin 1857
LEE Shepard 1857
GRAVES Ira 1860
17
WELCH William 1857
SAMPLE David N 1859
SAMPLE David N 1860
16
WRIGHT Andrew 1857
19
PIFER Joseph 1857
WRIGHT Andrew J 1857
ALDERTON Jacob 1857
HURLEY Joel 1859
20
MIDDAUGH John W 1857
HURLEY Joel 1859
21
ALDERTON James 1861
FORD Hiram R 1857
FORD Hiram R 1857
30
GOODRICH Alanson 1857
GOODRICH Alanson 1868
PAKE Urias 1857
PAKE Urias 1857
29
HEATHCOTE Joseph 1870
HEATHCOTE Joseph 1859
FARNSWORTH John 1875
MASON Lorenzo M 1854
28
MASON Lorenzo M 1854
GOODRICH Alanson 1857
31
CHRISTIAN Adolphus B 1857
WIGHT Buckminster 1852
WIGHT Buckminster 1852
PAKE William 1859
OSGOOD Cragure 1859
OSGOOD Crague 1859
32
MCINTOSH William W 1859
PRESLEY William 1860
CAMPBELL Horatio 1857
33
WOODS John L 1854
WOODS John L 1854

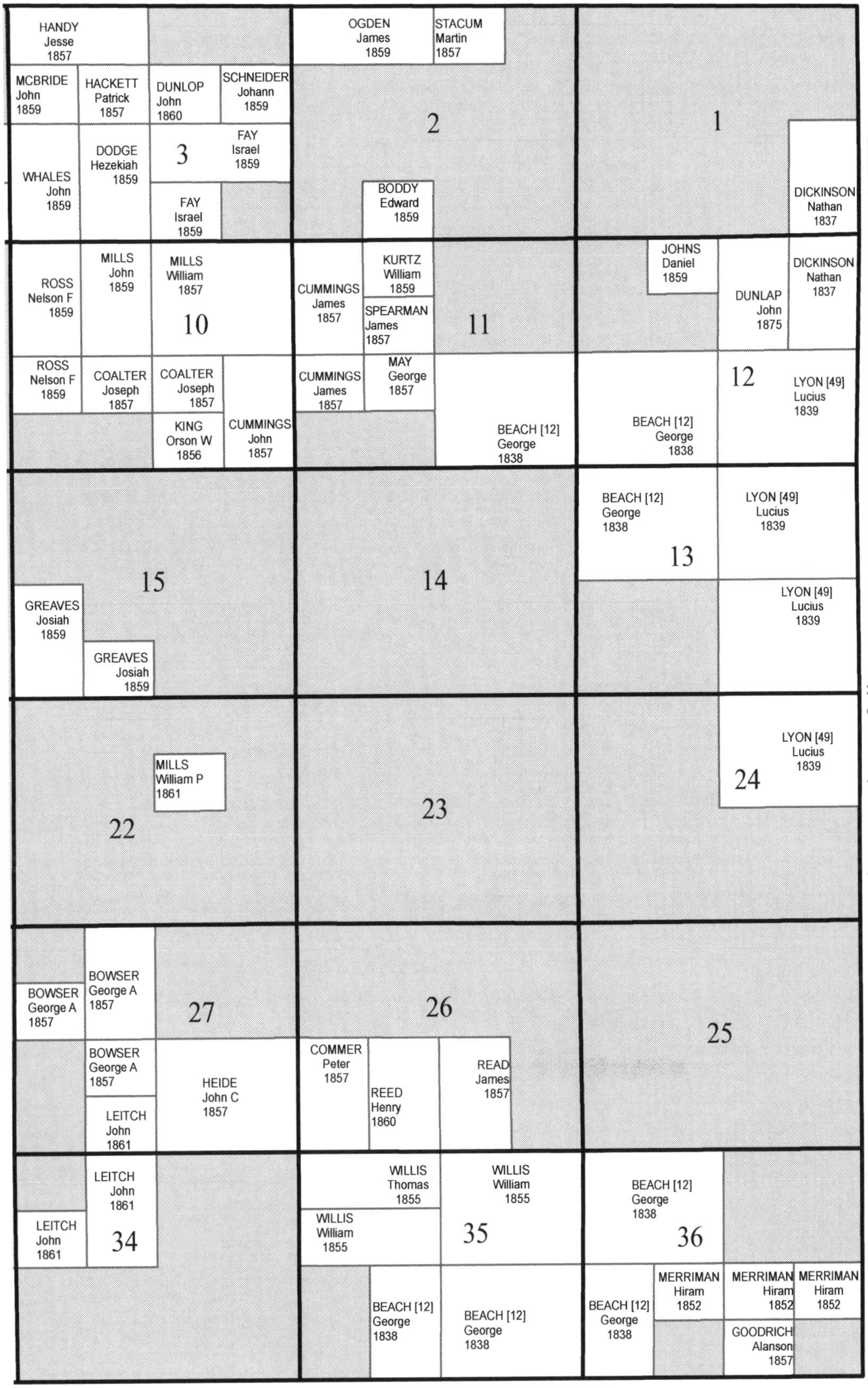

Helpful Hints

1. This Map's INDEX can be found on the preceding pages.
2. Refer to Map "C" to see where this Township lies within Sanilac County, Michigan.
3. Numbers within square brackets [ ] denote a multi-patentee land parcel (multi-owner). Refer to Appendix "C" for a full list of members in this group.
4. Areas that look to be crowded with Patentees usually indicate multiple sales of the same parcel (Re-issues) or Overlapping parcels. See this Township's Index for an explanation of these and other circumstances that might explain "odd" groupings of Patentees on this map.

Legend

- Patent Boundary
- Section Boundary
- No Patents Found (or Outside County)
- 1., 2., 3., ... Lot Numbers (when beside a name)
- [ ] Group Number (see Appendix "C")

Scale: Section = 1 mile X 1 mile (generally, with some exceptions)

Road Map

T13-N R15-E
Michigan-Toledo Strip Meridian

Map Group 9

Cities & Towns

Deckerville

Cemeteries

East Marion Cemetery
Mills Cemetery
Wright Cemetery

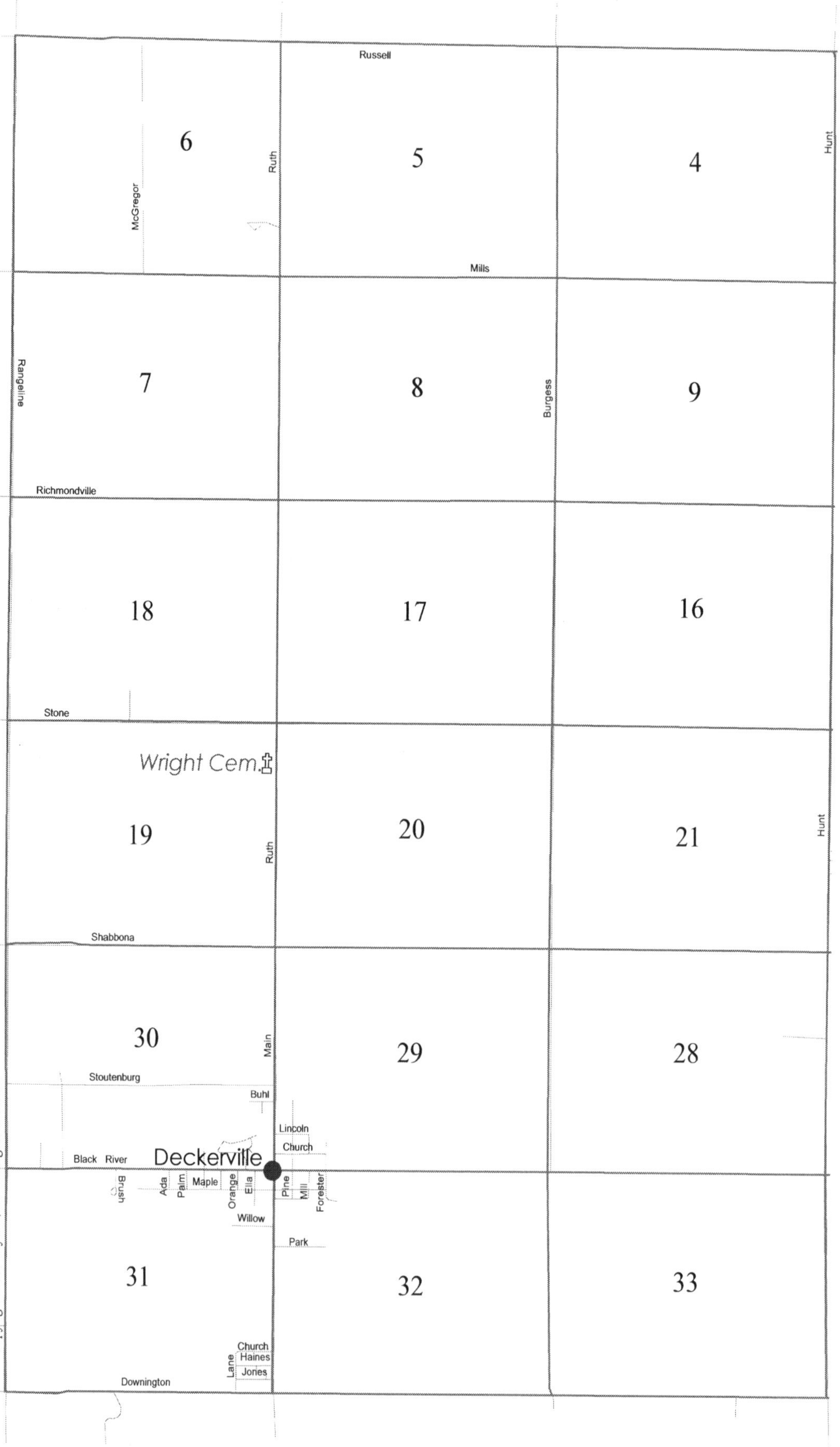

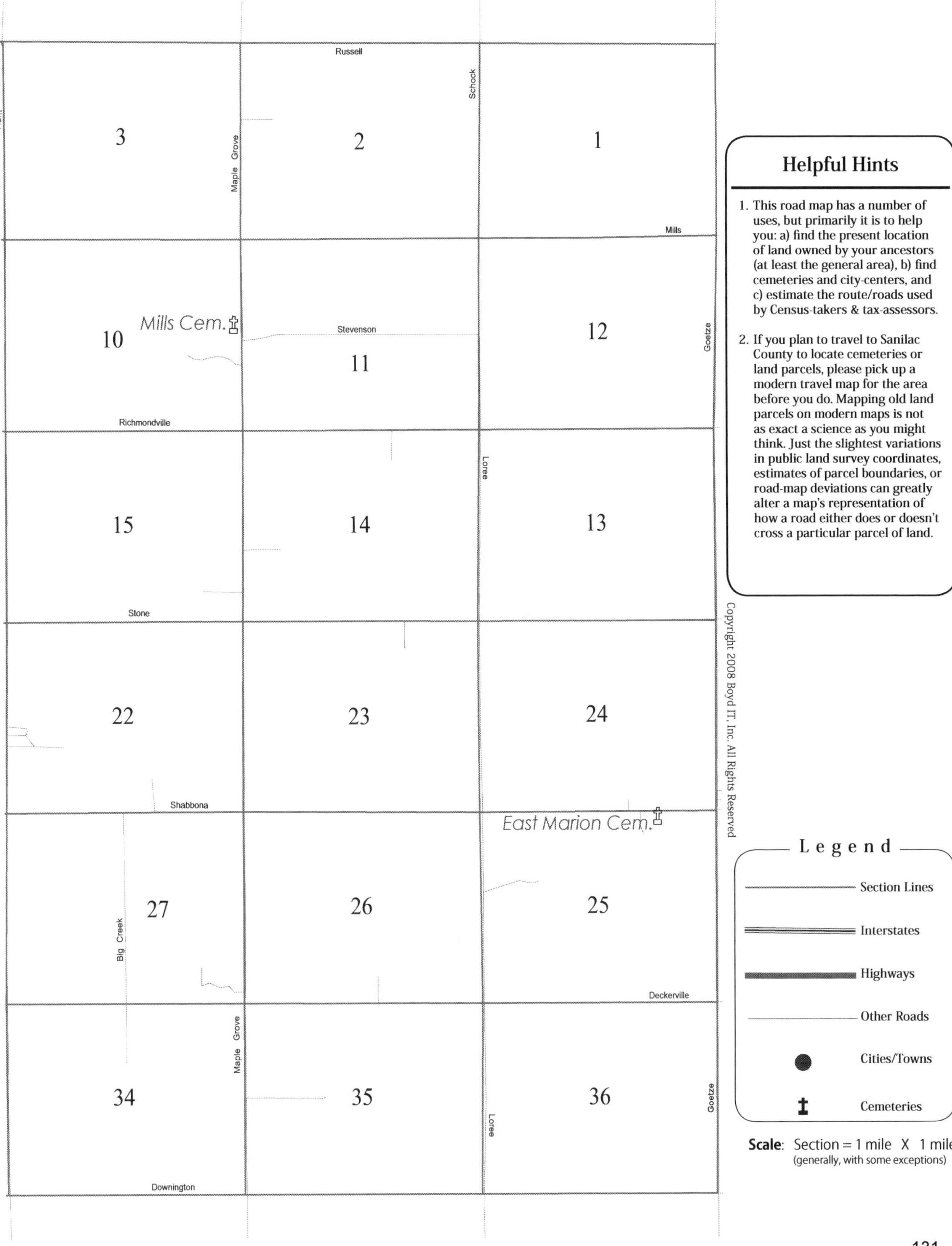
Russell
Schock
Maple Grove
Mills
Mills Cem.
Stevenson
Goetze
Richmondville
Loree
Stone
Shabbona
East Marion Cem.
Big Creek
Deckerville
Downington
3
2
1
10
11
12
15
14
13
22
23
24
27
26
25
34
35
36
Helpful Hints
1. This road map has a number of uses, but primarily it is to help you: a) find the present location of land owned by your ancestors (at least the general area), b) find cemeteries and city-centers, and c) estimate the route/roads used by Census-takers & tax-assessors.
2. If you plan to travel to Sanilac County to locate cemeteries or land parcels, please pick up a modern travel map for the area before you do. Mapping old land parcels on modern maps is not as exact a science as you might think. Just the slightest variations in public land survey coordinates, estimates of parcel boundaries, or road-map deviations can greatly alter a map's representation of how a road either does or doesn't cross a particular parcel of land.
Copyright 2008 Boyd IT, Inc. All Rights Reserved
Legend
Section Lines
Interstates
Highways
Other Roads
Cities/Towns
Cemeteries
Scale: Section = 1 mile X 1 mile
(generally, with some exceptions)

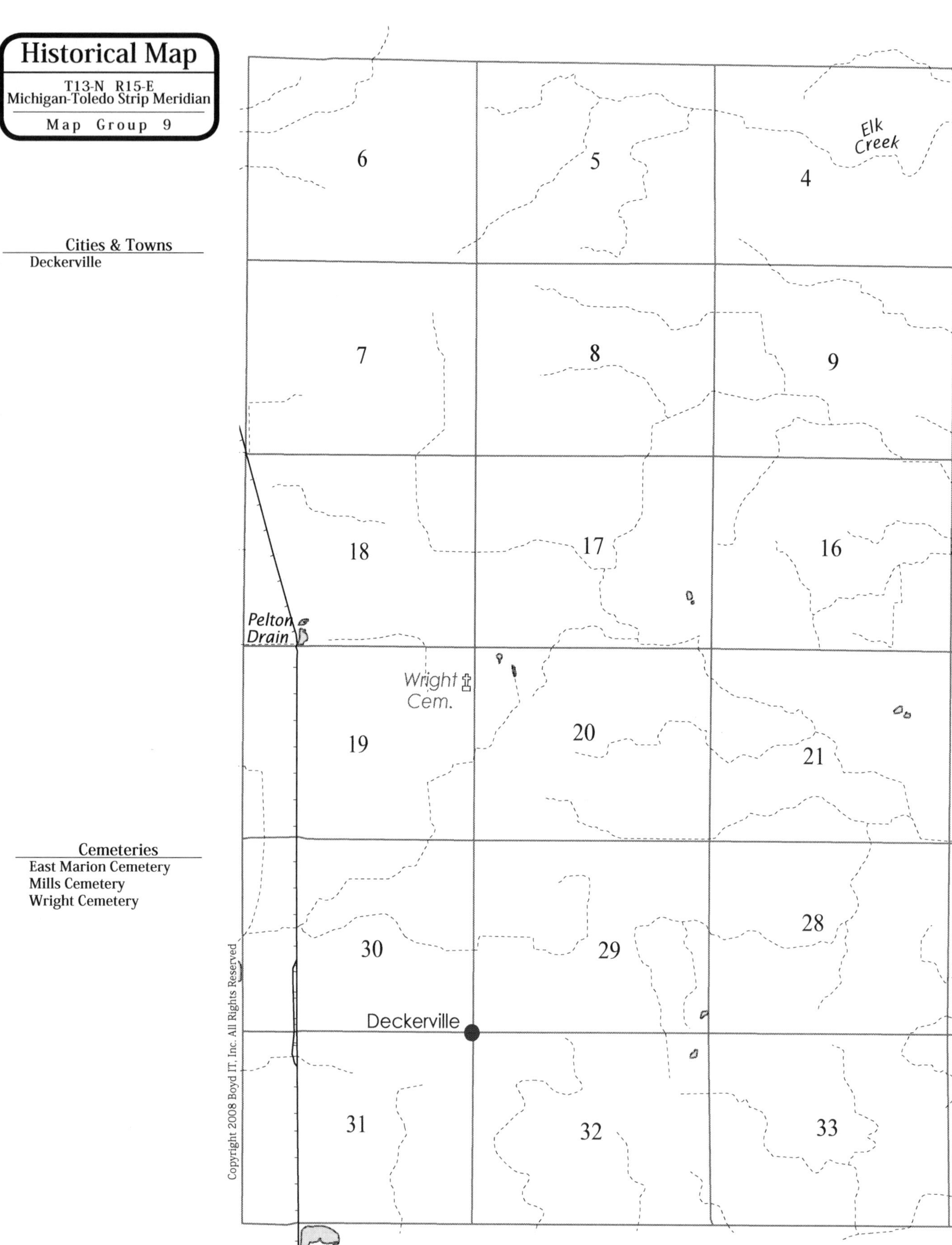
Historical Map
T13-N R15-E
Michigan-Toledo Strip Meridian
Map Group 9
Cities & Towns
Deckerville
Cemeteries
East Marion Cemetery
Mills Cemetery
Wright Cemetery
6
5
4
Elk Creek
7
8
9
18
17
16
Pelton Drain
Wright Cem.
19
20
21
30
29
28
Deckerville
31
32
33
Copyright 2008 Boyd IT, Inc. All Rights Reserved

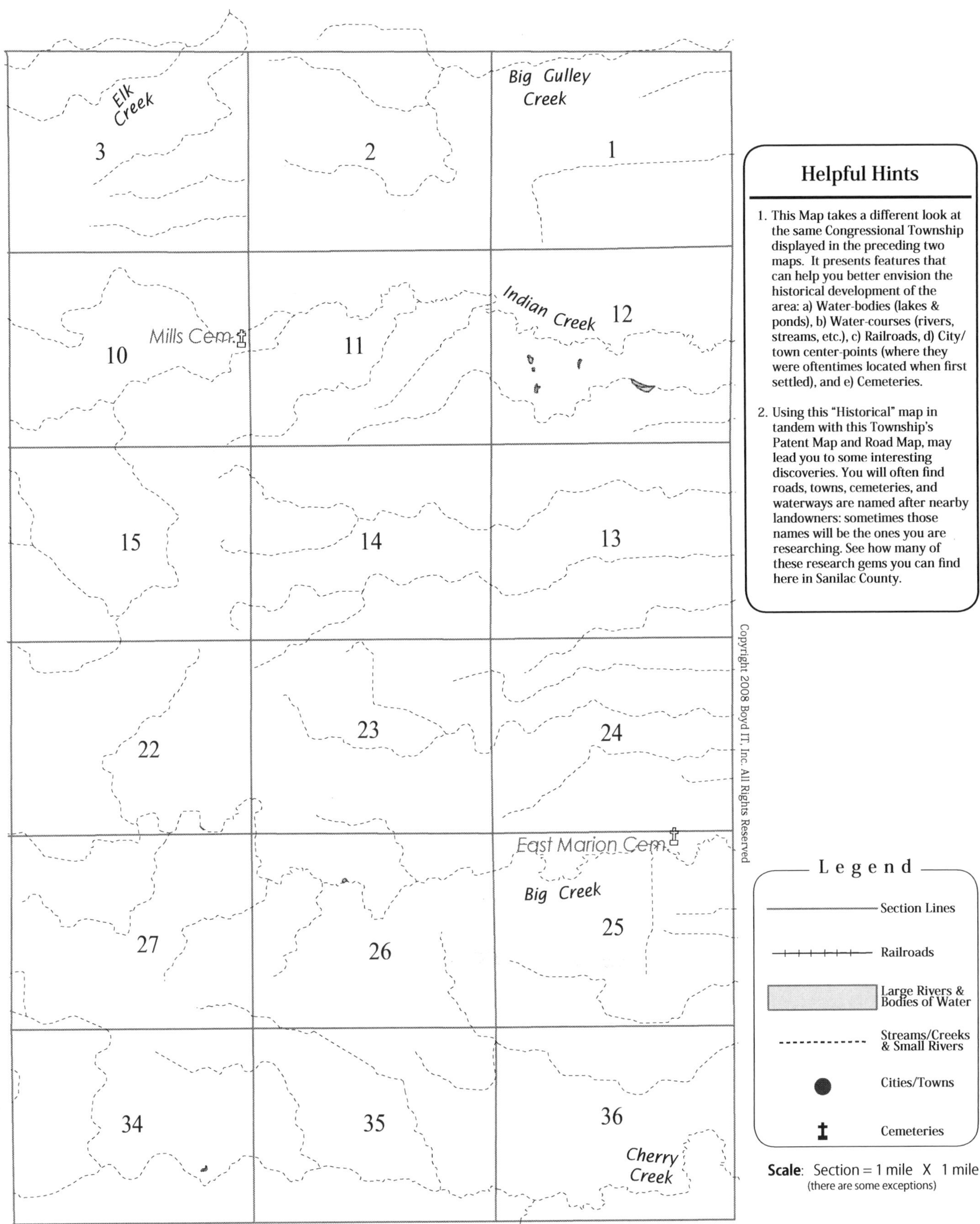

Helpful Hints

1. This Map takes a different look at the same Congressional Township displayed in the preceding two maps. It presents features that can help you better envision the historical development of the area: a) Water-bodies (lakes & ponds), b) Water-courses (rivers, streams, etc.), c) Railroads, d) City/town center-points (where they were oftentimes located when first settled), and e) Cemeteries.
2. Using this "Historical" map in tandem with this Township's Patent Map and Road Map, may lead you to some interesting discoveries. You will often find roads, towns, cemeteries, and waterways are named after nearby landowners: sometimes those names will be the ones you are researching. See how many of these research gems you can find here in Sanilac County.

Legend

- Section Lines
- Railroads
- Large Rivers & Bodies of Water
- Streams/Creeks & Small Rivers
- Cities/Towns
- Cemeteries

Scale: Section = 1 mile X 1 mile
(there are some exceptions)

Map Group 10: Index to Land Patents

Township 13-North Range 16-East (Michigan-Toledo Strip)

After you locate an individual in this Index, take note of the Section and Section Part then proceed to the Land Patent map on the pages immediately following. You should have no difficulty locating the corresponding parcel of land.

The "For More Info" Column will lead you to more information about the underlying Patents. See the *Legend* at right, and the "How to Use this Book" chapter, for more information.

LEGEND

"For More Info . . . " column

A = Authority (Legislative Act, See Appendix "A")
B = Block or Lot (location in Section unknown)
C = Cancelled Patent
F = Fractional Section
G = Group (Multi-Patentee Patent, see Appendix "C")
V = Overlaps another Parcel
R = Re-Issued (Parcel patented more than once)

(A & G items require you to look in the Appendixes referred to above. All other Letter-designations followed by a number require you to locate line-items in this index that possess the ID number found after the letter).

ID	Individual in Patent	Sec.	Sec. Part	Date Issued	Other Counties	For More Info . . .
1084	BALDWIN, James M	32	SWSW	1855-10-01		A1
1114	BALDWIN, Mary A	31	SESE	1855-10-01		A1
1079	BEACH, George	7	NE	1838-09-04		A1 G12
1080	" "	7	SW	1838-09-04		A1 G12
1079	BECKWITH, Alonzo S	7	NE	1838-09-04		A1 G12
1080	" "	7	SW	1838-09-04		A1 G12
1126	CROCKER, William A	28	W½NW	1837-08-16		A1 G25
1127	" "	29	NE	1837-08-16		A1 G25
1128	" "	29	NW	1837-08-16		A1 G25
1116	DICKINSON, Nathan	5	NE	1837-08-05		A1 F
1117	" "	5	NW	1837-08-05		A1 F
1118	" "	5	W½SW	1837-08-05		A1
1119	" "	6	SE	1837-08-05		A1
1120	" "	6	SW	1837-08-05		A1
1121	" "	7	NW	1837-08-05		A1
1079	" "	7	NE	1838-09-04		A1 G12
1080	" "	7	SW	1838-09-04		A1 G12
1073	DWIGHT, Francis	29	SE	1837-08-18		A1
1081	DWIGHT, George	19	SW	1837-08-18		A1
1094	EDMONDS, John W	18	NE	1837-08-16		A1
1095	" "	19	SE	1837-08-16		A1
1098	" "	7	SE	1837-08-16		A1
1093	" "	17	NW	1837-08-18		A1 F
1096	" "	30	NE	1837-08-18		A1 F
1097	" "	30	NW	1837-08-18		A1 F
1072	HAGGERTY, Clements C	28	SW	1837-08-18		A1
1085	HURD, Jarvis	32	E½NW	1837-11-02		A1
1086	" "	32	E½SW	1837-11-02		A1
1087	" "	32	NE	1837-11-02		A1
1088	" "	32	SE	1837-11-02		A1
1089	" "	33	SE	1837-11-02		A1 F
1090	" "	33	SW	1837-11-02		A1 F
1091	" "	33	W½NW	1837-11-02		A1 F
1092	" "	34		1837-11-02		A1 F
1101	LYON, Lucius	17	NE	1839-04-10		A1 G49
1102	" "	17	SE	1839-04-10		A1 G49
1103	" "	17	SW	1839-04-10		A1 G49
1104	" "	18	NW	1839-04-10		A1 G49
1105	" "	18	SE	1839-04-10		A1 G49
1106	" "	18	SW	1839-04-10		A1 G49
1107	" "	19	NE	1839-04-10		A1 G49
1108	" "	19	NW	1839-04-10		A1 G49
1109	" "	20		1839-04-10		A1 G49
1110	" "	21		1839-04-10		A1 G49 F
1111	" "	8	NE	1839-04-10		A1 G49
1112	" "	8	SE	1839-04-10		A1 G49

ID	Individual in Patent	Sec.	Sec. Part	Date Issued	Other Counties	For More Info . . .
1113	LYON, Lucius (Cont'd)	9		1839-04-10		A1 G49 F
1082	MERRIMAN, Hiram	31	NESE	1852-02-10		A1
1083	" "	31	NWSE	1852-02-10		A1
1101	PARKER, Daniel	17	NE	1839-04-10		A1 G49
1102	" "	17	SE	1839-04-10		A1 G49
1103	" "	17	SW	1839-04-10		A1 G49
1104	" "	18	NW	1839-04-10		A1 G49
1105	" "	18	SE	1839-04-10		A1 G49
1106	" "	18	SW	1839-04-10		A1 G49
1107	" "	19	NE	1839-04-10		A1 G49
1108	" "	19	NW	1839-04-10		A1 G49
1109	" "	20		1839-04-10		A1 G49
1110	" "	21		1839-04-10		A1 G49 F
1111	" "	8	NE	1839-04-10		A1 G49
1112	" "	8	SE	1839-04-10		A1 G49
1113	" "	9		1839-04-10		A1 G49 F
1122	RUMNEY, Robert	33	E½NW	1837-08-18		A1
1115	SCOTT, Moses W	28	SE	1837-08-12		A1
1074	STEEVENS, Frederick H	28	E½NW	1837-08-18		A1 F
1075	" "	28	NE	1837-08-18		A1 F
1076	" "	33	NE	1837-08-18		A1 F
1077	" "	5	E½SW	1837-08-18		A1 F
1078	" "	5	SE	1837-08-18		A1
1123	SWIFT, Samuel	29	SW	1837-08-18		A1
1124	" "	30	SE	1837-08-18		A1
1125	" "	30	SW	1837-08-18		A1
1126	WALDO, William B	28	W½NW	1837-08-16		A1 G25
1127	" "	29	NE	1837-08-16		A1 G25
1128	" "	29	NW	1837-08-16		A1 G25
1099	WHITE, Jonathan R	8	NW	1837-08-16		A1
1100	" "	8	SW	1837-08-16		A1

Patent Map

T13-N R16-E
Michigan-Toledo Strip Meridian

Map Group 10

Township Statistics

Parcels Mapped	:	57
Number of Patents	:	19
Number of Individuals	:	20
Patentees Identified	:	17
Number of Surnames	:	18
Multi-Patentee Parcels	:	18
Oldest Patent Date	:	8/5/1837
Most Recent Patent	:	10/1/1855
Block/Lot Parcels	:	0
Parcels Re - Issued	:	0
Parcels that Overlap	:	0
Cities and Towns	:	1
Cemeteries	:	0

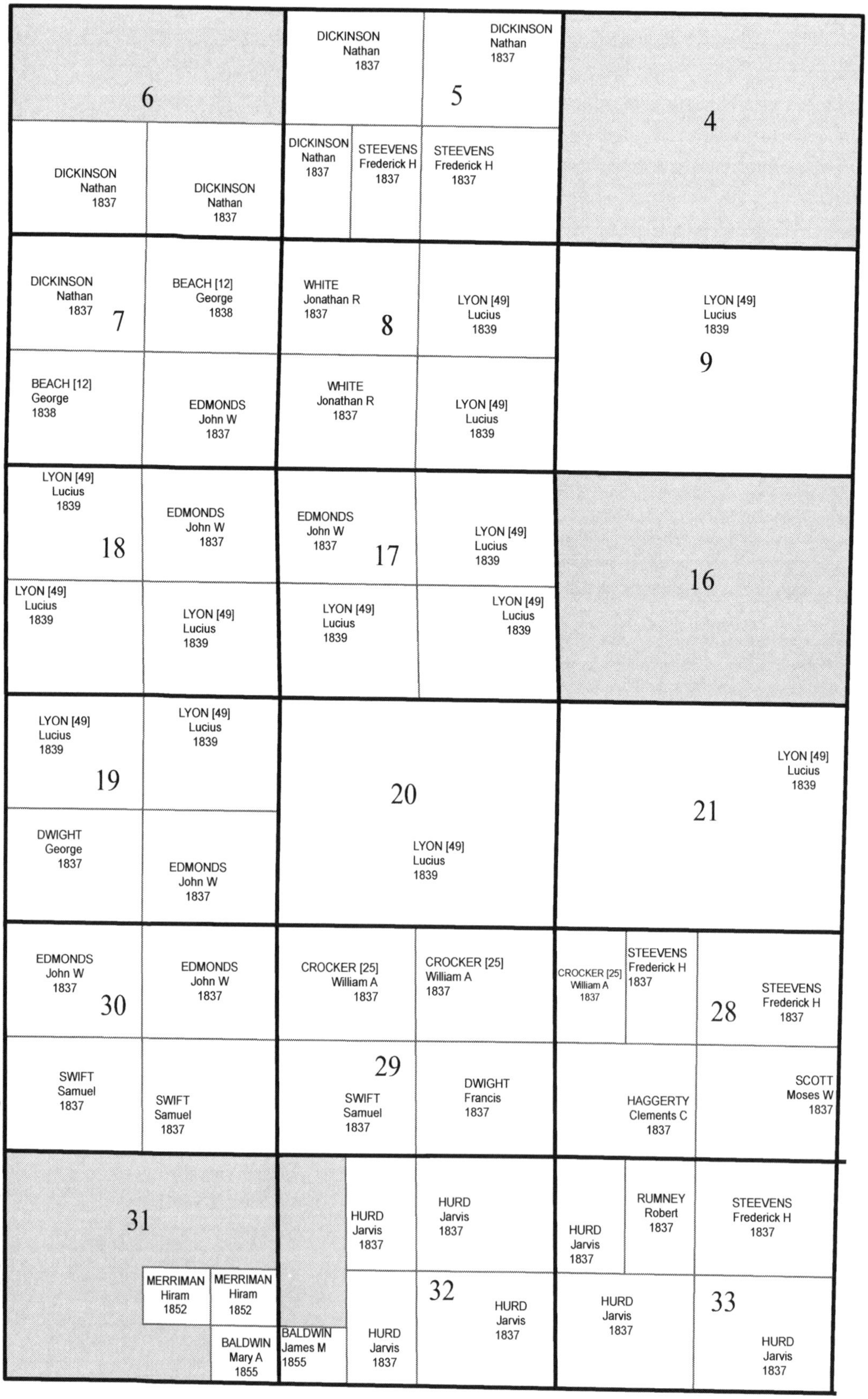

6
DICKINSON Nathan 1837
DICKINSON Nathan 1837

5
DICKINSON Nathan 1837
DICKINSON Nathan 1837
DICKINSON Nathan 1837
STEEVENS Frederick H 1837
STEEVENS Frederick H 1837

4

7
DICKINSON Nathan 1837
BEACH [12] George 1838
BEACH [12] George 1838
EDMONDS John W 1837

8
WHITE Jonathan R 1837
LYON [49] Lucius 1839
WHITE Jonathan R 1837
LYON [49] Lucius 1839

9
LYON [49] Lucius 1839

18
LYON [49] Lucius 1839
EDMONDS John W 1837
LYON [49] Lucius 1839
LYON [49] Lucius 1839

17
EDMONDS John W 1837
LYON [49] Lucius 1839
LYON [49] Lucius 1839
LYON [49] Lucius 1839

16

19
LYON [49] Lucius 1839
LYON [49] Lucius 1839
DWIGHT George 1837
EDMONDS John W 1837

20
LYON [49] Lucius 1839

21
LYON [49] Lucius 1839

30
EDMONDS John W 1837
EDMONDS John W 1837
SWIFT Samuel 1837
SWIFT Samuel 1837

29
CROCKER [25] William A 1837
CROCKER [25] William A 1837
SWIFT Samuel 1837
DWIGHT Francis 1837

28
CROCKER [25] William A 1837
STEEVENS Frederick H 1837
STEEVENS Frederick H 1837
HAGGERTY Clements C 1837
SCOTT Moses W 1837

31
MERRIMAN Hiram 1852
MERRIMAN Hiram 1852
BALDWIN Mary A 1855

32
BALDWIN James M 1855
HURD Jarvis 1837
HURD Jarvis 1837
HURD Jarvis 1837
HURD Jarvis 1837

33
HURD Jarvis 1837
RUMNEY Robert 1837
STEEVENS Frederick H 1837
HURD Jarvis 1837
HURD Jarvis 1837

Helpful Hints

1. This Map's INDEX can be found on the preceding pages.
2. Refer to Map "C" to see where this Township lies within Sanilac County, Michigan.
3. Numbers within square brackets [ ] denote a multi-patentee land parcel (multi-owner). Refer to Appendix "C" for a full list of members in this group.
4. Areas that look to be crowded with Patentees usually indicate multiple sales of the same parcel (Re-issues) or Overlapping parcels. See this Township's Index for an explanation of these and other circumstances that might explain "odd" groupings of Patentees on this map.

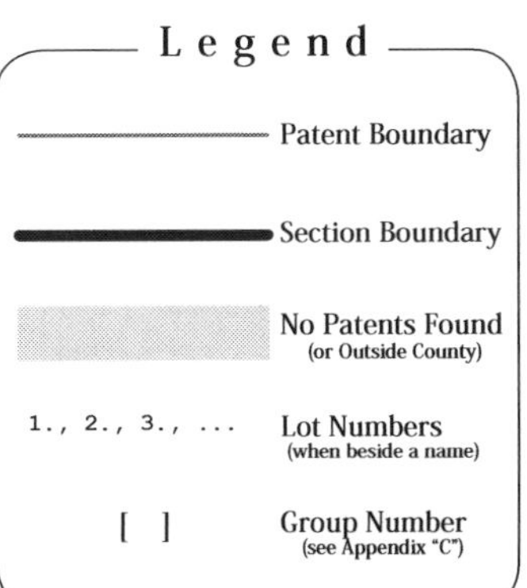

Scale: Section = 1 mile X 1 mile
(generally, with some exceptions)

34

HURD
Jarvis
1837

Road Map

T13-N R16-E
Michigan-Toledo Strip Meridian

Map Group 10

Cities & Towns

Richmondville

Cemeteries

None

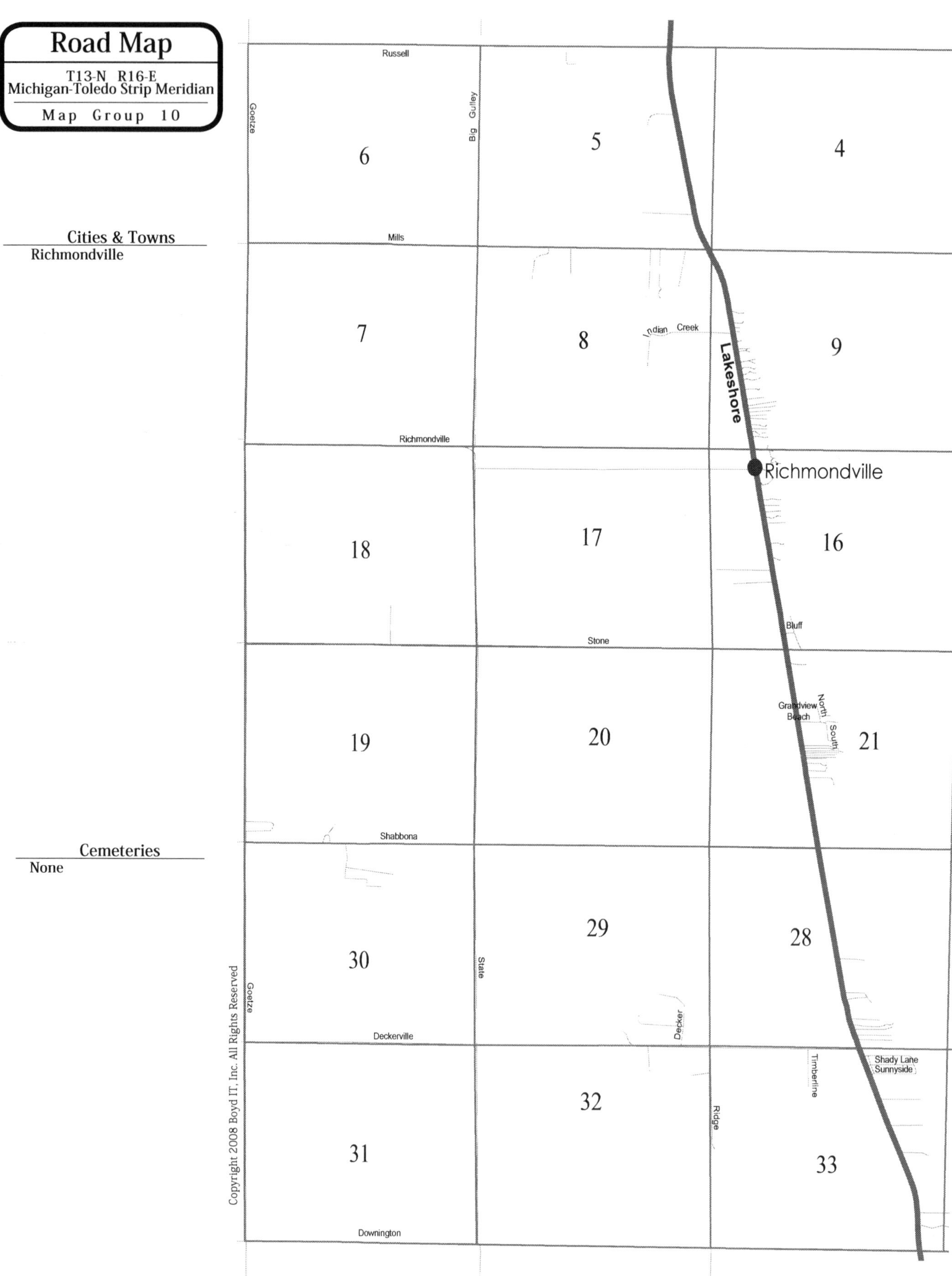

Helpful Hints

1. This road map has a number of uses, but primarily it is to help you: a) find the present location of land owned by your ancestors (at least the general area), b) find cemeteries and city-centers, and c) estimate the route/roads used by Census-takers & tax-assessors.

2. If you plan to travel to Sanilac County to locate cemeteries or land parcels, please pick up a modern travel map for the area before you do. Mapping old land parcels on modern maps is not as exact a science as you might think. Just the slightest variations in public land survey coordinates, estimates of parcel boundaries, or road-map deviations can greatly alter a map's representation of how a road either does or doesn't cross a particular parcel of land.

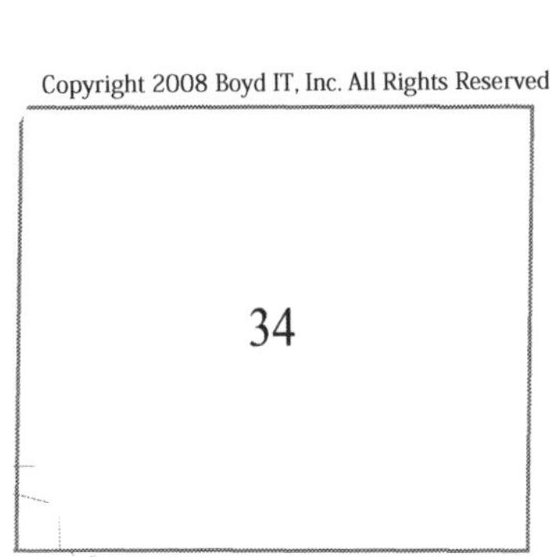

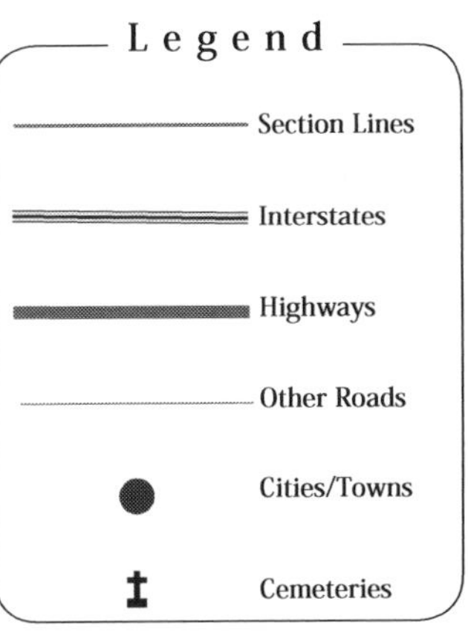

Scale: Section = 1 mile X 1 mile
(generally, with some exceptions)

Historical Map

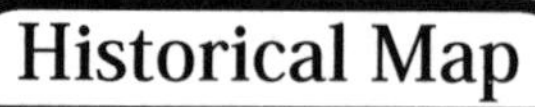

T13-N R16-E
Michigan-Toledo Strip Meridian

Map Group 10

Cities & Towns

Richmondville

Cemeteries

None

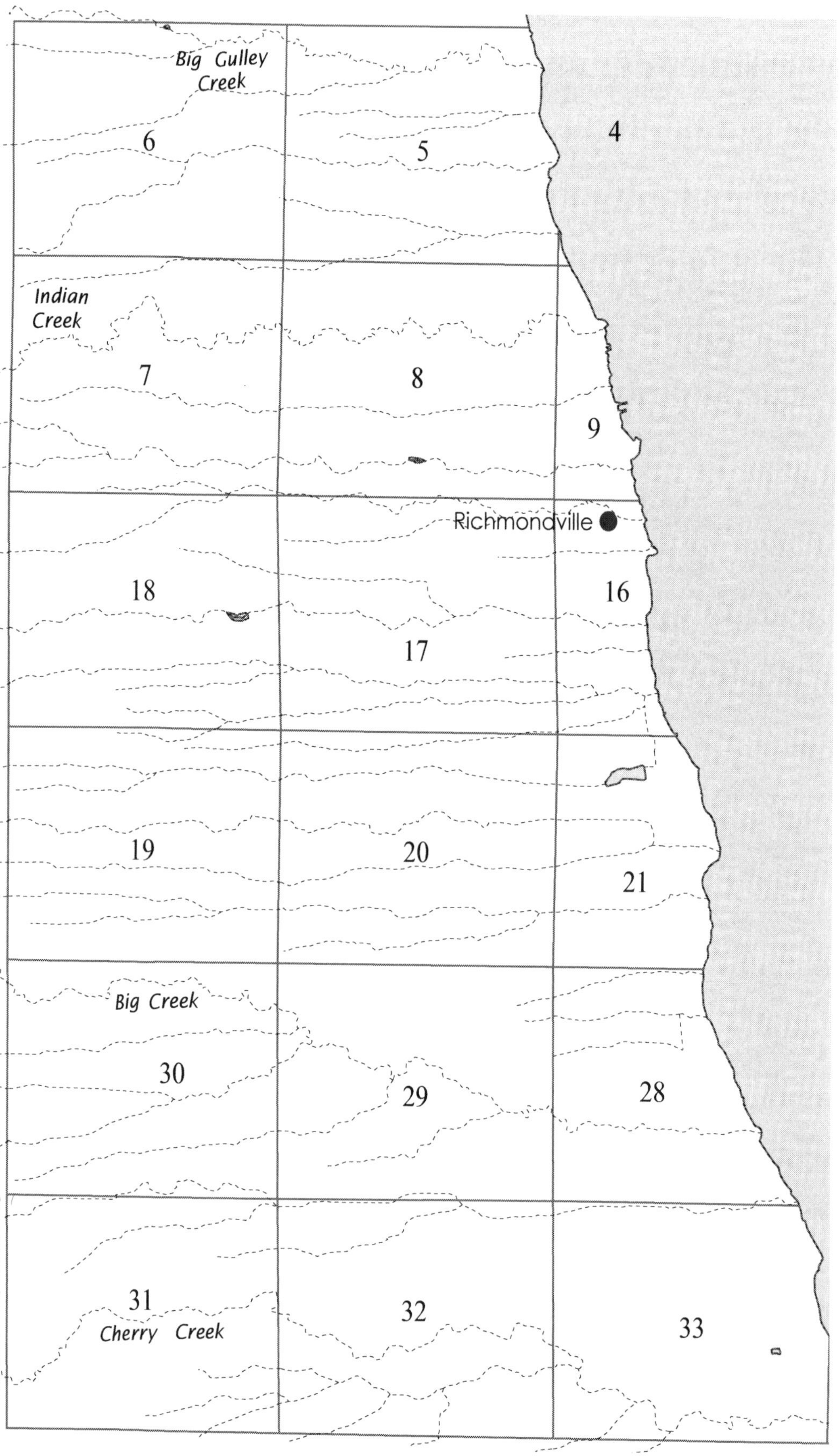

Lake Huron

34

Helpful Hints

1. This Map takes a different look at the same Congressional Township displayed in the preceding two maps. It presents features that can help you better envision the historical development of the area: a) Water-bodies (lakes & ponds), b) Water-courses (rivers, streams, etc.), c) Railroads, d) City/town center-points (where they were oftentimes located when first settled), and e) Cemeteries.
2. Using this "Historical" map in tandem with this Township's Patent Map and Road Map, may lead you to some interesting discoveries. You will often find roads, towns, cemeteries, and waterways are named after nearby landowners: sometimes those names will be the ones you are researching. See how many of these research gems you can find here in Sanilac County.

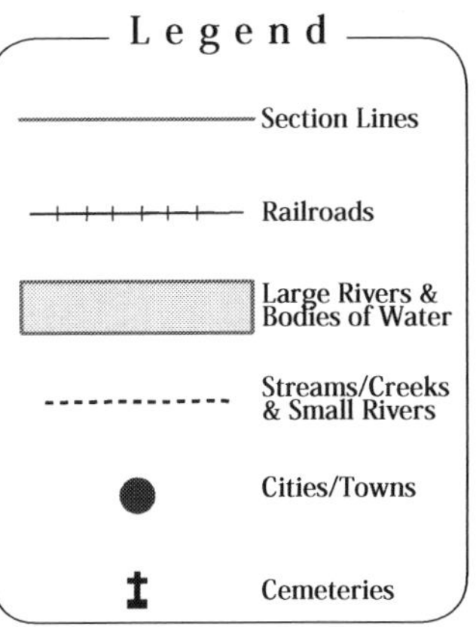

Scale: Section = 1 mile X 1 mile
(there are some exceptions)

Map Group 11: Index to Land Patents

Township 12-North Range 12-East (Michigan-Toledo Strip)

After you locate an individual in this Index, take note of the Section and Section Part then proceed to the Land Patent map on the pages immediately following. You should have no difficulty locating the corresponding parcel of land.

The "For More Info" Column will lead you to more information about the underlying Patents. See the *Legend* at right, and the "How to Use this Book" chapter, for more information.

LEGEND

"For More Info . . . " column

- **A** = Authority (Legislative Act, See Appendix "A")
- **B** = Block or Lot (location in Section unknown)
- **C** = Cancelled Patent
- **F** = Fractional Section
- **G** = Group (Multi-Patentee Patent, see Appendix "C")
- **V** = Overlaps another Parcel
- **R** = Re-Issued (Parcel patented more than once)

(A & G items require you to look in the Appendixes referred to above. All other Letter-designations followed by a number require you to locate line-items in this index that possess the ID number found after the letter).

ID	Individual in Patent	Sec.	Sec. Part	Date Issued	Other Counties	For More Info . . .
1162	ALCORN, John K	10	NWNE	1879-02-18		A1
1191	BASHFORD, Solomon A	12	NESE	1861-12-03		A1
1199	BISHOP, William J	8	E½NW	1877-05-15		A1
1159	BROWN, John	17	N½SE	1876-12-01		A2
1160	" "	17	S½NE	1876-12-01		A2
1129	BUCHANAN, Alexander	13	NESE	1855-10-01		A1 G14
1198	BURT, Wellington R	11	NWSW	1872-04-15		A1
1178	CASLER, Joshua	33	NWSE	1906-02-16		A2
1190	CAVEN, Robert	32	S½SW	1859-05-09		A1
1140	COUSE, Edward	8	NWNW	1872-08-10		A1
1156	CURTIS, Jay S	10	NENE	1859-10-10		A1
1157	" "	14	SESW	1859-10-10		A1
1158	" "	23	NESE	1859-10-10		A1
1143	DAVIS, Frank	10	NWSW	1883-01-20		A1
1148	FIELD, James	18	NWSE	1896-02-05		A2
1149	" "	18	SWNE	1896-02-05		A2
1186	FOX, Peter	9	E½SE	1877-03-20		A2
1187	" "	9	S½NE	1877-03-20		A2
1150	HAY, James	3	NENE	1855-10-01		A1 F
1144	HOWELL, George	13	NENE	1883-06-07		A2
1142	JOHNSON, Enos	12	E½NE	1875-09-01		A2
1139	KELLEY, David	1	W½NW	1891-10-13		A2
1163	KELLY, John	10	S½SE	1885-01-30		A1
1164	" "	10	S½SW	1885-01-30		A1
1151	KIPP, James	6	SW	1875-02-05		A2
1165	LAMB, John M	17	S½SE	1868-08-20		A1
1167	" "	25	NESE	1868-08-20		A1
1169	" "	30	W½SW	1868-08-20		A1 F
1171	" "	33	SWSE	1868-08-20		A1
1166	" "	20	NWNE	1869-11-15		A1
1170	" "	31	NENE	1869-11-15		A1
1168	" "	28	NWNE	1870-09-20		A1
1152	LEONARD, James	10	NESW	1867-07-01		A1
1153	" "	10	NWSE	1867-07-01		A1
1154	" "	11	NESW	1867-07-01		A1
1179	MANWARING, Joshua	33	NENW	1869-11-15		A1
1131	MCALPINE, Andrew	31	NESW	1877-04-05		A2
1132	" "	31	W½NW	1877-04-05		A2
1133	" "	31	W½SW	1877-04-05		A2
1200	MCKIE, William	3	NESW	1852-02-10		A1
1201	" "	3	NWSE	1852-02-10		A1
1172	MCPHEE, John	1	S½SE	1880-12-10		A2
1173	" "	1	S½SW	1880-12-10		A2
1174	MILLER, John	28	E½NE	1860-05-01		A1
1175	" "	28	SWNE	1860-05-01		A1
1206	MILLS, Williard	24	NWNW	1862-02-01		A1

ID	Individual in Patent	Sec.	Sec. Part	Date Issued	Other Counties	For More Info . . .
1194	MOORE, Tacy	35	SWSW	1867-07-01		A1
1136	MOSHIER, David H	7	SESW	1873-04-25		A2 F
1137	" "	7	SWSE	1873-04-25		A2 F
1138	" "	7	W½SW	1873-04-25		A2
1195	MOSHIER, Thomas	17	E½SW	1876-01-20		A2
1196	" "	17	SENW	1876-01-20		A2
1197	" "	17	SWSW	1876-01-20		A2
1202	MOSHIER, William	17	NWSW	1873-04-25		A2
1203	" "	17	SWNW	1873-04-25		A2
1204	" "	18	NESE	1873-04-25		A2
1205	" "	18	SENE	1873-04-25		A2
1180	PACE, Josiah	14	NESE	1862-02-01		A1
1176	PHILIPS, John	10	SENE	1872-04-15		A1
1181	PRATT, Levi	12	N½SW	1877-07-20		A2
1182	" "	12	NWSE	1877-07-20		A2
1135	SCHAFER, Christian	36	SW	1859-10-10		A1
1134	SILVERTHORN, Anson	18	NW	1883-06-07		A2 F
1183	SMITH, Oliver	32	N½SW	1860-05-01		A1
1184	" "	32	NW	1860-05-01		A1
1185	" "	32	S½NE	1860-05-01		A1
1188	SMITH, Philip	31	SESW	1860-05-01		A1
1189	" "	31	SWSE	1860-05-01		A1
1161	SOMMERHALDER, John J	35	NESE	1862-05-15		A1
1130	SOPER, Alfred	35	NWSE	1885-04-15		A1
1141	STEEL, Elias	7	NWNE	1871-11-15		A1
1129	STILSON, John	13	NESE	1855-10-01		A1 G14
1177	SWINSTON, John	31	NWSE	1872-11-05		A1
1155	TWIST, James M	34	SESE	1856-01-10		A1
1192	WALLIS, T O	14	E½NE	1864-01-05		A1
1193	" "	30	NENE	1864-01-05		A1
1145	YOUNG, George	17	NWNW	1873-04-25		A2
1146	" "	18	N½NE	1873-04-25		A2
1147	" "	7	SESE	1873-04-25		A2

Patent Map

T12-N R12-E
Michigan-Toledo Strip Meridian

Map Group 11

Township Statistics

Parcels Mapped	:	78
Number of Patents	:	56
Number of Individuals	:	46
Patentees Identified	:	45
Number of Surnames	:	43
Multi-Patentee Parcels	:	1
Oldest Patent Date	:	2/10/1852
Most Recent Patent	:	2/16/1906
Block/Lot Parcels	:	0
Parcels Re - Issued	:	0
Parcels that Overlap	:	0
Cities and Towns	:	2
Cemeteries	:	2

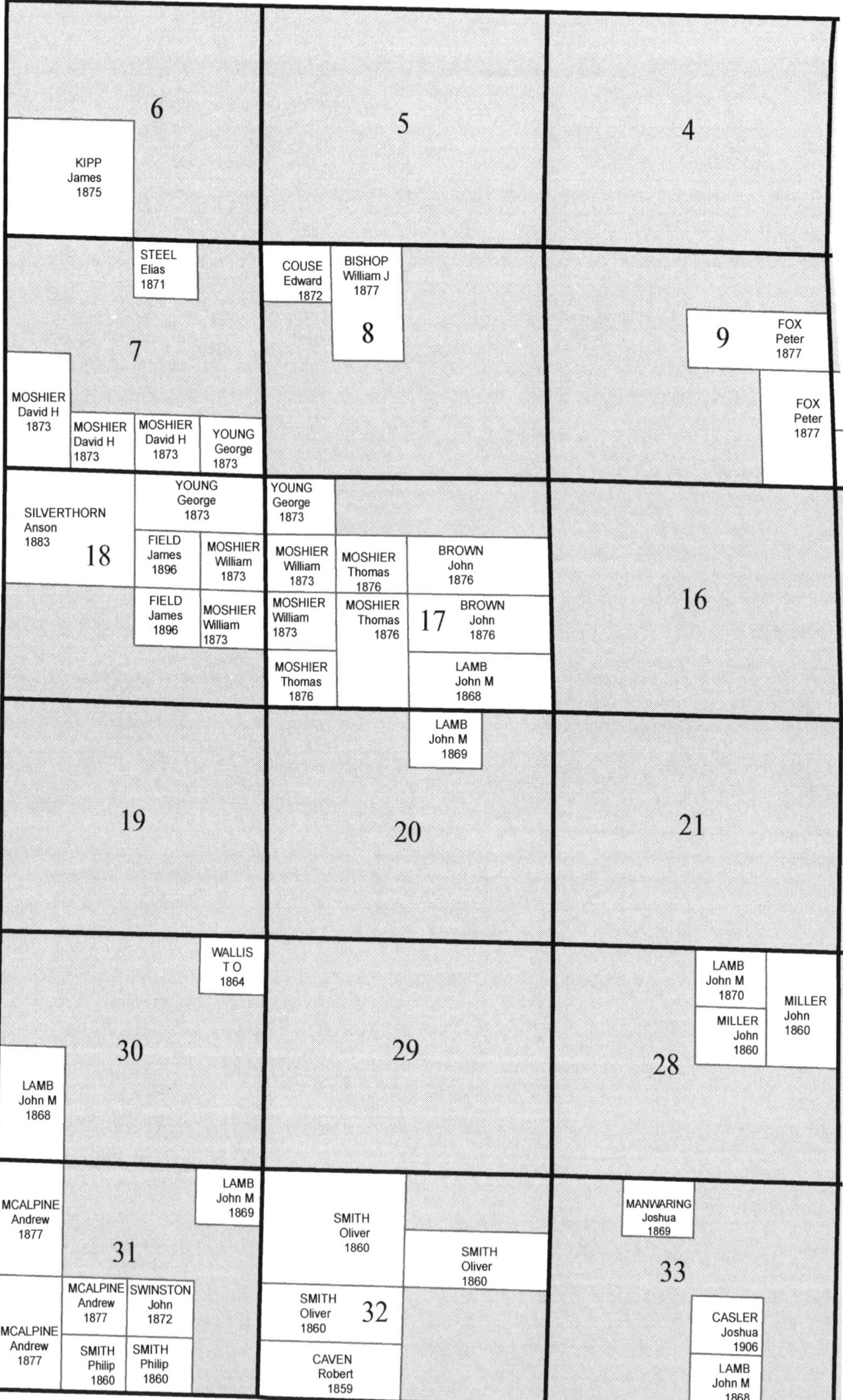

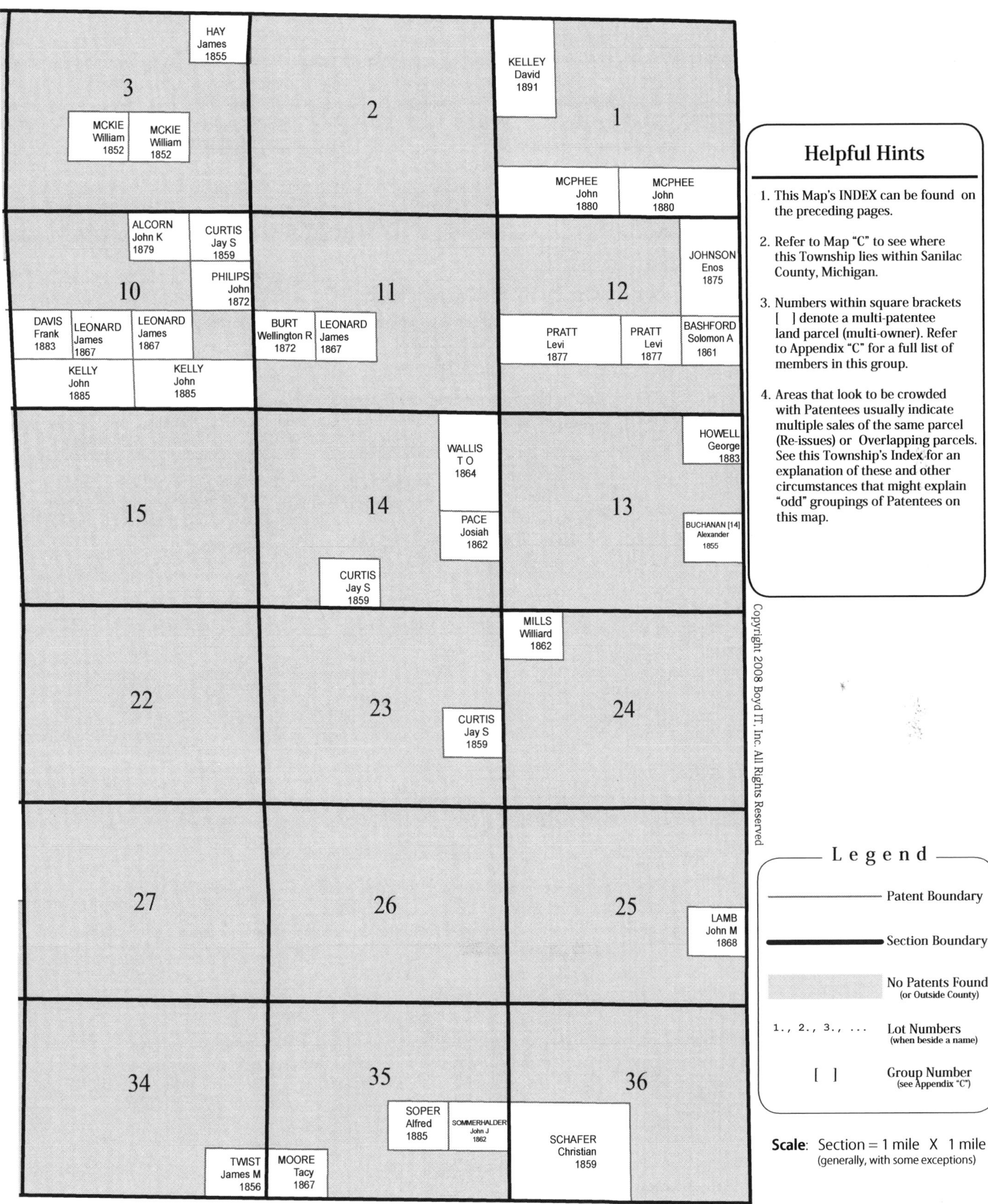

Helpful Hints

1. This Map's INDEX can be found on the preceding pages.
2. Refer to Map "C" to see where this Township lies within Sanilac County, Michigan.
3. Numbers within square brackets [ ] denote a multi-patentee land parcel (multi-owner). Refer to Appendix "C" for a full list of members in this group.
4. Areas that look to be crowded with Patentees usually indicate multiple sales of the same parcel (Re-issues) or Overlapping parcels. See this Township's Index for an explanation of these and other circumstances that might explain "odd" groupings of Patentees on this map.

Legend

- Patent Boundary
- Section Boundary
- No Patents Found (or Outside County)
- 1., 2., 3., ... Lot Numbers (when beside a name)
- [ ] Group Number (see Appendix "C")

Scale: Section = 1 mile X 1 mile (generally, with some exceptions)

Road Map

T12-N R12-E
Michigan-Toledo Strip Meridian

Map Group 11

Cities & Towns

Decker
Hemans

Cemeteries

Johnson Cemetery
Moshier Cemetery

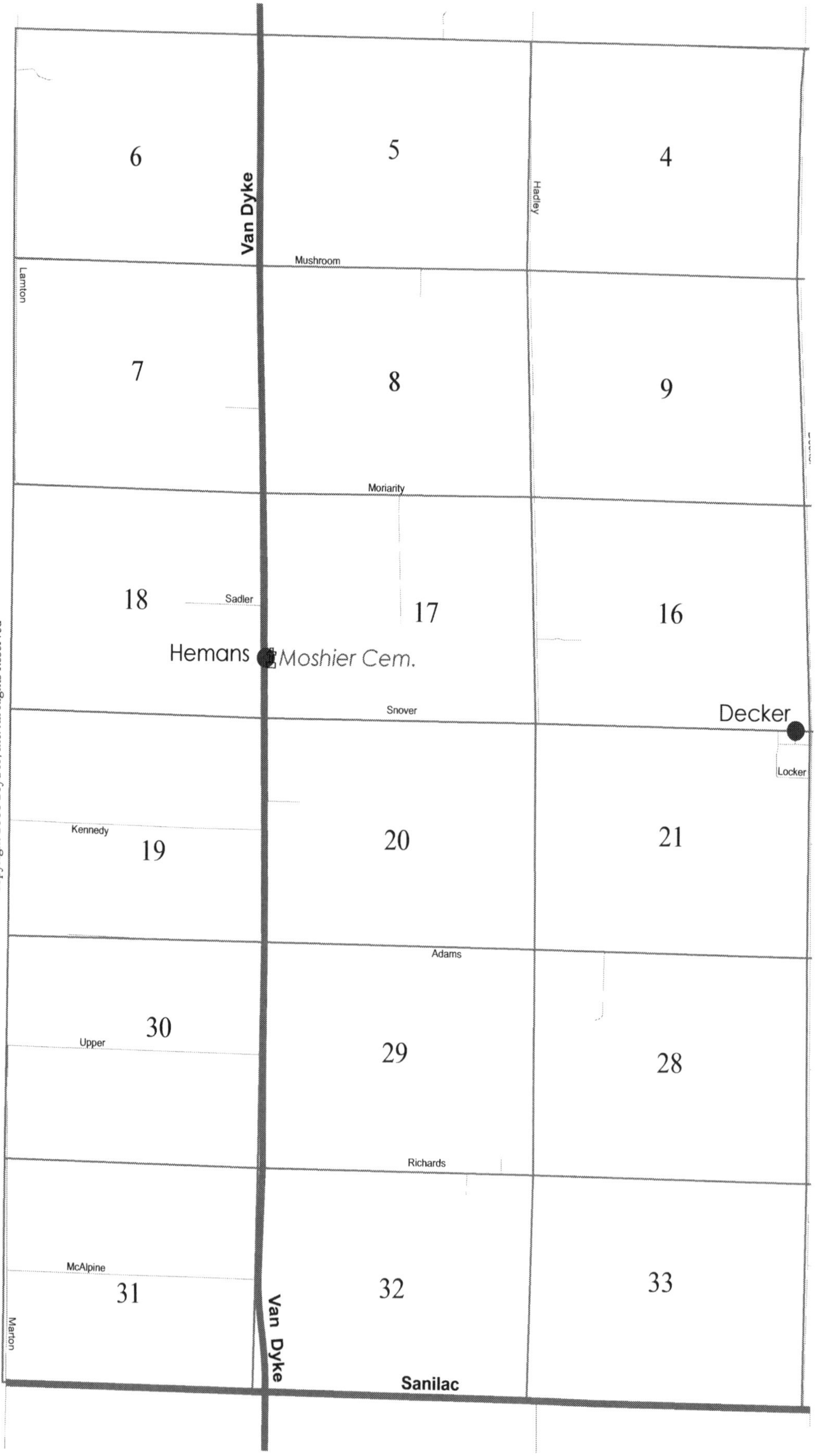

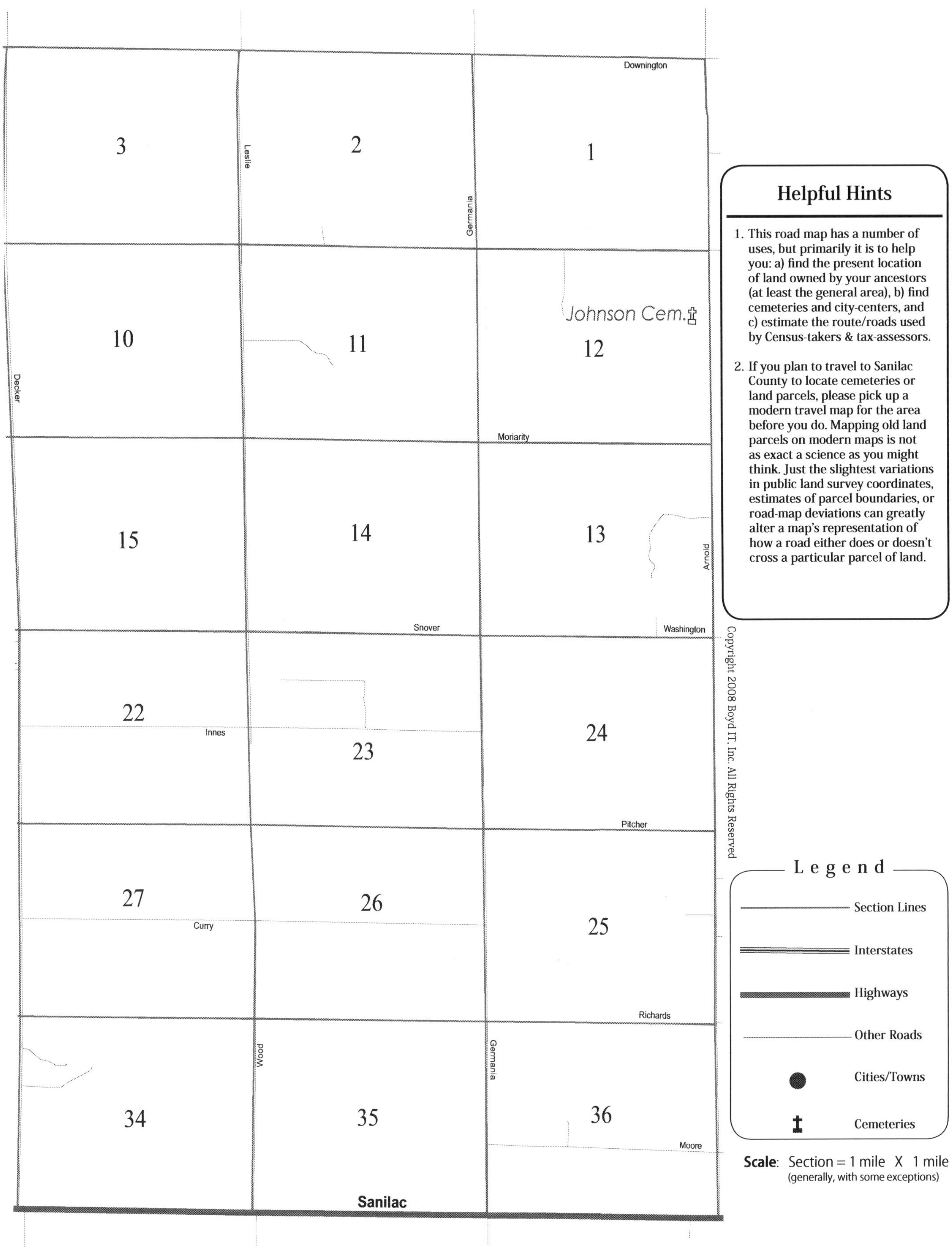

Helpful Hints

1. This road map has a number of uses, but primarily it is to help you: a) find the present location of land owned by your ancestors (at least the general area), b) find cemeteries and city-centers, and c) estimate the route/roads used by Census-takers & tax-assessors.
2. If you plan to travel to Sanilac County to locate cemeteries or land parcels, please pick up a modern travel map for the area before you do. Mapping old land parcels on modern maps is not as exact a science as you might think. Just the slightest variations in public land survey coordinates, estimates of parcel boundaries, or road-map deviations can greatly alter a map's representation of how a road either does or doesn't cross a particular parcel of land.

Legend

- Section Lines
- Interstates
- Highways
- Other Roads
- Cities/Towns
- Cemeteries

Scale: Section = 1 mile X 1 mile
(generally, with some exceptions)

Historical Map

T12-N R12-E
Michigan-Toledo Strip Meridian

Map Group 11

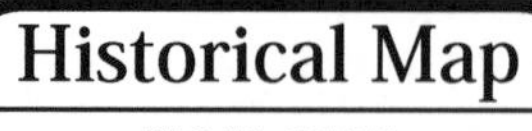

Cities & Towns

Decker
Hemans

Cemeteries

Johnson Cemetery
Moshier Cemetery

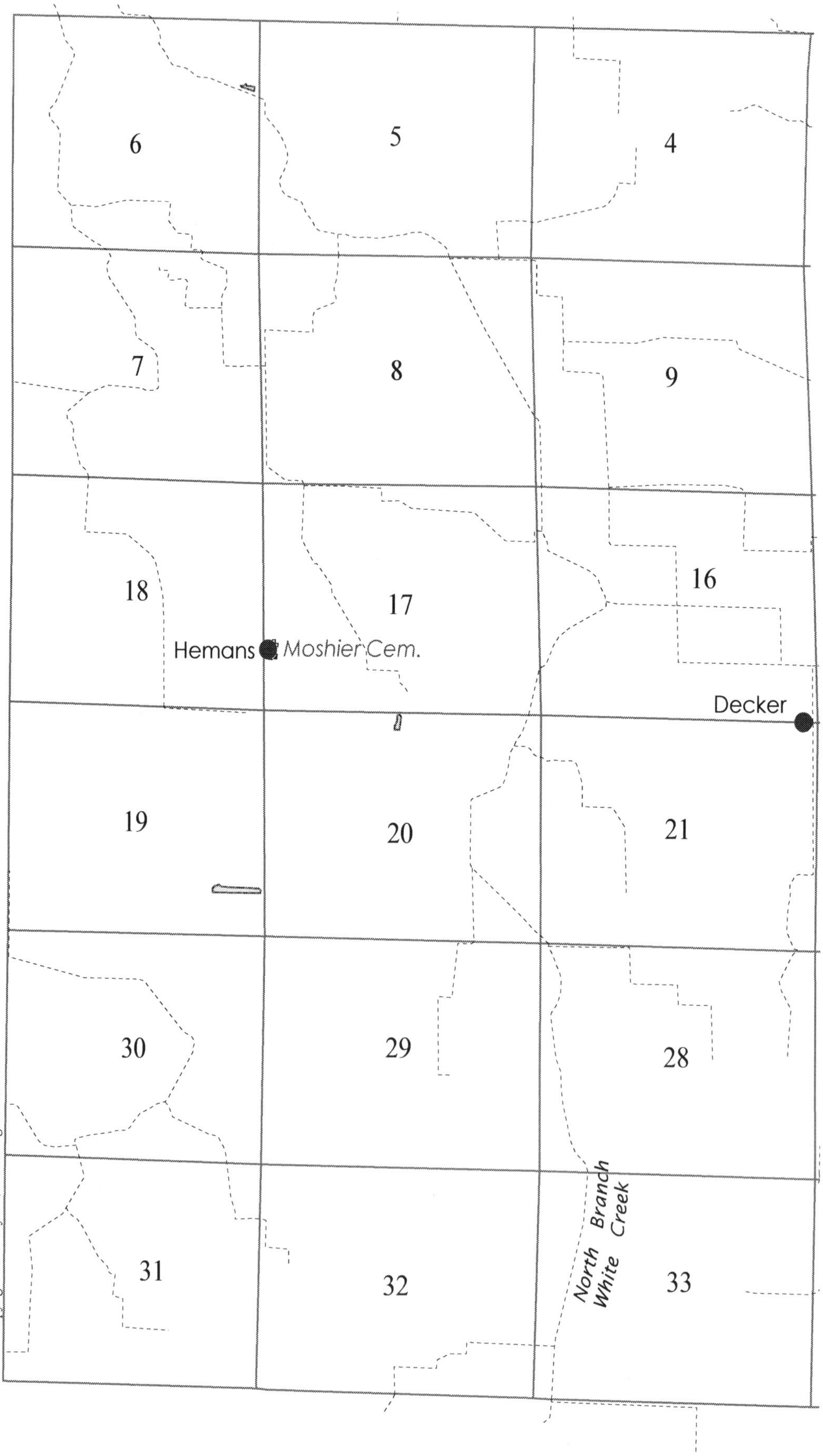

6
5
4
7
8
9
18
17
16
Hemans
Moshier Cem.
Decker
19
20
21
30
29
28
31
32
33
North Branch White Creek

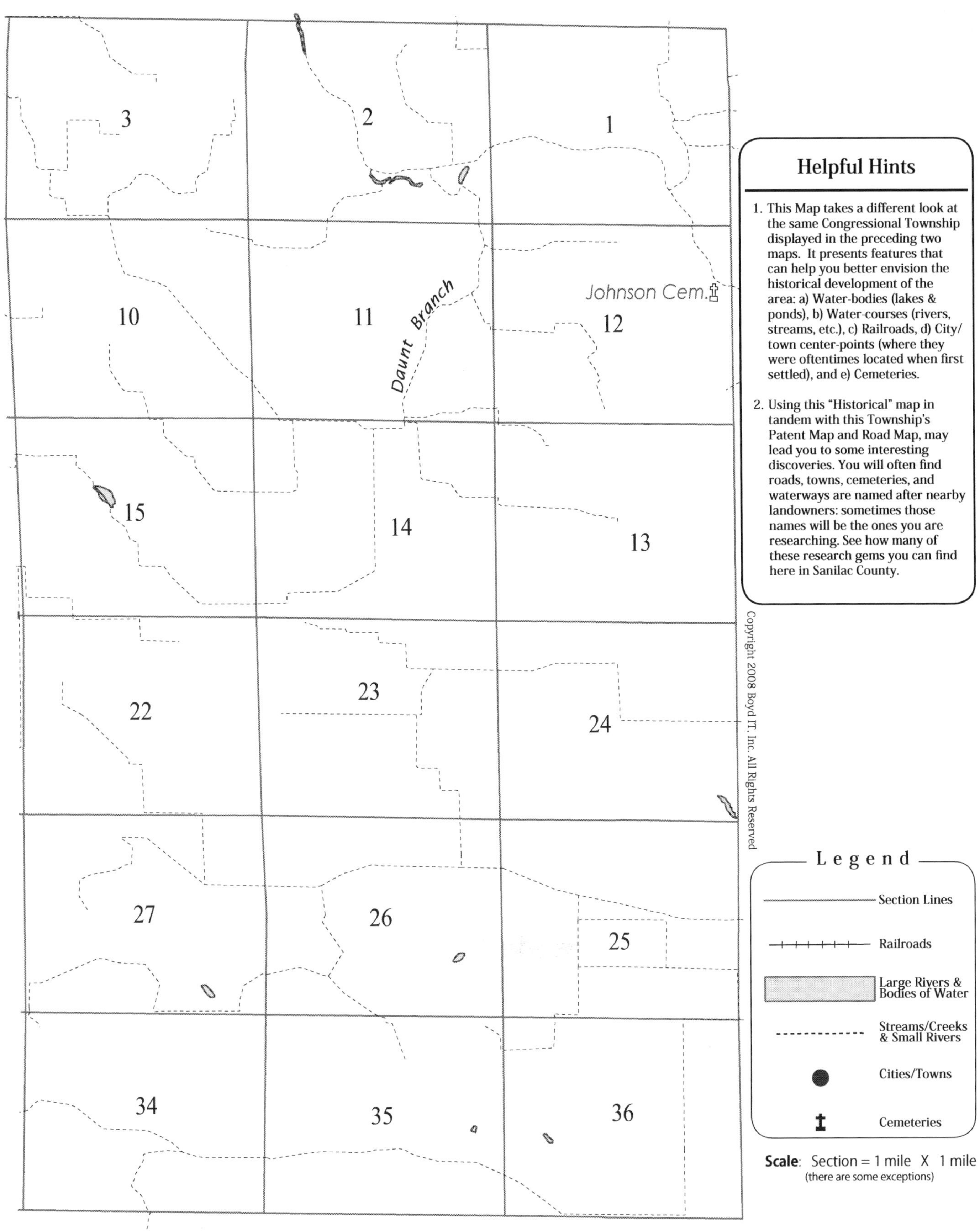

Helpful Hints

1. This Map takes a different look at the same Congressional Township displayed in the preceding two maps. It presents features that can help you better envision the historical development of the area: a) Water-bodies (lakes & ponds), b) Water-courses (rivers, streams, etc.), c) Railroads, d) City/town center-points (where they were oftentimes located when first settled), and e) Cemeteries.

2. Using this "Historical" map in tandem with this Township's Patent Map and Road Map, may lead you to some interesting discoveries. You will often find roads, towns, cemeteries, and waterways are named after nearby landowners: sometimes those names will be the ones you are researching. See how many of these research gems you can find here in Sanilac County.

Scale: Section = 1 mile X 1 mile
(there are some exceptions)

Map Group 12: Index to Land Patents

Township 12-North Range 13-East (Michigan-Toledo Strip)

After you locate an individual in this Index, take note of the Section and Section Part then proceed to the Land Patent map on the pages immediately following. You should have no difficulty locating the corresponding parcel of land.

The "For More Info" Column will lead you to more information about the underlying Patents. See the *Legend* at right, and the "How to Use this Book" chapter, for more information.

LEGEND

"For More Info . . . " column

A = Authority (Legislative Act, See Appendix "A")
B = Block or Lot (location in Section unknown)
C = Cancelled Patent
F = Fractional Section
G = Group (Multi-Patentee Patent, see Appendix "C")
V = Overlaps another Parcel
R = Re-Issued (Parcel patented more than once)

(A & G items require you to look in the Appendixes referred to above. All other Letter-designations followed by a number require you to locate line-items in this index that possess the ID number found after the letter).

ID	Individual in Patent	Sec.	Sec. Part	Date Issued	Other Counties	For More Info . . .
1318	ALLMAN, Wilmot	7	NESW	1872-12-30		A2
1319	" "	7	S½SW	1872-12-30		A2
1320	" "	7	SENW	1872-12-30		A2
1311	ARMSTRONG, Wesley	19	NW	1859-10-10		A1 F
1290	AVERY, Newell	28	SWNE	1870-06-10		A1 R1293
1291	" "	8	NENW	1872-04-15		A1 G4
1284	BATCHELDER, John W	6	N½NW	1869-11-15		A1
1312	BLASHILL, William	15	SESW	1883-06-07		A2
1212	BRODIE, Alexander	27	E½SW	1859-10-10		A1
1239	CADY, Edwin M	17	SENE	1864-01-05		A1
1276	CAMP, John	10	SWNE	1872-07-01		A2
1277	" "	10	W½SE	1872-07-01		A2
1216	CAMPBELL, Archa	19	SENE	1855-10-01		A1 G18
1217	" "	20	N½SW	1855-10-01		A1 G18
1218	" "	20	NWNE	1855-10-01		A1 G18
1219	" "	20	S½NW	1855-10-01		A1 G18
1220	" "	20	SESW	1855-10-01		A1 G18
1221	" "	29	NENW	1855-10-01		A1 G18
1222	" "	29	NESW	1855-10-01		A1 G18
1223	" "	29	NWSE	1855-10-01		A1 G18
1213	CLAPSADDLE, Alexander	4	E½NE	1873-04-25		A2 F
1214	" "	4	SWNE	1873-04-25		A2 F
1278	CLELAND, John	32	N½NW	1859-10-10		A1
1232	CONANT, Cornelius	36	E½NW	1898-03-08		A1
1233	" "	36	W½NE	1898-03-08		A1
1307	DAVIS, Simon P	9	SE	1872-07-01		A2
1266	DERR, James	1	NWSW	1883-06-07		A2 F
1267	" "	1	W½NW	1883-06-07		A2 F
1234	ERSKIN, E	12	NENW	1867-07-01		A1 G36
1236	ERSKINE, E	12	SWNW	1868-08-20		A1 G37
1235	" "	1	SESW	1869-07-01		A1 G37
1237	" "	14	SESW	1870-10-01		A1 G37
1234	ERSKINE, J	12	NENW	1867-07-01		A1 G36
1236	" "	12	SWNW	1868-08-20		A1 G37
1235	" "	1	SESW	1869-07-01		A1 G37
1237	" "	14	SESW	1870-10-01		A1 G37
1263	FIKE, Jackson	22	NE	1887-02-24		A2
1230	FRENCH, Charles J	15	NWSE	1875-05-10		A1
1264	HAIGHT, Jacob	35	NWNW	1860-11-21		A1
1268	HARTSHORN, James H	34	NW	1860-11-21		A1
1269	HAY, James	17	SWNE	1855-10-01		A1
1216	" "	19	SENE	1855-10-01		A1 G18
1270	" "	20	E½NE	1855-10-01		A1
1217	" "	20	N½SW	1855-10-01		A1 G18
1271	" "	20	NESE	1855-10-01		A1
1218	" "	20	NWNE	1855-10-01		A1 G18

ID	Individual in Patent	Sec.	Sec. Part	Date Issued	Other Counties	For More Info . . .
1219	HAY, James (Cont'd)	20	S½NW	1855-10-01		A1 G18
1220	" "	20	SESW	1855-10-01		A1 G18
1221	" "	29	NENW	1855-10-01		A1 G18
1222	" "	29	NESW	1855-10-01		A1 G18
1223	" "	29	NWSE	1855-10-01		A1 G18
1226	HAZEN, Caleb F	26	SWSW	1860-11-21		A1
1227	" "	27	SESE	1860-11-21		A1
1244	HENRY, Frederick	25	SESE	1885-04-15		A1
1300	HOLCOMB, Samuel	5	SWSW	1867-07-01		A1
1301	" "	8	NWNE	1867-07-01		A1
1302	" "	9	NWNE	1867-07-01		A1
1299	" "	31	SENW	1911-12-04		A1
1228	HOUSE, Chancey	10	E½NW	1872-03-20		A2
1229	" "	10	N½SW	1872-03-20		A2
1225	HUBBARD, Bela	2	W½SW	1868-08-20		A1 G47
1224	" "	3	NWNE	1868-08-20		A1
1245	HUBBARD, Frederick	3	SWNE	1868-08-20		A1
1265	INGRAHAM, James A	18	SW	1860-05-01		A1
1240	JOHNSON, Enos	7	NWSW	1875-09-01		A2
1241	" "	7	SWNW	1875-09-01		A2
1298	JOHNSON, Rufus	6	SESW	1865-10-02		A1
1275	JONES, John A	29	NWSW	1876-09-06		A2
1247	KELLAND, George	28	S½SE	1859-10-10		A1
1210	KELLY, Adam M	27	SWSW	1905-12-13		A2
1250	KIBBEE, Henry C	28	NESW	1864-01-05		A1
1251	" "	3	NWSW	1864-01-05		A1
1252	" "	32	NENE	1864-01-05		A1
1253	" "	33	NESW	1864-01-05		A1
1254	" "	33	SENW	1864-01-05		A1
1255	" "	5	E½SE	1864-01-05		A1
1256	" "	8	NWNW	1864-01-05		A1
1257	" "	9	SWSW	1864-01-05		A1
1258	KING, Henry C	27	NESE	1860-11-21		A1
1259	" "	27	W½SE	1860-11-21		A1
1225	KING, John E	2	W½SW	1868-08-20		A1 G47
1310	KIRBY, Vincent E	6	N½SW	1881-08-20		A2 F
1272	LEONARD, James	4	N½SE	1867-07-01		A1
1273	" "	5	NENE	1867-07-01		A1
1274	" "	8	SWSW	1867-07-01		A1
1308	LEWIS, Socrates	31	N½NE	1860-11-21		A1 F
1309	" "	31	N½NW	1860-11-21		A1
1215	MCDONALD, Alexander	36	NENE	1869-07-01		A1
1281	MILLER, John	21	SWNE	1864-01-05		A1
1282	" "	21	SWNW	1864-01-05		A1
1283	" "	8	SENW	1864-01-05		A1
1249	MOORE, George W	29	S½SW	1860-11-21		A1
1285	MOORE, Mortin	31	N½SE	1860-05-01		A1
1286	" "	31	S½NE	1860-05-01		A1
1287	" "	31	SESE	1860-05-01		A1
1288	" "	32	SWNW	1860-05-01		A1
1289	" "	32	W½SW	1860-05-01		A1
1296	MOORE, Robert	30	NENW	1872-12-30		A2
1297	" "	30	W½NE	1872-12-30		A2
1313	MOORE, William	5	SWNE	1888-10-18		A2
1314	MOORE, William S	21	SESE	1868-08-20		A1
1291	MURPHY, Simon J	8	NENW	1872-04-15		A1 G4
1293	NOBLE, Peter	28	SWNE	1867-07-01		A1 R1290
1292	" "	21	SWSE	1868-08-20		A1
1211	PACK, Albert	1	NESW	1869-07-01		A1
1208	PHILLIPS, Adaline	4	SENW	1869-07-01		A1
1209	" "	6	SENW	1869-07-01		A1
1304	REEVE, Selah	33	SESW	1855-10-01		A1
1305	" "	34	SESW	1855-10-01		A1
1306	" "	35	SWSE	1855-10-01		A1
1242	RUST, Ezra	19	N½NE	1861-12-03		A1
1315	SANBORN, William	20	W½SE	1860-05-01		A1
1316	" "	4	W½NW	1860-05-01		A1
1243	SEARS, Franklin	13	SWSW	1872-04-15		A1
1260	SHELDON, Henry	22	SESW	1878-02-13		A2
1261	" "	22	W½SE	1878-02-13		A2
1248	SHERWOOD, George	31	SWSE	1869-07-01		A1
1231	SOPER, Christopher J	7	NENW	1891-04-20		A1
1294	SPRING, Peter	8	NWSW	1882-12-01		A2

ID	Individual in Patent	Sec.	Sec. Part	Date Issued	Other Counties	For More Info . . .
1295	SPRING, Peter (Cont'd)	8	SWNW	1882-12-01		A2
1317	SPRING, William	4	W½SW	1883-06-07		A2
1262	STRONG, Henry T	17	NESE	1890-03-25		A2
1303	VIETS, Samuel W	34	NE	1860-11-21		A1
1279	WILDFONG, John L	33	SWSW	1859-10-10		A1
1207	WILLIAMS, Aaron	35	NENW	1861-07-01		A1
1238	WILLIAMS, Eauery	19	SWSE	1885-01-30		A2
1246	WILLIAMS, George H	31	SWNW	1885-05-20		A2
1280	WOODS, John L	5	SENE	1855-10-01		A1

Patent Map

T12-N R13-E
Michigan-Toledo Strip Meridian

Map Group 12

Township Statistics

Parcels Mapped	:	114
Number of Patents	:	91
Number of Individuals	:	67
Patentees Identified	:	66
Number of Surnames	:	56
Multi-Patentee Parcels	:	14
Oldest Patent Date	:	10/1/1855
Most Recent Patent	:	12/4/1911
Block/Lot Parcels	:	0
Parcels Re - Issued	:	1
Parcels that Overlap	:	0
Cities and Towns	:	2
Cemeteries	:	2

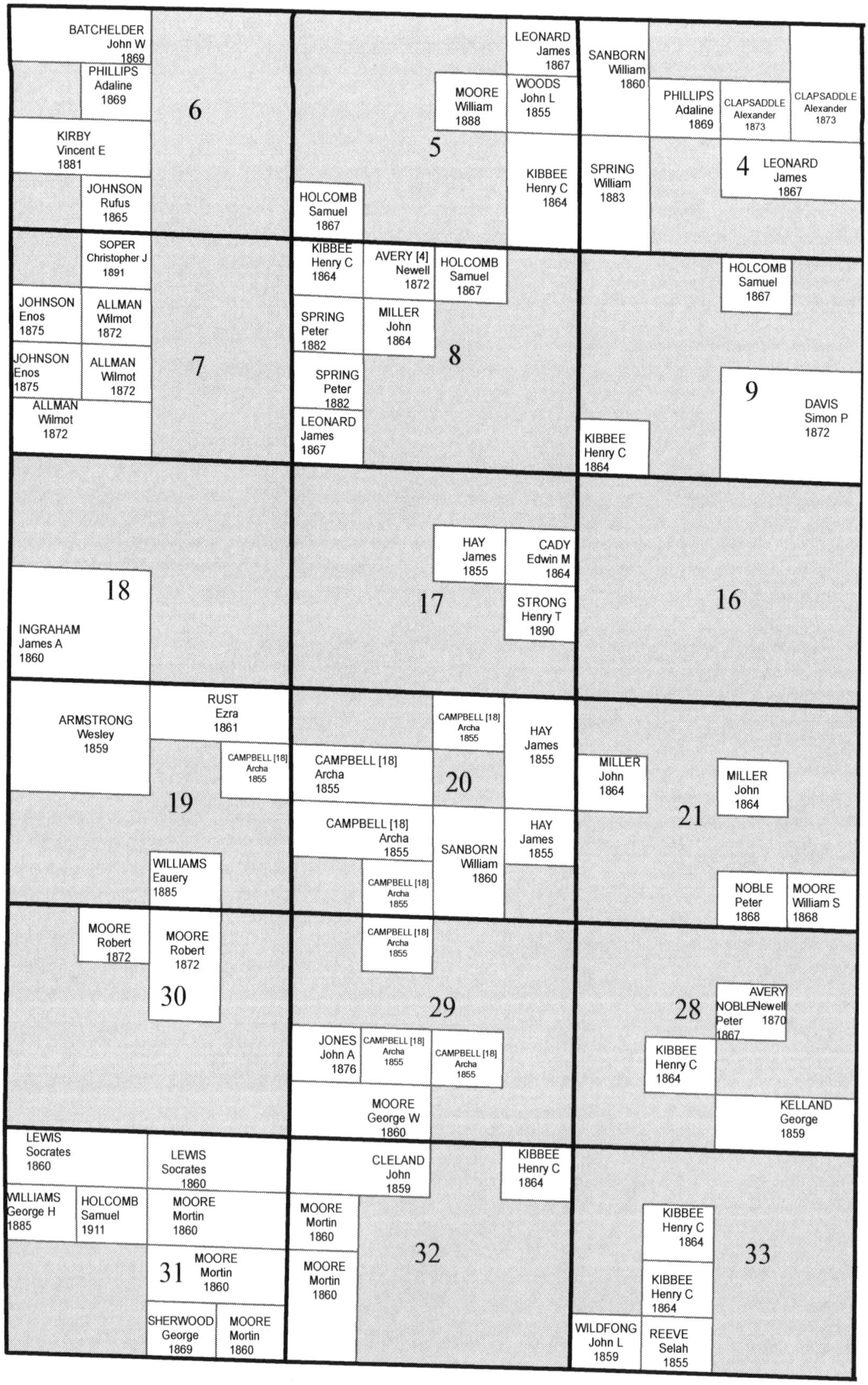

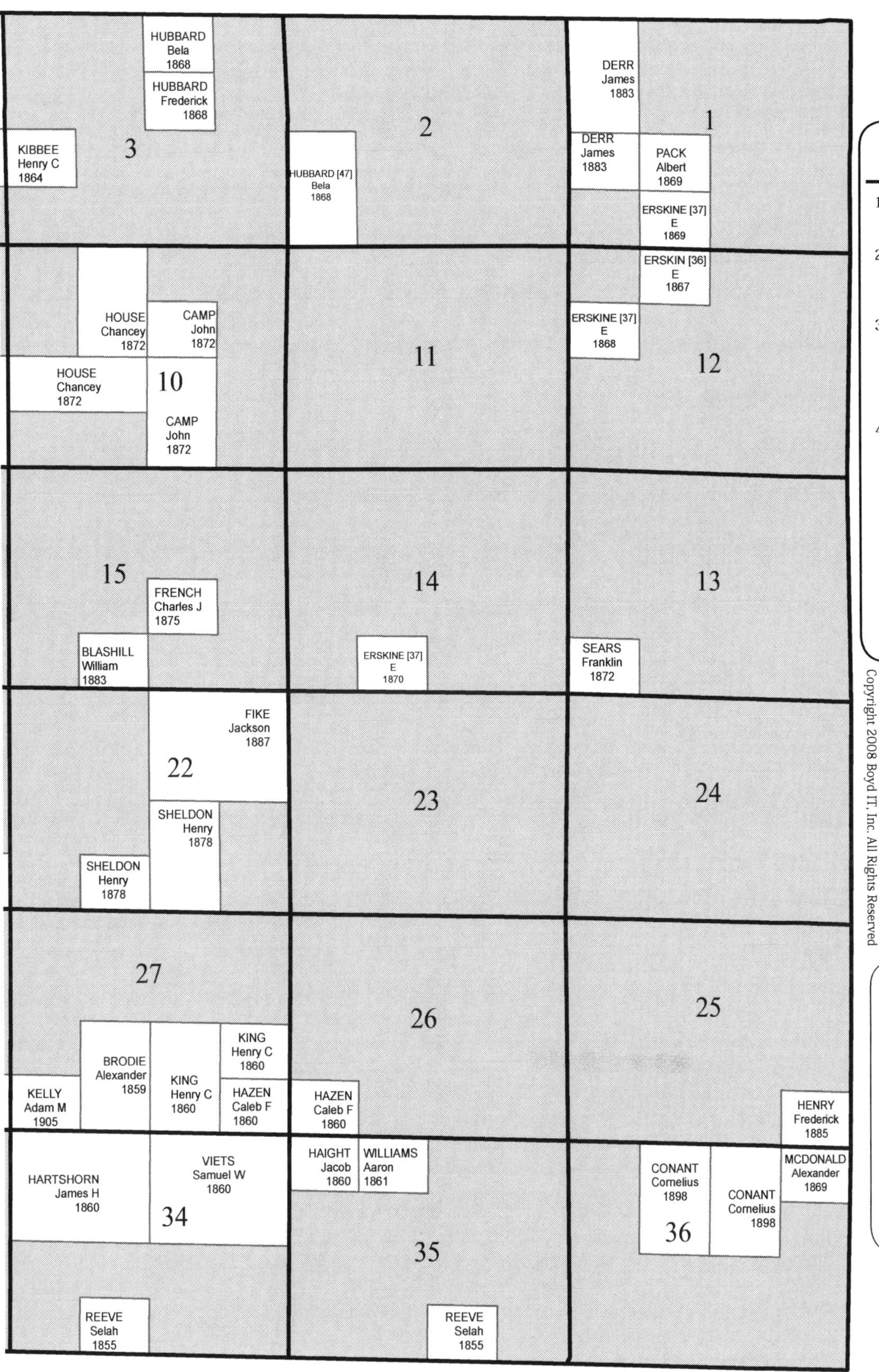

Helpful Hints

1. This Map's INDEX can be found on the preceding pages.
2. Refer to Map "C" to see where this Township lies within Sanilac County, Michigan.
3. Numbers within square brackets [ ] denote a multi-patentee land parcel (multi-owner). Refer to Appendix "C" for a full list of members in this group.
4. Areas that look to be crowded with Patentees usually indicate multiple sales of the same parcel (Re-issues) or Overlapping parcels. See this Township's Index for an explanation of these and other circumstances that might explain "odd" groupings of Patentees on this map.

Legend

- Patent Boundary
- Section Boundary
- No Patents Found (or Outside County)
- 1., 2., 3., ... Lot Numbers (when beside a name)
- [ ] Group Number (see Appendix "C")

Scale: Section = 1 mile X 1 mile (generally, with some exceptions)

Road Map

T12-N R13-E
Michigan-Toledo Strip Meridian

Map Group 12

Cities & Towns

Elmer
Snover

Cemeteries

Moore Cemetery
Snover Memorial Park

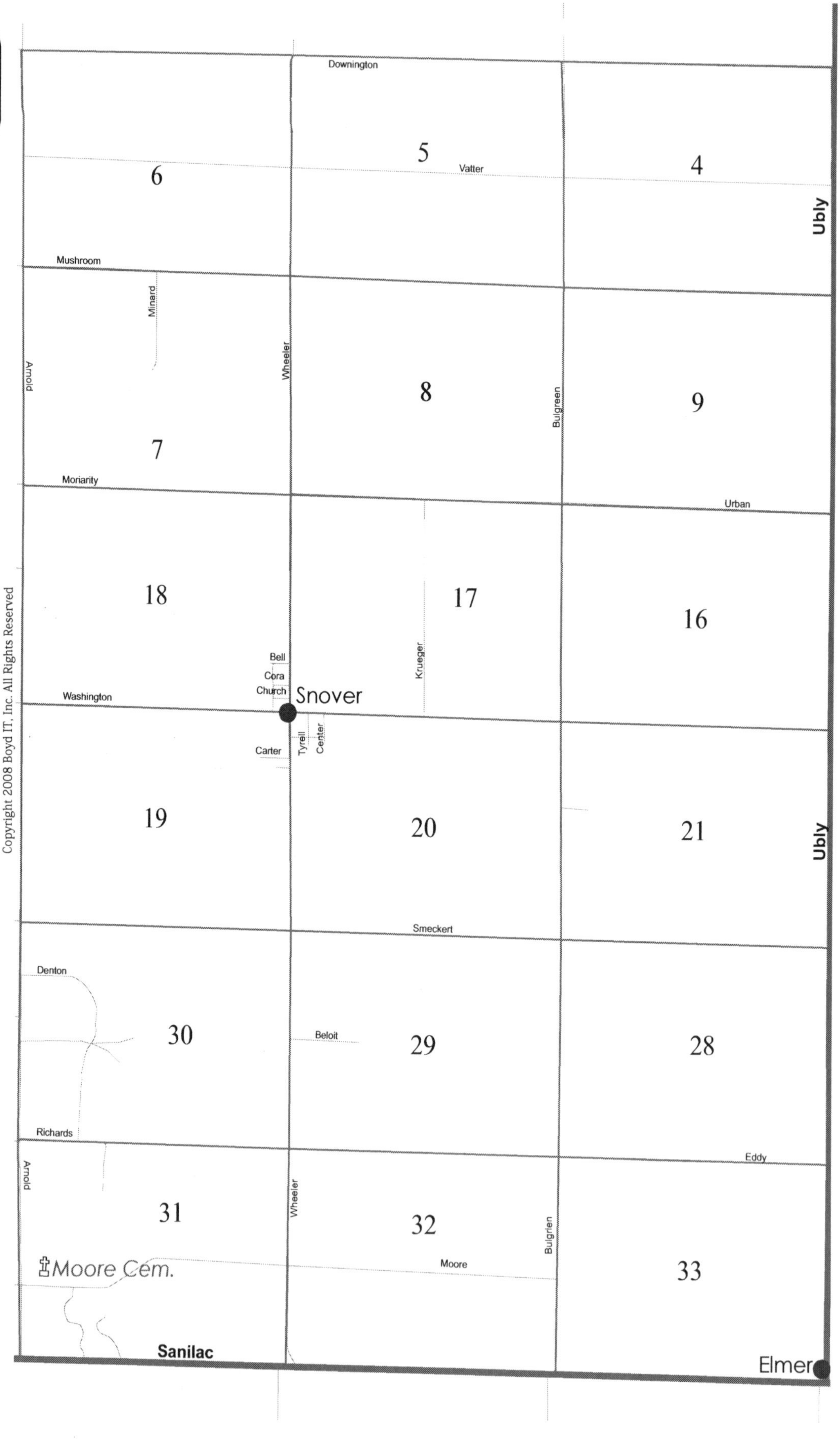

Downington
6
5
Vatter
4
Ubly
Mushroom
Minard
Arnold
Wheeler
8
Bulgreen
9
7
Moriarity
Urban
18
17
16
Krueger
Bell
Cora
Church
Washington
Snover
Carter
Tyrell
Center
19
20
21
Ubly
Smeckert
Denton
30
Beloit
29
28
Richards
Eddy
Arnold
Wheeler
31
32
Bulgrien
Moore Cem.
Moore
33
Sanilac
Elmer

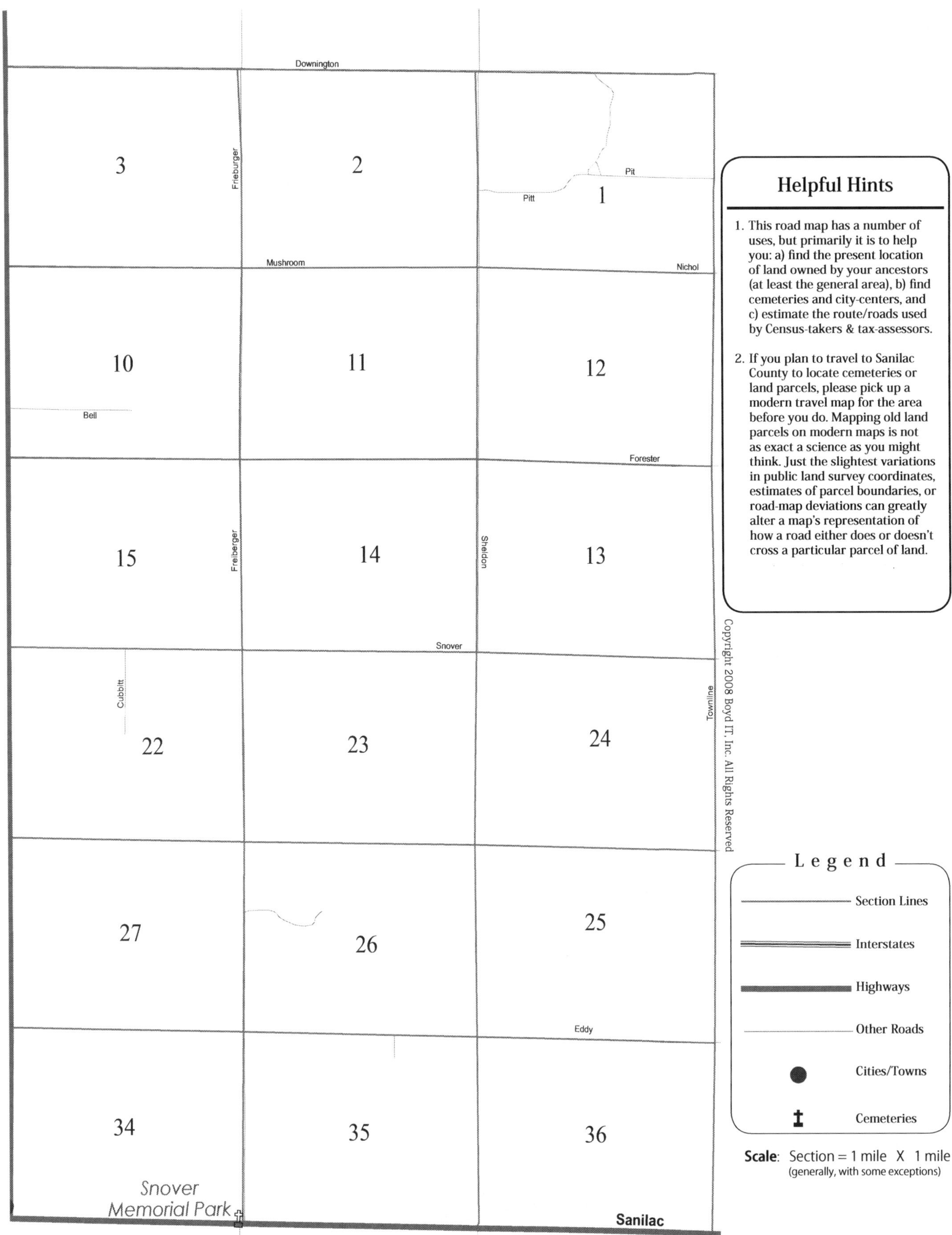

Helpful Hints

1. This road map has a number of uses, but primarily it is to help you: a) find the present location of land owned by your ancestors (at least the general area), b) find cemeteries and city-centers, and c) estimate the route/roads used by Census-takers & tax-assessors.

2. If you plan to travel to Sanilac County to locate cemeteries or land parcels, please pick up a modern travel map for the area before you do. Mapping old land parcels on modern maps is not as exact a science as you might think. Just the slightest variations in public land survey coordinates, estimates of parcel boundaries, or road-map deviations can greatly alter a map's representation of how a road either does or doesn't cross a particular parcel of land.

Legend

- Section Lines
- Interstates
- Highways
- Other Roads
- Cities/Towns
- Cemeteries

Scale: Section = 1 mile X 1 mile
(generally, with some exceptions)

Historical Map

T12-N R13-E
Michigan-Toledo Strip Meridian

Map Group 12

Cities & Towns

Elmer
Snover

Cemeteries

Moore Cemetery
Snover Memorial Park

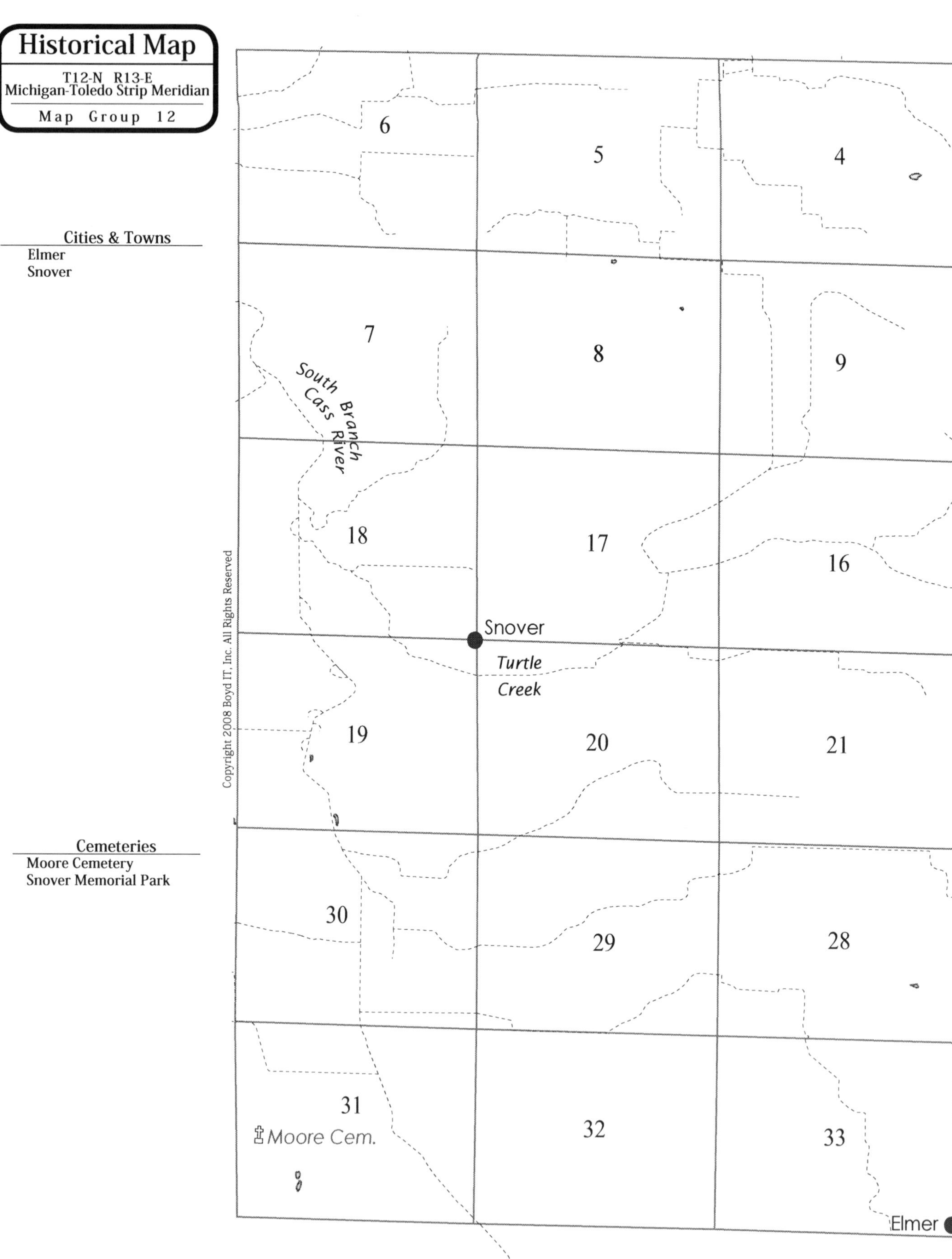

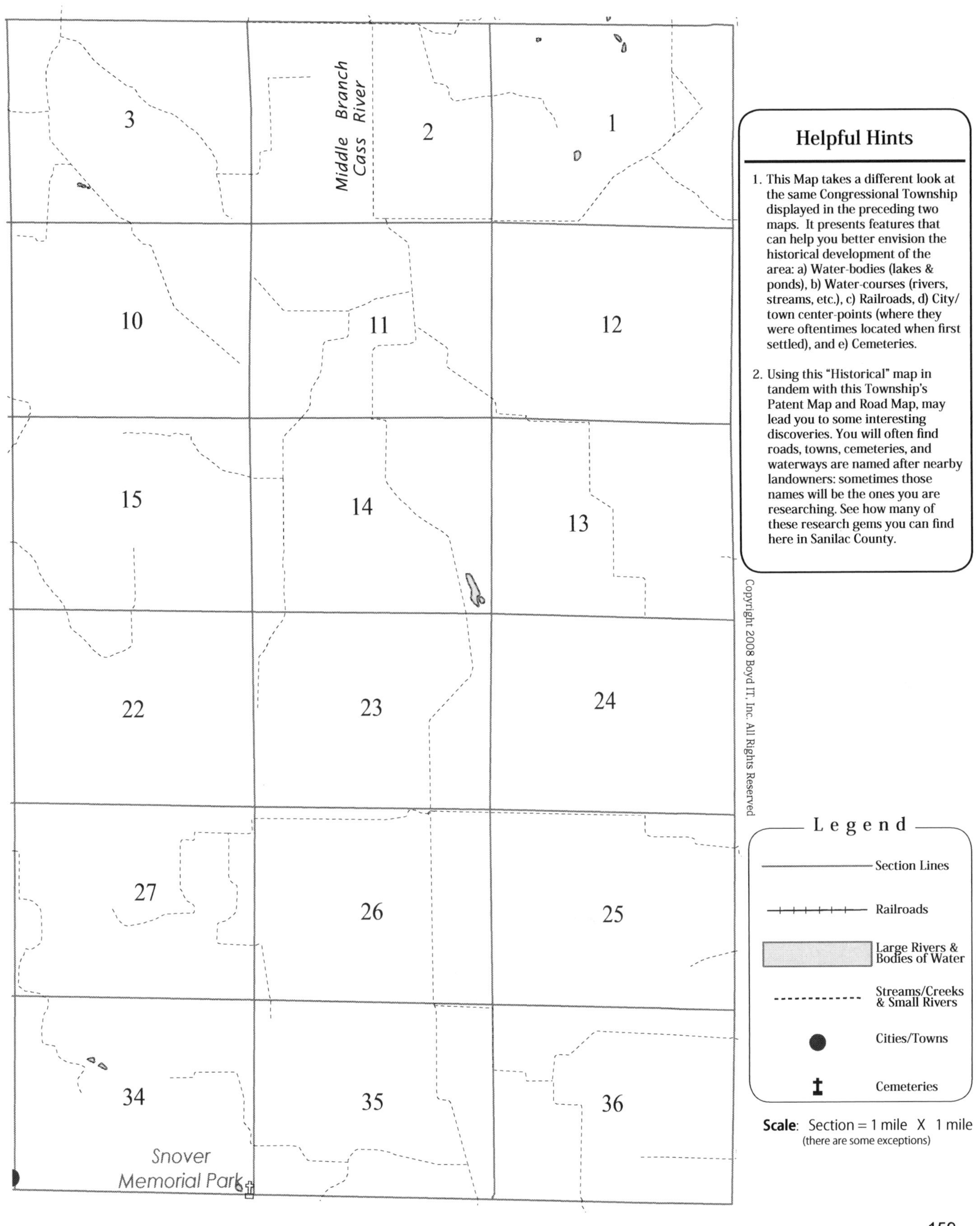

Helpful Hints

1. This Map takes a different look at the same Congressional Township displayed in the preceding two maps. It presents features that can help you better envision the historical development of the area: a) Water-bodies (lakes & ponds), b) Water-courses (rivers, streams, etc.), c) Railroads, d) City/town center-points (where they were oftentimes located when first settled), and e) Cemeteries.

2. Using this "Historical" map in tandem with this Township's Patent Map and Road Map, may lead you to some interesting discoveries. You will often find roads, towns, cemeteries, and waterways are named after nearby landowners: sometimes those names will be the ones you are researching. See how many of these research gems you can find here in Sanilac County.

Legend

- Section Lines
- Railroads
- Large Rivers & Bodies of Water
- Streams/Creeks & Small Rivers
- Cities/Towns
- Cemeteries

Scale: Section = 1 mile X 1 mile
(there are some exceptions)

Map Group 13: Index to Land Patents

Township 12-North Range 14-East (Michigan-Toledo Strip)

After you locate an individual in this Index, take note of the Section and Section Part then proceed to the Land Patent map on the pages immediately following. You should have no difficulty locating the corresponding parcel of land.

The "For More Info" Column will lead you to more information about the underlying Patents. See the *Legend* at right, and the "How to Use this Book" chapter, for more information.

LEGEND

"For More Info . . ." column

- **A** = Authority (Legislative Act, See Appendix "A")
- **B** = Block or Lot (location in Section unknown)
- **C** = Cancelled Patent
- **F** = Fractional Section
- **G** = Group (Multi-Patentee Patent, see Appendix "C")
- **V** = Overlaps another Parcel
- **R** = Re-Issued (Parcel patented more than once)

(A & G items require you to look in the Appendixes referred to above. All other Letter-designations followed by a number require you to locate line-items in this index that possess the ID number found after the letter).

ID	Individual in Patent	Sec.	Sec. Part	Date Issued	Other Counties	For More Info . . .
1360	ALEXANDER, James	33	W½NE	1875-11-20		A2
1387	BADGROW, Oliver	19	NESE	1888-10-18		A2
1321	BAILEY, Adam C	27	NWNW	1888-10-18		A2
1382	BARRY, Michael	9	E½NW	1884-08-09		A2
1383	" "	9	SWNW	1884-08-09		A2
1334	BERDEN, David	15	SWSW	1885-01-30		A2
1338	BERDEN, Edmund C	23	NWNW	1885-01-30		A2
1398	BIGNEY, Thomas	23	NENE	1861-12-03		A1
1349	BRIGHT, George	32	NENW	1883-11-20		A2
1350	" "	32	NESW	1883-11-20		A2
1351	" "	32	S½NW	1883-11-20		A2
1368	BROADBRIDGE, John	13	SWNW	1862-02-01		A1
1369	" "	13	W½SW	1862-02-01		A1
1403	CHIPMAN, William Y	10	N½NE	1861-07-01		A1
1404	" "	10	NENW	1861-07-01		A1
1405	" "	10	NWSE	1861-07-01		A1
1406	" "	10	SWNE	1861-07-01		A1
1361	CURN, James	11	SESE	1861-07-01		A1
1362	" "	12	SWSW	1861-07-01		A1
1363	" "	13	NWNW	1861-07-01		A1
1364	" "	14	NENE	1861-07-01		A1
1322	DERING, Adelia	31	W½NW	1883-01-20		A1 F
1323	" "	31	W½SW	1883-01-20		A1
1325	DEY, Alexander H	19	NWSE	1860-05-01		A1
1384	DOAN, Nathan	2	NWSE	1877-07-20		A2
1330	DOWNING, Alonzo	33	N½NW	1869-07-01		A1
1370	EDWARDS, John	28	N½SE	1885-01-30		A2
1371	" "	28	SWNE	1885-01-30		A2
1340	ENNEST, Elias	2	W½NE	1861-07-01		A1
1356	ENNEST, Jacob	14	E½SE	1860-11-21		A1
1357	" "	14	NWSE	1860-11-21		A1
1365	ENNEST, James	11	NESE	1860-10-01		A1
1336	ERSKINE, E	28	SENE	1866-09-01		A1 G37
1337	" "	7	SESE	1867-07-01		A1 G37
1336	ERSKINE, J	28	SENE	1866-09-01		A1 G37
1337	" "	7	SESE	1867-07-01		A1 G37
1353	FLETCHER, George	3	SENE	1859-10-10		A1
1352	" "	3	NENE	1861-07-01		A1 F
1366	FYE, James	22	SWNE	1890-01-27		A2
1358	GOODWIN, Jacob L	2	E½NE	1861-07-01		A1 F
1359	" "	2	E½SW	1861-07-01		A1 F
1326	HARPER, Alexander	11	E½NW	1860-11-21		A1
1327	" "	11	E½SW	1860-11-21		A1
1372	HARPER, John	3	E½NW	1861-12-03		A1 F
1373	" "	3	SWNW	1861-12-03		A1 F
1374	HENRY, John	30	W½SE	1887-09-07		A2

ID	Individual in Patent	Sec.	Sec. Part	Date Issued	Other Counties	For More Info . . .
1386	HENRY, Nicholas	30	N½SW	1880-10-01		A2 F
1324	HOCHSTETTER, Albert	8	NWNW	1870-06-10		A1
1354	HOSACK, George N	30	E½NW	1885-01-30		A2
1346	HUBBARD, F	19	SWSW	1867-07-01		A1
1347	HUBBARD, Frederick	20	SWSW	1868-08-20		A1
1348	" "	32	SESW	1868-08-20		A1
1401	JURN, William	30	S½SW	1882-12-01		A1 F
1402	KENNY, William	15	NWNW	1885-07-27		A2
1375	MAYES, John	22	NENW	1878-11-05		A2
1328	MCDONALD, Alexander R	36	SENE	1869-07-01		A1
1390	MCGINN, Sanis And	30	W½NW	1867-07-01		A1 F
1392	MCGINN, Senis And	19	NESW	1867-07-01		A1
1393	" "	20	NWSE	1867-07-01		A1
1394	" "	20	SESW	1867-07-01		A1
1395	MCGINN, Simms And	19	SENW	1868-08-20		A1
1396	" "	19	SESW	1868-08-20		A1
1397	" "	20	NESW	1868-08-20		A1
1377	MCGUGAN, John	3	W½NE	1861-07-01		A1
1376	" "	3	NWSE	1862-02-01		A1
1378	MILLER, John	6	SWSE	1864-01-05		A1
1355	MIZNER, Henry R	25	W½SW	1855-10-01		A1
1331	MOORE, Andrew	33	E½SW	1875-07-30		A2
1332	" "	33	S½NW	1875-07-30		A2
1339	MOORE, Edwin	20	NENW	1898-03-21		A2
1381	MOORE, Martin W	31	E½SW	1875-07-30		A2
1335	MORSE, E C	19	NWSW	1867-07-01		A1
1343	MORSE, Elijah	28	NESW	1868-08-20		A1
1344	" "	28	SENW	1868-08-20		A1
1341	MORSE, Elijah C	15	NENW	1868-08-20		A1
1342	" "	30	SWNE	1868-08-20		A1
1333	PARTRIDGE, Charles	20	NWSW	1873-05-20		A1
1345	QUAY, Eliza	14	NESW	1872-08-10		A1
1391	REEVE, Selah V	6	NWNW	1855-10-01		A1 F
1380	ROBERTS, Joseph	8	SWSW	1870-06-01		A1
1379	ROVOLT, John	32	N½SE	1885-01-30		A2
1385	SHARLOW, Nelson	4	NESE	1885-01-30		A1
1388	SMITH, Rollin C	28	NENW	1855-10-01		A1
1389	" "	28	NWNE	1855-10-01		A1
1329	STOCKWELL, Alonson J	2	W½SW	1862-02-01		A1
1367	STOVER, James	3	E½SW	1861-07-01		A1
1399	TAYLOR, William H	31	E½NW	1883-06-07		A2
1400	" "	31	NWNE	1883-06-07		A2

Patent Map

T12-N R14-E
Michigan-Toledo Strip Meridian

Map Group 13

Township Statistics

Parcels Mapped	:	86
Number of Patents	:	65
Number of Individuals	:	58
Patentees Identified	:	57
Number of Surnames	:	45
Multi-Patentee Parcels	:	2
Oldest Patent Date	:	10/1/1855
Most Recent Patent	:	3/21/1898
Block/Lot Parcels	:	0
Parcels Re - Issued	:	0
Parcels that Overlap	:	0
Cities and Towns	:	0
Cemeteries	:	0

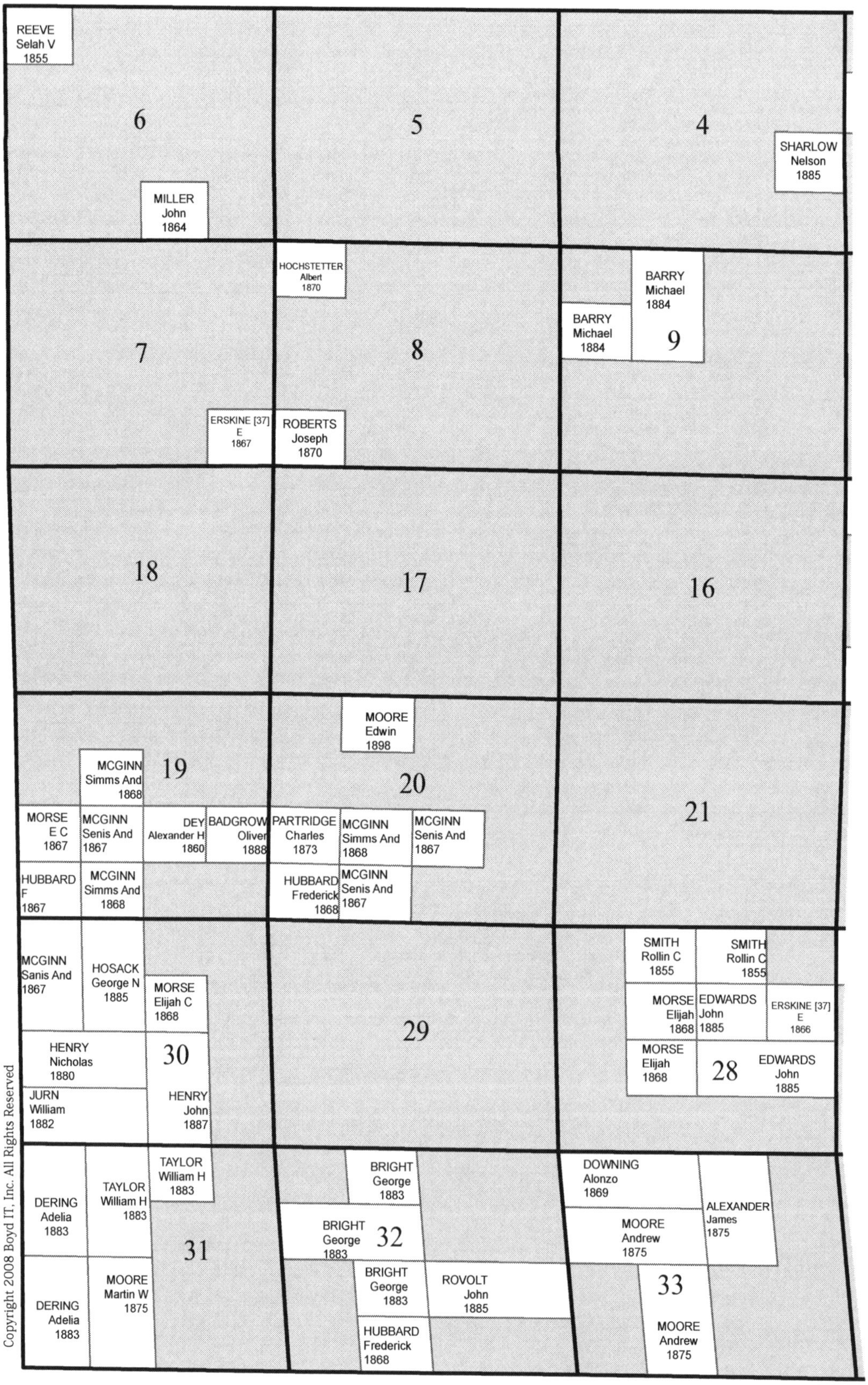

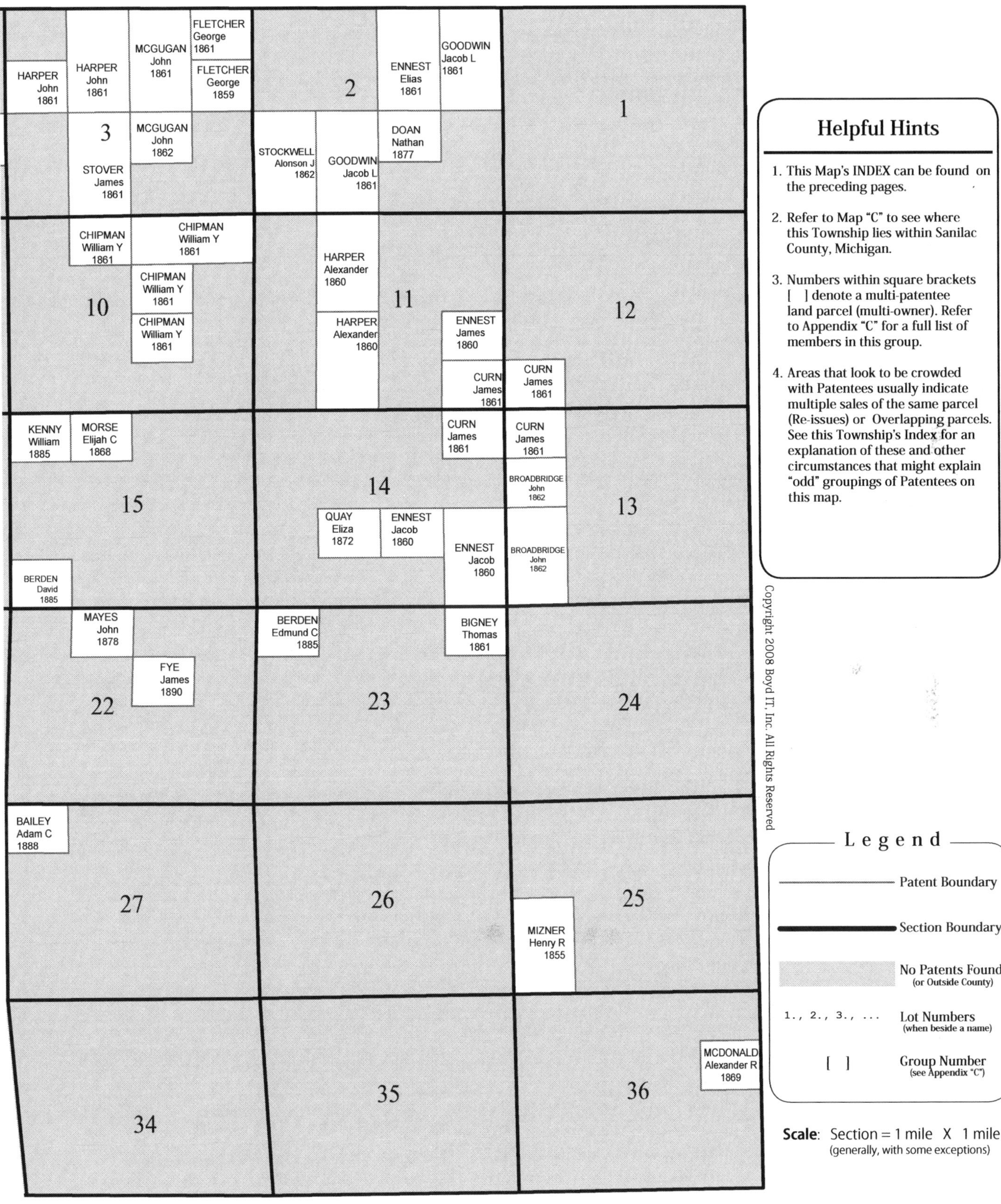

Helpful Hints

1. This Map's INDEX can be found on the preceding pages.
2. Refer to Map "C" to see where this Township lies within Sanilac County, Michigan.
3. Numbers within square brackets [ ] denote a multi-patentee land parcel (multi-owner). Refer to Appendix "C" for a full list of members in this group.
4. Areas that look to be crowded with Patentees usually indicate multiple sales of the same parcel (Re-issues) or Overlapping parcels. See this Township's Index for an explanation of these and other circumstances that might explain "odd" groupings of Patentees on this map.

Legend

- Patent Boundary
- Section Boundary
- No Patents Found (or Outside County)
- 1., 2., 3., ... Lot Numbers (when beside a name)
- [ ] Group Number (see Appendix "C")

Scale: Section = 1 mile X 1 mile (generally, with some exceptions)

Road Map

T12-N R14-E
Michigan-Toledo Strip Meridian

Map Group 13

Cities & Towns

None

Cemeteries

None

Copyright 2008 Boyd IT, Inc. All Rights Reserved

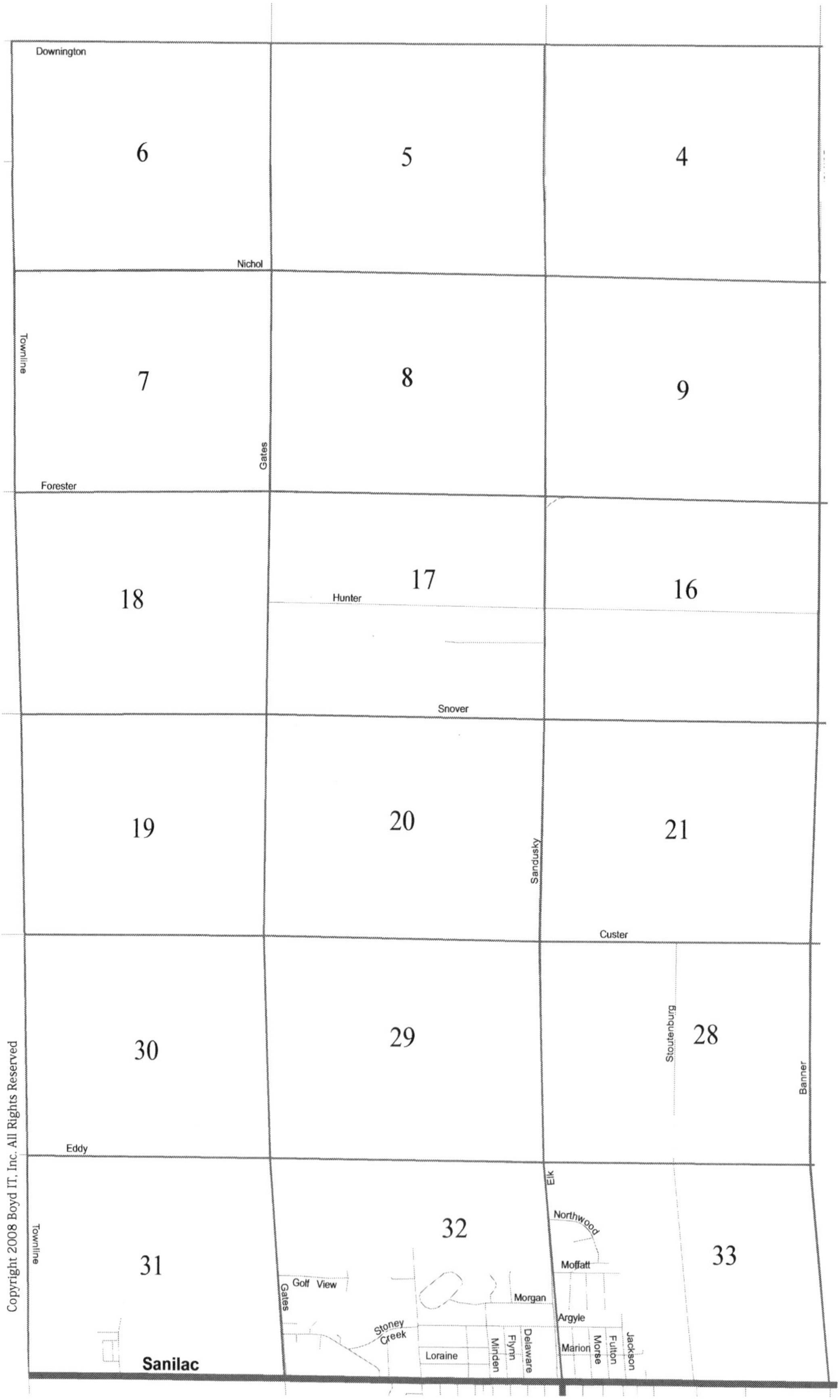

Helpful Hints

1. This road map has a number of uses, but primarily it is to help you: a) find the present location of land owned by your ancestors (at least the general area), b) find cemeteries and city-centers, and c) estimate the route/roads used by Census-takers & tax-assessors.

2. If you plan to travel to Sanilac County to locate cemeteries or land parcels, please pick up a modern travel map for the area before you do. Mapping old land parcels on modern maps is not as exact a science as you might think. Just the slightest variations in public land survey coordinates, estimates of parcel boundaries, or road-map deviations can greatly alter a map's representation of how a road either does or doesn't cross a particular parcel of land.

Legend

- Section Lines
- Interstates
- Highways
- Other Roads
- Cities/Towns
- Cemeteries

Scale: Section = 1 mile X 1 mile
(generally, with some exceptions)

Historical Map

T12-N R14-E
Michigan-Toledo Strip Meridian

Map Group 13

Cities & Towns
None

Cemeteries
None

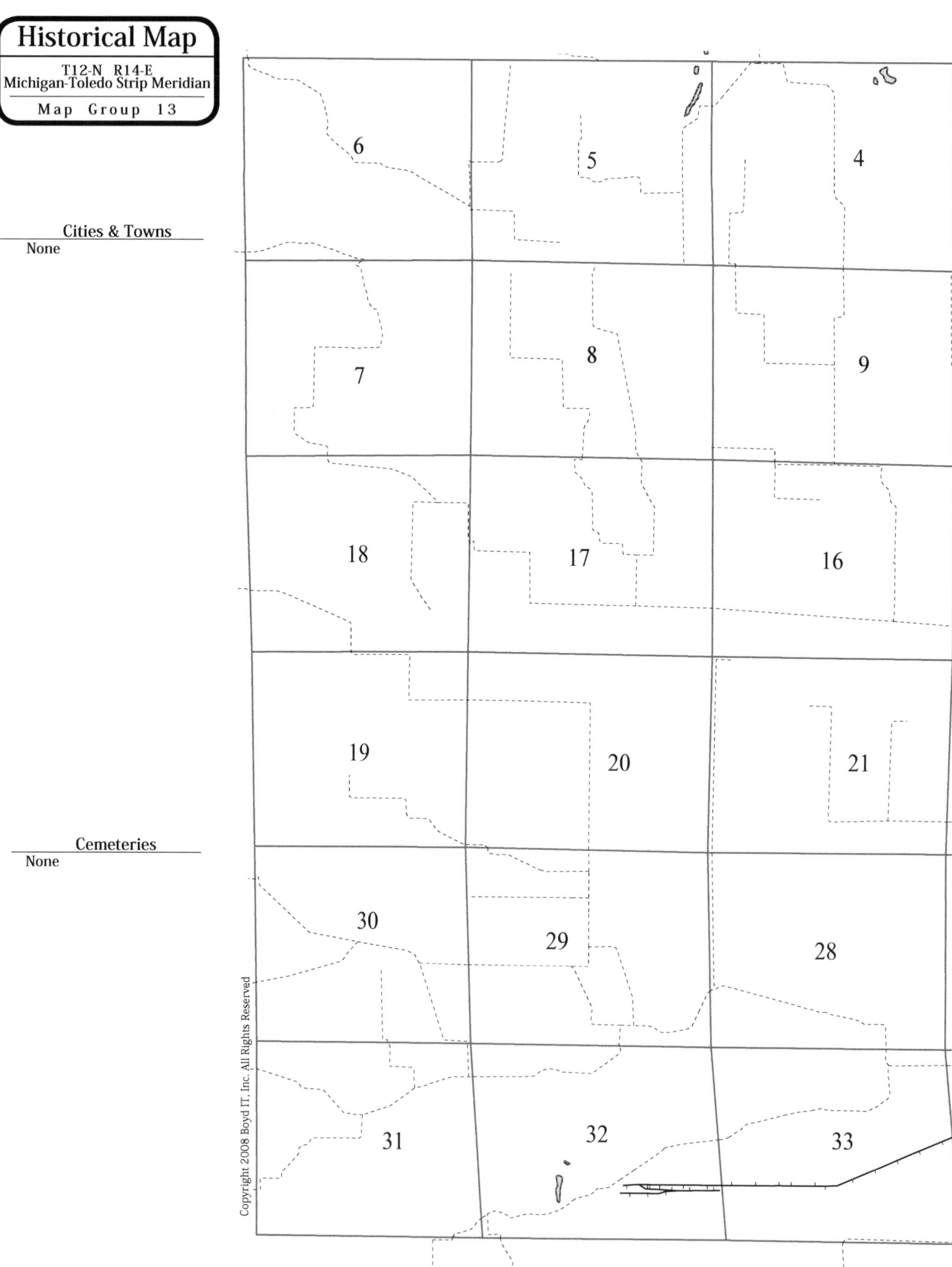

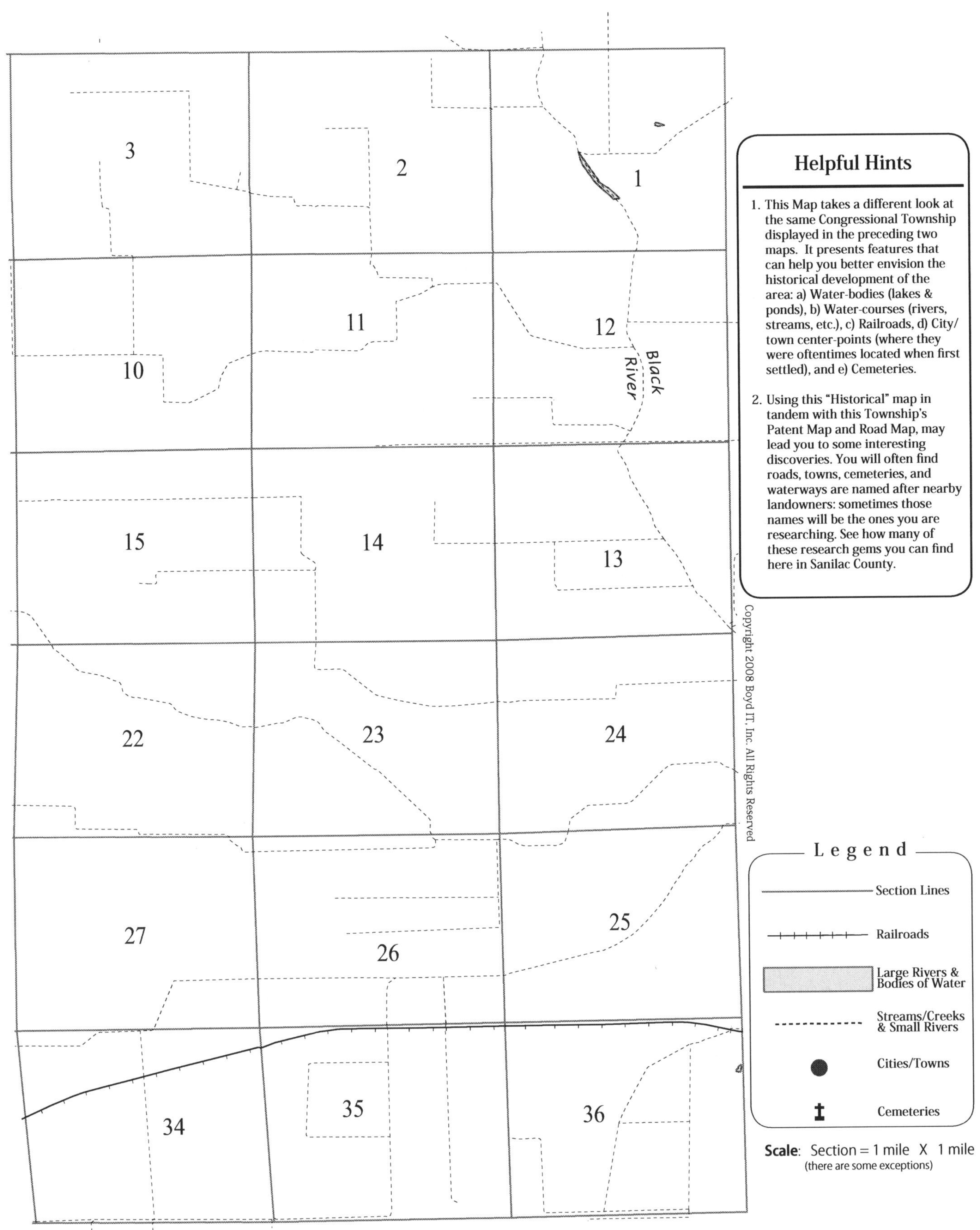

Helpful Hints

1. This Map takes a different look at the same Congressional Township displayed in the preceding two maps. It presents features that can help you better envision the historical development of the area: a) Water-bodies (lakes & ponds), b) Water-courses (rivers, streams, etc.), c) Railroads, d) City/town center-points (where they were oftentimes located when first settled), and e) Cemeteries.

2. Using this "Historical" map in tandem with this Township's Patent Map and Road Map, may lead you to some interesting discoveries. You will often find roads, towns, cemeteries, and waterways are named after nearby landowners: sometimes those names will be the ones you are researching. See how many of these research gems you can find here in Sanilac County.

Scale: Section = 1 mile X 1 mile
(there are some exceptions)

Map Group 14: Index to Land Patents

Township 12-North Range 15-East (Michigan-Toledo Strip)

After you locate an individual in this Index, take note of the Section and Section Part then proceed to the Land Patent map on the pages immediately following. You should have no difficulty locating the corresponding parcel of land.

The "For More Info" Column will lead you to more information about the underlying Patents. See the *Legend* at right, and the "How to Use this Book" chapter, for more information.

LEGEND

"For More Info . . . " column

A = Authority (Legislative Act, See Appendix "A")
B = Block or Lot (location in Section unknown)
C = Cancelled Patent
F = Fractional Section
G = Group (Multi-Patentee Patent, see Appendix "C")
V = Overlaps another Parcel
R = Re-Issued (Parcel patented more than once)

(A & G items require you to look in the Appendixes referred to above. All other Letter-designations followed by a number require you to locate line-items in this index that possess the ID number found after the letter).

ID	Individual in Patent	Sec.	Sec. Part	Date Issued	Other Counties	For More Info . . .
1421	BEACH, George	1	SW	1838-09-04		A1 G12
1422	" "	1	W½SE	1838-09-04		A1 G12
1423	" "	10	NE	1838-09-04		A1 G12
1424	" "	10	SE	1838-09-04		A1 G12
1425	" "	11		1838-09-04		A1 G12
1426	" "	12		1838-09-04		A1 G12
1427	" "	13	E½NW	1838-09-04		A1 G12
1428	" "	13	NE	1838-09-04		A1 G12
1429	" "	14		1838-09-04		A1 G12
1430	" "	15	NE	1838-09-04		A1 G12
1431	" "	15	SE	1838-09-04		A1 G12
1432	" "	2	NE	1838-09-04		A1 G12
1433	" "	2	SE	1838-09-04		A1 G12
1434	" "	2	SW	1838-09-04		A1 G12
1435	" "	22	NE	1838-09-04		A1 G12
1436	" "	24	SE	1838-09-04		A1 G12
1437	" "	24	SW	1838-09-04		A1 G12
1438	" "	25	NE	1838-09-04		A1 G12
1439	" "	25	NW	1838-09-04		A1 G12
1440	" "	3	SE	1838-09-04		A1 G12
1454	BEARD, John	28	NWNE	1852-02-10		A1
1477	BEATYS, Moses C	20	W½SE	1855-10-01		A1
1478	" "	27	N½SE	1855-10-01		A1
1479	" "	27	NESW	1855-10-01		A1
1480	" "	27	W½NE	1855-10-01		A1
1421	BECKWITH, Alonzo S	1	SW	1838-09-04		A1 G12
1422	" "	1	W½SE	1838-09-04		A1 G12
1423	" "	10	NE	1838-09-04		A1 G12
1424	" "	10	SE	1838-09-04		A1 G12
1425	" "	11		1838-09-04		A1 G12
1426	" "	12		1838-09-04		A1 G12
1427	" "	13	E½NW	1838-09-04		A1 G12
1428	" "	13	NE	1838-09-04		A1 G12
1429	" "	14		1838-09-04		A1 G12
1430	" "	15	NE	1838-09-04		A1 G12
1431	" "	15	SE	1838-09-04		A1 G12
1432	" "	2	NE	1838-09-04		A1 G12
1433	" "	2	SE	1838-09-04		A1 G12
1434	" "	2	SW	1838-09-04		A1 G12
1435	" "	22	NE	1838-09-04		A1 G12
1436	" "	24	SE	1838-09-04		A1 G12
1437	" "	24	SW	1838-09-04		A1 G12
1438	" "	25	NE	1838-09-04		A1 G12
1439	" "	25	NW	1838-09-04		A1 G12
1440	" "	3	SE	1838-09-04		A1 G12
1488	BISHOP, Thomas	27	S½SW	1855-10-01		A1

ID	Individual in Patent	Sec.	Sec. Part	Date Issued	Other Counties	For More Info . . .
1474	COCOMAN, Morris	6	N½NE	1856-01-10		A1
1475	" "	6	SENW	1857-10-30		A1
1476	" "	6	SWNE	1857-10-30		A1
1453	CONNOR, Jeremiah O	34	NW	1857-07-01		A1
1455	CRORY, John	32	SESW	1857-10-30		A1
1456	" "	32	SWSE	1859-05-09		A1 R1492
1441	CROSS, George	35	NWSE	1857-07-01		A1
1413	DECKER, Charles	22	NWSW	1852-02-10		A1
1414	" "	22	SWNW	1852-02-10		A1
1421	DICKINSON, Nathan	1	SW	1838-09-04		A1 G12
1422	" "	1	W½SE	1838-09-04		A1 G12
1423	" "	10	NE	1838-09-04		A1 G12
1424	" "	10	SE	1838-09-04		A1 G12
1425	" "	11		1838-09-04		A1 G12
1426	" "	12		1838-09-04		A1 G12
1427	" "	13	E½NW	1838-09-04		A1 G12
1428	" "	13	NE	1838-09-04		A1 G12
1429	" "	14		1838-09-04		A1 G12
1430	" "	15	NE	1838-09-04		A1 G12
1431	" "	15	SE	1838-09-04		A1 G12
1432	" "	2	NE	1838-09-04		A1 G12
1433	" "	2	SE	1838-09-04		A1 G12
1434	" "	2	SW	1838-09-04		A1 G12
1435	" "	22	NE	1838-09-04		A1 G12
1436	" "	24	SE	1838-09-04		A1 G12
1437	" "	24	SW	1838-09-04		A1 G12
1438	" "	25	NE	1838-09-04		A1 G12
1439	" "	25	NW	1838-09-04		A1 G12
1440	" "	3	SE	1838-09-04		A1 G12
1417	DODGE, Delia	32	NWSE	1854-06-15		A1
1494	DOZING, William	18	SWSE	1857-07-01		A1
1495	" "	19	NWNE	1857-07-01		A1
1467	DUCAT, Joseph	22	NENW	1857-07-01		A1
1445	FENTON, Hugh	17	SESW	1857-10-30		A1
1446	" "	17	W½SE	1857-10-30		A1
1481	FINLEY, Richard L	9	SESW	1859-05-09		A1
1482	" "	9	SWSE	1859-05-09		A1
1493	FINLEY, William A	18	SENW	1861-12-03		A1 F
1450	GRICE, James	10	SESW	1859-10-10		A1
1442	HALL, George	28	S½SE	1855-10-01		A1
1473	HEYMAN, Mark	30	SWNW	1890-04-16		A1
1489	KELSO, Thomas	27	SWNW	1857-10-30		A1
1447	KIDD, Hugh	21	E½NW	1855-10-01		A1
1448	" "	21	NWNE	1855-10-01		A1
1449	" "	21	SWNW	1855-10-01		A1
1457	KING, John	4	W½NE	1859-10-10		A1 F
1451	LANE, James	18	E½NE	1857-02-16		A1
1468	LAUREL, Josiah	4	NENE	1857-02-20		A1 F
1486	LAUREL, Theodore	1	NENW	1857-07-01		A1
1487	" "	36	SESW	1857-07-01		A1
1415	LENSE, Christian	5	S½NW	1857-07-01		A1
1418	LINCE, Edward	5	N½NW	1857-02-16		A1 F
1458	LUCAS, John	8	W½NE	1860-05-01		A1
1485	MASON, Sylvester P	28	SWNE	1857-10-30		A1
1416	MAXSON, Daniel R	8	E½NW	1860-05-01		A1
1459	MCGREGOR, John	18	NWNE	1867-07-01		A1
1490	MELVILLE, Thomas	3	SWSW	1859-10-10		A1 F
1484	MICHIGAN, State Of	10	SWNW	1913-02-25		A3
1443	MIZNER, Henry	27	E½NW	1855-10-01		A1
1444	MIZNER, Henry R	35	S½NE	1855-10-01		A1
1460	NICHOL, John	17	NESW	1860-05-01		A1
1461	" "	17	W½SW	1860-05-01		A1
1462	" "	18	E½SE	1860-05-01		A1
1483	NICHOLS, Samuel	17	SENW	1879-06-30		A2
1470	PALMER, Leonard	17	E½SE	1857-10-13		A1
1471	" "	20	NENE	1857-10-13		A1
1452	PICKARD, James	5	S½NE	1857-02-16		A1
1472	ROSBERRY, Levi	5	NENE	1857-07-01		A1 F
1496	ROSS, William	20	NENW	1855-10-01		A1
1497	" "	20	NESW	1855-10-01		A1
1498	" "	20	W½NE	1855-10-01		A1
1499	SNOWDIN, William	28	NESW	1857-10-30		A1
1491	STEBBINS, Thompson P	32	SESE	1852-02-10		A1

ID	Individual in Patent	Sec.	Sec. Part	Date Issued	Other Counties	For More Info . . .
1492	STEBBINS, Thompson P (Cont'd)	32	SWSE	1852-02-10		A1 R1456
1463	TUCKER, John	20	SENW	1857-10-30		A1
1464	" "	20	W½NW	1857-10-30		A1
1420	VACHI, Francis	8	SENE	1859-05-09		A1
1419	" "	8	NENE	1860-05-01		A1
1469	VACHI, Leander	4	SENW	1857-07-01		A1
1465	WELLS, John	10	NESW	1856-09-01		A1
1466	" "	22	SESW	1856-09-01		A1
1500	WHITNEY, William	5	E½SE	1856-01-10		A1
1501	" "	5	SWSE	1856-01-10		A1
1409	WIGHT, Buckminster	31	NESE	1852-02-10		A1
1410	" "	5	NWSE	1852-02-10		A1
1411	" "	6	NWNW	1852-02-10		A1 F
1412	" "	6	SESE	1852-02-10		A1
1407	WIXSON, Amos	20	NESE	1855-10-01		A1
1408	" "	20	SENE	1855-10-01		A1

Patent Map

T12-N R15-E
Michigan-Toledo Strip Meridian

Map Group 14

Township Statistics

Parcels Mapped	:	95
Number of Patents	:	60
Number of Individuals	:	51
Patentees Identified	:	49
Number of Surnames	:	47
Multi-Patentee Parcels	:	20
Oldest Patent Date	:	9/4/1838
Most Recent Patent	:	2/25/1913
Block/Lot Parcels	:	0
Parcels Re - Issued	:	1
Parcels that Overlap	:	0
Cities and Towns	:	2
Cemeteries	:	2

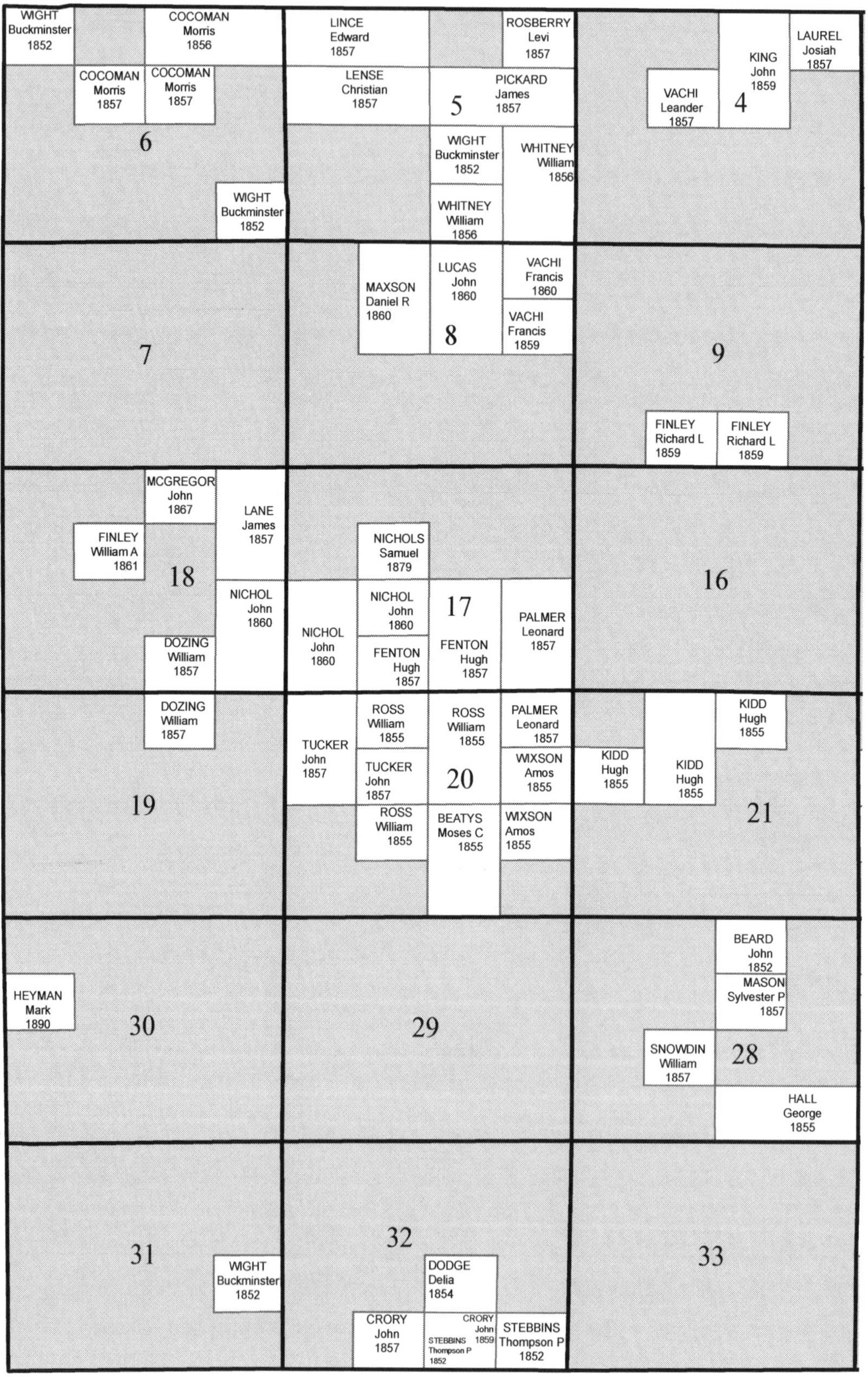

Helpful Hints

1. This Map's INDEX can be found on the preceding pages.
2. Refer to Map "C" to see where this Township lies within Sanilac County, Michigan.
3. Numbers within square brackets [ ] denote a multi-patentee land parcel (multi-owner). Refer to Appendix "C" for a full list of members in this group.
4. Areas that look to be crowded with Patentees usually indicate multiple sales of the same parcel (Re-issues) or Overlapping parcels. See this Township's Index for an explanation of these and other circumstances that might explain "odd" groupings of Patentees on this map.

Legend

- Patent Boundary
- Section Boundary
- No Patents Found (or Outside County)
- 1., 2., 3., ... Lot Numbers (when beside a name)
- [ ] Group Number (see Appendix "C")

Scale: Section = 1 mile X 1 mile (generally, with some exceptions)

Road Map

T12-N R15-E
Michigan-Toledo Strip Meridian

Map Group 14

Cities & Towns

Carsonville
McGregor

Cemeteries

Mount Lion Cemetery
Rosbury Cemetery

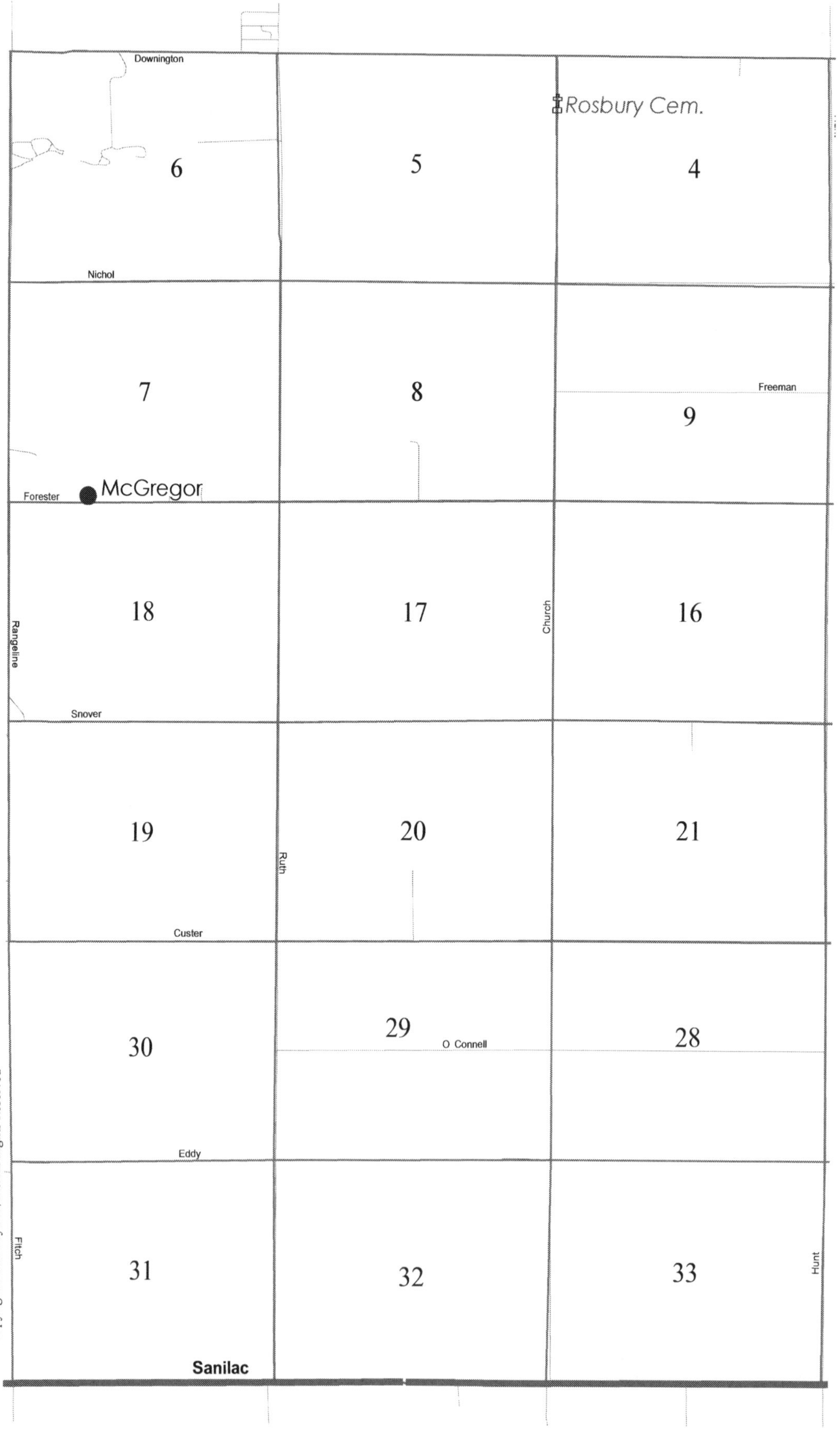

Downington
Hunt
3
2
1
Nichol
Goetze
10
11
Loree
12
Forester
Mount Lion Cem.
15
14
13
Snover
22
Maple Grove
23
24
Custer
27
26
25
Basler
Goetze
34
35
36
Cheryl
Main
Marsh
Arthur
High
Baird
Carsonville
Chandler
Sanilac

Helpful Hints

1. This road map has a number of uses, but primarily it is to help you: a) find the present location of land owned by your ancestors (at least the general area), b) find cemeteries and city-centers, and c) estimate the route/roads used by Census-takers & tax-assessors.
2. If you plan to travel to Sanilac County to locate cemeteries or land parcels, please pick up a modern travel map for the area before you do. Mapping old land parcels on modern maps is not as exact a science as you might think. Just the slightest variations in public land survey coordinates, estimates of parcel boundaries, or road-map deviations can greatly alter a map's representation of how a road either does or doesn't cross a particular parcel of land.

Legend

- Section Lines
- Interstates
- Highways
- Other Roads
- Cities/Towns
- Cemeteries

Scale: Section = 1 mile X 1 mile (generally, with some exceptions)

Historical Map

T12-N R15-E
Michigan-Toledo Strip Meridian

Map Group 14

Cities & Towns
Carsonville
McGregor

Cemeteries
Mount Lion Cemetery
Rosbury Cemetery

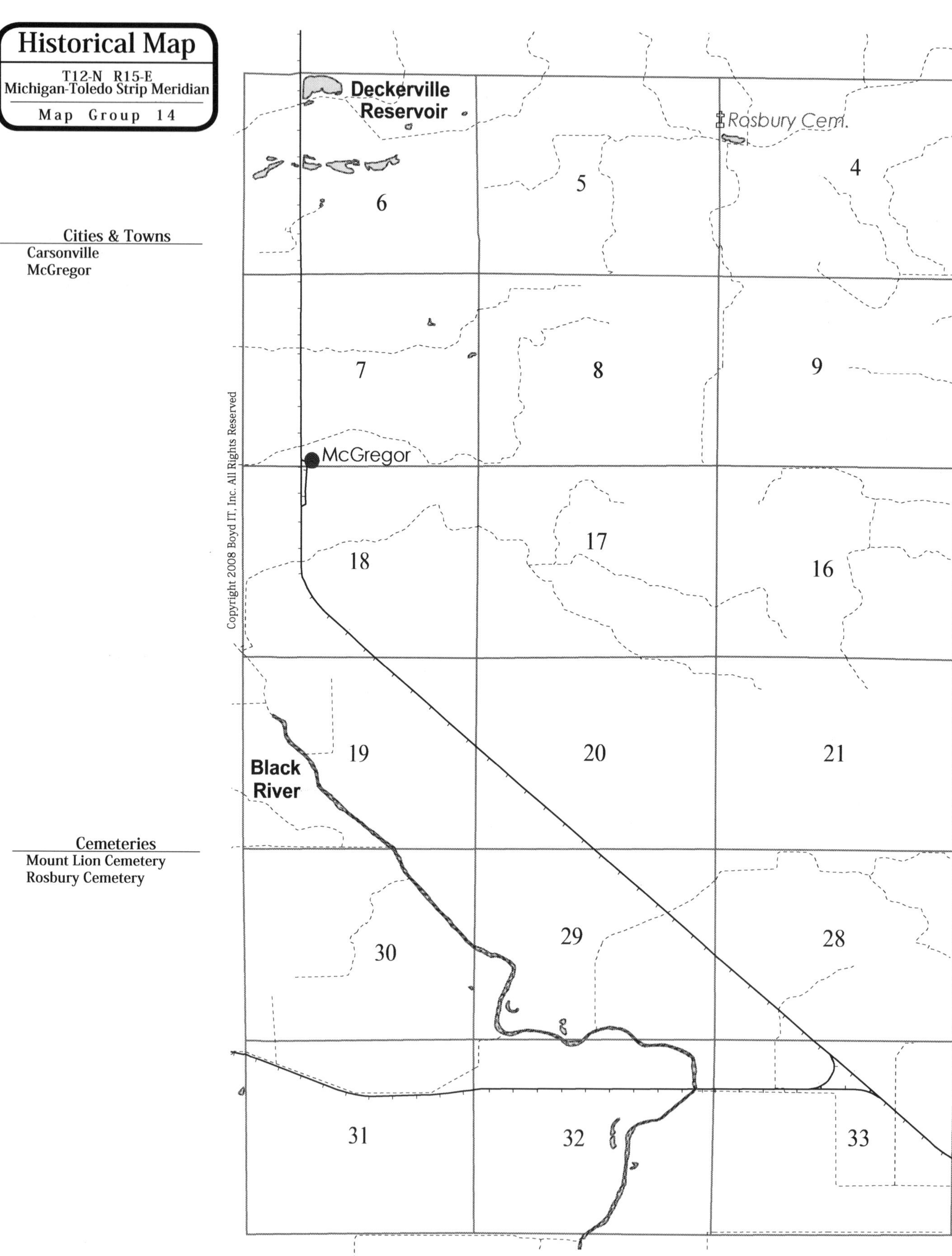

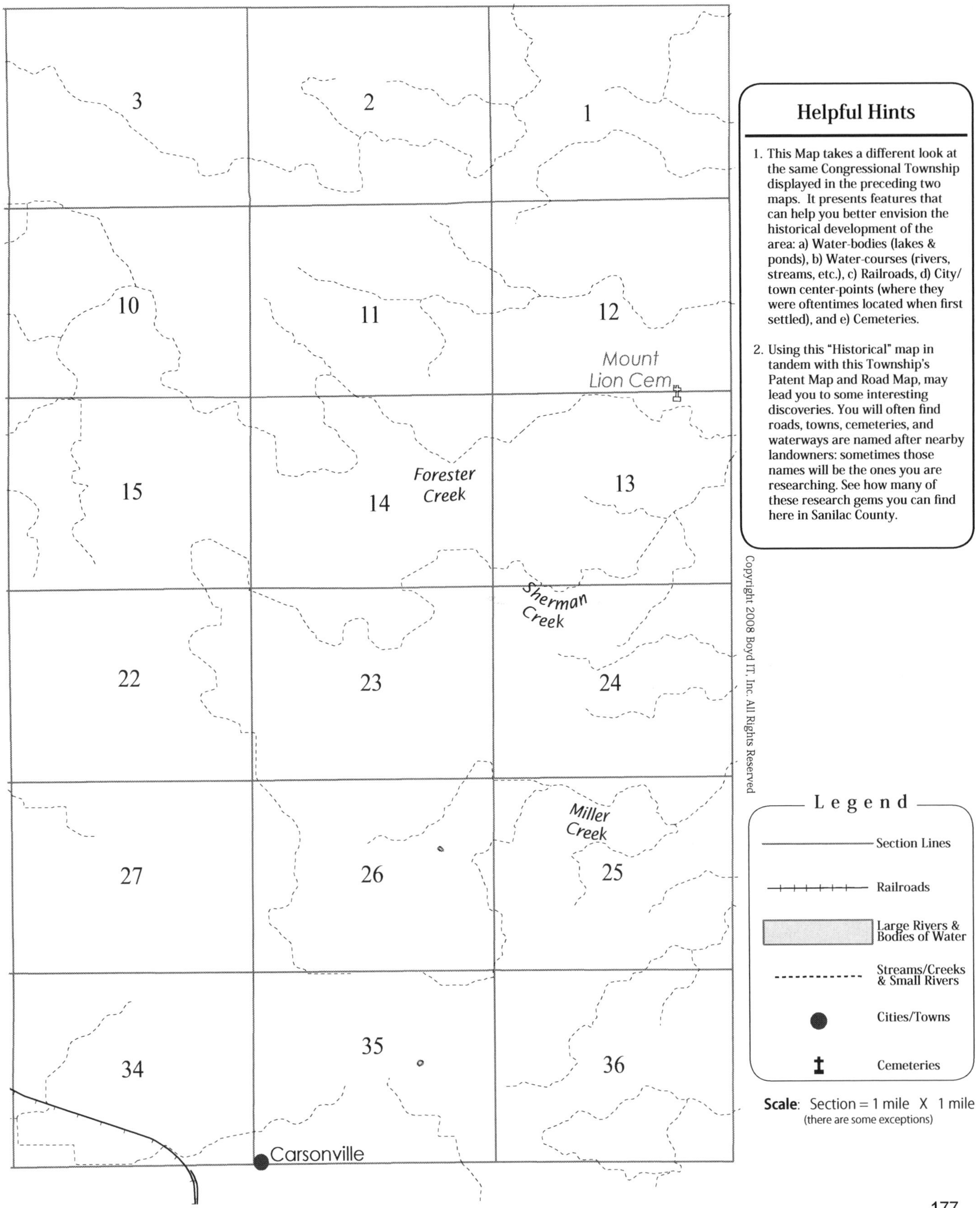
3
2
1
10
11
12
Mount
Lion Cem
15
14
Forester
Creek
13
Sherman
Creek
22
23
24
Miller
Creek
27
26
25
34
35
36
Carsonville
Helpful Hints
1. This Map takes a different look at the same Congressional Township displayed in the preceding two maps. It presents features that can help you better envision the historical development of the area: a) Water-bodies (lakes & ponds), b) Water-courses (rivers, streams, etc.), c) Railroads, d) City/town center-points (where they were oftentimes located when first settled), and e) Cemeteries.
2. Using this "Historical" map in tandem with this Township's Patent Map and Road Map, may lead you to some interesting discoveries. You will often find roads, towns, cemeteries, and waterways are named after nearby landowners: sometimes those names will be the ones you are researching. See how many of these research gems you can find here in Sanilac County.
Legend
Section Lines
Railroads
Large Rivers & Bodies of Water
Streams/Creeks & Small Rivers
Cities/Towns
Cemeteries
Scale: Section = 1 mile X 1 mile
(there are some exceptions)

Map Group 15: Index to Land Patents

Township 12-North Range 16-East (Michigan-Toledo Strip)

After you locate an individual in this Index, take note of the Section and Section Part then proceed to the Land Patent map on the pages immediately following. You should have no difficulty locating the corresponding parcel of land.

The "For More Info" Column will lead you to more information about the underlying Patents. See the *Legend* at right, and the "How to Use this Book" chapter, for more information.

LEGEND

"For More Info . . . " column

A = Authority (Legislative Act, See Appendix "A")
B = Block or Lot (location in Section unknown)
C = Cancelled Patent
F = Fractional Section
G = Group (Multi-Patentee Patent, see Appendix "C")
V = Overlaps another Parcel
R = Re-Issued (Parcel patented more than once)

(A & G items require you to look in the Appendixes referred to above. All other Letter-designations followed by a number require you to locate line-items in this index that possess the ID number found after the letter).

ID	Individual in Patent	Sec.	Sec. Part	Date Issued	Other Counties	For More Info . . .
1502	ALLEN, Adna	5	SENW	1861-12-03		A1
1592	ALLEN, William S	27	SENW	1854-06-15		A1
1593	" "	28	E½SE	1857-07-01		A1
1562	BALDWIN, Mary A	5	NWNE	1855-10-01		A1 F
1525	BEACH, George	19	SW	1838-09-04		A1 G12
1526	" "	19	W½SE	1838-09-04		A1 G12
1527	" "	21	NE	1838-09-04		A1 G12
1528	" "	21	NW	1838-09-04		A1 G12
1529	" "	22	NW	1838-09-04		A1 G12
1530	" "	32	E½SW	1838-09-04		A1 G12
1531	" "	32	SE	1838-09-04		A1 G12
1532	" "	7	SE	1838-09-04		A1 G12
1533	" "	7	SW	1838-09-04		A1 G12
1525	BECKWITH, Alonzo S	19	SW	1838-09-04		A1 G12
1526	" "	19	W½SE	1838-09-04		A1 G12
1527	" "	21	NE	1838-09-04		A1 G12
1528	" "	21	NW	1838-09-04		A1 G12
1529	" "	22	NW	1838-09-04		A1 G12
1530	" "	32	E½SW	1838-09-04		A1 G12
1531	" "	32	SE	1838-09-04		A1 G12
1532	" "	7	SE	1838-09-04		A1 G12
1533	" "	7	SW	1838-09-04		A1 G12
1555	BLACKMAIR, John M	19	E½SE	1853-11-01		A1
1509	BLINDBURY, Charles	20	SWNE	1852-02-10		A1
1587	BLINDBURY, Volney H	20	SENE	1852-02-10		A1
1583	BODDY, Samuel	34	E½NW	1856-01-10		A1
1519	BRACKENRIDGE, Edward A	20	NWNW	1854-06-15		A1
1570	BUGBEE, Oliver	20	SWNW	1852-02-10		A1
1541	BURCHAM, James	5	SWNW	1859-10-10		A1 F
1538	BURK, Hiram	8	NESE	1850-12-02		A1
1539	" "	8	NWSE	1850-12-02		A1
1510	BUTLER, Charles	10	E½SW	1837-08-21		A1 F
1511	" "	15	NE	1837-08-21		A1 F
1512	" "	20	S½	1837-08-21		A1 C
1513	" "	26	3	1923-06-27		A1
1514	" "	26	4	1923-06-27		A1
1550	CALKINS, Jerome	28	NWNW	1852-02-10		A1
1515	CLARKE, Charles	20	SENW	1852-02-10		A1
1551	CLIFTON, John	6	SE	1859-10-10		A1
1588	CROWELL, William E	15	NWNW	1850-12-02		A1
1552	CURRIE, John	33	NWSE	1852-02-10		A1
1542	DAVENPORT, James	34	NENE	1850-03-01		A1
1535	DEYOE, Heman	9	SWSW	1850-12-02		A1
1534	" "	29	SWSE	1856-09-01		A1
1566	DICKINSON, Nathan	10	N½	1837-08-05		A1 F
1567	" "	3		1837-08-05		A1 F

ID	Individual in Patent	Sec.	Sec. Part	Date Issued	Other Counties	For More Info . . .
1568	DICKINSON, Nathan (Cont'd)	4	E½SE	1837-08-05		A1
1569	" "	9	NE	1837-08-05		A1
1525	" "	19	SW	1838-09-04		A1 G12
1526	" "	19	W½SE	1838-09-04		A1 G12
1527	" "	21	NE	1838-09-04		A1 G12
1528	" "	21	NW	1838-09-04		A1 G12
1529	" "	22	NW	1838-09-04		A1 G12
1530	" "	32	E½SW	1838-09-04		A1 G12
1531	" "	32	SE	1838-09-04		A1 G12
1532	" "	7	SE	1838-09-04		A1 G12
1533	" "	7	SW	1838-09-04		A1 G12
1577	DIMOND, Reuben B	21	NWSW	1852-02-10		A1
1578	" "	22	NESW	1852-02-10		A1
1579	" "	22	SWSW	1852-02-10		A1
1507	EATON, Amos B	21	SE	1837-08-21		A1 C F
1520	ENNEST, Elias	27	W½NE	1859-05-09		A1
1553	FERRIS, John	8	NWNW	1862-10-01		A1
1554	GARVIN, John	6	NESW	1860-10-01		A1
1589	GARVIN, William	5	W½SW	1860-10-01		A1
1503	GOODRICH, Alanson	4	NENE	1852-02-10		A1
1504	" "	4	NENW	1852-02-10		A1
1505	" "	4	NWNE	1852-11-01		A1 F
1571	GOULD, Orvil A	7	SENE	1852-11-01		A1
1574	GOULD, Rascellas E	15	E½NW	1852-02-10		A1
1576	GOULD, Rassellas	10	NWSW	1850-12-02		A1
1575	GOULD, Rassellas E	27	SESE	1850-03-01		A1
1580	HALL, Richard H	10	SWSW	1850-12-02		A1 F
1590	HINKSON, William	21	SWSE	1850-12-02		A1
1563	HOMER, Michael	6	N½NE	1857-10-30		A1
1547	HURD, Jarvis	35	E½N½	1837-08-16		A1
1548	" "	35	S½	1837-08-16		A1
1561	HURD, Marshall F	34	SENE	1848-09-01		A1
1544	JOHNSON, James	5	SESW	1859-10-10		A1
1543	" "	5	NESW	1860-05-01		A1
1517	JOINER, Charles W	33	N½NE	1857-02-20		A1
1559	JONES, Josiah P	21	E½SE	1852-02-10		A1
1545	LANE, James	17	SWNW	1855-10-01		A1
1506	MARTINDALE, Alpheus	33	NESW	1852-02-10		A1
1516	MARTINDALE, Charles	28	SWSE	1867-02-16		A1
1546	MCINTOSH, James M	5	NENE	1859-10-10		A1 F
1556	MCMULDROCH, John	27	NENW	1856-09-01		A1
1582	MERCHANT, Rufus	33	NESE	1859-05-09		A1
1536	MIZNER, Henry R	32	W½SW	1854-06-15		A1
1537	" "	34	W½SW	1855-10-01		A1
1581	MUNFORD, Robert	22	SESW	1859-10-10		A1
1508	OLDFIELD, Anthony	21	NWSE	1852-02-10		A1
1557	PAGANETTI, John	17	SENW	1859-10-10		A1
1560	PAGANETTI, Margaret	17	NWSW	1885-01-30		A1
1591	PETERS, William	33	SENW	1856-09-01		A1
1585	RAYMOND, Uri	21	NESW	1855-10-01		A1
1586	" "	22	NWSW	1855-10-01		A1
1572	RYAN, Patrick	17	NESW	1857-02-20		A1
1573	" "	17	S½SW	1857-02-20		A1
1549	SPENCER, Jeremiah	4	SENE	1852-02-10		A1
1521	STEEVENS, Frederick H	15	SE	1837-08-07		A1 F
1522	" "	22	NE	1837-08-07		A1 F
1523	" "	23		1837-08-07		A1 F
1524	" "	26	N½	1837-08-07		A1 F
1564	TODD, Morris	28	NESW	1852-02-10		A1
1565	" "	28	SESW	1852-02-10		A1
1584	WARING, Thomas P	6	S½NW	1857-07-01		A1 F
1518	WATERBURY, David	27	NESE	1857-02-20		A1
1558	WATERBURY, John	20	NWSE	1852-02-10		A1
1540	WESLEY, Hiram	20	NENW	1859-10-10		A1

Patent Map

T12-N R16-E
Michigan-Toledo Strip Meridian

Map Group 15

Township Statistics

Parcels Mapped	:	92
Number of Patents	:	74
Number of Individuals	:	62
Patentees Identified	:	61
Number of Surnames	:	52
Multi-Patentee Parcels	:	9
Oldest Patent Date	:	8/5/1837
Most Recent Patent	:	6/27/1923
Block/Lot Parcels	:	2
Parcels Re - Issued	:	0
Parcels that Overlap	:	0
Cities and Towns	:	2
Cemeteries	:	0

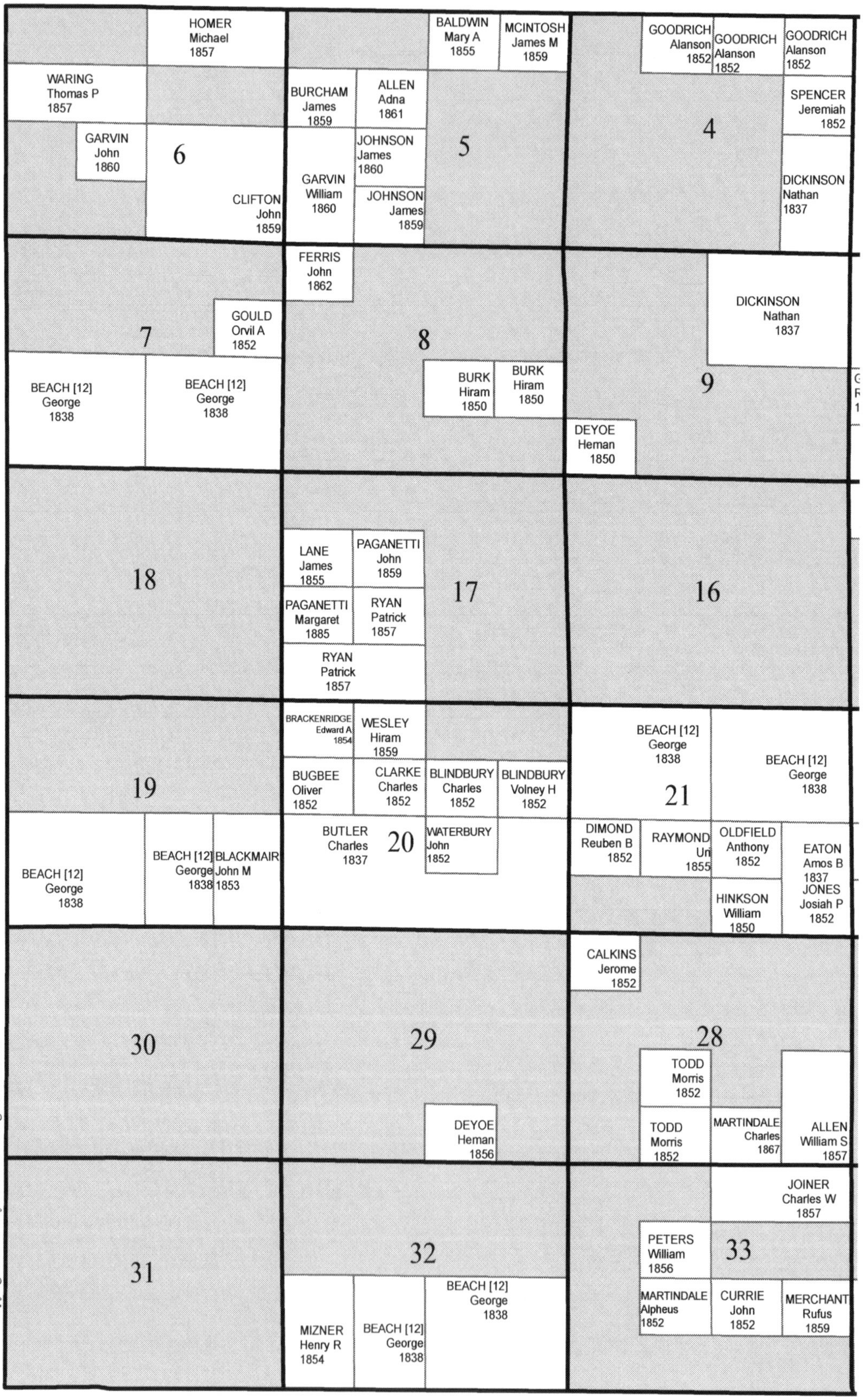

DICKINSON
Nathan
1837

3

10

DICKINSON
Nathan
1837

GOULD
Rassellas
1850

HALL
Richard H
1850

BUTLER
Charles
1837

CROWELL
William E
1850

GOULD
Rascellas E
1852

BUTLER
Charles
1837

15

STEEVENS
Frederick H
1837

BEACH [12]
George
1838

STEEVENS
Frederick H
1837

RAYMOND
Uri
1855

DIMOND
Reuben B
1852

22

DIMOND
Reuben B
1852

MUNFORD
Robert
1859

23

STEEVENS
Frederick H
1837

MCMULDROCH
John
1856

ALLEN
William S
1854

ENNEST
Elias
1859

STEEVENS
Frederick H
1837

27

WATERBURY
David
1857

GOULD
Rassellas E
1850

26

Lots-Sec. 26

3 BUTLER, Charles 1923
4 BUTLER, Charles 1923

BODDY
Samuel
1856

DAVENPORT
James
1850

HURD
Marshall F
1848

HURD
Jarvis
1837

35

34

MIZNER
Henry R
1855

HURD
Jarvis
1837

Helpful Hints

1. This Map's INDEX can be found on the preceding pages.
2. Refer to Map "C" to see where this Township lies within Sanilac County, Michigan.
3. Numbers within square brackets [ ] denote a multi-patentee land parcel (multi-owner). Refer to Appendix "C" for a full list of members in this group.
4. Areas that look to be crowded with Patentees usually indicate multiple sales of the same parcel (Re-issues) or Overlapping parcels. See this Township's Index for an explanation of these and other circumstances that might explain "odd" groupings of Patentees on this map.

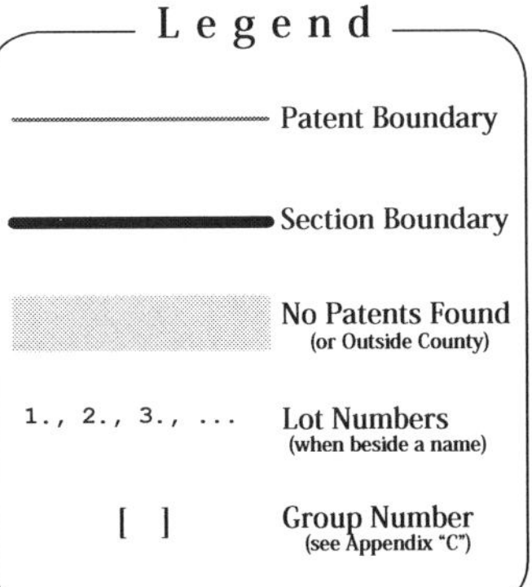

Scale: Section = 1 mile X 1 mile
(generally, with some exceptions)

Road Map

T12-N R16-E
Michigan-Toledo Strip Meridian

Map Group 15

Cities & Towns
Forester
Port Sanilac

Cemeteries
None

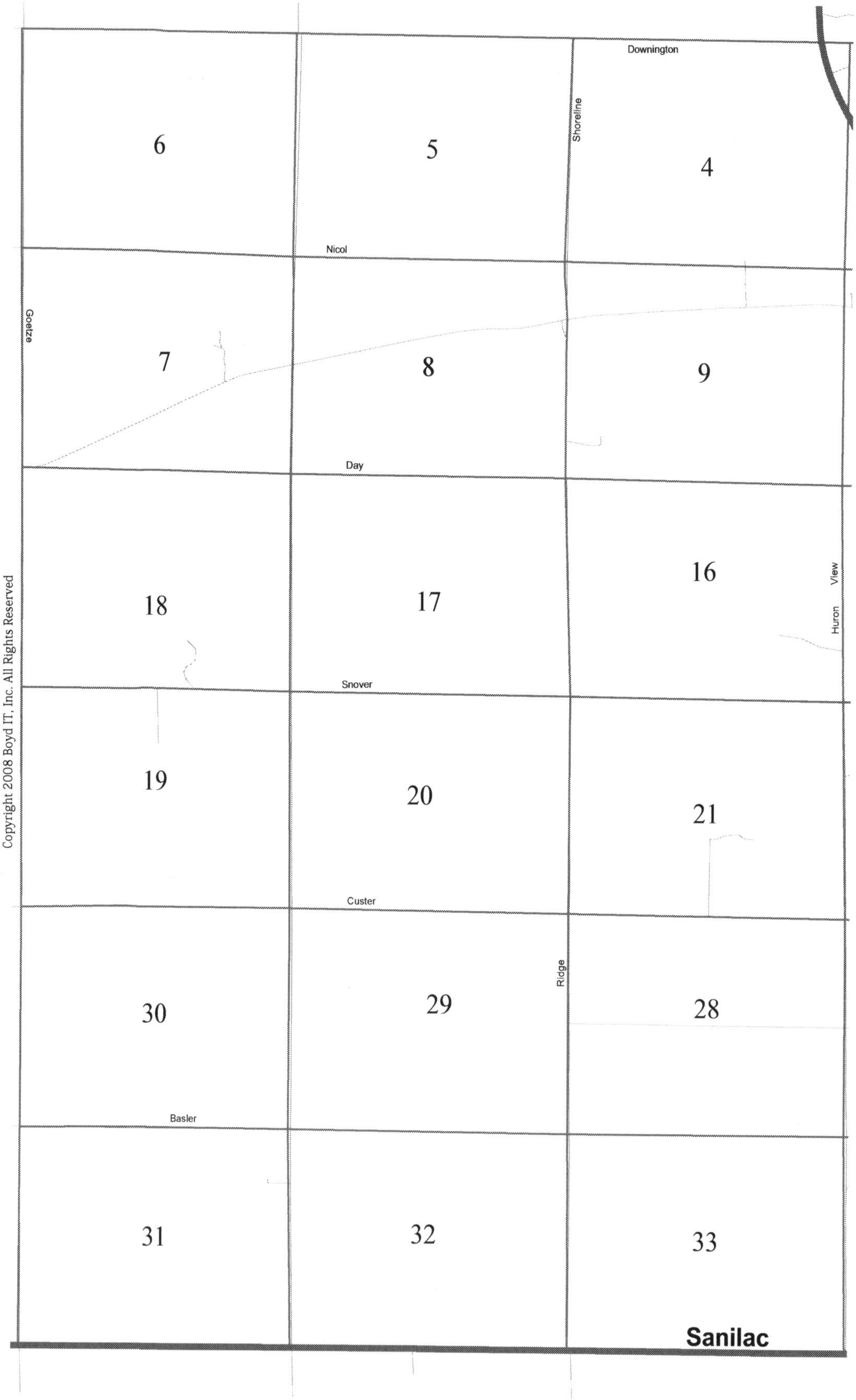

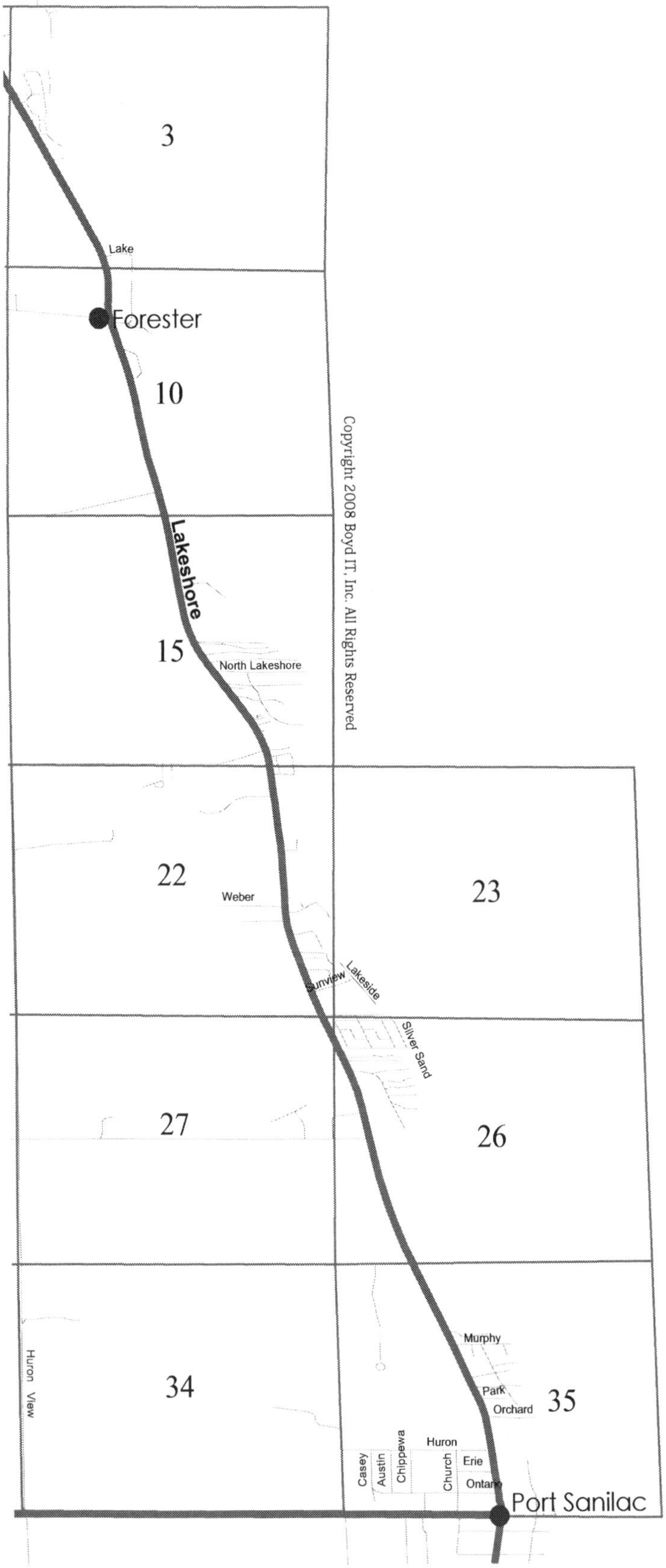

3
Lake
Forester
10
Lakeshore
15
North Lakeshore
22
Weber
23
Sunview
Lakeside
Silver Sand
27
26
34
Huron View
Murphy
Park
Orchard
35
Huron
Casey
Austin
Chippewa
Church
Erie
Ontario
Port Sanilac

Helpful Hints

1. This road map has a number of uses, but primarily it is to help you: a) find the present location of land owned by your ancestors (at least the general area), b) find cemeteries and city-centers, and c) estimate the route/roads used by Census-takers & tax-assessors.

2. If you plan to travel to Sanilac County to locate cemeteries or land parcels, please pick up a modern travel map for the area before you do. Mapping old land parcels on modern maps is not as exact a science as you might think. Just the slightest variations in public land survey coordinates, estimates of parcel boundaries, or road-map deviations can greatly alter a map's representation of how a road either does or doesn't cross a particular parcel of land.

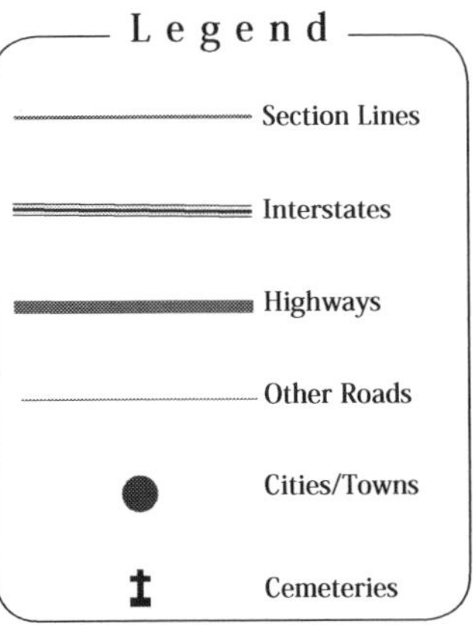

Scale: Section = 1 mile X 1 mile
(generally, with some exceptions)

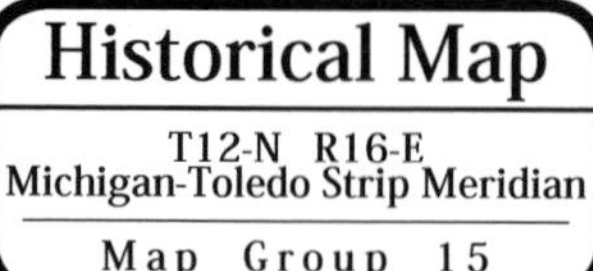

Cities & Towns

Forester
Port Sanilac

Cemeteries

None

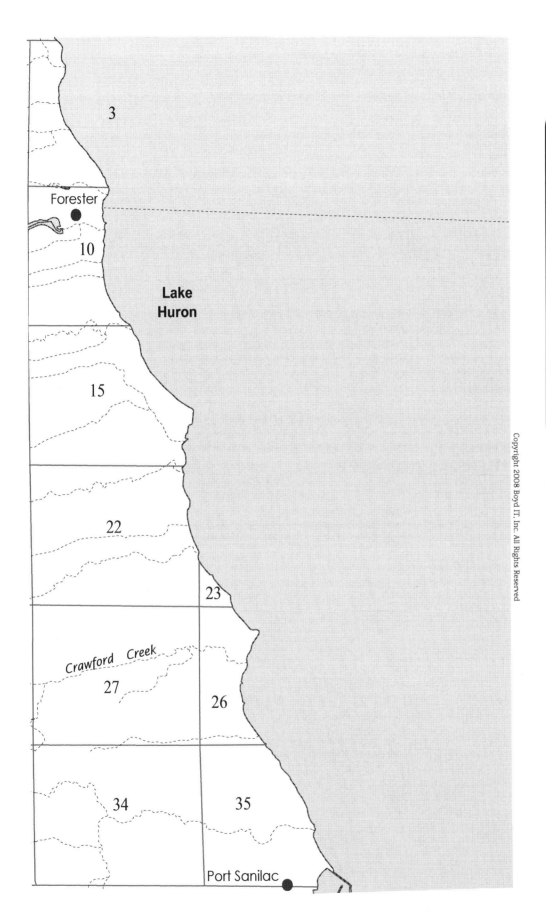

3
Forester
10
Lake Huron
15
22
23
Crawford Creek
27
26
34
35
Port Sanilac

Helpful Hints

1. This Map takes a different look at the same Congressional Township displayed in the preceding two maps. It presents features that can help you better envision the historical development of the area: a) Water-bodies (lakes & ponds), b) Water-courses (rivers, streams, etc.), c) Railroads, d) City/town center-points (where they were oftentimes located when first settled), and e) Cemeteries.

2. Using this "Historical" map in tandem with this Township's Patent Map and Road Map, may lead you to some interesting discoveries. You will often find roads, towns, cemeteries, and waterways are named after nearby landowners: sometimes those names will be the ones you are researching. See how many of these research gems you can find here in Sanilac County.

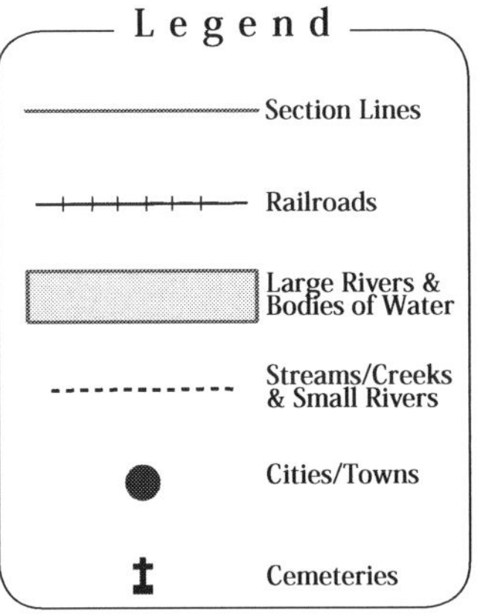

Scale: Section = 1 mile X 1 mile
(there are some exceptions)

Map Group 16: Index to Land Patents

Township 11-North Range 12-East (Michigan-Toledo Strip)

After you locate an individual in this Index, take note of the Section and Section Part then proceed to the Land Patent map on the pages immediately following. You should have no difficulty locating the corresponding parcel of land.

The "For More Info" Column will lead you to more information about the underlying Patents. See the *Legend* at right, and the "How to Use this Book" chapter, for more information.

LEGEND

"For More Info . . . " column

A = Authority (Legislative Act, See Appendix "A")
B = Block or Lot (location in Section unknown)
C = Cancelled Patent
F = Fractional Section
G = Group (Multi-Patentee Patent, see Appendix "C")
V = Overlaps another Parcel
R = Re-Issued (Parcel patented more than once)

(A & G items require you to look in the Appendixes referred to above. All other Letter-designations followed by a number require you to locate line-items in this index that possess the ID number found after the letter).

ID	Individual in Patent	Sec.	Sec. Part	Date Issued	Other Counties	For More Info . . .
1630	ANDERSON, Henry	21	W½NW	1859-05-09		A1
1674	BATCHELDER, John W	12	E½SW	1870-05-10		A1 G10
1602	BELDEN, Austin A	27	SW	1857-07-01		A1
1603	" "	34	NW	1857-07-01		A1
1653	BIEBER, Johann A	9	NENE	1861-12-10		A1
1654	" "	9	S½NE	1861-12-10		A1
1655	" "	9	SENW	1861-12-10		A1
1665	BISHOP, John H	31	W½SE	1859-05-09		A1
1664	" "	31	SW	1860-05-01		A1
1726	BISHOP, William J	4	NENW	1882-10-20		A2 F
1671	BLAKE, John J	30	SWNW	1859-05-09		A1
1717	BOTTOMLEY, Thomas	28	NWSE	1865-10-02		A1
1601	BURGER, Anton	36	W½SE	1857-07-01		A1
1607	BURMEISTER, Charles A	18	SWSW	1870-05-10		A1 F
1658	BYRNE, John	23	E½SW	1859-05-09		A1
1659	BYRNES, John	14	E½NW	1875-02-05		A2
1594	CARPENTER, Addison	6	E½SW	1860-05-01		A1
1595	" "	6	S½SE	1860-05-01		A1
1660	CARROLL, John	14	SWSW	1856-01-10		A1
1631	CAWOOD, Henry	23	W½SW	1859-05-09		A1
1634	CAWOOD, Horatio	14	W½NW	1860-05-01		A1
1661	CAWOOD, John	15	W½SE	1857-07-01		A1
1715	COFFEY, Rosanah	14	NWSW	1866-06-20		A1
1723	COFFY, William B	14	SESW	1885-11-25		A2
1608	COLE, Charles	25	N½SW	1859-10-10		A1
1609	" "	26	NESE	1859-10-10		A1
1639	COLE, James H	25	S½SW	1859-10-10		A1
1610	COOK, Charles	30	E½SE	1857-02-20		A1
1611	" "	31	E½NE	1857-02-20		A1
1614	COVIL, Elijah	1	SWSW	1877-07-20		A2
1615	" "	12	SENW	1877-07-20		A2
1616	" "	12	W½NW	1877-07-20		A2
1625	CRAMPTON, George	27	E½	1857-07-01		A1
1626	" "	34	SW	1857-07-01		A1
1633	CRAMPTON, Holmes	34	NE	1857-07-01		A1
1702	CUMMINGS, Redmon S	14	NESW	1855-10-01		A1
1703	" "	14	SE	1855-10-01		A1
1704	" "	14	W½NE	1855-10-01		A1
1705	" "	22	SENE	1855-10-01		A1
1706	" "	22	SENW	1855-10-01		A1
1707	" "	26	W½SE	1855-10-01		A1
1637	DALE, Hugh	35	W½SW	1856-01-10		A1
1635	" "	35	NW	1857-02-16		A1
1636	" "	35	W½NE	1857-02-16		A1
1627	DONALD, George	33	SE	1860-05-01		A1
1662	ELLIS, John	11	N½NE	1855-10-01		A1

ID	Individual in Patent	Sec.	Sec. Part	Date Issued	Other Counties	For More Info . . .
1719	ESELE, Wendelin	5	N½NE	1878-02-13		A2 F
1638	EVOY, James	29	N½NE	1860-05-01		A1
1712	FERGUSON, Robert	28	SWSW	1857-07-01		A1
1710	" "	28	N½SW	1857-10-30		A1
1711	" "	28	SESW	1857-10-30		A1
1713	" "	33	NW	1857-10-30		A1
1689	FISHER, Michael	26	SESE	1857-07-01		A1
1718	FITZPATRICK, Thomas	25	NW	1857-07-01		A1
1663	FOSTER, John	21	E½NW	1860-05-01		A1
1695	GOIT, Oliver S	33	N½SW	1860-05-01		A1
1699	GREEN, Philip	30	NE	1859-05-09		A1
1714	HADDOW, Robert	5	W½	1859-05-09		A1
1690	HAMILTON, Michael J	18	N½NE	1859-05-09		A1
1691	" "	18	S½NE	1860-05-01		A1
1621	HILLEBRAND, Franz	4	SWSE	1859-10-10		A1
1622	" "	9	NWNE	1859-10-10		A1
1604	HOBSON, Benjamin	32	S½	1857-02-20		A1
1725	HOFFMANN, William	13	W½NW	1862-05-15		A1
1724	" "	13	E½NW	1862-10-01		A1
1666	HOMUTH, John	4	N½SW	1860-05-01		A1
1667	" "	4	S½NW	1860-05-01		A1
1668	" "	5	N½SE	1860-05-01		A1
1669	" "	5	S½NE	1860-05-01		A1
1670	HOWIE, John	7	SW	1857-07-01		A1
1640	HUNTER, James	19	E½SW	1857-10-30		A1
1641	" "	19	NWSW	1857-10-30		A1
1642	" "	19	SE	1857-10-30		A1
1693	HUNTER, Neil	19	N	1857-10-30		A1
1674	JOHNSON, James S	12	E½SW	1870-05-10		A1 G10
1613	KEYS, David	36	SW	1857-10-30		A1
1612	" "	35	NENE	1861-12-10		A1
1708	KIRKPATRICK, Richard	35	N½SE	1859-05-09		A1
1709	" "	35	SENE	1859-10-10		A1
1680	KLEIN, Joseph	31	NENW	1859-05-09		A1
1681	" "	31	NWNE	1859-05-09		A1
1643	KNIGHT, James	15	E½SE	1859-05-09		A1
1644	" "	22	N½NE	1859-05-09		A1
1645	" "	22	SWNE	1859-05-09		A1
1672	LENNON, John	14	E½NE	1860-11-21		A1
1628	MACOMBER, George	26	W½	1857-07-01		A1
1694	MANS, Nicolaus	11	SWNE	1879-06-30		A2
1656	MANSS, Johannes	11	E½SE	1862-02-01		A1
1657	" "	12	W½SW	1862-02-01		A1
1696	MARVIN, Orson	6	N½SE	1860-05-01		A1
1697	" "	6	S½NE	1860-05-01		A1
1600	MCALPIN, Andrew	20	S½SW	1857-10-30		A1
1599	" "	20	N½SW	1859-05-09		A1
1673	MCALPIN, John	20	E½	1857-10-30		A1
1727	MCLEISH, William	22	N½NW	1859-05-09		A1
1728	" "	22	SWNW	1859-05-09		A1
1721	MONTGOMERY, William A	35	E½SW	1859-05-09		A1
1722	" "	35	S½SE	1859-05-09		A1
1692	MOONY, Michael	29	SE	1857-10-30		A1
1682	MORRIS, Joseph	18	NWSW	1859-10-10		A1 F
1596	NEUMANN, Alexander	8	NWSE	1859-10-10		A1
1683	NEUMANN, Joseph	8	N½SW	1859-05-09		A1
1684	NEWMAN, Joseph	7	SE	1860-05-01		A1
1685	" "	8	S½SW	1860-05-01		A1
1720	NEWMAN, Wenzel	18	W½NW	1861-07-01		A1
1629	NOTLEY, George	34	SE	1857-10-30		A1
1652	RATTRAY, James	21	SW	1857-10-30		A1
1716	ROGERS, Samuel	9	SWSW	1885-01-30		A2
1729	RUDD, William	29	W½	1857-10-30		A1
1605	SCHLEGEL, Carl	4	S½SW	1859-10-10		A1
1606	" "	5	S½SE	1859-10-10		A1
1686	SCHOLTZ, Joseph	30	S½SW	1859-10-10		A1 F
1687	SCHREIN, Joseph	31	SENW	1861-12-03		A1
1688	" "	31	SWNE	1861-12-03		A1
1698	SELTZER, Peter	2	W½NW	1881-05-03		A1
1624	SLADE, Frederick	21	N½NE	1857-07-01		A1
1700	SMITH, Philip	6	N½NE	1860-05-01		A1
1701	" "	6	NW	1860-05-01		A1
1730	SMITH, William	12	SE	1875-02-05		A2 C

ID	Individual in Patent	Sec.	Sec. Part	Date Issued	Other Counties	For More Info . . .
1617	TAMBURAT, Felix	13	E½SW	1861-12-10		A1 R1618
1617	" "	13	E½SW	1861-12-10		A1 C R1618
1618	" "	13	E½SW	1861-12-10		A1 R1617
1618	" "	13	E½SW	1861-12-10		A1 C R1617
1619	" "	13	W½SW	1861-12-10		A1
1620	" "	24	NWNW	1861-12-10		A1
1623	TATE, Frederick G	7	SENW	1910-12-19		A1 F
1646	TWISS, James M	3	NWSW	1857-10-30		A1
1647	" "	3	W½NW	1857-10-30		A1
1648	" "	4	E½NE	1857-10-30		A1
1649	" "	4	E½SE	1857-10-30		A1
1650	" "	4	NWNE	1857-10-30		A1
1651	TWIST, James M	3	NENE	1856-01-10		A1
1735	TYLDEN, Zimri	22	SE	1857-10-30		A1
1675	WALKER, John	1	NWSW	1867-07-01		A1
1731	WALKER, William	23	S½SE	1857-10-30		A1
1732	" "	24	S½SW	1857-10-30		A1
1733	" "	26	NE	1857-10-30		A1
1598	WALSH, Ambrose	3	S½SE	1876-11-03		A2
1734	WARPOOL, William	11	SW	1860-05-01		A1
1676	WELSH, John	33	NE	1857-10-30		A1
1597	WIGGINS, Alleyne H	28	S½SE	1856-09-01		A1
1677	WOOD, John	6	W½SW	1859-05-09		A1
1678	" "	7	NENW	1859-05-09		A1
1679	" "	7	W½NW	1859-05-09		A1
1632	WOOLLEY, Henry	2	NENE	1859-05-09		A1

Patent Map

T11-N R12-E
Michigan-Toledo Strip Meridian

Map Group 16

Township Statistics

Parcels Mapped	:	142
Number of Patents	:	106
Number of Individuals	:	90
Patentees Identified	:	89
Number of Surnames	:	79
Multi-Patentee Parcels	:	1
Oldest Patent Date	:	10/1/1855
Most Recent Patent	:	12/19/1910
Block/Lot Parcels	:	1
Parcels Re - Issued	:	1
Parcels that Overlap	:	0
Cities and Towns	:	0
Cemeteries	:	2

Helpful Hints

1. This Map's INDEX can be found on the preceding pages.
2. Refer to Map "C" to see where this Township lies within Sanilac County, Michigan.
3. Numbers within square brackets [ ] denote a multi-patentee land parcel (multi-owner). Refer to Appendix "C" for a full list of members in this group.
4. Areas that look to be crowded with Patentees usually indicate multiple sales of the same parcel (Re-issues) or Overlapping parcels. See this Township's Index for an explanation of these and other circumstances that might explain "odd" groupings of Patentees on this map.

Legend

- Patent Boundary
- Section Boundary
- No Patents Found (or Outside County)
- 1., 2., 3., ... Lot Numbers (when beside a name)
- [ ] Group Number (see Appendix "C")

Scale: Section = 1 mile X 1 mile (generally, with some exceptions)

Road Map

T11-N R12-E
Michigan-Toledo Strip Meridian

Map Group 16

Cities & Towns

None

Cemeteries

Germania Cemetery
McLeish Cemetery

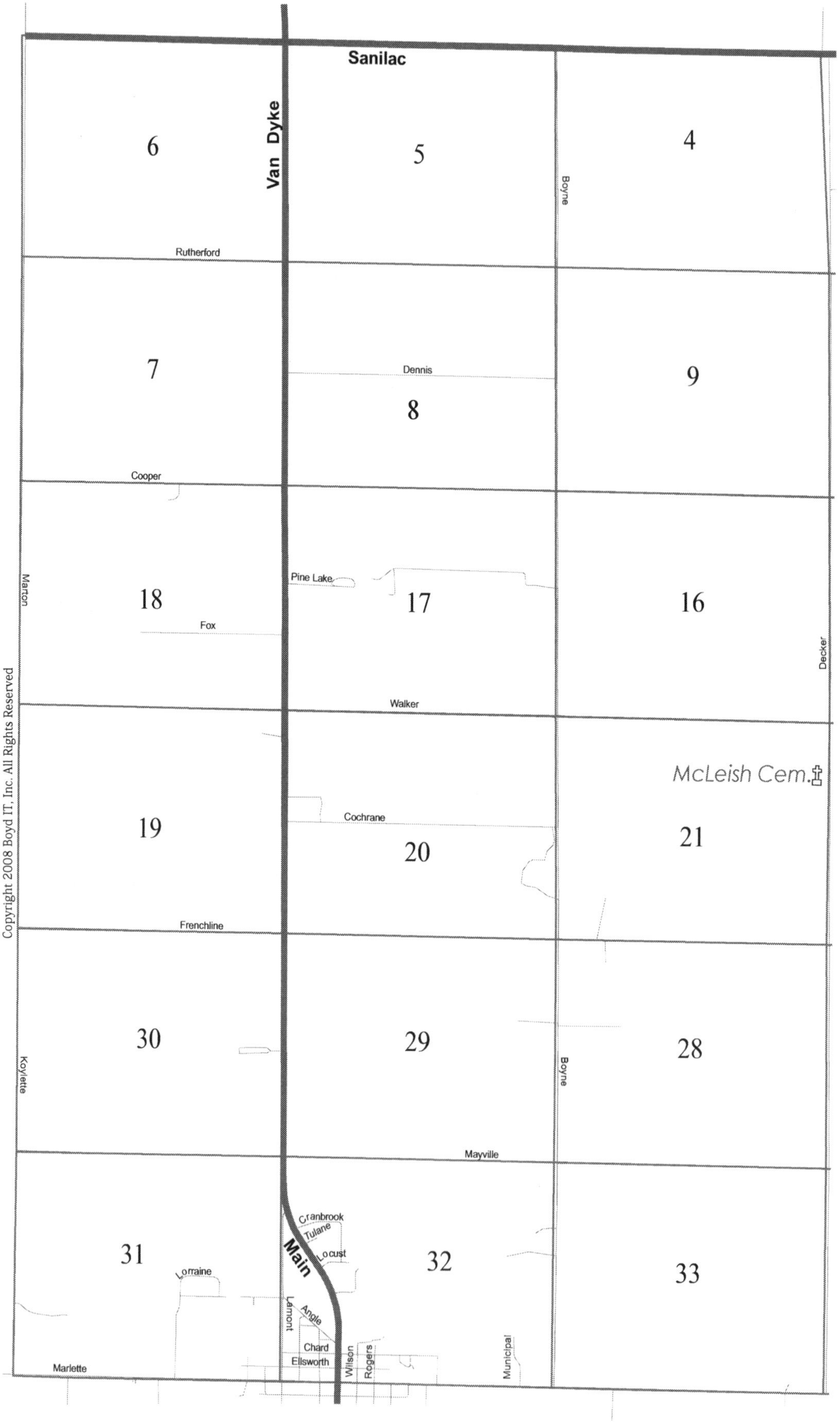

Helpful Hints

1. This road map has a number of uses, but primarily it is to help you: a) find the present location of land owned by your ancestors (at least the general area), b) find cemeteries and city-centers, and c) estimate the route/roads used by Census-takers & tax-assessors.

2. If you plan to travel to Sanilac County to locate cemeteries or land parcels, please pick up a modern travel map for the area before you do. Mapping old land parcels on modern maps is not as exact a science as you might think. Just the slightest variations in public land survey coordinates, estimates of parcel boundaries, or road-map deviations can greatly alter a map's representation of how a road either does or doesn't cross a particular parcel of land.

Legend

- Section Lines
- Interstates
- Highways
- Other Roads
- Cities/Towns
- Cemeteries

Scale: Section = 1 mile X 1 mile (generally, with some exceptions)

Historical Map

T11-N R12-E
Michigan-Toledo Strip Meridian

Map Group 16

Cities & Towns
None

Cemeteries
Germania Cemetery
McLeish Cemetery

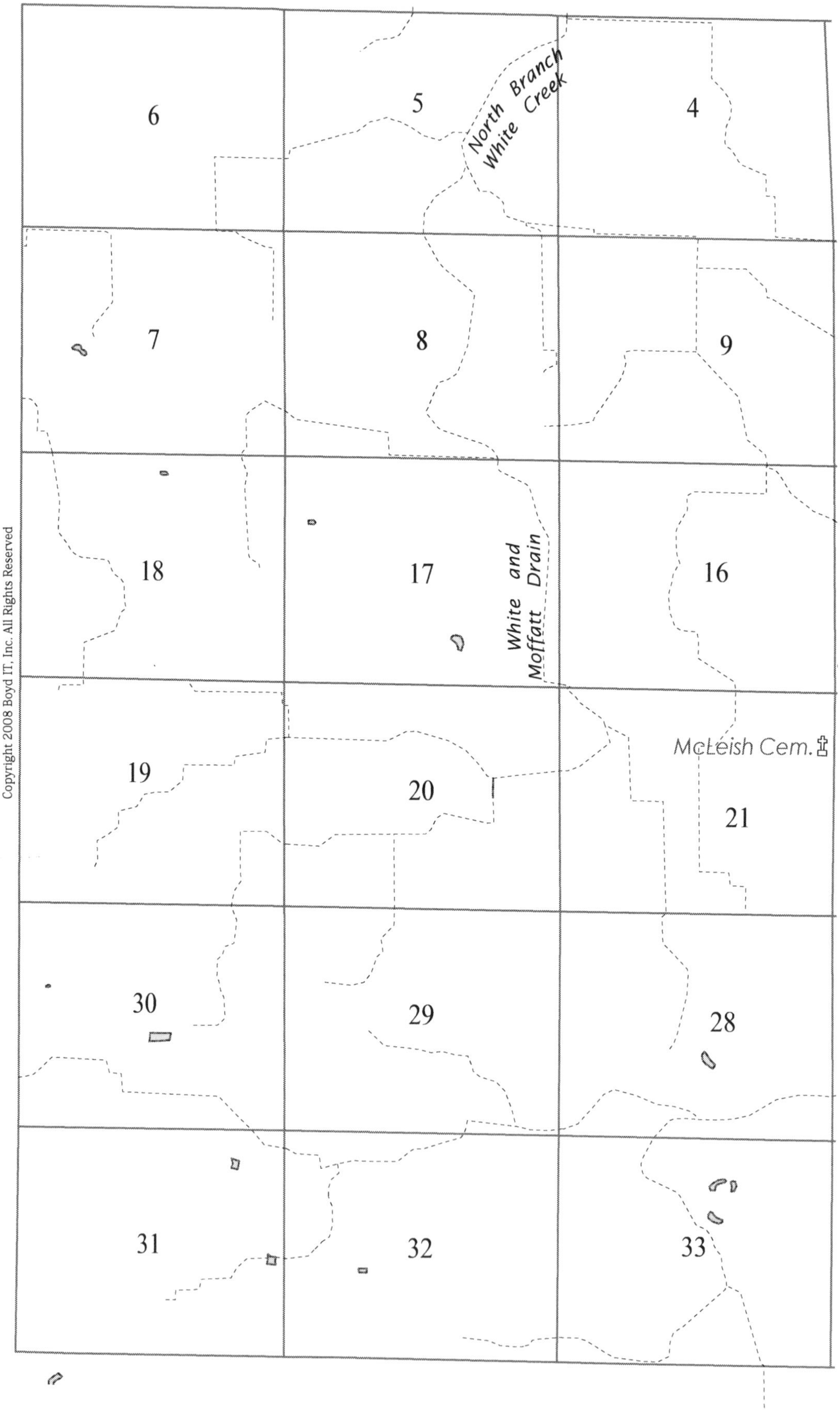

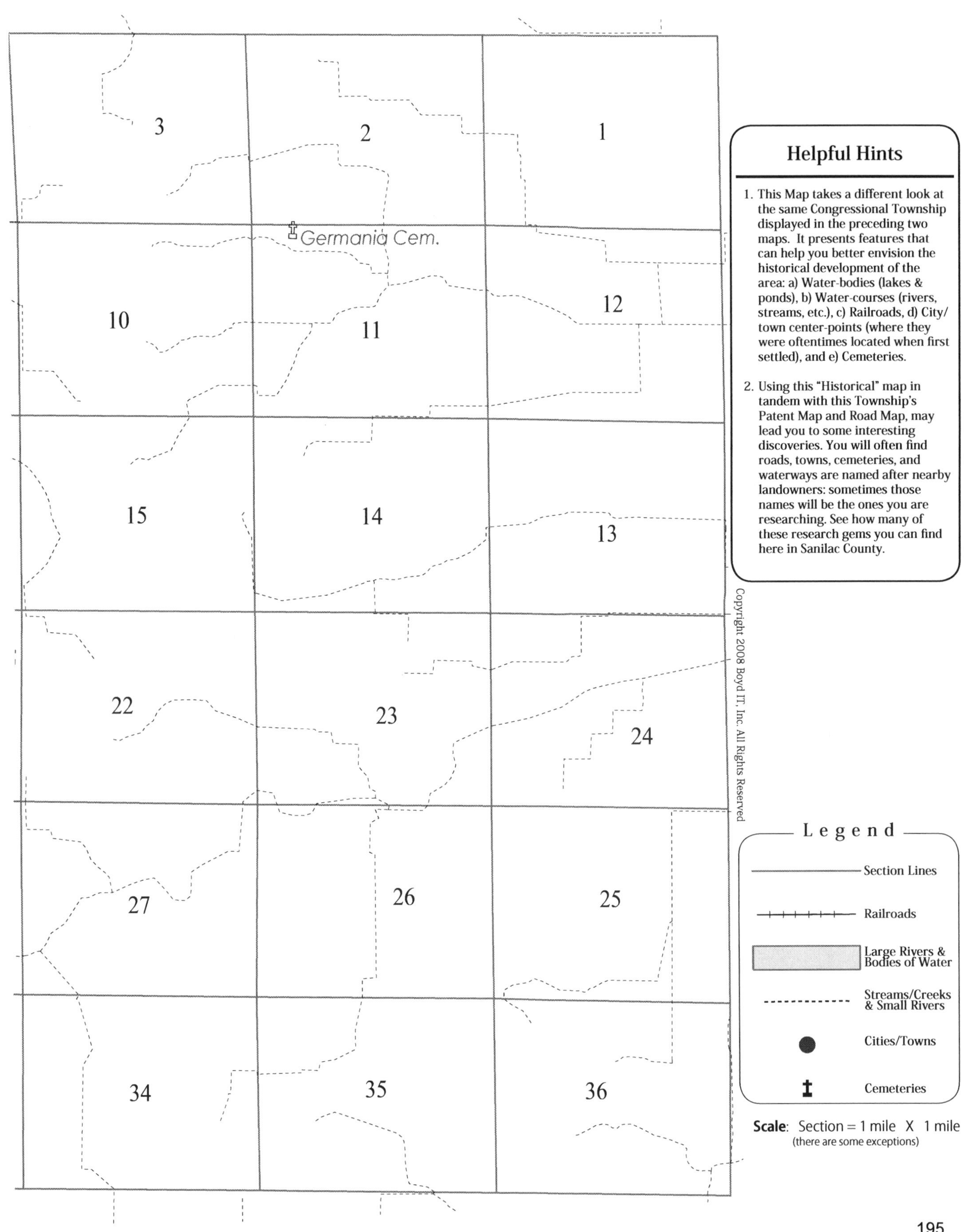

Helpful Hints

1. This Map takes a different look at the same Congressional Township displayed in the preceding two maps. It presents features that can help you better envision the historical development of the area: a) Water-bodies (lakes & ponds), b) Water-courses (rivers, streams, etc.), c) Railroads, d) City/town center-points (where they were oftentimes located when first settled), and e) Cemeteries.

2. Using this "Historical" map in tandem with this Township's Patent Map and Road Map, may lead you to some interesting discoveries. You will often find roads, towns, cemeteries, and waterways are named after nearby landowners: sometimes those names will be the ones you are researching. See how many of these research gems you can find here in Sanilac County.

Scale: Section = 1 mile X 1 mile
(there are some exceptions)

Map Group 17: Index to Land Patents

Township 11-North Range 13-East (Michigan-Toledo Strip)

After you locate an individual in this Index, take note of the Section and Section Part then proceed to the Land Patent map on the pages immediately following. You should have no difficulty locating the corresponding parcel of land.

The "For More Info" Column will lead you to more information about the underlying Patents. See the *Legend* at right, and the "How to Use this Book" chapter, for more information.

LEGEND

"For More Info . . . " column

A = Authority (Legislative Act, See Appendix "A")
B = Block or Lot (location in Section unknown)
C = Cancelled Patent
F = Fractional Section
G = Group (Multi-Patentee Patent, see Appendix "C")
V = Overlaps another Parcel
R = Re-Issued (Parcel patented more than once)

(A & G items require you to look in the Appendixes referred to above. All other Letter-designations followed by a number require you to locate line-items in this index that possess the ID number found after the letter).

ID	Individual in Patent	Sec.	Sec. Part	Date Issued	Other Counties	For More Info . . .
1736	ASH, Allen K	24	SESE	1864-01-05		A1
1747	BANKS, Frederick	21	NESW	1878-11-05		A2
1748	" "	21	NWSE	1878-11-05		A2
1749	BANKS, George H	21	NE	1876-01-20		A2
1781	BATCHELDER, John W	17	SESE	1869-11-15		A1 G10
1782	" "	28	W½SW	1869-11-15		A1 G10
1783	" "	29	SESE	1869-11-15		A1 G10
1742	DAVIS, Augustus	5	NWSW	1890-05-23		A2 G27
1743	" "	5	S½SW	1890-05-23		A2 G27
1744	" "	5	SWNW	1890-05-23		A2 G27
1742	DAVIS, Mary	5	NWSW	1890-05-23		A2 G27
1743	" "	5	S½SW	1890-05-23		A2 G27
1744	" "	5	SWNW	1890-05-23		A2 G27
1797	DICKSON, Richard	15	SWNW	1864-01-05		A1
1849	DOERING, William F	24	N½NE	1879-06-30		A2
1850	" "	24	N½NW	1879-06-30		A2
1848	DORING, William	12	SW	1873-04-25		A2
1745	ERSKINE, E	2	SESW	1869-07-01		A1 G37
1746	" "	25	NWNE	1870-10-01		A1 G37
1745	ERSKINE, J	2	SESW	1869-07-01		A1 G37
1746	" "	25	NWNE	1870-10-01		A1 G37
1795	FIKE, Nelson	11	SESE	1896-02-05		A2
1851	HARPER, William	5	SENE	1876-04-10		A2
1785	HARRIS, Joseph	20	SWSE	1890-04-16		A1
1752	HOWARD, Henry	25	SENW	1855-10-01		A1
1753	" "	26	NESE	1855-10-01		A1
1754	" "	9	SWSE	1864-01-05		A1
1836	HYSLOP, Walter	11	E½SW	1871-09-30		A2
1837	" "	11	W½SE	1871-09-30		A2
1781	JOHNSON, James S	17	SESE	1869-11-15		A1 G10
1782	" "	28	W½SW	1869-11-15		A1 G10
1783	" "	29	SESE	1869-11-15		A1 G10
1852	JOHNSON, William	12	E½NW	1875-11-20		A2
1853	" "	12	S½NE	1875-11-20		A2
1767	KIRKBRIDE, John	4	NWNE	1889-11-22		A2 F
1834	KIRKBRIDE, Thomas	10	NWSE	1873-04-25		A2
1835	" "	10	SWNE	1873-04-25		A2
1750	KOTZKE, Heinrich W	13	S½NE	1880-10-01		A2
1751	" "	13	S½NW	1880-10-01		A2
1766	LEE, John H	20	NWSE	1864-09-15		A1
1791	MASON, Lorenzo	25	NESW	1855-10-01		A1
1786	MASON, Lorenzo M	22	N½SW	1855-10-01		A1
1787	" "	22	NWSE	1855-10-01		A1
1788	" "	22	SESW	1855-10-01		A1
1789	" "	26	NWSE	1855-10-01		A1
1790	" "	36	NENW	1855-10-01		A1

ID	Individual in Patent	Sec.	Sec. Part	Date Issued	Other Counties	For More Info . . .
1761	MERRILL, Jarvis	17	NENW	1872-07-01		A2
1762	" "	17	W½NE	1872-07-01		A2
1763	" "	8	SWSE	1872-07-01		A2
1794	MERRILL, Mary	3	SESE	1867-07-01		A1
1842	MILLS, Wildman	24	SWSW	1870-09-20		A1
1839	" "	15	NWSE	1870-10-01		A1
1840	" "	15	SENE	1870-10-01		A1
1845	" "	35	NESW	1870-11-15		A1
1838	" "	14	SESE	1871-11-15		A1
1841	" "	24	NESE	1871-11-15		A1
1843	" "	25	SENE	1871-11-15		A1
1844	" "	35	NESE	1871-11-15		A1
1846	" "	36	NWSE	1871-11-15		A1
1847	" "	36	SWSW	1871-11-15		A1
1755	MINARD, James	10	E½NE	1872-07-01		A2
1756	" "	10	E½SE	1872-07-01		A2
1757	MOORE, James	5	NESW	1871-09-30		A2
1758	" "	5	NWSE	1871-09-30		A2
1759	" "	5	SENW	1871-09-30		A2
1760	" "	5	SWNE	1871-09-30		A2
1833	MOORE, Tacy	5	NWNW	1867-07-01		A1
1764	MYERS, Jesse	11	W½NE	1872-04-15		A1
1765	" "	2	W½SE	1872-04-15		A1
1739	NIXON, Andrew	3	S½NW	1872-04-15		A1
1771	NIXON, John	10	SESW	1873-05-20		A1
1772	" "	4	SESE	1873-05-20		A1
1796	NORRIS, Philetus W	13	NWNW	1869-11-15		A1
1854	OAKES, William	28	SWNW	1864-01-05		A1
1798	REEVE, Selah	10	NENW	1855-10-01		A1
1799	" "	10	NWNE	1855-10-01		A1
1801	" "	12	W½NW	1855-10-01		A1
1802	" "	13	NENW	1855-10-01		A1
1803	" "	13	NWNE	1855-10-01		A1
1804	" "	14	SW	1855-10-01		A1
1805	" "	15	NESE	1855-10-01		A1
1806	" "	15	NESW	1855-10-01		A1
1807	" "	2	W½NE	1855-10-01		A1 F
1808	" "	22	NESE	1855-10-01		A1
1809	" "	23	NENE	1855-10-01		A1
1810	" "	23	NW	1855-10-01		A1
1811	" "	23	W½NE	1855-10-01		A1
1812	" "	23	W½SW	1855-10-01		A1
1813	" "	26	NWNW	1855-10-01		A1
1814	" "	28	NESW	1855-10-01		A1
1815	" "	29	NESE	1855-10-01		A1
1816	" "	29	SENE	1855-10-01		A1
1817	" "	3	N½SE	1855-10-01		A1
1818	" "	3	N½SW	1855-10-01		A1
1819	" "	3	NENW	1855-10-01		A1 F
1820	" "	3	SWNE	1855-10-01		A1
1821	" "	35	E½NW	1855-10-01		A1
1822	" "	35	NWSE	1855-10-01		A1
1823	" "	35	SESE	1855-10-01		A1
1824	" "	35	SWNW	1855-10-01		A1
1825	" "	35	W½NE	1855-10-01		A1
1826	" "	36	SENE	1855-10-01		A1
1827	" "	4	E½NW	1855-10-01		A1
1828	" "	4	NESW	1855-10-01		A1
1829	" "	4	SWSE	1855-10-01		A1
1830	" "	9	N½NE	1855-10-01		A1
1831	" "	9	NWSE	1855-10-01		A1
1832	" "	9	SWNE	1855-10-01		A1
1800	" "	11	NENW	1856-01-10		A1
1792	ROBSON, Mark	25	NWSW	1885-01-30		A2
1793	" "	25	SWNW	1885-01-30		A2
1740	SELLARS, Archibald	14	E½NW	1871-09-30		A2
1741	" "	14	W½NE	1871-09-30		A2
1855	SMITH, William	12	SE	1876-01-20		A2
1773	STILSON, John	10	NESW	1864-01-05		A1
1774	" "	15	NENE	1864-01-05		A1
1775	" "	15	NENW	1864-01-05		A1
1776	" "	15	SWNE	1864-01-05		A1
1777	" "	21	NESE	1864-01-05		A1

ID	Individual in Patent	Sec.	Sec. Part	Date Issued	Other Counties	For More Info . . .
1778	STILSON, John (Cont'd)	21	SESW	1864-01-05		A1
1779	" "	21	SWSE	1864-01-05		A1
1780	" "	28	W½NE	1864-01-05		A1
1737	THOMAS, Alonzo	18	N½NE	1859-10-10		A1
1738	" "	7	S½SE	1859-10-10		A1
1856	WALKER, William	18	SENE	1868-08-20		A1
1784	WELLS, John	19	S½SE	1850-12-02		A1
1768	WILDFONG, John L	4	NWSW	1859-10-10		A1
1769	" "	4	W½NW	1859-10-10		A1
1770	WOODS, John L	22	NWNE	1857-02-20		A1

Patent Map

T11-N R13-E
Michigan-Toledo Strip Meridian

Map Group 17

Township Statistics

Parcels Mapped	:	121
Number of Patents	:	84
Number of Individuals	:	45
Patentees Identified	:	42
Number of Surnames	:	36
Multi-Patentee Parcels	:	8
Oldest Patent Date	:	12/2/1850
Most Recent Patent	:	2/5/1896
Block/Lot Parcels	:	0
Parcels Re - Issued	:	0
Parcels that Overlap	:	0
Cities and Towns	:	1
Cemeteries	:	2

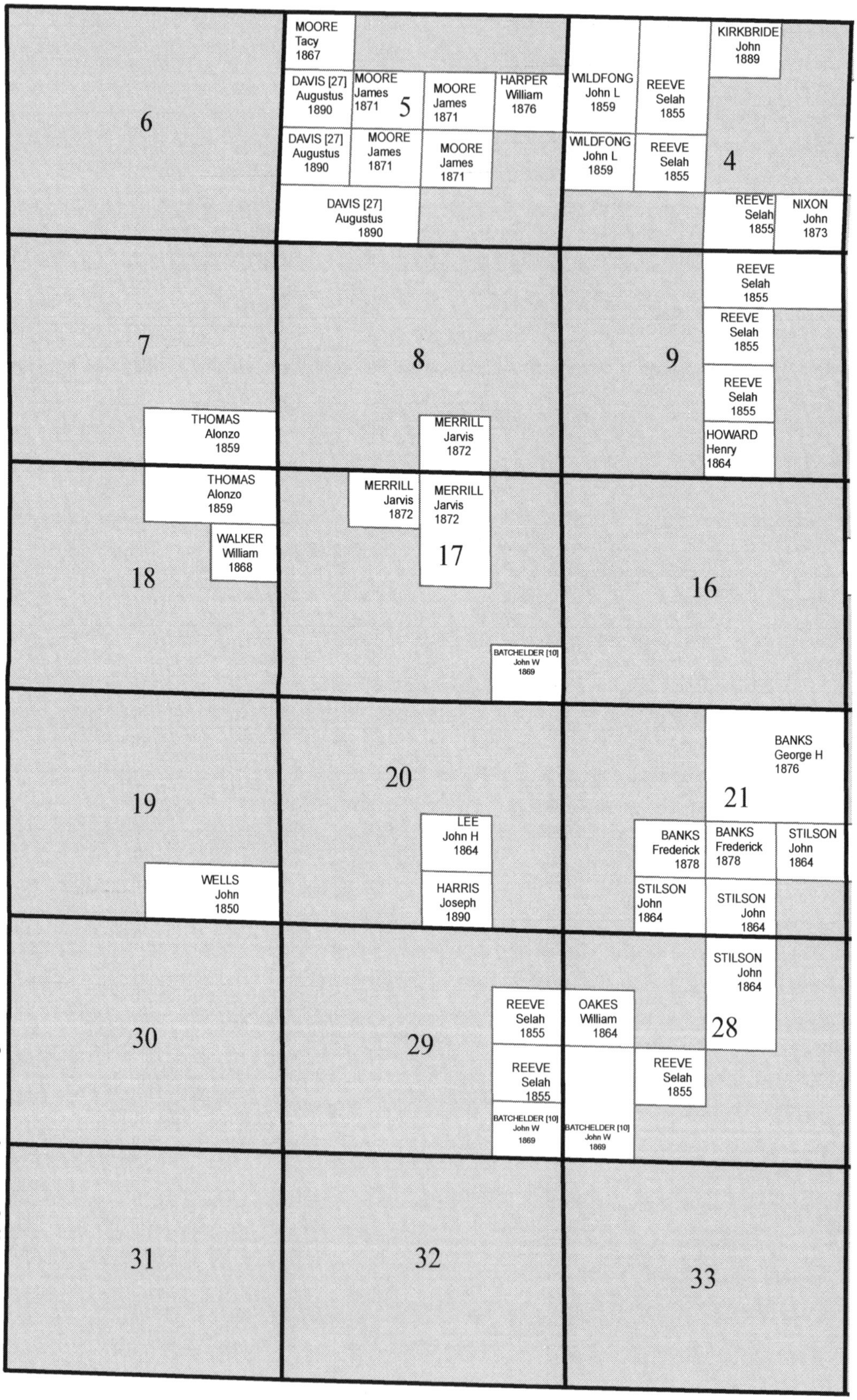

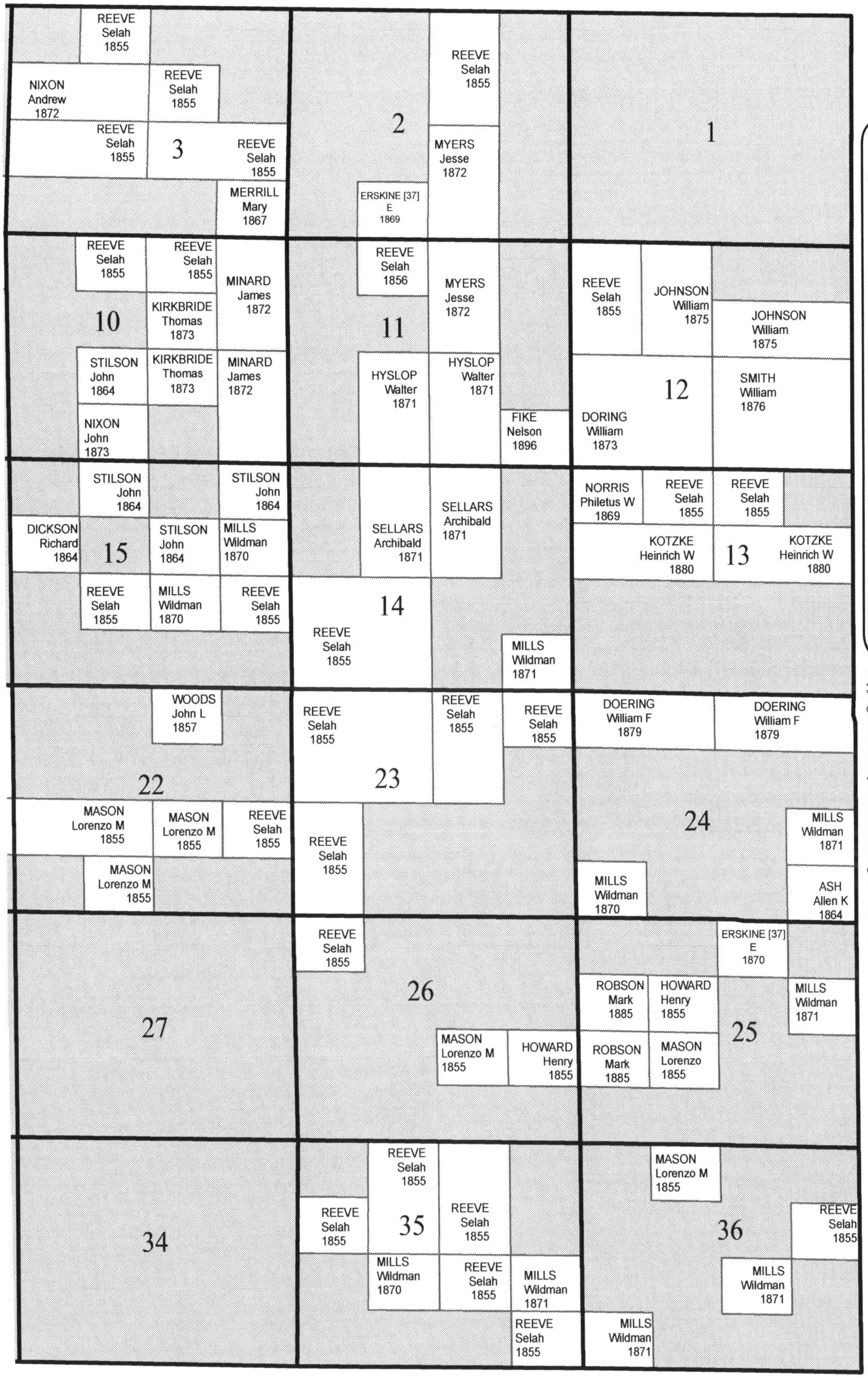

Helpful Hints

1. This Map's INDEX can be found on the preceding pages.
2. Refer to Map "C" to see where this Township lies within Sanilac County, Michigan.
3. Numbers within square brackets [ ] denote a multi-patentee land parcel (multi-owner). Refer to Appendix "C" for a full list of members in this group.
4. Areas that look to be crowded with Patentees usually indicate multiple sales of the same parcel (Re-issues) or Overlapping parcels. See this Township's Index for an explanation of these and other circumstances that might explain "odd" groupings of Patentees on this map.

Legend

- Patent Boundary
- Section Boundary
- No Patents Found (or Outside County)
- 1., 2., 3., ... Lot Numbers (when beside a name)
- [ ] Group Number (see Appendix "C")

Scale: Section = 1 mile X 1 mile (generally, with some exceptions)

Road Map

T11-N R13-E
Michigan-Toledo Strip Meridian

Map Group 17

Cities & Towns
Juhl

Cemeteries
Hyslop Cemetery
Juhl Cemetery

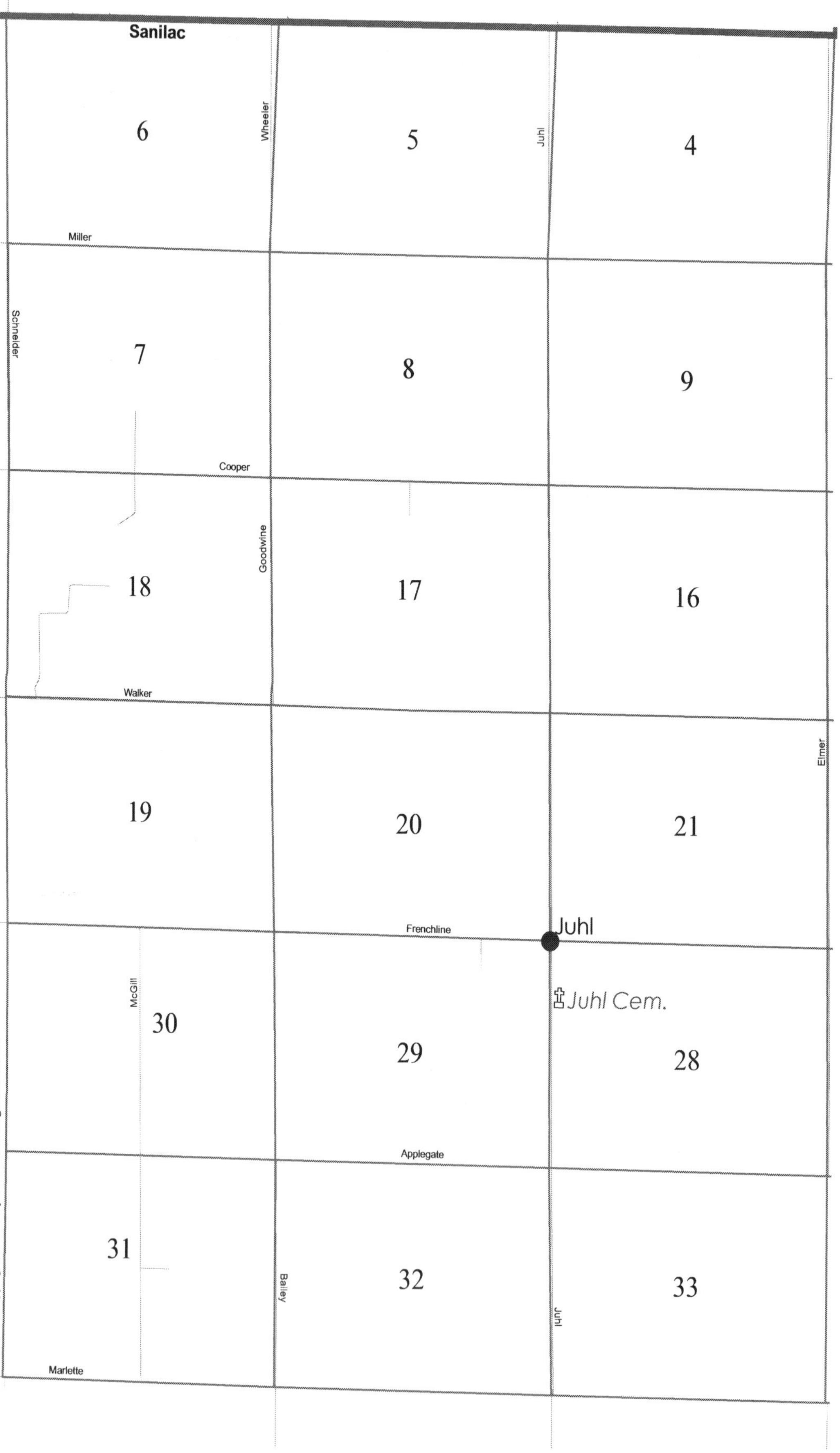

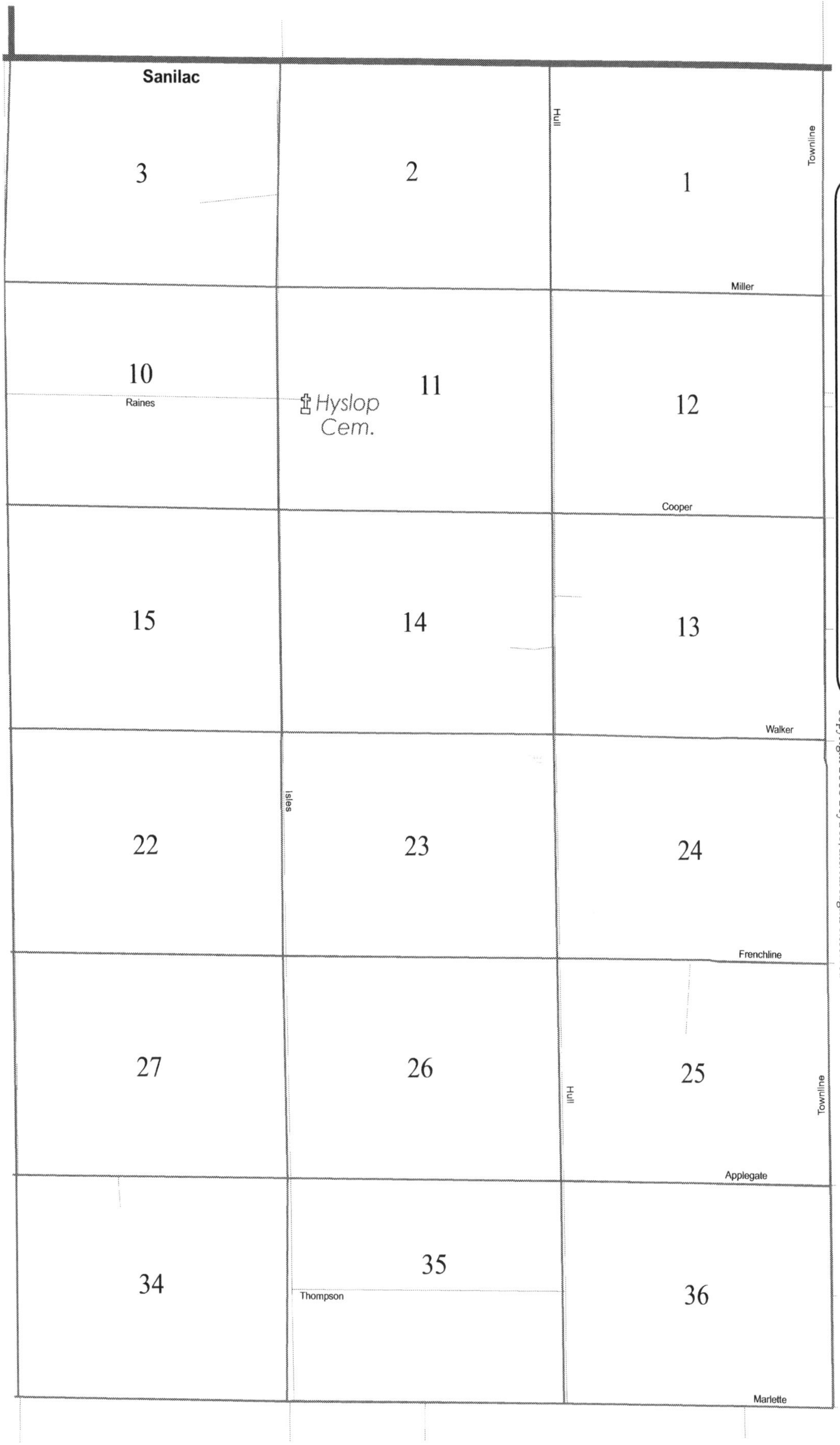

Sanilac

Hull

Townline

3

2

1

Miller

10

Raines

Hyslop Cem.

11

12

Cooper

15

14

13

Walker

Isles

22

23

24

Frenchline

27

26

Hull

25

Townline

Applegate

34

35

Thompson

36

Marlette

Helpful Hints

1. This road map has a number of uses, but primarily it is to help you: a) find the present location of land owned by your ancestors (at least the general area), b) find cemeteries and city-centers, and c) estimate the route/roads used by Census-takers & tax-assessors.
2. If you plan to travel to Sanilac County to locate cemeteries or land parcels, please pick up a modern travel map for the area before you do. Mapping old land parcels on modern maps is not as exact a science as you might think. Just the slightest variations in public land survey coordinates, estimates of parcel boundaries, or road-map deviations can greatly alter a map's representation of how a road either does or doesn't cross a particular parcel of land.

Legend

Section Lines

Interstates

Highways

Other Roads

Cities/Towns

Cemeteries

Scale: Section = 1 mile X 1 mile
(generally, with some exceptions)

Historical Map

T11-N R13-E
Michigan-Toledo Strip Meridian

Map Group 17

Cities & Towns
Juhl

Cemeteries
Hyslop Cemetery
Juhl Cemetery

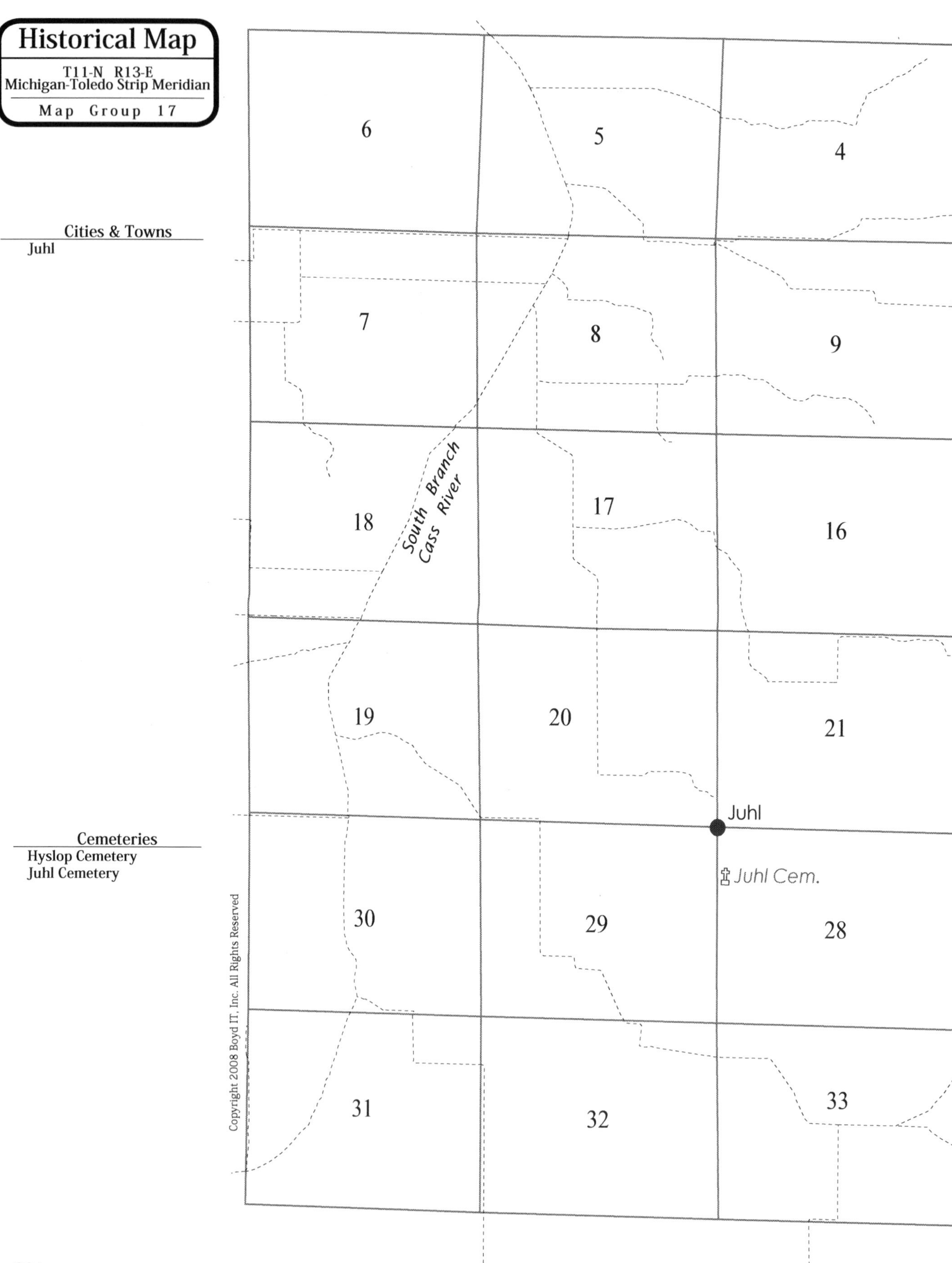

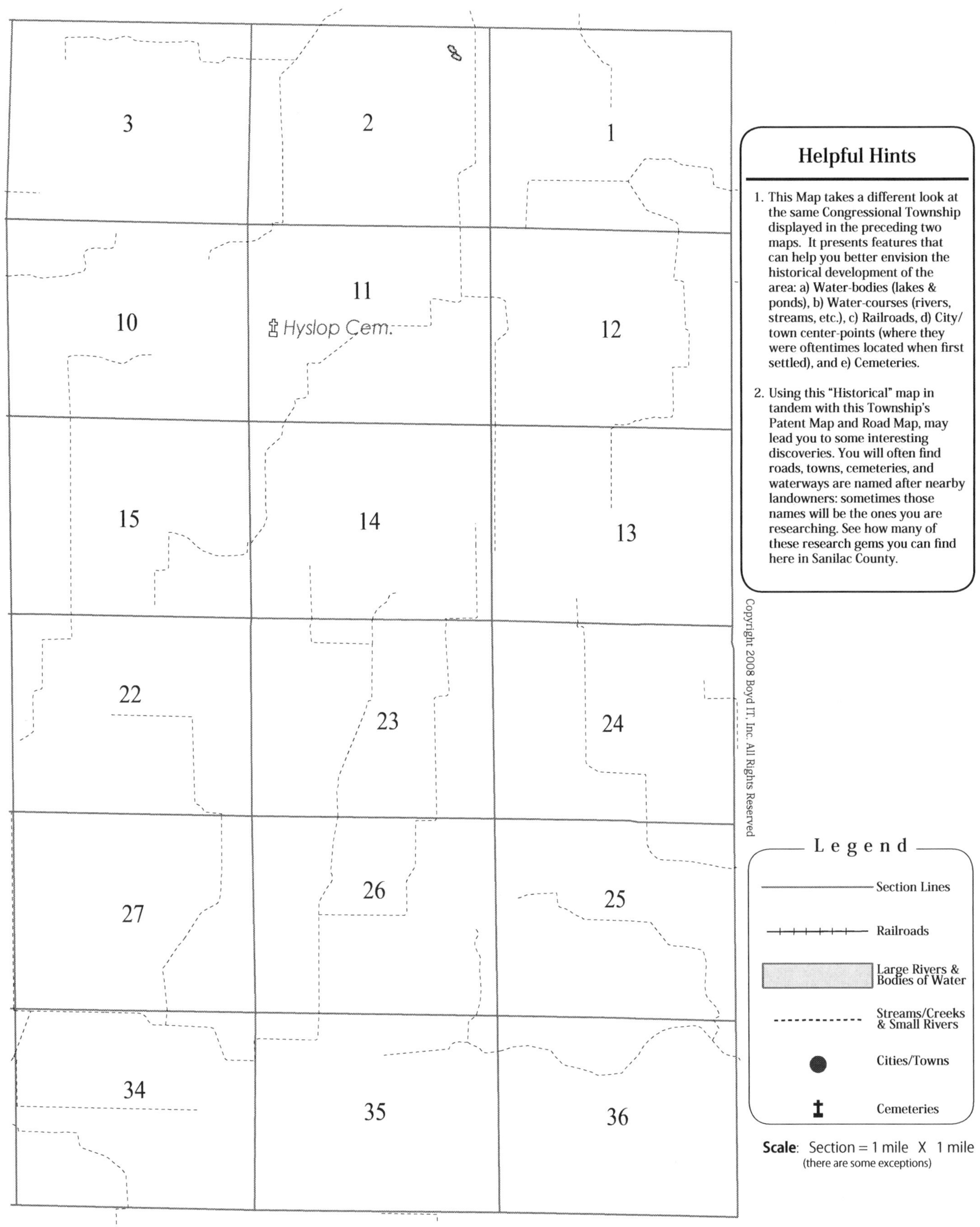
3
2
1
10
11
12
Hyslop Cem.
15
14
13
22
23
24
27
26
25
34
35
36
Helpful Hints
1. This Map takes a different look at the same Congressional Township displayed in the preceding two maps. It presents features that can help you better envision the historical development of the area: a) Water-bodies (lakes & ponds), b) Water-courses (rivers, streams, etc.), c) Railroads, d) City/town center-points (where they were oftentimes located when first settled), and e) Cemeteries.
2. Using this "Historical" map in tandem with this Township's Patent Map and Road Map, may lead you to some interesting discoveries. You will often find roads, towns, cemeteries, and waterways are named after nearby landowners: sometimes those names will be the ones you are researching. See how many of these research gems you can find here in Sanilac County.
Copyright 2008 Boyd IT, Inc. All Rights Reserved
Legend
Section Lines
Railroads
Large Rivers & Bodies of Water
Streams/Creeks & Small Rivers
Cities/Towns
Cemeteries
Scale: Section = 1 mile X 1 mile
(there are some exceptions)

Map Group 18: Index to Land Patents

Township 11-North Range 14-East (Michigan-Toledo Strip)

After you locate an individual in this Index, take note of the Section and Section Part then proceed to the Land Patent map on the pages immediately following. You should have no difficulty locating the corresponding parcel of land.

The "For More Info" Column will lead you to more information about the underlying Patents. See the *Legend* at right, and the "How to Use this Book" chapter, for more information.

LEGEND

"For More Info . . . " column

A = Authority (Legislative Act, See Appendix "A")
B = Block or Lot (location in Section unknown)
C = Cancelled Patent
F = Fractional Section
G = Group (Multi-Patentee Patent, see Appendix "C")
V = Overlaps another Parcel
R = Re-Issued (Parcel patented more than once)

(A & G items require you to look in the Appendixes referred to above. All other Letter-designations followed by a number require you to locate line-items in this index that possess the ID number found after the letter).

ID	Individual in Patent	Sec.	Sec. Part	Date Issued	Other Counties	For More Info . . .
1858	ASH, Allen K	18	NENE	1864-01-05		A1
1859	" "	19	NENE	1864-01-05		A1
1871	BABCOCK, Edward C	18	SW	1876-09-06		A2
1914	BELL, John	18	NW	1883-06-07		A2 F
1963	BENNETT, William	4	E½SW	1876-09-06		A2
1949	BLAKESLEY, Samuel	20	N½SE	1871-06-15		A2
1950	" "	20	N½SW	1871-06-15		A2
1946	BOYD, Robert	8	NESE	1878-05-16		A2
1947	" "	9	NWSW	1878-05-16		A2
1948	" "	9	S½SW	1878-05-16		A2
1880	BROCKWAY, Elliot T	32	NWNE	1853-11-01		A1
1872	CASH, Edward	34	NESW	1856-01-10		A1
1873	" "	34	SENW	1856-01-10		A1
1874	" "	34	SWNW	1856-01-10		A1
1875	" "	35	E½NE	1856-01-10		A1
1934	CHASE, Nathan B	36	SENW	1852-02-10		A1 G24
1932	CODDINGTON, Morris	25	N½NW	1872-03-20		A2
1933	" "	25	W½NE	1872-03-20		A2
1876	COREY, Elias B	7	SESW	1875-07-30		A2
1877	" "	7	SWSE	1875-07-30		A2
1878	" "	7	W½SW	1875-07-30		A2
1915	DARCY, John	29	N½NE	1861-12-03		A1
1916	" "	29	N½NW	1861-12-03		A1
1960	DAVIS, Wellington	34	E½NE	1852-02-10		A1
1961	" "	35	SENW	1852-02-10		A1
1962	" "	36	W½NW	1852-02-10		A1
1870	ERSKINE, E	6	SWSW	1869-07-01		A1 G37
1870	ERSKINE, J	6	SWSW	1869-07-01		A1 G37
1866	FLEMING, David	5	W½NW	1859-10-10		A1 F
1882	GILL, George	9	N½NW	1881-08-20		A2
1883	" "	9	NESW	1881-08-20		A2
1884	" "	9	SENW	1881-08-20		A2
1905	GORDON, James	21	NESW	1890-03-25		A2
1900	HAWKS, Henry W	19	W½NW	1877-04-05		A2
1901	" "	19	W½SW	1877-04-05		A2
1959	HENDERSON, Truman	1	NWSE	1875-11-20		A2
1955	HILL, Thomas	23	SESE	1885-01-30		A2
1956	" "	26	N½NE	1885-01-30		A2
1957	" "	26	NENW	1885-01-30		A2
1927	HIRSCHMAN, L	36	NENW	1865-10-02		A1
1935	HOUSE, Peter	24	NESE	1881-01-20		A2
1936	" "	24	S½SE	1881-01-20		A2
1937	" "	24	SESW	1881-01-20		A2
1889	HOWARD, Harry	6	NESW	1868-08-20		A1
1897	HOWARD, Henry	29	SESE	1855-10-01		A1
1898	" "	30	NESW	1855-10-01		A1 F

ID	Individual in Patent	Sec.	Sec. Part	Date Issued	Other Counties	For More Info . . .
1899	HOWARD, Henry (Cont'd)	30	S½NW	1855-10-01		A1 F
1892	" "	21	S½NE	1864-01-05		A1
1893	" "	21	SESW	1864-01-05		A1
1894	" "	21	SWSE	1864-01-05		A1
1895	" "	22	S½NW	1864-01-05		A1
1896	" "	29	NESE	1864-01-05		A1
1861	HUBBARD, Bela	5	E½NW	1868-08-20		A1 G47
1862	" "	8	W½SE	1869-07-01		A1 G47
1881	HUBBARD, Frederick	22	E½SW	1864-01-05		A1
1890	KIBBEE, Henry C	18	SENE	1864-01-05		A1
1891	" "	8	E½SW	1864-01-05		A1
1861	KING, John E	5	E½NW	1868-08-20		A1 G47
1862	" "	8	W½SE	1869-07-01		A1 G47
1869	LENTY, Dimaline	33	NWSE	1855-10-01		A1
1939	LICHTENBERG, Philipp	22	NWNW	1865-10-02		A1
1940	" "	26	NESW	1865-10-02		A1
1941	" "	27	SWNE	1865-10-02		A1
1942	" "	34	SESW	1865-10-02		A1
1943	" "	35	SESE	1865-10-02		A1
1928	MARRELL, Levi	6	NWSW	1869-07-01		A1 G50
1929	MASON, Lorenzo M	20	S½SW	1855-10-01		A1
1930	" "	27	NENW	1855-10-01		A1
1906	MCCLURE, James	29	E½SW	1861-12-03		A1
1907	" "	29	SENW	1861-12-03		A1
1908	" "	29	SWSE	1861-12-03		A1
1938	MCCORMACK, Philip	5	NE	1859-05-09		A1
1865	MCFARLAND, Consider	36	E½SE	1839-09-02		A1
1902	MOFFAT, Hugh	28	SWSE	1855-10-01		A1
1903	" "	28	W½NE	1855-10-01		A1
1904	" "	33	SENE	1855-10-01		A1
1931	MOORE, Martin W	6	E½NW	1875-07-30		A2
1913	MORRILL, Jesse A	8	NE	1872-07-01		A2
1964	OAKES, William	28	NWNW	1864-01-05		A1
1885	PACK, George	30	NESE	1852-11-01		A1
1886	" "	30	SENE	1852-11-01		A1
1887	" "	33	NWSW	1852-11-01		A1
1888	" "	35	NENW	1852-12-01		A1
1879	PARKINSON, Elisha E	15	SWSW	1885-01-30		A2
1958	POWER, Thomas	33	NW	1857-07-01		A1
1951	REEVE, Selah	21	NWSE	1855-10-01		A1
1952	" "	21	SENW	1855-10-01		A1
1953	" "	23	NENE	1855-10-01		A1
1954	" "	24	NENE	1855-10-01		A1
1860	RUST, Aloney	33	SWSE	1852-02-10		A1 G55 R1923
1860	RUST, David W	33	SWSE	1852-02-10		A1 G55 R1923
1911	SANBORN, James W	29	NWSW	1852-02-10		A1 G56
1912	" "	29	SWNW	1852-02-10		A1 G56
1934	" "	36	SENW	1852-02-10		A1 G24
1909	" "	29	NWSE	1852-11-01		A1
1910	" "	30	SWSW	1855-10-01		A1 F
1863	SMITH, Carl	18	NWSE	1882-10-20		A2
1864	" "	18	W½NE	1882-10-20		A2
1944	SMITH, Ralph C	12	NWNE	1865-10-02		A1
1945	" "	21	N½NE	1865-10-02		A1
1868	STEPHENS, David	24	SWSW	1865-10-02		A1
1867	STEPHENS, David S	23	SWNE	1864-01-05		A1
1924	STILSON, John	17	NWSE	1854-06-15		A1
1925	" "	30	NENE	1854-06-15		A1
1911	SWEETSER, Alvah	29	NWSW	1852-02-10		A1 G56
1912	" "	29	SWNW	1852-02-10		A1 G56
1926	VANDERBURGH, John	35	NWNE	1855-10-01		A1
1917	VANDERBURGH, John J	13	NESW	1855-10-01		A1
1918	" "	13	SENW	1855-10-01		A1
1919	" "	14	SESE	1855-10-01		A1
1920	" "	23	NWNE	1855-10-01		A1
1921	" "	27	NESE	1855-10-01		A1
1922	" "	27	SENE	1855-10-01		A1
1923	" "	33	SWSE	1855-10-01		A1 R1860
1857	VINCENT, Albion	36	SENE	1860-10-01		A1
1965	WARNER, William	1	NENE	1856-01-10		A1 F
1966	" "	4	NENW	1856-09-01		A1 F
1967	" "	4	NWNE	1856-09-01		A1 F
1928	WELCH, Samuel O	6	NWSW	1869-07-01		A1 G50

Patent Map

T11-N R14-E
Michigan-Toledo Strip Meridian

Map Group 18

Township Statistics

Parcels Mapped	:	111
Number of Patents	:	85
Number of Individuals	:	58
Patentees Identified	:	54
Number of Surnames	:	51
Multi-Patentee Parcels	:	8
Oldest Patent Date	:	9/2/1839
Most Recent Patent	:	3/25/1890
Block/Lot Parcels	:	0
Parcels Re - Issued	:	1
Parcels that Overlap	:	0
Cities and Towns	:	3
Cemeteries	:	2

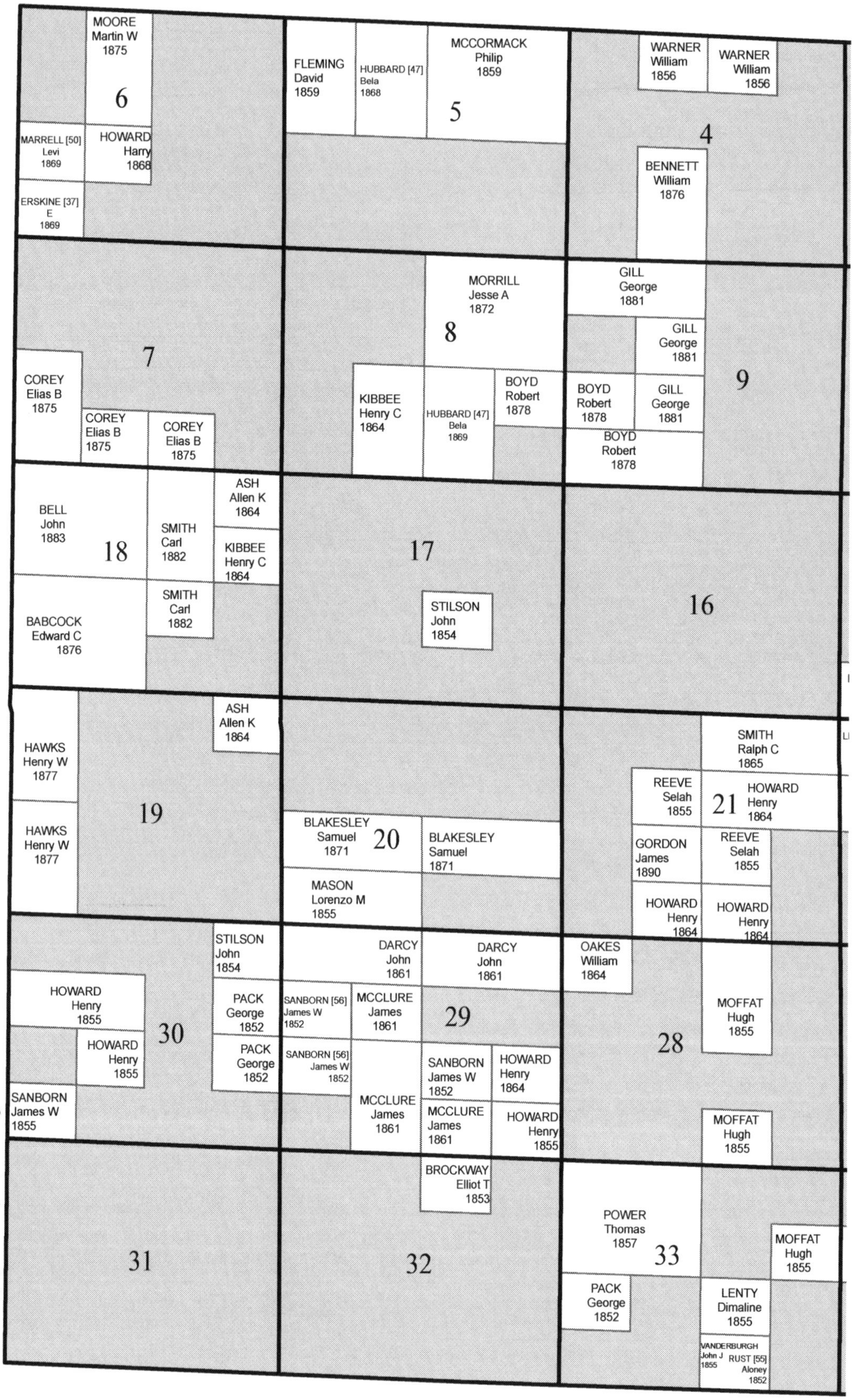

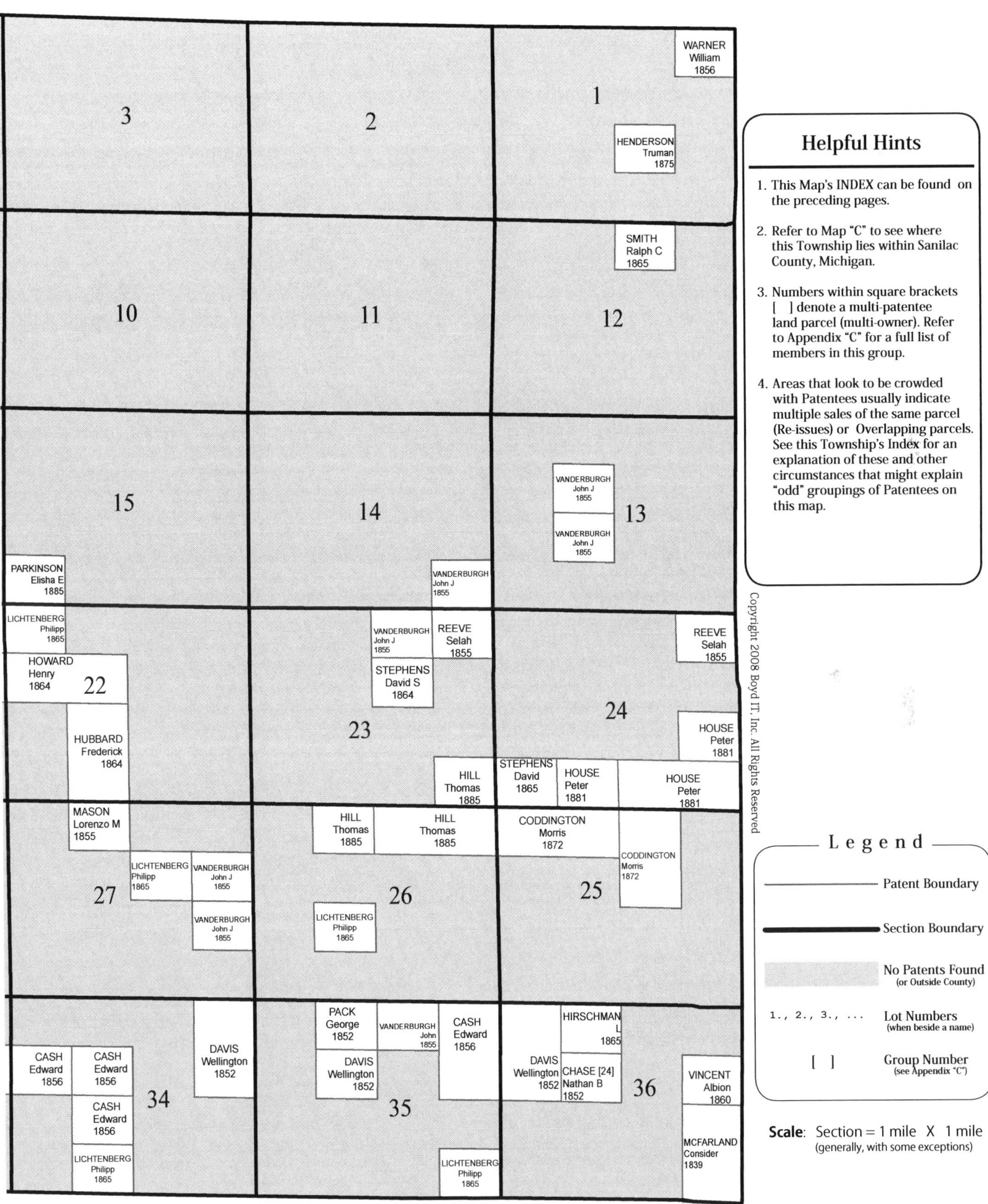

Helpful Hints

1. This Map's INDEX can be found on the preceding pages.
2. Refer to Map "C" to see where this Township lies within Sanilac County, Michigan.
3. Numbers within square brackets [ ] denote a multi-patentee land parcel (multi-owner). Refer to Appendix "C" for a full list of members in this group.
4. Areas that look to be crowded with Patentees usually indicate multiple sales of the same parcel (Re-issues) or Overlapping parcels. See this Township's Index for an explanation of these and other circumstances that might explain "odd" groupings of Patentees on this map.

Legend

- Patent Boundary
- Section Boundary
- No Patents Found (or Outside County)
- 1., 2., 3., ... Lot Numbers (when beside a name)
- [ ] Group Number (see Appendix "C")

Scale: Section = 1 mile X 1 mile (generally, with some exceptions)

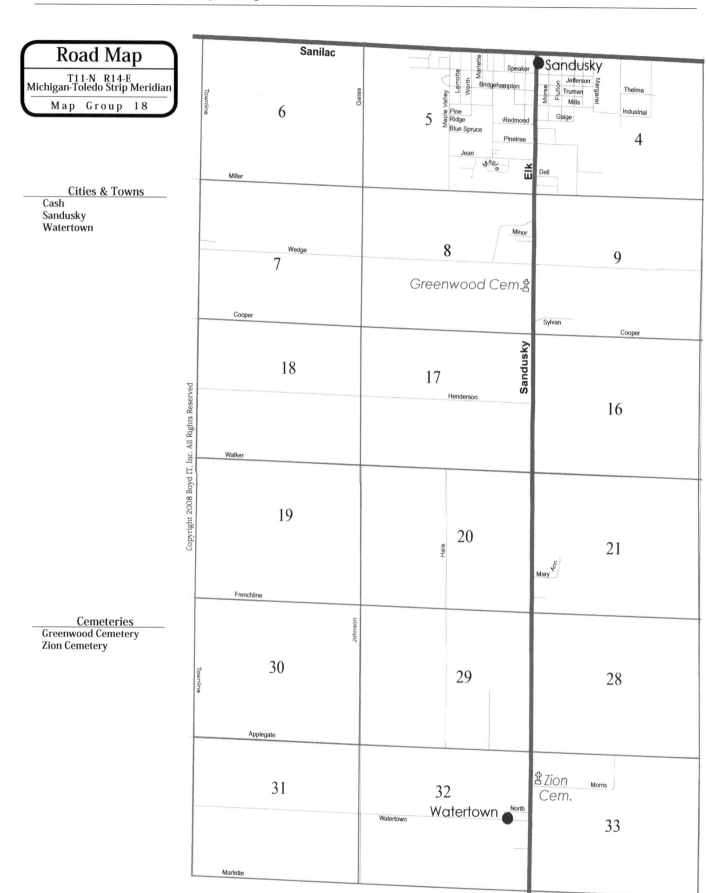

Road Map

T11-N R14-E
Michigan-Toledo Strip Meridian

Map Group 18

Cities & Towns

Cash
Sandusky
Watertown

Cemeteries

Greenwood Cemetery
Zion Cemetery

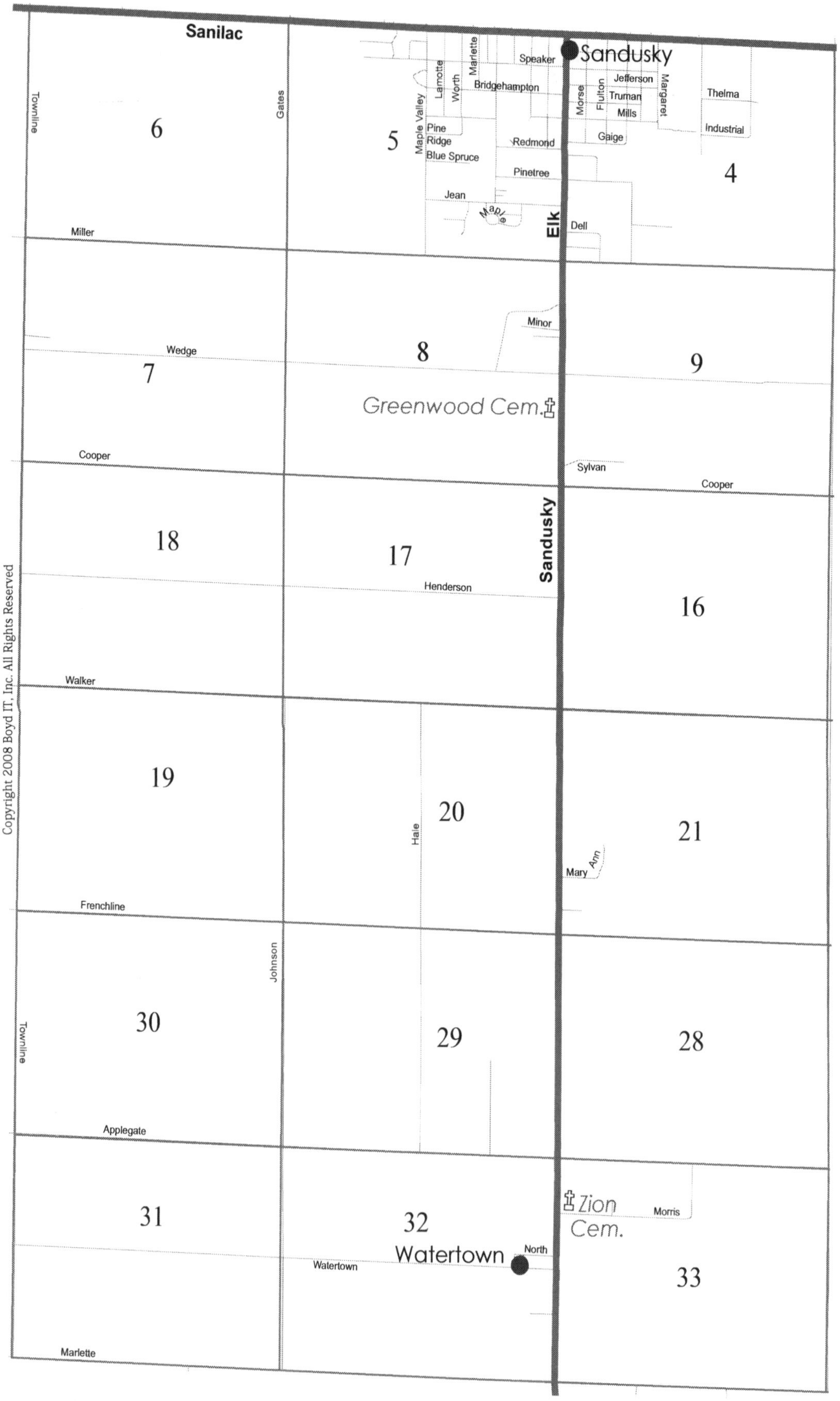

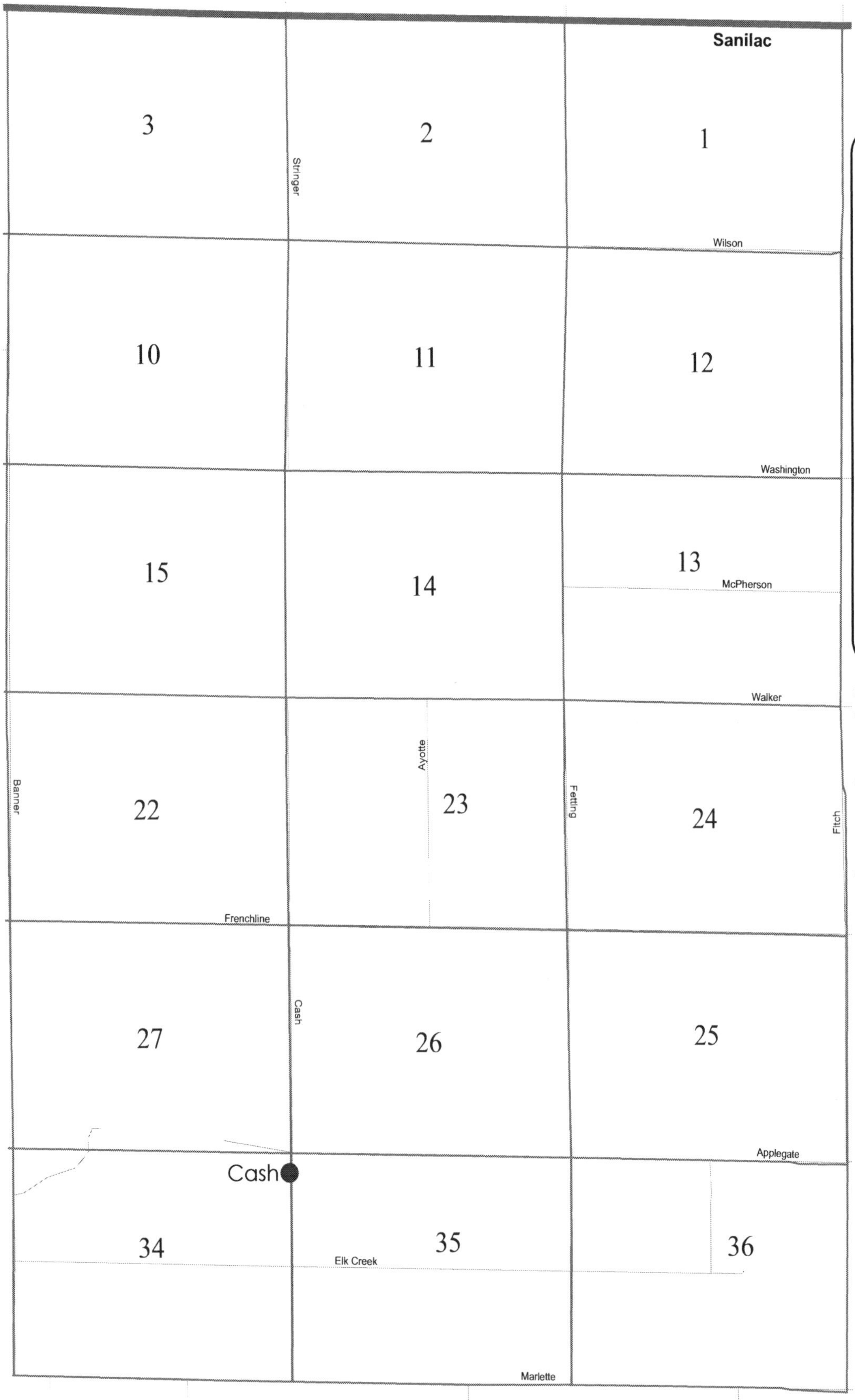

Sanilac

3
2
1
Stringer
Wilson
10
11
12
Washington
15
14
13
McPherson
Walker
Banner
22
Ayotte
23
Fetting
24
Fitch
Frenchline
27
Cash
26
25
Applegate
Cash
34
Elk Creek
35
36
Marlette

Helpful Hints

1. This road map has a number of uses, but primarily it is to help you: a) find the present location of land owned by your ancestors (at least the general area), b) find cemeteries and city-centers, and c) estimate the route/roads used by Census-takers & tax-assessors.

2. If you plan to travel to Sanilac County to locate cemeteries or land parcels, please pick up a modern travel map for the area before you do. Mapping old land parcels on modern maps is not as exact a science as you might think. Just the slightest variations in public land survey coordinates, estimates of parcel boundaries, or road-map deviations can greatly alter a map's representation of how a road either does or doesn't cross a particular parcel of land.

Legend

Section Lines
Interstates
Highways
Other Roads
Cities/Towns
Cemeteries

Scale: Section = 1 mile X 1 mile
(generally, with some exceptions)

Historical Map
T11-N R14-E
Michigan-Toledo Strip Meridian
Map Group 18
Cities & Towns
Sandusky
Watertown
Cash
Cemeteries
Greenwood Cemetery
Zion Cemetery
6
5
4
Sandusky
7
8
9
Greenwood Cem.
18
17
16
19
20
21
30
29
28
Beals and Frizzle Drain
31
32
33
Hale Drain
Zion Cem.
Watertown
Copyright 2008 Boyd IT, Inc. All Rights Reserved

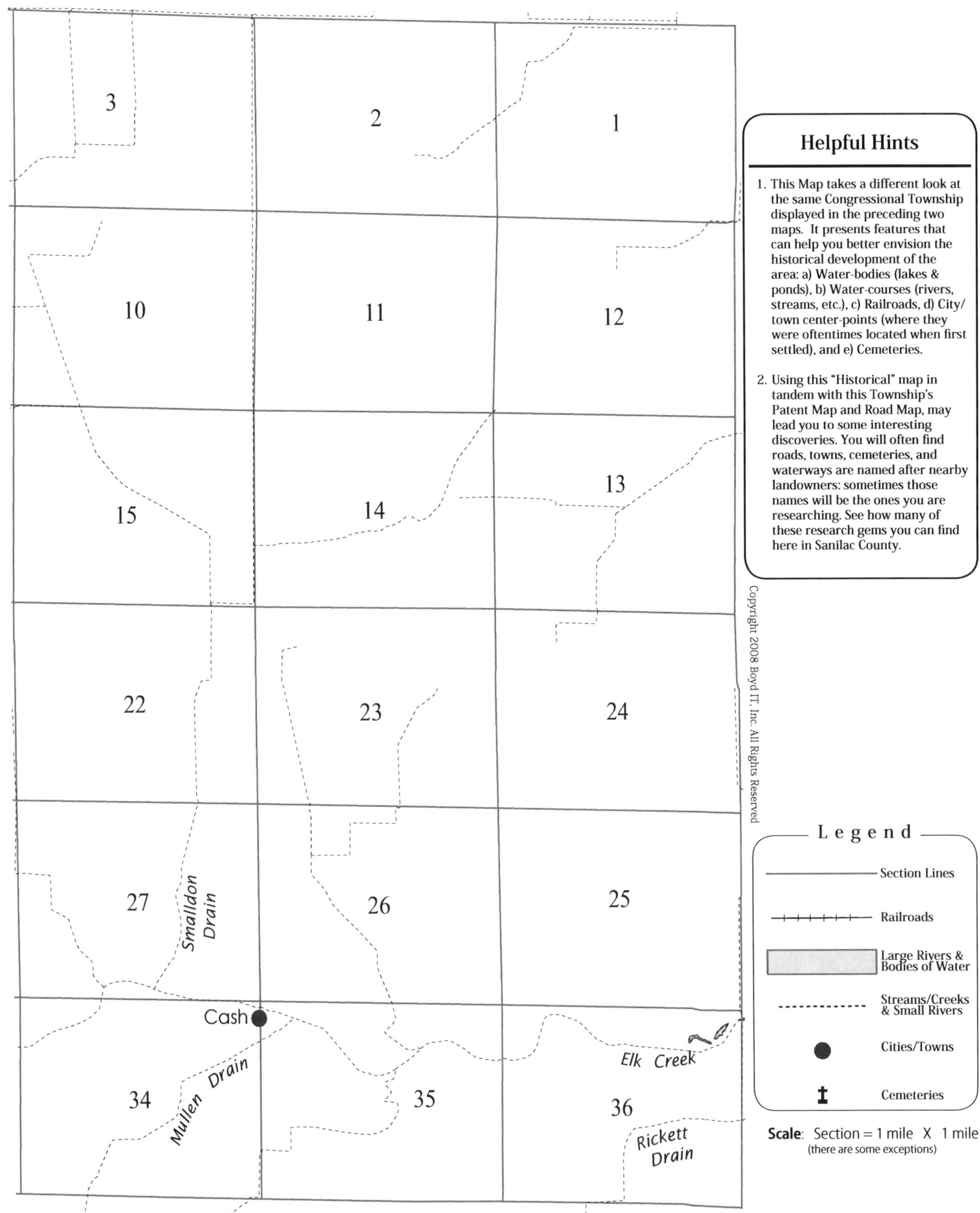
3
2
1
10
11
12
15
14
13
22
23
24
27
26
25
34
35
36
Smalldon Drain
Cash
Mullen Drain
Elk Creek
Rickett Drain
Helpful Hints
1. This Map takes a different look at the same Congressional Township displayed in the preceding two maps. It presents features that can help you better envision the historical development of the area: a) Water-bodies (lakes & ponds), b) Water-courses (rivers, streams, etc.), c) Railroads, d) City/town center-points (where they were oftentimes located when first settled), and e) Cemeteries.
2. Using this "Historical" map in tandem with this Township's Patent Map and Road Map, may lead you to some interesting discoveries. You will often find roads, towns, cemeteries, and waterways are named after nearby landowners: sometimes those names will be the ones you are researching. See how many of these research gems you can find here in Sanilac County.
Copyright 2008 Boyd IT, Inc. All Rights Reserved
Legend
Section Lines
Railroads
Large Rivers & Bodies of Water
Streams/Creeks & Small Rivers
Cities/Towns
Cemeteries
Scale: Section = 1 mile X 1 mile
(there are some exceptions)

Map Group 19: Index to Land Patents

Township 11-North Range 15-East (Michigan-Toledo Strip)

After you locate an individual in this Index, take note of the Section and Section Part then proceed to the Land Patent map on the pages immediately following. You should have no difficulty locating the corresponding parcel of land.

The "For More Info" Column will lead you to more information about the underlying Patents. See the *Legend* at right, and the "How to Use this Book" chapter, for more information.

LEGEND

"For More Info . . . " column

- **A** = Authority (Legislative Act, See Appendix "A")
- **B** = Block or Lot (location in Section unknown)
- **C** = Cancelled Patent
- **F** = Fractional Section
- **G** = Group (Multi-Patentee Patent, see Appendix "C")
- **V** = Overlaps another Parcel
- **R** = Re-Issued (Parcel patented more than once)

(A & G items require you to look in the Appendixes referred to above. All other Letter-designations followed by a number require you to locate line-items in this index that possess the ID number found after the letter).

ID	Individual in Patent	Sec.	Sec. Part	Date Issued	Other Counties	For More Info . . .
1975	ASH, Allen K	10	SWNE	1852-02-10		A1 V1999
2037	BAILEY, Mark T	35	S½NE	1854-06-15		A1
1968	BARTLETT, Addison	32	SESW	1848-07-01		A1
2032	BATCHELDER, John W	15	SENW	1870-05-10		A1 G10 V2003
2033	" "	15	W½SW	1870-05-10		A1 G10 R2039
2021	BEARD, John	3	NWNE	1852-02-10		A1
2022	" "	4	NENE	1852-02-10		A1
2014	BERNEY, Henry W	3	W½NW	1874-07-15		A1
2017	BUEL, Jacob W	26	W½SW	1852-02-10		A1
2010	BUELL, Grove N	32	SWSW	1848-07-01		A1
1978	CARSON, Arthur	5	E½NW	1857-07-01		A1 F
1979	" "	5	NWNW	1860-10-01		A1
2039	CHASE, Nathan B	15	W½SW	1849-02-01		A1 G23 R2033
2040	" "	21	NENE	1849-02-01		A1 G23
2041	" "	35	NENE	1850-03-01		A1 G23
2038	" "	15	E½SW	1852-02-10		A1 G24
2053	COMPANY, S Rothschild And	20	SENW	1865-10-02		A1
2054	" "	21	NESW	1865-10-02		A1
2055	" "	25	SESW	1865-10-02		A1
2056	" "	29	N½NE	1865-10-02		A1
2057	" "	4	NESE	1865-10-02		A1
2058	" "	4	NWNW	1865-10-02		A1 F
2048	DAVIS, Randall E	36	NWNW	1849-02-01		A1 G32
2070	DAVIS, Wellington	8	W½NW	1852-02-10		A1
1973	DWIGHT, Alfred	4	NWSW	1852-02-10		A1
1974	" "	5	NESE	1852-02-10		A1
1971	DWIGHT, Alfred A	4	SWNW	1848-07-01		A1
1972	" "	5	SENE	1848-07-01		A1
1970	" "	32	N½SW	1852-11-01		A1
1999	FARNSWORTH, Elon	10	NE	1837-05-01		A1 G38 V1975
2000	" "	10	SE	1837-05-01		A1 G38
2001	" "	10	SW	1837-05-01		A1 G38
2002	" "	14	W½NW	1837-05-01		A1 G38
2003	" "	15	E½NW	1837-05-01		A1 G38 V2032
2004	" "	15	NE	1837-05-01		A1 G38
2005	" "	25	E½SE	1837-08-02		A1 G38
2006	" "	36	E½NE	1837-08-02		A1 G38
1976	HADDOW, Archibald	6	E½NW	1860-05-01		A1
1977	" "	6	E½SW	1860-05-01		A1
2064	HALL, Silas C	2	SWNW	1855-10-01		A1
2062	" "	2	NESW	1856-01-10		A1
2066	" "	3	SWSE	1856-01-10		A1
2063	" "	2	NWSW	1856-09-01		A1
2065	" "	3	E½SE	1856-09-01		A1
2025	HOFFMAN, John M	9	SESW	1865-10-02		A1
2007	HUBBARD, Frederick	31	SESE	1864-01-05		A1

ID	Individual in Patent	Sec.	Sec. Part	Date Issued	Other Counties	For More Info . . .
2032	JOHNSON, James S	15	SENW	1870-05-10		A1 G10 V2003
2033	" "	15	W½SW	1870-05-10		A1 G10 R2039
2024	JONES, John	12	SWSW	1852-02-10		A1
2016	KAUFMANN, J	9	S½NW	1865-10-02		A1
2011	KNAPP, Henry	18	NENE	1865-10-02		A1
2047	LICHTENBERG, Philipp	19	NWNW	1865-10-02		A1
1982	LUCE, Benjamin	31	NENE	1852-02-10		A1
1981	LUCE, Benjamin F	9	SESE	1852-02-10		A1
1980	" "	9	NESE	1852-11-01		A1
2015	MANION, Hugh	1	E½NW	1854-06-15		A1
2035	MASON, Lorenzo M	30	SWSW	1855-10-01		A1
2072	MAYNARD, William	2	SWNE	1857-10-30		A1
1998	MCFARLAND, Consider	31	SW	1839-09-02		A1
2049	MCMILLAN, Robert	18	NESW	1865-10-02		A1
2050	" "	31	SWSE	1865-10-02		A1
1988	MERRILL, Charles	28	NENW	1852-02-10		A1
1989	" "	28	NWNE	1852-02-10		A1
2039	MILLER, John	15	W½SW	1849-02-01		A1 G23 R2033
2040	" "	21	NENE	1849-02-01		A1 G23
2041	" "	35	NENE	1850-03-01		A1 G23
2036	MILLS, Luther D	36	SESE	1852-02-10		A1
2008	MITCHELL, George	34	NE	1855-10-01		A1
2012	MIZNER, Henry R	2	E½NW	1855-10-01		A1
2013	" "	2	SESE	1855-10-01		A1
2045	NESTER, Patrick	23	NWSE	1857-02-20		A1
2046	" "	23	SWNE	1857-02-20		A1
2020	OCALLAGHAN, Jeremiah	31	N½SE	1855-10-01		A1
2026	ODLAUM, John	2	W½SE	1855-10-01		A1
2009	PACK, George	23	NWNE	1850-12-02		A1
2027	PARKIN, John	15	NESE	1860-11-21		A1
2071	POLAND, Wesley	10	N½NW	1861-07-01		A1
1993	REEVE, Christopher	26	NENW	1850-12-02		A1
1994	" "	26	NWNE	1850-12-02		A1
1992	" "	25	NESW	1852-02-10		A1
1995	" "	26	SWNE	1852-02-10		A1
1997	" "	9	N½NW	1852-02-10		A1
1990	" "	19	NWSW	1855-10-01		A1 F
1991	" "	19	SWNW	1855-10-01		A1 F
1996	" "	8	NENW	1856-01-10		A1
2060	REEVE, Selah	22	E½SW	1852-02-10		A1
2061	" "	28	E½NE	1852-02-10		A1
2028	RICE, John	18	E½NW	1855-10-01		A1
2029	" "	18	NWNE	1855-10-01		A1
2030	" "	7	SESE	1855-10-01		A1 F
2031	" "	7	SESW	1855-10-01		A1 F
2038	SANBORN, James W	15	E½SW	1852-02-10		A1 G24
2019	" "	21	NWSE	1852-11-01		A1
2018	" "	15	NWSE	1852-12-01		A1
2073	SANBORN, William	33	SENE	1856-09-01		A1
1969	SIBLEY, Alexander H	15	W½NW	1837-05-01		A1
1999	SIBLEY, Sylvester	10	NE	1837-05-01		A1 G38 V1975
2000	" "	10	SE	1837-05-01		A1 G38
2001	" "	10	SW	1837-05-01		A1 G38
2002	" "	14	W½NW	1837-05-01		A1 G38
2003	" "	15	E½NW	1837-05-01		A1 G38 V2032
2004	" "	15	NE	1837-05-01		A1 G38
2005	" "	25	E½SE	1837-08-02		A1 G38
2006	" "	36	E½NE	1837-08-02		A1 G38
2067	SKINNER, Thomas S	9	SWSE	1864-01-05		A1
2051	SMITH, Rollin C	4	NESW	1852-11-01		A1
2052	" "	5	NESW	1852-11-01		A1
2074	SNOWDEN, William	24	NWSE	1855-10-01		A1
2069	STEBBINS, Thompson P	5	N½NE	1852-02-10		A1
2068	TAYLOR, Thomas	3	NENW	1859-10-10		A1 F
1999	TROWBRIDGE, Charles C	10	NE	1837-05-01		A1 G38 V1975
2000	" "	10	SE	1837-05-01		A1 G38
2001	" "	10	SW	1837-05-01		A1 G38
1986	" "	11	NW	1837-05-01		A1
1987	" "	11	SW	1837-05-01		A1 V2023
2002	" "	14	W½NW	1837-05-01		A1 G38
2003	" "	15	E½NW	1837-05-01		A1 G38 V2032
2004	" "	15	NE	1837-05-01		A1 G38
2005	" "	25	E½SE	1837-08-02		A1 G38

ID	Individual in Patent	Sec.	Sec. Part	Date Issued	Other Counties	For More Info . . .
2006	TROWBRIDGE, Charles C (Cont'd)	36	E½NE	1837-08-02		A1 G38
2023	VANDERBURGH, John J	11	SESW	1855-10-01		A1 V1987
2042	WARD, Nathan	29	SE	1837-08-10		A1
2043	" "	30	E½SE	1837-08-10		A1
2044	" "	32	NW	1837-08-10		A1
2059	WARD, Samuel	32	NE	1837-08-10		A1
1985	WIGHT, Buckminster	2	SWSW	1849-02-01		A1
2048	" "	36	NWNW	1849-02-01		A1 G32
1984	" "	2	SESW	1852-11-01		A1
1983	" "	12	S½SE	1853-11-01		A1
2034	WIXSON, John	24	E½NW	1852-02-10		A1

Patent Map

T11-N R15-E
Michigan-Toledo Strip Meridian

Map Group 19

Township Statistics

Parcels Mapped	:	107
Number of Patents	:	90
Number of Individuals	:	61
Patentees Identified	:	59
Number of Surnames	:	54
Multi-Patentee Parcels	:	15
Oldest Patent Date	:	5/1/1837
Most Recent Patent	:	7/15/1874
Block/Lot Parcels	:	0
Parcels Re - Issued	:	1
Parcels that Overlap	:	6
Cities and Towns	:	1
Cemeteries	:	3

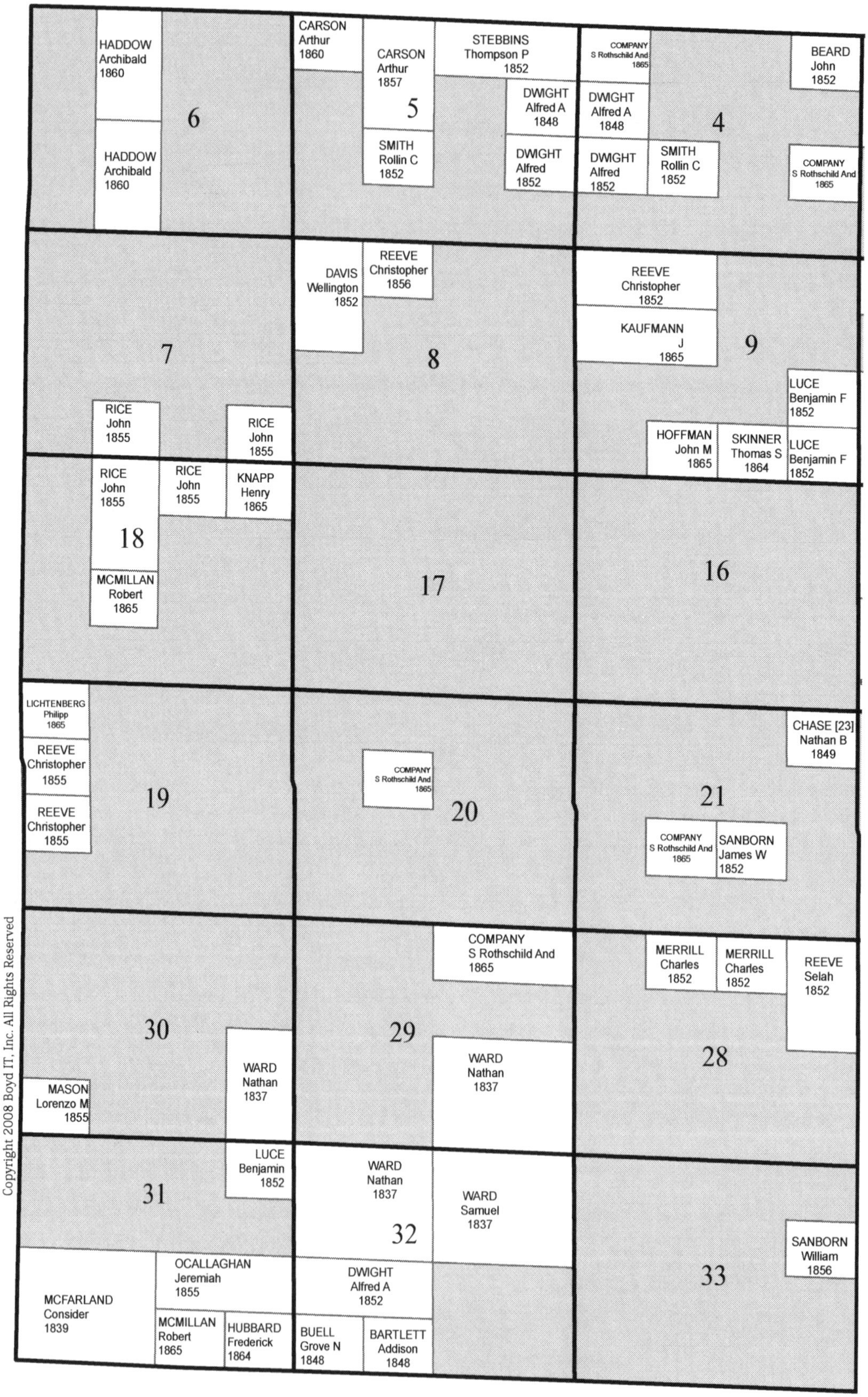

Helpful Hints

1. This Map's INDEX can be found on the preceding pages.
2. Refer to Map "C" to see where this Township lies within Sanilac County, Michigan.
3. Numbers within square brackets [ ] denote a multi-patentee land parcel (multi-owner). Refer to Appendix "C" for a full list of members in this group.
4. Areas that look to be crowded with Patentees usually indicate multiple sales of the same parcel (Re-issues) or Overlapping parcels. See this Township's Index for an explanation of these and other circumstances that might explain "odd" groupings of Patentees on this map.

Legend

- Patent Boundary
- Section Boundary
- No Patents Found (or Outside County)
- 1., 2., 3., ... Lot Numbers (when beside a name)
- [ ] Group Number (see Appendix "C")

Scale: Section = 1 mile X 1 mile (generally, with some exceptions)

Road Map

T11-N R15-E
Michigan-Toledo Strip Meridian

Map Group 19

Cities & Towns

Applegate

Cemeteries

Lee Cemetery
Saint Marys Cemetery
Steckley Cemetery

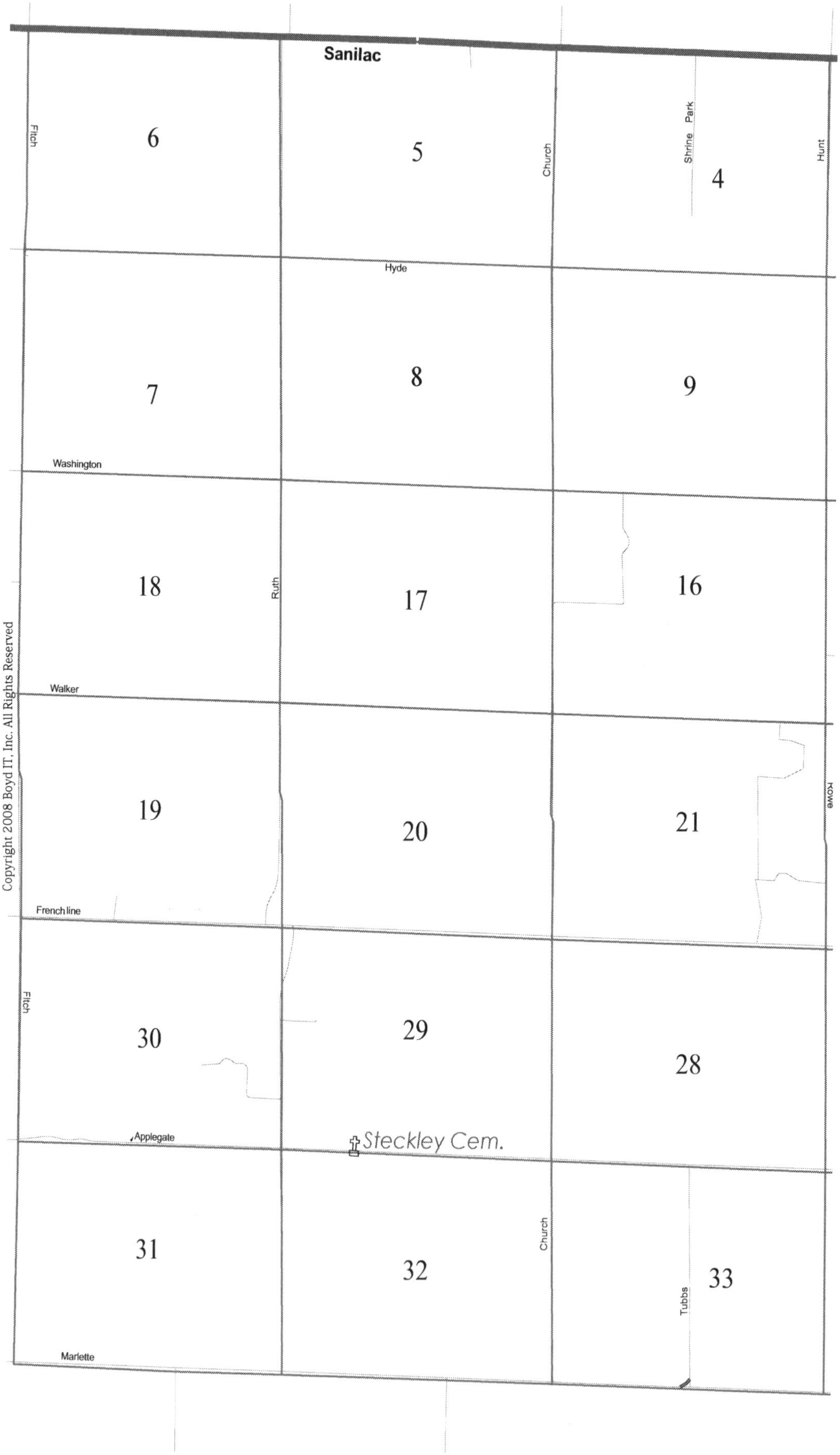

Sanilac
Fitch
6
5
Church
Shrine Park
4
Hunt
Hyde
7
8
9
Washington
18
Ruth
17
16
Walker
19
20
21
Howe
Frenchline
Fitch
30
29
28
Applegate
Steckley Cem.
31
32
Church
Tubbs
33
Marlette

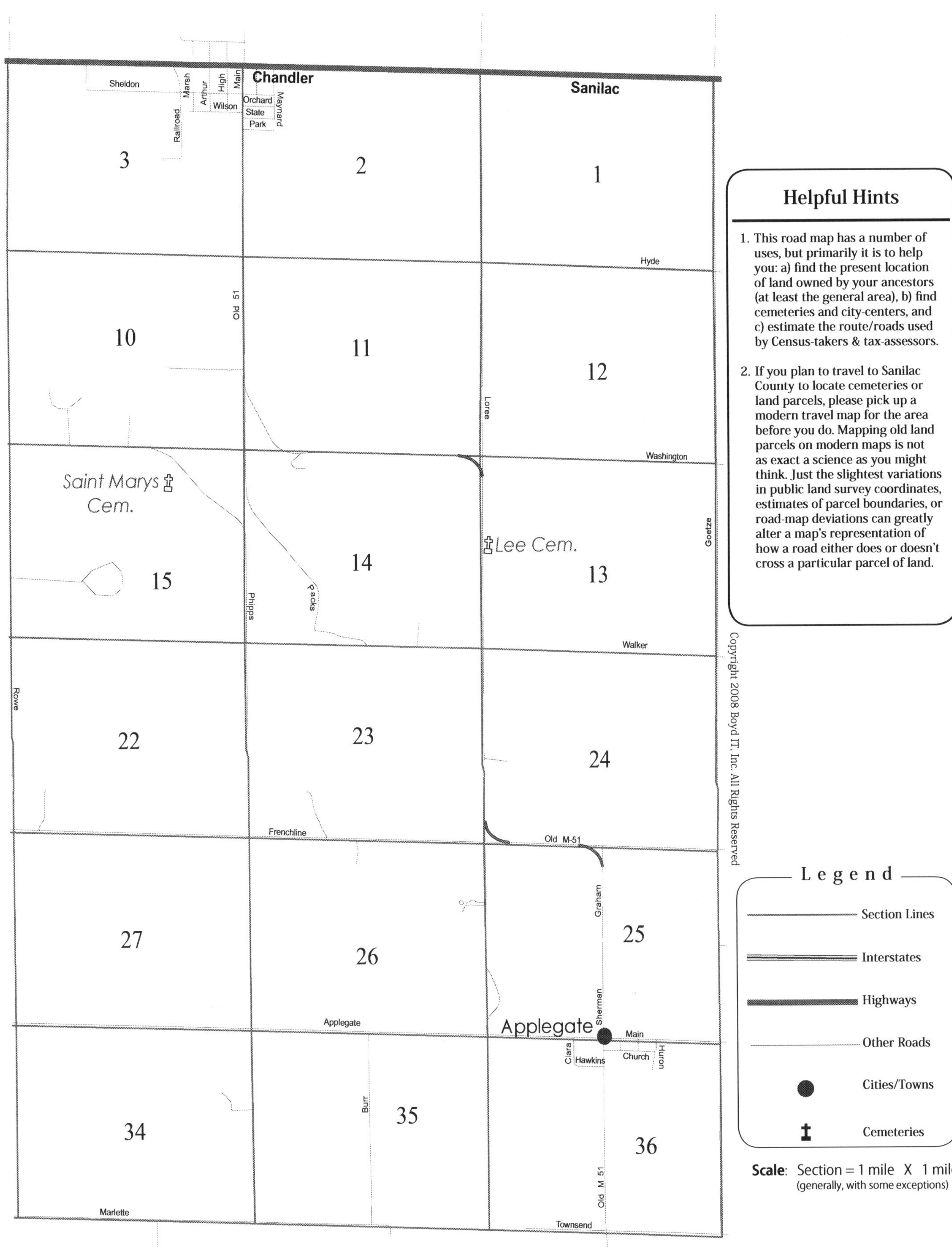
Chandler
Sanilac
Sheldon
Marsh
Arthur
High
Main
Wilson
Railroad
Orchard
State
Park
Maynard
3
2
1
Hyde
Old 51
10
11
12
Loree
Washington
Saint Marys Cem.
Lee Cem.
14
13
15
Goetze
Phipps
Packs
Walker
Rowe
22
23
24
Frenchline
Old M-51
Graham
27
26
25
Applegate
Applegate
Sherman
Main
Clara
Hawkins
Church
Huron
Burr
34
35
36
Old M 51
Marlette
Townsend
Helpful Hints
1. This road map has a number of uses, but primarily it is to help you: a) find the present location of land owned by your ancestors (at least the general area), b) find cemeteries and city-centers, and c) estimate the route/roads used by Census-takers & tax-assessors.
2. If you plan to travel to Sanilac County to locate cemeteries or land parcels, please pick up a modern travel map for the area before you do. Mapping old land parcels on modern maps is not as exact a science as you might think. Just the slightest variations in public land survey coordinates, estimates of parcel boundaries, or road-map deviations can greatly alter a map's representation of how a road either does or doesn't cross a particular parcel of land.
Legend
Section Lines
Interstates
Highways
Other Roads
Cities/Towns
Cemeteries
Scale: Section = 1 mile X 1 mile
(generally, with some exceptions)

Historical Map

T11-N R15-E
Michigan-Toledo Strip Meridian

Map Group 19

Cities & Towns
- Applegate

Cemeteries
- Lee Cemetery
- Saint Marys Cemetery
- Steckley Cemetery

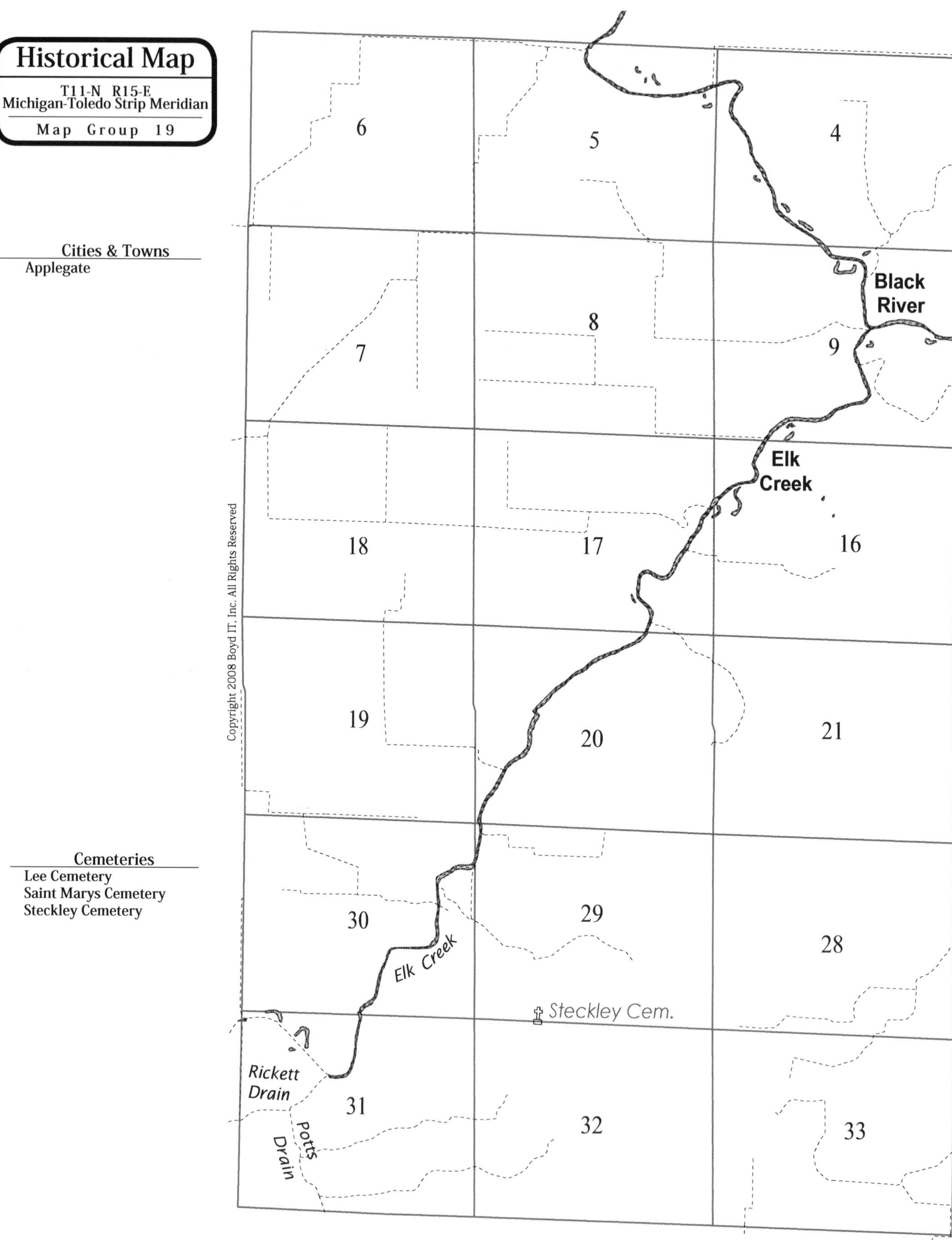

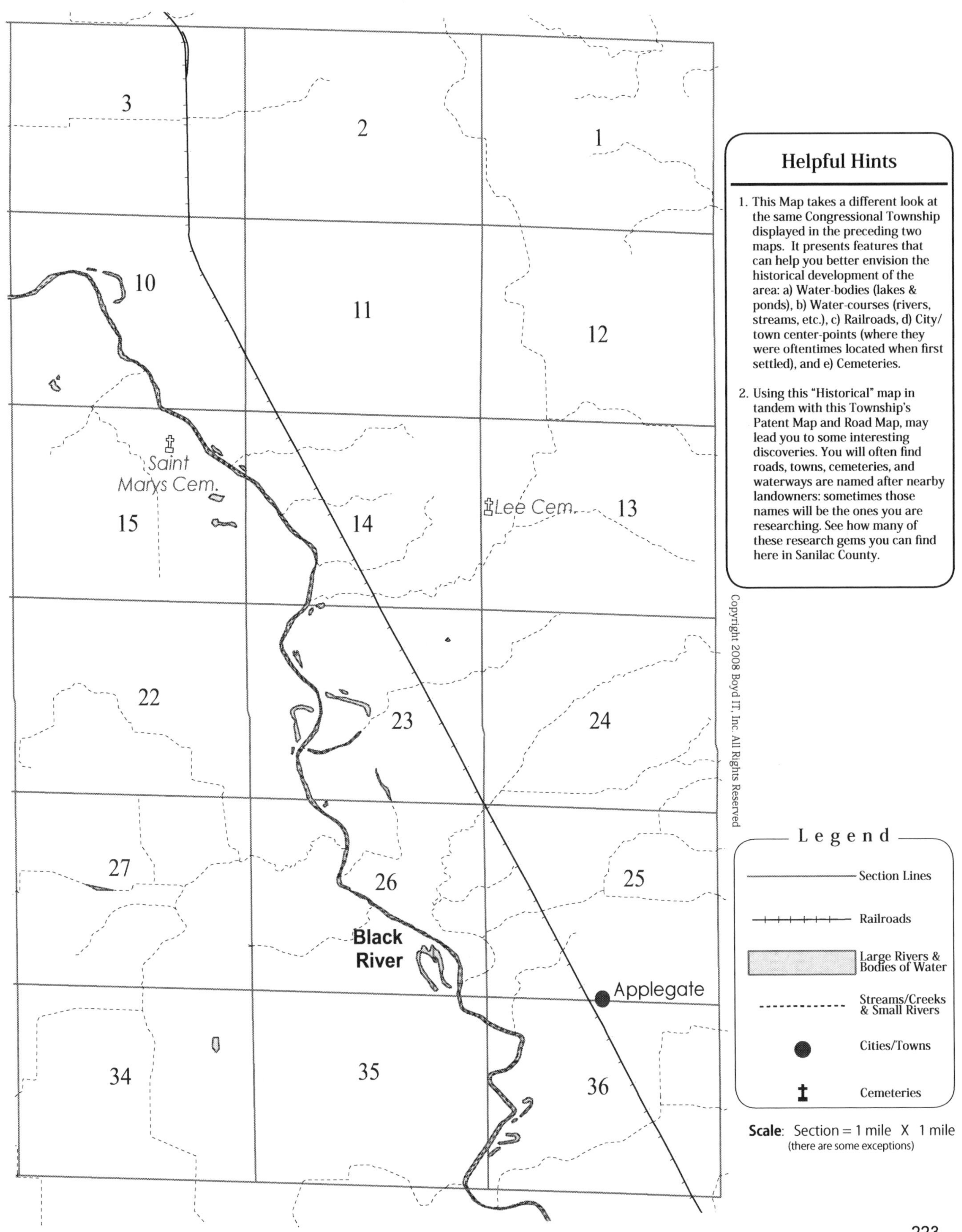
3
2
1
10
11
12
Saint
Marys Cem.
Lee Cem.
15
14
13
22
23
24
27
26
25
Black
River
Applegate
34
35
36
Helpful Hints
1. This Map takes a different look at the same Congressional Township displayed in the preceding two maps. It presents features that can help you better envision the historical development of the area: a) Water-bodies (lakes & ponds), b) Water-courses (rivers, streams, etc.), c) Railroads, d) City/town center-points (where they were oftentimes located when first settled), and e) Cemeteries.
2. Using this "Historical" map in tandem with this Township's Patent Map and Road Map, may lead you to some interesting discoveries. You will often find roads, towns, cemeteries, and waterways are named after nearby landowners: sometimes those names will be the ones you are researching. See how many of these research gems you can find here in Sanilac County.
Copyright 2008 Boyd IT, Inc. All Rights Reserved
Legend
Section Lines
Railroads
Large Rivers & Bodies of Water
Streams/Creeks & Small Rivers
Cities/Towns
Cemeteries
Scale: Section = 1 mile X 1 mile
(there are some exceptions)

Map Group 20: Index to Land Patents

Township 11-North Range 16-East (Michigan-Toledo Strip)

After you locate an individual in this Index, take note of the Section and Section Part then proceed to the Land Patent map on the pages immediately following. You should have no difficulty locating the corresponding parcel of land.

The "For More Info" Column will lead you to more information about the underlying Patents. See the *Legend* at right, and the "How to Use this Book" chapter, for more information.

LEGEND

"For More Info . . . " column

A = Authority (Legislative Act, See Appendix "A")
B = Block or Lot (location in Section unknown)
C = Cancelled Patent
F = Fractional Section
G = Group (Multi-Patentee Patent, see Appendix "C")
V = Overlaps another Parcel
R = Re-Issued (Parcel patented more than once)

(A & G items require you to look in the Appendixes referred to above. All other Letter-designations followed by a number require you to locate line-items in this index that possess the ID number found after the letter).

ID	Individual in Patent	Sec.	Sec. Part	Date Issued	Other Counties	For More Info . . .
2076	ABBOTT, Alvin B	17	SENW	1852-11-01		A1
2077	" "	17	SWNE	1852-11-01		A1
2137	ANDERSON, James	9	NWSE	1865-10-02		A1 G1 C R2138, 2179
2138	ARMSTRONG, James	9	NWSE	1867-05-11		A1 G2 R2137, 2179
2192	BAGG, Silas A	14	E½N½	1837-08-21		A1 G6 F
2123	BEACH, George	5	NE	1838-09-04		A1 G12 F
2123	BECKWITH, Alonzo S	5	NE	1838-09-04		A1 G12 F
2198	BINNINGA, Vallentin	22	NESE	1857-02-16		A1
2137	BLINDBERRY, V H	9	NWSE	1865-10-02		A1 G1 C R2138, 2179
2138	" "	9	NWSE	1867-05-11		A1 G2 R2137, 2179
2115	BODDY, Edward	8	E½NE	1852-02-10		A1
2108	BREADER, Christian	27	SENE	1854-06-15		A1
2171	BRYANT, Moses	32	SE	1837-08-21		A1 G13
2172	" "	33	W½SW	1837-08-21		A1 G13
2173	" "	35	E½S½	1837-08-21		A1 G13
2083	BUNKER, Charles	15	SE	1844-07-10		A1 G15
2084	" "	15	SW	1844-07-10		A1 G15
2085	" "	17	SE	1844-07-10		A1 G15
2086	" "	20	NE	1844-07-10		A1 G15
2087	" "	20	NW	1844-07-10		A1 G15
2088	" "	20	SE	1844-07-10		A1 G15
2089	" "	21	NW	1844-07-10		A1 G15
2090	" "	21	W½SW	1844-07-10		A1 G15
2091	" "	22	NW	1844-07-10		A1 G15
2092	" "	28	NW	1844-07-10		A1 G15
2093	" "	28	W½NE	1844-07-10		A1 G15
2094	" "	29	NE	1844-07-10		A1 G15
2095	" "	34	W½NE	1844-07-10		A1 G15
2096	" "	35	N½	1844-07-10		A1 G15
2097	" "	35	NWS½	1844-07-10		A1 G15
2083	BUNKER, Frederick R	15	SE	1844-07-10		A1 G15
2084	" "	15	SW	1844-07-10		A1 G15
2085	" "	17	SE	1844-07-10		A1 G15
2086	" "	20	NE	1844-07-10		A1 G15
2087	" "	20	NW	1844-07-10		A1 G15
2088	" "	20	SE	1844-07-10		A1 G15
2089	" "	21	NW	1844-07-10		A1 G15
2090	" "	21	W½SW	1844-07-10		A1 G15
2091	" "	22	NW	1844-07-10		A1 G15
2092	" "	28	NW	1844-07-10		A1 G15
2093	" "	28	W½NE	1844-07-10		A1 G15
2094	" "	29	NE	1844-07-10		A1 G15
2095	" "	34	W½NE	1844-07-10		A1 G15
2096	" "	35	N½	1844-07-10		A1 G15
2097	" "	35	NWS½	1844-07-10		A1 G15
2078	CAMPBELL, Archibald	32	NENE	1849-02-01		A1

ID	Individual in Patent	Sec.	Sec. Part	Date Issued	Other Counties	For More Info . . .
2113	CARLISLE, David	34	SESE	1848-09-01		A1
2133	CARNEY, Hill	27	SESE	1848-09-01		A1
2116	CLARK, Edward P	14	W½S½	1837-11-02		A1 F
2200	COLE, William	4	E½SE	1852-02-10		A1
2188	COMPANY, S Rothschild And	10	SESE	1865-10-02		A1
2202	CRAIG, William H	18	W½SE	1854-06-15		A1
2203	" "	7	W½SE	1854-06-15		A1
2139	DAVIS, James C	11	4	1852-02-10		A1 F
2123	DICKINSON, Nathan	5	NE	1838-09-04		A1 G12 F
2185	DONELLY, Robert	27	W½SW	1852-02-10		A1
2201	DOPP, William	21	NESE	1852-02-10		A1
2144	DUNLOP, John	32	NENW	1856-01-10		A1
2145	" "	32	NWNE	1856-01-10		A1
2194	EDMONDS, Thomas B	14	W½N½	1837-08-21		A1 F
2154	EINSIDER, Joseph	23	NWSW	1855-10-01		A1 F
2117	ELDRED, Elisha	23	3	1848-07-01		A1 F
2191	ERBE, Sebastian	22	SESE	1854-06-15		A1
2083	EWER, Peter F	15	SE	1844-07-10		A1 G15
2084	" "	15	SW	1844-07-10		A1 G15
2085	" "	17	SE	1844-07-10		A1 G15
2086	" "	20	NE	1844-07-10		A1 G15
2087	" "	20	NW	1844-07-10		A1 G15
2088	" "	20	SE	1844-07-10		A1 G15
2089	" "	21	NW	1844-07-10		A1 G15
2090	" "	21	W½SW	1844-07-10		A1 G15
2091	" "	22	NW	1844-07-10		A1 G15
2092	" "	28	NW	1844-07-10		A1 G15
2093	" "	28	W½NE	1844-07-10		A1 G15
2094	" "	29	NE	1844-07-10		A1 G15
2095	" "	34	W½NE	1844-07-10		A1 G15
2096	" "	35	N½	1844-07-10		A1 G15
2097	" "	35	NWS½	1844-07-10		A1 G15
2119	FARNSWORTH, Elon	30	W½SW	1837-08-02		A1 G38
2120	" "	31	W½NW	1837-08-02		A1 G38
2075	FINLAYSON, Alexander	2	NWNW	1852-12-01		A1 F
2190	GARDNER, Sarah	32	W½SW	1837-08-18		A1
2081	GIBSON, Chandler	2	2	1852-02-10		A1
2082	" "	2	3	1852-02-10		A1
2098	GLOVER, Charles G	28	SE	1837-08-18		A1
2099	" "	28	SW	1837-08-18		A1
2100	" "	29	SE	1837-08-18		A1
2101	" "	30	SE	1837-08-18		A1
2102	" "	31	E½NW	1837-08-18		A1
2103	" "	31	NE	1837-08-18		A1
2104	" "	31	W½SW	1837-08-18		A1
2105	" "	32	W½NW	1837-08-18		A1
2126	HADLEY, Henry G	11	1N½	1837-11-02		A1 F
2171	HADLEY, Timothy G	32	SE	1837-08-21		A1 G13
2172	" "	33	W½SW	1837-08-21		A1 G13
2173	" "	35	E½S½	1837-08-21		A1 G13
2147	HAGER, John	23	NW	1859-07-01		A1
2184	HALL, Richard H	33	NENW	1849-02-01		A1
2106	HAMMOND, Charles	34	E½NE	1839-07-09		A1 G44
2106	HAMMOND, John C	34	E½NE	1839-07-09		A1 G44
2146	HARDEN, John H	22	NWSW	1856-09-01		A1
2135	HARDER, Jacob	33	S½NW	1849-02-01		A1
2183	HARDER, Peter	22	SWSW	1857-07-01		A1
2175	HERRICK, Nelson	4	S½NE	1852-12-01		A1
2186	HICKEY, Robert	27	W½NE	1857-02-16		A1
2192	HIGGINS, Sylvester	14	E½N½	1837-08-21		A1 G6 F
2204	HINKSON, William	34	NESE	1848-09-01		A1
2160	HIRSCHMAN, L	17	NWSW	1865-10-02		A1
2177	HOGAN, Patrick	15	NENW	1849-02-01		A1
2179	" "	9	NWSE	1850-12-02		A1 C R2137, 2138
2178	" "	9	NESW	1852-12-18		A1
2161	HOWARD, Levi	22	SESW	1855-10-01		A1
2162	HURD, Marshall F	3	NWNE	1848-07-01		A1
2148	JEX, John	8	E½SE	1852-11-01		A1
2205	JOWETT, William	28	E½NE	1852-02-10		A1
2195	LAPPIN, Thomas	14	SES½	1837-08-21		A1 F
2196	" "	23	NE	1837-11-02		A1 F
2124	LESTER, George S	32	SENE	1850-02-20		A1
2193	LOSAYA, Stephen	10	NWNW	1852-02-10		A1

ID	Individual in Patent	Sec.	Sec. Part	Date Issued	Other Counties	For More Info . . .
2206	MARSHALL, William	17	N½NE	1852-12-01		A1
2163	MASKELL, Michael	26	3	1848-07-01		A1
2164	" "	3	SWNW	1852-02-10		A1
2189	MASTEN, Samuel	33	NWNW	1849-02-01		A1
2079	MCGREGOR, Archibald	2	4	1852-02-10		A1
2127	MIZNER, Henry R	6	NW	1854-06-15		A1 F
2128	" "	7	NESW	1854-06-15		A1
2129	" "	7	W½SW	1855-10-01		A1
2130	" "	9	SWSE	1855-10-01		A1
2180	NESTER, Patrick	18	NWNW	1856-01-10		A1
2151	PATTERSON, John W	21	SESE	1857-10-30		A1
2192	PETTY, Danforth	14	E½N½	1837-08-21		A1 G6 F
2106	PHELPS, Elihu	34	E½NE	1839-07-09		A1 G44
2125	PRATT, Grove	3	NENE	1852-02-10		A1
2197	RAYMOND, Uri	15	NENE	1855-10-01		A1
2176	ROBERTS, Nelson	18	SWNW	1852-02-10		A1
2107	ROBISON, Charles	14	NES½	1837-08-21		A1 F
2131	RUNKWITZ, Henry	15	S½NE	1857-02-20		A1
2132	" "	15	SENW	1857-02-20		A1
2110	SANBORN, Cummings	21	E½SW	1848-09-01		A1
2111	" "	21	W½NE	1848-09-01		A1
2112	" "	21	W½SE	1848-09-01		A1
2109	" "	17	SENE	1849-02-01		A1
2140	SANBORN, James W	18	E½NW	1852-11-01		A1
2181	SHIRLEY, Paul	11		1852-02-10		A1 F
2182	" "	15	W½NW	1855-10-01		A1
2119	SIBLEY, Sylvester	30	W½SW	1837-08-02		A1 G38
2120	" "	31	W½NW	1837-08-02		A1 G38
2192	STOWELL, Alexander	14	E½N½	1837-08-21		A1 G6 F
2141	SUTTON, James W	11	W½NW	1855-10-01		A1
2118	TAYLOR, Elisha	3	NWNW	1856-09-01		A1 F
2134	TEMISON, Hugh	22	SENE	1852-02-10		A1
2121	THROOP, Enos T	18	E½NE	1854-06-15		A1
2170	TODD, Morris	9	W½NW	1849-02-01		A1
2165	" "	11	3	1852-02-10		A1
2166	" "	15	NWNE	1852-02-10		A1
2167	" "	3	SESE	1852-02-10		A1 R2168
2169	" "	9	SESW	1852-02-10		A1
2168	" "	3	SESE	1852-11-01		A1 R2167
2119	TROWBRIDGE, Charles C	30	W½SW	1837-08-02		A1 G38
2120	" "	31	W½NW	1837-08-02		A1 G38
2136	VINCENT, Jacob L	34	N½SW	1857-02-16		A1
2156	WAHLY, Jurgen H	26	1	1852-02-10		A1 F
2157	" "	26	2	1852-02-10		A1 F
2158	" "	26	SENW	1852-02-10		A1
2159	WAHLY, Jurgen Henry	23	4	1852-02-10		A1 F
2114	WARD, Eber B	26	SWS½	1837-08-07		A1
2174	WARD, Nathan	29	SW	1837-08-10		A1
2208	WARD, Zael	26	4	1837-08-12		A1 F
2143	WATERBURY, John C	3	SENW	1852-02-10		A1
2199	WATKINS, Watson	2	1NE	1838-09-04		A1 F
2122	WELLS, Frederick L	19	SENE	1855-10-01		A1
2152	WELLS, John	19	NWSE	1852-02-10		A1
2080	WIGHT, Buckminster	19	W½NE	1853-11-01		A1
2155	WITHAM, Joseph G	9	W½SW	1852-02-10		A1
2149	WOODS, John L	21	NENE	1855-10-01		A1
2150	" "	21	SENE	1856-09-01		A1
2187	WRIGHT, Robert	10	N½SE	1857-07-01		A1
2207	WRIGHT, William	11	NWSW	1857-07-01		A1
2153	WYMAN, John	35	SWSW	1837-08-10		A1
2106	" "	34	E½NE	1839-07-09		A1 G44
2142	YATES, James	3	SENE	1853-11-01		A1 F

Patent Map

T11-N R16-E
Michigan-Toledo Strip Meridian

Map Group 20

Township Statistics

Parcels Mapped	:	134
Number of Patents	:	109
Number of Individuals	:	99
Patentees Identified	:	86
Number of Surnames	:	89
Multi-Patentee Parcels	:	25
Oldest Patent Date	:	8/2/1837
Most Recent Patent	:	5/11/1867
Block/Lot Parcels	:	13
Parcels Re - Issued	:	2
Parcels that Overlap	:	0
Cities and Towns	:	1
Cemeteries	:	4

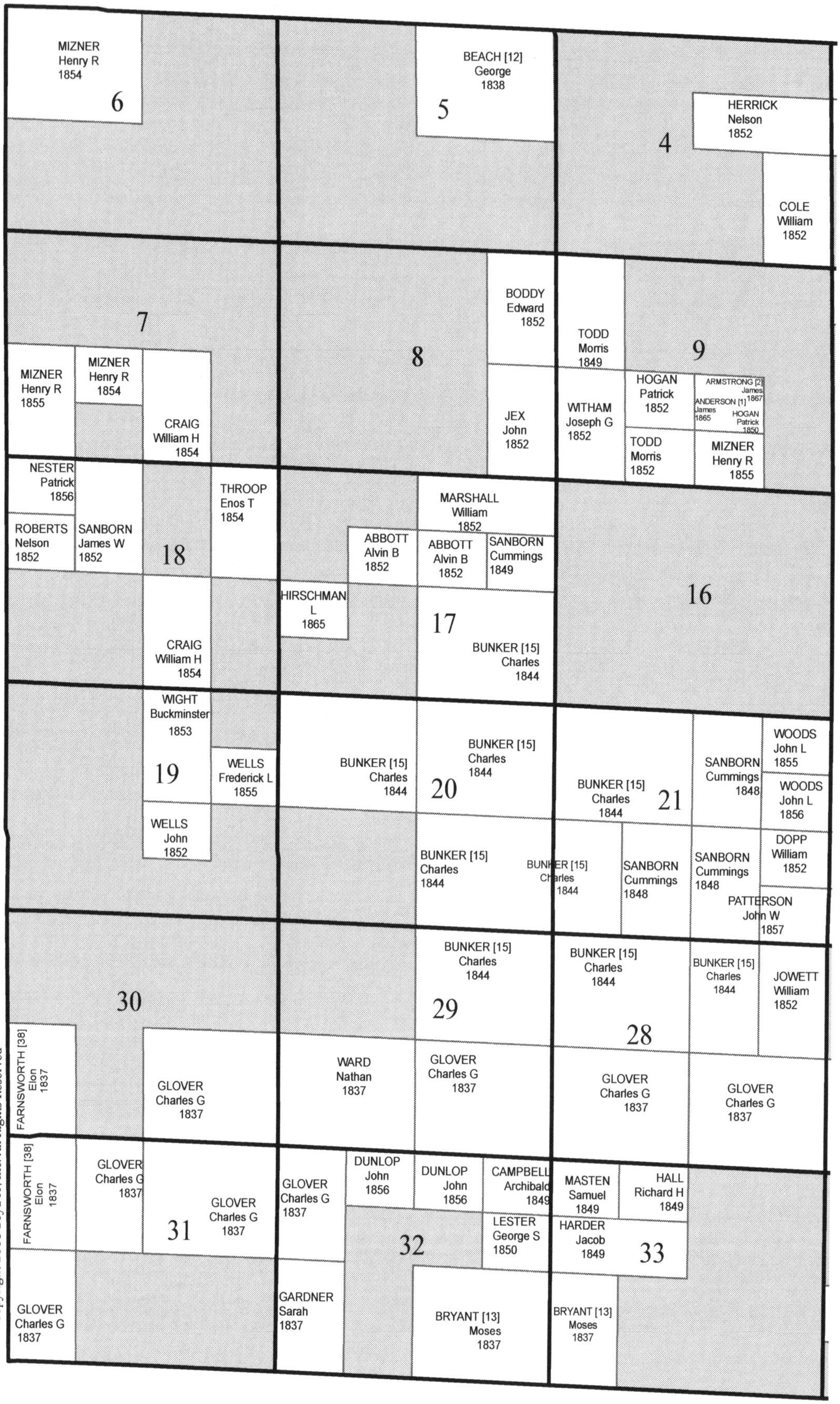

TAYLOR Elisha 1856
HURD Marshall F 1848
PRATT Grove 1852
FINLAYSON Alexander 1852
MASKELL Michael 1852
WATERBURY John C 1852
YATES James 1853

3

TODD Morris 1852
TODD Morris 1852

2

Lots-Sec. 2

1 WATKINS, Watson 1838
2 GIBSON, Chandler 1852
3 GIBSON, Chandler 1852
4 MCGREGOR, Archibald 1852

LOSAYA Stephen 1852

10

WRIGHT Robert 1857
COMPANY S Rothschild And 1865
SUTTON James W 1855
WRIGHT William 1857
SHIRLEY Paul 1852

11

Lots-Sec. 11

1 HADLEY, Henry G 1837
3 TODD, Morris 1852
4 DAVIS, James C 1852

SHIRLEY Paul 1855
HOGAN Patrick 1849
TODD Morris 1852
RAYMOND Uri 1855
RUNKWITZ Henry 1857
RUNKWITZ Henry 1857

15

BUNKER [15] Charles 1844
BUNKER [15] Charles 1844
EDMONDS Thomas B 1837
BAGG [6] Silas A 1837

14

CLARK Edward P 1837
ROBISON Charles 1837
LAPPIN Thomas 1837

BUNKER [15] Charles 1844
TEMISON Hugh 1852
HARDEN John H 1856

22

BINNINGA Vallentin 1857
HARDER Peter 1857
HOWARD Levi 1855
ERBE Sebastian 1854
HAGER John 1859
LAPPIN Thomas 1837

23

EINSIDER Joseph 1855

Lots-Sec. 23

3 ELDRED, Elisha 1848
4 WAHLY, Jurgen Henry 1852

HICKEY Robert 1857
BREADER Christian 1854

27

DONELLY Robert 1852
CARNEY Hill 1848
WAHLY Jurgen H 1852

26

WARD Eber B 1837

Lots-Sec. 26

1 WAHLY, Jurgen H 1852
2 WAHLY, Jurgen H 1852
3 MASKELL, Michael 1848
4 WARD, Zael 1837

BUNKER [15] Charles 1844
HAMMOND [44] Charles 1839
VINCENT Jacob L 1857

34

HINKSON William 1848
CARLISLE David 1848
BUNKER [15] Charles 1844

35

BUNKER [15] Charles 1844
WYMAN John 1837
BRYANT [13] Moses 1837

Helpful Hints

1. This Map's INDEX can be found on the preceding pages.
2. Refer to Map "C" to see where this Township lies within Sanilac County, Michigan.
3. Numbers within square brackets [ ] denote a multi-patentee land parcel (multi-owner). Refer to Appendix "C" for a full list of members in this group.
4. Areas that look to be crowded with Patentees usually indicate multiple sales of the same parcel (Re-issues) or Overlapping parcels. See this Township's Index for an explanation of these and other circumstances that might explain "odd" groupings of Patentees on this map.

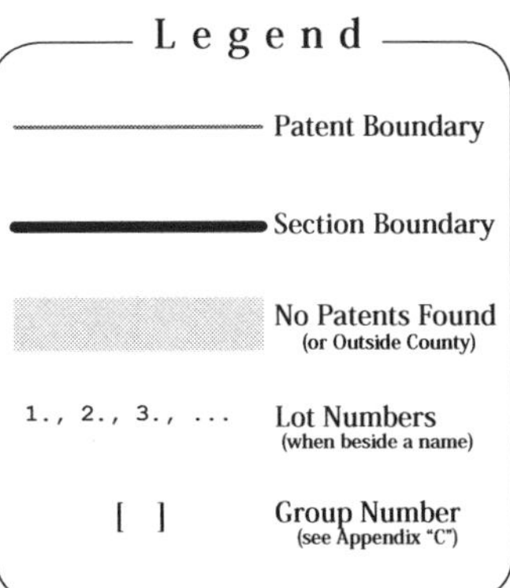

Scale: Section = 1 mile X 1 mile
(generally, with some exceptions)

Road Map

T11-N R16-E
Michigan-Toledo Strip Meridian

Map Group 20

Cities & Towns

Pine Hill (historical)

Cemeteries

Hoppenworth Cemetery
Ridge Cemetery
Saint John Cemetery
Saint Marys Cemetery

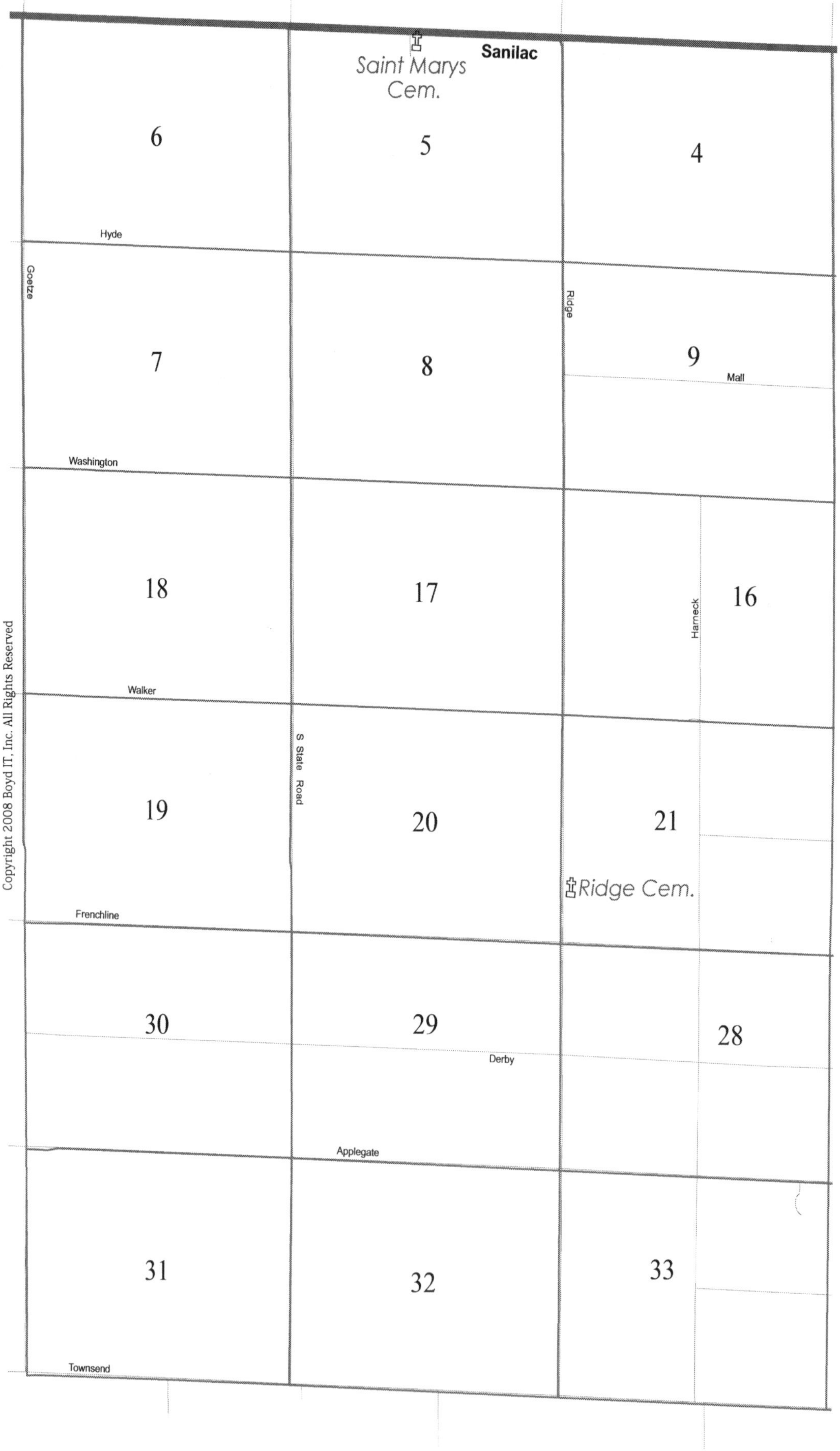

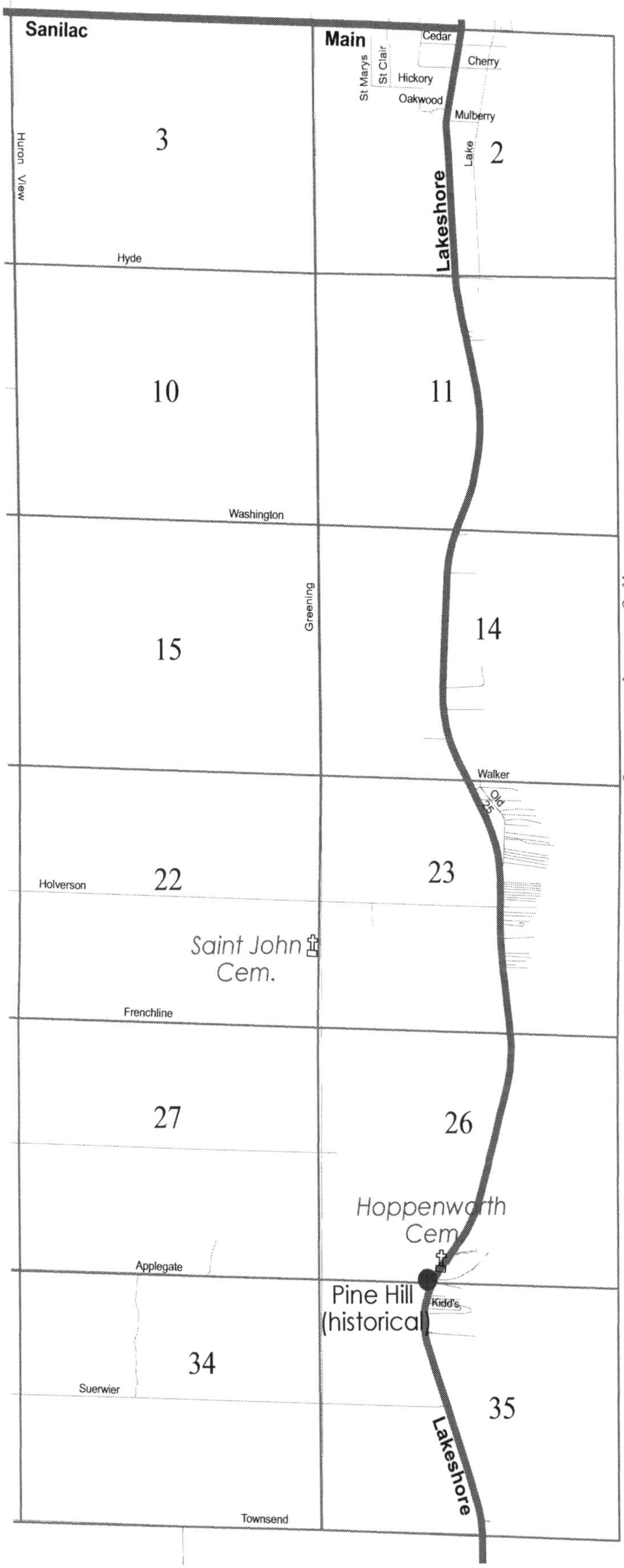

Sanilac
Main
Cedar
Cherry
St Marys
St Clair
Hickory
Oakwood
Mulberry
Lake
Huron View
Lakeshore
Hyde
Washington
Greening
Walker
Old 25
Holverson
Saint John Cem.
Frenchline
Hoppenwarth Cem.
Applegate
Pine Hill (historical)
Kidd's
Suerwier
Townsend
3 2 10 11 15 14 22 23 27 26 34 35

Helpful Hints

1. This road map has a number of uses, but primarily it is to help you: a) find the present location of land owned by your ancestors (at least the general area), b) find cemeteries and city-centers, and c) estimate the route/roads used by Census-takers & tax-assessors.

2. If you plan to travel to Sanilac County to locate cemeteries or land parcels, please pick up a modern travel map for the area before you do. Mapping old land parcels on modern maps is not as exact a science as you might think. Just the slightest variations in public land survey coordinates, estimates of parcel boundaries, or road-map deviations can greatly alter a map's representation of how a road either does or doesn't cross a particular parcel of land.

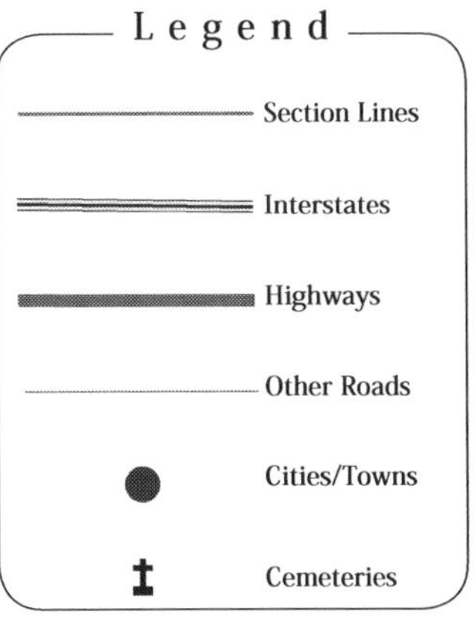

Scale: Section = 1 mile X 1 mile
(generally, with some exceptions)

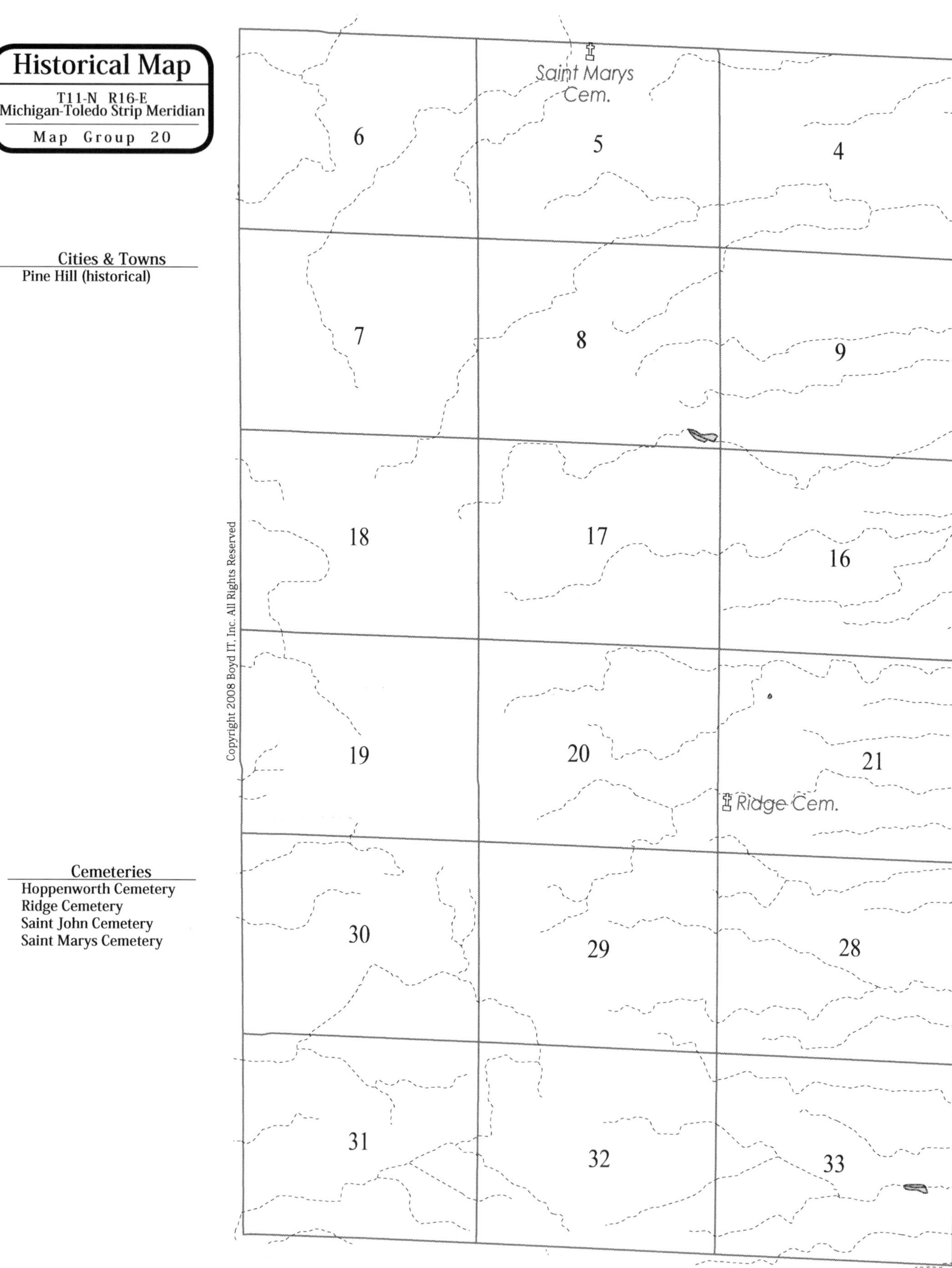
Historical Map
T11-N R16-E
Michigan-Toledo Strip Meridian
Map Group 20
Cities & Towns
Pine Hill (historical)
Cemeteries
Hoppenworth Cemetery
Ridge Cemetery
Saint John Cemetery
Saint Marys Cemetery
Saint Marys
Cem.
Ridge Cem.
6
5
4
7
8
9
18
17
16
19
20
21
30
29
28
31
32
33
Copyright 2008 Boyd IT, Inc. All Rights Reserved

3

2

Herron Creek

10

11

Mc Kenzie Creek

Lake Huron

15

14

22

23

Saint John Cem.

26

27

Hoppenworth Cem.

Pine Hill (historical)

34

35

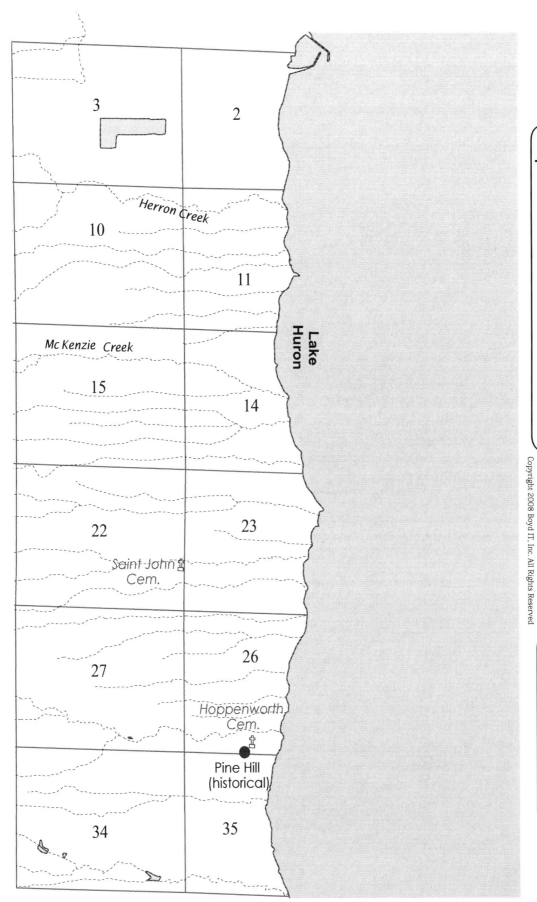

Helpful Hints

1. This Map takes a different look at the same Congressional Township displayed in the preceding two maps. It presents features that can help you better envision the historical development of the area: a) Water-bodies (lakes & ponds), b) Water-courses (rivers, streams, etc.), c) Railroads, d) City/town center-points (where they were oftentimes located when first settled), and e) Cemeteries.
2. Using this "Historical" map in tandem with this Township's Patent Map and Road Map, may lead you to some interesting discoveries. You will often find roads, towns, cemeteries, and waterways are named after nearby landowners: sometimes those names will be the ones you are researching. See how many of these research gems you can find here in Sanilac County.

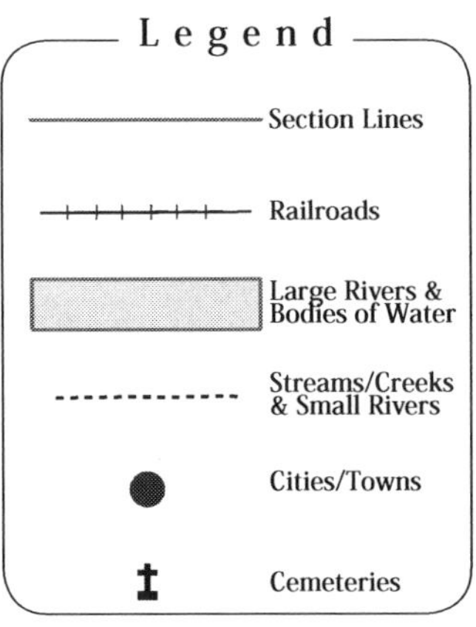

Scale: Section = 1 mile X 1 mile
(there are some exceptions)

Map Group 21: Index to Land Patents

Township 10-North Range 12-East (Michigan-Toledo Strip)

After you locate an individual in this Index, take note of the Section and Section Part then proceed to the Land Patent map on the pages immediately following. You should have no difficulty locating the corresponding parcel of land.

The "For More Info" Column will lead you to more information about the underlying Patents. See the *Legend* at right, and the "How to Use this Book" chapter, for more information.

LEGEND

"For More Info . . . " column

A = Authority (Legislative Act, See Appendix "A")
B = Block or Lot (location in Section unknown)
C = Cancelled Patent
F = Fractional Section
G = Group (Multi-Patentee Patent, see Appendix "C")
V = Overlaps another Parcel
R = Re-Issued (Parcel patented more than once)

(A & G items require you to look in the Appendixes referred to above. All other Letter-designations followed by a number require you to locate line-items in this index that possess the ID number found after the letter).

ID	Individual in Patent	Sec.	Sec. Part	Date Issued	Other Counties	For More Info . . .
2221	ABBOTT, Elon	5	NW	1859-10-10		A1 F
2222	" "	6	NE	1859-10-10		A1 F
2219	ABEL, Christian	14	S½SE	1861-12-10		A1
2265	AHEARN, Marten	1	NWNW	1861-07-01		A1 F
2266	AHEARN, Martin	1	NENW	1860-10-01		A1
2267	" "	1	S½NW	1860-10-01		A1
2295	BALDWIN, William C	8	W½SW	1870-06-01		A2
2253	BATCHELDER, John W	13	SESE	1870-05-10		A1 G10
2255	" "	7	E½NE	1870-05-10		A1 G10
2254	" "	15	N½SE	1870-06-10		A1 G10
2287	BEISANG, Stefan	1	NESE	1861-12-10		A1
2284	BELL, Samuel	5	S½NE	1860-05-01		A1
2223	BOWMAN, Ezekiel	9	NWNE	1867-02-16		A1
2238	BOWMAN, Israel	9	S½NW	1867-02-16		A1 V2268
2233	BRABBS, Isaac	8	N½SE	1856-01-10		A1
2234	" "	8	NE	1856-01-10		A1
2237	" "	8	SWSE	1856-01-10		A1
2235	" "	8	SESE	1856-09-01		A1
2236	" "	8	SESW	1856-09-01		A1
2268	BRADY, Patrick	9	NW	1857-07-01		A1 V2246, 2238
2239	BRAUN, Jacob	12	E½SW	1860-11-21		A1
2240	" "	12	NW	1860-11-21		A1
2241	" "	12	SWSW	1860-11-21		A1
2220	CAMPBELL, Colin	15	SWSW	1856-09-01		A1
2271	CUMMINGS, Redmon S	12	NWSW	1855-10-01		A1
2260	FIFIELD, Joseph	10	NWSE	1859-10-10		A1
2261	" "	10	SW	1859-10-10		A1
2262	" "	9	SESE	1859-10-10		A1
2296	GALLEY, William	4	SE	1860-10-01		A1
2249	GILLIGAN, John	17	N½NW	1860-10-01		A1
2227	GOETCHINS, Henry D	17	NE	1856-01-10		A1
2228	" "	17	NESE	1856-01-10		A1
2230	" "	17	W½SE	1856-01-10		A1
2229	" "	17	SESE	1856-09-01		A1
2263	HARNACK, Karl	5	N½NE	1862-02-01		A1 F
2242	HEARN, James A	12	S½NE	1861-07-01		A1
2243	" "	12	SE	1861-07-01		A1
2244	" "	13	NENE	1861-07-01		A1
2259	HOBSON, Jonathan	8	NESW	1861-12-03		A1
2285	HOWARD, Samuel	14	NWSE	1861-12-10		A1
2274	HULSART, Robert K	6	N½SW	1862-05-15		A1 F
2297	HULSART, William	5	SW	1860-05-01		A1
2298	" "	8	E½NW	1860-11-21		A1
2253	JOHNSON, James S	13	SESE	1870-05-10		A1 G10
2255	" "	7	E½NE	1870-05-10		A1 G10
2254	" "	15	N½SE	1870-06-10		A1 G10

ID	Individual in Patent	Sec.	Sec. Part	Date Issued	Other Counties	For More Info . . .
2248	LANGE, Johann R	14	NESW	1862-02-01		A1
2212	LIDDELL, Andrew A	15	N½SW	1856-01-10		A1
2213	" "	15	SESW	1856-01-10		A1
2250	MCGILL, John	6	SWSE	1867-07-01		A1
2251	" "	7	NWNW	1867-07-01		A1
2299	MCLEAN, William	17	SWSW	1860-05-01		A1
2275	MONTGOMERY, Robert	1	NE	1857-10-30		A1
2269	MORGAN, Quinton	10	NWNW	1857-02-20		A1
2270	" "	3	SW	1857-02-20		A1
2209	MURRAY, Alexander	3	NW	1860-05-01		A1
2210	" "	4	E½NE	1860-05-01		A1
2211	" "	4	NWNE	1860-05-01		A1
2215	PERKINS, Charles W	10	E½NW	1860-05-01		A1
2216	" "	10	SWNW	1860-05-01		A1
2217	" "	9	E½NE	1860-05-01		A1
2218	" "	9	SWNE	1860-05-01		A1
2252	RAMSAY, John	11	W½NW	1860-05-01		A1
2231	SAUDER, Henry	18	NWSW	1861-07-01		A1
2232	" "	18	W½NW	1861-07-01		A1
2214	SCHOLZ, August	15	NE	1860-10-01		A1
2293	SMITH, Trueworthy	10	NE	1857-02-16		A1
2294	" "	10	NESE	1857-02-16		A1
2300	SNOVER, William	17	S½NW	1860-11-21		A1
2301	" "	18	E½SE	1860-11-21		A1
2302	" "	18	SENE	1860-11-21		A1
2276	STEENSON, Robert	15	NENW	1860-11-21		A1
2277	STENSON, Robert	15	S½NW	1857-02-16		A1
2278	STINSON, Robert	15	NWNW	1856-01-10		A1
2264	VERDRIES, Lewis	6	NW	1859-10-10		A1 F
2256	WALKER, John	1	SESW	1857-10-30		A1
2257	" "	1	W½SW	1857-10-30		A1
2286	WALKER, Samuel	2	NENE	1870-06-01		A1
2288	WALKER, Thomas	2	N½SE	1857-02-16		A1 F
2289	" "	2	N½SW	1857-02-16		A1
2291	" "	2	S½NE	1857-02-16		A1 F
2292	" "	2	SWSW	1857-02-16		A1
2290	" "	2	NWNE	1861-07-01		A1 F
2272	WILLIAMS, Richard	14	S½NW	1861-07-01		A1
2273	" "	14	SWNE	1861-07-01		A1
2224	WILSON, George	17	E½SW	1860-05-01		A1
2225	" "	17	NWSW	1860-10-01		A1
2226	" "	9	SW	1873-04-25		A2 V2245, 2247
2245	WILSON, James	9	E½SW	1860-10-01		A1 V2226
2246	" "	9	N½NW	1860-10-01		A1 V2268
2247	" "	9	SWSW	1860-10-01		A1 V2226
2258	WILSON, John	4	SWNE	1859-10-10		A1 F
2279	WILSON, Robert	4	NW	1859-10-10		A1 F
2280	" "	4	NWSW	1860-05-01		A1
2281	" "	5	E½SE	1860-05-01		A1
2282	" "	5	NWSE	1860-05-01		A1
2283	" "	5	SWSE	1861-12-10		A1

Patent Map

T10-N R12-E
Michigan-Toledo Strip Meridian

Map Group 21

Township Statistics

Parcels Mapped	:	94
Number of Patents	:	61
Number of Individuals	:	51
Patentees Identified	:	50
Number of Surnames	:	43
Multi-Patentee Parcels	:	3
Oldest Patent Date	:	10/1/1855
Most Recent Patent	:	4/25/1873
Block/Lot Parcels	:	0
Parcels Re - Issued	:	0
Parcels that Overlap	:	6
Cities and Towns	:	1
Cemeteries	:	3

Note: the area contained in this map amounts to far less than a full Township. Therefore, its contents are completely on this single page (instead of a "normal" 2-page spread).

6: VERDRIES Lewis 1859; HULSART Robert K 1862; MCGILL John 1867; ABBOTT Elon 1859
7: MCGILL John 1867; BATCHELDER [10] John W 1870
18: SAUDER Henry 1861; SAUDER Henry 1861; SNOVER William 1860; SNOVER William 1860
5: ABBOTT Elon 1859; HULSART William 1860; HARNACK Karl 1862; WILSON Robert 1860; WILSON Robert 1861; BELL Samuel 1860; WILSON Robert 1860
8: BALDWIN William C 1870; HULSART William 1860; HOBSON Jonathan 1861; BRABBS Isaac 1856; BRABBS Isaac 1856; BRABBS Isaac 1856; BRABBS Isaac 1856; BRABBS Isaac 1856
17: WILSON George 1860; MCLEAN William 1860; GILLIGAN John 1860; SNOVER William 1860; WILSON George 1860; GOETCHINS Henry D 1856; GOETCHINS Henry D 1856; GOETCHINS Henry D 1856; GOETCHINS Henry D 1856
4: WILSON Robert 1860; WILSON Robert 1859; MURRAY Alexander 1860; WILSON John 1859; GALLEY William 1860; MURRAY Alexander 1860
9: WILSON James 1860; BRADY Patrick 1857; BOWMAN Israel 1867; WILSON George 1873; WILSON James 1860; WILSON James 1860; BOWMAN Ezekiel 1867; PERKINS Charles W 1860; PERKINS Charles W 1860; FIFIELD Joseph 1859
16
3: MURRAY Alexander 1860; MORGAN Quinton 1857
10: MORGAN Quinton 1857; PERKINS Charles W 1860; PERKINS Charles W 1860; FIFIELD Joseph 1859; FIFIELD Joseph 1859; SMITH Trueworthy 1857; SMITH Trueworthy 1857
15: STINSON Robert 1856; STENSON Robert 1857; STEENSON Robert 1860; LIDDELL Andrew A 1856; LIDDELL Andrew A 1856; CAMPBELL Colin 1856; SCHOLZ August 1860; BATCHELDER [10] John W 1870
2: WALKER Thomas 1857; WALKER Thomas 1857; WALKER Thomas 1861; WALKER Thomas 1857; WALKER Thomas 1857; WALKER Samuel 1870
11: RAMSAY John 1860
14: WILLIAMS Richard 1861; LANGE Johann R 1862; WILLIAMS Richard 1861; HOWARD Samuel 1861; ABEL Christian 1861
1: AHEARN Marten 1861; AHEARN Martin 1860; AHEARN Martin 1860; WALKER John 1857; WALKER John 1857; MONTGOMERY Robert 1857; BEISANG Stefan 1861
12: BRAUN Jacob 1860; CUMMINGS Redmon S 1855; BRAUN Jacob 1860; BRAUN Jacob 1860; HEARN James A 1861; HEARN James A 1861
13: HEARN James A 1861; BATCHELDER [10] John W 1870

Legend

(thin line)	Patent Boundary
(thick line)	Section Boundary
(shaded)	No Patents Found (or Outside County)
1., 2., 3., ...	Lot Numbers (when beside a name)
[ ]	Group Number (see Appendix "C")

Scale: Section = 1 mile X 1 mile
(generally, with some exceptions)

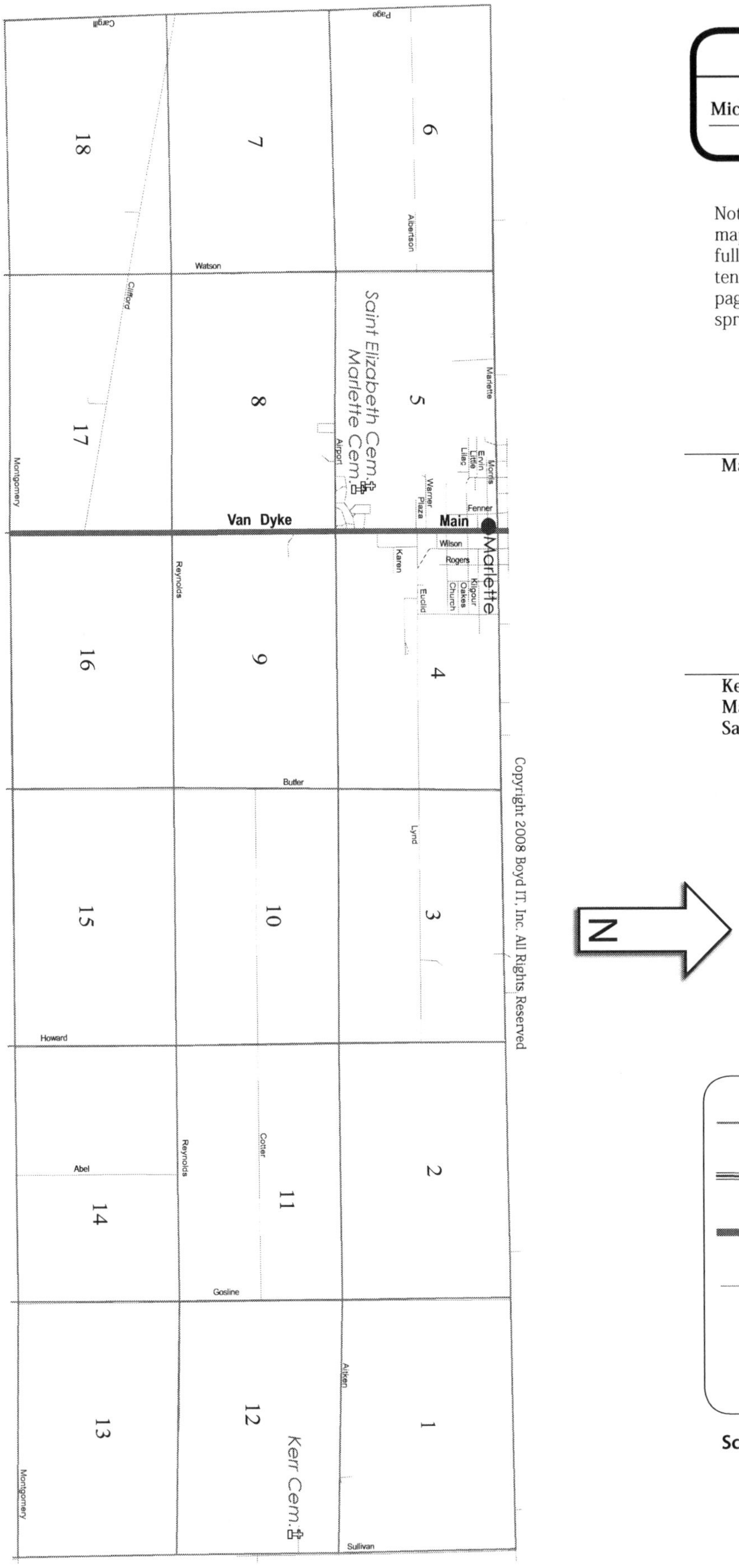

Road Map

T10-N R12-E
Michigan-Toledo Strip Meridian

Map Group 21

Note: the area contained in this map amounts to far less than a full Township. Therefore, its contents are completely on this single page (instead of a "normal" 2-page spread).

18 7 6
17 8 5
16 9 4
15 10 3
14 11 2
13 12 1

Cargill, Page, Albertson, Watson, Clifford, Marlette, Montgomery, Airport, Morris, Ervin, Little, Lilac, Warner, Plaza, Fenner, Van Dyke, Main, Wilson, Rogers, Karen, Kilgour, Oakes, Church, Euclid, Reynolds, Butler, Lynd, Howard, Abel, Cotter, Gosline, Aitken, Sullivan

Saint Elizabeth Cem.
Marlette Cem.
Marlette
Kerr Cem.

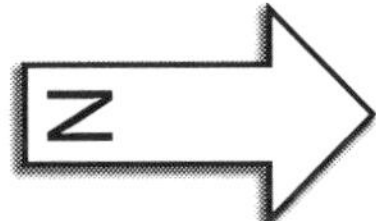

Cities & Towns

Marlette

Cemeteries

Kerr Cemetery
Marlette Cemetery
Saint Elizabeth Cemetery

Legend

- Section Lines
- Interstates
- Highways
- Other Roads
- Cities/Towns
- Cemeteries

Scale: Section = 1 mile X 1 mile
(generally, with some exceptions)

Historical Map

T10-N R12-E
Michigan-Toledo Strip Meridian

Map Group 21

Note: the area contained in this map amounts to far less than a full Township. Therefore, its contents are completely on this single page (instead of a "normal" 2-page spread).

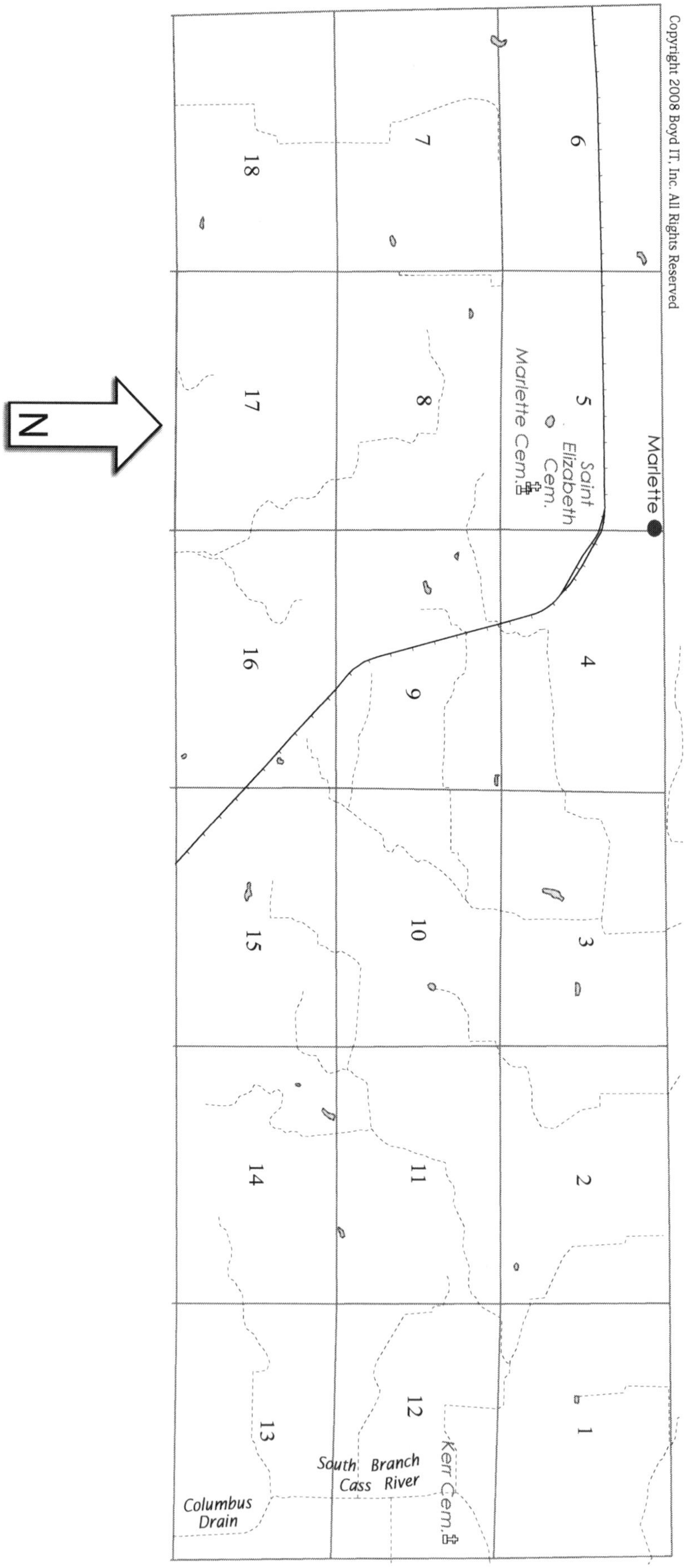

Cities & Towns

Marlette

Cemeteries

Kerr Cemetery
Marlette Cemetery
Saint Elizabeth Cemetery

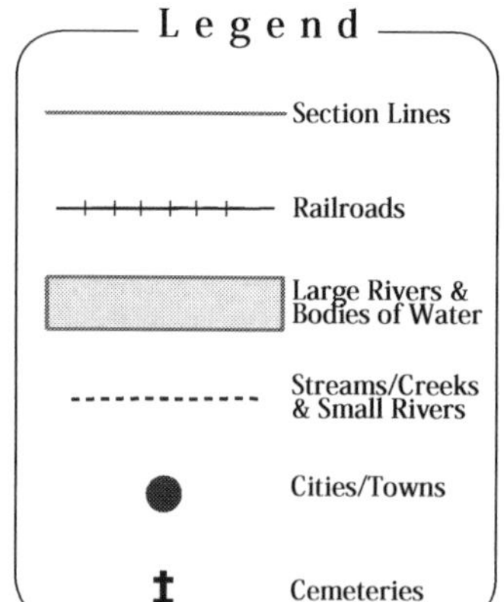

Scale: Section = 1 mile X 1 mile
(there are some exceptions)

N

6 7 18 5 8 17 4 9 16 3 10 15 2 11 14 1 12 13

Marlette
Saint Elizabeth Cem.
Marlette Cem.
South Branch Cass River
Kerr Cem.
Columbus Drain

Map Group 22: Index to Land Patents

Township 10-North Range 13-East (Michigan-Toledo Strip)

After you locate an individual in this Index, take note of the Section and Section Part then proceed to the Land Patent map on the pages immediately following. You should have no difficulty locating the corresponding parcel of land.

The "For More Info" Column will lead you to more information about the underlying Patents. See the *Legend* at right, and the "How to Use this Book" chapter, for more information.

LEGEND

"For More Info . . . " column

A = Authority (Legislative Act, See Appendix "A")
B = Block or Lot (location in Section unknown)
C = Cancelled Patent
F = Fractional Section
G = Group (Multi-Patentee Patent, see Appendix "C")
V = Overlaps another Parcel
R = Re-Issued (Parcel patented more than once)

(A & G items require you to look in the Appendixes referred to above. All other Letter-designations followed by a number require you to locate line-items in this index that possess the ID number found after the letter).

ID	Individual in Patent	Sec.	Sec. Part	Date Issued	Other Counties	For More Info . . .
2303	ABEL, Augustine	20	NESW	1890-05-20		A1
2337	BATCHELDER, John W	18	N½SE	1869-11-15		A1 G10
2338	BOOTHBY, Joseph	36	SESE	1857-10-30		A1
2371	BOTTOMLEY, Thomas H	33	NESE	1865-10-02		A1
2372	" "	34	NWSW	1865-10-02		A1
2365	CANEDY, Salmon S	8	E½	1861-12-10		A1
2377	CANEDY, William	9	S½	1861-12-10		A1
2311	DAVIS, Francis	20	N½NW	1878-02-13		A2 V2353, 2326
2369	DEUSHAM, Thomas	23	SENW	1864-10-15		A1
2359	DODGE, Pidesco R	4	W½SW	1883-01-20		A1
2366	DOLE, Sebastian	6	S½NW	1862-02-01		A1 F
2370	DONAHUE, Thomas	26	SWNW	1855-10-01		A1
2330	FALKENBURY, John J	27	SESE	1852-02-10		A1
2331	" "	34	NENE	1852-02-10		A1
2332	" "	35	E½NE	1852-02-10		A1
2333	" "	35	E½SE	1852-02-10		A1
2378	FITCH, William	36	N½SE	1857-07-01		A1
2379	" "	36	SWSE	1857-07-01		A1
2357	FOX, Patrick	23	SWSE	1861-07-01		A1
2358	" "	26	W½NE	1861-07-01		A1
2355	" "	10	SWNW	1862-11-13		A1
2356	" "	11	NENE	1864-01-05		A1
2308	HILL, Daniel	35	SWSW	1865-10-02		A1
2309	HOUSE, Daniel	36	SENE	1860-05-01		A1
2304	HUBBARD, Bela	11	NWSE	1868-08-20		A1 G47
2384	JENNY, William T	9	N½	1861-07-01		A1
2337	JOHNSON, James S	18	N½SE	1869-11-15		A1 G10
2328	KENGOTT, Gottlob	17	NE	1862-05-15		A1
2329	" "	17	NESE	1862-05-15		A1
2304	KING, John E	11	NWSE	1868-08-20		A1 G47
2344	KOLTS, Mathew J	33	NENE	1872-12-30		A2
2345	" "	34	SENW	1872-12-30		A2
2346	" "	34	W½NW	1872-12-30		A2
2339	MASON, Lorenzo M	1	NENE	1855-10-01		A1
2310	MCCREDIE, Edwin R	13	SWSW	1868-08-20		A1
2380	MCGREGOR, William	23	NESE	1871-09-30		A2
2340	MILLS, Luther D	25	NESE	1855-10-01		A1
2341	" "	25	S½SE	1855-10-01		A1
2342	" "	36	NENE	1855-10-01		A1
2343	" "	36	SENW	1855-10-01		A1
2376	MILLS, Wildman	21	NWNW	1869-07-01		A1
2373	MOSS, Truman	22	NWSE	1868-08-20		A1
2381	OAKES, William	7	NENE	1864-09-15		A1
2314	PACK, George	30	N½SW	1857-07-01		A1 F
2315	" "	30	NWNE	1857-07-01		A1
2316	PACK, George W	12	SESW	1855-10-01		A1

ID	Individual in Patent	Sec.	Sec. Part	Date Issued	Other Counties	For More Info . . .
2317	PACK, George W (Cont'd)	23	NWNW	1855-10-01		A1
2318	" "	33	NENW	1855-10-01		A1
2319	" "	33	NWNE	1855-10-01		A1
2320	" "	33	NWSE	1855-10-01		A1
2322	" "	33	SWNE	1855-10-01		A1
2321	" "	33	SENE	1860-10-01		A1
2367	REEVE, Selah	4	NENW	1855-10-01		A1
2368	" "	5	NENW	1855-10-01		A1 F
2349	ROCKWELL, Morris	19	S½NE	1883-06-07		A2
2350	" "	19	S½NW	1883-06-07		A2 F
2305	ROSS, Catharine	22	SESE	1878-11-05		A2
2306	" "	23	E½SW	1878-11-05		A2
2307	" "	23	SWSW	1878-11-05		A2
2382	RUSSELSMITH, William	17	NW	1861-12-10		A1
2383	" "	18	NE	1861-12-10		A1
2323	SCHWEIZER, Gottfried	17	E½SW	1862-05-15		A1
2324	" "	20	E½NE	1862-05-15		A1
2325	" "	20	N½SE	1862-05-15		A1
2326	" "	20	NENW	1862-05-15		A1 V2311
2327	" "	20	NWNE	1862-05-15		A1
2374	SEYMOUR, Walter	3	W½SW	1877-04-05		A2
2375	" "	4	E½SE	1877-04-05		A2
2360	SMITH, Ralph C	20	SESE	1865-10-02		A1
2361	" "	27	SESW	1865-10-02		A1
2362	" "	32	SESE	1865-10-02		A1
2363	" "	33	SENW	1865-10-02		A1
2351	SNELL, Nathan	17	W½SW	1861-07-01		A1
2352	" "	19	E½SE	1861-07-01		A1
2353	" "	20	W½NW	1861-07-01		A1 V2311
2354	" "	20	W½SW	1861-07-01		A1
2335	STILSON, John	5	NESW	1864-01-05		A1
2336	" "	5	NWSW	1866-06-20		A1
2364	STINSON, Robert E	8	NENW	1878-11-05		A2
2347	WHITAKER, Melville	3	SWNW	1883-06-07		A2
2348	" "	4	E½NE	1883-06-07		A2
2334	WOODS, John L	12	NESW	1864-01-05		A1
2313	ZAUNER, Franz X	6	SW	1859-10-10		A1 C F
2312	" "	6	N½NW	1861-08-03		A1 F

Patent Map

T10-N R13-E
Michigan-Toledo Strip Meridian

Map Group 22

Township Statistics

Parcels Mapped	:	82
Number of Patents	:	58
Number of Individuals	:	44
Patentees Identified	:	42
Number of Surnames	:	41
Multi-Patentee Parcels	:	2
Oldest Patent Date	:	2/10/1852
Most Recent Patent	:	5/20/1890
Block/Lot Parcels	:	0
Parcels Re - Issued	:	0
Parcels that Overlap	:	3
Cities and Towns	:	0
Cemeteries	:	1

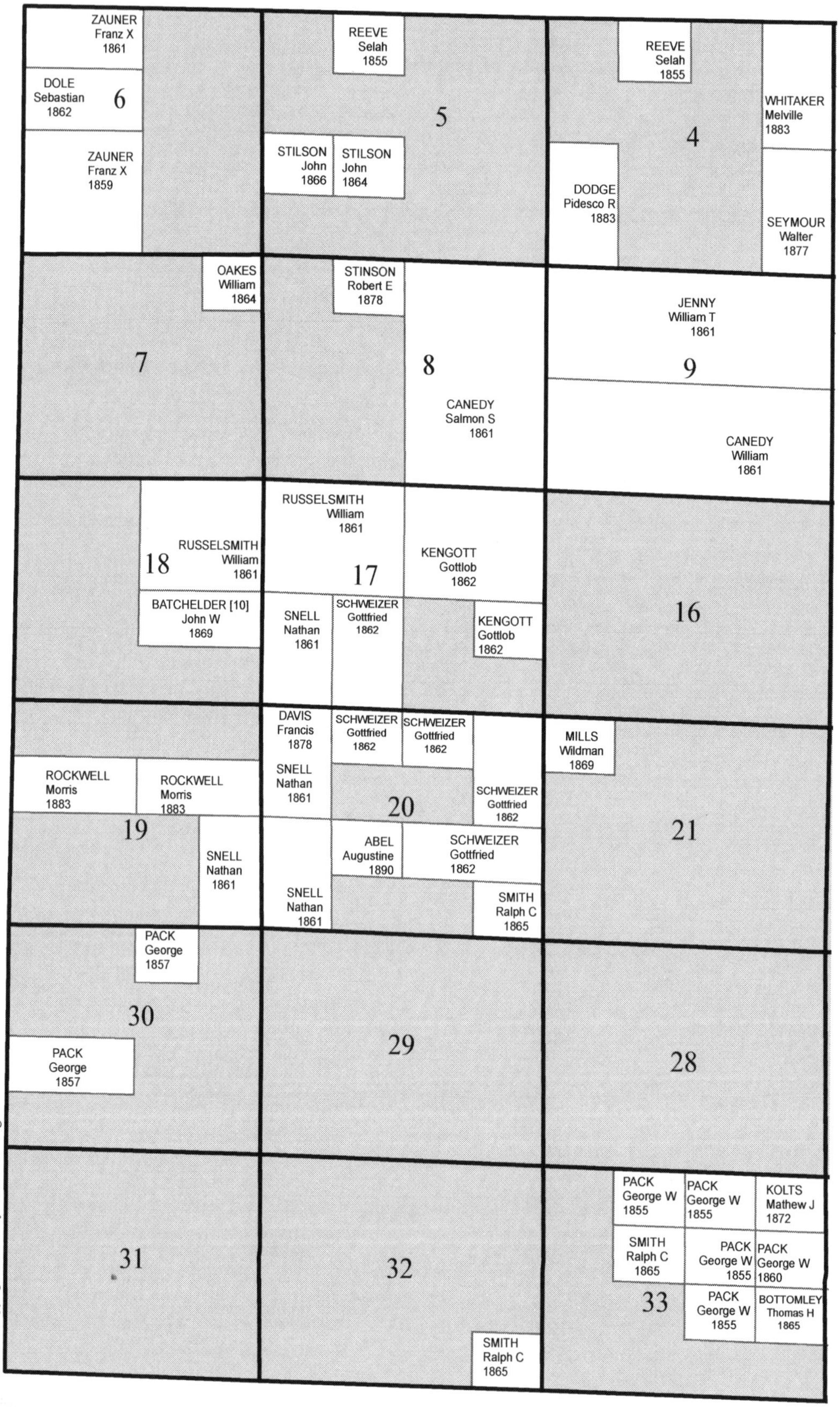

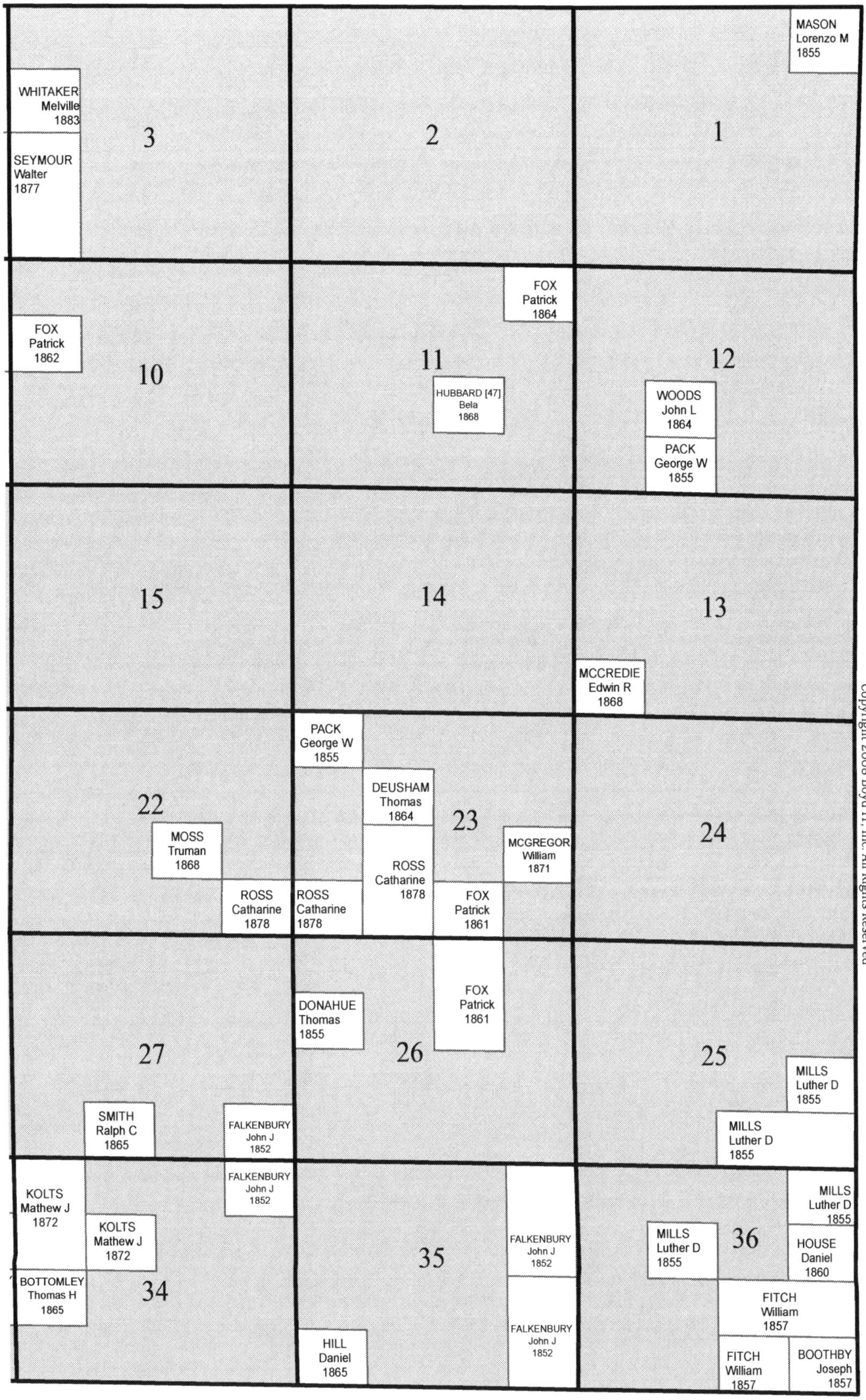

MASON Lorenzo M 1855
WHITAKER Melville 1883
SEYMOUR Walter 1877
3
2
1
FOX Patrick 1864
FOX Patrick 1862
10
11
12
HUBBARD [47] Bela 1868
WOODS John L 1864
PACK George W 1855
15
14
13
MCCREDIE Edwin R 1868
PACK George W 1855
DEUSHAM Thomas 1864
22
23
24
MOSS Truman 1868
MCGREGOR William 1871
ROSS Catharine 1878
ROSS Catharine 1878
ROSS Catharine 1878
FOX Patrick 1861
FOX Patrick 1861
DONAHUE Thomas 1855
27
26
25
MILLS Luther D 1855
MILLS Luther D 1855
SMITH Ralph C 1865
FALKENBURY John J 1852
FALKENBURY John J 1852
KOLTS Mathew J 1872
KOLTS Mathew J 1872
MILLS Luther D 1855
FALKENBURY John J 1852
MILLS Luther D 1855
36
HOUSE Daniel 1860
35
BOTTOMLEY Thomas H 1865
34
FITCH William 1857
FALKENBURY John J 1852
HILL Daniel 1865
FITCH William 1857
BOOTHBY Joseph 1857

Helpful Hints

1. This Map's INDEX can be found on the preceding pages.
2. Refer to Map "C" to see where this Township lies within Sanilac County, Michigan.
3. Numbers within square brackets [ ] denote a multi-patentee land parcel (multi-owner). Refer to Appendix "C" for a full list of members in this group.
4. Areas that look to be crowded with Patentees usually indicate multiple sales of the same parcel (Re-issues) or Overlapping parcels. See this Township's Index for an explanation of these and other circumstances that might explain "odd" groupings of Patentees on this map.

Legend

- Patent Boundary
- Section Boundary
- No Patents Found (or Outside County)
- 1., 2., 3., ... Lot Numbers (when beside a name)
- [ ] Group Number (see Appendix "C")

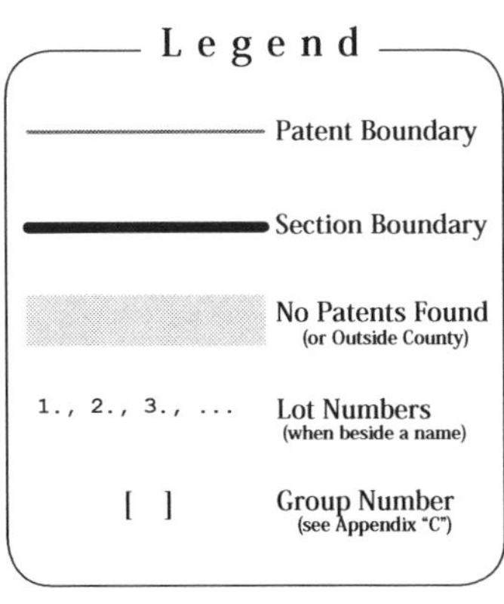

Scale: Section = 1 mile X 1 mile (generally, with some exceptions)

Road Map

T10-N R13-E
Michigan-Toledo Strip Meridian

Map Group 22

Cities & Towns
None

Cemeteries
Omard Cemetery

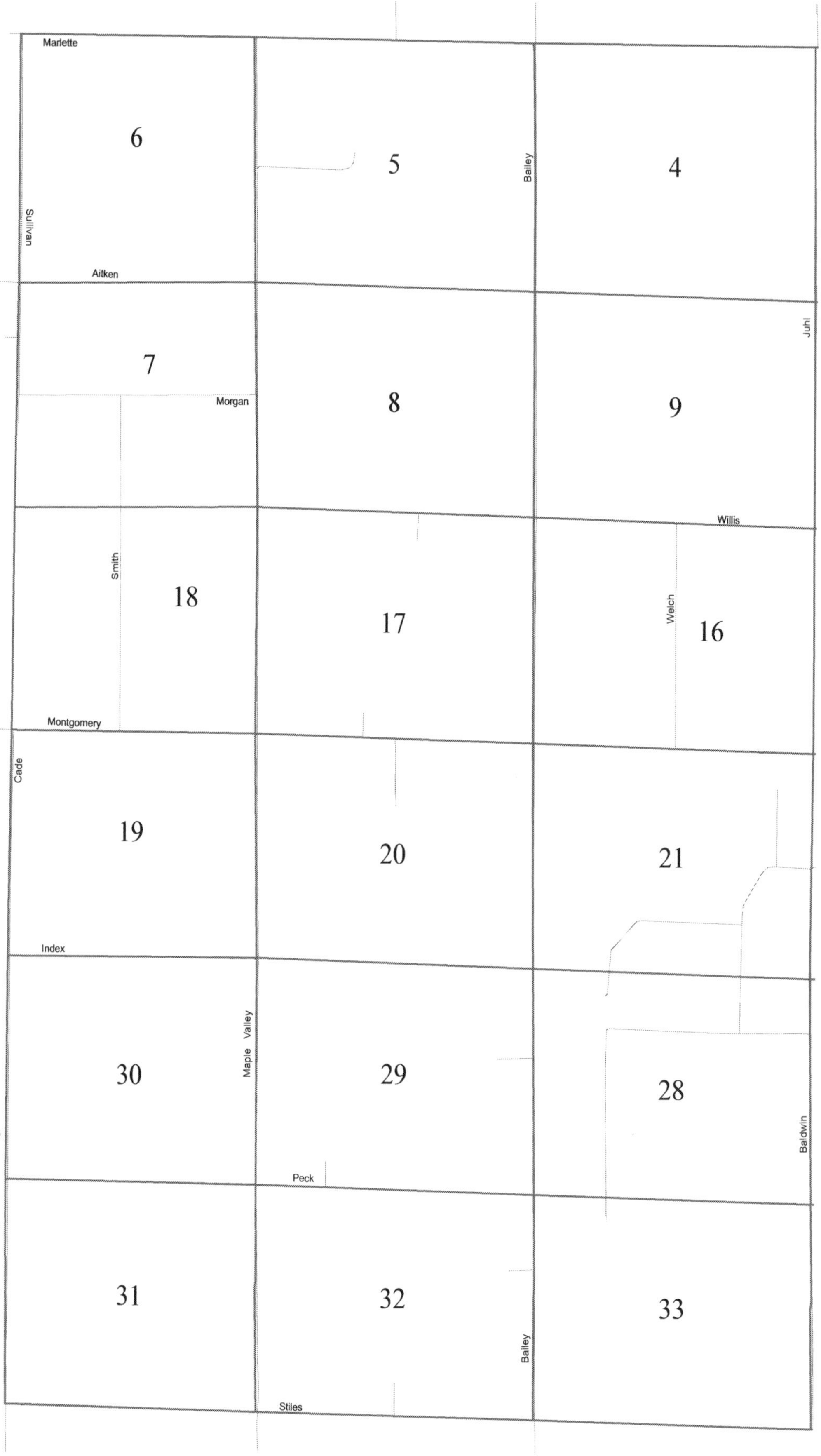

Marlette
3
Shepherd
2
Isles
1
Marsh
Aitkins
10
11
12
Millan
Stilson
15
Setter
14
13
Mowerson
Montgomery
22
Campbell
23
24
Harrington
27
Shepherd
26
Isles
25
Peck
Omard Cem.
34
35
Flynn
36
Stiles

Helpful Hints

1. This road map has a number of uses, but primarily it is to help you: a) find the present location of land owned by your ancestors (at least the general area), b) find cemeteries and city-centers, and c) estimate the route/roads used by Census-takers & tax-assessors.

2. If you plan to travel to Sanilac County to locate cemeteries or land parcels, please pick up a modern travel map for the area before you do. Mapping old land parcels on modern maps is not as exact a science as you might think. Just the slightest variations in public land survey coordinates, estimates of parcel boundaries, or road-map deviations can greatly alter a map's representation of how a road either does or doesn't cross a particular parcel of land.

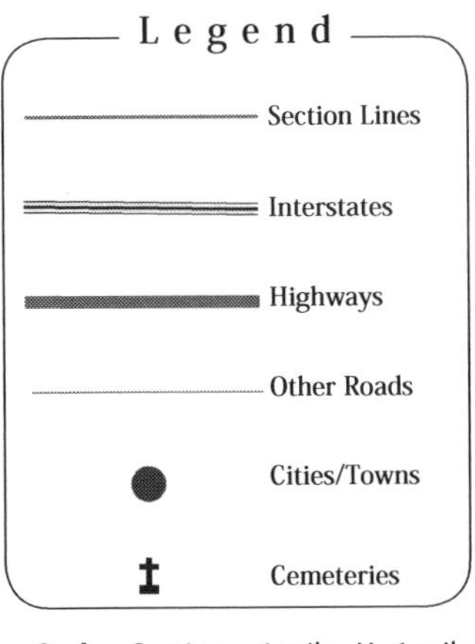

Scale: Section = 1 mile X 1 mile
(generally, with some exceptions)

Historical Map

T10-N R13-E
Michigan-Toledo Strip Meridian

Map Group 22

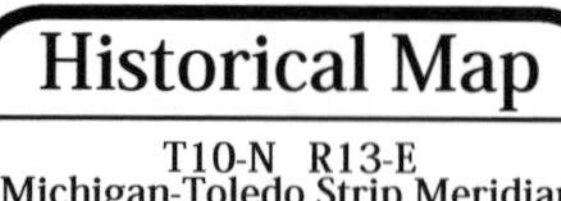

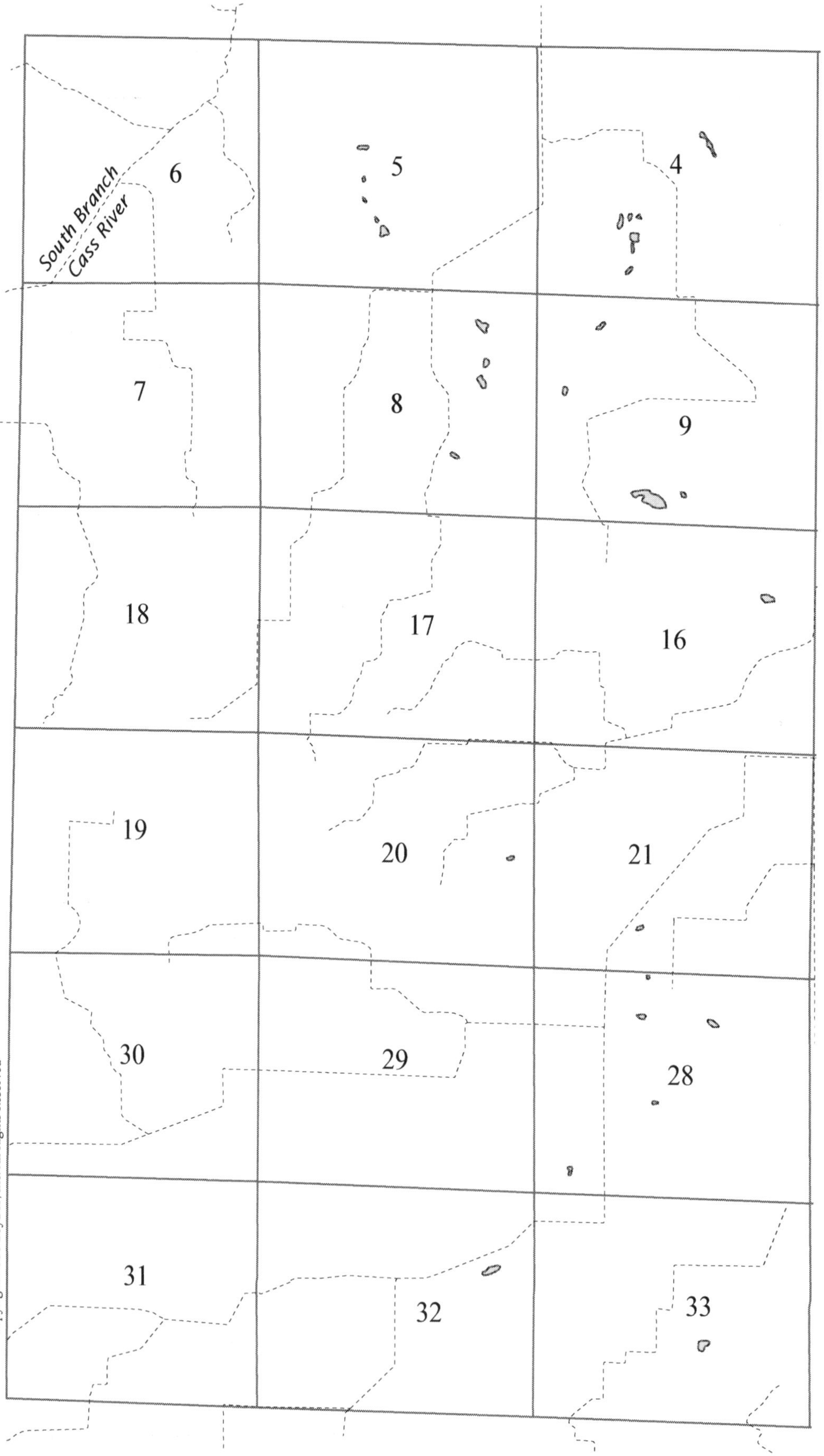

Cities & Towns

None

Cemeteries

Omard Cemetery

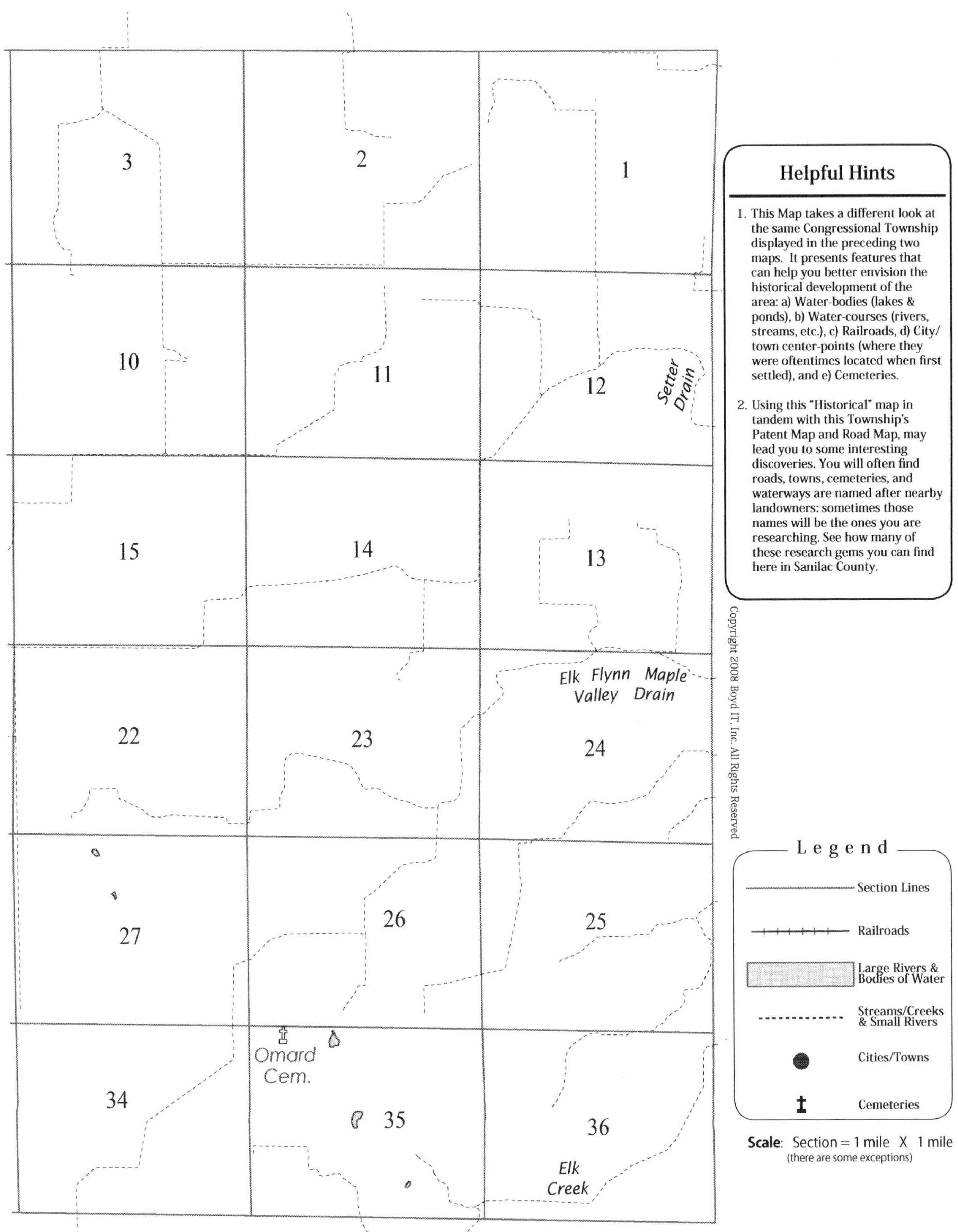

Helpful Hints

1. This Map takes a different look at the same Congressional Township displayed in the preceding two maps. It presents features that can help you better envision the historical development of the area: a) Water-bodies (lakes & ponds), b) Water-courses (rivers, streams, etc.), c) Railroads, d) City/town center-points (where they were oftentimes located when first settled), and e) Cemeteries.
2. Using this "Historical" map in tandem with this Township's Patent Map and Road Map, may lead you to some interesting discoveries. You will often find roads, towns, cemeteries, and waterways are named after nearby landowners: sometimes those names will be the ones you are researching. See how many of these research gems you can find here in Sanilac County.

Scale: Section = 1 mile X 1 mile
(there are some exceptions)

Map Group 23: Index to Land Patents

Township 10-North Range 14-East (Michigan-Toledo Strip)

After you locate an individual in this Index, take note of the Section and Section Part then proceed to the Land Patent map on the pages immediately following. You should have no difficulty locating the corresponding parcel of land.

The "For More Info" Column will lead you to more information about the underlying Patents. See the *Legend* at right, and the "How to Use this Book" chapter, for more information.

LEGEND

"For More Info . . . " column

A = Authority (Legislative Act, See Appendix "A")
B = Block or Lot (location in Section unknown)
C = Cancelled Patent
F = Fractional Section
G = Group (Multi-Patentee Patent, see Appendix "C")
V = Overlaps another Parcel
R = Re-Issued (Parcel patented more than once)

(A & G items require you to look in the Appendixes referred to above. All other Letter-designations followed by a number require you to locate line-items in this index that possess the ID number found after the letter).

ID	Individual in Patent	Sec.	Sec. Part	Date Issued	Other Counties	For More Info . . .
2401	ALLEN, Chancy	26	N½SW	1857-02-16		A1
2402	" "	27	N½SE	1857-02-16		A1
2436	ANDREWS, John L	5	SESW	1865-10-02		A1
2387	ASH, Allan K	9	NESW	1856-09-01		A1
2388	" "	9	NWSW	1856-09-01		A1
2390	ASH, Allen K	11	NENW	1853-11-01		A1
2409	AYLSWORTH, Ebenezer	5	SE	1861-12-03		A1
2398	BABCOCK, Amos	29	N½NW	1857-10-30		A1
2418	BACON, James H	5	SWNW	1854-06-15		A1
2462	BAILEY, Mark	29	SESW	1855-10-01		A1
2492	BAILIE, William	1	NWSW	1861-07-01		A1
2493	" "	1	S½SW	1861-07-01		A1
2494	" "	2	SESE	1861-07-01		A1
2415	BALL, James	11	SESE	1870-06-01		A2
2416	" "	12	SWSW	1870-06-01		A2
2482	BARNARD, Sherman S	5	NENE	1853-11-01		A1 G8 F
2483	" "	5	NWNE	1853-11-01		A1 G8 F
2484	" "	5	NWNW	1853-11-01		A1 G8 F
2429	BAUGHMAN, John C	9	NENW	1856-09-01		A1 G11
2410	BEACH, Elijah W	12	NWNE	1857-10-30		A1
2417	BEARD, James	7	NESE	1852-02-10		A1
2428	BEARD, John	8	NWSW	1852-02-10		A1
2495	BOYS, William	11	W½SW	1857-10-30		A1
2474	BRASEBRIDGE, Robert	26	E½NW	1867-02-16		A1
2475	" "	26	W½NE	1867-02-16		A1
2411	BROCKWAY, Elliot T	11	SENW	1853-11-01		A1
2482	BROOKS, Nathaniel W	5	NENE	1853-11-01		A1 G8 F
2483	" "	5	NWNE	1853-11-01		A1 G8 F
2484	" "	5	NWNW	1853-11-01		A1 G8 F
2405	BRYCE, David	33	S½NE	1857-07-01		A1
2485	BURTON, Thomas	1	SENE	1882-10-20		A2
2385	CAMPBELL, Alexander	9	SWNE	1856-09-01		A1
2403	CARLETON, Chester	11	SWNW	1853-11-01		A1
2466	CHASE, Nathan	26	SWSW	1852-02-10		A1
2467	" "	34	SWNE	1852-02-10		A1
2464	CHASE, Nathan B	3	W½SW	1850-12-02		A1 G24
2465	" "	30	W½NE	1850-12-02		A1 G24
2469	COCHRAN, Neil	6	W½SE	1862-05-15		A1
2430	DOUGLASS, John	2	5	1885-07-27		A2
2431	" "	2	SWNE	1885-07-27		A2
2486	DUNLEY, Thomas	32	E½SW	1861-07-01		A1
2472	EDWARDS, Richard H	1	SWSE	1862-02-01		A1
2389	FISH, Allen	2	W½SE	1853-11-01		A1
2498	HAMILTON, William	14	E½NW	1857-02-16		A1
2499	" "	14	NWSE	1857-02-16		A1
2500	" "	14	W½NE	1857-02-16		A1

ID	Individual in Patent	Sec.	Sec. Part	Date Issued	Other Counties	For More Info . . .
2479	HARDY, Samuel	29	NWSE	1860-05-01		A1
2432	HAYES, John	12	N½SW	1861-07-01		A1
2433	" "	12	NENE	1861-07-01		A1
2434	" "	12	NW	1861-07-01		A1
2435	" "	12	SWNE	1861-07-01		A1
2429	HUBBARD, Thomas	9	NENW	1856-09-01		A1 G11
2420	JOHNSON, James	31	S½NW	1856-01-10		A1
2419	" "	31	N½NW	1857-02-16		A1
2429	KING, John E	9	NENW	1856-09-01		A1 G11
2446	LAMBERT, Joseph	26	SWSE	1859-10-10		A1
2386	LEONARD, Alfred E	14	NWSW	1877-09-26		A1
2391	MACOMBER, Allen	28	SWNW	1855-10-01		A1
2392	" "	30	S½SE	1857-07-01		A1
2393	" "	31	NE	1857-07-01		A1
2394	" "	32	S½NW	1857-07-01		A1
2451	MASON, Lorenzo M	30	N½SW	1855-10-01		A1 F
2421	MCGRATH, James L	22	NWSE	1859-10-10		A1
2422	" "	22	SWNE	1859-10-10		A1
2438	MCLAREN, John	28	SESW	1860-05-01		A1
2447	MCLELLAN, Joseph	1	NWSE	1885-01-30		A2
2448	" "	1	S½NW	1885-01-30		A2
2449	" "	1	SWNE	1885-01-30		A2
2487	MILLER, Thomas	15	SESW	1867-02-16		A1
2488	" "	15	SWSE	1867-02-16		A1
2489	" "	22	NWNE	1867-02-16		A1
2452	MILLS, Luther D	14	NESW	1855-10-01		A1
2453	" "	21	SESW	1855-10-01		A1
2454	" "	22	E½SW	1855-10-01		A1
2455	" "	22	SENW	1855-10-01		A1
2456	" "	27	S½NE	1855-10-01		A1
2457	" "	28	NENW	1855-10-01		A1
2458	" "	30	S½NW	1855-10-01		A1
2459	" "	30	S½SW	1855-10-01		A1 F
2460	" "	33	N½SE	1855-10-01		A1
2461	" "	33	SENW	1855-10-01		A1
2463	MULLINS, Michael	11	N½NE	1861-12-10		A1
2480	PARKIN, Samuel	33	NENW	1860-05-01		A1
2439	POTTS, John	36	E½NE	1857-02-16		A1
2491	POTTS, Thomas	28	W½NE	1856-01-10		A1
2490	" "	28	N½SE	1857-02-16		A1
2414	ROBISON, Hiram	29	W½NE	1867-02-16		A1
2395	RUST, Aloney	3	5	1855-10-01		A1
2396	" "	3	SWNE	1855-10-01		A1 F
2440	RYAN, John	23	SENW	1857-02-20		A1
2441	RYANS, John	23	E½SW	1861-12-03		A1
2442	" "	23	W½SE	1861-12-03		A1
2423	SANBORN, James	26	SESW	1852-02-10		A1
2424	" "	34	SENE	1852-02-10		A1
2464	SANBORN, James W	3	W½SW	1850-12-02		A1 G24
2465	" "	30	W½NE	1850-12-02		A1 G24
2427	" "	24	NESE	1852-02-10		A1 G56
2425	" "	3	1	1853-11-01		A1 F
2426	" "	3	2	1853-11-01		A1 F
2476	SCOLLAY, Robert	36	SWSE	1856-01-10		A1
2450	SMITH, Lernerd	30	NESE	1855-10-01		A1
2470	SMITH, R C	4	NWNE	1864-01-05		A1
2471	" "	4	S½NW	1864-01-05		A1
2481	SPENCER, Samuel	36	SW	1857-07-01		A1
2404	STEINER, Christian	6	N½NE	1898-04-27		A2
2413	STEVENS, Harmon L	22	SWNW	1852-02-10		A1
2444	STILSON, John	10	W½SW	1855-10-01		A1
2443	" "	10	SWNW	1860-05-01		A1
2427	SWEETSER, Alvah	24	NESE	1852-02-10		A1 G56
2397	" "	6	N½NW	1854-06-15		A1
2496	TOBIN, William D	14	SENE	1865-10-02		A1
2497	" "	2	1	1865-10-02		A1
2412	VAN CAMP, EZRA	21	W½NW	1857-02-16		A1
2468	VAN NEST, NATHANIEL	29	SWSW	1857-02-20		A1
2473	VARNUM, Richard M	4	W½SE	1861-12-03		A1
2445	WARREN, John	6	S½NE	1856-01-10		A1
2477	WHEELER, Robert	36	E½NW	1855-10-01		A1
2478	" "	36	W½NE	1855-10-01		A1
2399	WIGHT, Buckminster	22	W½SW	1852-02-10		A1

ID	Individual in Patent	Sec.	Sec. Part	Date Issued	Other Counties	For More Info . . .
2400	WIGHT, Buckminster (Cont'd)	28	NENE	1852-02-10		A1
2407	WILLSON, David	21	NWSW	1857-02-20		A1
2406	" "	21	NWNE	1857-10-30		A1
2408	WILSON, David	27	NWNW	1861-09-02		A1
2437	WOODS, John L	8	SENW	1864-01-05		A1

Patent Map

T10-N R14-E
Michigan-Toledo Strip Meridian

Map Group 23

Township Statistics

Parcels Mapped	116
Number of Patents	91
Number of Individuals	73
Patentees Identified	71
Number of Surnames	67
Multi-Patentee Parcels	7
Oldest Patent Date	12/2/1850
Most Recent Patent	4/27/1898
Block/Lot Parcels	5
Parcels Re - Issued	0
Parcels that Overlap	0
Cities and Towns	1
Cemeteries	1

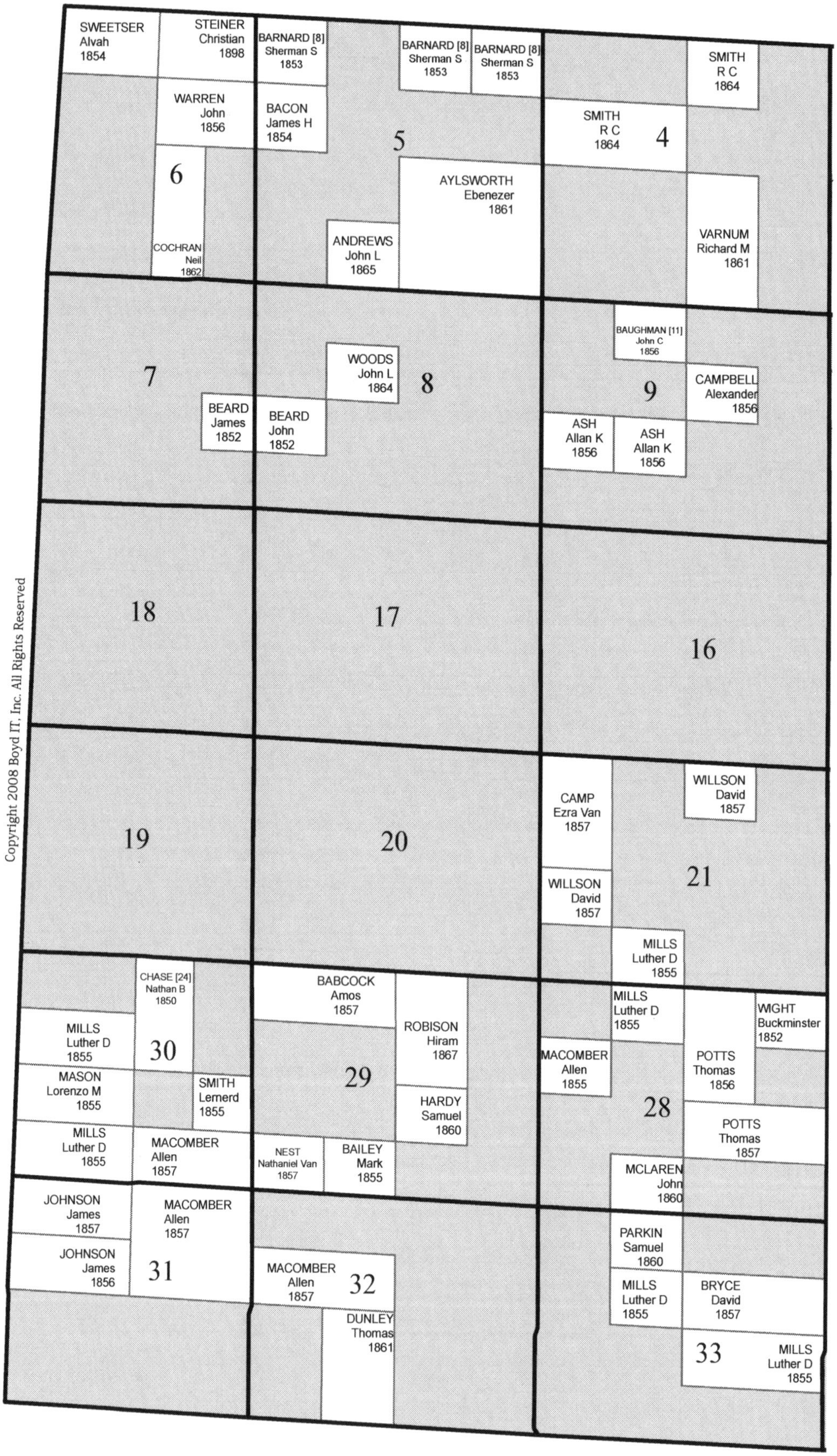

SWEETSER Alvah 1854
STEINER Christian 1898
WARREN John 1856
6
COCHRAN Neil 1862
BARNARD [8] Sherman S 1853
BACON James H 1854
5
BARNARD [8] Sherman S 1853
BARNARD [8] Sherman S 1853
AYLSWORTH Ebenezer 1861
ANDREWS John L 1865
SMITH R C 1864
SMITH R C 1864
4
VARNUM Richard M 1861
7
BEARD James 1852
WOODS John L 1864
8
BEARD John 1852
BAUGHMAN [11] John C 1856
9
CAMPBELL Alexander 1856
ASH Allan K 1856
ASH Allan K 1856
18
17
16
19
20
CAMP Ezra Van 1857
WILLSON David 1857
WILLSON David 1857
21
MILLS Luther D 1855
CHASE [24] Nathan B 1850
MILLS Luther D 1855
30
MASON Lorenzo M 1855
SMITH Lernerd 1855
MILLS Luther D 1855
MACOMBER Allen 1857
BABCOCK Amos 1857
ROBISON Hiram 1867
29
HARDY Samuel 1860
NEST Nathaniel Van 1857
BAILEY Mark 1855
MILLS Luther D 1855
WIGHT Buckminster 1852
MACOMBER Allen 1855
POTTS Thomas 1856
28
POTTS Thomas 1857
MCLAREN John 1860
JOHNSON James 1857
MACOMBER Allen 1857
JOHNSON James 1856
31
MACOMBER Allen 1857
32
DUNLEY Thomas 1861
PARKIN Samuel 1860
MILLS Luther D 1855
BRYCE David 1857
33
MILLS Luther D 1855

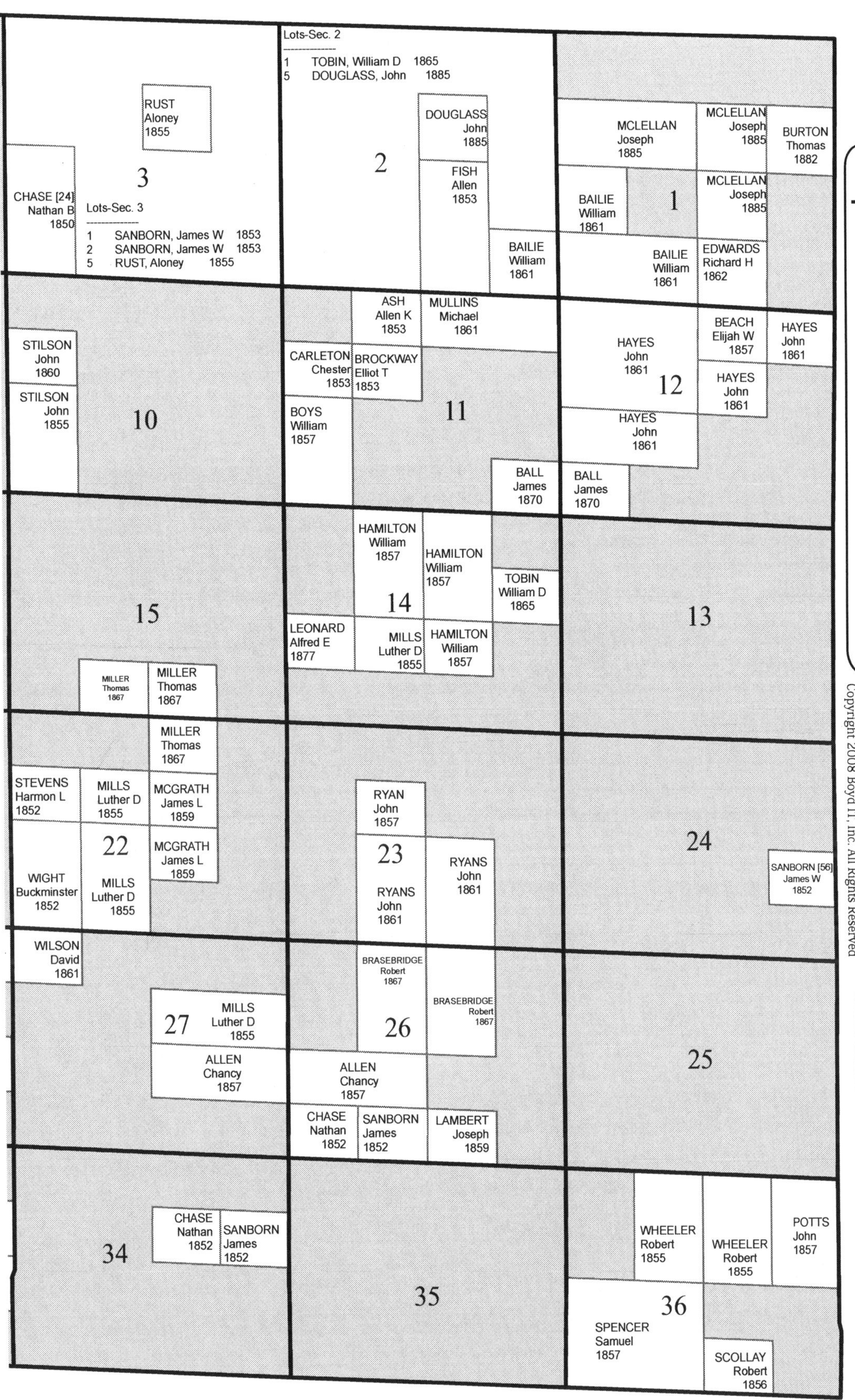

Helpful Hints

1. This Map's INDEX can be found on the preceding pages.
2. Refer to Map "C" to see where this Township lies within Sanilac County, Michigan.
3. Numbers within square brackets [ ] denote a multi-patentee land parcel (multi-owner). Refer to Appendix "C" for a full list of members in this group.
4. Areas that look to be crowded with Patentees usually indicate multiple sales of the same parcel (Re-issues) or Overlapping parcels. See this Township's Index for an explanation of these and other circumstances that might explain "odd" groupings of Patentees on this map.

Legend

- Patent Boundary
- Section Boundary
- No Patents Found (or Outside County)
- 1., 2., 3., ... Lot Numbers (when beside a name)
- [ ] Group Number (see Appendix "C")

Scale: Section = 1 mile X 1 mile (generally, with some exceptions)

Road Map

T10-N R14-E
Michigan-Toledo Strip Meridian

Map Group 23

Cities & Towns

Peck

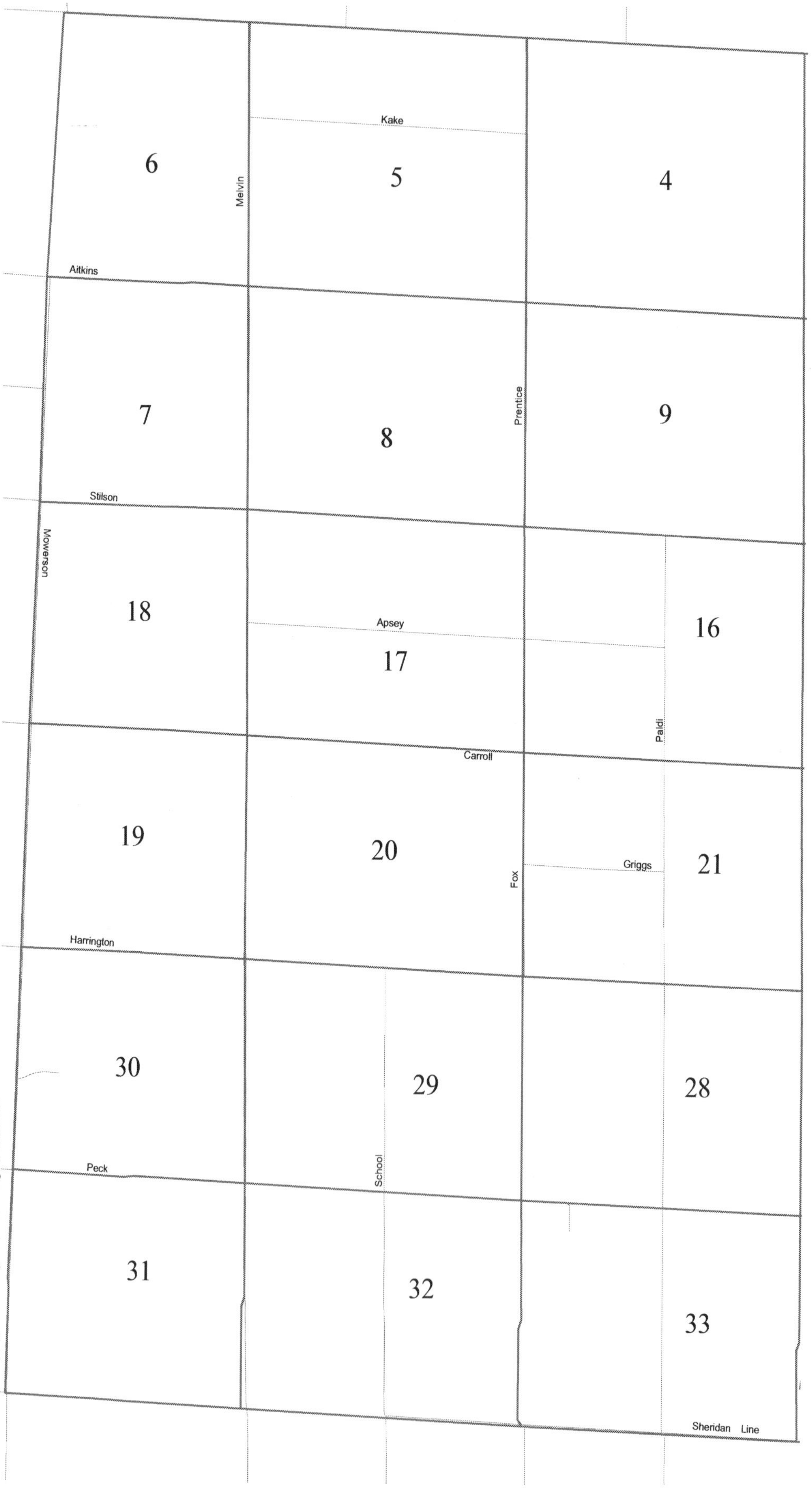

Cemeteries

Mount Hope Cemetery

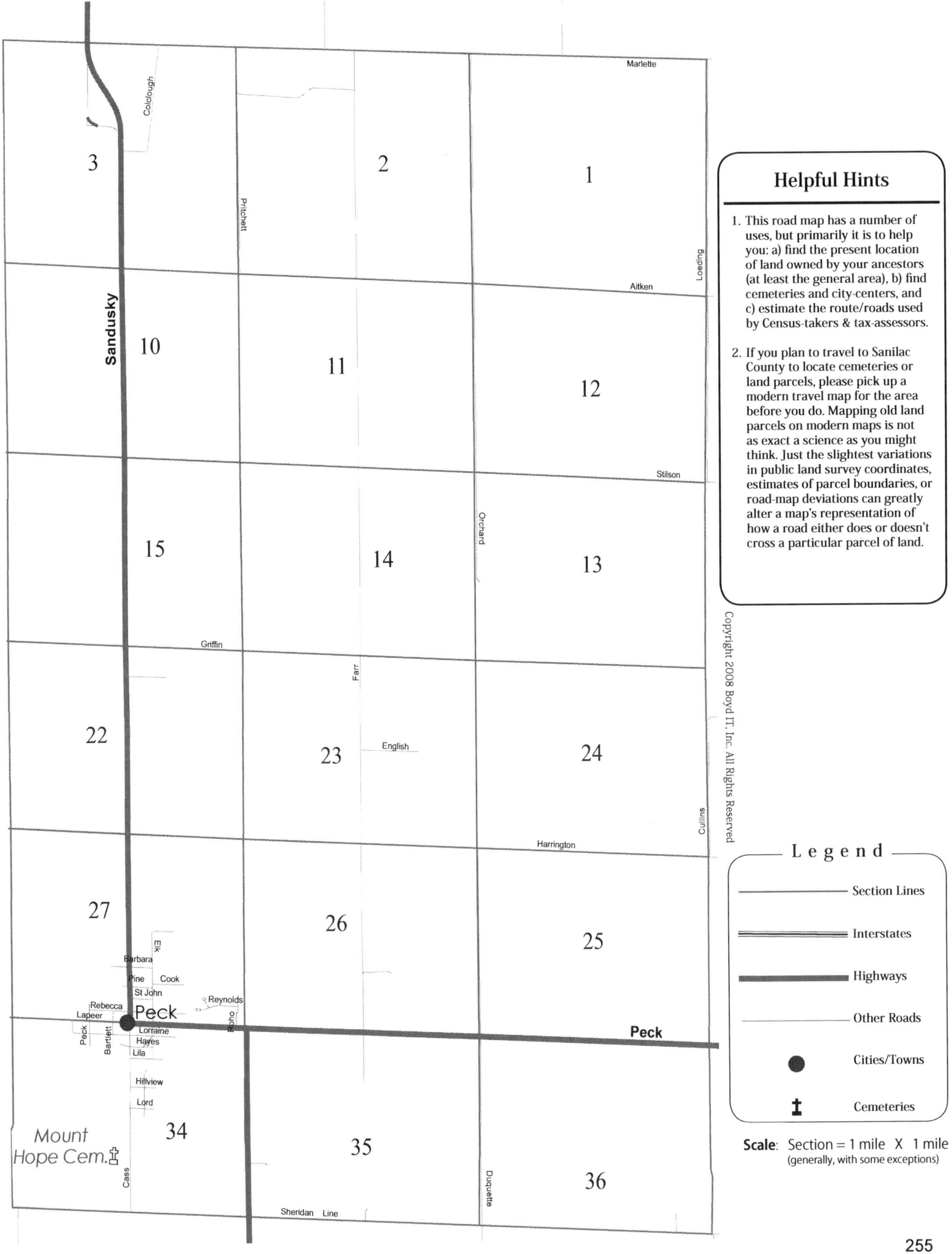

Helpful Hints

1. This road map has a number of uses, but primarily it is to help you: a) find the present location of land owned by your ancestors (at least the general area), b) find cemeteries and city-centers, and c) estimate the route/roads used by Census-takers & tax-assessors.

2. If you plan to travel to Sanilac County to locate cemeteries or land parcels, please pick up a modern travel map for the area before you do. Mapping old land parcels on modern maps is not as exact a science as you might think. Just the slightest variations in public land survey coordinates, estimates of parcel boundaries, or road-map deviations can greatly alter a map's representation of how a road either does or doesn't cross a particular parcel of land.

Historical Map

T10-N R14-E
Michigan-Toledo Strip Meridian

Map Group 23

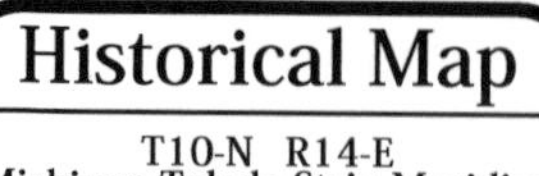

Cities & Towns

Peck

Cemeteries

Mount Hope Cemetery

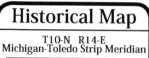

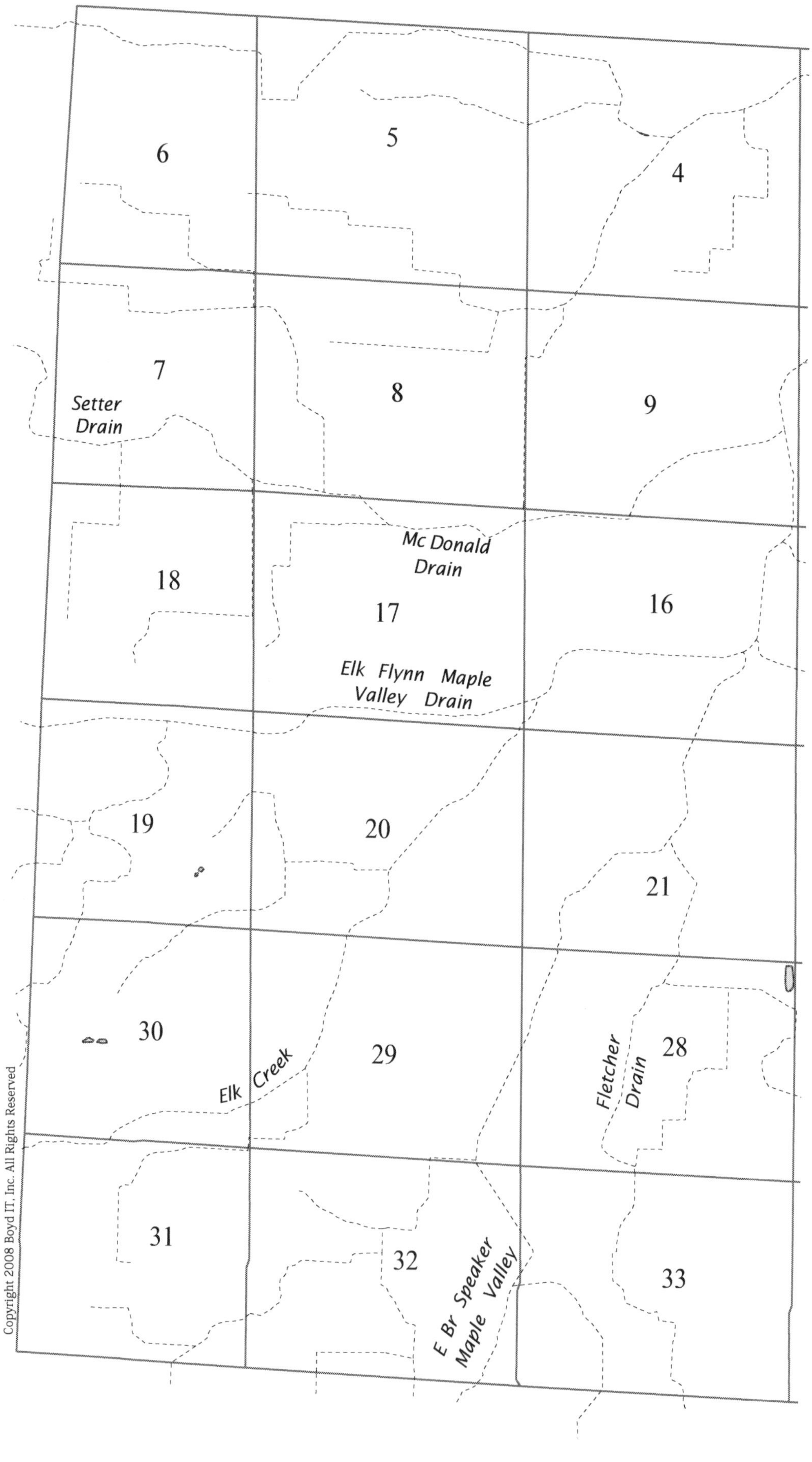

6
5
4
7
Setter Drain
8
9
18
Mc Donald Drain
17
16
Elk Flynn Maple Valley Drain
19
20
21
30
Elk Creek
29
Fletcher Drain
28
31
32
E Br Speaker Maple Valley
33

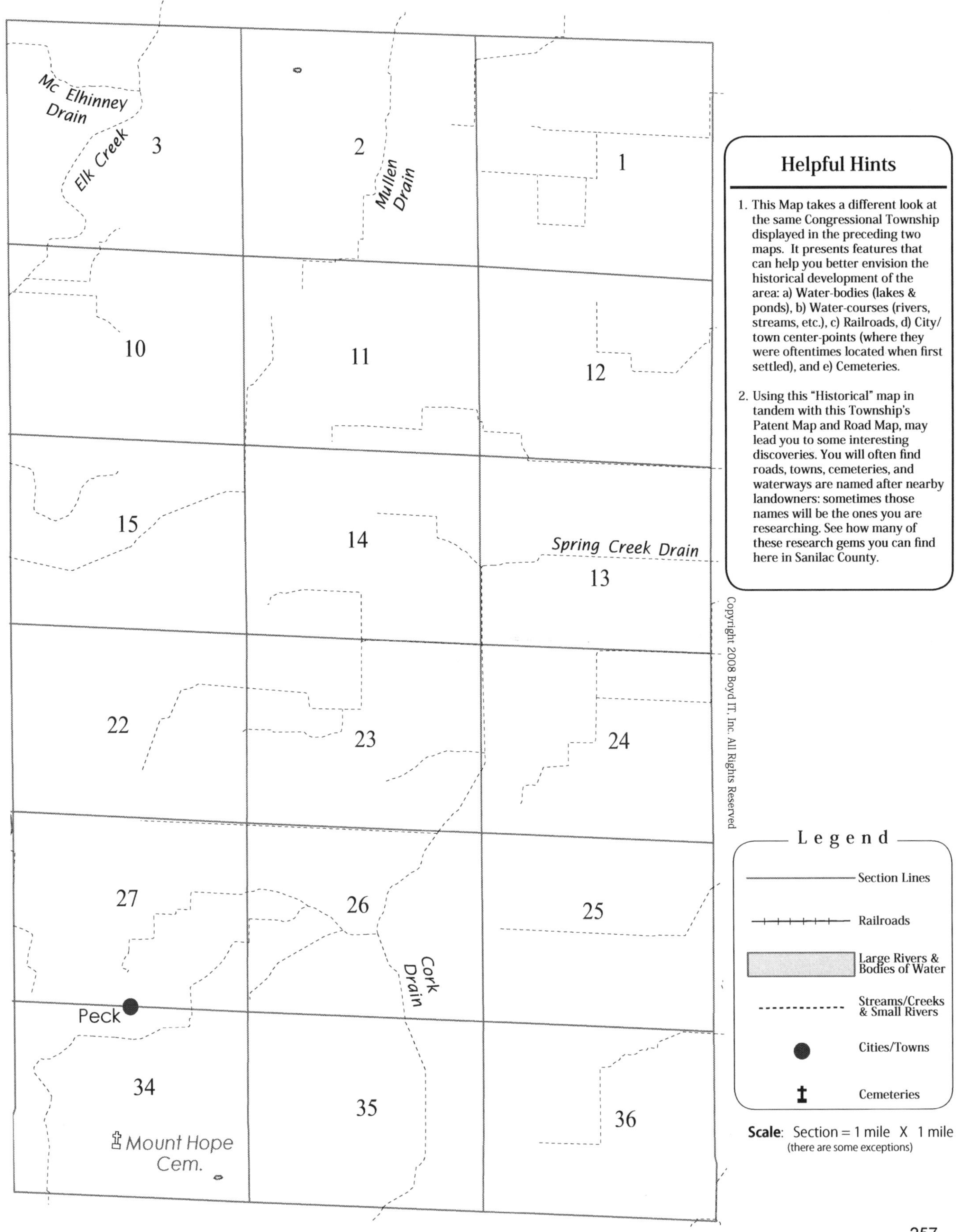

Helpful Hints

1. This Map takes a different look at the same Congressional Township displayed in the preceding two maps. It presents features that can help you better envision the historical development of the area: a) Water-bodies (lakes & ponds), b) Water-courses (rivers, streams, etc.), c) Railroads, d) City/town center-points (where they were oftentimes located when first settled), and e) Cemeteries.
2. Using this "Historical" map in tandem with this Township's Patent Map and Road Map, may lead you to some interesting discoveries. You will often find roads, towns, cemeteries, and waterways are named after nearby landowners: sometimes those names will be the ones you are researching. See how many of these research gems you can find here in Sanilac County.

Legend

- Section Lines
- Railroads
- Large Rivers & Bodies of Water
- Streams/Creeks & Small Rivers
- Cities/Towns
- Cemeteries

Scale: Section = 1 mile X 1 mile
(there are some exceptions)

Map Group 24: Index to Land Patents

Township 10-North Range 15-East (Michigan-Toledo Strip)

After you locate an individual in this Index, take note of the Section and Section Part then proceed to the Land Patent map on the pages immediately following. You should have no difficulty locating the corresponding parcel of land.

The "For More Info" Column will lead you to more information about the underlying Patents. See the *Legend* at right, and the "How to Use this Book" chapter, for more information.

LEGEND

"For More Info . . . " column

- **A** = Authority (Legislative Act, See Appendix "A")
- **B** = Block or Lot (location in Section unknown)
- **C** = Cancelled Patent
- **F** = Fractional Section
- **G** = Group (Multi-Patentee Patent, see Appendix "C")
- **V** = Overlaps another Parcel
- **R** = Re-Issued (Parcel patented more than once)

(A & G items require you to look in the Appendixes referred to above. All other Letter-designations followed by a number require you to locate line-items in this index that possess the ID number found after the letter).

ID	Individual in Patent	Sec.	Sec. Part	Date Issued	Other Counties	For More Info . . .
2523	ABBIHL, David	36	W½SE	1860-05-01		A1
2579	ACHESON, Robert	35	N½SE	1860-11-21		A1
2580	" "	35	NESW	1860-11-21		A1
2581	" "	35	W½NE	1860-11-21		A1
2612	BANCROFT, William S	25	NESW	1854-06-15		A1
2547	BENNETT, John	32	NWNW	1867-02-16		A1
2571	BRENNAN, Michael	32	S½NW	1860-05-01		A1
2602	BROWN, William	26	SENW	1854-06-15		A1
2525	BRUCE, Eli	13	SWSE	1855-06-15		A1
2541	BUEL, Jacob W	1	4	1852-02-10		A1
2542	" "	4	5	1852-02-10		A1
2543	" "	4	6	1852-02-10		A1
2549	CAMERON, John	34	NWSE	1857-02-16		A1
2548	" "	34	E½SE	1859-10-10		A1
2524	CASH, Edward	6	5	1856-01-10		A1
2507	CHASE, Anthony M	4	2	1848-07-01		A1 G22
2508	" "	4	3	1848-07-01		A1 G22
2509	" "	5	3	1848-07-01		A1 G22
2507	CHASE, Nathan B	4	2	1848-07-01		A1 G22
2508	" "	4	3	1848-07-01		A1 G22
2509	" "	5	3	1848-07-01		A1 G22
2591	COMPANY, S Rothschild And	2	NENE	1865-10-02		A1
2592	" "	4	8	1878-02-13		A1
2575	DAVIS, Randall E	12	SWSE	1850-12-02		A1 G31
2574	" "	32	NWSW	1854-06-15		A1 G30
2600	DAVIS, Wellington	1	NW	1852-02-10		A1 F
2601	" "	1	SENW	1852-02-10		A1
2519	DECKER, Daniel	20	SWNE	1852-02-10		A1
2597	DENSHAM, Thomas	26	NWNW	1861-12-03		A1
2598	DENSHAW, Thomas	14	NESW	1866-09-03		A1
2576	DIAMOND, Reuben	12	SESE	1852-02-10		A1
2603	DOUGLASS, William	12	SESW	1860-11-21		A1
2604	" "	13	NENW	1860-11-21		A1
2605	" "	13	S½NW	1860-11-21		A1
2502	ERSKINE, Alexander	15	N½SW	1857-02-20		A1
2503	" "	15	SWNW	1857-02-20		A1
2550	ERSKINE, John	20	NESE	1857-07-01		A1
2551	" "	20	S½SE	1857-07-01		A1
2606	HALE, William	29	E½SE	1857-02-16		A1
2529	HALWERSON, Halwer	31	NENW	1852-02-10		A1
2530	" "	31	NWNE	1852-02-10		A1
2593	HAMILTON, Samuel W	12	SWSW	1852-02-10		A1
2594	" "	13	NWNW	1852-02-10		A1
2595	" "	14	NENE	1852-02-10		A1
2607	HINKSON, William	2	E½SW	1849-02-01		A1
2536	HOOLE, Henry	6	NWSW	1889-06-06		A2 F

ID	Individual in Patent	Sec.	Sec. Part	Date Issued	Other Counties	For More Info . . .
2537	HOOLE, Henry (Cont'd)	6	SWNW	1889-06-06		A2 F
2540	HULVERSON, Hulver	34	N½SW	1857-02-16		A1
2538	HULVORSON, Henry	34	SESW	1857-07-01		A1
2539	" "	34	SWSE	1857-07-01		A1
2553	HUNTER, John	22	SE	1857-02-20		A1
2552	" "	22	E½NE	1859-05-09		A1
2582	HUNTER, Robert	31	N½SE	1859-10-10		A1
2583	" "	31	NESW	1859-10-10		A1 F
2584	" "	31	SWSE	1859-10-10		A1
2585	" "	31	SWSW	1859-10-10		A1 F
2586	" "	31	W½SW	1859-10-10		A1 F
2587	JOLLY, Robert	29	W½SE	1854-06-15		A1
2588	" "	31	E½NE	1854-06-15		A1
2565	JONES, Joseph	35	W½SW	1857-10-30		A1
2510	KING, Archibald	28	W½NW	1861-12-03		A1
2526	KING, George	29	NWSW	1857-02-20		A1
2527	" "	29	SWNW	1857-10-30		A1
2554	KING, John	21	NENE	1860-10-01		A1
2608	KING, William	29	NENE	1857-02-16		A1
2609	KINY, William	29	W½NE	1856-01-10		A1
2501	LEINS, Agustin	13	N½NE	1861-07-01		A1
2511	LEINS, Augustin	13	S½NE	1860-11-21		A1
2567	LEINS, Kaspar	13	N½SE	1861-09-02		A1
2573	LICHTENBERG, Philipp	4	NWNW	1865-10-02		A1
2555	LOOBY, John	11	NWSW	1861-07-01		A1
2512	LUCE, Benjamin F	24	SESW	1852-02-10		A1
2558	MASON, John	4	SESW	1860-11-21		A1
2559	" "	4	SWSE	1860-11-21		A1
2556	" "	4	N½SE	1861-07-01		A1
2557	" "	4	N½SW	1861-12-10		A1
2589	MCCLURE, Robert	29	NWNW	1860-05-01		A1
2560	MCDONALD, John	36	SESE	1864-09-15		A1
2518	MCFARLAND, Consider	5	N½NE	1839-09-02		A1
2514	MERRILL, Charles	21	SESE	1852-02-10		A1
2515	" "	22	SESW	1852-02-10		A1
2516	" "	22	SWSW	1852-02-10		A1
2517	" "	27	E½NW	1852-02-10		A1
2613	MILLS, William S	26	NESE	1855-10-01		A1
2520	ORTON, Daniel	29	SESW	1857-02-16		A1
2528	PACK, Greene	1	SESW	1869-07-01		A1
2610	PALMER, William P	14	SESW	1863-06-05		A1
2611	" "	23	NENW	1863-06-05		A1
2506	PAUL, Andrew	27	NESE	1860-05-01		A1
2561	POTTS, John	31	NWNW	1857-02-20		A1 F
2596	REEVE, Selah	1	1	1852-12-01		A1 F
2599	ROBB, Thomas	25	SENW	1861-12-10		A1
2504	RUST, Aloney	36	SWSW	1852-02-10		A1 G55
2505	" "	4	1	1852-02-10		A1 G55
2504	RUST, David W	36	SWSW	1852-02-10		A1 G55
2505	" "	4	1	1852-02-10		A1 G55
2577	SEAL, Richard	31	SENW	1867-02-16		A1
2578	" "	31	SWNE	1867-02-16		A1
2544	SOMERVILLE, James	30	E½NE	1859-10-10		A1
2532	STEVENS, Harmon L	32	SWSW	1852-02-10		A1
2533	" "	33	NWSW	1852-02-10		A1
2531	" "	31	SESE	1854-06-15		A1
2574	" "	32	NWSW	1854-06-15		A1 G30
2534	" "	34	SWSW	1854-06-15		A1
2575	STEVENS, Matthew	12	SWSE	1850-12-02		A1 G31
2570	STEVENSON, Mathew W	30	NWSE	1850-12-02		A1
2568	" "	12	NWSE	1852-11-01		A1
2569	" "	12	SWNE	1852-11-01		A1
2546	STEWART, James	9	S½NE	1860-11-21		A1
2545	" "	9	N½NE	1861-07-01		A1
2614	STEWART, William	4	SESE	1861-07-01		A1
2566	SULLIVAN, Joseph	11	SENW	1861-12-03		A1
2562	WALLACE, John	33	NESE	1855-10-01		A1
2563	" "	35	SESE	1855-10-01		A1
2564	" "	36	NWSW	1855-10-01		A1
2590	WELLS, Rufus	27	SESW	1853-11-01		A1
2535	WIGHT, Henry A	10	SWSW	1860-10-01		A1
2513	WIXSON, Benjamin	26	SESE	1852-11-01		A1
2522	YAKE, Daniel	22	SWNW	1855-10-01		A1

ID	Individual in Patent	Sec.	Sec. Part	Date Issued	Other Counties	For More Info . . .
2521	YAKE, Daniel (Cont'd)	15	S½SW	1857-07-01		A1
2572	ZOLL, Peter G	14	S½NE	1859-10-10		A1

Patent Map

T10-N R15-E
Michigan-Toledo Strip Meridian

Map Group 24

Township Statistics

Parcels Mapped	:	114
Number of Patents	:	93
Number of Individuals	:	73
Patentees Identified	:	71
Number of Surnames	:	61
Multi-Patentee Parcels	:	7
Oldest Patent Date	:	9/2/1839
Most Recent Patent	:	6/6/1889
Block/Lot Parcels	:	10
Parcels Re - Issued	:	0
Parcels that Overlap	:	0
Cities and Towns	:	0
Cemeteries	:	0

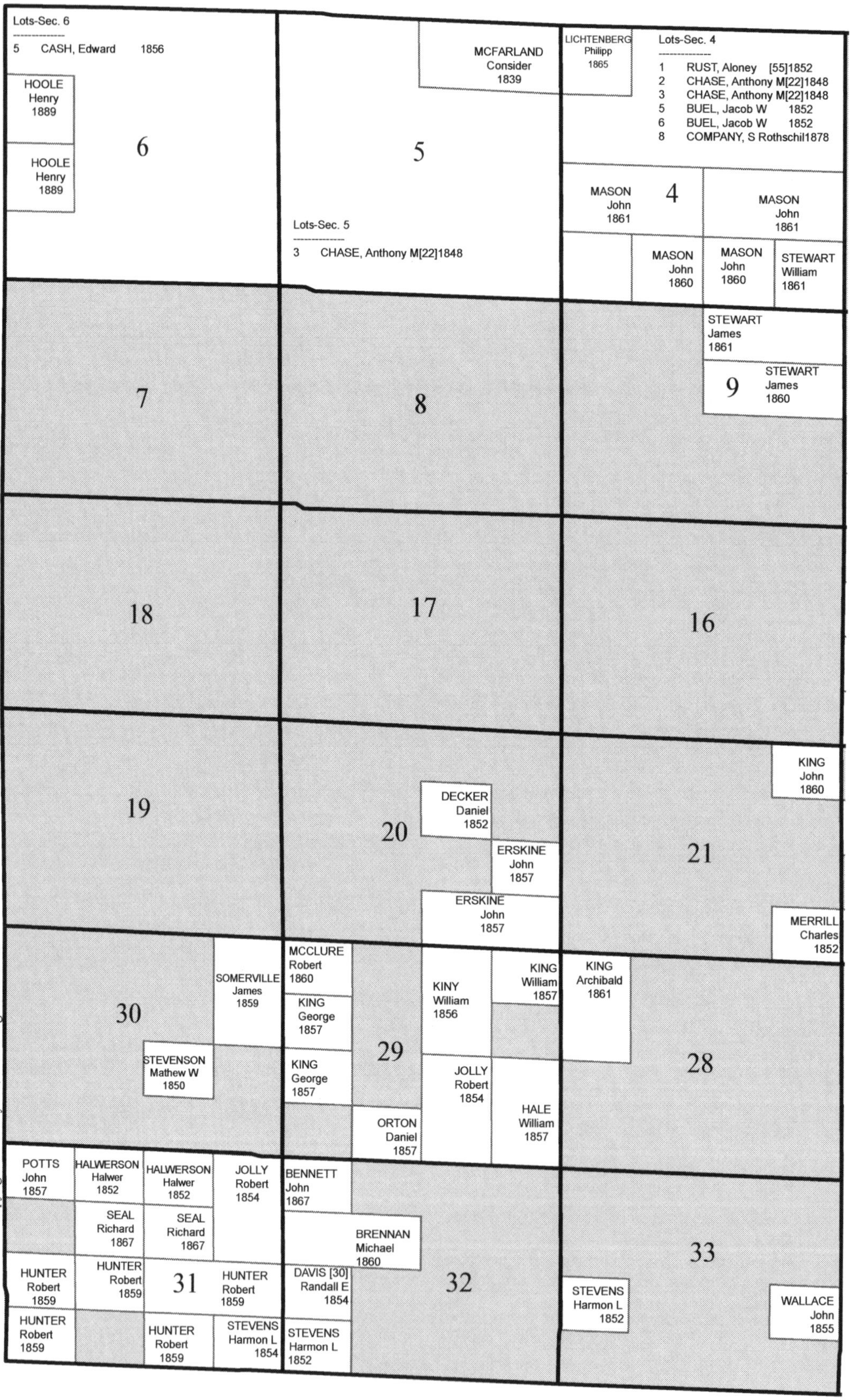

Lots-Sec. 6
5 CASH, Edward 1856

HOOLE Henry 1889
HOOLE Henry 1889
6

MCFARLAND Consider 1839
5
Lots-Sec. 5
3 CHASE, Anthony M[22]1848

LICHTENBERG Philipp 1865
Lots-Sec. 4
1 RUST, Aloney [55]1852
2 CHASE, Anthony M[22]1848
3 CHASE, Anthony M[22]1848
5 BUEL, Jacob W 1852
6 BUEL, Jacob W 1852
8 COMPANY, S Rothschil1878

MASON John 1861
4
MASON John 1861
MASON John 1860
MASON John 1860
STEWART William 1861

7
8
STEWART James 1861
9
STEWART James 1860

18
17
16

19
20
DECKER Daniel 1852
ERSKINE John 1857
ERSKINE John 1857
21
KING John 1860
MERRILL Charles 1852

30
SOMERVILLE James 1859
STEVENSON Mathew W 1850
MCCLURE Robert 1860
KING George 1857
KING George 1857
29
ORTON Daniel 1857
KINY William 1856
KING William 1857
JOLLY Robert 1854
HALE William 1857
KING Archibald 1861
28

POTTS John 1857
HALWERSON Halwer 1852
HALWERSON Halwer 1852
JOLLY Robert 1854
SEAL Richard 1867
SEAL Richard 1867
HUNTER Robert 1859
HUNTER Robert 1859
31
HUNTER Robert 1859
HUNTER Robert 1859
HUNTER Robert 1859
STEVENS Harmon L 1854
BENNETT John 1867
BRENNAN Michael 1860
DAVIS [30] Randall E 1854
STEVENS Harmon L 1852
32
33
STEVENS Harmon L 1852
WALLACE John 1855

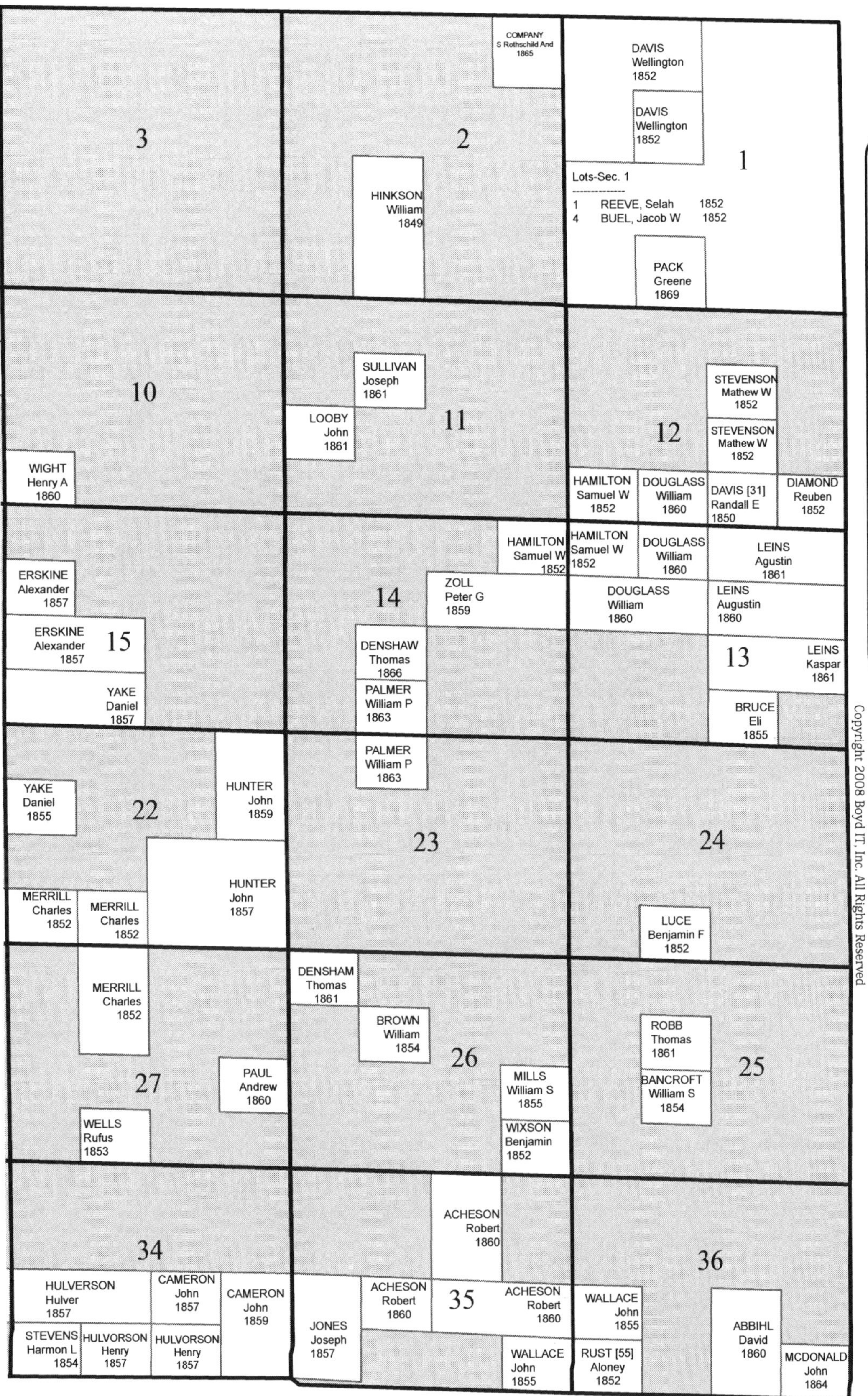

Helpful Hints

1. This Map's INDEX can be found on the preceding pages.
2. Refer to Map "C" to see where this Township lies within Sanilac County, Michigan.
3. Numbers within square brackets [ ] denote a multi-patentee land parcel (multi-owner). Refer to Appendix "C" for a full list of members in this group.
4. Areas that look to be crowded with Patentees usually indicate multiple sales of the same parcel (Re-issues) or Overlapping parcels. See this Township's Index for an explanation of these and other circumstances that might explain "odd" groupings of Patentees on this map.

Legend

———	Patent Boundary
▬▬▬	Section Boundary
(shaded)	No Patents Found (or Outside County)
1., 2., 3., ...	Lot Numbers (when beside a name)
[ ]	Group Number (see Appendix "C")

Scale: Section = 1 mile X 1 mile (generally, with some exceptions)

Road Map

T10-N R15-E
Michigan-Toledo Strip Meridian

Map Group 24

Cities & Towns
None

Cemeteries
None

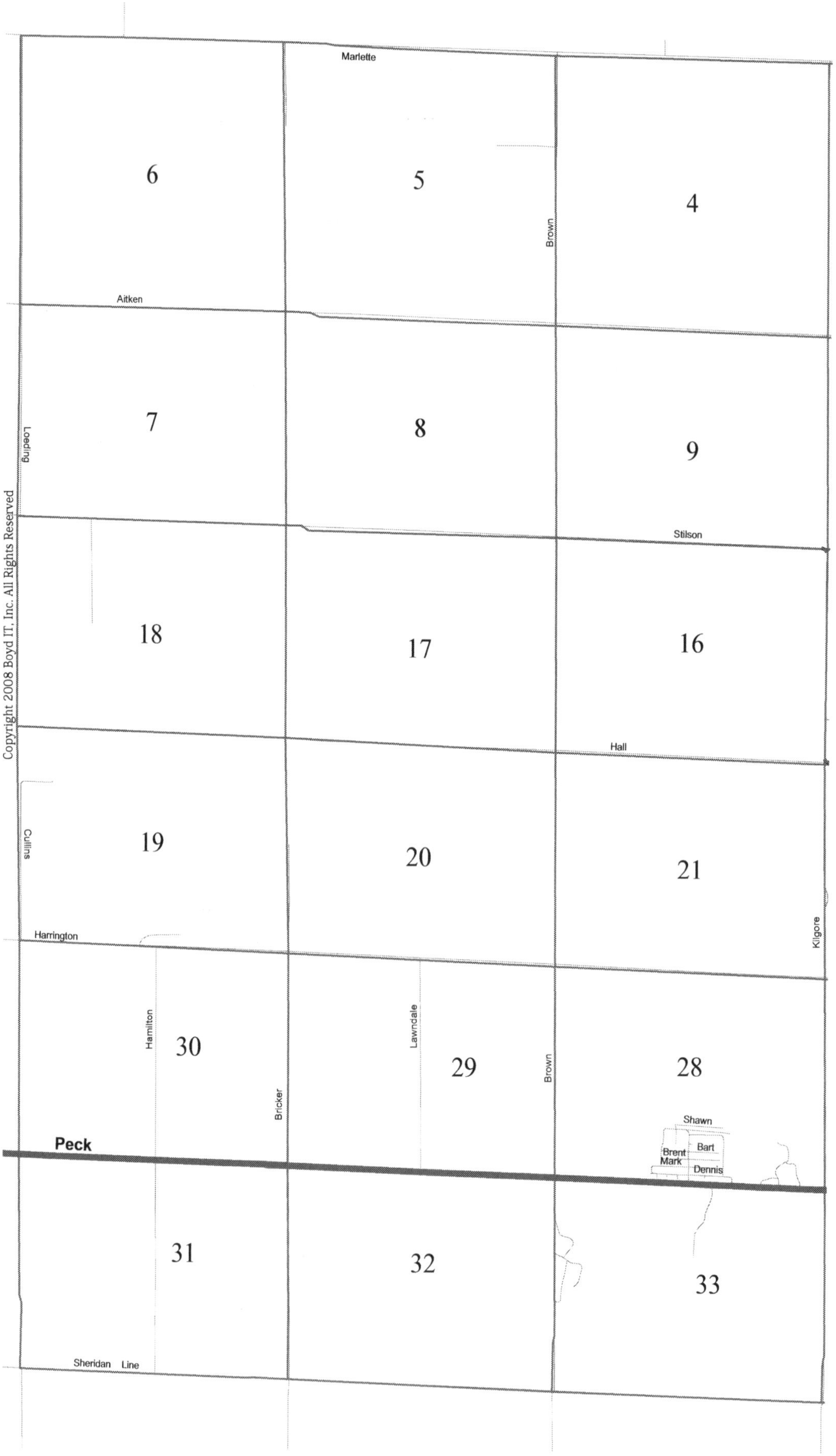

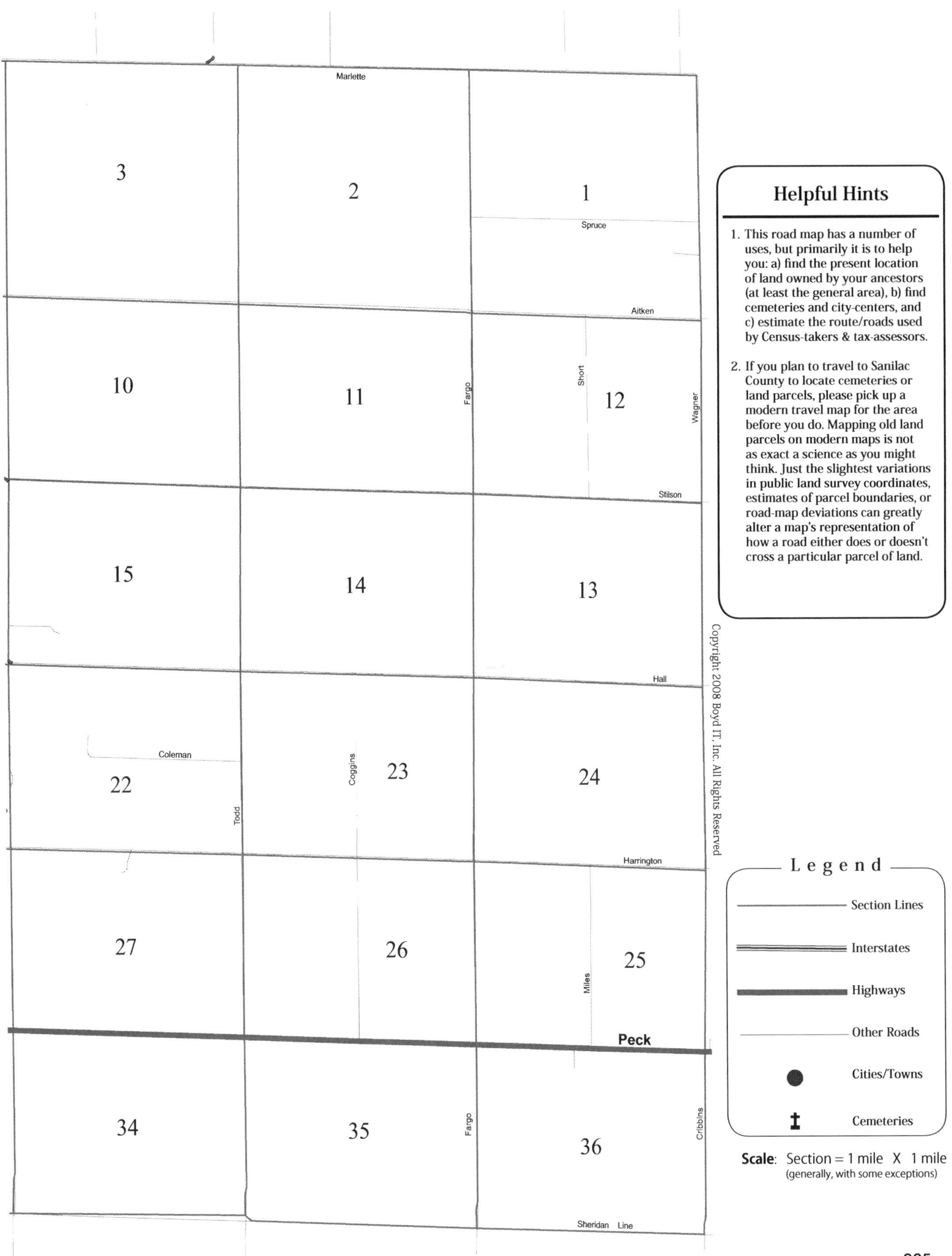

Helpful Hints

1. This road map has a number of uses, but primarily it is to help you: a) find the present location of land owned by your ancestors (at least the general area), b) find cemeteries and city-centers, and c) estimate the route/roads used by Census-takers & tax-assessors.

2. If you plan to travel to Sanilac County to locate cemeteries or land parcels, please pick up a modern travel map for the area before you do. Mapping old land parcels on modern maps is not as exact a science as you might think. Just the slightest variations in public land survey coordinates, estimates of parcel boundaries, or road-map deviations can greatly alter a map's representation of how a road either does or doesn't cross a particular parcel of land.

Legend

- Section Lines
- Interstates
- Highways
- Other Roads
- Cities/Towns
- Cemeteries

Scale: Section = 1 mile X 1 mile
(generally, with some exceptions)

Historical Map

T10-N R15-E
Michigan-Toledo Strip Meridian

Map Group 24

Cities & Towns
None

Cemeteries
None

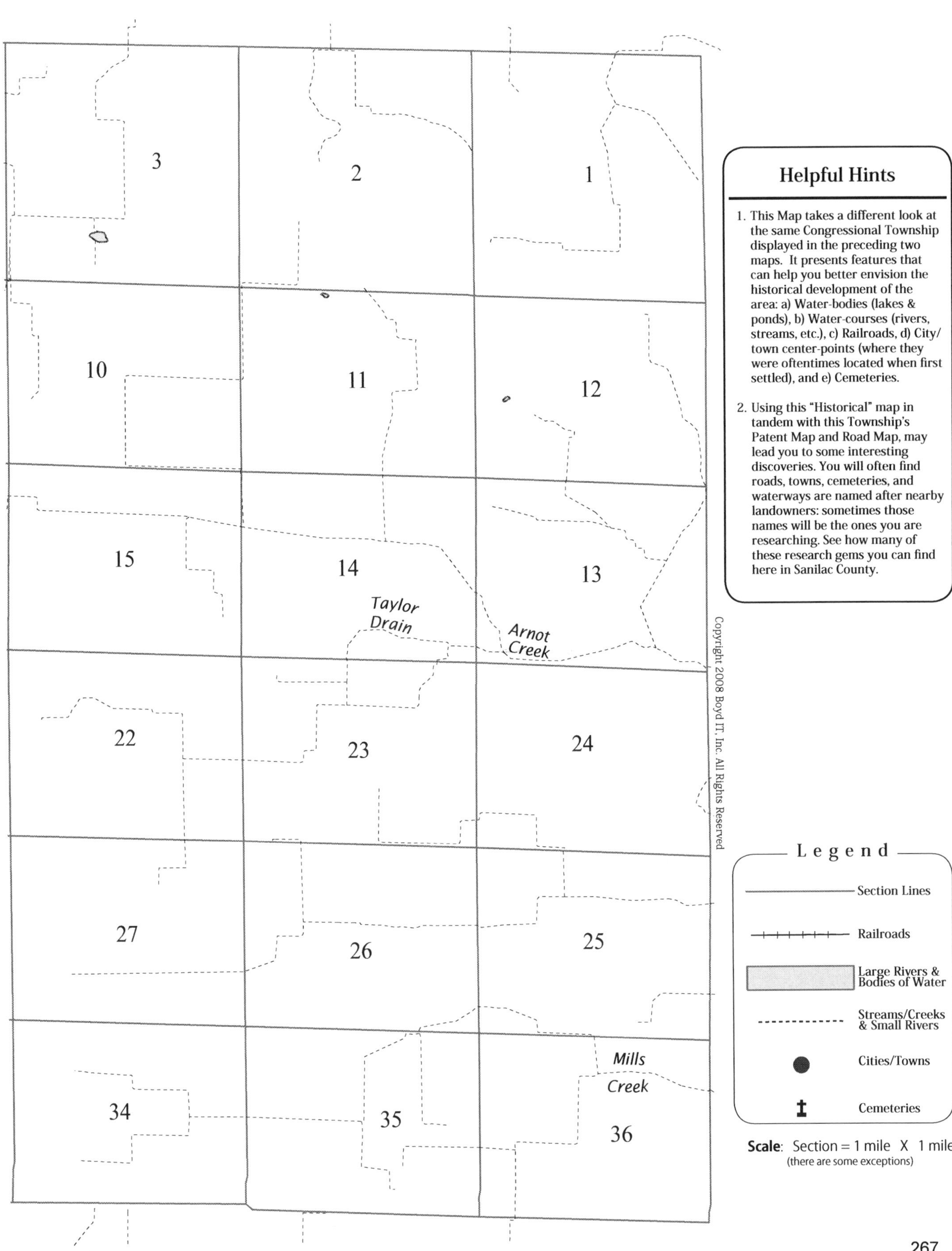
3
2
1
10
11
12
15
14
13
Taylor Drain
Arnot Creek
22
23
24
27
26
25
34
35
36
Mills Creek
Copyright 2008 Boyd IT, Inc. All Rights Reserved
Helpful Hints
1. This Map takes a different look at the same Congressional Township displayed in the preceding two maps. It presents features that can help you better envision the historical development of the area: a) Water-bodies (lakes & ponds), b) Water-courses (rivers, streams, etc.), c) Railroads, d) City/town center-points (where they were oftentimes located when first settled), and e) Cemeteries.
2. Using this "Historical" map in tandem with this Township's Patent Map and Road Map, may lead you to some interesting discoveries. You will often find roads, towns, cemeteries, and waterways are named after nearby landowners: sometimes those names will be the ones you are researching. See how many of these research gems you can find here in Sanilac County.
Legend
Section Lines
Railroads
Large Rivers & Bodies of Water
Streams/Creeks & Small Rivers
Cities/Towns
Cemeteries
Scale: Section = 1 mile X 1 mile
(there are some exceptions)

Map Group 25: Index to Land Patents

Township 10-North Range 16-East (Michigan-Toledo Strip)

After you locate an individual in this Index, take note of the Section and Section Part then proceed to the Land Patent map on the pages immediately following. You should have no difficulty locating the corresponding parcel of land.

The "For More Info" Column will lead you to more information about the underlying Patents. See the *Legend* at right, and the "How to Use this Book" chapter, for more information.

LEGEND

"For More Info . . . " column

A = Authority (Legislative Act, See Appendix "A")
B = Block or Lot (location in Section unknown)
C = Cancelled Patent
F = Fractional Section
G = Group (Multi-Patentee Patent, see Appendix "C")
V = Overlaps another Parcel
R = Re-Issued (Parcel patented more than once)

(A & G items require you to look in the Appendixes referred to above. All other Letter-designations followed by a number require you to locate line-items in this index that possess the ID number found after the letter).

ID	Individual in Patent	Sec.	Sec. Part	Date Issued	Other Counties	For More Info . . .
2689	ARMSTRONG, James B	29	SESW	1844-07-10		A1
2690	" "	29	W½SE	1848-09-01		A1
2743	ASHLEY, Peter W	11	SWSE	1850-03-01		A1
2742	" "	11	NWSW	1852-02-10		A1 R2630
2636	BAKER, Arnst	18	SWNW	1857-07-01		A1
2637	" "	18	W½SW	1857-07-01		A1
2751	BAKER, Russell	28	SESW	1844-07-10		A1
2763	BANCROFT, William L	8	W½SE	1854-06-15		A1
2765	BANCROFT, William S	17	W½NE	1854-06-15		A1
2718	BISBEE, Lawson	28	SESE	1844-07-10		A1
2702	BLAKE, John	27	E½NE	1844-07-10		A1
2634	BOTSFORD, Amzi B	24	SWSW	1837-08-21		A1
2734	BRYANT, Moses	22	W½NW	1837-08-21		A1 G13
2735	" "	22	W½SW	1837-08-21		A1 G13
2685	BUEL, Jacob	30	NWNW	1848-07-01		A1
2686	BUELL, Jacob	18	SESW	1848-07-01		A1
2737	BUGBEE, Oliver	31	SESE	1850-12-02		A1
2738	" "	31	SWNW	1850-12-02		A1
2739	" "	32	NESW	1850-12-02		A1
2740	" "	32	SWSW	1850-12-02		A1
2643	BUNKER, Charles	1	7NE	1844-07-10		A1 G15 F
2644	" "	1	E½SE	1844-07-10		A1 G15
2645	" "	1	NW	1844-07-10		A1 G15 F
2646	" "	1	S½NE	1844-07-10		A1 G15 V2715
2647	" "	2	NE	1844-07-10		A1 G15 F
2648	" "	2	NW	1844-07-10		A1 G15 F
2649	" "	3	NE	1844-07-10		A1 G15 F
2643	BUNKER, Frederick R	1	7NE	1844-07-10		A1 G15 F
2644	" "	1	E½SE	1844-07-10		A1 G15
2645	" "	1	NW	1844-07-10		A1 G15 F
2646	" "	1	S½NE	1844-07-10		A1 G15 V2715
2647	" "	2	NE	1844-07-10		A1 G15 F
2648	" "	2	NW	1844-07-10		A1 G15 F
2649	" "	3	NE	1844-07-10		A1 G15 F
2716	BURLINGGAME, Joseph	11	S½SW	1840-11-10		A1
2699	CARRINGTON, Joel	12	SESE	1837-08-15		A1
2700	" "	36	W½NE	1837-08-18		A1
2684	CASE, Israel P	27	W½NW	1844-07-10		A1
2703	CASTER, John	33	SENE	1848-07-01		A1
2736	CHASE, Nathan B	33	NWNW	1848-09-01		A1
2669	CICOTTE, Francis	25	E½NW	1837-08-16		A1
2670	" "	25	E½SW	1837-08-16		A1
2672	" "	25	W½SE	1837-08-16		A1
2668	" "	13	SE	1837-08-18		A1
2671	" "	25	NE	1837-08-18		A1
2615	COBURN, Abner	14	NW	1837-05-01		A1

ID	Individual in Patent	Sec.	Sec. Part	Date Issued	Other Counties	For More Info . . .
2616	COBURN, Abner (Cont'd)	14	W½NE	1837-05-01		A1
2619	" "	23	E½NE	1837-05-01		A1
2620	" "	23	E½SE	1837-05-01		A1
2621	" "	31	4	1837-05-01		A1 F
2623	" "	35	E½SE	1837-05-01		A1
2624	" "	35	NE	1837-05-01		A1
2625	" "	35	NW	1837-05-01		A1
2626	" "	35	W½SE	1837-05-01		A1
2627	" "	36	E½SW	1837-05-01		A1 V2758
2628	" "	36	SE	1837-05-01		A1
2629	" "	36	W½SW	1837-05-01		A1 V2758
2617	" "	22	E½NE	1837-08-14		A1
2618	" "	22	E½SE	1837-08-14		A1
2622	" "	34	E½SE	1837-08-14		A1
2749	COURTNEY, Richard	33	NENE	1844-07-10		A1
2719	DAVIS, Lodowick L	10	SESE	1844-07-10		A1
2746	DAVIS, Randal E	31	NESW	1850-12-02		A1 G28
2747	" "	31	SENW	1850-12-02		A1 G28
2744	" "	29	NESE	1852-02-10		A1
2745	" "	30	SESW	1852-02-10		A1
2748	" "	19	SESE	1852-11-01		A1 G29
2654	DECKER, Charles	26	NWSE	1850-12-02		A1 V2665
2653	" "	20	SWSE	1852-02-10		A1
2655	" "	29	NENE	1852-02-10		A1
2720	DICKSON, Maria A	33	NWNE	1844-07-10		A1
2733	DOWNING, Miner	27	W½SE	1837-11-02		A1
2691	DROWN, James	3	NWSW	1850-03-01		A1
2635	EDDY, Andrew	31	SESW	1856-09-01		A1 F
2643	EWER, Peter F	1	7NE	1844-07-10		A1 G15 F
2644	" "	1	E½SE	1844-07-10		A1 G15
2645	" "	1	NW	1844-07-10		A1 G15 F
2646	" "	1	S½NE	1844-07-10		A1 G15 V2715
2647	" "	2	NE	1844-07-10		A1 G15 F
2648	" "	2	NW	1844-07-10		A1 G15 F
2649	" "	3	NE	1844-07-10		A1 G15 F
2658	FARNSWORTH, Elon	13	NE	1837-05-01		A1 G38
2659	" "	14	SE	1837-05-01		A1 G38
2660	" "	14	SW	1837-05-01		A1 G38
2661	" "	23	NW	1837-05-01		A1 G38
2662	" "	23	SW	1837-05-01		A1 G38
2663	" "	23	W½NE	1837-05-01		A1 G38
2664	" "	23	W½SE	1837-05-01		A1 G38
2665	" "	26		1837-05-01		A1 G38
2704	FEAD, John	33	S½NW	1850-03-01		A1
2759	FOELSZ, William	30	E½NW	1857-07-01		A1
2693	GEEL, James M	18	W½SE	1837-05-03		A1
2694	" "	32	E½SE	1837-05-03		A1
2734	HADLEY, Timothy G	22	W½NW	1837-08-21		A1 G13
2735	" "	22	W½SW	1837-08-21		A1 G13
2679	HALL, Horace	33	NENW	1848-06-01		A1
2656	HAMMOND, Charles	1	N½N½NE	1839-07-09		A1 G44
2656	HAMMOND, John C	1	N½N½NE	1839-07-09		A1 G44
2687	HARDER, Jacob	11	NENW	1849-02-01		A1
2753	HOPKINS, Seth J	2	NWSW	1848-06-01		A1
2760	HOWARD, William	10	NE	1837-08-02		A1
2761	" "	2	SWSW	1837-08-02		A1
2762	" "	3	SESE	1837-08-02		A1
2731	HUCKINS, Miles	27	E½SW	1840-11-10		A1
2732	" "	27	W½SW	1840-11-10		A1
2730	" "	27	E½NW	1844-07-10		A1
2755	HUCKINS, Thomas	34	E½NW	1840-11-10		A1
2756	" "	34	W½NW	1840-11-10		A1
2708	HUGHES, John M	25	E½SE	1837-08-16		A1
2641	LUCE, Benjamin	15	E½SE	1848-07-01		A1
2638	LUCE, Benjamin F	11	NESW	1848-07-01		A1
2639	" "	11	SENW	1848-07-01		A1
2640	" "	18	NESW	1852-12-01		A1 F
2677	LYON, Hiram	3	NESE	1837-08-21		A1
2678	" "	3	W½SE	1837-08-21		A1
2709	MATTESON, John	12	NESE	1838-09-04		A1
2692	MATTISON, James L	34	NENE	1837-11-02		A1
2657	MCMILLEN, Charles	10	NWSE	1850-12-02		A1
2750	MIDDAUGH, Robert	30	SWNW	1857-02-20		A1 F

ID	Individual in Patent	Sec.	Sec. Part	Date Issued	Other Counties	For More Info . . .
2741	MILLS, Orromel E	30	NWSW	1857-07-01		A1
2766	MILLS, William S	18	NWNW	1855-10-01		A1
2721	MIZNER, Mary Gouverneur	10	NESE	1848-08-21		A1 G53
2682	MOFFAT, Hugh	31	W½SW	1854-05-29		A1 F
2680	" "	19	SWNW	1854-06-15		A1 F
2681	" "	19	W½SW	1854-06-15		A1 F
2752	MUNRO, Samuel W	34	SWSE	1840-11-10		A1
2754	MUNRO, Solomon	27	E½SE	1848-06-01		A1
2717	ORVIS, Josiah H	3	E½SW	1837-08-21		A1
2757	PARKER, Thomas	11	SESE	1849-02-01		A1
2656	PHELPS, Elihu	1	N½N½NE	1839-07-09		A1 G44
2710	PHILIPS, John P	32	NWNW	1848-06-01		A1
2667	PIERCE, Ephraim	29	NESW	1844-07-10		A1
2683	PORTER, Ira	36	E½NE	1837-08-16		A1
2630	PRATT, Alvah S	11	NWSW	1848-07-01		A1 R2742
2695	PROVOST, James	10	SWSE	1848-09-01		A1
2676	RUDEL, Henry	7	W½NW	1857-07-01		A1
2767	SAMPLE, William	33	E½SW	1849-02-01		A1
2768	" "	33	W½SW	1850-03-01		A1
2746	SANBORN, Cummings	31	NESW	1850-12-02		A1 G28
2747	" "	31	SENW	1850-12-02		A1 G28
2688	SHARP, Jacob	15	NENE	1844-07-10		A1
2696	SHELDEN, James	34	W½NE	1837-11-02		A1
2711	SHELL, John	34	SENE	1844-07-10		A1
2758	SHEPHARD, William F	36	SW	1837-08-18		A1 V2627, 2629
2658	SIBLEY, Sylvester	13	NE	1837-05-01		A1 G38
2659	" "	14	SE	1837-05-01		A1 G38
2660	" "	14	SW	1837-05-01		A1 G38
2661	" "	23	NW	1837-05-01		A1 G38
2662	" "	23	SW	1837-05-01		A1 G38
2663	" "	23	W½NE	1837-05-01		A1 G38
2664	" "	23	W½SE	1837-05-01		A1 G38
2665	" "	26		1837-05-01		A1 G38
2721	SPENCER, William	10	NESE	1848-08-21		A1 G53
2764	STAFFORD, William R	19	NWNW	1852-02-10		A1 F
2673	STEEL, Gilbert	3	5NW	1850-03-01		A1 F
2674	" "	3	SWNW	1850-03-01		A1 F
2675	STEVENS, Harmon L	30	E½SE	1852-02-10		A1
2722	STEVENSON, Mathew	18	NENW	1852-02-10		A1
2723	STEVENSON, Mathew W	20	NENW	1849-02-01		A1
2748	" "	19	SESE	1852-11-01		A1 G29
2724	" "	7	NWNE	1852-11-01		A1
2725	" "	7	SWSE	1852-11-01		A1
2727	STEVENSON, Matthew	19	NENW	1850-12-02		A1
2726	" "	18	SENW	1852-02-10		A1
2746	STEVENSON, Matthew W	31	NESW	1850-12-02		A1 G28
2747	" "	31	SENW	1850-12-02		A1 G28
2728	" "	31	NENW	1852-02-10		A1
2729	" "	7	E½NW	1852-02-10		A1 F
2666	THROOP, Enos T	32	NWNE	1854-06-15		A1
2658	TROWBRIDGE, Charles C	13	NE	1837-05-01		A1 G38
2659	" "	14	SE	1837-05-01		A1 G38
2660	" "	14	SW	1837-05-01		A1 G38
2661	" "	23	NW	1837-05-01		A1 G38
2662	" "	23	SW	1837-05-01		A1 G38
2663	" "	23	W½NE	1837-05-01		A1 G38
2664	" "	23	W½SE	1837-05-01		A1 G38
2650	" "	25	W½NW	1837-05-01		A1
2651	" "	25	W½SW	1837-05-01		A1
2665	" "	26		1837-05-01		A1 G38
2652	" "	35	SW	1837-05-01		A1
2642	WIGHT, Buckminster	17	NESW	1849-02-01		A1
2712	WILSON, John	8	S½SW	1854-06-15		A1
2697	WISSON, Jesse	17	SESW	1853-11-01		A1
2632	WIXSON, Amos	34	NWSE	1844-07-10		A1
2633	" "	34	SW	1844-07-10		A1
2631	" "	33	SWNE	1848-09-01		A1
2698	WIXSON, Jesse	20	NWNE	1852-11-01		A1
2713	WIXSON, John	17	E½NE	1848-09-01		A1
2714	" "	17	E½SE	1848-09-01		A1
2707	WOODS, John L	3	SWSW	1852-02-10		A1
2705	" "	17	SENW	1854-06-15		A1
2706	" "	17	W½SE	1854-06-15		A1

ID	Individual in Patent	Sec.	Sec. Part	Date Issued	Other Counties	For More Info . . .
2701	WRIGHT, John A	15	SENE	1844-07-10		A1
2715	WYMAN, John	1	SENE	1837-08-10		A1 V2646
2656	" "	1	N½N½NE	1839-07-09		A1 G44

Patent Map

T10-N R16-E
Michigan-Toledo Strip Meridian

Map Group 25

Township Statistics

Parcels Mapped	:	154
Number of Patents	:	127
Number of Individuals	:	93
Patentees Identified	:	87
Number of Surnames	:	79
Multi-Patentee Parcels	:	22
Oldest Patent Date	:	5/1/1837
Most Recent Patent	:	7/1/1857
Block/Lot Parcels	:	3
Parcels Re - Issued	:	1
Parcels that Overlap	:	6
Cities and Towns	:	1
Cemeteries	:	4

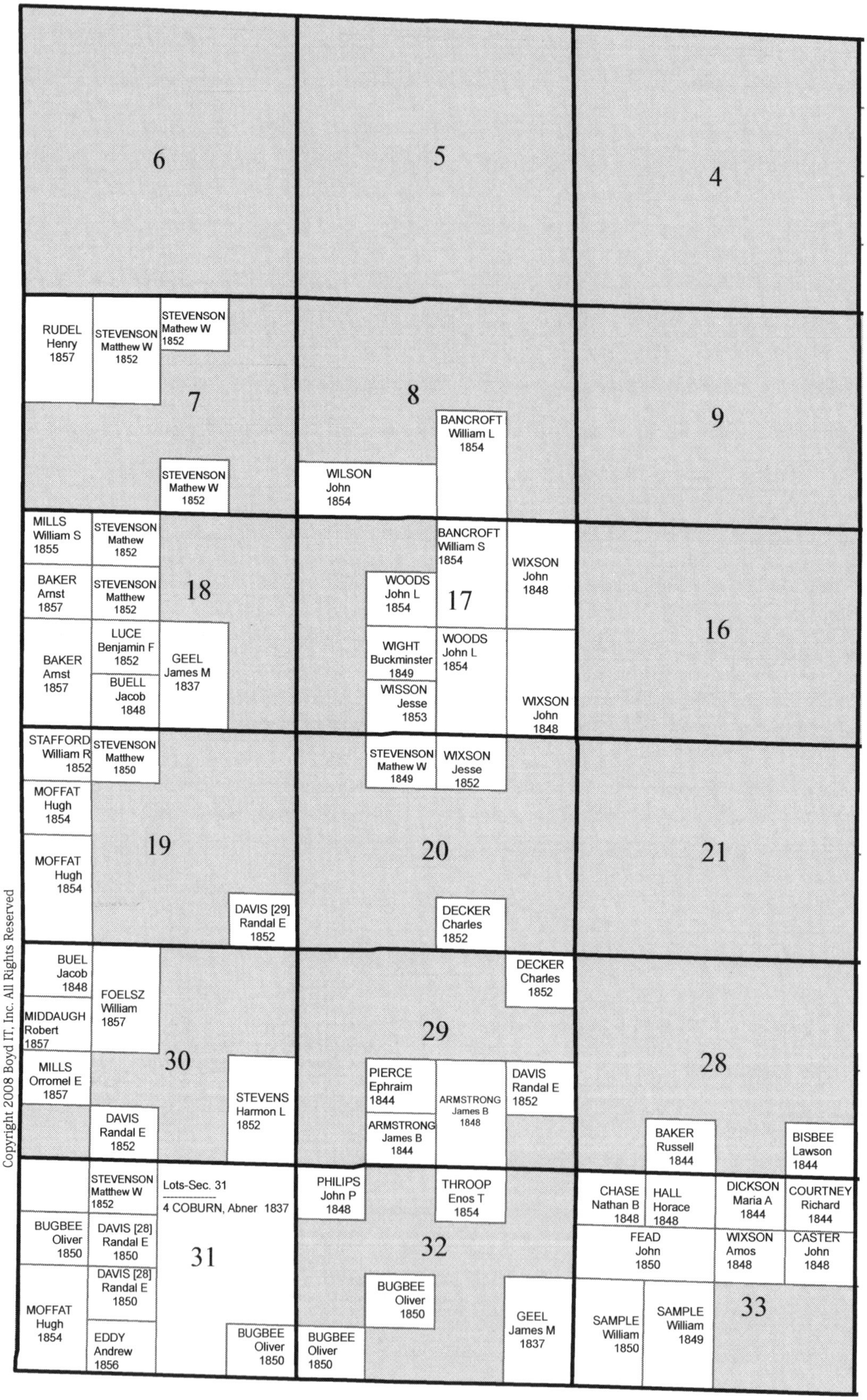

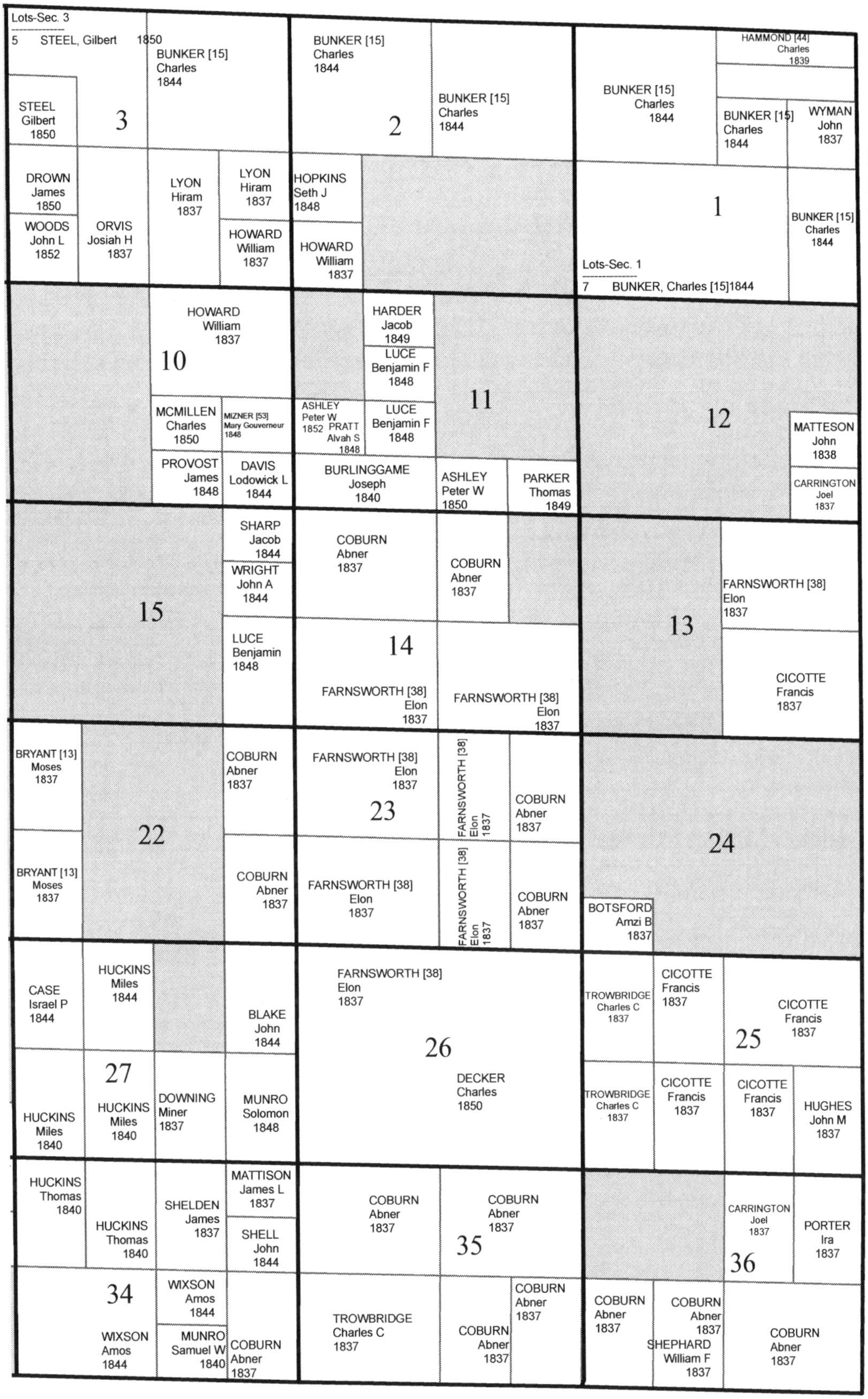

Helpful Hints

1. This Map's INDEX can be found on the preceding pages.
2. Refer to Map "C" to see where this Township lies within Sanilac County, Michigan.
3. Numbers within square brackets [ ] denote a multi-patentee land parcel (multi-owner). Refer to Appendix "C" for a full list of members in this group.
4. Areas that look to be crowded with Patentees usually indicate multiple sales of the same parcel (Re-issues) or Overlapping parcels. See this Township's Index for an explanation of these and other circumstances that might explain "odd" groupings of Patentees on this map.

Legend

- Patent Boundary
- Section Boundary
- No Patents Found (or Outside County)
- 1., 2., 3., ... Lot Numbers (when beside a name)
- [ ] Group Number (see Appendix "C")

Scale: Section = 1 mile X 1 mile (generally, with some exceptions)

Road Map

T10-N R16-E
Michigan-Toledo Strip Meridian

Map Group 25

Cities & Towns

Croswell

Cemeteries

Huckins Cemetery
Long Cemetery
Mount Hope Cemetery
Saint Denis Cemetery

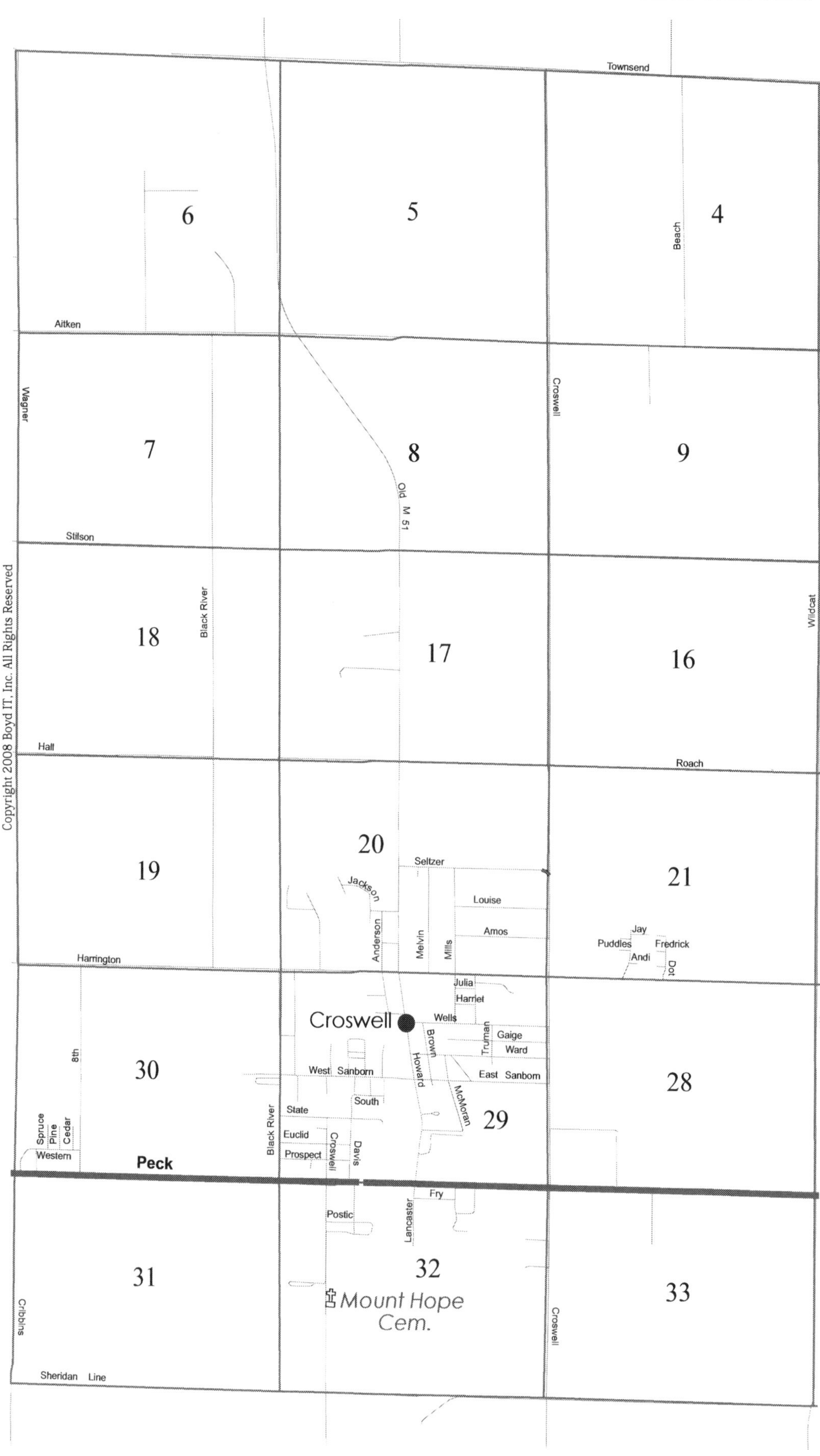

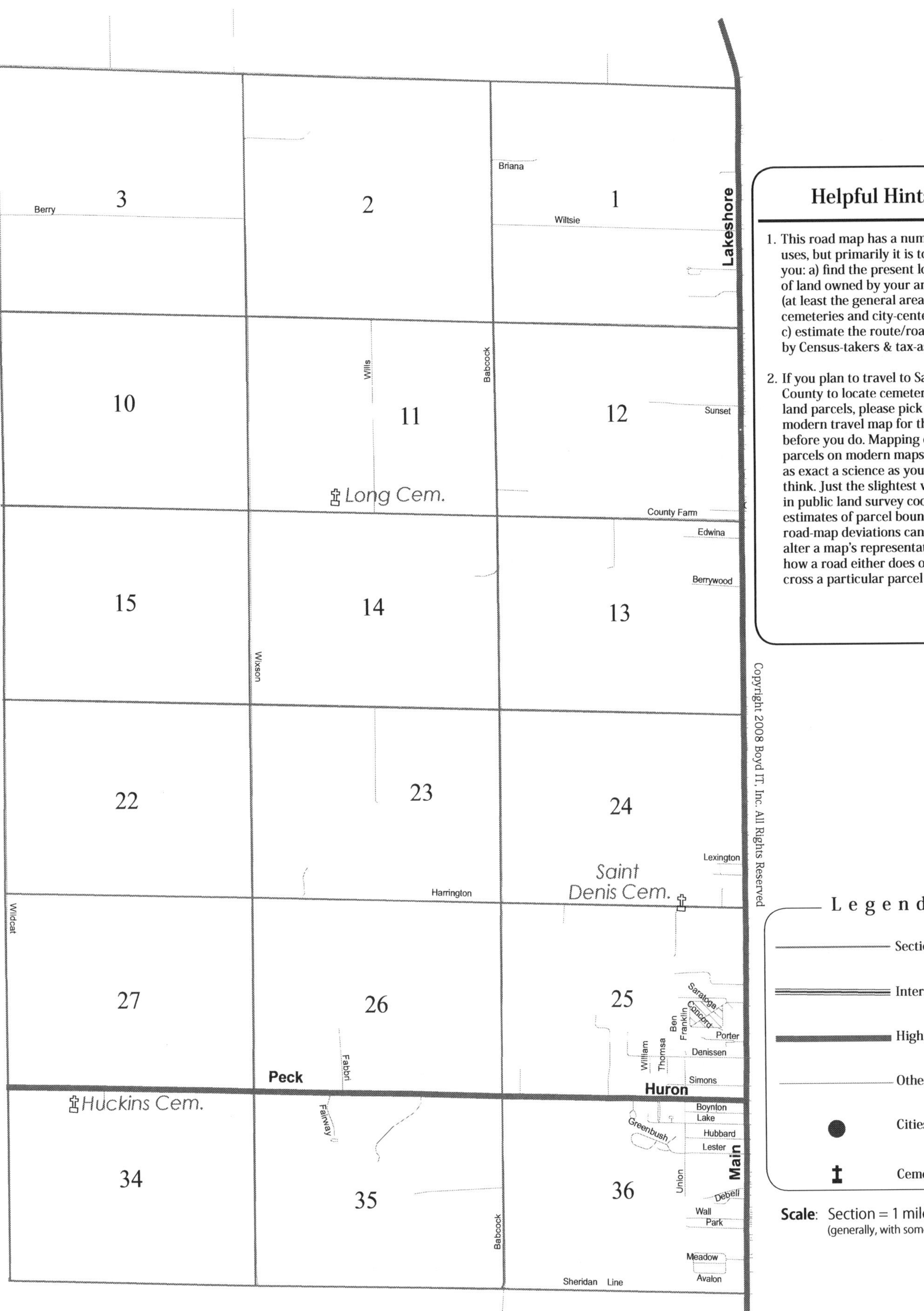

Helpful Hints

1. This road map has a number of uses, but primarily it is to help you: a) find the present location of land owned by your ancestors (at least the general area), b) find cemeteries and city-centers, and c) estimate the route/roads used by Census-takers & tax-assessors.

2. If you plan to travel to Sanilac County to locate cemeteries or land parcels, please pick up a modern travel map for the area before you do. Mapping old land parcels on modern maps is not as exact a science as you might think. Just the slightest variations in public land survey coordinates, estimates of parcel boundaries, or road-map deviations can greatly alter a map's representation of how a road either does or doesn't cross a particular parcel of land.

Legend

- Section Lines
- Interstates
- Highways
- Other Roads
- Cities/Towns
- Cemeteries

Scale: Section = 1 mile X 1 mile (generally, with some exceptions)

Historical Map

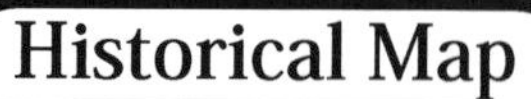

T10-N R16-E
Michigan-Toledo Strip Meridian

Map Group 25

Cities & Towns

Croswell

Cemeteries

Huckins Cemetery
Long Cemetery
Mount Hope Cemetery
Saint Denis Cemetery

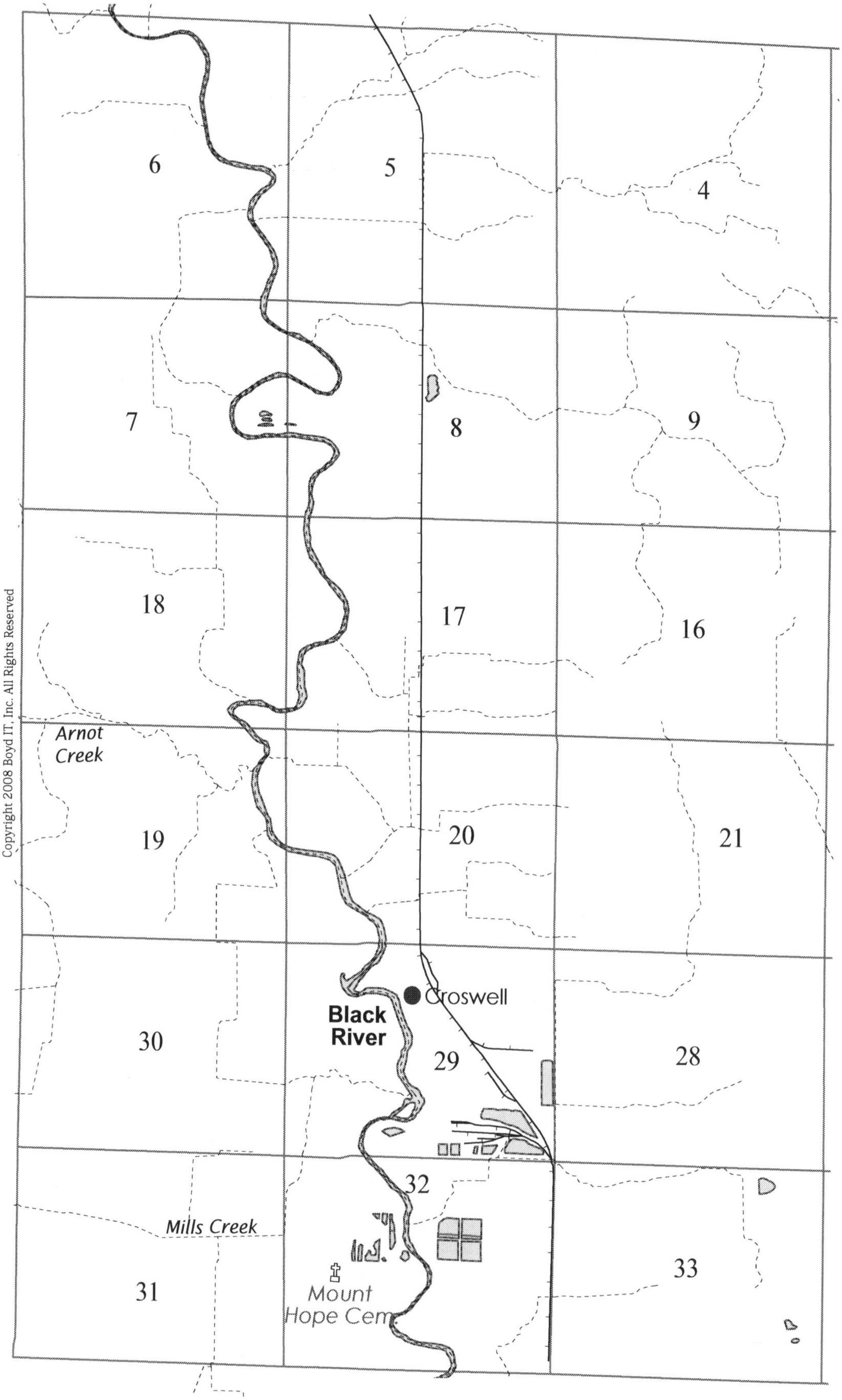

6
5
4
7
8
9
18
17
16
Arnot Creek
19
20
21
30
Croswell
Black River
29
28
32
Mills Creek
31
Mount Hope Cem
33

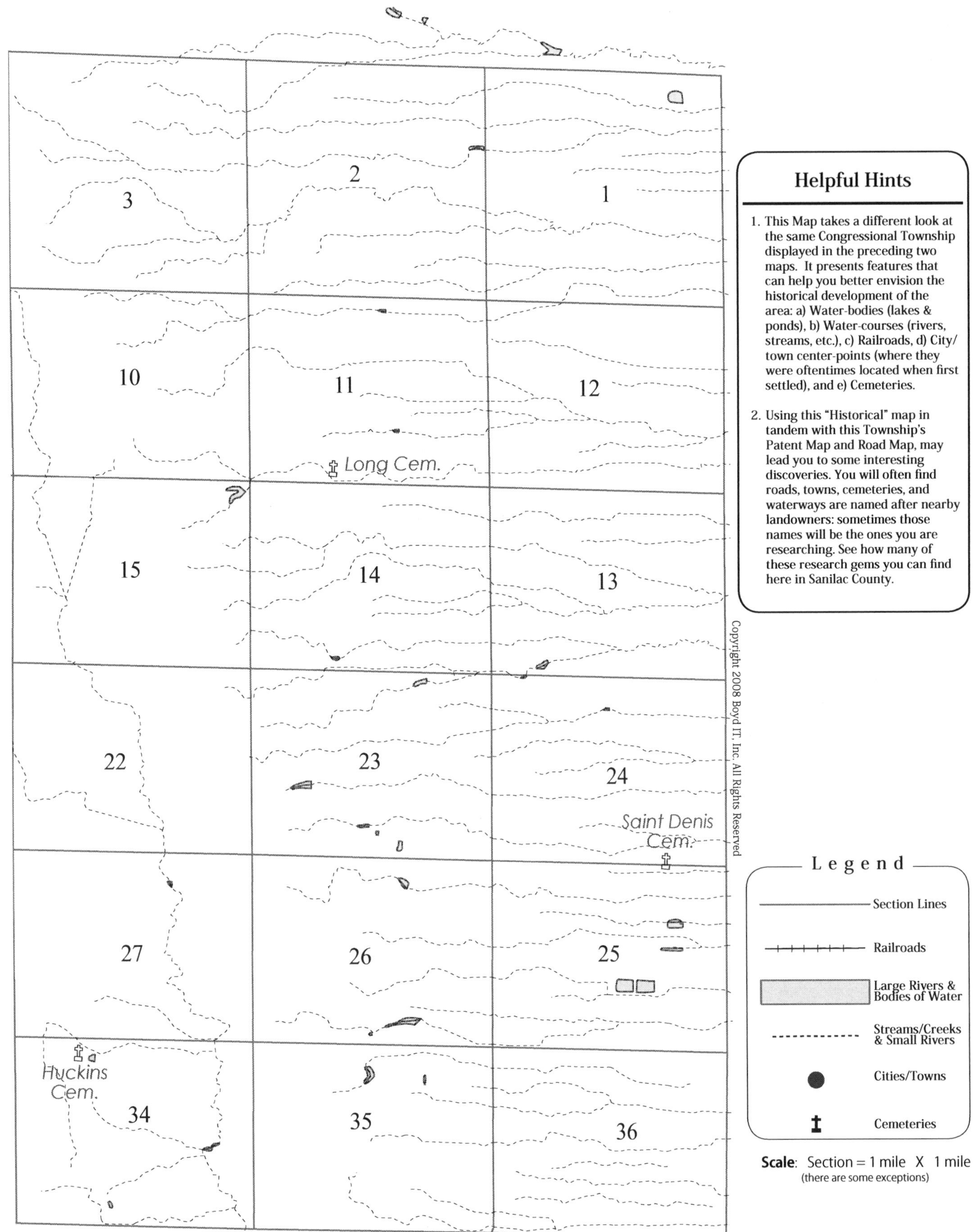

Helpful Hints

1. This Map takes a different look at the same Congressional Township displayed in the preceding two maps. It presents features that can help you better envision the historical development of the area: a) Water-bodies (lakes & ponds), b) Water-courses (rivers, streams, etc.), c) Railroads, d) City/town center-points (where they were oftentimes located when first settled), and e) Cemeteries.

2. Using this "Historical" map in tandem with this Township's Patent Map and Road Map, may lead you to some interesting discoveries. You will often find roads, towns, cemeteries, and waterways are named after nearby landowners: sometimes those names will be the ones you are researching. See how many of these research gems you can find here in Sanilac County.

Map Group 26: Index to Land Patents

Township 10-North Range 17-East (Michigan-Toledo Strip)

After you locate an individual in this Index, take note of the Section and Section Part then proceed to the Land Patent map on the pages immediately following. You should have no difficulty locating the corresponding parcel of land.

The "For More Info" Column will lead you to more information about the underlying Patents. See the *Legend* at right, and the "How to Use this Book" chapter, for more information.

LEGEND

"For More Info . . . " column

A = Authority (Legislative Act, See Appendix "A")
B = Block or Lot (location in Section unknown)
C = Cancelled Patent
F = Fractional Section
G = Group (Multi-Patentee Patent, see Appendix "C")
V = Overlaps another Parcel
R = Re-Issued (Parcel patented more than once)

(A & G items require you to look in the Appendixes referred to above. All other Letter-designations followed by a number require you to locate line-items in this index that possess the ID number found after the letter).

ID	Individual in Patent	Sec.	Sec. Part	Date Issued	Other Counties	For More Info . . .
2769	AYRAULT, Allen	19		1837-08-21		A1 F
2770	" "	7		1837-08-21		A1 F
2772	CICOTT, Francis	30	N	1837-08-18		A1 F
2771	HAMMOND, Charles	6		1839-07-09		A1 G44 F
2771	HAMMOND, John C	6		1839-07-09		A1 G44 F
2777	MIZNER, Lancing B	18		1837-08-18		A1 F
2771	PHELPS, Elihu	6		1839-07-09		A1 G44 F
2773	PORTER, Ira	31	2	1837-04-10		A1 F
2774	" "	31	3	1837-04-10		A1 F
2775	" "	31	N	1837-05-05		A1 F
2776	SMITH, John	30	S½	1837-08-16		A1 F
2771	WYMAN, John	6		1839-07-09		A1 G44 F

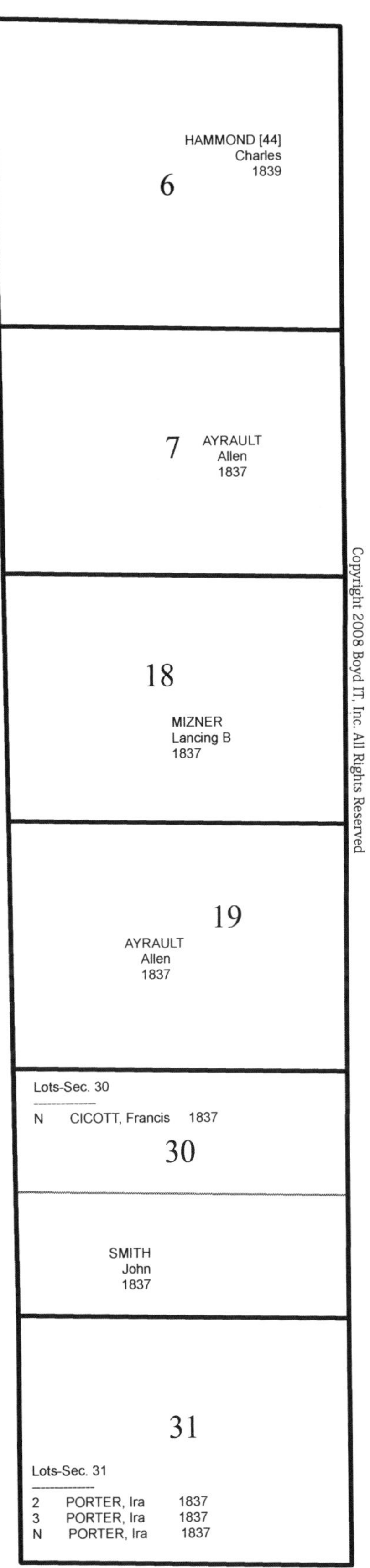

Patent Map

T10-N R17-E
Michigan-Toledo Strip Meridian

Map Group 26

Township Statistics

Parcels Mapped	:	9
Number of Patents	:	8
Number of Individuals	:	9
Patentees Identified	:	6
Number of Surnames	:	8
Multi-Patentee Parcels	:	1
Oldest Patent Date	:	4/10/1837
Most Recent Patent	:	7/9/1839
Block/Lot Parcels	:	4
Parcels Re - Issued	:	0
Parcels that Overlap	:	0
Cities and Towns	:	1
Cemeteries	:	0

Note: the area contained in this map amounts to far less than a full Township. Therefore, its contents are completely on this single page (instead of a "normal" 2-page spread).

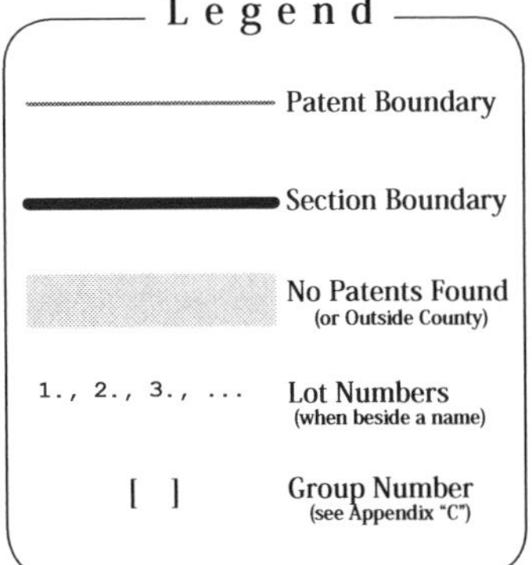

Scale: Section = 1 mile X 1 mile
(generally, with some exceptions)

Road Map

T10-N R17-E
Michigan-Toledo Strip Meridian

Map Group 26

Note: the area contained in this map amounts to far less than a full Township. Therefore, its contents are completely on this single page (instead of a "normal" 2-page spread).

Cities & Towns

Lexington

Cemeteries

None

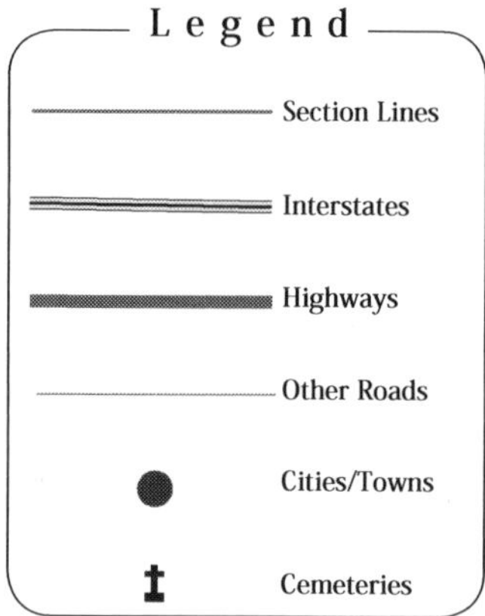

Scale: Section = 1 mile X 1 mile
(generally, with some exceptions)

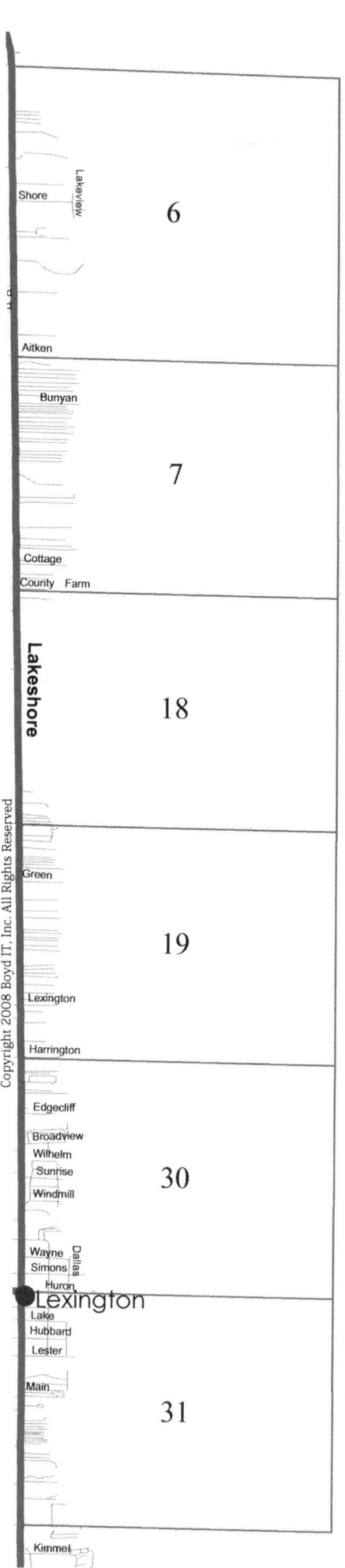

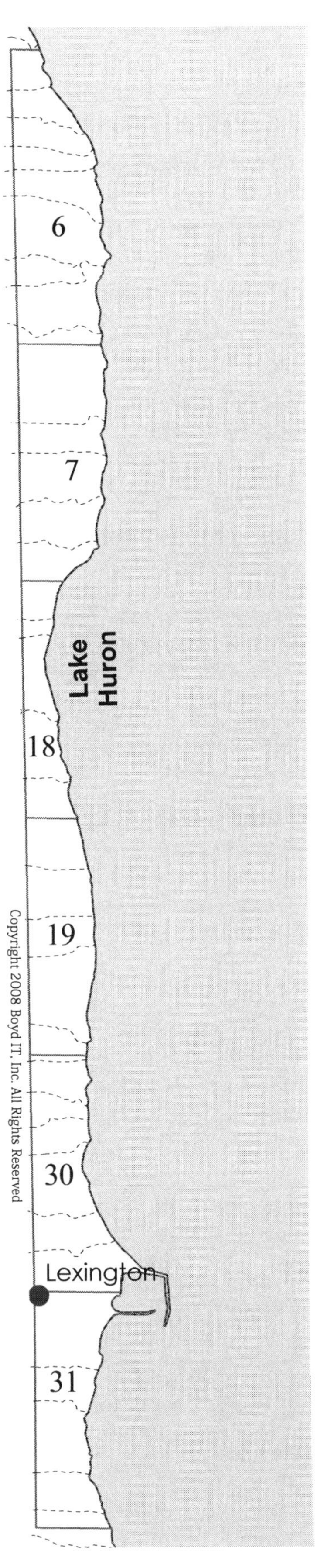

Historical Map

T10-N R17-E
Michigan-Toledo Strip Meridian

Map Group 26

Note: the area contained in this map amounts to far less than a full Township. Therefore, its contents are completely on this single page (instead of a "normal" 2-page spread).

Cities & Towns

Lexington

Cemeteries

None

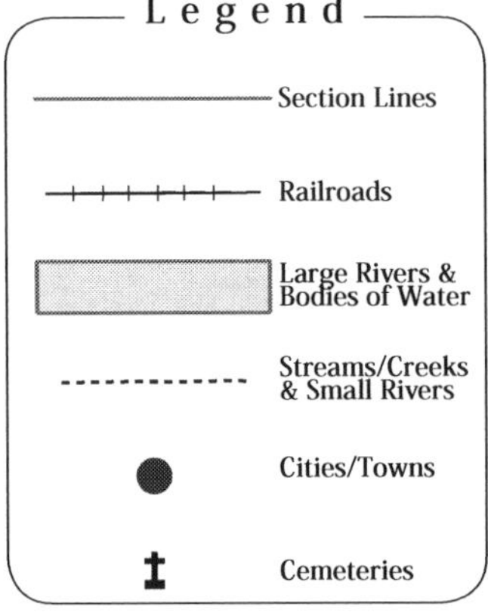

Scale: Section = 1 mile X 1 mile
(there are some exceptions)

Map Group 27: Index to Land Patents

Township 9-North Range 13-East (Michigan-Toledo Strip)

After you locate an individual in this Index, take note of the Section and Section Part then proceed to the Land Patent map on the pages immediately following. You should have no difficulty locating the corresponding parcel of land.

The "For More Info" Column will lead you to more information about the underlying Patents. See the *Legend* at right, and the "How to Use this Book" chapter, for more information.

LEGEND

"For More Info . . . " column

A = Authority (Legislative Act, See Appendix "A")
B = Block or Lot (location in Section unknown)
C = Cancelled Patent
F = Fractional Section
G = Group (Multi-Patentee Patent, see Appendix "C")
V = Overlaps another Parcel
R = Re-Issued (Parcel patented more than once)

(A & G items require you to look in the Appendixes referred to above. All other Letter-designations followed by a number require you to locate line-items in this index that possess the ID number found after the letter).

ID	Individual in Patent	Sec.	Sec. Part	Date Issued	Other Counties	For More Info . . .
2811	ANDREWS, Hiram	24	SESE	1856-09-01		A1
2855	ATKINSON, Obrien J	17	S½NE	1868-08-20		A1 G3
2854	AVERY, Newell	6	NESE	1855-10-01		A1
2863	BARNARD, Sherman S	25	SESW	1852-02-10		A1 G9
2864	" "	25	W½SW	1852-02-10		A1 G9
2865	" "	26	SESE	1852-02-10		A1 G9
2836	BECKETT, John H	23	E½SE	1857-10-30		A1
2837	" "	23	SWSE	1857-10-30		A1
2872	BRADLEY, Thomas	8	SWNE	1871-09-30		A2
2828	BROWN, John	18	W½NW	1857-07-01		A1
2829	" "	7	SW	1857-07-01		A1
2830	" "	7	W½NW	1857-07-01		A1 V2838
2857	BROWN, Robert	18	E½NW	1857-07-01		A1
2858	" "	18	SW	1857-07-01		A1
2859	" "	18	W½NE	1857-07-01		A1
2843	BROWNE, John S	8	W½NW	1870-05-20		A2
2814	BRYCE, Hutchison J	8	W½SW	1875-05-05		A2
2860	BRYCE, Robert	6	W½SW	1870-05-20		A2
2789	CARLETON, Chester	30	SWSW	1854-06-15		A1
2790	" "	31	NWNW	1854-06-15		A1 F
2881	CARTER, William J	27	NENE	1857-10-30		A1
2844	CAVE, Joseph B	6	SWNW	1861-07-01		A1 F
2863	COE, Israel	25	SESW	1852-02-10		A1 G9
2864	" "	25	W½SW	1852-02-10		A1 G9
2865	" "	26	SESE	1852-02-10		A1 G9
2877	CUMMINGS, William	3	NWNW	1870-06-01		A2
2878	" "	4	E½NE	1870-06-01		A2
2879	" "	4	NESE	1870-06-01		A2
2873	CUNNINGHAM, Thomas	3	NESW	1861-07-01		A1
2816	DANCEY, James	4	SESE	1861-12-03		A1
2817	" "	4	W½SE	1861-12-03		A1
2822	DE GROAT, JAMES R	20	S½NW	1887-09-07		A2
2856	DEAN, Ransom	20	SWSW	1885-01-30		A1
2788	DECKER, Charles	6	NWNW	1854-06-15		A1 F
2831	DELL, John	20	N½NW	1878-02-13		A1
2832	" "	20	NWNE	1878-02-13		A1
2845	DESOTELL, Joseph	30	E½	1857-07-01		A1
2833	EARLES, John	34	NENE	1857-02-20		A1
2834	" "	35	N½NW	1857-02-20		A1
2835	" "	35	SENW	1857-02-20		A1
2785	EASTMAN, Alfred S	3	NWSE	1878-11-05		A2
2868	ECKARDT, Theodor	4	SWNW	1862-02-01		A1 F
2869	" "	5	S½NE	1862-02-01		A1 F
2802	FARRELL, Edward	8	E½NW	1857-10-30		A1
2818	FOLEY, James	26	E½SW	1857-02-20		A1
2875	FOLEY, Timothy	26	SWSW	1857-02-20		A1

ID	Individual in Patent	Sec.	Sec. Part	Date Issued	Other Counties	For More Info . . .
2876	FOLEY, Timothy (Cont'd)	27	SESE	1857-02-20		A1
2783	GYSTER, Abraham	18	E½SE	1888-05-16		A2
2847	HILL, Joseph	3	SWNE	1860-10-01		A1
2846	" "	2	SWNW	1870-09-20		A2
2880	HODGKINS, William	22	W½SW	1870-05-20		A2
2807	HUBBARD, Frederick	3	NESE	1860-10-01		A1
2808	" "	3	SENE	1860-10-01		A1
2806	LACASSE, Francis	25	SWSE	1857-02-20		A1
2805	" "	25	SESE	1857-07-01		A1
2839	MARIN, John	12	NESE	1868-08-20		A1
2803	MARSHALL, Elizabeth	14	NWSE	1885-01-30		A1
2882	MARTINDALE, William	31	SWNW	1857-10-30		A1
2883	" "	31	W½SW	1857-10-30		A1
2819	MASDAN, James	5	N½NE	1861-12-03		A1
2820	MASDEN, James	4	NWNW	1870-11-18		A2
2849	MASON, Lorenzo M	30	NWSW	1855-10-01		A1
2853	MCCABE, Mark	8	NWNE	1857-10-30		A1
2855	MCGINN, John W	17	S½NE	1868-08-20		A1 G3
2841	MCRAE, John	30	NWNW	1870-05-20		A2
2842	" "	30	S½NW	1870-05-20		A2
2840	" "	30	E½SW	1870-06-10		A2
2850	MILLS, Luther D	11	E½SW	1855-10-01		A1
2851	" "	11	SENW	1855-10-01		A1
2852	" "	11	SWNE	1855-10-01		A1
2884	MILLS, William S	2	NWNW	1855-10-01		A1 F
2810	NEWTON, Harris	15	W½SW	1837-11-02		A1
2784	PHELPS, Abram	28	S½NW	1866-06-20		A1
2821	PREVOST, James	26	SWSE	1859-10-10		A1
2866	ROCKWELL, Stephen Y	23	N½SW	1856-09-01		A1
2867	" "	23	S½SW	1857-10-30		A1
2778	SABIN, Aaron D	36	N½NE	1857-07-01		A1
2779	" "	36	NENW	1857-07-01		A1
2855	SIMMS, Walter	17	S½NE	1868-08-20		A1 G3
2809	SMITH, Gillis	18	W½SE	1881-05-03		A1
2812	STEINHOFF, Hiram	25	N½SE	1857-02-20		A1
2813	" "	25	NESW	1857-02-20		A1
2827	STEVENS, Jeremiah W	28	NESW	1870-10-01		A1
2870	STEVENS, Thomas B	8	E½SW	1857-10-30		A1
2871	" "	8	W½SE	1857-10-30		A1
2782	SUMNER, Able B	32	SWNE	1878-02-13		A1
2848	THAYER, Lemuel	3	N½NE	1861-07-01		A1
2804	VAN DUSEN, ELIZABETH	18	E½NE	1870-06-01		A2
2862	VAN DUSEN, ROBERT	8	NENE	1871-09-30		A2
2815	VANDUSEN, Isaac	8	SENE	1857-10-30		A1
2823	WATERS, James	31	E½SW	1857-02-20		A1 F
2824	" "	31	N½SE	1857-02-20		A1
2825	" "	31	SWNE	1857-02-20		A1 F
2826	" "	31	SWSE	1857-02-20		A1
2791	WHITMAN, David	12	SESE	1855-10-01		A1
2792	" "	13	E½NE	1855-10-01		A1
2793	" "	25	NENE	1855-10-01		A1
2794	" "	25	SWNE	1855-10-01		A1
2795	" "	26	NWSE	1855-10-01		A1
2796	" "	26	NWSW	1855-10-01		A1
2797	" "	26	SENW	1855-10-01		A1
2798	" "	26	SWNE	1855-10-01		A1
2799	" "	3	NENW	1855-10-01		A1
2800	" "	4	SENW	1855-10-01		A1
2801	" "	4	SWNE	1855-10-01		A1
2786	WIGHT, Buckminster	35	SWSE	1852-02-10		A1
2787	" "	36	SWNW	1852-02-10		A1
2861	WILLOUGHBY, Robert T	33	E½SW	1891-08-24		A1
2838	WILSON, John H	7	S½NW	1857-07-01		A1 V2830
2874	WILSON, Thomas	34	SENE	1867-07-01		A1
2780	YORKE, Aaron	26	N½NW	1857-02-20		A1
2781	" "	26	SWNW	1857-02-20		A1

Patent Map

T9-N R13-E
Michigan-Toledo Strip Meridian

Map Group 27

Township Statistics

Parcels Mapped	:	107
Number of Patents	:	81
Number of Individuals	:	67
Patentees Identified	:	64
Number of Surnames	:	60
Multi-Patentee Parcels	:	4
Oldest Patent Date	:	11/2/1837
Most Recent Patent	:	8/24/1891
Block/Lot Parcels	:	0
Parcels Re - Issued	:	0
Parcels that Overlap	:	2
Cities and Towns	:	2
Cemeteries	:	2

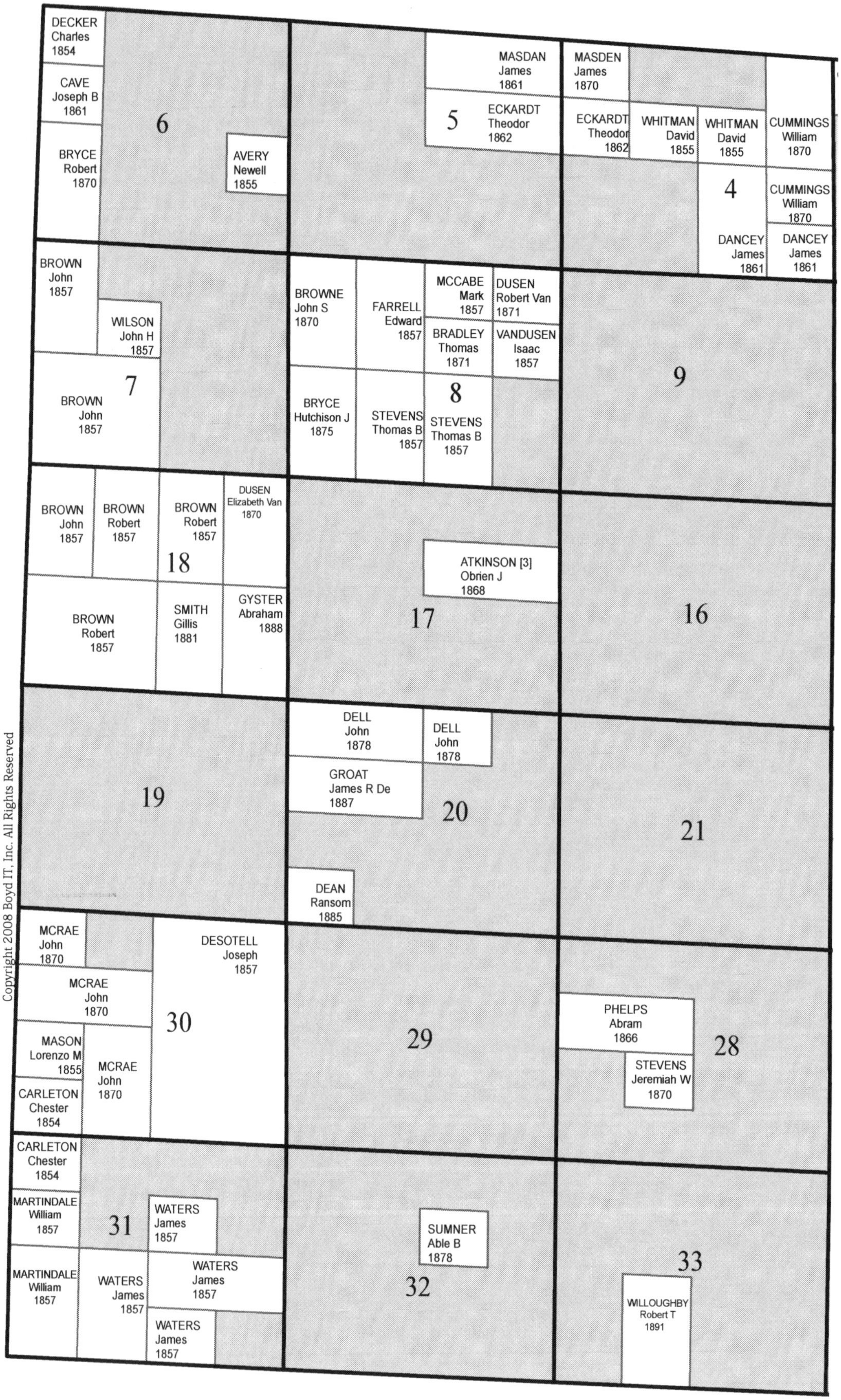

Helpful Hints

1. This Map's INDEX can be found on the preceding pages.
2. Refer to Map "C" to see where this Township lies within Sanilac County, Michigan.
3. Numbers within square brackets [ ] denote a multi-patentee land parcel (multi-owner). Refer to Appendix "C" for a full list of members in this group.
4. Areas that look to be crowded with Patentees usually indicate multiple sales of the same parcel (Re-issues) or Overlapping parcels. See this Township's Index for an explanation of these and other circumstances that might explain "odd" groupings of Patentees on this map.

Legend

- Patent Boundary
- Section Boundary
- No Patents Found (or Outside County)
- 1., 2., 3., ... Lot Numbers (when beside a name)
- [ ] Group Number (see Appendix "C")

Scale: Section = 1 mile X 1 mile (generally, with some exceptions)

Road Map

T9-N R13-E
Michigan-Toledo Strip Meridian

Map Group 27

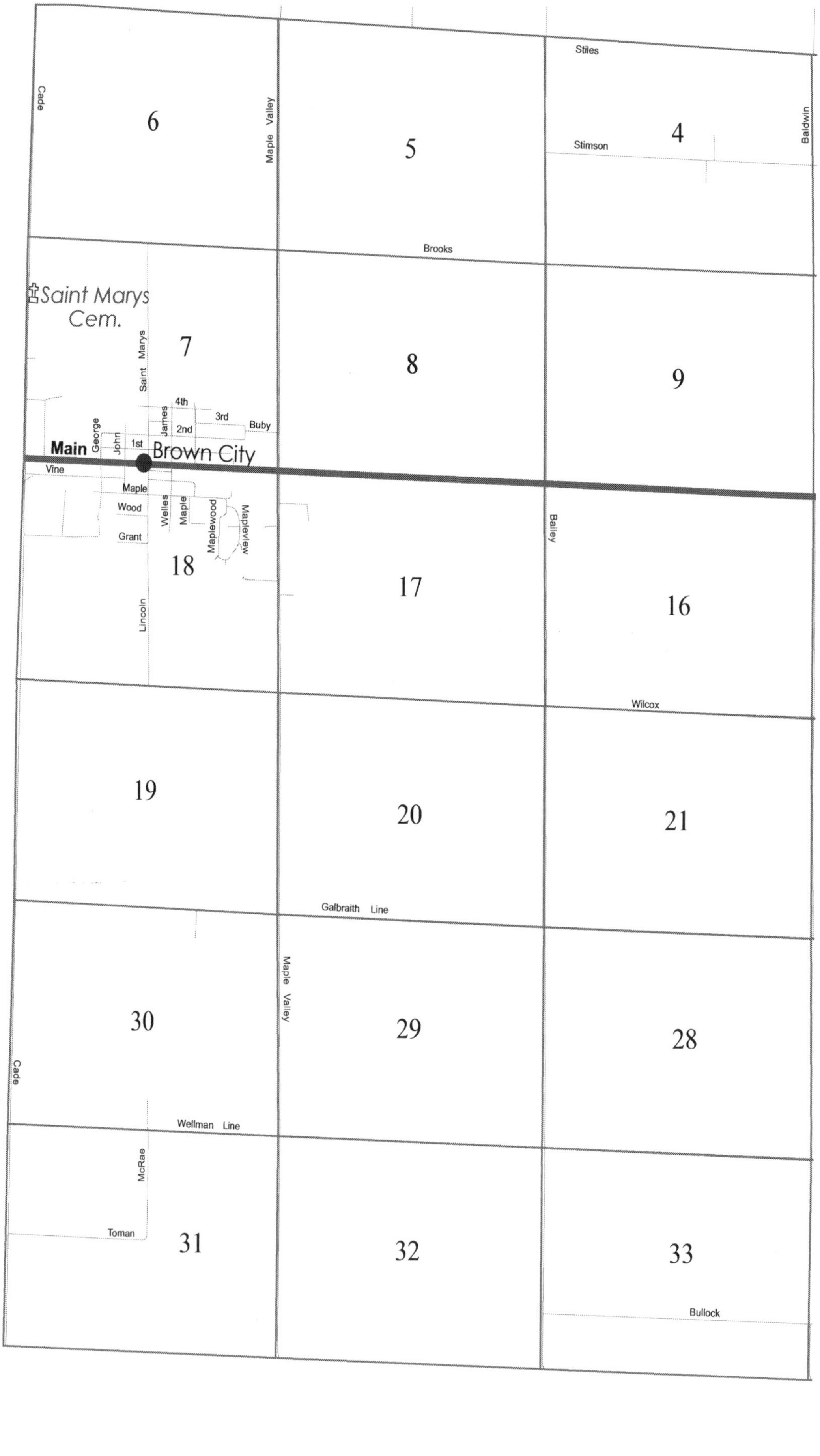

Cities & Towns

Brown City
Valley Center

Cemeteries

Saint Marys Cemetery
Valley Center Cemetery

Stiles
Cade
6
Maple Valley
5
Stimson
4
Baldwin
Brooks
Saint Marys Cem.
7
Saint Marys
8
9
4th
3rd
James
2nd
Buby
George
John
1st
Main
Brown City
Vine
Maple
Wood
Welles
Maple
Maplewood
Mapleview
Grant
Bailey
18
17
16
Lincoln
Wilcox
19
20
21
Galbraith Line
Maple Valley
30
29
28
Cade
Wellman Line
McRae
Toman
31
32
33
Bullock

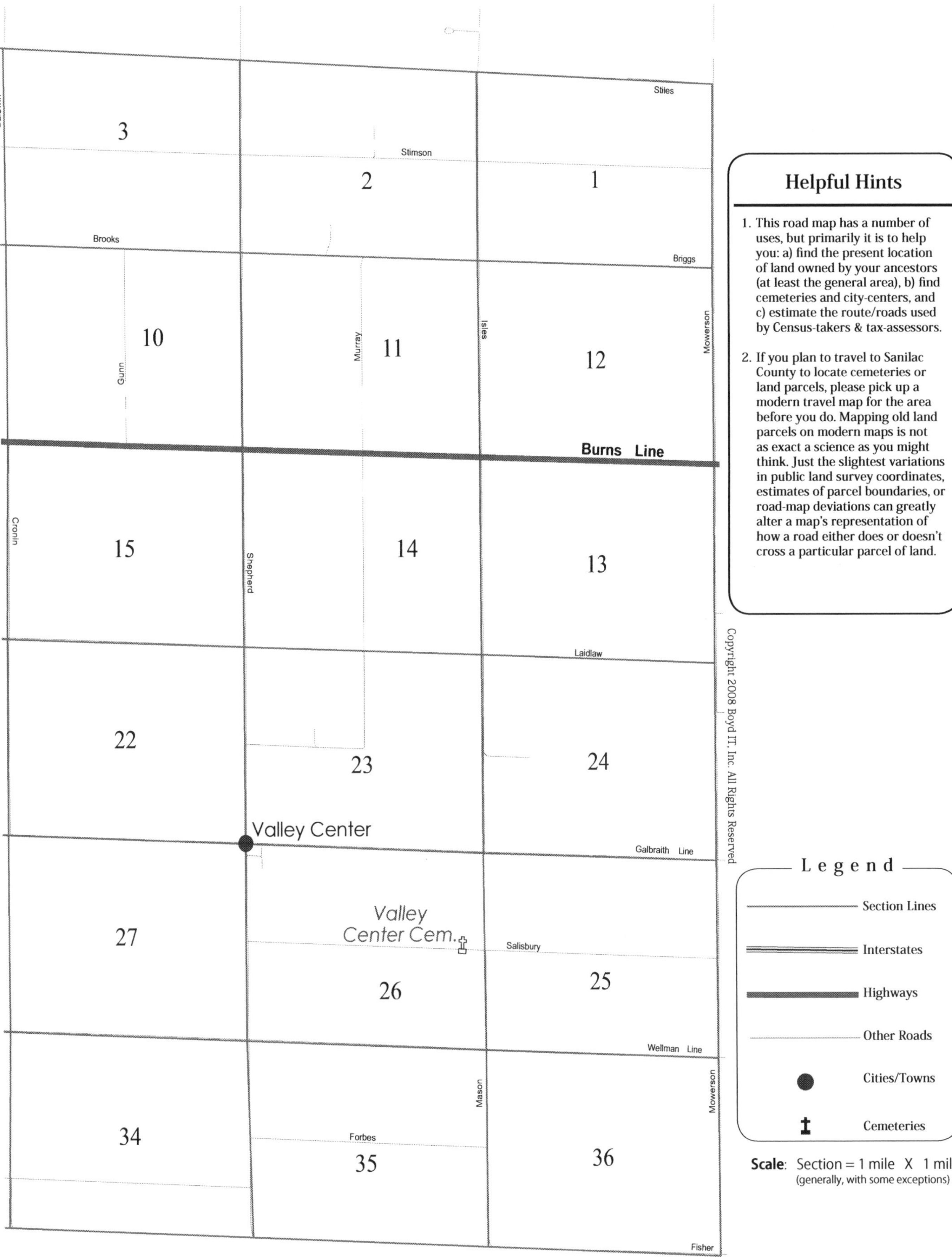

Helpful Hints

1. This road map has a number of uses, but primarily it is to help you: a) find the present location of land owned by your ancestors (at least the general area), b) find cemeteries and city-centers, and c) estimate the route/roads used by Census-takers & tax-assessors.

2. If you plan to travel to Sanilac County to locate cemeteries or land parcels, please pick up a modern travel map for the area before you do. Mapping old land parcels on modern maps is not as exact a science as you might think. Just the slightest variations in public land survey coordinates, estimates of parcel boundaries, or road-map deviations can greatly alter a map's representation of how a road either does or doesn't cross a particular parcel of land.

Historical Map

T9-N R13-E
Michigan-Toledo Strip Meridian

Map Group 27

Cities & Towns
Brown City
Valley Center

Cemeteries
Saint Marys Cemetery
Valley Center Cemetery

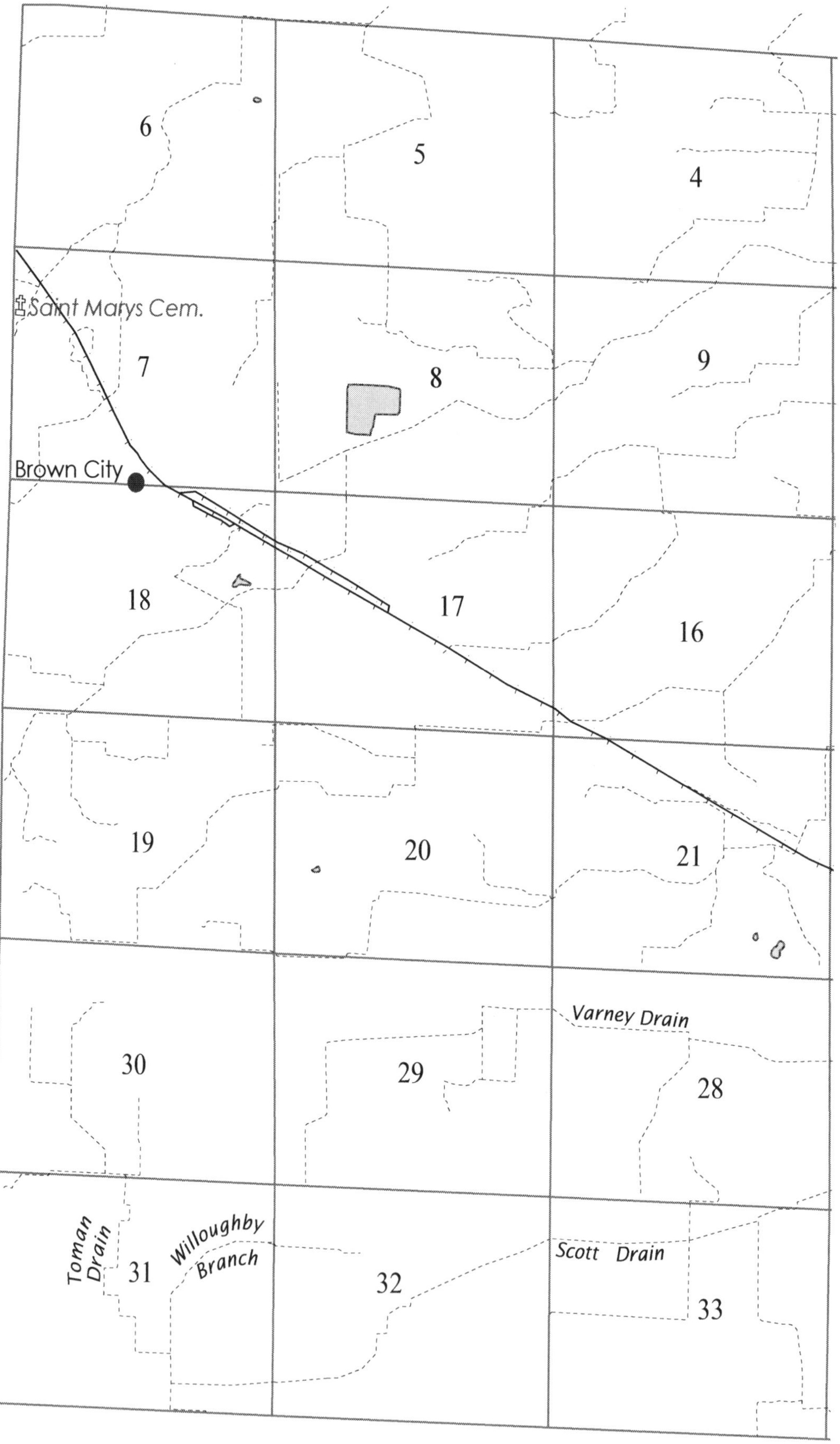

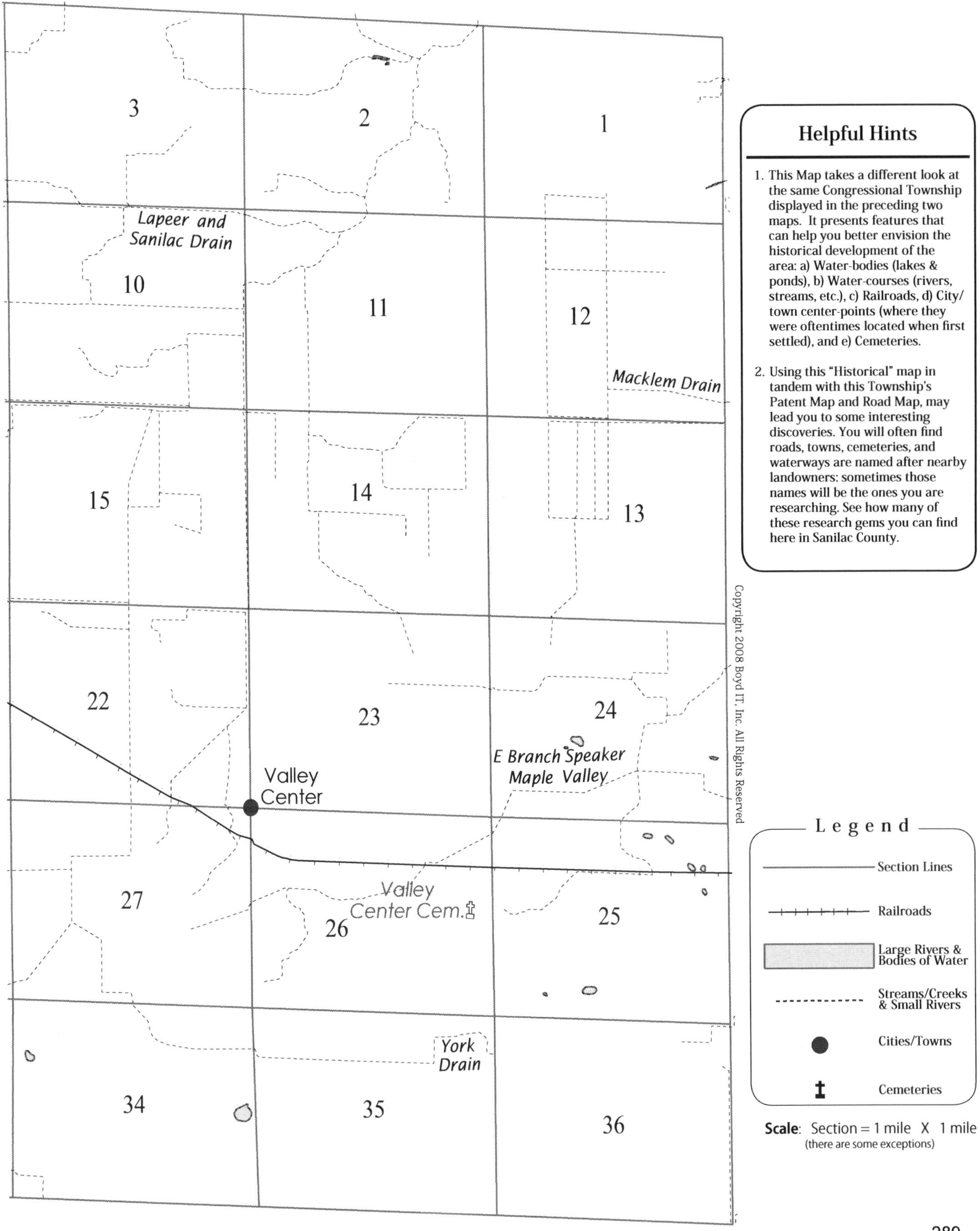

Helpful Hints

1. This Map takes a different look at the same Congressional Township displayed in the preceding two maps. It presents features that can help you better envision the historical development of the area: a) Water-bodies (lakes & ponds), b) Water-courses (rivers, streams, etc.), c) Railroads, d) City/town center-points (where they were oftentimes located when first settled), and e) Cemeteries.
2. Using this "Historical" map in tandem with this Township's Patent Map and Road Map, may lead you to some interesting discoveries. You will often find roads, towns, cemeteries, and waterways are named after nearby landowners: sometimes those names will be the ones you are researching. See how many of these research gems you can find here in Sanilac County.

Scale: Section = 1 mile X 1 mile
(there are some exceptions)

Map Group 28: Index to Land Patents

Township 9-North Range 14-East (Michigan-Toledo Strip)

After you locate an individual in this Index, take note of the Section and Section Part then proceed to the Land Patent map on the pages immediately following. You should have no difficulty locating the corresponding parcel of land.

The "For More Info" Column will lead you to more information about the underlying Patents. See the *Legend* at right, and the "How to Use this Book" chapter, for more information.

LEGEND

"For More Info . . . " column

A = Authority (Legislative Act, See Appendix "A")
B = Block or Lot (location in Section unknown)
C = Cancelled Patent
F = Fractional Section
G = Group (Multi-Patentee Patent, see Appendix "C")
V = Overlaps another Parcel
R = Re-Issued (Parcel patented more than once)

(A & G items require you to look in the Appendixes referred to above. All other Letter-designations followed by a number require you to locate line-items in this index that possess the ID number found after the letter).

ID	Individual in Patent	Sec.	Sec. Part	Date Issued	Other Counties	For More Info . . .
2967	ANDERSON, Hiram	36	NWNE	1856-01-10		A1
3037	BARNARD, Sherman S	36	NESE	1852-02-10		A1 G9
3038	" "	36	NWSE	1852-02-10		A1 G9
3039	" "	36	S½NE	1852-02-10		A1 G9
2950	BEAL, Ezekiel	35	E½NE	1853-11-01		A1
2951	" "	35	E½SE	1853-11-01		A1
2953	" "	35	NWNE	1853-11-01		A1
2954	" "	35	SWSE	1853-11-01		A1
2956	" "	36	NW	1853-11-01		A1
2957	" "	36	W½SW	1853-11-01		A1
2952	" "	35	N½NW	1855-10-01		A1
2955	" "	36	NESW	1855-10-01		A1
3025	BEAL, Richard	13	SWSE	1854-06-15		A1
3026	" "	26	W½SE	1855-10-01		A1
3040	BEAL, Simon	26	SWNE	1853-11-01		A1
2974	BEARD, James	33	SENE	1849-02-01		A1
2975	" "	33	W½NE	1849-02-01		A1
3011	BROCKWAY, Lewis	26	NWNW	1850-03-01		A1
3012	" "	27	NENE	1850-03-01		A1
2885	BUTTERFIELD, Abner	30	S½SE	1857-07-01		A1
2976	CALHOUN, James	25	SESE	1850-03-01		A1
2977	" "	36	NENE	1850-03-01		A1
2926	CARLTON, Chester	34	NESE	1852-02-10		A1
3017	CHASE, Nathan B	2	W½NW	1852-02-10		A1 G24 F
3018	" "	3	E½NW	1852-02-10		A1 G24 F
3019	" "	3	NE	1852-02-10		A1 G24 F
2983	CLAYTON, John	30	N½SE	1857-02-16		A1
2984	" "	30	NENE	1857-02-16		A1
2985	" "	30	S½NE	1857-02-16		A1
2886	COBURN, Abner	33	SE	1837-05-01		A1
2887	" "	33	SW	1837-05-01		A1 V2995
2888	" "	34	SW	1837-05-01		A1
3037	COE, Israel	36	NESE	1852-02-10		A1 G9
3038	" "	36	NWSE	1852-02-10		A1 G9
3039	" "	36	S½NE	1852-02-10		A1 G9
3024	COFFINGER, Philip D	30	SW	1857-02-16		A1 F
2962	COLBORN, Hanford	20	S½NW	1855-10-01		A1 F
2963	" "	21	SENW	1855-10-01		A1
2964	" "	21	SWNE	1855-10-01		A1
3028	COMPANY, S Rothschild And	1	E½NE	1865-10-02		A1 F
2986	CONDON, John	12	NWSW	1861-07-01		A1
2948	COOK, Eve	2	SESW	1856-09-01		A1
2949	" "	8	NESE	1856-09-01		A1
3031	COOK, Samuel	17	E½SE	1856-09-01		A1
2989	DAVIS, John	21	SESW	1856-09-01		A1
3014	DAVIS, Nancy	19	N½SW	1856-01-10		A1

ID	Individual in Patent	Sec.	Sec. Part	Date Issued	Other Counties	For More Info . . .
3016	DAVIS, Nancy (Cont'd)	19	NWSE	1856-01-10		A1
3015	" "	19	NESE	1857-07-01		A1
3023	DAVIS, Patrick	33	NWNW	1856-09-01		A1
2990	DEGRAW, John	1	NWSE	1861-12-03		A1
2991	" "	1	W½NE	1861-12-03		A1
3044	DOWLING, William H	24	SESE	1854-06-15		A1 G33
3045	" "	25	NESE	1854-06-15		A1 G33
3046	" "	26	SESW	1854-06-15		A1 G33
2930	DUDLEY, Daniel D	29	SENW	1855-10-01		A1 G34
2893	FISH, Allen	26	SENW	1852-12-01		A1
2894	" "	33	NENE	1852-12-01		A1
2889	" "	12	NENE	1854-06-15		A1
2890	" "	13	NWSW	1854-06-15		A1
2891	" "	14	NESE	1854-06-15		A1
2892	" "	14	SENE	1854-06-15		A1
2895	" "	24	N½NE	1854-06-15		A1 G39
2896	" "	24	NWNW	1854-06-15		A1 G39
2895	FISH, Henry	24	N½NE	1854-06-15		A1 G39
2896	" "	24	NWNW	1854-06-15		A1 G39
3044	FORBES, John C	24	SESE	1854-06-15		A1 G33
3045	" "	25	NESE	1854-06-15		A1 G33
3046	" "	26	SESW	1854-06-15		A1 G33
3013	GILLETT, Martin S	34	W½NW	1848-07-01		A1
3021	GOODWIN, Newlove	12	NESW	1861-07-01		A1
3022	" "	12	NWSE	1861-07-01		A1
2978	GRANDY, James	3	NESE	1859-10-10		A1
2927	HAEBERLE, Christian	1	SESW	1862-02-01		A1
2995	HALL, John K	33	SESW	1856-01-10		A1 V2887
2979	HAYNES, James	13	E½NE	1850-12-02		A1
2980	" "	20	NWSW	1850-12-02		A1
2965	HEEBENER, Harmon	14	SWNW	1856-01-10		A1
2946	HOLBERT, Ephraim	18	N½SW	1870-05-20		A2 F
2947	" "	18	SWSW	1870-05-20		A2 F
2930	HUNT, Henry C	29	SENW	1855-10-01		A1 G34
2992	IRVING, John	35	W½SW	1857-02-16		A1
2993	JONES, John	34	SENW	1848-09-01		A1 R2994
2994	" "	34	SENW	1848-09-01		A1 R2993
2988	JONES, John D	34	SWSE	1850-03-01		A1
2987	" "	29	SWNE	1850-12-02		A1
2898	LEE, Benjamin	2	E½NW	1857-02-16		A1
2899	" "	2	W½NE	1857-02-16		A1
2900	" "	35	SESW	1857-02-16		A1 R2972
2968	LEE, Hiram	15	SE	1857-02-20		A1
3010	LOCK, Levi	27	NESE	1855-10-01		A1
2973	LOCKE, Hosea	26	W½SW	1857-07-01		A1
2996	MCMAHON, John	23	NESW	1854-06-15		A1
2997	" "	23	S½NE	1854-06-15		A1
2998	" "	23	SENW	1854-06-15		A1
2921	MERRILL, Charles	28	NESW	1850-12-02		A1
2923	" "	28	SWNE	1850-12-02		A1
2903	" "	13	NWSE	1852-02-10		A1
2904	" "	13	SWSW	1852-02-10		A1
2905	" "	14	NENW	1852-02-10		A1
2906	" "	14	NWSW	1852-02-10		A1
2907	" "	14	SESE	1852-02-10		A1
2908	" "	14	SESW	1852-02-10		A1
2909	" "	15	SWSW	1852-02-10		A1
2911	" "	20	E½NW	1852-02-10		A1
2912	" "	21	NWNW	1852-02-10		A1
2914	" "	23	NENE	1852-02-10		A1
2915	" "	23	NWNW	1852-02-10		A1
2916	" "	24	NESW	1852-02-10		A1
2917	" "	24	SENW	1852-02-10		A1
2919	" "	25	SENW	1852-02-10		A1
2920	" "	25	SESW	1852-02-10		A1
2922	" "	28	SESW	1852-02-10		A1
2924	" "	29	NESE	1852-02-10		A1
2925	" "	29	NWSE	1852-02-10		A1
2910	" "	17	SWSW	1852-11-01		A1
2913	" "	22	NESW	1852-11-01		A1
2918	" "	25	NESW	1852-11-01		A1
2999	MILLER, John	15	NESW	1854-06-15		A1
3047	MOORE, William S	6	N½SE	1860-11-21		A1 F

ID	Individual in Patent	Sec.	Sec. Part	Date Issued	Other Counties	For More Info . . .
3048	MOORE, William S (Cont'd)	6	N½SW	1860-11-21		A1 F
3049	" "	6	SE	1860-11-21		A1 F
2897	PAISLEY, Andrew	34	SESE	1857-02-16		A1
2958	PERKINS, George	14	NESW	1852-02-10		A1
2959	" "	14	NWSE	1852-02-10		A1
2960	" "	14	SWNE	1852-02-10		A1
2961	" "	25	NWSE	1852-02-10		A1
3032	PITTS, Samuel	23	NWNE	1855-10-01		A1
3033	" "	24	NENW	1855-10-01		A1
3034	" "	24	SWNW	1855-10-01		A1
2981	ROBINSON, James	12	NESE	1862-05-15		A1
2940	RUST, David W	14	SENW	1852-02-10		A1
3029	SALSBURY, Samson	18	E½NE	1857-07-01		A1
3030	" "	7	E½SE	1857-07-01		A1
2928	SANBORN, Cummings	27	SENE	1852-11-01		A1
2929	" "	27	W½NW	1852-11-01		A1
3017	SANBORN, James W	2	W½NW	1852-02-10		A1 G24 F
3018	" "	3	E½NW	1852-02-10		A1 G24 F
3019	" "	3	NE	1852-02-10		A1 G24 F
2944	SHILL, Edward	12	SENW	1861-12-10		A1
2945	" "	12	SWNE	1861-12-10		A1
3027	SISCHO, Rutsey M	12	SWSW	1860-11-21		A1
2934	SMITH, David C	17	NWSW	1857-10-30		A1
2935	" "	17	SWNW	1857-10-30		A1
2936	" "	18	E½SE	1857-10-30		A1
2942	SMITH, Ebenezer	20	W½NW	1870-05-20		A2
3043	SMITH, William C	34	NENW	1852-02-10		A1
2937	STEPHENS, David F	23	NENW	1852-02-10		A1
2938	" "	26	NENW	1852-02-10		A1
2939	" "	26	NWNE	1852-02-10		A1
2966	STEPHENS, Henry	32	SESE	1850-03-01		A1
3000	STEPHENS, John	27	SWSE	1852-02-10		A1
2943	STEVENS, Ebenezer	8	SESW	1857-02-20		A1
2982	STEVENS, Jeremiah W	18	NENW	1872-03-20		A2
3020	STEVENS, Nehemiah	23	S½SW	1855-10-01		A1
3002	TOOL, John	9	NENW	1859-05-09		A1
3001	" "	5	SENE	1860-10-01		A1 F
3003	" "	9	SWNE	1864-01-05		A1
3035	TOOL, Sarah	5	E½NW	1856-09-01		A1 F
3036	" "	8	NESW	1856-09-01		A1
3041	TRAINER, Terrence	19	SENW	1857-10-20		A1 F
3042	" "	19	SWNE	1857-10-20		A1 F
3005	WELLS, John	22	W½SE	1852-02-10		A1
3006	" "	26	NESW	1852-02-10		A1
3007	" "	27	NENW	1852-02-10		A1
3008	" "	27	NWNE	1852-02-10		A1
3004	" "	15	NWSW	1852-11-01		A1
3009	" "	36	S½SE	1852-12-01		A1
2969	WHEELOCK, Hiram	28	E½NE	1849-02-01		A1
2970	" "	28	W½SE	1849-02-01		A1
2971	" "	33	NENW	1849-02-01		A1
2972	" "	35	SESW	1849-02-01		A1 R2900
2941	WHITMAN, David	18	S½NW	1855-10-01		A1 F
2931	WHITNEY, Daniel	4	E½NW	1855-10-01		A1 G58 F
2932	" "	4	E½SW	1855-10-01		A1 G58 F
2933	" "	4	W½SE	1855-10-01		A1 G58
2931	WHITNEY, John W	4	E½NW	1855-10-01		A1 G58 F
2932	" "	4	E½SW	1855-10-01		A1 G58 F
2933	" "	4	W½SE	1855-10-01		A1 G58
2901	WIGHT, Buckminster	6	S½SW	1852-02-10		A1
2902	" "	7	S½NW	1852-02-10		A1 F

Patent Map

T9-N R14-E
Michigan-Toledo Strip Meridian

Map Group 28

Township Statistics

Parcels Mapped	:	165
Number of Patents	:	126
Number of Individuals	:	77
Patentees Identified	:	72
Number of Surnames	:	60
Multi-Patentee Parcels	:	15
Oldest Patent Date	:	5/1/1837
Most Recent Patent	:	3/20/1872
Block/Lot Parcels	:	0
Parcels Re - Issued	:	2
Parcels that Overlap	:	2
Cities and Towns	:	2
Cemeteries	:	0

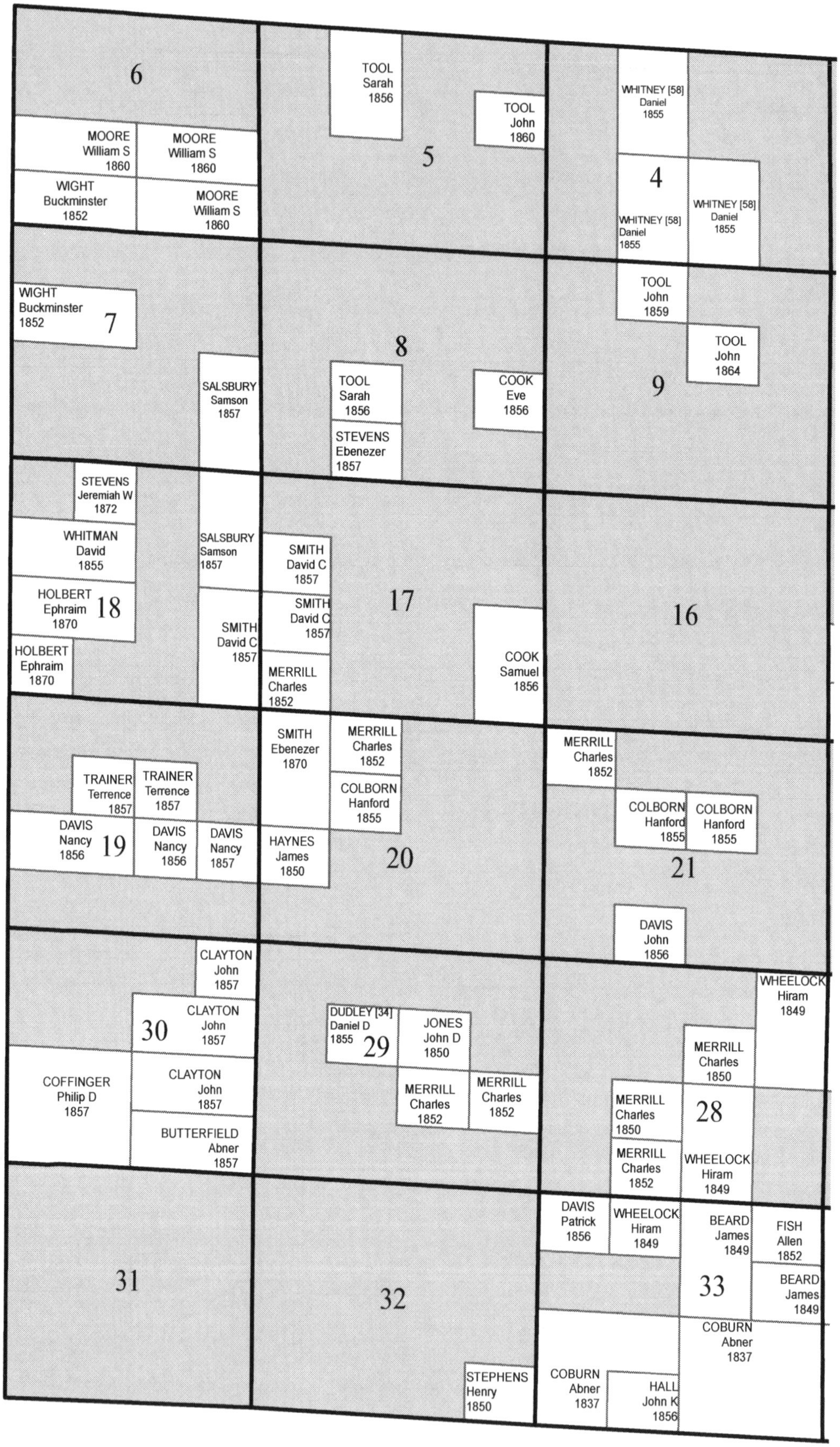

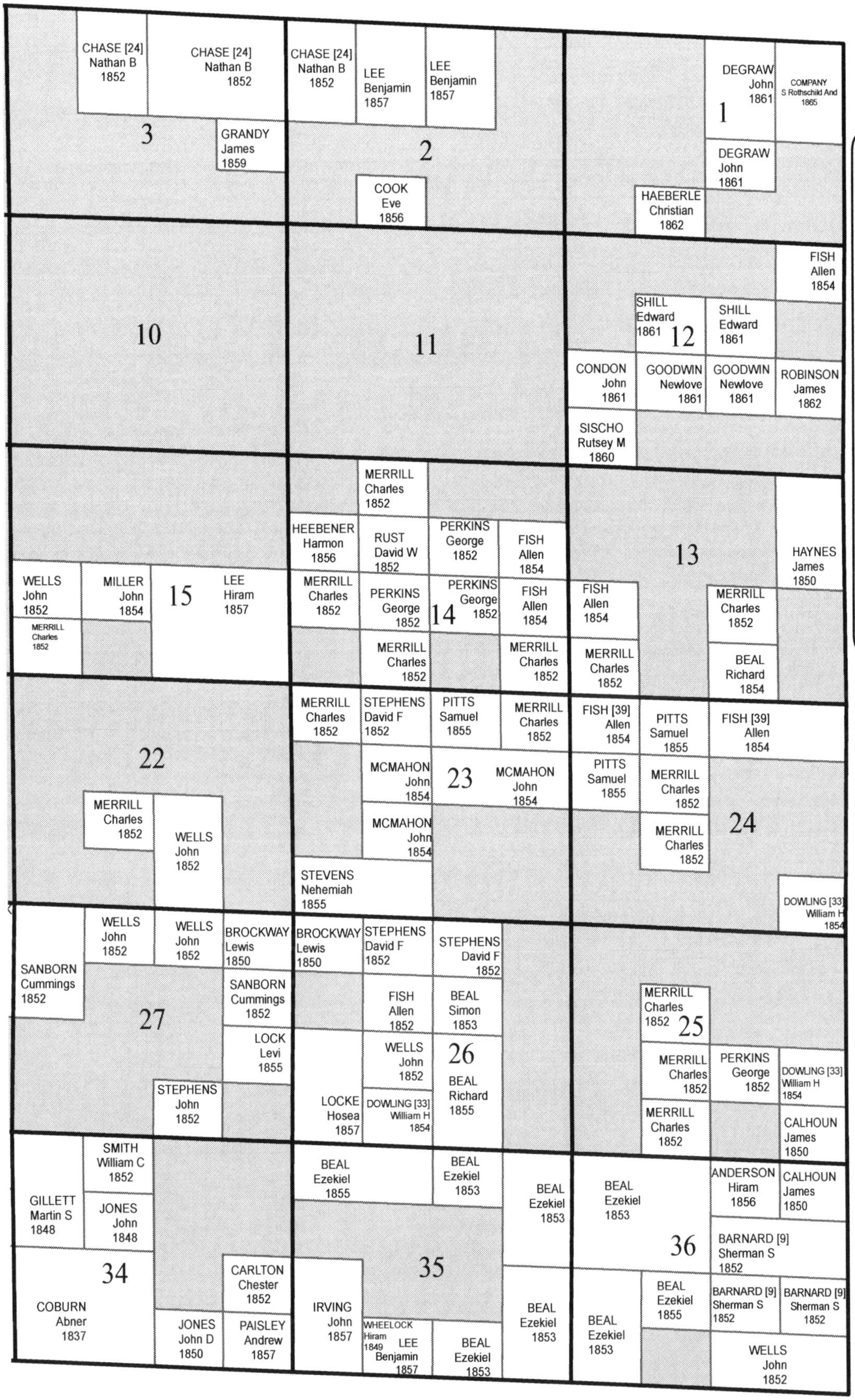

3
CHASE [24] Nathan B 1852
CHASE [24] Nathan B 1852
GRANDY James 1859

2
CHASE [24] Nathan B 1852
LEE Benjamin 1857
LEE Benjamin 1857
COOK Eve 1856

1
DEGRAW John 1861
COMPANY S Rothschild And 1865
DEGRAW John 1861
HAEBERLE Christian 1862

10

11

12
FISH Allen 1854
SHILL Edward 1861
SHILL Edward 1861
CONDON John 1861
GOODWIN Newlove 1861
GOODWIN Newlove 1861
ROBINSON James 1862
SISCHO Rutsey M 1860

15
WELLS John 1852
MILLER John 1854
LEE Hiram 1857
MERRILL Charles 1852

14
MERRILL Charles 1852
HEEBENER Harmon 1856
RUST David W 1852
PERKINS George 1852
FISH Allen 1854
MERRILL Charles 1852
PERKINS George 1852
PERKINS George 1852
FISH Allen 1854
MERRILL Charles 1852
MERRILL Charles 1852

13
HAYNES James 1850
FISH Allen 1854
MERRILL Charles 1852
MERRILL Charles 1852
BEAL Richard 1854

22
MERRILL Charles 1852
WELLS John 1852

23
MERRILL Charles 1852
STEPHENS David F 1852
PITTS Samuel 1855
MERRILL Charles 1852
MCMAHON John 1854
MCMAHON John 1854
MCMAHON John 1854
STEVENS Nehemiah 1855

24
FISH [39] Allen 1854
PITTS Samuel 1855
FISH [39] Allen 1854
PITTS Samuel 1855
MERRILL Charles 1852
MERRILL Charles 1852
DOWLING [33] William H 1854

27
WELLS John 1852
WELLS John 1852
BROCKWAY Lewis 1850
SANBORN Cummings 1852
SANBORN Cummings 1852
LOCK Levi 1855
STEPHENS John 1852

26
BROCKWAY Lewis 1850
STEPHENS David F 1852
STEPHENS David F 1852
FISH Allen 1852
BEAL Simon 1853
WELLS John 1852
BEAL Richard 1855
LOCKE Hosea 1857
DOWLING [33] William H 1854

25
MERRILL Charles 1852
MERRILL Charles 1852
PERKINS George 1852
DOWLING [33] William H 1854
MERRILL Charles 1852
CALHOUN James 1850

34
SMITH William C 1852
GILLETT Martin S 1848
JONES John 1848
CARLTON Chester 1852
COBURN Abner 1837
JONES John D 1850
PAISLEY Andrew 1857

35
BEAL Ezekiel 1855
BEAL Ezekiel 1853
BEAL Ezekiel 1853
IRVING John 1857
WHEELOCK Hiram 1849
LEE Benjamin 1857
BEAL Ezekiel 1853
BEAL Ezekiel 1853

36
BEAL Ezekiel 1853
ANDERSON Hiram 1856
CALHOUN James 1850
BARNARD [9] Sherman S 1852
BEAL Ezekiel 1855
BARNARD [9] Sherman S 1852
BARNARD [9] Sherman S 1852
BEAL Ezekiel 1853
WELLS John 1852

Helpful Hints

1. This Map's INDEX can be found on the preceding pages.
2. Refer to Map "C" to see where this Township lies within Sanilac County, Michigan.
3. Numbers within square brackets [ ] denote a multi-patentee land parcel (multi-owner). Refer to Appendix "C" for a full list of members in this group.
4. Areas that look to be crowded with Patentees usually indicate multiple sales of the same parcel (Re-issues) or Overlapping parcels. See this Township's Index for an explanation of these and other circumstances that might explain "odd" groupings of Patentees on this map.

Legend

Patent Boundary
Section Boundary
No Patents Found (or Outside County)
1., 2., 3., ... Lot Numbers (when beside a name)
[ ] Group Number (see Appendix "C")

Scale: Section = 1 mile X 1 mile (generally, with some exceptions)

Road Map

T9-N R14-E
Michigan-Toledo Strip Meridian

Map Group 28

Cities & Towns

Melvin
Speaker

Cemeteries

None

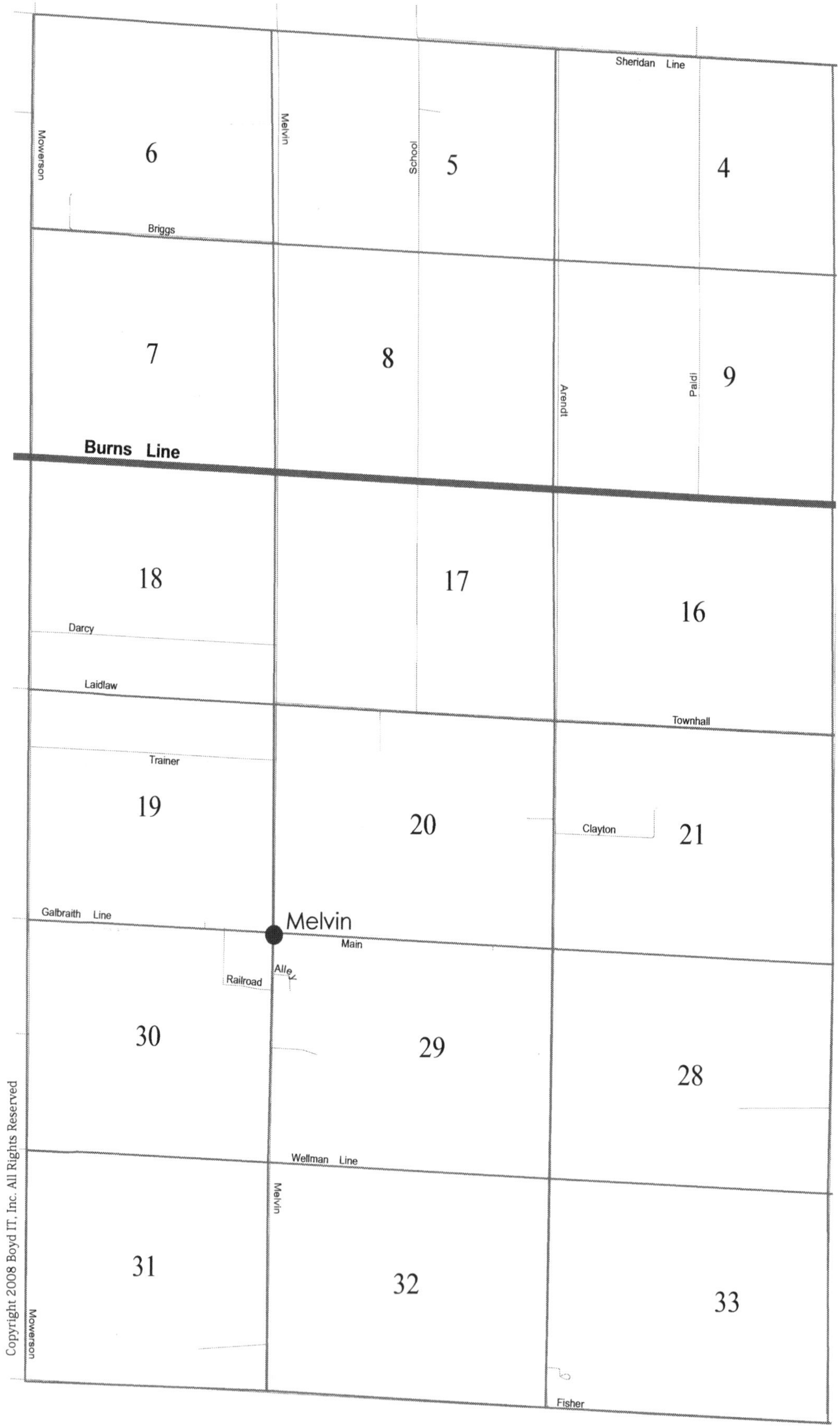

Sheridan Line
Mowerson
Melvin
School
6
5
4
Briggs
7
8
Arendt
Paldi
9
Burns Line
18
17
16
Darcy
Laidlaw
Townhall
Trainer
19
20
Clayton
21
Galbraith Line
Melvin
Main
Railroad
Alley
30
29
28
Wellman Line
Melvin
31
32
33
Mowerson
Fisher

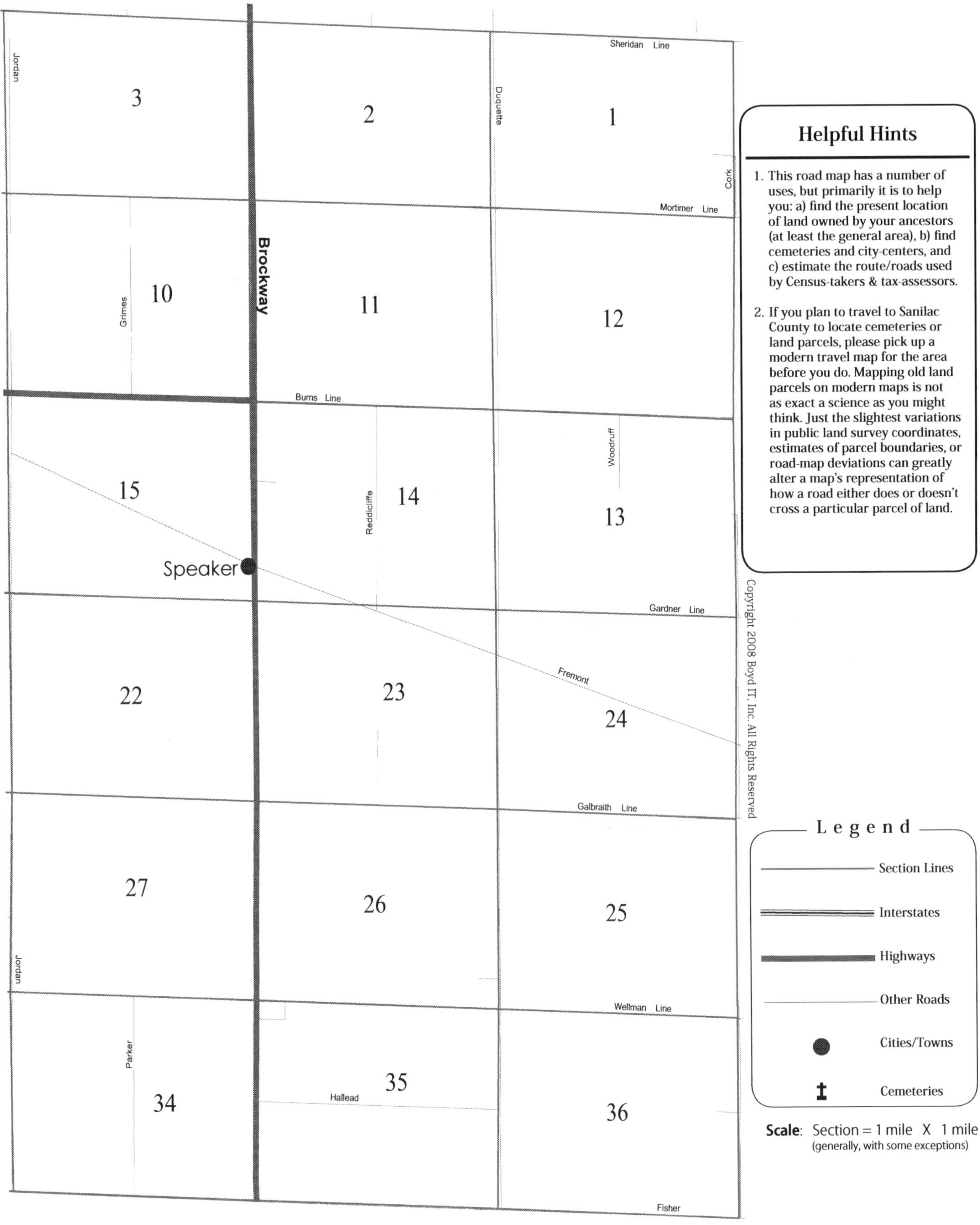
Jordan
3
2
Duquette
1
Sheridan Line
Cork
Mortimer Line
Brockway
Grimes
10
11
12
Burns Line
Woodruff
15
Reddicliffe
14
13
Speaker
Gardner Line
Fremont
22
23
24
Galbraith Line
27
26
25
Jordan
Wellman Line
Parker
34
Hallead
35
36
Fisher
Copyright 2008 Boyd IT, Inc. All Rights Reserved
Helpful Hints
1. This road map has a number of uses, but primarily it is to help you: a) find the present location of land owned by your ancestors (at least the general area), b) find cemeteries and city-centers, and c) estimate the route/roads used by Census-takers & tax-assessors.
2. If you plan to travel to Sanilac County to locate cemeteries or land parcels, please pick up a modern travel map for the area before you do. Mapping old land parcels on modern maps is not as exact a science as you might think. Just the slightest variations in public land survey coordinates, estimates of parcel boundaries, or road-map deviations can greatly alter a map's representation of how a road either does or doesn't cross a particular parcel of land.
Legend
Section Lines
Interstates
Highways
Other Roads
Cities/Towns
Cemeteries
Scale: Section = 1 mile X 1 mile
(generally, with some exceptions)

Historical Map

T9-N R14-E
Michigan-Toledo Strip Meridian

Map Group 28

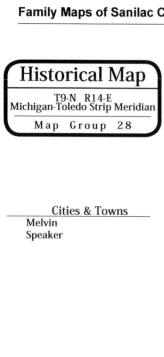

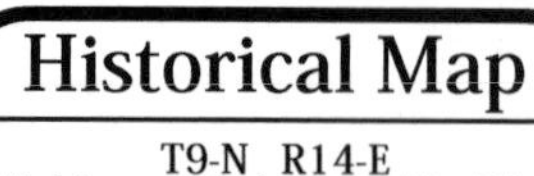

Cities & Towns

Melvin
Speaker

Cemeteries

None

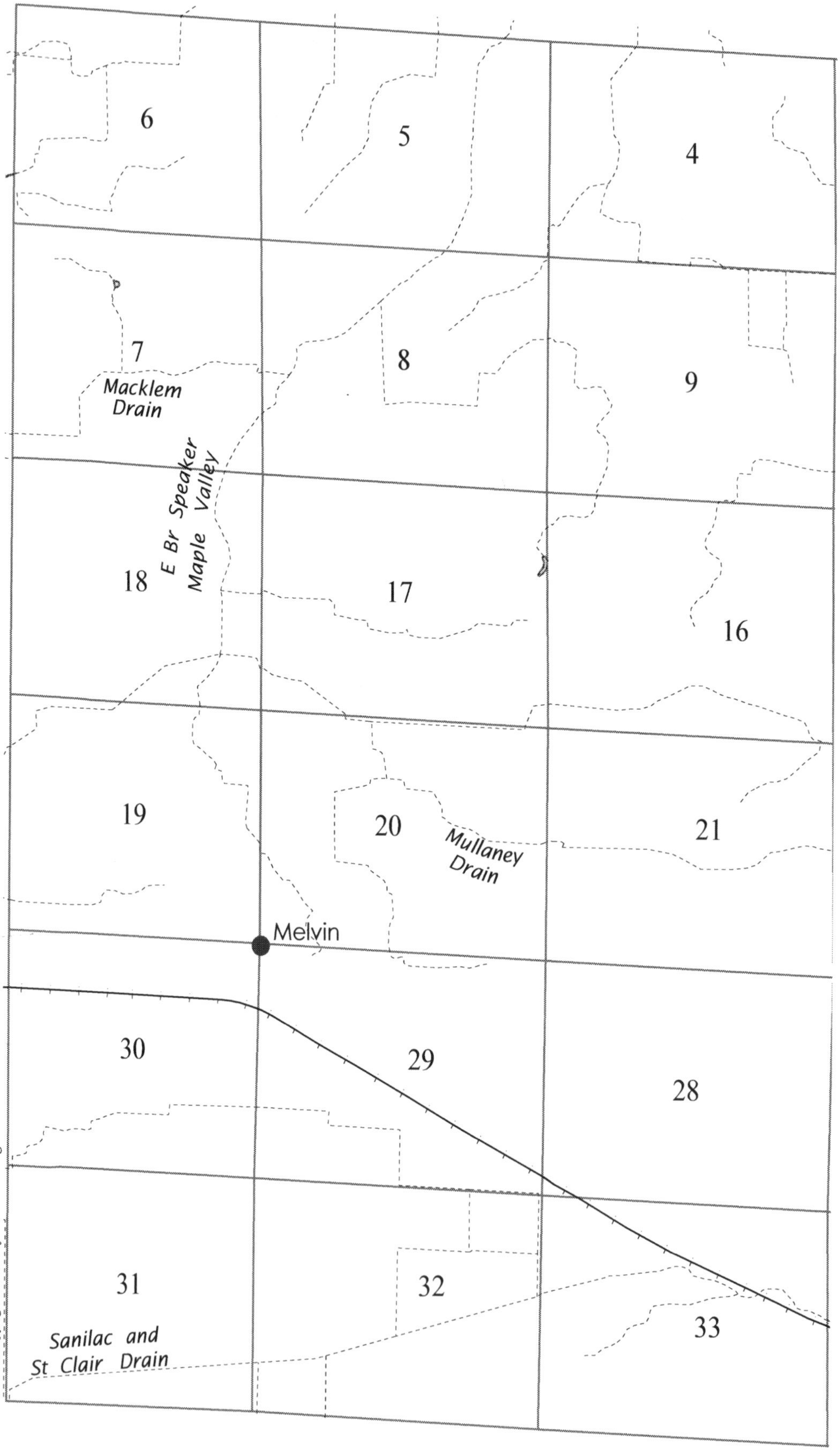

6
5
4
7
8
9
Macklem Drain
E Br Speaker Maple Valley
18
17
16
19
20
21
Mullaney Drain
Melvin
30
29
28
31
32
33
Sanilac and St Clair Drain

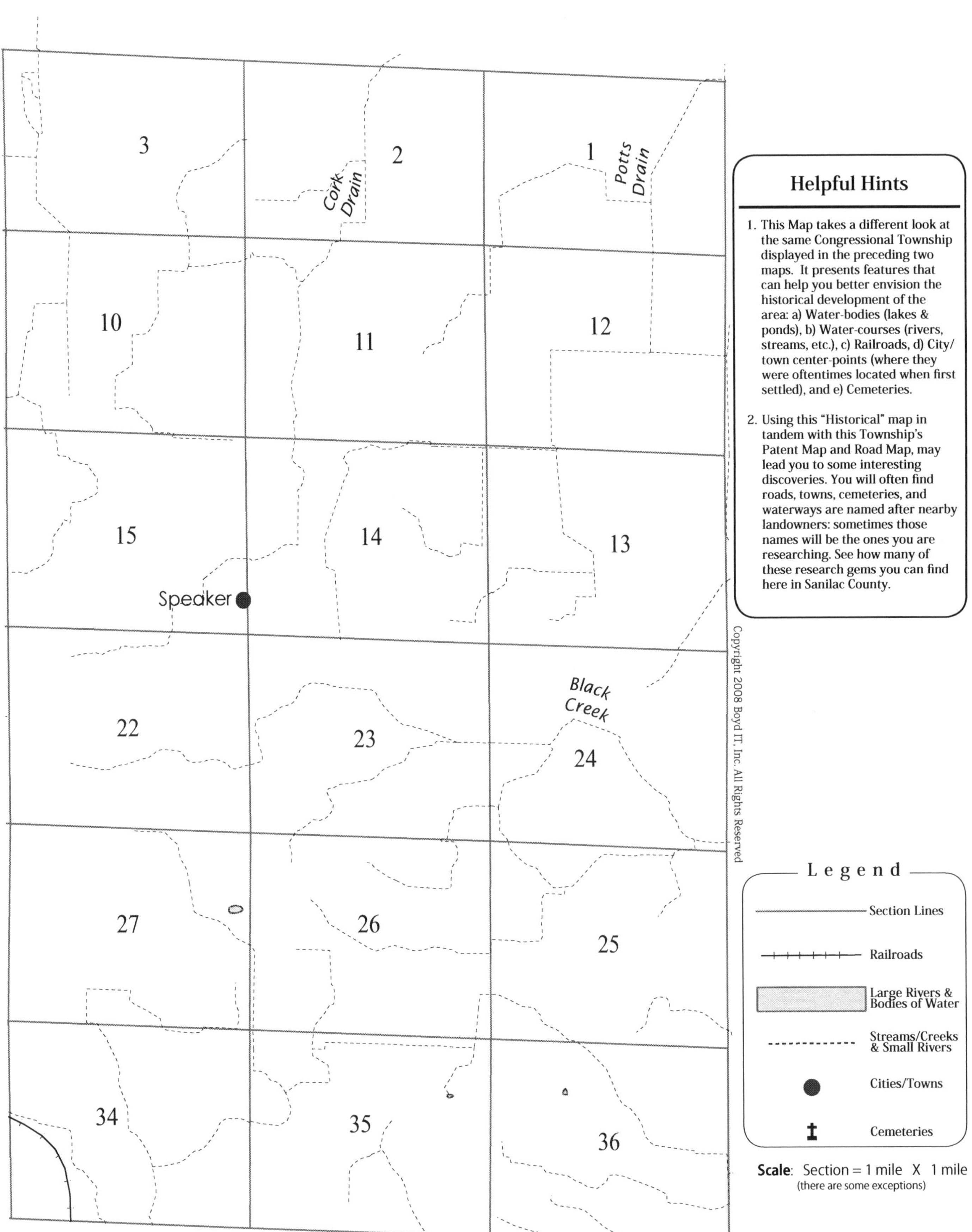
3
2
1
Cork Drain
Potts Drain
10
11
12
15
14
13
Speaker
22
23
24
Black Creek
27
26
25
34
35
36
Copyright 2008 Boyd IT, Inc. All Rights Reserved
Helpful Hints
1. This Map takes a different look at the same Congressional Township displayed in the preceding two maps. It presents features that can help you better envision the historical development of the area: a) Water-bodies (lakes & ponds), b) Water-courses (rivers, streams, etc.), c) Railroads, d) City/town center-points (where they were oftentimes located when first settled), and e) Cemeteries.
2. Using this "Historical" map in tandem with this Township's Patent Map and Road Map, may lead you to some interesting discoveries. You will often find roads, towns, cemeteries, and waterways are named after nearby landowners: sometimes those names will be the ones you are researching. See how many of these research gems you can find here in Sanilac County.
Legend
Section Lines
Railroads
Large Rivers & Bodies of Water
Streams/Creeks & Small Rivers
Cities/Towns
Cemeteries
Scale: Section = 1 mile X 1 mile
(there are some exceptions)

Map Group 29: Index to Land Patents

Township 9-North Range 15-East (Michigan-Toledo Strip)

After you locate an individual in this Index, take note of the Section and Section Part then proceed to the Land Patent map on the pages immediately following. You should have no difficulty locating the corresponding parcel of land.

The "For More Info" Column will lead you to more information about the underlying Patents. See the *Legend* at right, and the "How to Use this Book" chapter, for more information.

LEGEND

"For More Info . . . " column

A = Authority (Legislative Act, See Appendix "A")
B = Block or Lot (location in Section unknown)
C = Cancelled Patent
F = Fractional Section
G = Group (Multi-Patentee Patent, see Appendix "C")
V = Overlaps another Parcel
R = Re-Issued (Parcel patented more than once)

(A & G items require you to look in the Appendixes referred to above. All other Letter-designations followed by a number require you to locate line-items in this index that possess the ID number found after the letter).

ID	Individual in Patent	Sec.	Sec. Part	Date Issued	Other Counties	For More Info . . .
3092	AITKEN, James	23	E½NW	1857-07-01		A1
3093	" "	23	SWNW	1857-07-01		A1
3052	AITKIN, Andrew	1	SESE	1857-10-30		A1
3147	AVERY, Newell	19	SWNW	1854-06-15		A1
3148	" "	20	NWSW	1854-06-15		A1
3146	" "	13	S½SE	1855-10-01		A1
3150	" "	32	SWSE	1855-10-01		A1
3149	" "	24	N½NE	1856-01-10		A1
3163	BARNARD, Sherman S	31	SWSW	1852-02-10		A1 G9
3151	BOISE, Peter	12	N½SE	1856-01-10		A1
3152	" "	12	S½SE	1857-10-30		A1
3166	BOTTOMLEY, Thomas H	9	SESW	1865-10-02		A1
3065	BRANAGAN, Edward	19	E½SE	1857-02-20		A1
3066	" "	20	SWSW	1857-02-20		A1
3067	BRANNAGAN, Edward	30	NENE	1857-02-20		A1
3135	BROCKWAY, Lewis	31	NWNW	1850-12-02		A1 F
3081	BROWN, Freeman W	30	S½NE	1867-02-16		A1
3138	BURNS, Moses	11	E½NW	1857-07-01		A1
3139	" "	11	SW	1857-07-01		A1
3165	BYERS, Thomas	29	SW	1857-02-16		A1
3143	CHASE, Nathan B	24	SESE	1849-02-01		A1 G23
3140	" "	23	NESE	1850-03-01		A1
3144	" "	25	SWNW	1850-03-01		A1 G23
3145	" "	26	SWSW	1850-03-01		A1 G23
3141	" "	25	NWSW	1852-02-10		A1
3142	" "	36	NESE	1852-02-10		A1 G24
3163	COE, Israel	31	SWSW	1852-02-10		A1 G9
3085	COLBORN, Hanford	33	NWNE	1852-12-01		A1
3086	" "	34	SENW	1852-12-01		A1
3133	COMSTOCK, Joseph B	27	SWSE	1852-12-01		A1
3134	" "	34	NWNE	1852-12-01		A1
3090	CROCKERD, Hugh	27	NENW	1852-11-01		A1
3154	DAVIS, Randall E	3	E½NW	1854-06-15		A1 G30 F
3155	" "	4	W½NE	1854-06-15		A1 G30 F
3173	DOWLING, William H	19	SWSW	1854-06-15		A1 G33
3156	ELWIN, Robert	12	N½NE	1857-10-30		A1
3094	ERITY, James G	1	NESE	1855-10-01		A1 G35
3050	FISH, Allen	17	SWNW	1856-01-10		A1 G39
3050	FISH, Henry	17	SWNW	1856-01-10		A1 G39
3173	FORBES, John C	19	SWSW	1854-06-15		A1 G33
3102	GALBRAITH, John	25	NWNW	1852-11-01		A1
3103	" "	27	SENE	1852-11-01		A1
3104	GILBRAITH, John	33	NESE	1852-12-01		A1
3171	GRANT, William	20	SESW	1856-01-10		A1
3172	" "	30	E½SW	1857-10-30		A1 F
3174	GRAY, William H	19	SESW	1859-10-10		A1

ID	Individual in Patent	Sec.	Sec. Part	Date Issued	Other Counties	For More Info . . .
3175	GRAY, William H (Cont'd)	19	SWSE	1859-10-10		A1
3164	HARRIS, Silas	21	SESE	1857-02-16		A1
3095	HARTEN, James	12	E½SW	1857-10-30		A1
3096	HAYNES, James	7	NESE	1850-12-02		A1
3097	" "	7	SENE	1850-12-02		A1
3160	JONES, Selden A	23	E½SW	1852-11-01		A1
3161	" "	23	NWSE	1852-11-01		A1
3162	" "	23	SWSW	1852-11-01		A1
3176	JURY, William	30	SE	1857-02-16		A1
3107	LEVAGOOD, John	9	SWNW	1855-10-01		A1
3157	MARECK, Robert	20	SESE	1857-02-16		A1
3158	" "	28	NWNW	1857-02-16		A1
3159	" "	29	NENE	1857-02-16		A1
3136	MASON, Lorenzo M	30	NWNW	1854-06-15		A1
3169	MCCARTHY, Timothy	4	NWSW	1856-09-01		A1
3167	" "	10	E½NW	1867-02-16		A1
3168	" "	10	N½NE	1867-02-16		A1
3108	MCDONALD, John	1	NE	1864-09-15		A1
3109	" "	1	NWSE	1864-09-15		A1
3064	MCINNIS, Donald	3	W½NE	1857-10-30		A1 F
3055	MERRILL, Charles	28	NWNE	1852-02-10		A1
3056	" "	35	NWNW	1852-11-01		A1
3054	" "	18	NWNE	1852-12-01		A1
3094	MILES, Cyrus	1	NESE	1855-10-01		A1 G35
3062	" "	14	SE	1855-10-01		A1
3143	MILLER, John	24	SESE	1849-02-01		A1 G23
3144	" "	25	SWNW	1850-03-01		A1 G23
3145	" "	26	SWSW	1850-03-01		A1 G23
3111	" "	9	SWSE	1854-06-15		A1
3110	" "	31	SESW	1855-10-01		A1
3091	MOFFAT, Hugh	1	NW	1854-06-15		A1 F
3059	NICHOLS, Chauncy C	25	SWSW	1852-12-01		A1
3057	NORMANDIE, Charles	30	S½NW	1867-02-16		A1 F
3058	" "	30	W½SW	1867-02-16		A1 F
3137	OBRIEN, Michael	15	NENE	1856-09-01		A1
3170	PARKER, Willard	24	NESE	1852-02-10		A1
3068	ROBINSON, Edwin	34	N½SE	1870-05-20		A2
3098	ROBINSON, James	24	SENE	1861-12-03		A1
3180	ROBINSON, William W	9	N½SE	1861-12-03		A1
3051	RUST, Aloney	13	SWNW	1852-02-10		A1 G55
3051	RUST, David W	13	SWNW	1852-02-10		A1 G55
3060	SANBORN, Cummings	24	SWSW	1850-03-01		A1
3061	" "	31	SWNW	1852-02-10		A1
3142	SANBORN, James W	36	NESE	1852-02-10		A1 G24
3100	" "	27	SWNW	1852-12-01		A1
3101	" "	28	NWSE	1852-12-01		A1
3063	SARSFIELD, David B	20	SWSE	1857-02-16		A1
3114	SAUNDERS, John	31	NESE	1857-02-16		A1
3115	" "	31	SENE	1857-02-16		A1
3116	" "	32	NWNW	1857-02-16		A1
3117	" "	32	S½NW	1857-02-16		A1
3118	" "	32	W½SW	1857-02-16		A1
3177	SCOTT, William	17	NESE	1856-01-10		A1
3178	" "	21	NWSE	1857-10-30		A1
3179	" "	21	S½NE	1857-10-30		A1
3079	SHELL, Frederick	22	N½SE	1857-07-01		A1
3080	" "	22	N½SW	1857-07-01		A1
3119	SHELL, John	22	SWSW	1857-02-16		A1
3120	" "	27	NWNW	1857-02-16		A1
3121	" "	28	E½NE	1857-02-16		A1
3053	SHRIGLEY, Benjamin	21	NENE	1857-02-16		A1
3099	SLY, James	1	SWSE	1861-12-10		A1
3122	SPRING, John	32	E½NE	1857-02-20		A1
3073	STEVENS, Frederick H	25	E½NW	1838-04-20		A1
3074	" "	25	E½SW	1838-04-20		A1
3075	" "	25	NE	1838-04-20		A1
3076	" "	25	SE	1838-04-20		A1
3077	" "	36	E½NW	1838-04-20		A1
3078	" "	36	NE	1838-04-20		A1
3082	STEVENS, George	22	SESW	1857-02-16		A1
3087	STEVENS, Harmon L	5	E½NW	1852-02-10		A1 F
3088	" "	6	E½NE	1852-02-10		A1 F
3154	" "	3	E½NW	1854-06-15		A1 G30 F

ID	Individual in Patent	Sec.	Sec. Part	Date Issued	Other Counties	For More Info . . .
3155	STEVENS, Harmon L (Cont'd)	4	W½NE	1854-06-15		A1 G30 F
3112	STEVENS, John R	30	NENW	1857-07-01		A1
3113	" "	30	NWNE	1857-07-01		A1
3083	TEMPLE, George	21	SW	1857-07-01		A1
3084	TEMPLE, Godfrey	7	NWNE	1877-03-20		A2
3123	TEMPLE, John	7	SESE	1877-03-20		A2
3153	THIBODEAU, Peter	22	SWNW	1857-02-16		A1
3126	TODD, John	3	SE	1857-07-01		A1
3124	" "	2	W½SW	1859-10-10		A1
3125	" "	3	E½NE	1859-10-10		A1
3130	WALLACE, John	32	E½SE	1855-10-01		A1
3131	" "	33	NWSW	1855-10-01		A1
3127	" "	1	N½SW	1856-01-10		A1
3128	" "	1	SESW	1856-01-10		A1
3129	" "	12	NW	1856-01-10		A1
3089	WARD, Haroy	22	NWNW	1857-02-16		A1
3132	WELLS, John	23	SENE	1854-06-15		A1
3105	WELSH, John L	22	E½NW	1867-02-16		A1
3069	WHITE, Frederick F	14	SWSW	1853-11-01		A1
3070	" "	26	SESW	1853-11-01		A1
3071	" "	32	NWNE	1853-11-01		A1
3072	" "	34	NESW	1853-11-01		A1
3106	WOODS, John L	6	NWNE	1854-06-15		A1 F
3181	YAKE, William	21	E½NW	1857-07-01		A1

Patent Map

T9-N R15-E
Michigan-Toledo Strip Meridian

Map Group 29

Township Statistics

Parcels Mapped	:	132
Number of Patents	:	103
Number of Individuals	:	78
Patentees Identified	:	76
Number of Surnames	:	67
Multi-Patentee Parcels	:	11
Oldest Patent Date	:	4/20/1838
Most Recent Patent	:	3/20/1877
Block/Lot Parcels	:	0
Parcels Re - Issued	:	0
Parcels that Overlap	:	0
Cities and Towns	:	1
Cemeteries	:	1

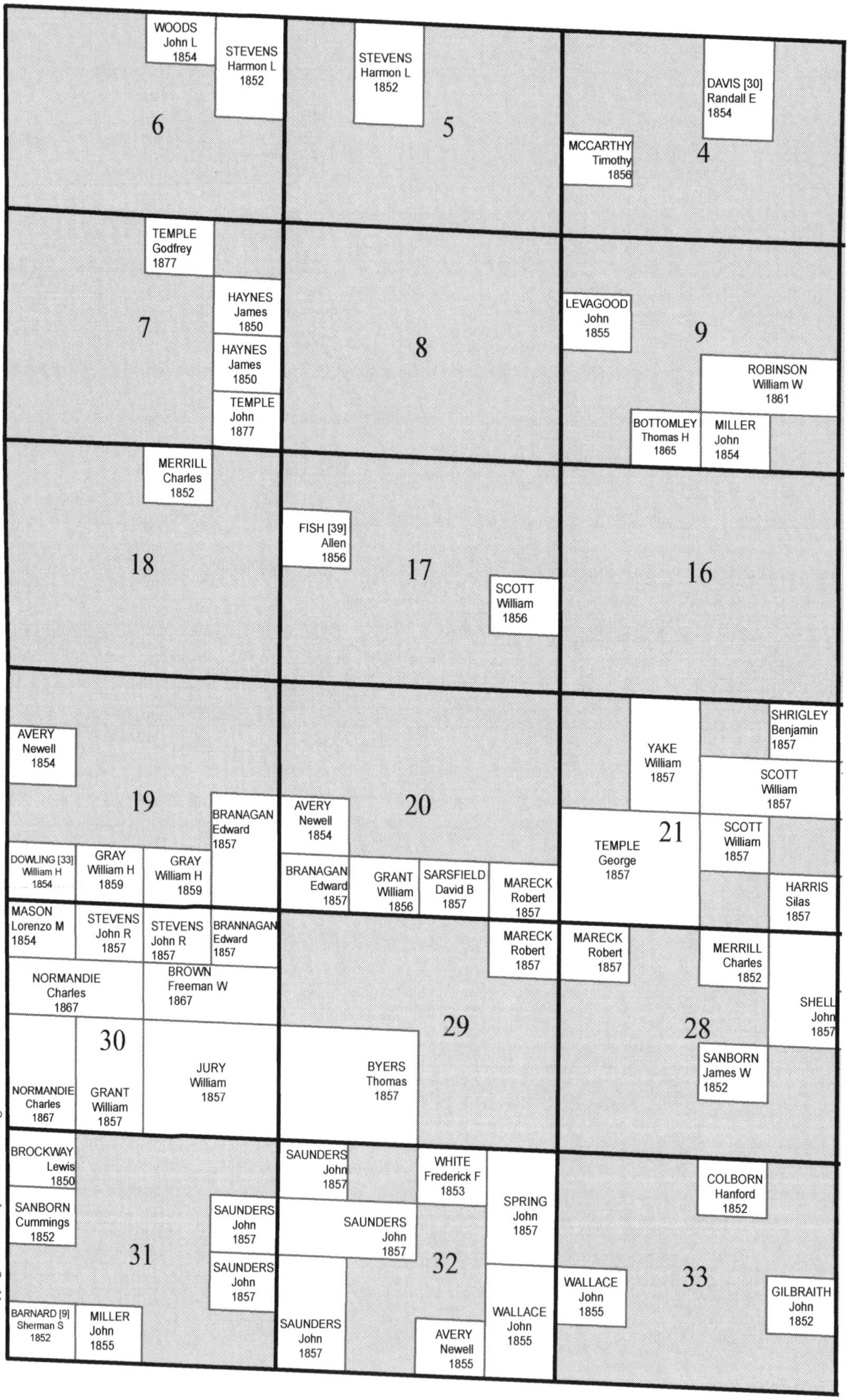

Helpful Hints

1. This Map's INDEX can be found on the preceding pages.
2. Refer to Map "C" to see where this Township lies within Sanilac County, Michigan.
3. Numbers within square brackets [ ] denote a multi-patentee land parcel (multi-owner). Refer to Appendix "C" for a full list of members in this group.
4. Areas that look to be crowded with Patentees usually indicate multiple sales of the same parcel (Re-issues) or Overlapping parcels. See this Township's Index for an explanation of these and other circumstances that might explain "odd" groupings of Patentees on this map.

Legend

- Patent Boundary
- Section Boundary
- No Patents Found (or Outside County)
- 1., 2., 3., ... Lot Numbers (when beside a name)
- [ ] Group Number (see Appendix "C")

Scale: Section = 1 mile X 1 mile (generally, with some exceptions)

Road Map

T9-N R15-E
Michigan-Toledo Strip Meridian

Map Group 29

Cities & Towns
Roseburg

Cemeteries
Fremont Cemetery

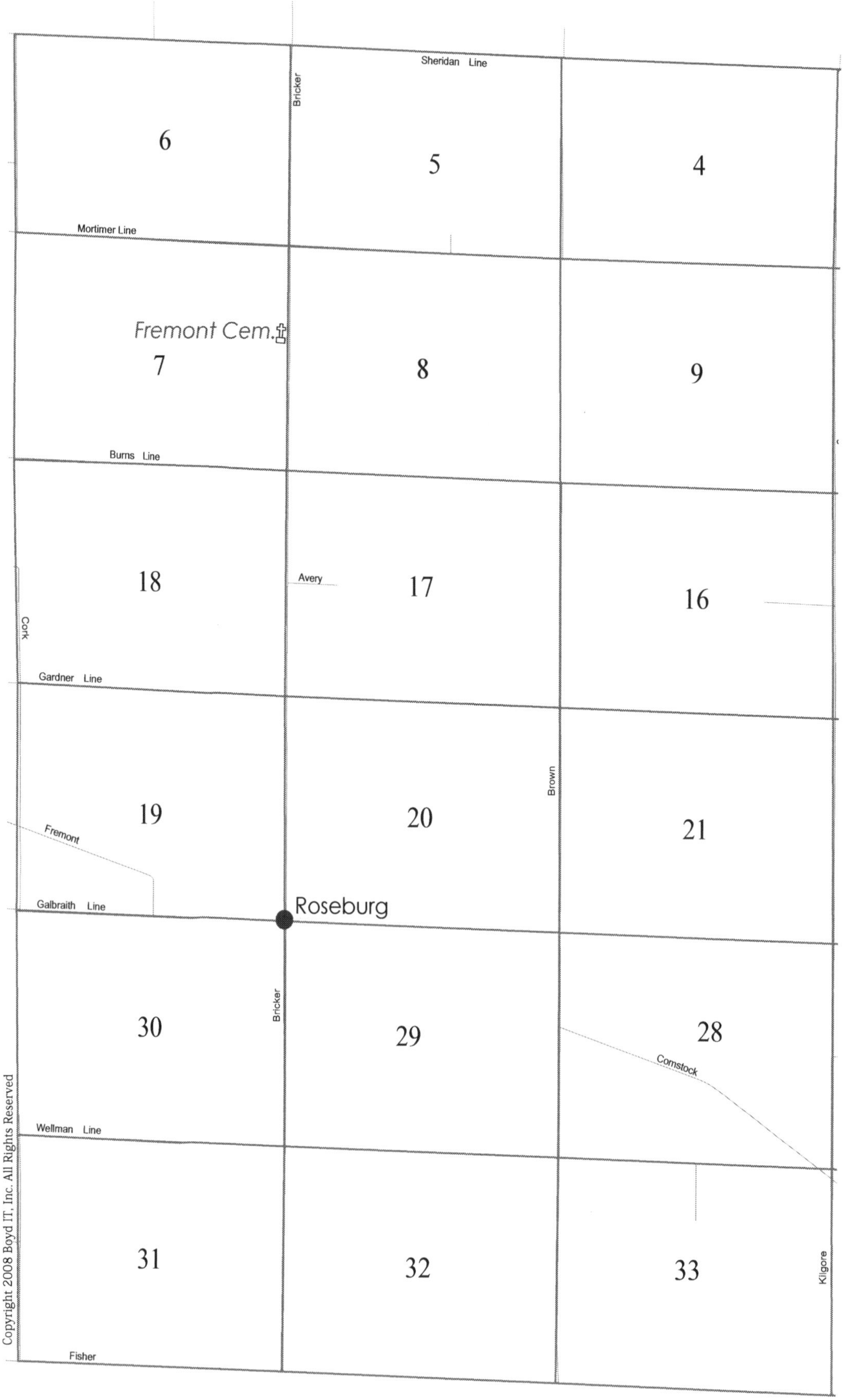

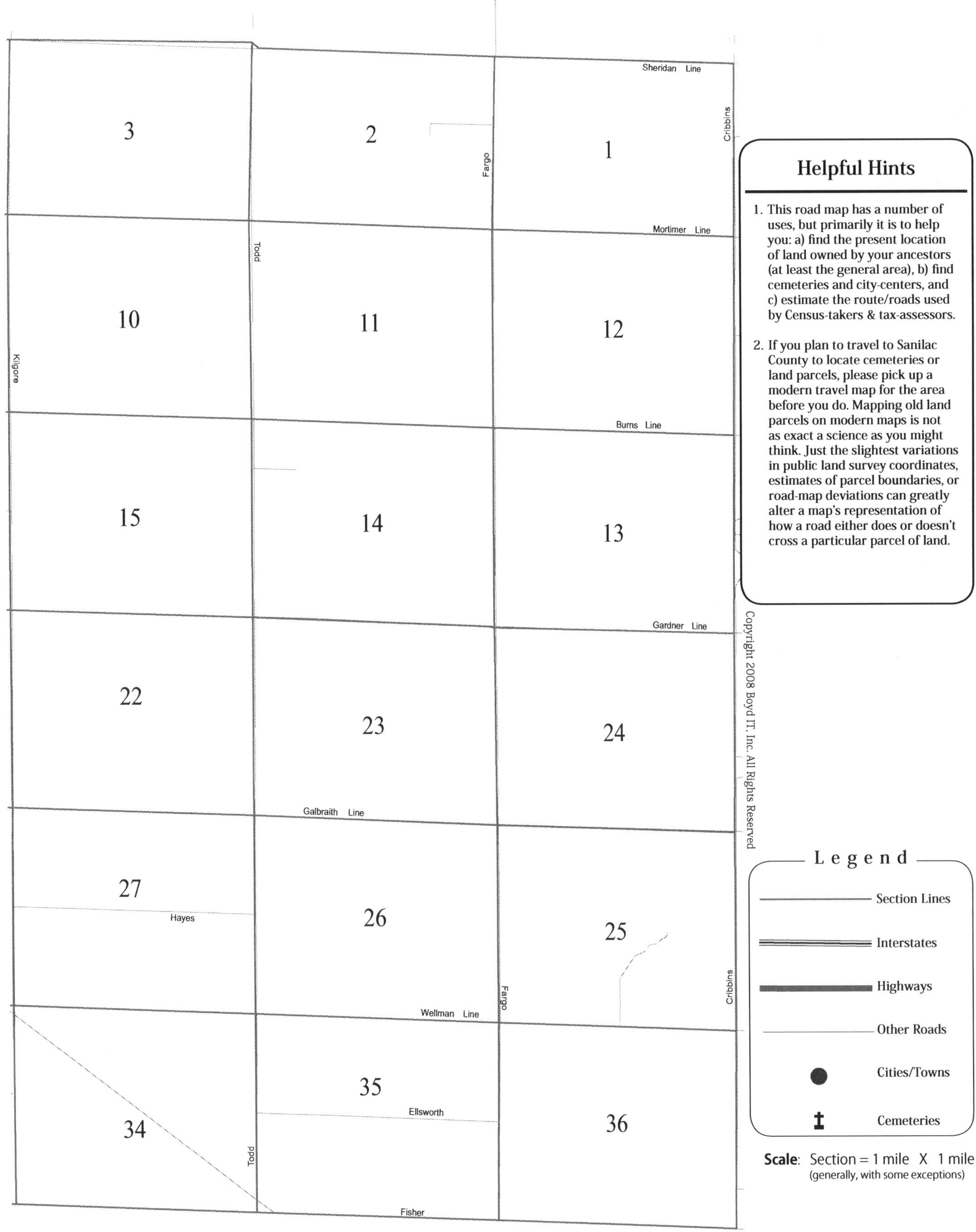
Sheridan Line
Cribbins
Fargo
Mortimer Line
Todd
Kilgore
Burns Line
Gardner Line
Galbraith Line
Hayes
Wellman Line
Ellsworth
Fisher
3
2
1
10
11
12
15
14
13
22
23
24
27
26
25
34
35
36
Helpful Hints
1. This road map has a number of uses, but primarily it is to help you: a) find the present location of land owned by your ancestors (at least the general area), b) find cemeteries and city-centers, and c) estimate the route/roads used by Census-takers & tax-assessors.
2. If you plan to travel to Sanilac County to locate cemeteries or land parcels, please pick up a modern travel map for the area before you do. Mapping old land parcels on modern maps is not as exact a science as you might think. Just the slightest variations in public land survey coordinates, estimates of parcel boundaries, or road-map deviations can greatly alter a map's representation of how a road either does or doesn't cross a particular parcel of land.
Copyright 2008 Boyd IT, Inc. All Rights Reserved
Legend
Section Lines
Interstates
Highways
Other Roads
Cities/Towns
Cemeteries
Scale: Section = 1 mile X 1 mile
(generally, with some exceptions)

Historical Map

T9-N R15-E
Michigan-Toledo Strip Meridian

Map Group 29

Cities & Towns
Roseburg

Cemeteries
Fremont Cemetery

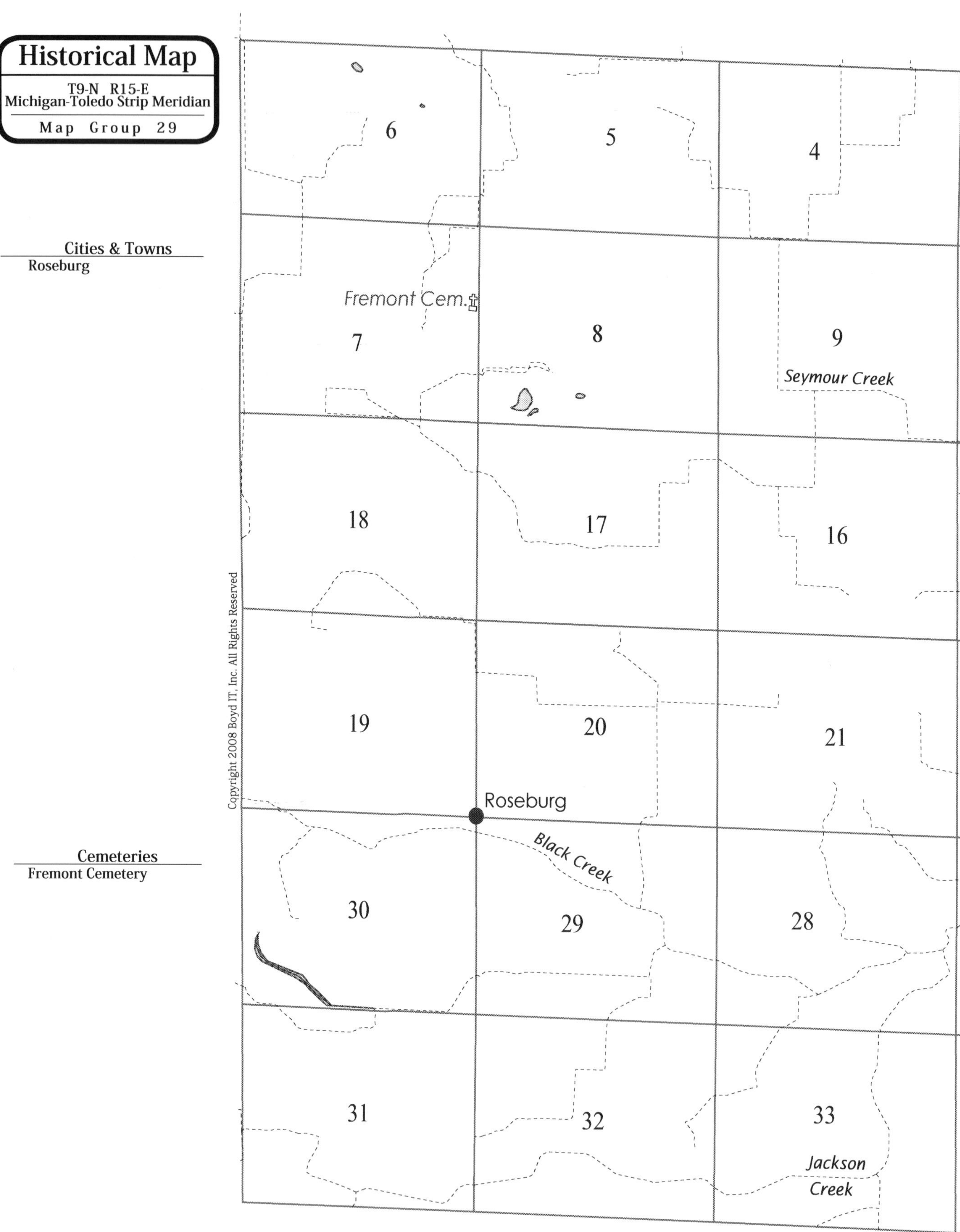

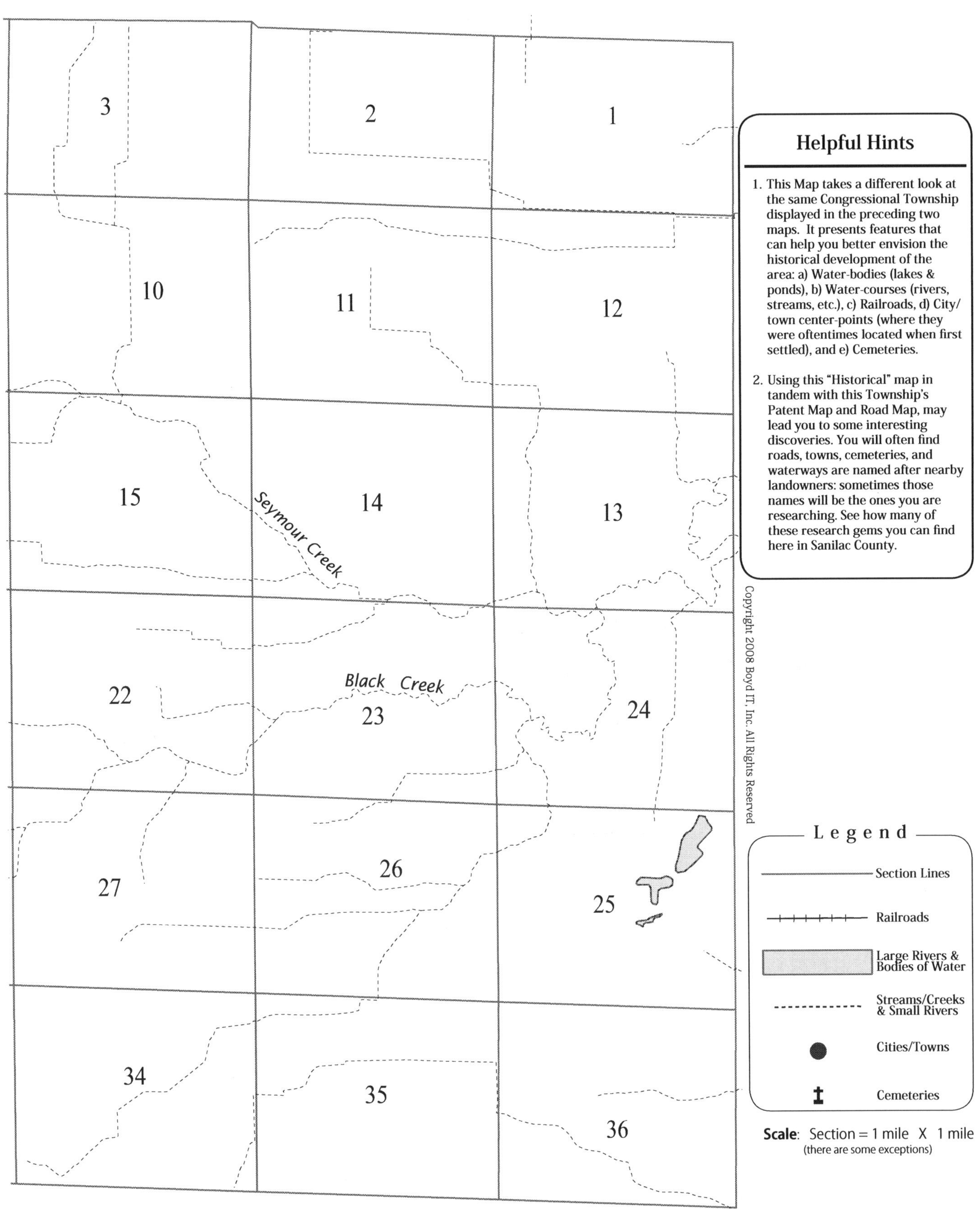
3
2
1
10
11
12
15
14
13
Seymour Creek
22
23
24
Black Creek
27
26
25
34
35
36
Helpful Hints
1. This Map takes a different look at the same Congressional Township displayed in the preceding two maps. It presents features that can help you better envision the historical development of the area: a) Water-bodies (lakes & ponds), b) Water-courses (rivers, streams, etc.), c) Railroads, d) City/town center-points (where they were oftentimes located when first settled), and e) Cemeteries.
2. Using this "Historical" map in tandem with this Township's Patent Map and Road Map, may lead you to some interesting discoveries. You will often find roads, towns, cemeteries, and waterways are named after nearby landowners: sometimes those names will be the ones you are researching. See how many of these research gems you can find here in Sanilac County.
Copyright 2008 Boyd IT, Inc. All Rights Reserved
Legend
Section Lines
Railroads
Large Rivers & Bodies of Water
Streams/Creeks & Small Rivers
Cities/Towns
Cemeteries
Scale: Section = 1 mile X 1 mile
(there are some exceptions)

Map Group 30: Index to Land Patents

Township 9-North Range 16-East (Michigan-Toledo Strip)

After you locate an individual in this Index, take note of the Section and Section Part then proceed to the Land Patent map on the pages immediately following. You should have no difficulty locating the corresponding parcel of land.

The "For More Info" Column will lead you to more information about the underlying Patents. See the *Legend* at right, and the "How to Use this Book" chapter, for more information.

LEGEND

"For More Info . . . " column

- **A** = Authority (Legislative Act, See Appendix "A")
- **B** = Block or Lot (location in Section unknown)
- **C** = Cancelled Patent
- **F** = Fractional Section
- **G** = Group (Multi-Patentee Patent, see Appendix "C")
- **V** = Overlaps another Parcel
- **R** = Re-Issued (Parcel patented more than once)

(A & G items require you to look in the Appendixes referred to above. All other Letter-designations followed by a number require you to locate line-items in this index that possess the ID number found after the letter).

ID	Individual in Patent	Sec.	Sec. Part	Date Issued	Other Counties	For More Info . . .
3409	ALLAN, William	18	E½NE	1857-02-16		A1
3410	" "	18	SWNE	1857-02-16		A1
3401	ALLEN, Thomas	19	S½SE	1857-02-16		A1
3402	" "	19	SESW	1857-02-16		A1 F
3254	ANDERSON, Daniel	6	E½SW	1857-07-01		A1
3255	" "	6	NW	1857-07-01		A1
3348	ANDREWS, John J	28	NESE	1840-11-10		A1
3349	" "	28	SWSE	1840-11-10		A1
3380	AVERY, Newell	18	W½NW	1855-10-01		A1 F
3381	" "	19	W½NW	1855-10-01		A1 F
3207	AYRAULT, Allen	11	E½SW	1837-08-21		A1 V3185
3215	BAKER, Amaziah	26	NWNW	1848-07-01		A1
3396	BAKER, Seneca	24	SESW	1844-07-12		A1
3394	BARDWELL, Rufus	27	NWSE	1848-06-01		A1
3395	" "	34	SWNE	1849-02-01		A1
3407	BEACH, William A	10	NE	1837-08-18		A1
3408	" "	10	SE	1837-08-18		A1
3383	BENNAWAY, Peter	22	SESE	1850-12-02		A1
3239	BHONONE, Charles	35	NWNE	1852-02-10		A1
3226	BOTSFORD, Amzi B	11	W½SW	1837-08-21		A1 V3185
3405	BROWN, Walter	35	NENE	1852-11-01		A1
3274	BROWNING, Francis P	17	E½NW	1835-10-15		A1
3275	" "	17	E½SW	1835-10-15		A1
3373	BUEL, Mary	3	NE	1840-11-10		A1 F
3265	BURCH, Elijah	17	W½SE	1837-08-18		A1
3266	" "	36	NESE	1837-08-21		A1
3360	BURTCH, Jonathan	13	N½NE	1837-04-01		A1
3359	" "	1	S½NE	1837-05-01		A1 F
3362	" "	35	SE	1837-05-01		A1 G17
3361	" "	36	SW	1837-05-01		A1 G16
3371	CARRINGTON, Mark	5	NWSW	1850-12-02		A1 G19
3244	CARROLL, Charles H	33	E½SE	1837-08-15		A1 G20
3245	" "	34	E½NE	1837-08-15		A1 G20
3246	" "	34	SE	1837-08-15		A1 G20
3247	" "	34	SW	1837-08-15		A1 G20
3248	" "	35	W½NW	1837-08-15		A1 G20
3240	" "	32	E½SW	1838-04-18		A1 G21
3241	" "	32	SE	1838-04-18		A1 G21
3242	" "	33	SW	1838-04-18		A1 G21
3243	" "	33	W½SE	1838-04-18		A1 G21
3334	CARROLL, John	27	E½SW	1838-09-04		A1
3335	" "	35	SENE	1850-03-01		A1
3336	" "	35	SWNE	1850-03-01		A1
3244	CARROLL, William Thomas	33	E½SE	1837-08-15		A1 G20
3245	" "	34	E½NE	1837-08-15		A1 G20
3246	" "	34	SE	1837-08-15		A1 G20

ID	Individual in Patent	Sec.	Sec. Part	Date Issued	Other Counties	For More Info . . .
3247	CARROLL, William Thomas (Cont'd)	34	SW	1837-08-15		A1 G20
3248	" "	35	W½NW	1837-08-15		A1 G20
3228	CHASE, Anthony M	28	NWNE	1844-07-10		A1
3379	CHASE, Nathan	29	NENW	1848-07-01		A1
3377	CHASE, Nathan B	18	W½SW	1848-07-01		A1
3378	" "	17	NESE	1850-12-02		A1 G23
3273	CICOTTE, Francis	15	NE	1837-08-16		A1
3289	CLARK, George	18	NESW	1857-02-16		A1 F
3290	" "	18	SENW	1857-02-16		A1
3337	CLARKE, John	18	E½SE	1837-08-21		A1
3338	" "	27	NE	1837-08-21		A1
3370	CLEAVELAND, Luther J	14	NWNE	1855-10-01		A1
3411	CLINE, William	35	NWSW	1852-11-01		A1
3182	COBURN, Abner	1	N½NE	1837-05-01		A1 F
3183	" "	1	NW	1837-05-01		A1 F
3184	" "	11	E½NE	1837-05-01		A1
3186	" "	11	W½NE	1837-05-01		A1
3187	" "	11	W½SE	1837-05-01		A1
3189	" "	12	W½NE	1837-05-01		A1
3190	" "	12	W½SE	1837-05-01		A1
3191	" "	13	NW	1837-05-01		A1
3192	" "	14	NW	1837-05-01		A1
3193	" "	14	SW	1837-05-01		A1
3194	" "	2	E½SE	1837-05-01		A1
3195	" "	2	NE	1837-05-01		A1
3199	" "	30	E½SW	1837-05-01		A1
3200	" "	30	SE	1837-05-01		A1
3188	" "	12	E½SE	1837-05-03		A1
3198	" "	2	W½SE	1837-05-03		A1
3201	" "	31	SW	1837-05-03		A1
3202	" "	31	W½NW	1837-05-03		A1
3203	" "	31	W½SE	1837-05-03		A1
3196	" "	2	NW	1837-08-14		A1 F
3197	" "	2	SW	1837-08-14		A1
3185	" "	11	SW	1837-08-18		A1 V3207, 3226
3258	COOK, David	22	NENW	1844-07-10		A1
3315	CORNELL, Hiram	4	SE	1844-07-10		A1
3403	COXE, Thomas	26	NWSW	1850-03-01		A1
3301	CRAMPTON, Henry B	20	W½NW	1837-08-07		A1
3302	" "	6	NE	1837-08-07		A1
3319	CROCKET, James	8	W½SE	1857-07-01		A1
3285	CUMMINGS, Gaylord	12	NENE	1837-08-21		A1
3386	DAVIS, Phineas	17	W½SW	1906-05-01		A1
3398	DAVIS, Simon P	5	N½NW	1857-07-01		A1
3399	DE GROATE, STEPHEN C	29	E½NE	1840-11-10		A1
3305	DELAVAN, Henry W	20	E½NW	1837-08-16		A1
3306	" "	20	NE	1837-08-16		A1
3307	" "	20	SW	1837-08-16		A1
3308	" "	29	SE	1837-08-16		A1
3309	" "	29	SW	1837-08-16		A1
3310	" "	32	NE	1837-08-16		A1
3311	" "	32	NW	1837-08-16		A1
3312	" "	33	NE	1837-08-16		A1
3313	" "	33	NW	1837-08-16		A1
3314	" "	34	NW	1837-08-16		A1
3339	DEVINE, John	25	SENE	1852-02-10		A1
3387	DIMOND, Reuben B	13	NWSW	1852-02-10		A1
3388	" "	14	NENE	1852-02-10		A1
3227	DURR, Andreas	21	W½SW	1838-09-04		A1
3320	ERITY, James G	6	W½SW	1855-10-01		A1 G35
3267	FARNSWORTH, Elon	36	NW	1837-08-21		A1 G38
3208	FISH, Allen	36	W½SE	1852-02-10		A1
3318	FRALICK, Jacob	27	SENW	1848-07-01		A1
3340	GALBRAITH, John	20	E½SE	1840-10-10		A1
3341	" "	21	E½SW	1840-10-10		A1
3342	" "	21	SE	1840-10-10		A1
3346	" "	28	SW	1840-10-10		A1
3344	" "	24	SWSW	1840-11-10		A1
3343	" "	24	NWSW	1844-07-10		A1
3345	" "	28	NENE	1844-07-10		A1
3412	GALBRAITH, William	20	W½SE	1840-11-10		A1
3413	" "	29	NWNE	1840-11-10		A1
3325	GEEL, James M	17	W½NE	1837-04-01		A1 G42

ID	Individual in Patent	Sec.	Sec. Part	Date Issued	Other Counties	For More Info . . .
3321	GEEL, James M (Cont'd)	5	E½SW	1837-05-03		A1
3322	" "	5	N½NE	1837-05-03		A1
3323	" "	5	S½NW	1837-05-03		A1
3324	" "	8	E½NW	1837-05-03		A1
3347	GRAHAM, John	10	S½NW	1848-07-01		A1
3414	GRAHAM, William	10	N½NW	1844-07-10		A1
3240	GRANGER, Josephus	32	E½SW	1838-04-18		A1 G21
3241	" "	32	SE	1838-04-18		A1 G21
3242	" "	33	SW	1838-04-18		A1 G21
3243	" "	33	W½SE	1838-04-18		A1 G21
3415	GUTHRIE, William	19	SENE	1857-07-01		A1
3416	" "	19	SENW	1857-07-01		A1
3417	" "	19	W½NE	1857-07-01		A1
3212	HALL, Almira	9	SENW	1850-03-01		A1
3316	HALL, Ira	9	NENW	1850-03-01		A1
3350	HANES, John R	26	NENW	1850-03-01		A1
3351	" "	26	SWNW	1850-03-01		A1
3418	HANES, William	23	SWSE	1850-03-01		A1
3303	HANSEN, Henry	9	SWNW	1857-02-16		A1
3304	HARDING, Henry	17	W½NW	1857-07-01		A1
3256	HARRINGTON, Daniel	13	SENE	1844-07-10		A1
3352	HAYNES, John R	23	NENW	1850-12-02		A1
3213	HEDRICK, Alphred	25	SWNW	1850-12-02		A1
3375	HICKEY, Morris	25	NENE	1852-02-10		A1
3382	HOLLISTER, Norton	25	W½SE	1844-07-10		A1
3268	JONES, Enoch	1	SW	1838-04-20		A1 G48
3269	" "	11	E½SE	1838-04-20		A1 G48
3270	" "	12	NW	1838-04-20		A1 G48
3271	" "	12	SW	1838-04-20		A1 G48
3367	KE_Y_KE_SIK,	31	E½SE	1837-08-21		A1
3214	KING, Alvinza	25	NENW	1848-07-01		A1
3249	KINNE, Chester D	28	NWSE	1840-11-10		A1
3250	" "	28	SWNE	1840-11-10		A1
3391	KNOX, Robert	28	SENE	1840-11-10		A1
3390	" "	21	SWNW	1844-07-10		A1
3331	LEONHARD, Johann G	28	W½NW	1838-09-04		A1
3332	LEONHARD, Johann W	28	E½NW	1838-09-04		A1
3291	LESTER, George S	26	SWSW	1852-02-10		A1
3317	LOUNT, Ira	25	SENW	1853-11-01		A1
3268	LUCE, Bartlett A	1	SW	1838-04-20		A1 G48
3269	" "	11	E½SE	1838-04-20		A1 G48
3270	" "	12	NW	1838-04-20		A1 G48
3271	" "	12	SW	1838-04-20		A1 G48
3371	LUCE, Benjamin F	5	NWSW	1850-12-02		A1 G19
3234	" "	7	NWSE	1852-02-10		A1
3233	" "	5	SENE	1852-12-01		A1 F
3392	LYNN, Robert	10	SWSW	1848-07-01		A1
3282	MAIRE, Frederick	18	NENW	1857-07-01		A1
3283	" "	7	SESW	1857-07-01		A1
3284	" "	7	W½SW	1857-07-01		A1
3369	MASON, Lorenzo M	17	NENE	1852-02-10		A1
3374	MASTERSON, Michael	3	SESE	1837-11-02		A1
3259	MCCLURE, David	21	NWNW	1844-07-10		A1
3393	MCCLURE, Robert	27	W½SW	1838-09-04		A1
3389	MCGRATH, Richard	25	NESE	1852-02-10		A1
3320	MILES, Cyrus	6	W½SW	1855-10-01		A1 G35
3378	MILLER, John	17	NESE	1850-12-02		A1 G23
3376	NAGESIK,	27	S½SE	1837-08-21		A1
3419	NICHOLSON, William	22	W½SE	1838-09-04		A1
3384	NISBET, Peter	21	NE	1840-11-10		A1
3262	NORTHRUP, Duthan	7	SENE	1854-06-15		A1
3366	ORVIS, Josiah S	13	NESW	1837-08-21		A1
3406	ORVIS, Willard	13	SWNE	1837-08-21		A1
3325	PARMELY, Lemuel	17	W½NE	1837-04-01		A1 G42
3420	PEASLEE, William	36	SWNE	1854-06-15		A1
3326	POTTS, James	5	NWSE	1857-07-01		A1
3251	REEVE, Christopher	8	SESE	1852-02-10		A1
3353	RYEN, John	28	SESE	1838-09-04		A1
3253	SANBORN, Cummings	24	SWSE	1850-03-01		A1
3252	" "	14	SWNE	1850-12-02		A1
3327	SANBORN, James	30	NWNE	1850-12-02		A1
3263	SANDERSON, Edward	36	SESE	1857-07-01		A1
3232	SCHULZ, August	19	NESE	1857-07-01		A1

ID	Individual in Patent	Sec.	Sec. Part	Date Issued	Other Counties	For More Info . . .
3261	SHELL, David	23	SESE	1844-07-10		A1
3260	" "	21	NENW	1848-07-01		A1
3355	SHELL, John	22	E½SW	1844-07-10		A1
3354	" "	17	SESE	1848-06-01		A1
3356	" "	25	NWNW	1848-07-01		A1
3372	SHELL, Mark	15	SENW	1844-07-10		A1
3385	SHELL, Peter	15	E½SW	1844-07-10		A1
3361	SIBLEY, Sylvester	36	SW	1837-05-01		A1 G16
3400	" "	1	SE	1837-08-07		A1
3267	" "	36	NW	1837-08-21		A1 G38
3362	SILBEY, Sylvester	35	SE	1837-05-01		A1 G17
3230	SLY, Asa M	34	NWNE	1848-07-01		A1
3229	" "	23	SWSW	1849-02-01		A1
3293	SMITH, George	22	W½SW	1840-11-10		A1
3292	" "	22	SWNE	1848-07-01		A1
3294	" "	23	SESW	1850-03-01		A1
3422	SMITH, William	22	W½NW	1844-07-10		A1
3421	" "	22	SENW	1848-07-01		A1
3277	STEEVENS, Frederick H	30	E½NE	1837-05-01		A1
3276	" "	29	W½NW	1838-04-20		A1
3278	" "	31	E½NW	1838-04-20		A1 F
3279	" "	31	NE	1838-04-20		A1 F
3368	STEPHENS, Kinyon	27	W½NW	1844-07-10		A1
3211	STEVENS, Allen R	25	NWNE	1849-02-01		A1
3209	" "	23	NWNW	1855-10-01		A1
3210	" "	23	SWNW	1855-10-01		A1
3231	STEVENS, Asa	13	SESW	1856-01-10		A1
3280	STEVENS, Frederick H	30	W½NW	1838-04-20		A1
3281	" "	30	W½SW	1838-04-20		A1
3358	STEVENS, Jonathan B	24	NWSE	1855-10-01		A1
3397	STEVENS, Seneca J	27	NENW	1848-07-01		A1
3328	SWAFFER, James	18	W½SE	1857-02-16		A1
3295	TERRIL, George	12	SENE	1837-08-21		A1
3333	THEABO, John A	25	SESE	1854-06-15		A1
3272	THEBOULT, Enos	30	NENW	1850-12-02		A1
3267	TROWBRIDGE, Charles C	36	NW	1837-08-21		A1 G38
3357	VAN CAMP, JOHN	27	NESE	1849-02-01		A1
3404	VAN CAMP, TUNIS	18	NWNE	1857-07-01		A1
3296	WARD, George	4	NE	1844-07-10		A1 F
3297	" "	9	NWNW	1852-02-10		A1
3286	WEBSTER, George C	7	NESW	1857-07-01		A1
3287	" "	7	SENW	1857-07-01		A1 F
3288	" "	7	W½NW	1857-07-01		A1
3206	WILLITS, Abram	30	SENW	1856-01-10		A1 C R3205
3205	WILLITS, Abram W	30	SENW	1857-03-10		A1 F R3206
3204	WILLITTS, Abraham W	30	SWNE	1850-12-02		A1
3222	WIXSON, Amos	3	NW	1844-07-10		A1 F
3219	" "	15	W½NW	1848-06-01		A1
3220	" "	15	W½SW	1848-06-01		A1
3216	" "	10	N½SW	1848-07-01		A1
3217	" "	15	NENW	1848-07-01		A1
3218	" "	15	SE	1848-07-01		A1
3221	" "	29	SENW	1848-07-01		A1
3223	" "	4	SW	1848-07-01		A1
3224	" "	9	N½SE	1848-07-01		A1
3225	" "	9	NE	1848-07-01		A1
3235	WIXSON, Benjamin	4	N½NW	1848-09-01		A1
3236	" "	4	SENW	1848-09-01		A1
3237	" "	4	SWNW	1849-02-01		A1
3238	" "	9	NESW	1850-03-01		A1
3329	WIXSON, Joel	21	SENW	1848-09-01		A1
3330	" "	23	SENW	1855-10-01		A1
3363	WIXSON, Joshua	3	NESE	1844-07-10		A1
3364	" "	3	SW	1844-07-10		A1
3365	" "	3	W½SE	1844-07-10		A1
3264	WOODRUFF, Edward	10	SESW	1848-07-01		A1
3257	WOODWARD, Daniel	32	W½SW	1837-04-15		A1
3298	WRIGHT, George	26	NENE	1848-06-01		A1
3299	" "	26	NWNE	1848-07-01		A1
3300	" "	26	SENE	1848-07-01		A1

Patent Map

T9-N R16-E
Michigan-Toledo Strip Meridian

Map Group 30

Township Statistics

Parcels Mapped	:	241
Number of Patents	:	194
Number of Individuals	:	136
Patentees Identified	:	133
Number of Surnames	:	108
Multi-Patentee Parcels	:	20
Oldest Patent Date	:	10/15/1835
Most Recent Patent	:	5/1/1906
Block/Lot Parcels	:	0
Parcels Re - Issued	:	1
Parcels that Overlap	:	3
Cities and Towns	:	1
Cemeteries	:	4

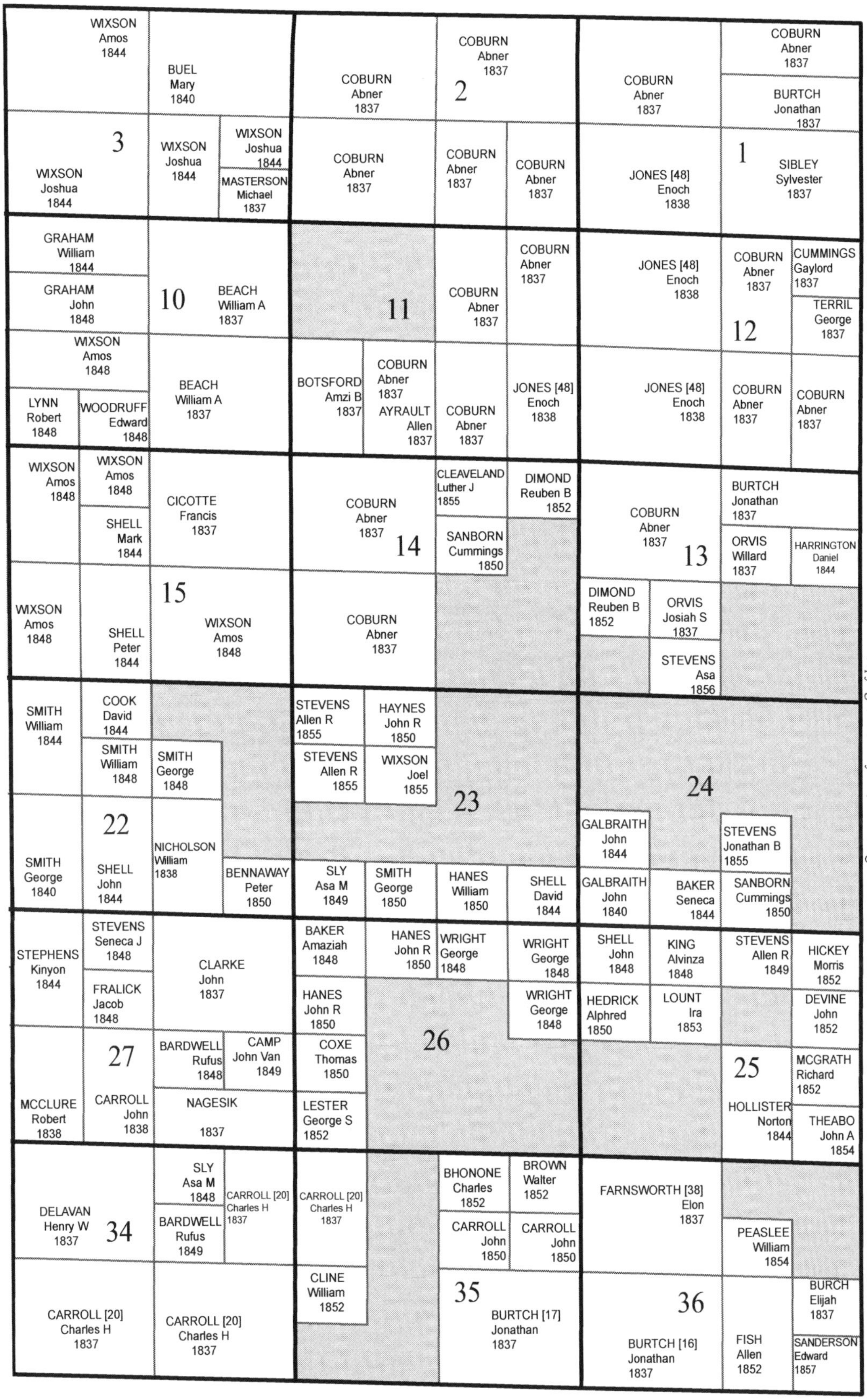

Helpful Hints

1. This Map's INDEX can be found on the preceding pages.
2. Refer to Map "C" to see where this Township lies within Sanilac County, Michigan.
3. Numbers within square brackets [ ] denote a multi-patentee land parcel (multi-owner). Refer to Appendix "C" for a full list of members in this group.
4. Areas that look to be crowded with Patentees usually indicate multiple sales of the same parcel (Re-issues) or Overlapping parcels. See this Township's Index for an explanation of these and other circumstances that might explain "odd" groupings of Patentees on this map.

Legend

- Patent Boundary
- Section Boundary
- No Patents Found (or Outside County)
- 1., 2., 3., ... Lot Numbers (when beside a name)
- [ ] Group Number (see Appendix "C")

Scale: Section = 1 mile X 1 mile (generally, with some exceptions)

Road Map

T9-N R16-E
Michigan-Toledo Strip Meridian

Map Group 30

Cities & Towns

Amadore

Cemeteries

Carmen Cemetery
Lakeview Cemetery
Wixson Cemetery
Worth Township Cemetery

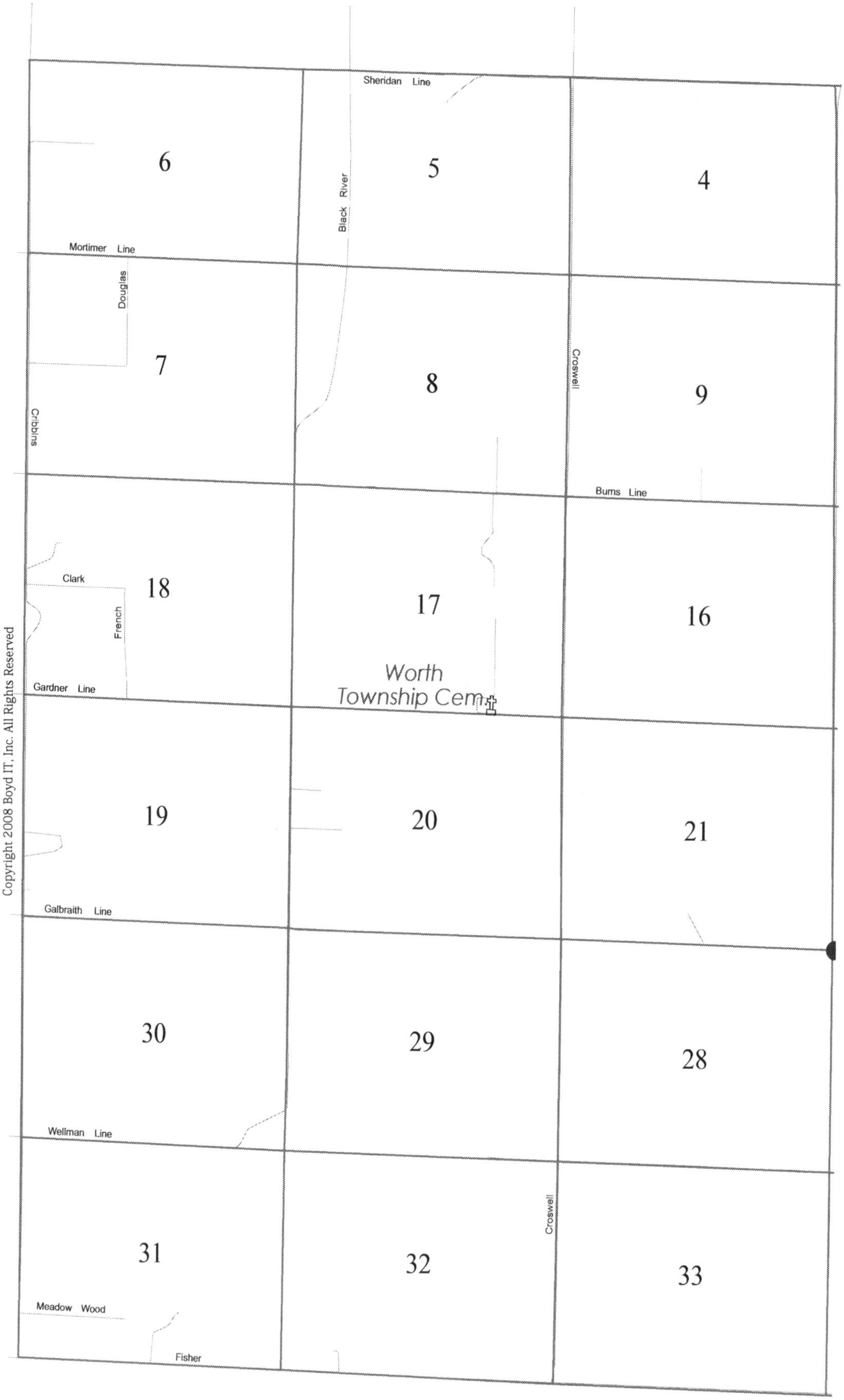

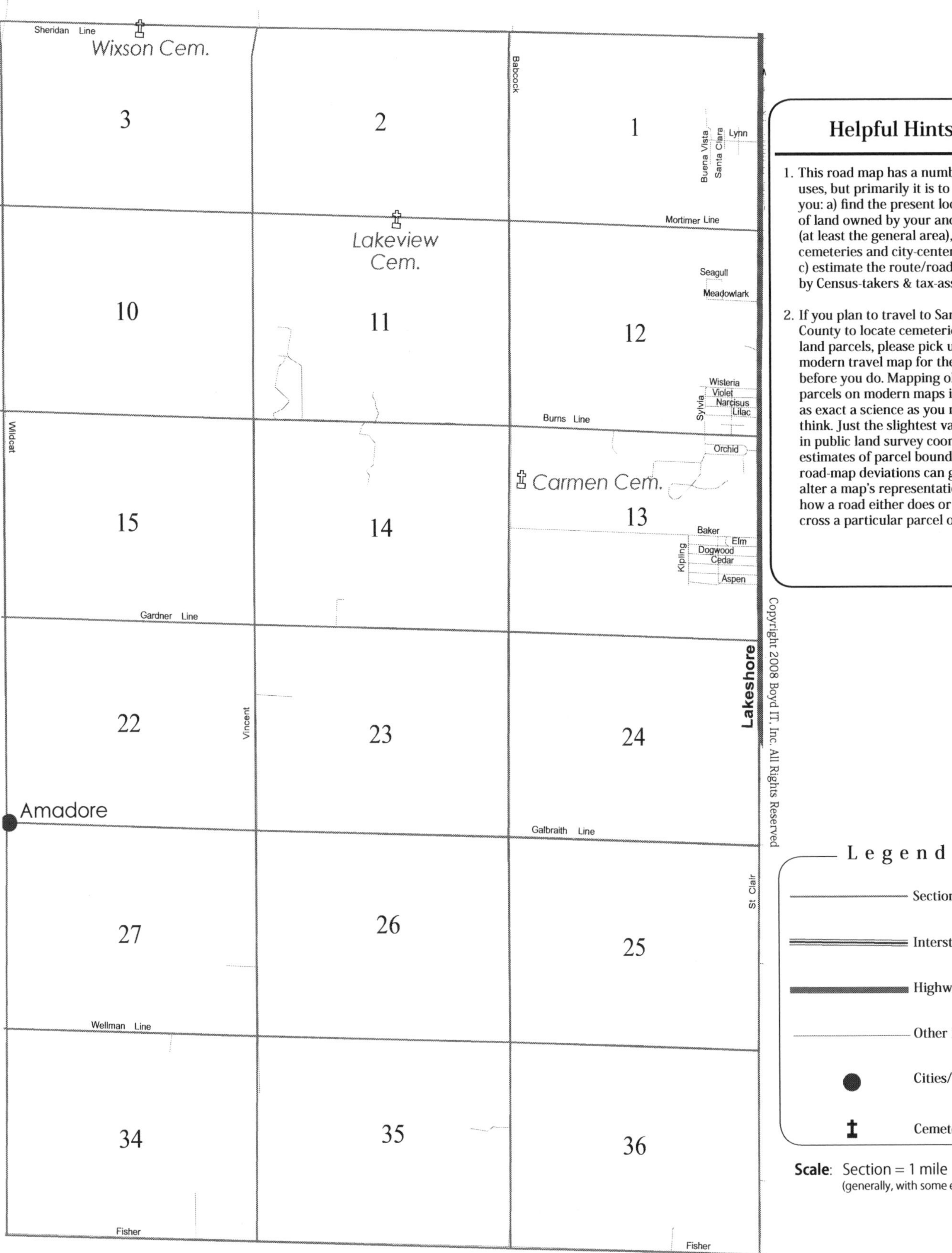

Helpful Hints

1. This road map has a number of uses, but primarily it is to help you: a) find the present location of land owned by your ancestors (at least the general area), b) find cemeteries and city-centers, and c) estimate the route/roads used by Census-takers & tax-assessors.
2. If you plan to travel to Sanilac County to locate cemeteries or land parcels, please pick up a modern travel map for the area before you do. Mapping old land parcels on modern maps is not as exact a science as you might think. Just the slightest variations in public land survey coordinates, estimates of parcel boundaries, or road-map deviations can greatly alter a map's representation of how a road either does or doesn't cross a particular parcel of land.

Legend

- Section Lines
- Interstates
- Highways
- Other Roads
- Cities/Towns
- Cemeteries

Scale: Section = 1 mile X 1 mile
(generally, with some exceptions)

Historical Map

T9-N R16-E
Michigan-Toledo Strip Meridian

Map Group 30

Cities & Towns
Amadore

Cemeteries
Carmen Cemetery
Lakeview Cemetery
Wixson Cemetery
Worth Township Cemetery

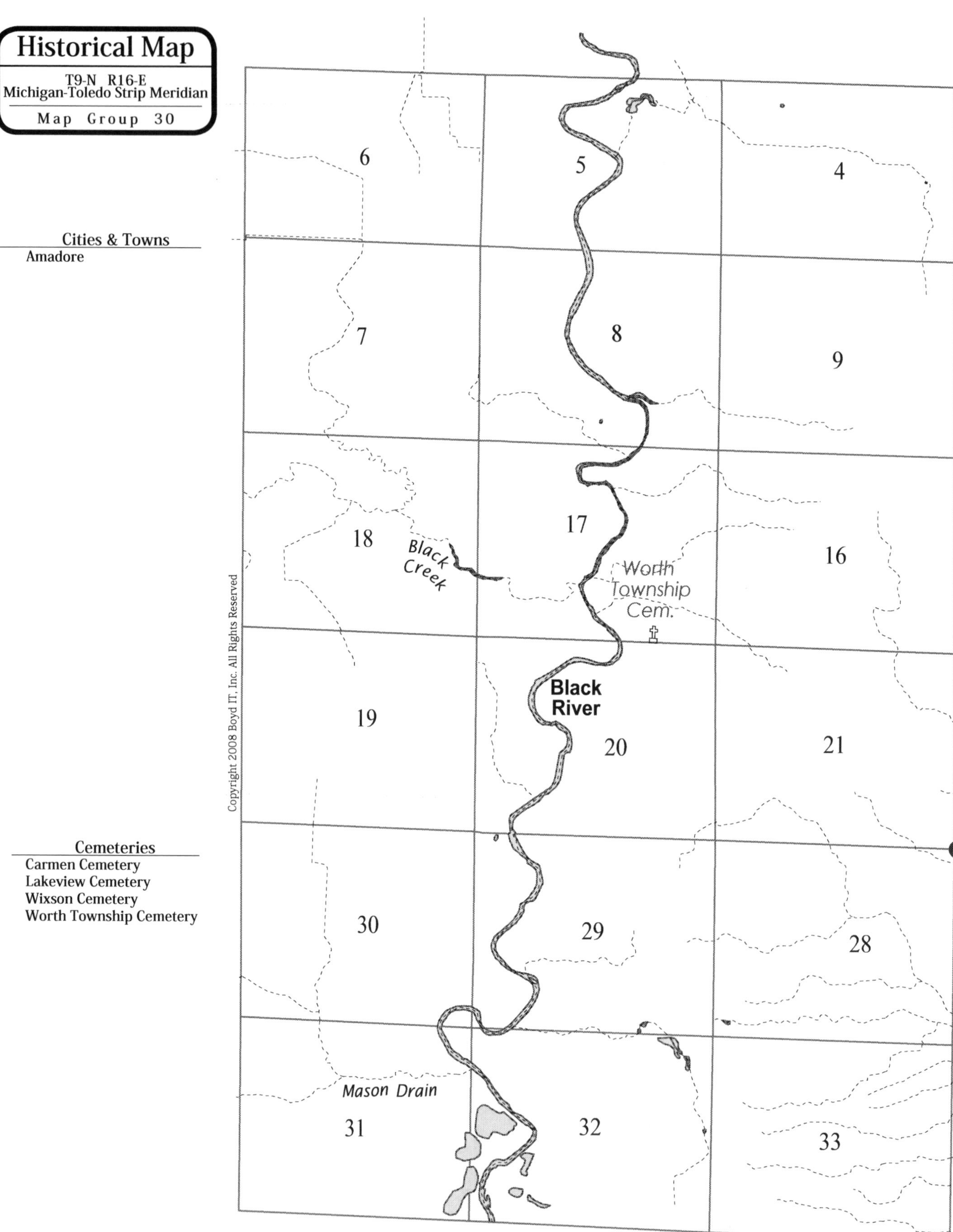

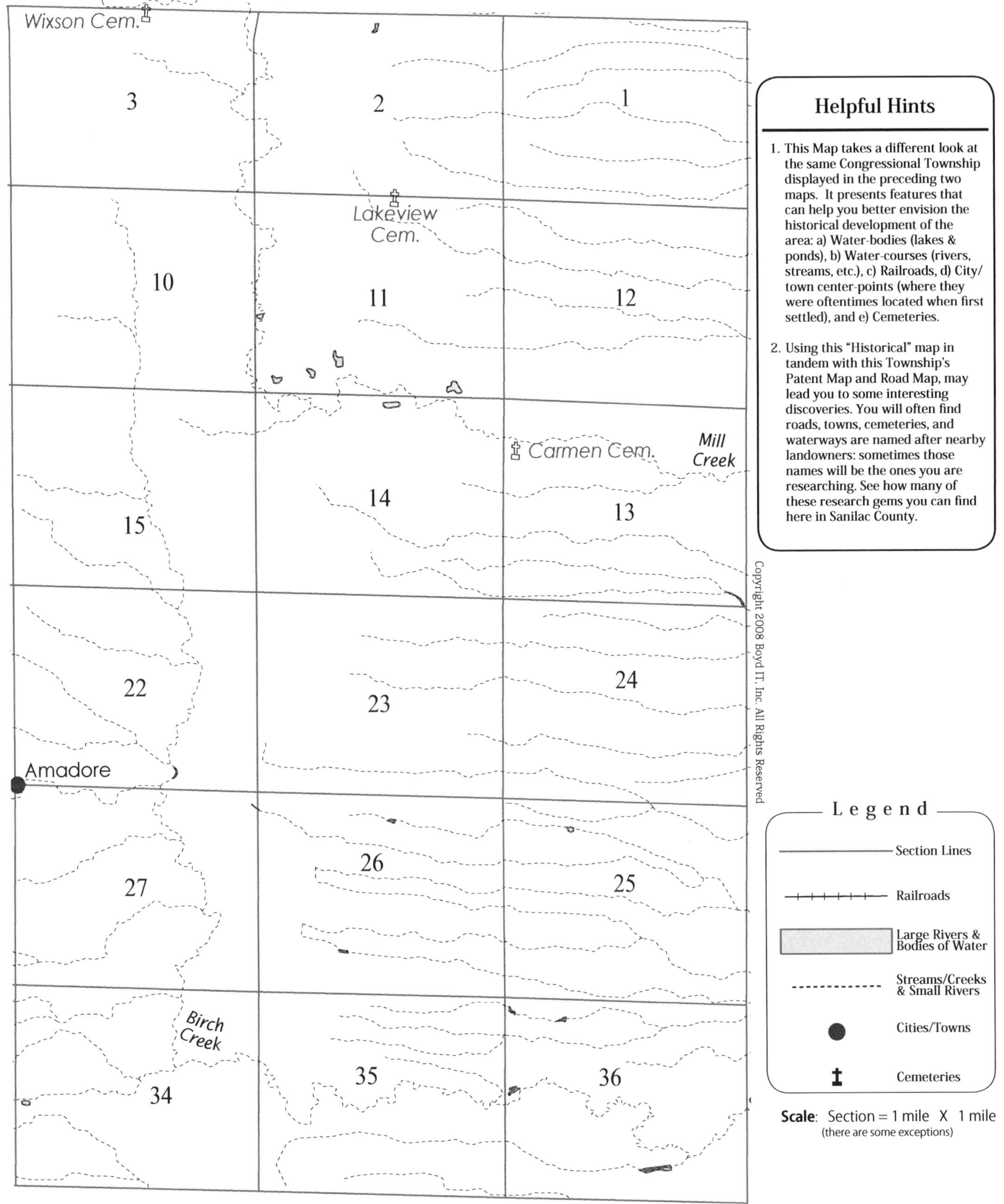

Helpful Hints

1. This Map takes a different look at the same Congressional Township displayed in the preceding two maps. It presents features that can help you better envision the historical development of the area: a) Water-bodies (lakes & ponds), b) Water-courses (rivers, streams, etc.), c) Railroads, d) City/town center-points (where they were oftentimes located when first settled), and e) Cemeteries.
2. Using this "Historical" map in tandem with this Township's Patent Map and Road Map, may lead you to some interesting discoveries. You will often find roads, towns, cemeteries, and waterways are named after nearby landowners: sometimes those names will be the ones you are researching. See how many of these research gems you can find here in Sanilac County.

Scale: Section = 1 mile X 1 mile
(there are some exceptions)

Map Group 31: Index to Land Patents

Township 9-North Range 17-East (Michigan-Toledo Strip)

After you locate an individual in this Index, take note of the Section and Section Part then proceed to the Land Patent map on the pages immediately following. You should have no difficulty locating the corresponding parcel of land.

The "For More Info" Column will lead you to more information about the underlying Patents. See the *Legend* at right, and the "How to Use this Book" chapter, for more information.

LEGEND

"For More Info . . . " column

A = Authority (Legislative Act, See Appendix "A")
B = Block or Lot (location in Section unknown)
C = Cancelled Patent
F = Fractional Section
G = Group (Multi-Patentee Patent, see Appendix "C")
V = Overlaps another Parcel
R = Re-Issued (Parcel patented more than once)

(A & G items require you to look in the Appendixes referred to above. All other Letter-designations followed by a number require you to locate line-items in this index that possess the ID number found after the letter).

ID	Individual in Patent	Sec.	Sec. Part	Date Issued	Other Counties	For More Info . . .
3426	AYRAULT, Allen	18	N½S½	1837-08-21		A1 F
3427	" "	30	N½NE	1837-08-21		A1
3428	" "	7	N	1837-08-21		A1 F
3429	BUTLER, Charles	30	S½NE	1837-08-21		A1 F
3430	" "	30	SE	1837-08-21		A1
3431	" "	31	SWSE	1837-08-21		A1
3435	CARRINGTON, Joel	6	N	1837-04-10		A1 F
3447	CHASE, Nathan	31	SESE	1837-08-15		A1 F
3436	CLARK, John	31	N½SE	1837-08-16		A1 F
3437	" "	31	NE	1837-08-16		A1 F
3423	COBURN, Abner	18	W½NW	1837-05-03		A1 F
3424	" "	7	S½	1837-05-03		A1 F
3453	CONAT, William	31	NWNW	1855-10-01		A1
3452	" "	31	NENW	1856-01-10		A1
3449	DIAMOND, Reuben B	6	S	1837-08-16		A1
3454	HALL, William	19	NWSW	1853-11-01		A1
3425	HOGAN, Abraham	31	SWNW	1844-07-10		A1
3448	HOLLISTER, Norton	31	NESW	1844-07-10		A1
3442	KELSEY, Joseph L	19	SE	1838-09-04		A1 F
3451	MILLS, William C	18	E½NW	1839-08-03		A1
3443	ORVIS, Josiah S	19	NENW	1837-08-21		A1
3444	" "	19	S	1838-09-04		A1 F
3450	ORVIS, Willard	18	S	1837-08-21		A1 F
3445	OWEN, Leonard S	31	NWSW	1837-08-21		A1
3446	" "	31	SENW	1837-08-21		A1
3434	PORTER, Ira	6	N½3SW	1837-04-10		A1 F
3433	REYNOLDS, George	30	NENW	1852-02-10		A1
3432	SANDERSON, Edward	31	S½SW	1857-07-01		A1
3438	VAN CAMP, JOHN	19	SWSW	1852-02-10		A1
3439	" "	30	NWNW	1852-02-10		A1
3441	" "	30	SWNW	1855-10-01		A1
3440	" "	30	SW	1856-01-10		A1

Lots-Sec. 6
N PORTER, Ira 1837
N CARRINGTON, Joel 1837

6

DIAMOND Reuben B 1837

Lots-Sec. 7
N AYRAULT, Allen 1837

7

COBURN Abner 1837

MILLS William C 1839

COBURN Abner 1837

18

AYRAULT Allen 1837

ORVIS Willard 1837

ORVIS Josiah S 1837

19

HALL William 1853

ORVIS Josiah S 1838

KELSEY Joseph L 1838

CAMP John Van 1852

CAMP John Van 1852

REYNOLDS George 1852

AYRAULT Allen 1837

CAMP John Van 1855

30

BUTLER Charles 1837

BUTLER Charles 1837

CAMP John Van 1856

CONAT William 1855

CONAT William 1856

CLARK John 1837

HOGAN Abraham 1844

OWEN Leonard S 1837

31

OWEN Leonard S 1837

HOLLISTER Norton 1844

CLARK John 1837

SANDERSON Edward 1857

BUTLER Charles 1837

CHASE Nathan 1837

32

Patent Map

T9-N R17-E
Michigan-Toledo Strip Meridian

Map Group 31

Township Statistics

Parcels Mapped	:	32
Number of Patents	:	28
Number of Individuals	:	20
Patentees Identified	:	20
Number of Surnames	:	19
Multi-Patentee Parcels	:	0
Oldest Patent Date	:	4/10/1837
Most Recent Patent	:	7/1/1857
Block/Lot Parcels	:	3
Parcels Re - Issued	:	0
Parcels that Overlap	:	0
Cities and Towns	:	5
Cemeteries	:	0

Note: the area contained in this map amounts to far less than a full Township. Therefore, its contents are completely on this single page (instead of a "normal" 2-page spread).

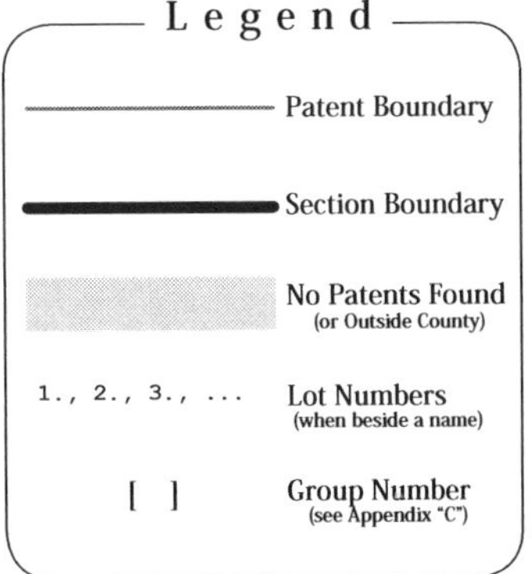

Scale: Section = 1 mile X 1 mile
(generally, with some exceptions)

Road Map

T9-N R17-E
Michigan-Toledo Strip Meridian

Map Group 31

Note: the area contained in this map amounts to far less than a full Township. Therefore, its contents are completely on this single page (instead of a "normal" 2-page spread).

Cities & Towns

Birch Beach
Blue Water Beach
Great Lakes Beach
Huronia Heights
Lexington Heights

Cemeteries

None

Kimmel
Meloche
Highview
6
Chippewa
Belair
Kilkare
Roger
7
Crest
Cherry
Hill
Zenith
Yale
Vine
Walbridge
Satinwood
Worth
Rosewood
Pine
Nymph
Oak
Lexington Heights
Maple
Laurel
Juniper
Woodside
Ivy
Grove
Forest
Huron
Bay
18
Elm
Dogwood
Cedar
Birchcrest
Aspen
Great Lakes Beach
Willow
Shoreward
Lakewood
Woodland
Portal
Huronia Heights
Elmwood
Maplewood
Southwood
Beechwood
Birchtree
Blue Water Beach
Blue Water
Cardinal
Sunset
Woodbine
Joy
Dian
19
Birch Beach
Lakeshore
St Clair
30
Roehl
31
32
Hollister
Copyright 2008 Boyd IT, Inc. All Rights Reserved

Legend
Section Lines
Interstates
Highways
Other Roads
Cities/Towns
Cemeteries

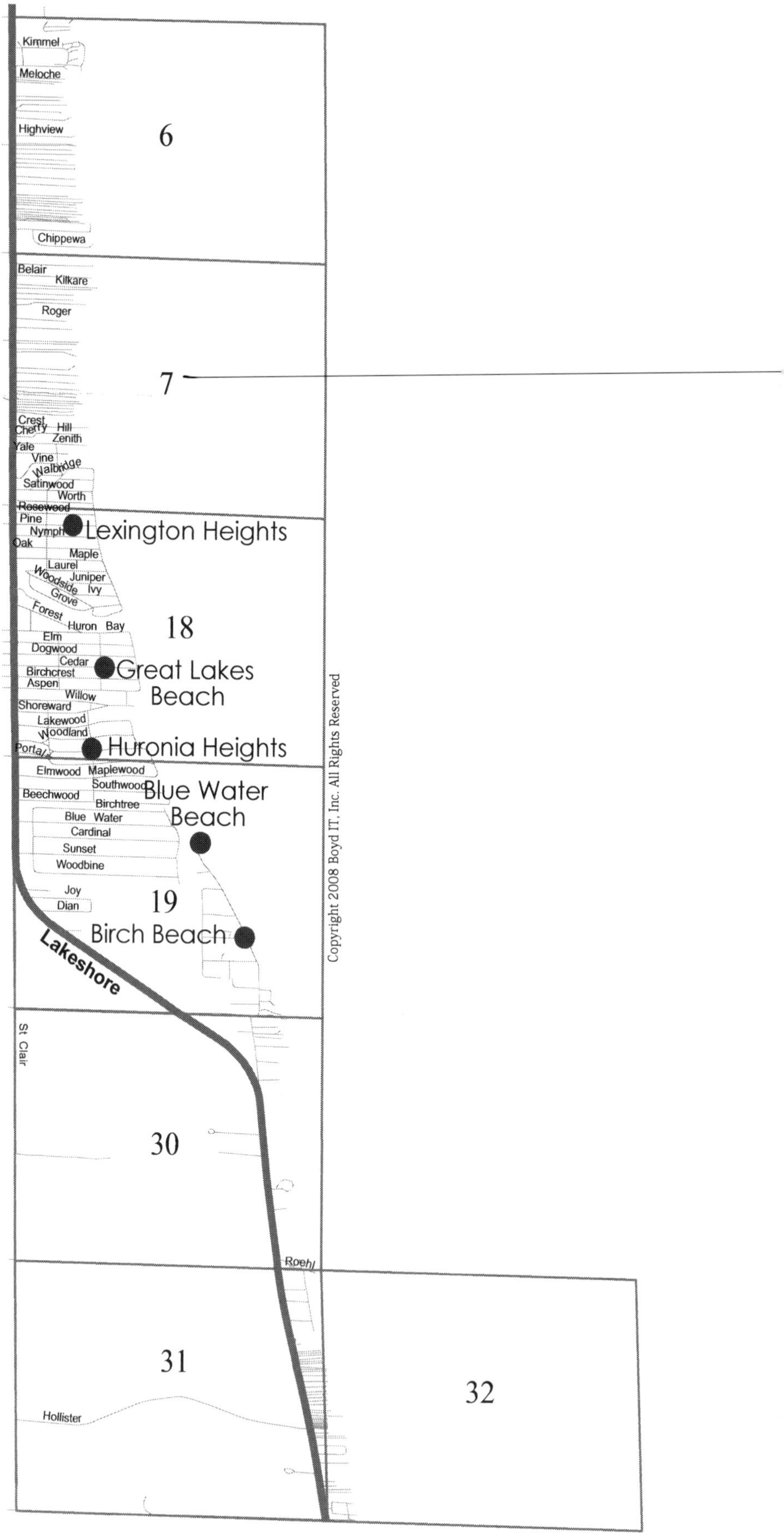

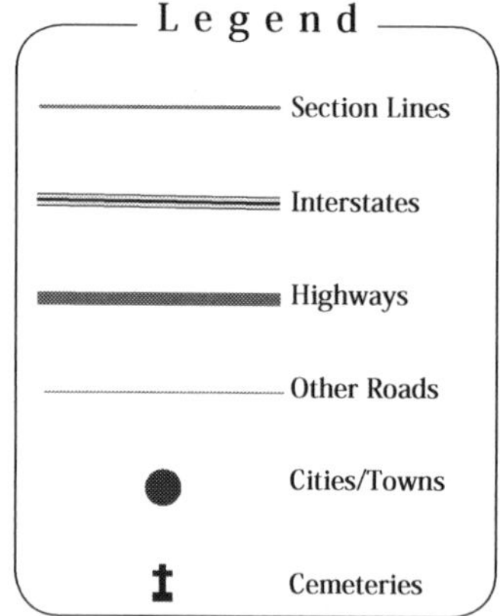

Scale: Section = 1 mile X 1 mile
(generally, with some exceptions)

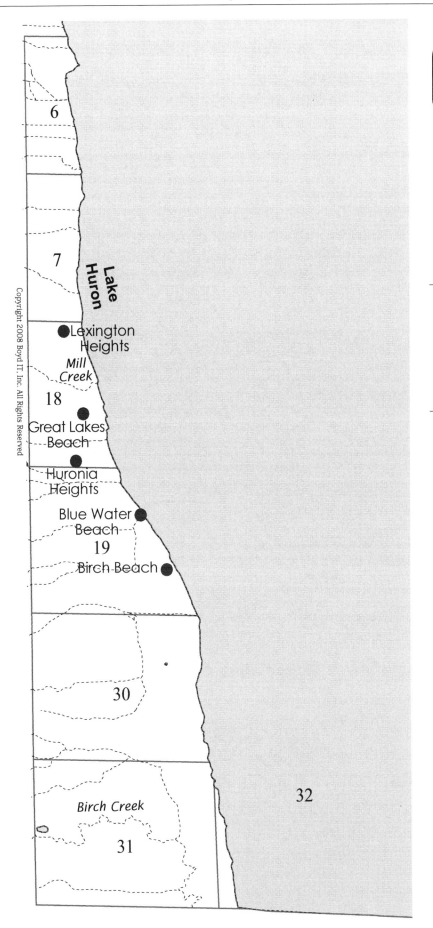

6
7
Lake Huron
Lexington Heights
Mill Creek
18
Great Lakes Beach
Huronia Heights
Blue Water Beach
19
Birch Beach
30
Birch Creek
31
32

Historical Map

T9-N R17-E
Michigan-Toledo Strip Meridian

Map Group 31

Note: the area contained in this map amounts to far less than a full Township. Therefore, its contents are completely on this single page (instead of a "normal" 2-page spread).

Cities & Towns

Birch Beach
Blue Water Beach
Great Lakes Beach
Huronia Heights
Lexington Heights

Cemeteries

None

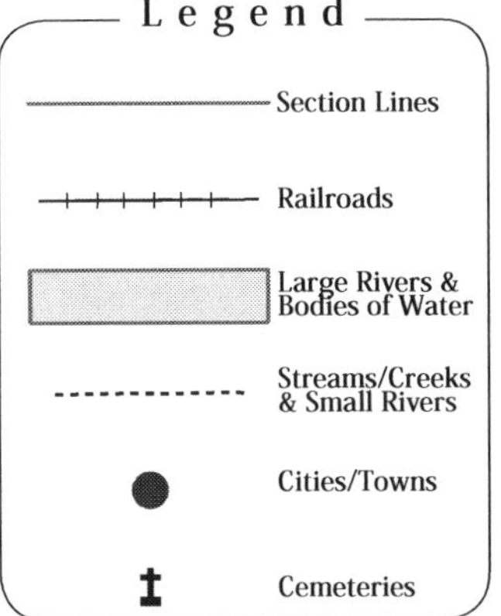

Scale: Section = 1 mile X 1 mile
(there are some exceptions)

Appendices

Appendix A - Acts of Congress Authorizing the Patents Contained in this Book

The following Acts of Congress are referred to throughout the Indexes in this book. The text of the Federal Statutes referred to below can usually be found on the web. For more information on such laws, check out the publishers's web-site at *www.arphax.com,* go to the "Research" page, and click on the "Land-Law" link.

Ref. No.	Date and Act of Congress	Number of Parcels of Land
1	April 24, 1820: Sale-Cash Entry (3 Stat. 566)	3060
2	May 20, 1862: Homestead EntryOriginal (12 Stat. 392)	393
3	September 28, 1850: Swamp Land Grant-Patent (9 Stat. 519)	1

Appendix B - Section Parts (Aliquot Parts)

The following represent the various abbreviations we have found thus far in describing the parts of a Public Land Section. Some of these are very obscure and rarely used, but we wanted to list them for just that reason. A full section is 1 square mile or 640 acres.

Section Part	Description	Acres
<none>	Full Acre (if no Section Part is listed, presumed a full Section)	640
<1-??>	A number represents a Lot Number and can be of various sizes	?
E½	East Half-Section	320
E½E½	East Half of East Half-Section	160
E½E½SE	East Half of East Half of Southeast Quarter-Section	40
E½N½	East Half of North Half-Section	160
E½NE	East Half of Northeast Quarter-Section	80
E½NENE	East Half of Northeast Quarter of Northeast Quarter-Section	20
E½NENW	East Half of Northeast Quarter of Northwest Quarter-Section	20
E½NESE	East Half of Northeast Quarter of Southeast Quarter-Section	20
E½NESW	East Half of Northeast Quarter of Southwest Quarter-Section	20
E½NW	East Half of Northwest Quarter-Section	80
E½NWNE	East Half of Northwest Quarter of Northeast Quarter-Section	20
E½NWNW	East Half of Northwest Quarter of Northwest Quarter-Section	20
E½NWSE	East Half of Northwest Quarter of Southeast Quarter-Section	20
E½NWSW	East Half of Northwest Quarter of Southwest Quarter-Section	20
E½S½	East Half of South Half-Section	160
E½SE	East Half of Southeast Quarter-Section	80
E½SENE	East Half of Southeast Quarter of Northeast Quarter-Section	20
E½SENW	East Half of Southeast Quarter of Northwest Quarter-Section	20
E½SESE	East Half of Southeast Quarter of Southeast Quarter-Section	20
E½SESW	East Half of Southeast Quarter of Southwest Quarter-Section	20
E½SW	East Half of Southwest Quarter-Section	80
E½SWNE	East Half of Southwest Quarter of Northeast Quarter-Section	20
E½SWNW	East Half of Southwest Quarter of Northwest Quarter-Section	20
E½SWSE	East Half of Southwest Quarter of Southeast Quarter-Section	20
E½SWSW	East Half of Southwest Quarter of Southwest Quarter-Section	20
E½W½	East Half of West Half-Section	160
N½	North Half-Section	320
N½E½NE	North Half of East Half of Northeast Quarter-Section	40
N½E½NW	North Half of East Half of Northwest Quarter-Section	40
N½E½SE	North Half of East Half of Southeast Quarter-Section	40
N½E½SW	North Half of East Half of Southwest Quarter-Section	40
N½N½	North Half of North Half-Section	160
N½NE	North Half of Northeast Quarter-Section	80
N½NENE	North Half of Northeast Quarter of Northeast Quarter-Section	20
N½NENW	North Half of Northeast Quarter of Northwest Quarter-Section	20
N½NESE	North Half of Northeast Quarter of Southeast Quarter-Section	20
N½NESW	North Half of Northeast Quarter of Southwest Quarter-Section	20
N½NW	North Half of Northwest Quarter-Section	80
N½NWNE	North Half of Northwest Quarter of Northeast Quarter-Section	20
N½NWNW	North Half of Northwest Quarter of Northwest Quarter-Section	20
N½NWSE	North Half of Northwest Quarter of Southeast Quarter-Section	20
N½NWSW	North Half of Northwest Quarter of Southwest Quarter-Section	20
N½S½	North Half of South Half-Section	160
N½SE	North Half of Southeast Quarter-Section	80
N½SENE	North Half of Southeast Quarter of Northeast Quarter-Section	20
N½SENW	North Half of Southeast Quarter of Northwest Quarter-Section	20
N½SESE	North Half of Southeast Quarter of Southeast Quarter-Section	20

Section Part	Description	Acres
N½SESW	North Half of Southeast Quarter of Southwest Quarter-Section	20
N½SESW	North Half of Southeast Quarter of Southwest Quarter-Section	20
N½SW	North Half of Southwest Quarter-Section	80
N½SWNE	North Half of Southwest Quarter of Northeast Quarter-Section	20
N½SWNW	North Half of Southwest Quarter of Northwest Quarter-Section	20
N½SWSE	North Half of Southwest Quarter of Southeast Quarter-Section	20
N½SWSE	North Half of Southwest Quarter of Southeast Quarter-Section	20
N½SWSW	North Half of Southwest Quarter of Southwest Quarter-Section	20
N½W½NW	North Half of West Half of Northwest Quarter-Section	40
N½W½SE	North Half of West Half of Southeast Quarter-Section	40
N½W½SW	North Half of West Half of Southwest Quarter-Section	40
NE	Northeast Quarter-Section	160
NEN½	Northeast Quarter of North Half-Section	80
NENE	Northeast Quarter of Northeast Quarter-Section	40
NENENE	Northeast Quarter of Northeast Quarter of Northeast Quarter	10
NENENW	Northeast Quarter of Northeast Quarter of Northwest Quarter	10
NENESE	Northeast Quarter of Northeast Quarter of Southeast Quarter	10
NENESW	Northeast Quarter of Northeast Quarter of Southwest Quarter	10
NENW	Northeast Quarter of Northwest Quarter-Section	40
NENWNE	Northeast Quarter of Northwest Quarter of Northeast Quarter	10
NENWNW	Northeast Quarter of Northwest Quarter of Northwest Quarter	10
NENWSE	Northeast Quarter of Northwest Quarter of Southeast Quarter	10
NENWSW	Northeast Quarter of Northwest Quarter of Southwest Quarter	10
NESE	Northeast Quarter of Southeast Quarter-Section	40
NESENE	Northeast Quarter of Southeast Quarter of Northeast Quarter	10
NESENW	Northeast Quarter of Southeast Quarter of Northwest Quarter	10
NESESE	Northeast Quarter of Southeast Quarter of Southeast Quarter	10
NESESW	Northeast Quarter of Southeast Quarter of Southwest Quarter	10
NESW	Northeast Quarter of Southwest Quarter-Section	40
NESWNE	Northeast Quarter of Southwest Quarter of Northeast Quarter	10
NESWNW	Northeast Quarter of Southwest Quarter of Northwest Quarter	10
NESWSE	Northeast Quarter of Southwest Quarter of Southeast Quarter	10
NESWSW	Northeast Quarter of Southwest Quarter of Southwest Quarter	10
NW	Northwest Quarter-Section	160
NWE½	Northwest Quarter of Eastern Half-Section	80
NWN½	Northwest Quarter of North Half-Section	80
NWNE	Northwest Quarter of Northeast Quarter-Section	40
NWNENE	Northwest Quarter of Northeast Quarter of Northeast Quarter	10
NWNENW	Northwest Quarter of Northeast Quarter of Northwest Quarter	10
NWNESE	Northwest Quarter of Northeast Quarter of Southeast Quarter	10
NWNESW	Northwest Quarter of Northeast Quarter of Southwest Quarter	10
NWNW	Northwest Quarter of Northwest Quarter-Section	40
NWNWNE	Northwest Quarter of Northwest Quarter of Northeast Quarter	10
NWNWNW	Northwest Quarter of Northwest Quarter of Northwest Quarter	10
NWNWSE	Northwest Quarter of Northwest Quarter of Southeast Quarter	10
NWNWSW	Northwest Quarter of Northwest Quarter of Southwest Quarter	10
NWSE	Northwest Quarter of Southeast Quarter-Section	40
NWSENE	Northwest Quarter of Southeast Quarter of Northeast Quarter	10
NWSENW	Northwest Quarter of Southeast Quarter of Northwest Quarter	10
NWSESE	Northwest Quarter of Southeast Quarter of Southeast Quarter	10
NWSESW	Northwest Quarter of Southeast Quarter of Southwest Quarter	10
NWSW	Northwest Quarter of Southwest Quarter-Section	40
NWSWNE	Northwest Quarter of Southwest Quarter of Northeast Quarter	10
NWSWNW	Northwest Quarter of Southwest Quarter of Northwest Quarter	10
NWSWSE	Northwest Quarter of Southwest Quarter of Southeast Quarter	10
NWSWSW	Northwest Quarter of Southwest Quarter of Southwest Quarter	10
S½	South Half-Section	320
S½E½NE	South Half of East Half of Northeast Quarter-Section	40
S½E½NW	South Half of East Half of Northwest Quarter-Section	40
S½E½SE	South Half of East Half of Southeast Quarter-Section	40

Section Part	Description	Acres
S½E½SW	South Half of East Half of Southwest Quarter-Section	40
S½N½	South Half of North Half-Section	160
S½NE	South Half of Northeast Quarter-Section	80
S½NENE	South Half of Northeast Quarter of Northeast Quarter-Section	20
S½NENW	South Half of Northeast Quarter of Northwest Quarter-Section	20
S½NESE	South Half of Northeast Quarter of Southeast Quarter-Section	20
S½NESW	South Half of Northeast Quarter of Southwest Quarter-Section	20
S½NW	South Half of Northwest Quarter-Section	80
S½NWNE	South Half of Northwest Quarter of Northeast Quarter-Section	20
S½NWNW	South Half of Northwest Quarter of Northwest Quarter-Section	20
S½NWSE	South Half of Northwest Quarter of Southeast Quarter-Section	20
S½NWSW	South Half of Northwest Quarter of Southwest Quarter-Section	20
S½S½	South Half of South Half-Section	160
S½SE	South Half of Southeast Quarter-Section	80
S½SENE	South Half of Southeast Quarter of Northeast Quarter-Section	20
S½SENW	South Half of Southeast Quarter of Northwest Quarter-Section	20
S½SESE	South Half of Southeast Quarter of Southeast Quarter-Section	20
S½SESW	South Half of Southeast Quarter of Southwest Quarter-Section	20
S½SESW	South Half of Southeast Quarter of Southwest Quarter-Section	20
S½SW	South Half of Southwest Quarter-Section	80
S½SWNE	South Half of Southwest Quarter of Northeast Quarter-Section	20
S½SWNW	South Half of Southwest Quarter of Northwest Quarter-Section	20
S½SWSE	South Half of Southwest Quarter of Southeast Quarter-Section	20
S½SWSE	South Half of Southwest Quarter of Southeast Quarter-Section	20
S½SWSW	South Half of Southwest Quarter of Southwest Quarter-Section	20
S½W½NE	South Half of West Half of Northeast Quarter-Section	40
S½W½NW	South Half of West Half of Northwest Quarter-Section	40
S½W½SE	South Half of West Half of Southeast Quarter-Section	40
S½W½SW	South Half of West Half of Southwest Quarter-Section	40
SE	Southeast Quarter Section	160
SEN½	Southeast Quarter of North Half-Section	80
SENE	Southeast Quarter of Northeast Quarter-Section	40
SENENE	Southeast Quarter of Northeast Quarter of Northeast Quarter	10
SENENW	Southeast Quarter of Northeast Quarter of Northwest Quarter	10
SENESE	Southeast Quarter of Northeast Quarter of Southeast Quarter	10
SENESW	Southeast Quarter of Northeast Quarter of Southwest Quarter	10
SENW	Southeast Quarter of Northwest Quarter-Section	40
SENWNE	Southeast Quarter of Northwest Quarter of Northeast Quarter	10
SENWNW	Southeast Quarter of Northwest Quarter of Northwest Quarter	10
SENWSE	Souteast Quarter of Northwest Quarter of Southeast Quarter	10
SENWSW	Southeast Quarter of Northwest Quarter of Southwest Quarter	10
SESE	Southeast Quarter of Southeast Quarter-Section	40
SESENE	SoutheastQuarter of Southeast Quarter of Northeast Quarter	10
SESENW	Southeast Quarter of Southeast Quarter of Northwest Quarter	10
SESESE	Southeast Quarter of Southeast Quarter of Southeast Quarter	10
SESESW	Southeast Quarter of Southeast Quarter of Southwest Quarter	10
SESW	Southeast Quarter of Southwest Quarter-Section	40
SESWNE	Southeast Quarter of Southwest Quarter of Northeast Quarter	10
SESWNW	Southeast Quarter of Southwest Quarter of Northwest Quarter	10
SESWSE	Southeast Quarter of Southwest Quarter of Southeast Quarter	10
SESWSW	Southeast Quarter of Southwest Quarter of Southwest Quarter	10
SW	Southwest Quarter-Section	160
SWNE	Southwest Quarter of Northeast Quarter-Section	40
SWNENE	Southwest Quarter of Northeast Quarter of Northeast Quarter	10
SWNENW	Southwest Quarter of Northeast Quarter of Northwest Quarter	10
SWNESE	Southwest Quarter of Northeast Quarter of Southeast Quarter	10
SWNESW	Southwest Quarter of Northeast Quarter of Southwest Quarter	10
SWNW	Southwest Quarter of Northwest Quarter-Section	40
SWNWNE	Southwest Quarter of Northwest Quarter of Northeast Quarter	10
SWNWNW	Southwest Quarter of Northwest Quarter of Northwest Quarter	10

Section Part	Description	Acres
SWNWSE	Southwest Quarter of Northwest Quarter of Southeast Quarter	10
SWNWSW	Southwest Quarter of Northwest Quarter of Southwest Quarter	10
SWSE	Southwest Quarter of Southeast Quarter-Section	40
SWSENE	Southwest Quarter of Southeast Quarter of Northeast Quarter	10
SWSENW	Southwest Quarter of Southeast Quarter of Northwest Quarter	10
SWSESE	Southwest Quarter of Southeast Quarter of Southeast Quarter	10
SWSESW	Southwest Quarter of Southeast Quarter of Southwest Quarter	10
SWSW	Southwest Quarter of Southwest Quarter-Section	40
SWSWNE	Southwest Quarter of Southwest Quarter of Northeast Quarter	10
SWSWNW	Southwest Quarter of Southwest Quarter of Northwest Quarter	10
SWSWSE	Southwest Quarter of Southwest Quarter of Southeast Quarter	10
SWSWSW	Southwest Quarter of Southwest Quarter of Southwest Quarter	10
W½	West Half-Section	320
W½E½	West Half of East Half-Section	160
W½N½	West Half of North Half-Section (same as NW)	160
W½NE	West Half of Northeast Quarter	80
W½NENE	West Half of Northeast Quarter of Northeast Quarter-Section	20
W½NENW	West Half of Northeast Quarter of Northwest Quarter-Section	20
W½NESE	West Half of Northeast Quarter of Southeast Quarter-Section	20
W½NESW	West Half of Northeast Quarter of Southwest Quarter-Section	20
W½NW	West Half of Northwest Quarter-Section	80
W½NWNE	West Half of Northwest Quarter of Northeast Quarter-Section	20
W½NWNW	West Half of Northwest Quarter of Northwest Quarter-Section	20
W½NWSE	West Half of Northwest Quarter of Southeast Quarter-Section	20
W½NWSW	West Half of Northwest Quarter of Southwest Quarter-Section	20
W½S½	West Half of South Half-Section	160
W½SE	West Half of Southeast Quarter-Section	80
W½SENE	West Half of Southeast Quarter of Northeast Quarter-Section	20
W½SENW	West Half of Southeast Quarter of Northwest Quarter-Section	20
W½SESE	West Half of Southeast Quarter of Southeast Quarter-Section	20
W½SESW	West Half of Southeast Quarter of Southwest Quarter-Section	20
W½SW	West Half of Southwest Quarter-Section	80
W½SWNE	West Half of Southwest Quarter of Northeast Quarter-Section	20
W½SWNW	West Half of Southwest Quarter of Northwest Quarter-Section	20
W½SWSE	West Half of Southwest Quarter of Southeast Quarter-Section	20
W½SWSW	West Half of Southwest Quarter of Southwest Quarter-Section	20
W½W½	West Half of West Half-Section	160

Appendix C - Multi-Patentee Groups

The following index presents groups of people who jointly received patents in Sanilac County, Michigan. The Group Numbers are used in the Patent Maps and their Indexes so that you may then turn to this Appendix in order to identify all the members of the each buying group.

Group Number 1
ANDERSON, James; BLINDBERRY, V H

Group Number 2
ARMSTRONG, James; BLINDBERRY, V H

Group Number 3
ATKINSON, Obrien J; MCGINN, John W; SIMMS, Walter

Group Number 4
AVERY, Newell; MURPHY, Simon J

Group Number 5
AVERY, Sewell; EDDY, Edwin

Group Number 6
BAGG, Silas A; HIGGINS, Sylvester; PETTY, Danforth; STOWELL, Alexander

Group Number 7
BAILEY, Calvin P; HURD, Jarvis

Group Number 8
BARNARD, Sherman S; BROOKS, Nathaniel W

Group Number 9
BARNARD, Sherman S; COE, Israel

Group Number 10
BATCHELDER, John W; JOHNSON, James S

Group Number 11
BAUGHMAN, John C; HUBBARD, Thomas; KING, John E

Group Number 12
BEACH, George; BECKWITH, Alonzo S; DICKINSON, Nathan

Group Number 13
BRYANT, Moses; HADLEY, Timothy G

Group Number 14
BUCHANAN, Alexander; STILSON, John

Group Number 15
BUNKER, Charles; BUNKER, Frederick R; EWER, Peter F

Group Number 16
BURTCH, Jonathan; SIBLEY, Sylvester

Group Number 17
BURTCH, Jonathan; SILBEY, Sylvester

Group Number 18
CAMPBELL, Archa; HAY, James

Group Number 19
CARRINGTON, Mark; LUCE, Benjamin F

Group Number 20
CARROLL, Charles H; CARROLL, William Thomas

Group Number 21
CARROLL, Charles H; GRANGER, Josephus

Group Number 22
CHASE, Anthony M; CHASE, Nathan B

Group Number 23
CHASE, Nathan B; MILLER, John

Group Number 24
CHASE, Nathan B; SANBORN, James W

Group Number 25
CROCKER, William A; WALDO, William B

Group Number 26
DAVIS, Alfred; HUBINGER, John J; WILLCOX, Byron; WILLCOX, George

Group Number 27
DAVIS, Augustus; DAVIS, Mary

Group Number 28
DAVIS, Randal E; SANBORN, Cummings; STEVENSON, Matthew W

Group Number 29
DAVIS, Randal E; STEVENSON, Mathew W

Group Number 30
DAVIS, Randall E; STEVENS, Harmon L

Group Number 31
DAVIS, Randall E; STEVENS, Matthew

Group Number 32
DAVIS, Randall E; WIGHT, Buckminster

Group Number 33
DOWLING, William H; FORBES, John C

Group Number 34
DUDLEY, Daniel D; HUNT, Henry C

Group Number 35
ERITY, James G; MILES, Cyrus

Group Number 36
ERSKIN, E; ERSKINE, J

Group Number 37
ERSKINE, E; ERSKINE, J

Group Number 38
FARNSWORTH, Elon; SIBLEY, Sylvester; TROWBRIDGE, Charles C

Group Number 39
FISH, Allen; FISH, Henry

Group Number 40
FLEMING, William; MOORE, Franklin; MOORE, Stephen

Group Number 41
FRENCH, Charles J; PAPST, R

Group Number 42
GEEL, James M; PARMELY, Lemuel

Group Number 43
GREGG, David; HOYT, William

Group Number 44
HAMMOND, Charles; HAMMOND, John C; PHELPS, Elihu; WYMAN, John

Group Number 45
HOWARD, Henry; HOWARD, John

Group Number 46
HOWARD, John T; SINCLAIR, Alexander

Group Number 47
HUBBARD, Bela; KING, John E

Group Number 48
JONES, Enoch; LUCE, Bartlett A

Group Number 49
LYON, Lucius; PARKER, Daniel

Group Number 50
MARRELL, Levi; WELCH, Samuel O

Group Number 51
MCGINN, John W; SIMMS, Walter

Group Number 52
MCLACHLAN, Andrew; WHEELER, Alonzo

Group Number 53
MIZNER, Mary Gouverneur; SPENCER, William

Group Number 54
MORSE, Timothy; WOODS, John L

Group Number 55
RUST, Aloney; RUST, David W

Group Number 56
SANBORN, James W; SWEETSER, Alvah

Group Number 57
SMITH, Catharine; SMITH, John

Group Number 58
WHITNEY, Daniel; WHITNEY, John W

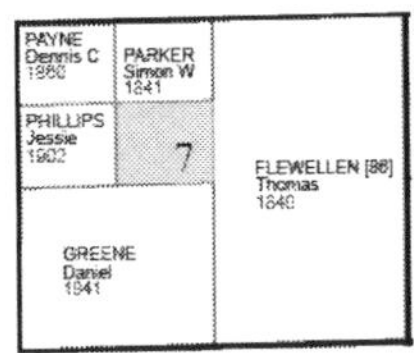

Extra! Extra! (about our Indexes)

We purposefully do not have an all-name index in the back of this volume so that our readers do not miss one of the best uses of this book: finding misspelled names among more specialized indexes.

Without repeating the text of our "How-to" chapter, we have nonetheless tried to assist our more anxious researchers by delivering a short-cut to the two county-wide Surname Indexes, the second of which will lead you to all-name indexes for each Congressional Township mapped in this volume :

Surname Index (whole county, with number of parcels mapped) ....page 18
Surname Index (township by township) ....just following

For your convenience, the "How To Use this Book" Chart on page 2 is repeated on the reverse of this page.

We should be releasing new titles every week for the foreseeable future. We urge you to write, fax, call, or email us any time for a current list of titles. Of course, our web-page will always have the most current information about current and upcoming books.

Arphax Publishing Co.
2210 Research Park Blvd.
Norman, Oklahoma 73069
(800) 681-5298 toll-free
(405) 366-6181 local
(405) 366-8184 fax
info@arphax.com

www.arphax.com

How to Use This Book - A Graphical Summary

Part I
"The Big Picture"

Map A ▸ *Counties in the State*
Map B ▸ *Surrounding Counties*
Map C ▸ *Congressional Townships (Map Groups) in the County*
Map D ▸ *Cities & Towns in the County*
Map E ▸ *Cemeteries in the County*
Surnames in the County ▸ *Number of Land-Parcels for Each Surname*
Surname/Township Index ▸ Directs you to Township Map Groups in Part II

The Surname/Township Index can direct you to any number of **Township Map Groups**

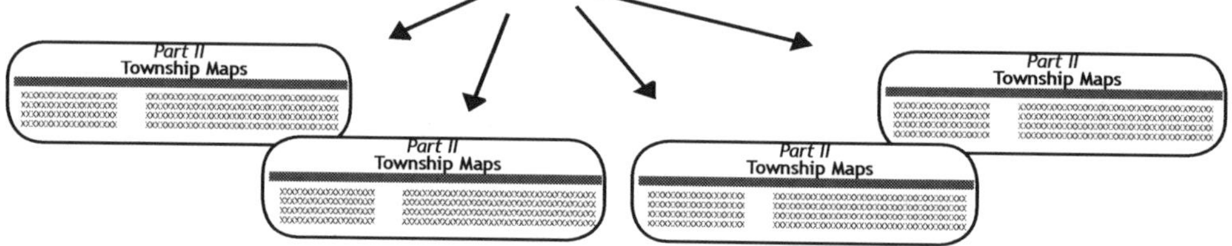

Part II
Township Map Groups
(1 for each Township in the County)

Each Township Map Group contains all four of of the following tools . . .

Land Patent Index ▸ *Every-name Index of Patents Mapped in this Township*
Land Patent Map ▸ *Map of Patents as listed in above Index*
Road Map ▸ *Map of Roads, City-centers, and Cemeteries in the Township*
Historical Map ▸ *Map of Railroads, Lakes, Rivers, Creeks, City-Centers, and Cemeteries*

Appendices

Appendix A ▸ *Congressional Authority enabling Patents within our Maps*
Appendix B ▸ *Section-Parts / Aliquot Parts (a comprehensive list)*
Appendix C ▸ *Multi-patentee Groups (Individuals within Buying Groups)*

Made in the USA
Lexington, KY
06 December 2019